THE WORKS OF GERRARD WINSTANLEY

THE WORKS OF
GERRARD WINSTANLEY

WITH AN APPENDIX OF DOCUMENTS
RELATING TO THE DIGGER MOVEMENT

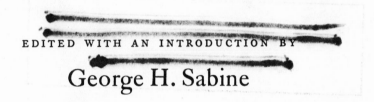

EDITED WITH AN INTRODUCTION BY

George H. Sabine

NEW YORK

RUSSELL & RUSSELL · INC

1965

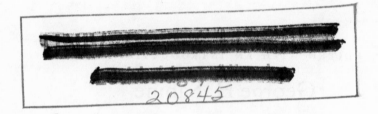

PREFACE

I N THIS EDITION I have reprinted all the works known to have been written by Gerrard Winstanley except his three earliest pamphlets; of these I have printed abstracts. The omission was partly to save space and partly because less interest attaches to books written before Winstanley's discovery of communism. I have printed the complete text of one of his religious tracts written before *The New Law of Righteousnes,* in which he first announced his communism. In the Appendix I have reprinted several pamphlets or broadsides connected with the Digger Movement which were pretty certainly not written by Winstanley, though some of them have been attributed to him.

The text is reproduced from the original editions. It seemed to me that any attempt to modernize Winstanley's English would produce a hybrid that was neither Winstanley nor modern. Some of the pamphlets were hastily printed and contained a number of misprints which it would have been mere pedantry to reproduce. I have corrected these and I have occasionally altered the punctuation, which is sometimes very erratic, where it interfered with a ready perception of the sense. My rule has been to make as few changes as possible. I have not dared to meddle with Winstanley's references to Scripture, though some of the citations are probably wrong; I distrust my ability to decide what he would have thought the symbolic meaning of a text.

I wish to make the following acknowledgments for help that I have received in the course of my work.

I must express a special debt of gratitude to Professor William Haller, of Columbia University, who resigned the intention to edit an edition of Winstanley in order to leave the field open for me. The contributions which Professor Haller's works have made to the history of Puritanism are such that his claim to reserve any part of the subject for himself would never have been challenged by me. In addition, he has allowed me to use notes made by himself or by his students. Bibliographical notes made by Miss Altha E. Terry have been very useful.

I acknowledge with thanks the permission given me by the Royal Historical Society to reprint from the *Clarke Papers* the two letters sent to Fairfax in December and the Digger Song which is reprinted in the Appendix. I thank Miss D. L. Powell, the Honorary Secretary of the Surrey Record Society, for transcribing the record of the suits at Kingston, and Mr. C. W. Winstanley, of 84 Home Park Road, Wimbledon Park, S.W. 19, for two references to Winstanley in contemporary records.

For the privilege of having film-photographs made of books in their possession I wish to thank the Seligman Library at Columbia University, the British Museum, and the libraries of the Princeton Theological Seminary, the University of Cincinnati, and the University of Chicago. I am indebted to Professor Wallace Notestein for helping me to get films and to the Yale University Library for lending me films that belong to their collection. Mr. D. G. Wing, from his continuation of the Short Title Catalogue, has given information about the location of copies of Winstanley's books.

The most signal help that I have had in preparing the volume came from my wife, Winifred Sabine, who read for me all the news sheets of relevant dates in the Thomason and the Burney Collections at the British Museum. My daughter, Janet Sabine, has helped me greatly with the difficult task of reading the proofs.

George H. Sabine

Ithaca, New York
July 15, 1940

CONTENTS

INTRODUCTION

POLITICAL PHILOSOPHY is not, characteristically, the product of the study or the laboratory. It occurs rather as an incident or a by-product of action, and even when it is produced by scholars, its authors have one eye on the forum. When political philosophy is produced in quantities, it is a sure symptom that society is going through a period of stress and strain. Political philosophies are secreted —to paraphrase a famous comparison of substantive and procedural law—in the interstices of political and social crisis. Of this there is no better illustration than the period of the Puritan Revolution. Here within the span of a few years—flanked on the one side by a longer period of preparation and on the other by a period of restabilization— occurred the most extraordinary outpouring of political philosophy that the modern world has seen. For it was the first of the modern revolutionary eras: a time in which all the intellectual, religious, moral, social, and political traditions were broken apart and put together in a new pattern. It produced political theories by great scholars, Hobbes and Harrington, and after an interval, Locke. But it produced also a great mass of popular writing on the subject indicative of the disturbance that was taking place in the minds of thousands of obscure men. As a symptom of what was taking place and as a sign of the future this popular political theorizing was hardly less important than the work of scholars.

Of these popular political philosophies much the most interesting is that which grew up in connection with the Leveller party and its plans for reestablishing constitutional government after the Revolution. Beside the large literature of pamphlets and manifestoes, there is one unique document, the report of the Putney debates in the Army Council, between the agitators from the regiments and the officers of

Cromwell's staff.[1] Here one finds the *verbatim* report of a discussion, unpremeditated and unrehearsed, between men in the midst of a revolutionary crisis. The debates afford a glimpse into the minds of private soldiers in Cromwell's army and some first-hand knowledge of the more radical ideas about constitutional government which prevailed among political-minded Englishmen in the less prosperous section of the middle class. These ideas form a surprisingly coherent plan of democratic radicalism, both in respect of its philosophy of individual natural rights and also in respect of the political apparatus by which democrats later tried to give their philosophy effect.

Side by side with this movement of Leveller democracy and originating on its fringes was the communistic movement of Gerrard Winstanley, whose works form the subject of this study. By comparison Winstanley's effort to found a socialist community for cultivating the common land was a very minor matter. The Levellers were a political party, numerous enough to compel at least the appearance of consideration from persons in authority. Their leader, John Lilburne, was a master of popular agitation with a genius for dramatizing himself before the public as the embodiment of the people's liberties. Their ideas were suitable for the platform of a party devoted to radical democratic reforms. Winstanley's movement was negligible in size, probably never more than fifty or sixty in the group at Cobham, and while other similar groups sprang up elsewhere in imitation of this, they never made a party. The ideas behind Winstanley's communism were not such as could ever have made an effective party. And Winstanley himself, it must be admitted, showed no evidence of possessing the practical political capacity that can be sensed in some of the army agitators. In spite of these disparities, Leveller democracy and Winstanley's utopian socialism are companion pieces, representing as they do the earliest examples of these two rival types of modern revolutionary radicalism.

The contrast between the two was not chiefly in respect to their practicability. That was a matter of degree, since in a sense both were utopian. The Leveller party accomplished none of its designs,

---

[1] *The Clarke Papers*, edited by C. H. Firth, Vols. I and II, Camden Society Publications, N.S. Nos. 49 and 54, Cambridge, 1891, 1894. The debates have been reprinted, in an improved text, by A. S. P. Woodhouse, *Puritanism and Liberty*, London, 1938.

and when later democratic movements realized what the Levellers planned, the results were not much like the expectations. Both movements were nearly as much religious as they were political. In Winstanley's case this is obvious; he was a mystic and his communism was revealed to him in a trance. But it would be a mistake to suppose that the Levellers were less religious than he, merely because their religion took a different form. Every revolution gets its drive from ideas that, psychologically speaking, are religious in their effects on human motivation. The Puritan Revolution made no pretenses about these ideas: it took them for what they were. In addition, the public questions about which a revolutionist was concerned were as likely to be ecclesiastical as political. It is probably true that, even when the Revolution was at its height, there were ten Puritans who were interested in reforming the church for one who cared what happened to the government of England. Finally, in the seventeenth century, theology came close to being a universal language, and among the large mass of Puritans Calvinism was the accepted form of theology. It is hopelessly unhistorical to take the seventeenth-century radical out of the religious and theological context in which, as a matter of fact, he did his thinking and his acting. And this holds good of the Levellers as it does of Winstanley. Anyone who wants to understand John Lilburne is ill advised if he forgets that Lilburne was a bitter opponent of prelacy before he ever thought of agitating for the reform of Parliament. In the case of Winstanley, communism was merely the last step in his rejection of beliefs held in common by the great mass of Puritans, however much they might differ among themselves about the details of those beliefs. But what put Winstanley outside the Puritanism of the Revolution was not a loss of religion, but another kind of religious experience.

What distinguished Winstanley's communism from the political philosophy of the Levellers was the thorough-going difference of principle between them. The most interesting phase of their history is to see these two types of political radicalism taking shape and forming each its own body of suitable philosophical ideas. Each, as it becomes internally coherent, rejects the other. The Leveller, as one can see from the Putney debates, was a political individualist. The object of his reforms was to safeguard personal and civil liberties. These liberties he conceived as inalienable rights inherent in every human being and inseparable from the idea of freely acting personality. The critical points in a political program were for him the suffrage and the bill of rights; the first to insure that government should be responsive to the popular will, the second to keep even a popular government from intruding upon the inviolable domain of individual right. In short, the Leveller was a democrat, and his political philosophy already embodied the social ideals of democracy: freedom of opportunity for the individual, prevention of monopoly by a liberal government. Among the rights to be respected and safeguarded by such a government is the inviolability of property. Already the Leveller notions of reform pretty clearly suggested the program characteristic of radical democracy: the separation, as complete as may be, of political action from interference with the working of the economic system.

There was scarcely a proposition in this summary account of Leveller doctrines from which Winstanley would not have dissented. Only in desiring that the Revolution should do its work thoroughly on English law and government, and in his reliance on the suffrage and frequent elections, did he follow the Leveller program. His ethics included no such belief in the moral excellence of aggressive individualism as was implicit in Leveller philosophy, and this, I believe, was a result of a quite different religious conviction that separated Winstanley from the characteristic moral ideals of Calvinism. Perhaps, too, Winstanley's own private failure in the rough-and-tumble of business may have given his moral valuations a twist: initiative and enterprise seemed to him fine names for greed and cunning. It seemed to him impossible that a free and peaceful society could be held together by the impulses that were responsible for oppression and war. Against the aggressive and acquisitive and competitive tendencies in human nature, as Winstanley thought, the principle of mutual aid and cooperation did continual battle. Only the latter, as it succeeds in keeping the family going, makes human life possible at all. Only its extension over the whole range of human relationships can bring into being a society that is really devoted to the democratic ideals of equity and reason. Accordingly it seemed to Winstanley to be a contradiction in terms to look for a free political system in a society that still harbored poverty. For political and legal oppression arose, as he thought, precisely from the relationships of property that put some men within the economic power of others.

It is Winstanley's grasp of this idea that put him outside the circle of Leveller political philosophy. His claim to a place, though a small one, in the history of political philosophy is that he tried to visualize a social system of a different sort, in accordance with the ethical principles that he had come to believe. The denunciation of abuses, economic as well as political, is a normal part of every revolutionary crisis. The fact that Winstanley found picturesque ways of calling landlords thieves and lawyers rascals does not distinguish him from a thousand other writers of his time, or of times before and after. The point is that he tried to frame for himself a different idea of property and a different idea of the relationship between property and government from those that existed or from those accepted by the other social philosophies that he knew. In short, he tried to plan a socialist society. In this respect it is well not to expect too much. Winstanley was a man of little education, a small tradesman with no experience of large affairs or of public questions. He had a keen appreciation of craftsmanship but very little conception of economics. His platform for a communistic society is not very complete, but it is complete enough to rank as the first socialist utopia formed in the hope of becoming a party program. Beyond any doubt it was the product of an intense moral and religious experience, and Winstanley achieved a really great degree of clarity in setting out the differences that put him in opposition to the prevalent qualities of Puritan thought and belief. In this respect he is a figure of not inconsiderable historical interest because he brings to light one of the less known phases of ethical thought in the age of the Revolution. It is moreover a phase not without significance in the later history of English morals and religion. It is the purpose of this Introduction to offer a summary of these phases of Winstanley's communism.

WINSTANLEY'S BIOGRAPHY

Very little is known with certainty of Winstanley's life except what may be gathered from the occasional biographical remarks that occur in his writings. There is no doubt that he was born in Lancashire, for he addressed his first published work, *The Mysterie of God,* to his "beloved countrymen" of that County. In the *Registers of the Parish Church of Wigan, 1580–1625*,[1] there is an entry showing that "Garrard, son of Edward Winstanlie" was baptized on July 10, 1609. Though Winstanley was a rather common family name[2] in the southern part of the County, this entry may very well record the birth of the Digger leader. If so, he was forty years old when the work at St. George's Hill began.

From his own statements it is clear that Winstanley was bred a tradesman and was engaged in business in London at the beginning of the Civil Wars. In the London Marriage Licenses in the Bishop of London's Register[3] occurs an entry showing that on September 28, 1640, Jerrard Winstanley was married to Susan King. It is quite certain from the address to the City of London at the beginning of *A Watch-word* that Winstanley had been admitted to the liberty of the City and had suffered bankruptcy as a consequence of the financial stress that accompanied the Civil Wars. He appears to have been engaged in some branch of the cloth industry and was probably a member of one of the City Companies.[4] Certainly he admired the Companies and modeled the regulation of trade in his *Law of Freedom* partly upon them. After his failure in business it was necessary for Winstanley to accept the hospitality of friends in Surrey. This move apparently was made at once, since he says that he was present in Kingston and saw Francis Drake, his future opponent at St. George's Hill, take the Covenant, presumably in 1643. In 1649, when he launched his communist project, Winstanley evidently was making a precarious living by pasturing his neighbors' cattle.

The key to Winstanley's communistic philosophy lay in his re-

---

[1] P. 74. Publications of the Lancashire Parish Register Society.

[2] In the Registers published (for seventy-seven parishes) the name Gerrard Winstanley occurs three times; the other two cannot refer to the right person.

[3] *Index Library*, Vol. LXII. For this reference I am indebted to Mr. C. W. Winstanley.

[4] At the Public Record Office there is a record of a suit in Chancery Proceedings, Reynardson's Division, dated October 20, 1660, by Jerrard Winstanley of Cobham, co. Surrey, in which he states that in April, 1641, being then a citizen of London, he had dealings with one Richard Allsworth for "fustions dimmities and lynnin cloth and such like commodities". He states also that his books were lost or destroyed in the late war. There appears to be no record of Winstanley in the books of the Drapers Company; possibly he was a Mercer or a Merchant Taylor. This reference also was given to me by Mr. C. W. Winstanley.

ligious experience, and though all that he wrote refers directly or indirectly to that subject, there are only a few events, and no dates for these, that can be established. He says in his *New Law of Righteousnes*, the book in which he first announced his communism, that formerly he had been "a strict professor and goer to church", which probably refers to membership in one of the more conventional religious congregations. At some time prior to his first publication, he had become a Baptist, since in *Truth Lifting up its Head* he says that he had undergone "the ordinance of dipping".[5] It is not unlikely that he had been one of the lay preachers in whom the Baptist sect abounded and who formed one of the most scandalous features of that body, in the eyes of more conservative Christians. The skill with which Winstanley varied the arguments in his pamphlets to suit the audience he was addressing suggests that he may have had experience in the art of *ex tempore* preaching. Like other Baptists, he not infrequently compares these unlearned "prophesiers" with the disciples of Christ and speaks with bitterness of the attempts by Parliament to suppress the preaching of the unordained. It is evident, however, that his Baptist connection was a thing of the past before Winstanley's writing began. He never refers to baptism with water as other than a non-essential form "after the flesh", to be contrasted with the baptism of the spirit, which he had come to regard as the true substance of that rite. In *The New Law of Righteousnes* he contrasts himself with those "that still live in dipping in water" and who still consider the observance of other Gospel forms important. If he ever had practiced more or less regular preaching in Baptist conventicles, he had evidently abandoned it by 1648 for a still more informal kind of religious discourse in occasional private gatherings: "not customarily to make a trade of it, for fleshly ends, but occasionally as the Light is pleased to manifest himself in me".[6] His *Mysterie of God* was written to prove the doctrine of universal salvation, that even the

---

[5] This form of the rite began to be practiced in England in 1641; Champlin Burrage, *The Early English Dissenters*, Cambridge, 1912, Vol. I, pp. 330 ff.

[6] *The New Law of Righteousnes*, p. 2 (bracketed paging). There is a difference, at least of emphasis, between *The Mysterie of God* and *The Saints Paradice*, which were written within a few months of each other in 1648. In the former Winstanley enlarges upon the necessity that preaching should set forth the "experimental" knowledge of the preacher; in the latter he renounced formal teaching altogether, since the only true teacher is the spirit which is in every man.

damned shall be rescued from Hell at the end, which was heretical doctrine from the point of view of the Arminian Baptists, and was still worse from the standpoint of Baptists who retained the stricter Calvinist theology.

It is clear, therefore, that before 1648 Winstanley had already passed beyond the Baptist sect and had become what I think would properly be called a Seeker, in the terminology of the day. That is, he had ceased to be a "goer to church" at all, because he was unable to find religious satisfaction in any existing religious body. Like Joseph Salmon he had heard a "voice from the throne of the Heavenly Almightiness: Arise and depart, for this is not your rest".[7] It was no uncommon experience in the mid-seventeenth century. The early records of the Quakers show many cases of men and women who "passed through all the professions", and "whose custom it was when met together neither to preach nor pray vocally, but to read the Scriptures and discourse of religion, expecting a further manifestation".[8] Such persons and such groups made no inconsiderable portion of those who were ready to accept the teaching of George Fox. Moreover, it is obvious that the Baptists furnished a great many of these believers in the immanence of God and discarders of the Christian ordinances; the early histories of the English Baptists are filled with complaints on this score.[9] Consequently, Winstanley's religious development was in some degree typical; many men and women in England were passing through a characteristic religious evolution which took them first out of the larger and more stable religious bodies, like the Episcopalians or the Presbyterians, into Independency, then into some Baptist congregation, and ultimately beyond the limits of any organized community.

This was, however, no growth of indifference to religion. In truth

[7] *Heights in Depths and Depths in Heights.* Per me Jo. Salmon. London, 1651, p. 12. Salmon was not a very well-balanced person, but his religious autobiography is a record of the kind of spiritual pilgrimage that many wiser men went through.

[8] *The First Publishers of Truth.* Being early records (now first printed) of the Introduction of Quakerism into the Counties of England and Wales. Edited by Norman Penney. London, 1907, pp. 16, 18, 48, 52. On the relation of such groups in Yorkshire to Fox's early teaching there, see W. C. Braithwaite, *The Beginnings of Quakerism*, London, 1912, ch. 3.

[9] *E.g.*, Adam Taylor, *The History of the English General Baptists*, London, 1818, Vol. I, p. 157. Cf. W. T. Whitley, *A History of British Baptists*, London, 1923, pp. 84 f.

it was exactly the reverse. The Seeker awaited a new revelation from above, either a new disciple gifted like the disciples of Christ to found a new church, or more often a new discipleship spiritually revealed in the inner experience of every believer. It was experience of this latter sort that terminated Winstanley's seeking and brought him finally to a state of peace and religious satisfaction. The record of the change, so far as he ever wrote it, is in his two early pamphlets, *The Breaking of the Day of God* and *The Saints Paradice*, the titles of which were evidently meant to be descriptive. It is clear that Winstanley passed through "spiritual burnings", such as George Fox describes in the opening pages of his *Journal* and such as fill the religious autobiographies of so many men of this time. Fears and anxieties, consciousness of sin, the temptations of the flesh, the horror of death, the dread of devils and spirits and apparitions—all these Winstanley enumerates with a vividness which shows clearly that he was recounting his own experience. In the end he arrived at tranquility in the consciousness of a personal revelation—an "experimental" knowledge of God within him, which supersedes the "imaginary" knowledge of the letter and the external law of ordinances and ceremonial, and which he conceived to be the cause of a complete moral transfiguration.

> I myself have known nothing but what I received by tradition from the mouths and pen of others; I worshipped a God, but I neither knew who he was nor where he was, so that I lived in the dark, being blinded by the imagination of my flesh, and by the imagination of such as stand up to teach the people to know the Lord and yet have no knowledge of the Lord themselves, but as they have received by hearsay, from their books and other men's words. . . . I do not write anything as to be a teacher of you, for I know you have a teacher within yourselves (which is the Spirit) and when your flesh is made subject to him, he will teach you all things and bring all things to your remembrance, so that you shall not need to run after men for instruction. . . . And this is the Spirit, or Father, which as he made the globe and every creature, so he dwells in every creature, but supremely in man. . . . I have yielded to let these few experiences come abroad, and partly unwilling, because I

see more clearly into these secrets than before I writ them, which teaches me to rejoice in silence, to see the Father so abundantly at work; and it shall cease speedily for men to stand up as they do to teach one another, for everyone shall be taught of him.[10]

The essence of Winstanley's "experimental" religion, therefore, was intuition or vision of a mystical sort, precisely such as George Fox describes as the "openings" of the Lord to him. These intuitions were to his mind, as to Fox's, completely self-authenticating, and therefore radically different from the "imaginary" knowledge of books, or authority, or tradition, or of logical inference. From his own account it is clear that, on occasion, he was subject to trances, which indeed are a normal part of the experience of those whose religious perceptions take this mystical form. It is characteristic also that what Winstanley regarded as his mission, the teaching and the practice of communism, should have begun with a command imparted to him in such a trance, as George Fox's effective ministry in Yorkshire began with his vision of "a great people in white raiment by a river-side, coming to the Lord." [11] The story of Winstanley's trance and of the voice that commanded, "Work together, Eat bread together", is told in *The New Law of Righteousnes*, which was published at the end of January, 1649. That this experience was the immediate occasion of his organizing a communist group to cultivate the common at St. George's Hill appears from his reference to this book in the address which precedes *A Watch-word*, and also from the first of the manifestoes issued by the Diggers, *The True Levellers Standard Advanced*. There can be no doubt that Winstanley quite sincerely regarded his communism as a revelation of spiritual truth, whose very existence vouched for its validity and authority. In the course of his movement he presented an argument in several guises, rational or Scriptural, but in his own mind his communism had its inception in what he took to be a direct revelation. For him it neither had nor needed any other support.

Of Winstanley's life after the publication of his *Law of Freedom* in 1652 nothing is known. It appears that he was still living at Cobham in 1660,[12] and since he was then able to institute a suit in Chan-

---

[10] *The Saints Paradice*, address.

[11] *Journal*, edited by Rufus M. Jones, Philadelphia, 1906, Vol. I, p. 150.

[12] Above, note 4.

cery, he must have recovered a tolerable degree of prosperity. The statement that in his later life Winstanley became a Quaker has no evidence to support it.[13] His mysticism did not come into being as a compensation for the failure of his political and social projects, as has sometimes been imagined. In the seventeenth century any kind of political radicalism was far more likely to begin in religious non-conformity. This was certainly the case with Winstanley. The best Quaker historians find no evidence of any external relationship or interchange between Winstanley and the Quakers, despite the close similarity of his religious experience to that of George Fox and the first generation of the Friends.[14] Such experiences existed far and wide in seventeenth-century England. They were spread largely by sermons, either heard or read, and by conversation and discussion. Even a very high degree of similarity carries no implication of direct influence.

WINSTANLEY'S COMMUNIST SOCIETY AT COBHAM

On the first day of April, 1649, a little band of some half dozen poor men, all resident either at Cobham or Walton-upon-Thames, appeared upon the common land at St. George's Hill and began to dig the ground and to prepare it for sowing parsnips, carrots, and beans. The Hill lies to the south of the Thames in Surrey, some seven or eight miles southwest from Kingston, and the line dividing the parishes of Walton and Cobham crosses it. Today it is the site of a prosperous suburban real-estate development, well grown with trees, but in 1649 it was an unenclosed and rather barren heath. The leaders of the movement were Gerrard Winstanley and William Everard. They continued their work on the days following, inviting all and sundry to join them in their new venture, which was nothing less than a design to cultivate the common land for the support of the needy. The plan had been announced some two months before, at the end of January, in Winstanley's little book entitled *The New Law of Righteousnes*, in which he had set forth the command, re-

---

[13] It was a speculation by Eduard Bernstein and G. P. Gooch, based upon the erroneous date assigned in the catalogue of the Thomason Library to *The Saints Paradice*. Bernstein, *Cromwell and Communism*, Engl. trans., London, 1930, p. 132; Gooch, *English Democratic Ideas in the Seventeenth Century*, second edition, p. 190.

[14] Rufus M. Jones, *Studies in Mystical Religion*, London, 1909, p. 494.

ceived in a trance, to "work together; eat bread together". In it he
had stated his intention to carry the command into action, "when
the Lord doth show me the place and manner, how he will have us
that are called the common people, to manure and work the common
lands". Now, at the beginning of April, he had received the divine
mandate for which he was waiting, and with such followers as he
could find, amounting within a week or two to some twenty persons,
he had begun his mission.

The venture was less surprising than it seems in more settled
times, nor need one be greatly astonished that Winstanley's divine
commission, under the circumstances, should have taken the form it
did. In general his movement was an off-shoot of the great Leveller
agitation which had begun with the Putney debates in the Army
Council in the autumn of 1647, and which, after subsiding during the
Second Civil War, had flared up again shortly before the execution
of the King. In December, 1648, the Leveller leader, John Lilburne,
had tried to gain the cooperation of Ireton and the officers of the
Army in a revision of the Agreement of the People, and the negotiations had broken down after creating in Lilburne's mind a firm conviction that Ireton had duped him. Lilburne had dissociated himself
from the emasculated version (as he thought it) of the Agreement
which the Council of Officers presented to Parliament in January.
And on March 28, 1649, Lilburne and his associates, Walwyn, Prince,
and Overton, had been committed to the Tower for their angry
charges against the Council in the second part of *England's New
Chains*. In April events were shaping up for the Leveller rising in
the Army which finally ended at Burford on May 14.[1] The sense
of betrayal felt by the Levellers, and their distrust of the officers and
gentry, may be gauged from the pamphlet, *More Light Shining in
Buckingham-shire*,[2] which almost certainly reflects the atmosphere
of feeling to which Winstanley was exposed at this time. It is quite
true that his social philosophy was fundamentally different from that

---

[1] For an account of the Levellers between February and May, 1649, see S. R.
Gardiner, *The Commonwealth and Protectorate*, London, 1894, Vol. I, ch. 2. For
the period of the Putney debates, see A. S. P. Woodhouse, *Puritanism and Liberty*,
London, 1938, Introduction, Section II.

[2] Appendix, p. 627. Note also the sympathy expressed for the Diggers in the resolutions adopted at Aylesbury early in May, 1649, and printed at the end of *A Declaration of the Wel-affected*, Appendix, p. 646.

which prevailed among the Levellers, and also that Winstanley was aware of the difference. But in his own mind he distinguished himself as the "true leveller", the real disciple of Christ who was the "chief leveller". For Winstanley levelling meant nothing less than a complete reconstruction of society, not merely its political reform, and before all else the destruction of "the thieving art of buying and selling".

This economic turn in Winstanley's religious mysticism was not surprising in a man whose sympathies were deeply enlisted by the miseries and deprivations of the poor. The disorders of the Civil War had been a crushing burden upon English industry both in the country and the cities, and with the disorganization of business came widespread unemployment. The enclosure of common land to the detriment of the poor was a grievance commonly condemned by Leveller petitions in 1647 and 1648.[3] The news sheets published during 1649 contain accounts from many parts of England of conditions bordering on famine and pestilence. Winstanley's native Lancashire suffered very severely. More than once the Mayor and Aldermen in London tried to fix the price of bread. Throughout the years 1649 and 1650 the subject appeared repeatedly in Parliament, the misery and discontent among the poorer people being a manifest threat of disorder and rioting, not to say of insurrection. In March, 1649, the Common Council in London and the Justices of the Peace in the counties were ordered to prevent speculation in foods and to supply the poor with corn and coal. No fewer than four parliamentary committees that year were appointed to consider plans for "setting the poor on work".[4] Finally, in 1650, Parliament appropriated £1000 to the City for the relief and employment of the poor.

Under these circumstances it was natural that men should have conceived of the use of the common lands, and more especially of the church and crown lands that had been confiscated, as an additional source of supply. Nor was Winstanley the only person whose mind ran in that direction. Almost as he began his work at St. George's Hill that much-devising man, Peter Chamberlen, published

---

[3] See the documents reprinted by A. S. P. Woodhouse in *Puritanism and Liberty*, London, 1938, pp. 338, 339, 436. Cf. *More Light Shining in Buckingham-shire*, pp. 3, 10 (bracketed paging).

[4] *Commons Journal*, Vol. VI, pp. 137, 167, 201, 374, 416, 481.

a plan for turning the confiscated land into a "joint-stock" to benefit the poor and enrich the nation.[5] A wiser and a better man than Chamberlen, Samuel Hartlib, published and republished a pamphlet on the state of the poor and the possibility of increasing employment, during the year when Winstanley was trying to launch the communistic tilling of the common land.[6] Hartlib ended as follows:

> To conclude, for the better relief of the poor, it was well observed of one, who said that England had many hundreds of acres of waste and barren lands, and many thousands of idle hands; if both these might be improved, England by God's blessing would grow to be a richer nation than it is now by far.

It is not really surprising, then, that the inner light should have opened to Winstanley the vision of a society in which there should be no beggars, or that the utilization of available land for social purposes should have seemed to him to be the solution of the problem of poverty and unemployment.

The Digging at St. George's Hill met such a reception from the landowners and other people of the locality as might be expected. The Diggers were taken by the country-people and shut up in the church at Walton until they were released by a Justice of the Peace, and on another occasion a crowd of a hundred men carried them to Kingston, where they were again released. By twentieth-century standards the English Revolution was astonishingly mild and easygoing. After some two weeks, however, there was an effort to invoke other than the powers of local government. Under date of April 16, one Henry Sanders, of Walton-upon-Thames, lodged an information with the Council of State,[7] giving a rather alarmist account of the Diggers' intentions, which is not borne out either by the pacific tone of their pronouncements or by anything that happened later.

[5] *The Poore Mans Advocate, or Englands Samaritan*, dated April 3, 1649. There is an article on Chamberlen in *D.N.B.* He abounded in "projects", medical, religious, and social, and had the distinction of being a millenarian in 1654 and the King's physician after the Restoration.

[6] *London's Charitie stilling the Poore Orphan's Cry*, dated September 3, 1649; and *Londons Charity inlarged*, April 15, 1650. Hartlib was a German resident of London, a friend of Milton, and the author of many tracts on the improvement of education and of agriculture.

[7] Sanders's letter is printed in *The Clarke Papers*, Vol. II, pp. 210 f. It is reprinted by L. H. Berens, *The Digger Movement*, London, 1906, pp. 34 f.

Bradshaw, the President of the Council, forwarded Sanders's letter to Fairfax with a request that he send a force of horse to disperse the Diggers, lest a local disturbance become a cover for the activity of "a malignant and disaffected party".[8] At the same time the Council of State directed the Justices of the Peace near Cobham to proceed against the promoters of riotous meetings.[9] Fairfax did as he was asked, and under date of April 19, Captain John Gladman reported from Kingston that he had visited the Diggers and had found the business "not worth the writing nor yet taking notice of: I wonder the Council of State should be so abused with informations".[10] He stated also that Winstanley and Everard had agreed to report their doings and purposes to the General, and they did so at Whitehall on April 20.[11] On the same day the first of the Digger manifestoes was issued, with fifteen signers, *The True Levellers Standard Advanced*. This document clearly stated that they were acting on the authority of a revelation, that, of course, which Winstanley had reported in *The New Law of Righteousnes*.

These proceedings made a nine-days wonder and they were widely reported in the news sheets of the time, but for the most part the news writers appear to have known nothing beyond what was reported to the Council of State and what transpired at Whitehall when Winstanley and Everard visited Fairfax.[12] This interview must have been picturesque. Like the Quakers later, the two Diggers refused to remove their hats in the General's presence, "because he was but their fellow-creature". They proclaimed themselves to be "of the race of the Jews", that is, of the chosen people or saints, and said that they relied on God to make the barren land fruitful. Their pur-

[8] Bradshaw's letter also is printed in *The Clarke Papers*, Vol. II, pp. 209 f., and is reprinted by Berens, *op. cit.*, pp. 35 f. The matter is reported in Bulstrode Whitelocke's *Memorials* under date of April 17, 1649.

[9] *Calendar of State Papers*, Domestic, 1649–1650, p. 95.

[10] *The Clarke Papers*, Vol. II, pp. 211 f., Berens, *op. cit.*, p. 36.

[11] The interview is reported at length in Whitelocke's *Memorials* under date of April 20, but Whitelocke copied his account almost *verbatim* from a pamphlet entitled *The Declaration and Standard of the Levellers of England delivered in a Speech* . . . *by Mr. Everard*, London, Imprinted for G. Laurenson, April 23, 1649. Reprinted by Berens, *op. cit.*, pp. 37 f.

[12] The most circumstantial account, which seems to depend on an eye-witness from Surrey, is in *The Kingdoms Faithfull and Impartiall Scout*, April 20–27. One gathers that the Diggers were repeatedly driven off by the country-people and as repeatedly came back to their work again.

pose, they said, was to remove the worse than Egyptian bondage imposed on England by the Norman yoke and to restore the ancient community of enjoying the fruits of the earth, without however breaking enclosures or meddling with private property. It is clear from these early accounts that at the start William Everard, rather than Winstanley, was regarded as the leading spirit in the movement. Everard was definitely "queer". Gladman in his report to Fairfax had described him as "no other than a mad man". From the address to *Truth Lifting up its Head above Scandals* it is apparent that Everard and Winstanley had religious associations that preceded their plan for a communistic society.[13] Though Everard's name appears first among the signers of *The True Levellers Standard Advanced*, he does not appear among those who signed the second manifesto, the *Declaration from the Poor Oppressed People of England*, in June, or at any time thereafter. In the news sheets for May it was repeatedly stated that he had joined the mutinous regiments near Oxford, which were defeated at Burford on May 14.[14] Whatever became of Everard, there is practically no doubt that the ideas and the leadership of the communistic movement belonged wholly to Gerrard Winstanley.

The next information about the communistic colony in Surrey comes at the end of May, when Lord Fairfax, returning to London from Guildford, stopped at St. George's Hill to see and talk to the Diggers.[15] There were then twelve men at work and some barley was sprouting, though some of the crops had been trampled by the country-people. It seems pretty clear that Fairfax was loath to bring the Army into a matter which he rightly regarded as belonging to the civil authorities. Early in June some of the soldiers quartered at Walton joined the local people in a raid on the Diggers, and on the ninth, Winstanley handed to the General the *Letter to the Lord Fairfax* complaining of this ill-treatment. Apparently Fairfax prom-

---

[13] See the note on Everard below, p. 103.

[14] For example, *Mercurius Brittanicus*, May 8–15; *The Kingdoms Faithfull and Impartiall Scout*, May 10. Since, however, he is sometimes called "Captain" Everard, there may be a confusion of identities.

[15] This interview was reported in a news sheet entitled *The Speeches of the Lord Generall Fairfax . . . to the Diggers at St. Georges Hill*, May 31, 1649. In fact, only one page refers to this subject. The interview is mentioned in several other news sheets.

ised that the soldiers should keep hands off, for in the letter which
Winstanley wrote the following December, he says that the soldiers
had not molested the Diggers for a half year past. In the meantime,
however, the relations of the communist colony to the local landowners were growing more strained. On June 1 the Diggers issued their
second manifesto, *A Declaration from the Poor Oppressed People
of England*. The number of signers has now risen from fifteen to
forty-five. They assert that they mean to cut and sell the wood on
the common to finance their work, and they give notice that they will
prevent the landlords from cutting the wood.[16] A few days later the
local owners retaliated with a piece of organized hooliganism, which
the Diggers reported in *A Declaration of the Bloudie and Unchristian Acting of William Star and John Taylor*. For obvious reasons
the threat to take the landlords' rights of commonage was regarded
as more serious than merely digging up an acre or two of heath,
which probably had no value for purposes of cultivation.

With affairs in this somewhat threatening posture, the more responsible of the local landlords decided to substitute legal duress
for the more dangerous methods of the mob. On June 23 four suits
asking damages for trespass were begun against the Diggers in the
Court of Record at Kingston, which by the Charter of the Borough
had jurisdiction in the Hundreds of Elmbridge, Copthorne, and Effingham, west of the town. Winstanley aired the grievance of these
suits in July and August, in *An Appeal to the House of Commons*
and *A Watch-word to the City of London*, but since he complains
that he was never shown the declarations, it is likely that he did not
know exactly what the court's action had been. Some of his statements are not quite correct. However, the record is available,[17] and

---

[16] *Mercurius Republicus*, May 22–29, reports a near-riot in which the Diggers
were prevented from cutting wood, "the horses hurt and killed that were to draw
the same away".

[17] The suits are Nos. 159–162, entered on June 23, 1649, in the Court of Record
Book, now in the Guildhall at Kingston-upon-Thames; indexed as B. Judicial, I.
Court of Record Books, No. 10, 21 Charles I to 1658, in Surrey Record Society,
No. XXIX: *Borough Records*, by Miss D. L. Powell, p. 49. I am indebted to Miss
Powell, the Honorary Secretary of the Society, for a transcript of the record. No. 159
was against John Barker, Thomas Starre, and William *****ll (probably Hoggrill),
but Barker's name is stricken out; damages £4 and judgment on August 25 against
the manucaptor, since the defendants cannot be found. No. 160 is against Henry
Bickerstaffe, Edward Longhurst, and John Barker; damages £10 and judgment

by putting this with Winstanley's statements, a complete picture of what happened can be pieced together. The suits were brought by Thomas, Lord Wenman, Sir Ralph Verney, and Richard Winwood, who must for some reason have been in legal possession of the Manor of Walton; the property belonged to Francis Drake,[18] whom Winstanley clearly regarded as responsible for the suits. Winstanley persistently refused to employ a lawyer, a stand which he doubtless took on principle, as he refused to remove his hat before Fairfax, and as the Quakers refused to take an oath. The statement which he offered to the court (later printed in *A Watch-word*) was a pamphlet rather than a proper pleading, and the court naturally refused to accept it. His non-appearance was technical, since he says that in fact he went to court on three days. The court accordingly gave damages in the sum of £10, with plaintiffs' costs of 29s. 1d. The cows which he was pasturing were taken in execution, but had to be released because they were not his property. Winstanley boasts that he never satisfied the judgment. It is pretty obvious from his account of the affair that the purpose of the suits was not to recover damages but to harass the Diggers and break up their community.

Whether because of these suits or for some other reason, the Diggers in the autumn left their first situation on Francis Drake's land and moved over into Cobham Manor, which was the property of John Platt [19] (or his wife), the rector at West Horsley. The crops planted in the spring had been destroyed but the Diggers planned to prepare the land and plant a crop of winter grain, and they had built four houses. From this time forward Platt appears in Winstanley's writings as his chief opponent. Evidently the state of affairs became more troubled. On October 10 the Council of State, on information of a tumultuous meeting at Cobham, again directed Fairfax to send troops to support the Justices of the Peace.[20] The news

---

against the manucaptor, who produced Bickerstaffe and had him committed to prison in execution for damages. No. 161 is against Henry Barton, Samuel Webb, and Abraham Pennard *alias* Goodgroome; no further action on this suit. No. 162 is against Winstanley; he is recorded as not appearing and was given a day successively on July 7, 14, and 21. A jury assessed damages of £10 and costs on July 28, and a writ of execution issued on August 11.

[18] See the note on these men below, p. 319.

[19] See the note on Platt below, p. 346.

[20] *Calendar of State Papers*, Domestic, 1649–1650, p. 335.

sheets report a petty riot, in which about fifty Diggers refused to disperse at the command of the Justices of the Peace, and state that they are to be indicted at the next Quarter Sessions.[21] Platt, so Winstanley says, spent two weeks at Army Headquarters trying to persuade Fairfax to send soldiers to Cobham, which he finally did, but ordered them merely to support the sheriff. About the end of November, however, some of the soldiers joined with the gentry in destroying two houses that the Diggers had built, and this occasioned the letters of protest that were sent to Fairfax in December. At this time also Winstanley again went to Whitehall to see Fairfax. On the first of January he published his *New-Yeers Gift for the Parliament and Armie*, which reviews the efforts made during the preceding months to disperse the Diggers and includes also some of his most vigorous statements of his religious communism.

> This great Leveller, Christ our king of righteousness in us, shall cause men to beat their swords into plowshares and spears into pruning hooks, and nations shall learn war no more, and everyone shall delight to let each other enjoy the pleasures of the earth, and shall hold each other no more in bondage. Then what will become of your power? Truly he must be cast out for a murtherer and I pity you for the torment your spirit must go through, if you be not forearmed, as you are abundantly forewarned from all places; but I look upon you as part of the creation who must be restored, and the spirit may give you wisdom to foresee a danger, as he hath admonished divers of your rank already to leave those high places and to lie quiet and wait for the breaking forth of the powerful day of the Lord. Farewell, once more. Let Israel go free.[22]

Winstanley himself had achieved the serenity of waiting upon the Lord, which was a characteristic part of his religion: "I have writ; I have acted; I have peace."

In the meantime the Diggers had pushed forward their work with remarkable vigor, intending that the spring of 1650 should see the first achievement of their communal cultivation of the common land. Writing in April Winstanley says that they had eleven acres of grain

---

[21] *A Brief Relation*, October 16; *Mercurius Elencticus*, October 15–22.
[22] *New-Yeers Gift*, p. 43 (bracketed paging).

growing and had built six or seven houses. On the whole it seems pretty clear that, as a consequence of Winstanley's determination and enthusiasm, the communist society at Cobham accomplished more than the historians have usually implied.[23] They were encouraged that spring by a similar venture in Northamptonshire [24] and another, as they say, in Kent. At the end of March they issued a new manifesto, *An Appeale to all Englishmen,* which bore twenty-five signatures, and they circulated an appeal for funds among their sympathizers in the surrounding country. At the same time, however, their local opponents, led by John Platt, became correspondingly active. They turned the cattle into the growing grain, and with a good deal of brutality, it seems, they destroyed the houses and turned the Diggers, women and children, out upon the heath. Winstanley's last argument, which is really an admission of defeat, was published on April 9, 1650: *An Humble Request.*

At some time which I have not been able to determine, the threat of the preceding autumn to take criminal proceedings against the Diggers was carried into effect. At the Public Record Office there is an indictment, endorsed *billa vera,* against Winstanley and fourteen other Diggers for disorderly and unlawful assembly, reciting that on April 1, 1649, being so assembled, "ad tunc et ibidem apud Cobham praedictam in comitatu praedicto terram ibidem vi et armis, etc., riotose routose et illicite effodierunt, anglice did digge up." [25] Unfortunately, apart from the indictments, there are no other records of Surrey Assizes extant for this date; [26] consequently it is not possible to say what further action was taken, but the return of a true bill is *prima facie* evidence that a prosecution followed. The bundle in which the indictment occurs is endorsed "Winter Sessions, 1649 and 1651", which suggests that the indictment was probably returned

[23] S. R. Gardiner, *The Commonwealth and Protectorate,* London, 1894, Vol. I, pp. 48 f.

[24] Appendix, p. 649.

[25] Assizes: Home Circuit, File 35, Bdle 90. Those named in the indictment, besides Winstanley, are Henry Barton, Thomas Starr, John Heyman, William Everard, John Palmer, James Hall, William Comes, Adam Knight, Thomas Edsaw (Edcer), Richard Goodgreene (Goodgroome), Henry Bickerstaffe, Richard Medley (Maidley), William Boggerell (Hoggrill), and Edward Longhurst.

[26] Guide to Archives and other Collections of Documents relating to Surrey: *The Public Record Office.* By M. S. Guiseppi. Surrey Record Society, No. XXIV, pp. Aa 59 f.

in January, 1650. Winstanley, however, never refers to it, which is surprising if it occurred before the writing of the *Humble Request*, in view of the publicity he gave to the civil suits of the preceding summer. Apart from the date endorsed on the bundle of indictments, I should have been inclined to infer that the Diggers were indicted at the Easter Quarter Sessions in 1650. If so, this was the last step in the dissolution of the communistic society at Cobham and the conclusion of Winstanley's effort to cultivate the common land.

WINSTANLEY'S ANTECEDENTS AND CONNECTIONS

Winstanley asserted repeatedly that he derived his beliefs from no man and from no book. It is obvious that this cannot be literally true, but it is certain that Winstanley was quite sincere in saying it. As has already been said, he was subject to flashes of insight which he attributed to an inner Light or a divine voice and his communistic experiment was directly induced by such an experience. In his writings he never cites any book but the Bible, and he never mentions any person, except William Everard, with whom he had been associated. It is therefore quite impossible to trace specific influences which contributed to his religious convictions or formed the antecedents of his communism. Winstanley was no scholar and probably had little occasion to be critical about the origin of his ideas; I should infer that he was a less bookish man even than the great Leveller agitator, John Lilburne, who improved his terms in prison with a considerable amount of reading. Like the early Quakers, to whom of all his contemporaries he was intellectually most akin, he combined a great amount of energy and determination in action with a highly developed power of introspection and of religious contemplation. It is almost certainly the case that he absorbed his ideas largely from sermons—that enormously powerful agency of Puritan publicity [1]— from the "prophesying" of laymen in the conventicles, and from private discussion and conversation. Hence it was easy for him to imagine that his thought was spontaneous.

This characteristic of indefiniteness and lack of personal attachment is typical of English thought in the mid part of the seventeenth century, perhaps most typical of all of the decade of the 1640's. The

---

[1] This phase of the period has been well presented by William Haller in his *Rise of Puritanism*, New York, 1938.

Puritanism of Thomas Cartwright and his successors at the close of
the sixteenth century is individual and easy to identify. The same is
true of strains of continental thought more akin to Winstanley: the
mysticism of Jakob Boehme or the religious individualism of Acontio,
which in the earlier part of the seventeenth century can be safely
attributed to those men or a few disciples influenced by them. In
respect to this kind of ideas, however, the seventeenth century was
very definitely a period of popularization. The pulpit and a popular
press of astonishing productivity, at least in comparison with any preceding age, rapidly spread both religious and political thought to a
multitude of obscure and uneducated men. And as the ideas traveled,
their individuality was worn off; by 1648 it is practically impossible
to tell where any popular writer got his ideas, unless he provides the
autobiographical clues, and even then it is not certain that he knows.
On the other hand, the 1640's are too early for any organization of
the religious denominations that lay to the left of Independency.
Nothing is harder than to tell what a writer like Thomas Edwards
meant by words like Anabaptist, Antinomian, Familist, or Ranter, and
while he probably took little enough trouble to find out what the
persons that he vilified really believed, the task was not too easy. In
the less stable denominations there were as yet no standards for
membership and no general organization. The history of congregations is a story of continuous division, and occasionally of recombina-
tion of the parts, largely according to the personal influence of individual preachers. All sorts of religious sects multiplied amazingly
after about 1645. Even the Baptists had no national organization
until the 1650's, though several congregations joined in adopting a
confession of faith in 1644. The Quakers had no effective national
organization until after 1660. To ask where Winstanley "belonged"
in 1648 in respect to religious affiliation is therefore meaningless;
there was not as yet any place where he could belong.

Nevertheless, Winstanley certainly did not stand alone. It is quite
possible to trace similarities, though not influences, between him and
certain religious currents of the time, though no one except Winstanley made religion the occasion for a communistic theory of society. As was said above, Winstanley had at some time been allied
with a Baptist congregation, though he had abandoned the connection before 1648. In substantial respects, however, he continued to

hold convictions in common with the Baptists. One of these was his frequently stated belief in toleration and a rooted objection to any interference by magistrates with freedom of religious belief or practice. The Baptists supported this position far more consistently than the Independents, who were the only other religious body of the time that supported it at all. Their conception of the church was out-and-out separatist, "a company of visible saints, called and separated from the world by the word and Spirit of God".[2] The belief that every Christian must be consciously "called" and separated from the world by a personal experience was the ground for the belief in adult baptism. This emphasis upon what Winstanley called "experimental" religion was the reason why the Baptist congregations were a chief recruiting ground of those who, like himself, came to regard the experience as all in all, superseding both organization and the practice of fixed religious rites. The Baptists themselves condemned in 1650 precisely the tendency illustrated by Winstanley, to regard Scriptural history as "but a letter" and the ordinances as "but fleshly forms", and to replace them with "a God within, and a Christ within, and a word within".[3] For the Baptists, though they required few ceremonies, were as tenacious of those they did require as any other religious denomination, and despite their emphasis on experience, they did not as a rule depart from the rigid acceptance of Scriptural authority which was characteristic of other Puritans. Most of them were Calvinist in their theology, though there were General Baptist congregations that denied particular election. It is not difficult to see, then, why for Winstanley his Baptist connection was only a temporary halt on the road to a religion without forms and without dogmas. As Robert Baillie said, instancing Roger Williams and John Saltmarsh, "Very many of the Anabaptists are now turned Seekers, denying the truth of any church upon earth for many ages past . . . any Church discipline at all, or any Church act, Church state, or Church ordinance whatsoever."[4]

The respect in which Winstanley probably owed most to his Baptist antecedents, however, was his belief that the restoration and ref-

[2] Baptist Confession of 1644, Section 33; E. B. Underhill, *Confessions of Faith and other Public Documents illustrative of the History of the Baptist Churches of England*, London, 1854, p. 39.

[3] *Heart-Bleedings for Professors Abominations*; Underhill, *op. cit.*, p. 295.

[4] *Anabaptism*, London, 1647, pp. 96 f.

ormation of religion depend upon the poor and the unlearned, the condemned and ridiculed, "the despised sons and daughters of Zion", in whom the Spirit is rising up. This idea recurs repeatedly in Winstanley's religious tracts and it may very well have led him to the belief that social regeneration would come by the communistic association of the poor laborers and landless peasants. "You are the despised ones of the world, yet the blessing is in you and shall spread forth to fill the world." These are the words with which he prefaced the revelation of his communism in *The New Law of Righteousnes*. A similar idea, though quite without reference to communism or any social project, occurs in Baptist writers and in others akin to the Baptists.

> The voice of Jesus Christ reigning in his Church comes first from the multitude . . . God uses the common people and the multitude to proclaim that the Lord God Omnipotent reigneth. As when Christ came at first the poor received the Gospel . . . so in the reformation of religion . . . it was the common people that first came to look after Christ. . . . You that are of the meaner rank, common people, be not discouraged; for God intends to make use of the common people in the great work of proclaiming the kingdom of his Son. . . . The voice that will come of Christ's reigning is like to begin from those that are the multitude, that are so contemptible, especially in the eyes and account of Antichrist's spirits and prelacy: the vulgar multitude, the common people—what more condemned in their mouths than they? [5]

This is the form in which class-feeling became most definitely conscious in the seventeenth century. In the 1640's the Baptists as a group were certainly constituted mostly from the poorer part of the urban tradesmen and workers. They were looked down upon for that reason, and very naturally they retorted by trying to change a badge of contempt into a mark of honor. The Baptist clergy was generally

---

[5] *A Glimpse of Sions Glory*, London, 1641; reprinted in A. S. P. Woodhouse, *Puritanism and Liberty*, London, 1938, p. 234. William Haller attributes the pamphlet to the Baptist clergyman Hanserd Knollys; *The Rise of Puritanism*, New York, 1938, p. 270. Cf. the similar idea in John Goodwin's *Anti-Cavalierisme*, 1642; quoted by J. W. Allen, *English Political Thought, 1603–1660*, Vol. I, London, 1938, p. 476. Goodwin was not a Baptist but like them he became an extreme Separatist.

reproached by Episcopalians, Presbyterians, and Independents alike as unlearned and uncouth, "mechanick preachers". The Baptists in turn condemned the established clergy as tithe-takers who preach for lucre. They often made a virtue of leaving their clergy to support themselves by a trade, and they regularly opened their meetings to the "prophesying" of any layman who was moved to speak, not excluding women. They deliberately defended the right of the un-ordained to preach, if they were "gifted and enobled by the Spirit", a practice which Parliament tried repeatedly and unsuccessfully to suppress. Winstanley shared with the Baptists, and perhaps first got from them, his detestation of those who make a trade of preaching. With this went what Robert Baillie called "their declared rage against universities and all societies of learning", of course as training schools for the clergy, which also appears to the full in Winstanley. It is difficult to imagine where, in the seventeenth century, he could more readily have found the rudiments of a sense of class-antagonism than in the left wing religious groups, though the Baptists as a class (apart from those who joined the Fifth Monarchy movement) had no radical views whatever, either about government or property.[6]

When Winstanley first appears in print, in his *Mysterie of God*, it is to defend the heresy of universalism, the belief that in the end even the damned shall be rescued from hell by the mercy of God. Perhaps it is not altogether fanciful to connect this belief also with a kind of religious sentimentalism that grew out of the agitation of the masses. In the seventeenth century it never arrived at any kind of denominational organization, and consequently it does not relate Winstanley to any group that can be identified. The belief recurred sporadically in the decade before 1650 but with sufficient frequency so that teaching "that all men shall be saved" was made actionable by the Ordinance for the Punishing of Blasphemies and Heresies.[7] It was mentioned several times by Thomas Edwards in his list of

[6] They were accused of harboring subversive ideas often enough to have defended themselves against the charge. *A Declaration by Congregational Societies in and about the City of London, as well of those Commonly called Anabaptists as others*, London, 1647; reprinted in E. B. Underhill, *op. cit.*, p. 273. There are sections on liberty, magistracy, "propriety", and polygamy.

[7] The Bill was before Parliament for about a year and a half and was finally passed in 1648; see W. K. Jordan, *The Development of Religious Toleration in England, 1640-1660*, pp. 90 ff.

sectarian heresies.[8] The belief in universal salvation appears to have been only a passing phase of Winstanley's thought, because eschatology in any form quickly lost interest for him. Still, this particular belief was a consequence of two other ideas that formed a permanent part of his religious metaphysics. The first of these was the belief that the world is governed by the power of universal love; given this belief it is hard to think that any part of the creation can be irretrievably damned. The second is the belief that the unfolding of this cosmic power of love runs through a series of stages that end with universal salvation. Thus history is turned into a succession of revelations or manifestations of divine love which mark the rise of the soul toward God. This is an almost universal aspect of religious mysticism.[9] It was neither difficult nor illogical for Winstanley, in his *Mysterie of God*, to extend the plan by supposing a final stage beyond the last judgment, in which even the damned would be released out of hell. It grew from a conviction that no creature of God could be beyond the reach of the love of God. Only evil as such, "the Serpent", is ineradicably opposed to God and must therefore remain in hell forever.

It is perfectly apparent that at a critical point in the development of his religious thought Winstanley was powerfully affected by some form of religious mysticism. By mysticism in this connection is meant the belief that God manifests Himself to man by an inner Light or clairvoyance, transcending either sensuous or rational knowledge, and consequently with a certainty which transcends the authority either of Scripture or of the church. The revelations of the Light are conceived as an experience which each individual can and must enjoy for himself, the teaching of any other person being by comparison thin and insubstantial, a mere form of "hearsay". Such a belief had, of course, recurred again and again in the history of Christianity, and also in the history of Protestantism, though it was more akin to

---

[8] Edwards connected it with a pamphlet called *The Fulnesse of God's Love Manifested*, by L. S. (1643): *Gangraena*, Part I, p. 30; with one entitled *Divine Light Manifesting the Love of God unto the Whole World* (1646): *Gangraena*, Part III, pp. 10, 11, 13; and with John Saltmarsh's *Free Grace, or the Flowings of Christs Blood* (1645): *Gangraena*, Part II, p. 2. Richard Coppin published several pamphlets teaching this doctrine after 1649; see the article in *D.N.B.*

[9] The idea of a progressive revelation was elaborately developed by John Saltmarsh in his *Sparkles of Glory, or some Beams of the Morning Star*, London, 1647.

Lutheran than to Calvinist Protestantism. Since in the sixteenth and seventeenth centuries it was unthinkable that Protestant mystics should seek to recreate monastic institutions, there was a corresponding modification of the plan of mystical contemplation. The mystic remained in the world, though in thought he set himself apart from it. The mystical experience which is here in question had therefore a second property: it was not exclusively contemplative and it did not end primarily in a kind of esoteric knowledge. The inner light was conceived as a means of spiritual, and consequently of moral, regeneration, a source of Christian strength and of righteous living which flowed continually and which the illuminated man tapped again and again in the midst of his quite ordinary pursuits. With the light, therefore, it was common to contrast the dark, the flesh with the spirit, as two powers that contended continually for mastery, within man and indeed within all nature. Scriptural history, and even the whole outward form of nature, were often conceived as a type or a parable or a visible manifestation of the inward struggle between the regenerating power of spirit and the degenerating power of darkness and flesh. Mysticism as here used, therefore, had three properties: the consciousness of inner Light, its saving power against inner darkness, and the belief that every man reenacts in his own experience the cosmic drama in which the Light becomes victorious over darkness.

Certainly mysticism in this sense was involved in everything that Winstanley either said or did; it was for him the essence of religion and the root from which he consciously derived his communism. Precisely how he came in contact with this sort of religious faith cannot be determined, but there is in truth no mystery here, for there were plenty of sources open to him in England in the 1640's. In the case of George Fox, whose *Journal* is an infinitely fuller record of biographical detail than exists for Winstanley, the precise sources of his substantially similar mysticism are also undiscoverable. This type of religious faith was, to be sure, a minor phase of English Puritanism, kept in abeyance probably by the dominance of Calvinist rationalism, which was always unfriendly to any form of mystical experience. Nevertheless it had existed in England before Winstanley was born, and there is unquestionable evidence of its spread before and during the time at which his ideas were taking form. Since none of these possible sources can be certainly connected with Winstanley, there is no need to do more than refer to them, stressing the general features of their doctrine and passing over their individual differences.

In the sixteenth century the Netherlands had, of course, been a fertile seed-bed of mystical sects, and any number of Englishmen with strongly marked religious interests had lived there. One such sect, the Family of Love, founded by Henry Niclaes, or Nicholas, was transplanted to England, where it existed sporadically in small religious communities throughout the seventeenth century. Very little is known about the English societies of the Family of Love, and that only in the distorted form reported by their enemies, but a number of Niclaes's works in English translation were reprinted beginning in 1646.[10] It is possibly significant that these translations, like several others of the works mentioned in the pages immediately following, were published by Giles Calvert, who was also Winstanley's publisher. Calvert was already notorious in 1646 as a sectary and a publisher of unlicensed books, and in the 1650's he became the chief publisher of Quaker books.[11] Historians of early Quakerism like Rufus M. Jones and W. C. Braithwaite believe that some relationship existed between Familist groups and groups that became Quaker, and possibly between the Familists and George Fox himself, though it is no longer possible to discover where the points of contact were.

The essence of the Familists' doctrine was the power of inward illumination: man deified and God hominified. By virtue of this inner light, they believed that it was possible for men to recover the original purity which Adam had before the Fall. According to report they were accustomed to share their property within the community. The illumination manifests itself in history in successive "breakings through" of the spirit. According to Robert Baillie they taught that the Scriptures are allegories, the ordinances of religion are "meat for

---

[10] An account of the Family of Love by Edmond Jessop, who had personal knowledge of the sect, is quoted in Champlin Burrage's *Early English Dissenters*, Cambridge, 1912, Vol. I, pp. 212 ff. There is a good account of Niclaes in R. M. Jones, *Studies in Mystical Religion*, London, 1909, ch. 18. On English translations of Niclaes's works see William Haller, *Tracts on Liberty in the Puritan Revolution*, New York, 1934, Vol. I, p. 43.

[11] Thomas Edwards, *Gangraena*, Part II, p. 9; Part III, p. 62. There is a short biography of Calvert in Henry R. Plomer, *Dictionary of Booksellers and Printers, 1641–1667*, p. 42.

babes", and the good and evil angels are merely good and bad impulses in the mind of man. Winstanley held all these beliefs, or at
least beliefs that a Presbyterian like Baillie would have thought in-
distinguishable from them. Baillie associated teaching of this sort
with Giles Randall, who "for some years has preached peaceably at
the Spittle, to as great a multitude of people as follows any Sectary
about the City".[12] There is not the least difficulty in supposing, therefore, that Winstanley heard this or other like preaching, as Professor
Haller believes to have been the case with William Walwyn.[13]

The works of Henry Niclaes were not the only books of mystical
religion which gained currency in England at this time. In 1645 the
much better known books of Jakob Boehme began to be published
in English translation.[14] An English version of *The Vision of God*,
by Nicholas of Cusa, was published in 1646, and of the *Theologia
Germanica* in 1648, under the auspices of the same Giles Randall
who has just been mentioned.[15] This translation of *The Vision of
God* appears to have been actually made by another popular clergyman of a few years before, John Everard, who had preached at St.
Martin's-in-the-Fields and later at Kensington, where he attracted
great audiences by his sermons. Everard, though himself a scholar and
apparently the intimate of well-to-do patrons, seems to have meant
his sermons to be attractive to the poor and humble. The editor of
his sermons says he was "familiar even with the meanest, and if willing to be taught he was as willing to instruct and teach them, and
they were upon this account more welcome to him than lords or
princes." [16] These sermons, which were not published until 1653,
were probably very influential in popularizing and publicizing the
ideas of continental mystics, such as Boehme and Sebastian Franck,

---

[12] *Anabaptism*, London, 1647, pp. 102 ff.

[13] *Tracts on Liberty*, Vol. I, p. 44. A tract entitled *The Power of Love*, published
in 1643, is a pretended Familist sermon which Professor Haller believes to have
been written by Walwyn; it is reprinted, *op. cit.*, Vol. II, p. 271. Walwyn was not
himself a Familist, or indeed a mystic of any kind, but was willing to turn sectarian
enthusiasm in the direction of social reform.

[14] R. M. Jones, *Spiritual Reformers in the Sixteenth and Seventeenth Centuries*,
London, 1914, ch. 12; there is a list of translations, p. 213, note.

[15] *Ibid.*, pp. 253 ff.

[16] *The Gospel-treasury Opened*, To the Reader. The editor was Rapha Harford.
I have used an edition published in London, 1679.

whose works had been until this time available in England only to scholars. Everard's editor describes his preaching in words that Winstanley would have been glad to apply to himself.

> He would often say that he desired and thirsted to be acquainted with men who had experience of Christ rather than men of notions or speculations, that desired to act more than to talk; and he did also in his public preaching often aver that, though they were never so mean, poor, and despised by the world, yet if they were but acquainted with such experimental truths as these, they were more welcome to him than so many princes and potentates.[17]

The central thought in Everard's sermons is the familiar idea of all mysticism: God in the whole creation and God in man.

> Never look nor never expect outwardly to find God, for God dwells within; nor expect not outwardly to hear God, for God dwells in his temple within; there he preacheth and there he teacheth.[18]

And Christ lives in every man, the "beggarly fellows" as well as the rich or the learned. Without denying the letter of Scripture, Everard still treats the Gospel story as an allegory whose mystical meaning is to be found in the inner experience of every man, "insomuch that whatever any man hath known in the letter and history of [Christ], that he knows the same within him, as truly done actually in his own soul as ever Christ did anything without him." [19] The Scripture is a type of the cosmic spiritual drama, and Christ and Satan, Heaven and Hell, are actually present in the soul.

> For there is no part of holy writ but is fulfilled always, in all times in every part thereof, either in every member of the church or in the enemies of the church at one time or other. Always the same things are in fulfilling, in doing, throughout all ages.[20]

---

[17] *Ibid.*, The Epistle Dedicatory.
[18] The Rending of the Vail; *ibid.*, Part I, p. 45.
[19] The Star in the East; *ibid.*, p. 67.
[20] The Dead and Killing Letter; *ibid.*, p. 358.

It was this sort of teaching in which literal-minded Calvinists saw the denial of Scripture, of religious ordinances, and of creeds. And in truth by implication they were denied. Under the stress of the Revolution Winstanley and his kind merely drew deductions that Everard a few years before had seen no occasion to draw.

There were at least two other influential clergymen who were famous in the 1640's as teachers of a mysticism akin to Everard's. These were John Saltmarsh and William Dell, whom Richard Baxter mentions as the two most influential preachers that he saw in Cromwell's Army.[21] What commended these men to Cromwell was chiefly their forthright stand in favor of religious toleration, and this position in turn depended partly upon the relatively small weight that they gave to the forms and ordinances of religion as compared with the inward experience. Saltmarsh's tract entitled *The Smoke in the Temple* (1646) dealt with possible means for reconciling the various English religious bodies (other than the Catholics and Episcopalians). His most significant work was called *Sparkles of Glory* (1647); both these books were published by Giles Calvert. *Sparkles of Glory* dealt with two current questions then receiving much attention in Parliament, the imposing of penalties to enforce conformity to Presbyterianism and the prevention of preaching by unordained laymen. Saltmarsh attacked Presbyterianism at its doctrinal center, the belief "that there is a very model [of belief and church government] in the letter of Scriptures to be discovered" and "that the setting up of such a form is an immediate way of fixing God and his Spirit upon it". The latter belief, he says, "is indeed a finer kind of idolatry, to conceive that God enters into outward things, and conveys his all glorious and Almighty Spirit by them, when as they are only signs, figures, and images of more spiritual things".[22] The substance of Saltmarsh's argument is the all-sufficiency of the "quickening Spirit" or inward revelation of God, which makes the true church consist in unity or incorporation with God. "The sons of men taken into this glory of the Son of God are that new or second creation, that New Jerusalem, which came down from God." [23] Hence all forms or

---

[21] *Reliquiae* (1696), pp. 56 f. There is a brief account of Saltmarsh and Dell in R. M. Jones, *Studies in Mystical Religion*, ch. 20.

[22] *Sparkles of Glory*, Address to the Reader.

[23] *Ibid.*, p. 10.

ordinances or even creeds have much less importance than Presbyterians, Independents, and Baptists attach to them. "All things in the visible churches of the nations were, and are, in the absence of the Spirit and of gifts, administered by arts and sciences and grammatical knowledge of tongues and languages." [24] Like Winstanley Saltmarsh pictures the whole history of religion as a contrast of flesh and spirit, the two Adams or two seeds, manifesting themselves primarily as the struggle of good and evil in man. Neither God nor the Devil is far away, either in space or time, but are omnipresent forces. The history of mankind is therefore a succession of "ministrations", or manifestations, which "types out" the experience of every Christian.

William Dell is best known for the strong stand which he took against the utility of university education as a way of training the clergy, this being the more remarkable since he was, between 1650 and 1660, the Master of Caius College, Cambridge. This matter will be referred to later in connection with Winstanley's ideas of education. Here it is important only to notice that this estimate of education was derived from the idea that a "spiritual" ministry, being dependent upon experience of the inward working and revelation of God, could not be supplied, or perhaps even fostered, by an education in languages, the arts and sciences, and divinity. This was a conclusion shared by Saltmarsh and indeed by all exponents of the inner light, and it affected profoundly Winstanley's ideas about the proper aim and content of public education. In general Dell's conception of religion was very like Saltmarsh's: since it depends upon a unique experience, forms and outward conformity are relatively insignificant. In 1646 he preached a sermon before the House of Commons on the reformation of the church, the gist of which is that civil authority, being necessarily confined in its action to that which concerns outward conduct, has nothing to do with true reform. "The reforming word is the word within us." In a pamphlet which he addressed to the House of Commons in 1649 [25] he further contrasted the true church

[24] *Ibid.*, p. 45.

[25] *Right Reformation, or the Reformation of the Church of the New Testament* (1646). *Select Works of William Dell*, London, 1773, p. 105. *The Way of True Peace and Unity in the True Church of Christ* (1649). *Works*, p. 145. This pamphlet is reprinted in A. S. P. Woodhouse, *Puritanism and Liberty*, p. 302. Both these works were originally published by Giles Calvert.

with any outward regulations either by Parliament or by ecclesiastical officers.

> The right church then is not the whole multitude of the people, whether good or bad, that join together in an outward form or way of worship. . . . But the church I speak of is the true church of the New Testament, which I say is not any outward or visible society, gathered together in the consent or use of outward things . . . but it is a spiritual and invisible fellowship, gathered in the unity of faith, hope, and love. . . . Wherefore it is wholly hid from carnal eyes, neither hath the world any knowledge or judgment of it.[26]

Within such a society there is absolute equality and no distinction of rank or power, a conception which in Winstanley's mind may well have germinated in the vision of a communistic society.

> In the kingdoms of men some have greater estates than others and are in higher honor and authority; and this breeds envy and emulation and strife and distance, etc., but in the Son's kingdom . . . all that are counted worthy to dwell therein do alike inherit all things.[27]

In Dell's opinion there is no reason why Christians should contend about forms, laws, or power; such matters, he thinks, may be left to each congregation to settle according to its own ideas. The distinction between clergy and laity ought to be laid aside. The only penalty which the church can inflict is to exclude the unworthy from its membership.

John Everard, Saltmarsh, and Dell were all scholars, bred at Cambridge in the academic tradition of the day, though their power lay in the influence of their preaching upon unlearned men. Winstanley had a meagre education, though he must have been a man of considerable intellectual power and of very great moral energy. In these respects he stood closest, as has already been said, to George Fox and the men who, under his leadership, became the first generation of Quakers. Fox's leadership, however, grew from the fact that

[26] *Works*, p. 157.
[27] *Works*, p. 177.

he found many persons like-minded with himself, not from the in-
doctrination of his followers.[28] For an understanding of Winstanley
this fact is important, since it shows that the sense of a spiritual illumination was a common experience in the later 1640's, shared by
many men of little learning and of humble position, and therefore
likely to be communicated in ways that can no longer be traced. Those
who gathered to the teaching of Fox were but a small part of those
whose religious experience was of this type. The writings of William
Dewsbury, James Nayler, Francis Howgill, and Edward Burrough
are filled with passages telling how "the Lord discovered to me the
deceits of all these men in England that were seeking the kingdom
of Heaven in outward observations". Any of these passages could be
transplanted into one of Winstanley's tracts without producing the
least sense of incongruity. In the case of these works there can be no
question of influence upon Winstanley, since they belong to the decade of the 1650's.[29] The resemblance, however, is astonishingly close
in respect of all the characteristics of the mystical experience here in
question. It is closest of all perhaps in the case of George Fox himself, whose sense of "Christ within", of worship as communion with
God, and of such communion as an inward source of serenity and
energy seems almost identical with Winstanley's conception of religion.[30] The substantial difference between the two men lay not at all
in their religious ideas, but in Fox's absorption in his mission and his
apparent indifference to the public questions that in 1649 were shaking the foundations of English society. Winstanley, on the other hand,
came to be dominated by his desire to create a social and economic
utopia out of the Revolution.

   In order to understand Winstanley, however, it is less important

---

   [28] There is, for example, a kind of spiritual autobiography in William Dewsbury's
Faithful Testimony, London, 1689, pp. 44–56, referring to experiences that occurred
as early as 1645.

   [29] It has sometimes been supposed that Winstanley influenced the early Quakers,
but the historians of the movement find no proof of it. See R. M. Jones, *Studies in
Mystical Religion*, p. 494. Nathaniel Stephens says that *The New Law of Righteousnes*
was still in circulation among mystical persons of his acquaintance in 1656. *A Plain
and Easie Calculation of the Name, Mark, and Number of the Name of the Beast*,
London, 1656, p. 267.

   [30] There is an excellent account of Fox's principles in R. M. Jones, *George Fox*,
London, 1930, ch. 5, or in W. C. Braithwaite, *The Beginnings of Quakerism*, London,
1912, chs. 2–4.

to emphasize differences between him and others of the group to which he belonged than to stress the fact that the group existed and that it differed in fundamental respects from the rest of what is loosely called Puritanism. Motivated as it was by religious mysticism, this group was different, and was profoundly conscious of being different, from Presbyterians, Independents, and even from most English Baptists. When they asserted the sufficiency of "experimental" religion, Winstanley, Fox, Saltmarsh, and Dell knew exactly what they meant to reject. The vain "imaginary knowledge" that Winstanley condemned, the "speculations" that Everard said led more to talk than to action, the "notions" which Quaker writers accused their opponents of purveying, "so as your pride, lust, riot, and oppression may be exalted",[31] were merely different names for that imposing edifice of Calvinist theology, which supplied the intellectual underpinning for all the other religious groups that lay to the left of the Episcopalians. Attempts to define Puritanism are not very profitable, and in actual usage the word now means practically nothing. In my judgment, however, no reasonable clarity can be attained unless a line is observed at least between mystics like Winstanley and the Quakers, and those who, like all Calvinists and nearly all Baptists, thought it essential to maintain a creed, a church discipline, and the outlines of rational theology. For Calvinism, whatever may now be thought of its premises, was in its method rationalistic; it was a lawyer-like analysis and interpretation of Scriptural texts, as if they were clauses in a charter. And this whole operation is exactly what the mystics rejected. It is quite true that all Christians have always admitted that religion ought to be personally experienced as well as rationally justified. The mystics, however, denied that any rational support was required for an experience which, in itself, was altogether self-authenticating. The effects of this denial were very profound, and, interestingly enough, they were far more destructive of clericalism, ecclesiasticism, dogmatism, and supernaturalism than any frontal attack on Calvinist theology could possibly have been in the seventeenth century. These effects will be traced in the exposition of Winstanley's religious argument for communism.

[31] James Nayler, *A Salutation to the Seed of God* (1655); *A Collection of Sundry Books*, etc., London, 1716, p. 243.

WINSTANLEY'S RELIGIOUS ARGUMENT

Winstanley nowhere set out in logical order an outline of the religious convictions which, as he believed, led inevitably to communism as their social corollary. This was in part due to the fact that his writings are pamphlets, written as occasion demanded, and in part to the fact that his convictions were in process of formation, not in the stage of being logically systematized. It is quite clear that he would have regarded this last stage, if he had reached it, as a mark of degeneration and not of progress. Winstanley's communism belonged to the class of prophetical writing, with no delusions about a "scientific" proof—the contemporary analogue would have been a theological proof—of the validity of human aspirations. Nevertheless, it is not difficult to arrange in a logical order the chief headings of his argument, which is in fact not very complicated. The propositions are repeated again and again throughout his works. After the revelation recorded in *The New Law of Righteousnes*, which turned his interest definitely toward the social implications of his religion, his train of thought is complete, though he varied the presentation of his case somewhat to adapt it to the audience he was addressing. *The Law of Freedom*, which was published a year and a half after the attempt to cultivate the common land had failed, is somewhat different from the works produced in the course of the controversy. Here Winstanley is trying to set out a rounded communist constitution that he hoped might commend itself to Cromwell. As his reliance on statesmanship has perforce grown, so his millenarian hopes have correspondingly shrunk. But even with this change of interest and purpose, there is no change of the convictions that lay behind Winstanley's communism.

The premise from which Winstanley's thought began, often stated but never argued, was his belief that the events of the Puritan Revolution were part of a tremendous change that was altering the whole status of human life. It is to be a real reformation, affecting to their roots all the relationships of men in society. As such it has a cosmic rather than a national significance, though it has the latter too. England, he hopes—speaking in the congenial chiliastic imagery of *Revelation* and the *Book of Daniel*—will be the tenth part of the city

Babylon that falls off first from the Beast. In the troubles that ac-
company and follow the Civil Wars, and more especially in the contempt and persecution visited upon the sectaries, he sees the rage of
the evil powers, in man and the world, against the power of spiritual
reformation, which in the end is certain to overcome them. The sectaries, therefore, have a quite extraordinary significance; the persecution of the "mechanick preachers" is part of the persecution which
the synagogue visited upon the equally humble disciples of Jesus, and
which the world, the flesh, and the devil always visit upon the saints.
The subtle craft, the unparalleled hypocrisy, and the cruelty expressed
against the saints (i.e., the sectaries) are an expression of the angels
of darkness let loose in the spirits of men. The bright appearing of
God in the saints, casting down all forms and customs of the beast
(i.e., religious law) is what torments the world today. For the saints
are about to partake of the glory of the city of God. The present is a
transitional stage—the dividing of time—between one cosmic era and
another, in which the rule of divine love will finally be consummated
on earth. Hence a true reformation concerns not the church alone
but will extend to government and all the social relationships on which
government depends. Magistrates will "love and delight to be exe-
cuting justice for the good and safety of the commonwealth". God
has cast England into the fire: hence the troubles of the times and
hence also the greatness of the triumph that awaits the spirit of love
and truth.

Winstanley's language, it should be observed, was more extraordinary than the idea he had to express. Millenarian hopes and imagery
are a normal accompaniment of every revolution. They are expressed
in the figures of speech which, in the circumstances, come easiest to
the pen—the New Jerusalem, democratic liberty and equality, or the
classless society. However expressed, they represent the religious
aspect of the revolution: the symbols that serve to release men's energies, that wear the guise of ultimate ends, and that always remove
farther into the future when one tries to approach them. In Puritan
England there was no effort to disguise the fact that these symbols
were religious, and their natural imagery came from the Bible. In
some degree most men, and by no means the most visionary, shared
ideas like those that Winstanley expressed. Cromwell's letters show

that he habitually regarded himself as acting under the guidance of God to accomplish the designs of Providence. In the course of the discussion in the Army Council with the Levellers he said:

> I am one of those whose heart God hath drawn out to wait for some extraordinary dispensations, according to those promises that he hath held forth of things to be accomplished in the later times, and I cannot but think that God is beginning of them.[1]

Milton's pamphlets, especially those on the reform of the church, include many passages holding out extravagant hopes of the regeneration, both of church and of government, that is impending in England. The Fifth Monarchy movement produced a great outcropping of works that set forth the chiliastic hopes from which that movement grew, though such ideas were not wanting at any time after 1642.[2] As usual it was the groups on the extreme left wing of the revolution that abounded most in millenarian expectations. In this respect, then, Winstanley was merely typical, both of his time and also of the place that he occupied in the Puritan Revolution.

It is characteristic of Winstanley, and also of others who were most given to these expectations, that they looked for the literal and, so to speak, the physical realization of the Kingdom of God on earth. It is a mere trick of self-seeking priests, he thought, to fob men off with hopes of a better life beyond the grave, or with "spiritual" meanings of Scriptural promises, instead of urging them to create the New Jerusalem here and now. Flesh judges it right that some should be poor and others rich and powerful, but in the light of equity and reason it is right that all should have freedom and subsistence. It dishonors the Maker that there should be oppressing tyrants, especially among Christians who make a verbal profession of love while in action they deny it. Fleshly dominion of one over all shall cease, and the eye of flesh shall see it. The visions of the Apocalypse thus become literal prophecies of that which is about to be. The saving distinction which Calvinists usually drew between the realms of nature and grace was quite obliterated. In 1647 the Baptist Thomas

---

[1] A. S. P. Woodhouse, *Puritanism and Liberty*, p. 103; *The Clarke Papers*, Vol. I, pp. 378 f.

[2] A number of typical passages are quoted by Louise F. Brown, *Baptists and Fifth Monarchy Men*, Washington, 1912, pp. 14 ff.

Collier preached a sermon at Army Headquarters which in part might have been uttered by Winstanley.

> It's true that we have had, and still have, exceeding low and carnal thoughts of heaven, looking on it as a glorious place above the firmament, out of sight, and not to be enjoyed till after this life. But God himself is the Saints' kingdom, their enjoyment, their glory. Where God is manifesting himself, there is his and the Saints' kingdom, and that is in the Saints.

In the new Heaven and the new earth that will thus arise, "The nations shall become the nations of Christ, and the government shall be in the hands of the saints." [3]

It was not the case, however, that Winstanley belonged with the Fifth Monarchy Men in the implications that he attached to a government in the hands of the saints. The rule of the saints became a synonym for government that was censorious, meddlesome, illiberal, and reactionary, devoted to establishing on earth not the kingdom of love but the dominance of a church, a dogma, and a discipline. This is the character that messianism in politics has always tended to assume, and the character that Puritanism often did assume. So far as can be judged of a man who never had to take the responsibility for any actual rule, Winstanley had no leanings whatever in this direction. In his *Law of Freedom* there is no suggestion that he wished to give the suffrage to the saints, meaning thereby persons of one religious profession as distinct from another. He was saved, I think, by the completeness with which he had broken away from any doctrinal or theological standard of religion. He believed, naively no doubt, that a life of Christian love was about to transform the whole economic and political organization of society, but he expected also a complete transformation of human nature. He did not believe that some, already in possession of the light, could force it on others. The all-sufficiency of the mystical experience, carried to its logical conclusion, destroyed church and clergy, and with them tests of orthodoxy and rationalized systems of the supernatural. The result, though it seems paradoxical, was something that might almost be described as secularism tinged with a religious motivation.

---

[3] The sermon is reprinted in A. S. P. Woodhouse's *Puritanism and Liberty*, Appendix, p. 390.

The second premise of Winstanley's religious argument, and the one which was central to all that he had to say, was his belief in the Light, or the Christ within—a divinely given insight or intuition working a moral reformation—as the essential part of religion. So much has already been said on this point that there is little need to add more; there is no limit to the number of citations that could be given from Winstanley's works, if there were any object in multiplying them. In contrast with "experimental" religion he places the "imaginary power"—parallel with John Everard's contrast of religious action with "notions and speculations"—by which Winstanley means school divinity, especially Calvinist theology, and all that he conceived to flow from it. There was of course nothing distinctive merely in the belief that religious experience is unique; Christians of every group agreed to that, and even a man so hard-headed as Ireton might assert that, "Everyone hath a spirit within him." But for Winstanley, and for the mystics and the Quakers, the experience becomes all in all. It supersedes the whole system of doctrine built up by inference from Scripture: the supposed truths of metaphysics and cosmology, the plan of church-government, and the ethical rules supposed to be demonstrable by piecing together Biblical texts. In a word it did away with all that made the clergy a learned profession, and Quakerism merely drew the logical conclusion when it abolished the distinction between clergy and laity. To this Winstanley added another inference when he argued that the abolition of the clergy implied also a thoroughgoing change in social organization. The "imaginary power", according to Winstanley, had four branches: the preaching "universative" power, the kingly power, the power of lawyers, and the art of buying and selling. Of these the clergy is the chief, and all fall if it falls. The universal power of love which rules in the creation, if once it is given first place in human life, must reform all human relationships and hence both the economic and political organization of society.

If Winstanley had been a speculative metaphysician, he would have been a pantheist. Some such conception is characteristic of mysticism, which of necessity sets aside any such rigid conception of God's personality as is required by theism. God is an indwelling power in nature and in man. Winstanley, in the address which precedes *Truth Lifting up its Head*, expressly adopts the word "Reason" in place of God, because the latter suggests a being apart from nature and from man, a being whose action is imagined to be far away or long ago, rather than an omnipresent power whose action is immediately felt. It would certainly be an error to infer that this implied any rationalistic (in the sense of non-religious) intention on Winstanley's part. Reason is, for him, merely a neutral word for "the incomprehensible spirit" from which the creation flowed and which continually works in it, "that living power of light that is in all things". He often calls it also "universal love". It manifests itself in the unconscious teleology of all living things, but especially in man by leading him to govern his actions according to justice, wisdom, and righteousness; if reason rules in a man, he will never trespass against his fellow-creature. There was plenty of authority for such a use of the word in the mystical tradition which Winstanley somehow tapped. The opposite of reason for him is "imagination", the false idea of separateness from God and one's fellows, that issues in covetousness and self-seeking, and fills men with fears, doubts, wars, divisions, and lust. From imagination proceeds the letter that killeth; from reason or love proceeds the spirit that maketh alive.

The struggle between reason and imagination—the higher and the lower natures—which every man experiences in his own being, is but a part of the cosmic struggle between light and darkness, God and the Devil, that goes on continually in the world. This struggle, and the final victory of light, is a standard theme of mystical experience, as it is with Winstanley and George Fox and as it was with Jakob Boehme. To this way of thinking it is more than an analogy, for there is a literal identification of reason with God, and of evil inclinations with the devil. The cosmic drama is reenacted in every man and is continually repeated in human society. Both God and the devil are literally within the soul. Winstanley is quite explicit in saying that it was the discovery of this fact that first set him free from the fears and anxieties, the dread of the supernatural that had assailed him, which forms an almost normal antecedent to the state of mystical exaltation. It is accordingly characteristic of this conception that it pictures history as successive stages in the struggle, or as "risings-up" of the spirit against the flesh. Winstanley tries his hand more than once at periodizing history, especially the Scriptural story and the history of the church, in the light of this idea, as Saltmarsh had done in his *Sparkles of Glory* and as many others did. It ought to be noted that the idea behind this read-

ing of history is essentially millenarian. It in no way implies progress
or a gradual development but the contrary. The "outpourings" of
the spirit come when "the time has been fulfilled" and they invariably
lead up to a perfect stage in which the light will be fully triumphant,
a new heaven and a new earth.

In the case of Winstanley the identification of inner and outer, of
evil in man and evil in nature, was carried in his earlier pamphlets to
the most naive extreme. In *The New Law of Righteousnes* he supposed that the corruption of the flesh in evil men literally infected the
whole of nature. Their decaying bodies, after they were dead and
buried, corrupted the plants and through them imparted the poison
of evil to the beasts that fed upon the plants. The very elements, and
all bodies that are composed of them, are disordered by man's rejection of the spirit. In *The Mysterie of God* he supposed that when
the spirit recovers its sway in man, as he expects that it is about to do,
all the creatures other than man will be dissolved, since there will be
no further need for food. It seems pretty clear that this conception of
the close sympathetic relation between man and nature played a considerable part in the beginning of his communism. From the first of
the Digger manifestoes, *The True Levellers Standard Advanced*, it
appears that he confidently expected the reestablishing of the rule of
community and love among men to increase automatically the fertility
of the barren land. In fact, without such a belief, his communism was
hardly workable, since it implied that a large part of the English population would be fed from the produce of land that had not previously
been arable. This mystical element in Winstanley's thought had become less prominent when he wrote *The Law of Freedom;* in that work
he assumes the existence of a considerable amount of nationalized
land got from the confiscated estates of the King, the royalists, and
the clergy.

In Winstanley's rather simple-minded metaphysics, then, the visible world is quite literally the garment of God, and God is the moving
spirit in the world, manifested in the sun, moon, and stars, in plants and
animals, but especially in human history. This universal power is present in every man and is able completely to transform human nature.
All that is required is that men should be aware, directly and immediately, of the light that is within them and, being aware, should follow
its dictates. This for Winstanley is the essence of all religion, its only

necessary condition and its all-sufficient condition. It is, however, not an easy condition, for not only the temptations of the flesh but also the forms and outward observances that imagination creates stand between men and the direct apprehension of truth and righteousness. It does not appear that Winstanley thought of this experience as a transcendent vision, momentarily attained, which sometimes lifts the mystic into another world. Like the Quakers he thought of it rather as an experience repeatedly enjoyed and continuously affording strength and guidance in quite everyday affairs. The beginning of religion is the knowledge that there is within one the capacity for such experience and guidance; the practice of religion consists in having habitual recourse to it, and everything else belongs among things indifferent.

> When men suck content from creatures, as from men's learning, gifts, customs, prayers, or forms of worship, and think they shall never have comfort unless they enjoy these outward helps, this is to prefer the broken cisterns before the fountains. . . . He cannot meditate nor understand till God come into him; he cannot speak till God give utterance; he feels his heart barren of understanding, of love, of peace; he feels and sees nothing in him but only a thirsting soul after God, whom his secret thoughts tell him is able to satisfy him, if he please but to manifest himself. . . . The experience and writings of prophets, apostles, and saints are dry shells to me and cannot comfort, unless God, whom my soul breathes after, give to me likewise some experiences of his love, as he gave to them, and then I shall have joy; yea, and my joy then will be fulfilled, and not till then.[4]

All Winstanley's reflection upon the religious and social problems of his day, which eventuated in his communism, was little more than an effort to carry through, relentlessly and to their final conclusions, the implications of this fundamental insight. These implications were devastating for all existing forms of faith and ecclesiastical institution, and also, as he came to believe, for all existing political and economic institutions, since he supposed that the latter must stand or fall with the former. In truth, his procedure, though simple-minded and without much grasp of the complexities of the phenomena he was trying to deal with, was surprisingly logical and thorough-going. Without

---

[4] *The Breaking of the Day of God*, 1648, pp. 51 f.

trying to reproduce the many repetitions and digressions into which he fell, I shall summarize his chief deductions relative to the authority of Scripture, the nature of the church, and the position of the clergy.

Winstanley's belief in the sufficiency of an experimental religion, consistently carried out, made a clean sweep of the mythology of the Christian tradition, and more particularly of Protestant bibliolatry. By placing the whole religious drama within the setting of the human mind, the mystics quite destroyed the external or, so to speak, the physical existence of those entities upon which all doctrinal forms of Christianity depended. Christ and the Devil, Winstanley says over and over again, are not forces outside human nature; they are the impulsions and inclinations, respectively, of good and evil—the flesh and the spirit—which every man experiences as the controlling motives of his own action. The Devil is not "a middle power between God and me, but it is the power of my proud flesh". And "the power of the perfect law taking hold thereupon threw me under sorrow and sealed up my misery, and this is utter darkness".[5] Heaven and hell are therefore literally within the soul, not places far off. Similarly, Christ is the regenerating power of goodness within every man, not the historical character who lived long ago in Palestine.

> And therefore if you expect or look for the resurrection of Jesus Christ, you must know that the spirit within the flesh is the Jesus Christ, and you must see, feel, and know from himself his own resurrection within you, if you expect life and peace by him.[6]
>
> So that you do not look for a God now, as formerly you did, to be [in] a place of glory beyond the sun, moon, and stars, nor imagine a divine being you know not where, but you see him ruling within you, and not only in you, but you see him to be the spirit and power that dwells in every man and woman; yea, in every creature, according to his orb, within the globe of the creation.[7]

In the second place, the belief in the all-sufficiency of direct experience destroyed the importance of a literal interpretation of Scripture. For Winstanley Scripture was valuable as a record of experiences enjoyed

[5] *The Saints Paradice* (edition of 85 pp.), pp. 21–23.
[6] *Ibid.*, p. 54.
[7] *Ibid.*, pp. 55 f.

by spiritually minded men in other times and places. To the Scripture stories, such for example as the story of the Gadarine swine, he attached, especially in his earlier writings, a considerable symbolic importance as typifying spiritual truths. After the first two or three of his pamphlets, his inclination to look for far-fetched symbolic meanings in them seems to have decreased, and at no time did he attach much importance to their literal truth. More and more he reserved elaborate citations of Scriptural authority for arguments addressed to those who presumably regarded this as an effective kind of proof, such as the paper addressed to John Platt which he inserted in *An Humble Request*. In order to be rightly interpreted or even recognized it requires the same kind of immediate experience that enabled its authors to write it. It is at the most an aid, not a substitute, and Winstanley clearly looked forward to a time when "none shall need to turn over books and writings to get knowledge". This distinction between the "experimental" knowledge of religion and "hearsay" knowledge from reading or from hearing a teacher was made habitually by George Fox.

> I told him [Cromwell] that all Christendom (so-called) had the Scriptures, but they wanted the power and Spirit that those had who gave forth the Scriptures; and that was the reason they were not in fellowship with the Son, nor with the Father, nor with the Scriptures, nor with one another.[8]

This willingness to dispense with the literal interpretation of Scripture was enough by itself to put Winstanley outside the main intellectual current of Puritanism. Presbyterians, Independents, and Baptists differed from one another in the deductions, with reference either to doctrine or to church-government, which they drew from Scripture, but they were quite in agreement on two points, first, that Scripture contained, either directly or by implication, a complete body of doctrine and practice, and second, that no doctrine or practice was binding upon Christians unless it were justified by the authority of Scripture. The differences between these groups of Puritan Protestants, therefore, were in a sense intellectually superficial. They might have been healed by the development of a sufficiently complete and a sufficiently learned system of theological science, something that these bodies all professed to look forward to. The superiority of Calvinism over other forms of

[8] *Journal*, edited by R. M. Jones, Vol. I, p. 214.

Protestant theology lay in the fact that it went about as far as it was humanly possible to go in constructing this kind of system. On the other hand, the form of religious faith represented by Winstanley and the Quakers was a forthright challenge to the whole principle of Biblical theology. It flatly denied that there was any such system of learned doctrine, or that it would be significant if it could be constructed. The whole theological project ends in nothing except "imaginary, book-studying, university divinity", as Winstanley calls it, a mass of dark interpretations and glosses upon the Scriptural records of an experience which, taken by itself, is self-sufficient and self-explanatory.

The implications of this position for scholarship and for public education will have to be examined later in connection with Winstanley's views of such matters in his *Law of Freedom*. Here it is necessary only to refer briefly to its implications with reference to the church and the clergy. From Winstanley's point of view the true church is exclusively a spiritual body, the whole company of the saints who have experienced salvation and have been morally regenerated by the inward operation of reason or the law of righteousness. No outward organization is required, and it needs no visible marks or signs to distinguish it from the world. It has no doctrinal tests, and certainly no mandate from magistrates to teach any creed or apply any discipline. It requires no rites or ordinances or set forms of worship, and if any congregation uses such forms, they have at the most only a symbolic meaning which might equally well be expressed in other ways, or indeed might equally well remain without formal expression. Winstanley set forth most fully his views upon the ordinances of religion in *Truth Lifting up its Head above Scandals*, where he defended himself against the charge of denying such ordinances altogether. Here it seems apparent that he had dispensed with every form of religious service except the meeting and communion of like-minded persons, and perhaps the "prophesying" of those whom the spirit might move. He expressly denies that baptism, except in the mystical sense of baptism by the spirit, is essential. Preaching from texts or from "imaginary beliefs" is worse than useless. Prayer, if it is "a declaration of the heart", is permissible, but words are "the remotest part of prayer"; its essence consists in acting righteously and in the "reasonings of the heart", that is, in reflection and self-examination. The observance of set days, as of the Sabbath, is a formality, and the notion that a whole parish can be called a church is a grotesque misunderstanding of the term. These views are, of course, substantially identical with those of George Fox and with the practice of the Quakers. But Winstanley's emphasis is on the negations. I believe it to be true to say that he saw no need even for that minimum of organization by which Fox preserved the Quakers as a recognizable religious body.

From this view of the church it follows that the clergy, as a distinct class of professionally trained persons, simply disappears. There is no place for it, since every man must experience the revelation of the inner light for himself. Moreover, there is no secular training which appreciably contributes to the attainment of such an experience: it is *sui generis* and therefore quite different from any form of worldly skill or learning. Hence the conventional requirements for ordination, and the university training designed to fulfill those requirements, are of no value in preparing men to teach spiritual truths. Like the Baptists generally, Winstanley repeatedly insists that the founder of Christianity and his apostles were simple, uneducated men—fishermen, tentmakers, and publicans—unskilled in those arts and sciences which have become the mainstay of university education. In this he exactly agreed with William Dell, who said:

> It is one of the grossest errors that ever reigned under Antichrist's kingdom to affirm that universities are the fountain of ministers of the Gospel, which do only proceed out of Christ's flock.[9]

For Winstanley, what he calls the "preaching universative power" is not only an error; it is part of a general conspiracy by the "zealous professors" of organized religion to keep down those risings of the spirit in the poor and despised ones of the earth that threaten their titles and their special privileges. It would be quite impossible to exaggerate the violence of Winstanley's anti-clericalism. The "ecclesiastical bastardly power got in fornication with the kings of the earth" he sometimes describes as an invention of secular rulers to support their tyrannous power, but more often he represents kings themselves as the dupes of cunning priests. In *The Law of Freedom* he does not hesitate to classify the clergy with those who practice witchcraft.

Thus for Winstanley the church as an organization, the clergy as a

[9] *The Stumbling-Stone, wherein the University is Reproved,* 1653; *Christ's Spirit,* Germantown, Penna., 1760, p. 155.

distinct class, and theology as a learned profession all disappear before a conception of religion that strips it of all sacerdotal and institutional elements. By what may seem at first sight a paradox, the very universality of religious experience in the life of the saint gives to Winstanley's personal philosophy a tone of secularism. Religion has for him no necessary connotation of supernaturalism, though it depends throughout upon an idealist or spiritualist conception of nature and man. Even personal immortality has ceased to be a matter of moment to him. He obviously believed that nothing is known about it; he had become convinced, no doubt both by experience and observation, that the omnipresent fear of damnation among the Puritans was a fruitful source of mental disorder; he believed that the hope of heaven had been used with cynical premeditation to turn men's thoughts away from tyranny and exploitation and to prevent them from applying the suitable remedies in this world for their ills and wrongs. In short, religion was for him a way of life, not a ceremonial, a profession, or a metaphysic. And as a way of life, though it required a continuous recourse to mystical communion with God, it did not exclude the application of intelligence or science to any problem either of individual or of social life.

In concluding this section, it is necessary to say something about the ethical implications that Winstanley attached to his religious beliefs. This is difficult because Winstanley certainly would not have understood a distinction between religion and ethics nor the possibility of one without the other. On the other hand, he undoubtedly did believe that the differences between himself and other religious groups of his time had the most important ethical consequences. His communism was neither more nor less than the expression of that belief. There is nothing harder, however, than to say precisely how religious beliefs pass over into moral conduct, for the transition is not made by logic and often is not such as an outside observer would infer that it ought to be. Philosophers have said that Calvinist predestination ought to have sapped the sources of individual initiative and vigorous action, but anyone who has studied the seventeenth-century Calvinists knows that it had the opposite effect. Similarly, a mystic ought, by conventional standards, to be visionary and incompetent, but the Quakers certainly were far from that. Even in Winstanley's case, though his communistic society was visionary, it was no mean accomplishment under the circumstances to keep the experiment going for a year and to spread his case before the public as he did. In moral matters it is a kind of logic of the emotions that connects belief with action.

Winstanley's ethics, like that of the Quakers, had a quality which might be called, for want of better terms, quietism or pacificism. It does not appear that Winstanley was literally a pacifist, in the sense that he thought it wrong to bear arms. He was undoubtedly a pacifist, however, so far as concerned the realization of his communism. God, he says, puts no weapons into the hands of his saints to fight against reproaches, oppression, poverty, and temptation. The Levellers will not conquer by the sword, for Christ, who is the head Leveller, fights only with the sword of love, and this in the end will throw down all government and ministry that is lifted up by the imagination. In the end, Christ, the law of universal love, will reign, and this will be true magistracy, the light of truth, reason, humility, and peace. Like George Fox—and this was the root of Quaker pacificism—Winstanley distrusted the efficacy of force to accomplish any permanent moral results, and this was altogether in accord with the belief that morality begins with a change of heart. Hence the root of moral regeneration is a kind of passivity, submissiveness to the better impulse that will rise if it be given the chance, a silence and a waiting until the wiser thought and action ripens.

> Tell a man that he hath no knowledge and no faith of God, and his heart swells presently and thinks you wrong him; tell him his own human learning and workings is abomination to the Lord and that he must lay aside his beloved actings and wait only upon God for knowledge and faith, and his heart swells and cannot endure to hear of waiting upon God: and truly God is more honored by our waiting than by the multitude of our self-actings. . . . For the flesh grudges to give God his liberty to do with his own what he will, and the flesh would have something in itself; it hath a secret grudging to acknowledge all wisdom, faith, and life must be given of God, and that his actings can get nothing.[10]

This sense of waiting and receiving, I have no doubt, is an authentic moral experience, quite apart from Winstanley's antiquated terminology. There is a type of mind, as William James has said, that finds itself able to tap unsuspected sources of energy by dipping below the

---

[10] *The Breaking of the Day of God*, 1648, pp. 72 f.

surface-play of consciousness. It was very different, however, from the typical moral experience that lay behind Calvinism—as different as Winstanley's religion was from Presbyterianism or Independency. Calvinism, I think, was a quasi-military ethics in which the fundamental virtues were conceived to be obedience and loyalty to the commands of the sovereign ruler of the world. The attribute of that ruler which Calvinists were most inclined to stress was not love but power or possibly justice. The relationship was rigidly personal. It required the unswerving devotion and the strict responsibility of every man to his divine superior, and perhaps for that very reason it implied his equality with all the other servants of God. Its moral effect was to steel men in the fight against evil, to discipline their energies and harden their endurance, sometimes to the point of harshness and cruelty. It was a form of moral individualism that stressed the virtues of enterprise and activity and self-assertion. Hence the political affinity of Calvinist ethics, when it showed itself as a radical movement in the Puritan Revolution, was with the democratic radicalism of the main body of the Levellers, of which the best extant record is the debates in the Army Council at Putney. For the social philosophy of democratic radicalism was built upon the postulate of inalienable natural rights, among which the right to own property acquired by one's exertions was not the least. From such a social philosophy communism was necessarily excluded.

It would be quite wrong to imply that the moral quietism or passivity of Winstanley and the Quakers carried with it a lack of vigor or pertinacity. In their case mysticism was neither a doctrine of moral defeat, an escape from a too harsh reality, nor a withdrawal from effective action on the level of everyday affairs. This ethics too may be called individualism, since every man must find out for himself the secret of his own being, without benefit of institutions or of clergy. But the secret that he discovers is not his self-sufficiency but rather his dependence upon subconscious powers that take possession of him and act through him. The relationship is not a personal one of loyalty to an omnipotent ruler, but one of reliance upon forces greater than himself that he nevertheless finds in himself. The outcome of moral reflection is felt not as self-assertion but rather as self-abnegation. Hence the fundamental fact of social ethics is not individual enterprise and self-preservation but rather the preservation of community and the responsibility of the strong for the weak. This Winstanley called the law of universal love. In all but words he thus arrived at the formula of all the utopian socialisms: From each according to his powers; to each according to his needs.

Winstanley differed from Fox and the Quakers chiefly in believing that this consciousness of human brotherhood must at once become the principle of a new form of community. For him true religion required the immediate creation of a society that substituted community and mutual aid for individualism and competition. He could not content himself with a religious experience that ended with a change of a personal morality, nor imagine a moral reform that did not include the elimination of poverty and the removal of political oppression. Both these, he believed, grew from the single root of self-love and covetousness, or individual aggressiveness, which issued in the tyranny of kings and rulers, the monopoly of the means of production by the landlords, the clerical pretensions of the hireling preachers, and the chicanery of lawyers, who played jackal to kings, landlords, and clergy alike. Because these had all one root Winstanley could not envisage a political reform which was not at the same time economic, or a form of civil liberty that could coexist with poverty and economic dependence. Hence he looked to the English Revolution, pledged by Parliament and the people to a "real reformation", to make the earth a common treasury and England a community in which the king of righteousness should rule in every heart.

WINSTANLEY'S POLITICAL ARGUMENT

When Winstanley sets out a formal outline of his argument for communism, he sometimes speaks of a threefold proof: by direct revelation, by the citation of Scripture, and by reason. The religious beliefs behind his trust in the inner Light have been described in the preceding section. Winstanley's offer to prove his case by the authority of Scripture was never, in my opinion, more than the acceptance of what was at the time a conventional form of argument. In his *Letter to the Lord Fairfax* he said that the issues raised had to be settled not by Scripture but by the law in men's hearts. The third line of proof, that based upon reason and equity, was borrowed by Winstanley from the pattern of argumentation built up for the Levellers by writers such as Lilburne, Overton, and Walwyn. In a measure it was second-hand—an effort, so to speak, to talk in the political vernacular—though certainly not insincere. Winstanley must of course have known about the Leveller agitation that had been going on since 1647, but there is nothing in his early pamphlets to show that he was concerned with it. His use of stereotyped Leveller arguments was not in itself either interesting or important. The question is, how far he perceived the differences of principle that separated his communism from the democratic radicalism of the Leveller program. The answer, I think, is that both sides were surprisingly clear-headed about the contrast. Lilburne repudiated Winstanley in his *Legal Fundamentall Liberties,* and Winstanley marked off his communist group as the "True Levellers".

In asserting that equity and right reason are the foundation of all morally binding laws Winstanley was merely taking a position that in one way or another is taken by every party which backs a revolutionary reform. The Levellers had used the argument again and again, in attacking one abuse or another, that no law can be really binding unless it is just and equitable. Richard Overton, for example, in the *Remonstrance* which he addressed to Parliament in 1646, had demanded a general revision of English Law in the light of reason:

> Ye know, the laws of this nation are unworthy a free people and deserve from first to last to be considered and seriously debated and reduced to an agreement with common equity and right reason, which ought to be the form and life of every government.[1]

With this Winstanley of course agreed, as he agreed in regarding the Revolution as the occasion for a complete overhauling of English law and institutions. But in calling himself a "true Leveller" he recorded the judgment that the political reforms sought by Lilburne and his party were superficial. Winstanley often says that the object of the Revolution is to restore men's "birthright", and like the Levellers, he does not trouble to distinguish at all sharply between the birthright of an Englishman and the rights of man. Sometimes the Digger manifestoes assert that the object of their movement is to recover for Englishmen their right to use the land of England. Sometimes they claim the "creation-right" of every man to gain his living from the earth, which by the law of righteousness is a common treasury for all human

---

[1] The pamphlet is reprinted in William Haller's *Tracts on Liberty in the Puritan Revolution,* New York, 1934, Vol. III, p. 351; the passage quoted is on p. 365.

beings. In these respects Winstanley's social philosophy agreed with that of the Levellers in appealing to a fundamental law of equity lying behind the positive law.

This resemblance, however, is superficial, since no revolutionist could fail to assert the justice of what he desired. Behind the resemblance there was a fundamental difference between Winstanley and the Levellers. Winstanley was clearly aware that he could not effectively claim a right to subsistence as an individual liberty. The Levellers, on the other hand, were in principle democrats. The purpose of their philosophy was to erect barriers against the incursions of bad law and bad government into those private rights which they considered fundamental to human liberty. Hence their plan of reform included bills of rights embodied in a written constitution which Parliament was expressly forbidden to change. Among the disabilities that they proposed to lay on Parliament was that of "abolishing propriety".[2] In general the Levellers thought of reform as equalizing civil and political liberties, abolishing monopoly, and opening up opportunity to equal competition. For them natural law meant individual rights, and natural equity meant that all men individually should be protected in the exercise of their rights.

Winstanley's conception of social reform was quite different. It is true that he objected to the private ownership of land because it permitted a few men to monopolize what justly belonged to all, but he had no notion of correcting the injustice by increasing the number of landowners, or by making private ownership possible to everyone. His communism was an effort to envisage a different kind of social system. His argument is that the common land is communally owned. Ideally his plan implied that land and all the means of production should be nationalized, and this is certainly the end he looked forward to, though he was opposed to the violent expropriation of private owners. The "creation-right" to subsistence, therefore, was a communal and not an individual right. Accordingly, Winstanley could not possibly identify equity with individual liberty. In *The Law of Freedom*, where he gave the most carefully planned statement of his theory, he based his com-

[2] The Leveller petition of September 11, 1648; reprinted by A. S. P. Woodhouse, *Puritanism and Liberty*, p. 340. The Second Agreement of the People, Article VII, contained a list of matters upon which Parliament was not to act, Woodhouse, *ibid.*, p. 361.

munism upon the difference between two types of society, the monarchy and the commonwealth. In substance this amounted to the contrast between an individualist, acquisitive, competitive society and a cooperative society. Reduced to a single sentence Winstanley's argument is simply that the latter is morally superior because it grows from the better impulses of human nature. It is not built upon individual enterprise but upon mutual aid and protection.

The political argument that Winstanley perhaps uses most frequently is drawn from the Solemn League and Covenant—the oath taken in 1643 by Parliament and people "to amend our lives and each one to go before another in the example of a real reformation". This might seem like an *ad hoc* argument, unless it be remembered that Winstanley never conceived of any social or political reform that did not have its origin in a religious transformation. Obviously his interpretation of the Covenant had nothing whatever to do with the actual political purposes of that document when it was framed. He took it as creating nothing less than a solemn personal obligation on every subscriber to effect a real reformation in England, with all that was implied by that expression. To Winstanley's mind it meant nothing less than an effort to realize "the pure law of righteousness". He acknowledged the obligation in his own conduct: apparently his refusal to employ a lawyer when he was sued for damages at Kingston was based on the belief that the administration of the law as it existed was an iniquitous institution which could not be supported by anyone who meant to amend his life in the interest of a real reformation. It was clearly the intention of the Digger community to boycott the courts and the magistracy as being unsuitable to a Christian society, just as they renounced the use of force as an unchristian way of gaining their ends. They say that they are willing to answer for any unlawful act that they commit, but they will not appeal to the courts for protection even against the unlawful acts of their assailants. In presenting his communistic platform to Cromwell Winstanley, of course, abandoned this attitude. At the same time he still believed the strongest argument for his communism to be the contention that it was implied in the express intent of the nation to effect a true reformation. If this were honestly meant, he urged, there was no place to stop short of a completely Christian society in which covetousness, the root of all inequality, was altogether grubbed up. All bad government, all war and all misery, Winstanley believed, arise from the acquisitiveness which is chiefly represented by the private ownership of land. Hence there can be no real reformation unless the land is restored to its rightful condition as a common treasury for all men. True religion, he says, is to make restitution of the land.

Often, however, Winstanley gives to the Covenant a much more specific meaning than this: he construes it as a contract between Parliament and the common people for prosecuting the war against the King to recover England's fundamental liberties. Parliament, he says, persuaded the people to take up arms by the promise that each should enjoy his right; some gave military service, some gave free quarter to troops, and all gave taxes. Parliament, Winstanley assumes, represents specifically the gentry and the clergy; their legislation shows that they mean to look after the interests of those classes. The question is whether they will "cozen" the poor commoners of their part of the bargain. Of all liberties the most fundamental is access to the land. This the gentry already enjoy in their enclosures, and Winstanley is willing to leave them in possession. But to complete the bargain the common people ought to have the common land, since this is the very least that can be given in recognition of their "creation-right". Everyone, Winstanley says, desires and struggles for land—gentry, clergy, and commons alike. Hence there can be no talk of restoring the fundamental liberties of Englishmen unless all are given the right to use the land of England. The most interesting part of the argument is its frank assumption that English government is controlled by a class in its own interest, even though Parliament legally represents the nation. The only question is whether the class in control means to live up to the contract implied in the National Covenant or whether the gentry mean to pursue their own interests at the cost of being "covenant-breakers". There is in Winstanley's writing a good deal that would now be called "class-consciousness", but he invariably repudiates the use of force as a way of securing the commoners' rights.

Winstanley addressed another argument to Parliament based not upon the Covenant but upon the legislation passed after the execution of the King declaring that monarchy was abolished and that England was a "free commonwealth". This formed, I believe, Winstanley's most important political argument, since it turned upon his belief that there are two opposed kinds of society and consequently two kinds of government. The "kingly power" is based upon greed and force, and therefore corresponds with private ownership of the land, while "true commonwealth-government" is based upon cooperation and therefore corresponds with making the land a "common treasury". Winstanley's argument amounts to showing that Parliament has contradicted itself. By its own act it has "cast out the kingly power", but it has also passed an act "to uphold the old law". By the latter he meant the act authorizing the courts to continue administering the law in force when the King died, but issuing writs in the name of the Keepers of the Liberty of England instead of the King. This, Winstanley argued, is absolutely illogical, if it does not cloak a hypocritical design to change the possessor of the kingly power without changing the thing itself. For the "old law" was merely the will of the Norman conqueror, and Charles's title to the throne was merely as the successor to William. Hence, if the kingly power were really cast out, the whole fabric of legal tyranny ought to go with it. The Civil Wars, he argued, had been fought not to remove the King but to reform a tyrannous system. This identification of tyranny with the Norman Power was a common form of Leveller argument. Winstanley merely adopted it. It had been fully developed by Overton in his *Remonstrance* in 1646 and by John Hare in several pamphlets published in 1647. In fact it was merely one phase of an argument that was common to all the anti-royalist parties and not to the Levellers alone: the mythical presumption that there had once been a free constitution in England which it was the purpose of the Civil War to restore.

Winstanley, however, made his own use of the Leveller argument against the Norman Power. At the conquest, Winstanley supposes, William turned the English out of their land and put his own soldiers in their place. In general, he thinks, all private ownership of land rests on cunning, robbery, and violence; the Norman conquest was merely the case that most concerns England. The lords of manors are the successors of William's "colonels", and the freeholders of the Norman common soldiers. They are merely the beneficiaries of a successful theft, and in consequence they are wholly lacking in title to their land, if the kingly power were really to be cast out. But the power of the landowners has two accessory supporters. These are the lawyers and the clergy. Both, Winstanley thinks, were set up by William to bolster his power. The lawyers were a deliberately created engine of oppression, made possible by keeping the law in French and Latin, and employed to twist its meaning by cunning and chicanery to the interest of the landowning gentry, who alone have money to pay them.

> England is a prison; the varieties of subtleties in the laws preserved by the sword are the bolts, bars, and doors of the prison; the lawyers are the jailors; and poor men are the prisoners.[3]

The privileges of the clergy also were designed expressly to support the conqueror's yoke. William gave them tithes "to preach him up"; they persuaded the people to fancy

> That true freedom lay in hearing them preach, and to enjoy that heaven which, they say, every man who believes their doctrine shall enjoy after he is dead. And so [they] tell us of a heaven and hell after death, which neither they nor we know what will be, so that the whole world is at a loss in the true knowledge thereof.[4]

According to Winstanley, therefore, the casting out of the kingly power, if carried out completely, would carry with it the lords of manors, tithing priests, bad laws and bad judges, and cunning lawyers.

Over against this representation of kingly government under the Norman yoke Winstanley places government in a free commonwealth, which Parliament has declared England to be. In his controversial tracts he nowhere undertakes to describe this kind of government or to make clear the contrast in principle which distinguished monarchy and commonwealth. This, however, is his point of departure in *The Law of Freedom*, and there can be no doubt that the distinction between the two types of society is the logical foundation upon which his communism ought to rest. In the controversial tracts he contents himself with arguing that Parliament's pledge is not fulfilled so long as the "old law" remains in force or so long as the landlords are permitted to retain both their enclosures and control of the commons as well. So long as the "creation-right" of access to the land is denied, there can be no pretense that law and government are really based upon equity and reason. The English are not a free people until the poor have the right at least to plant and sow the common land. Equally, he added later, Parliament ought to see to it that the confiscated estates, the king's lands, and the lands of bishops and deans, are not permitted

---

[3] *A New-Yeers Gift*, p. 10 (bracketed paging).
[4] *The Law of Freedom*, p. 20 (bracketed paging).

to fall into the hands of private owners but are kept for the use of the poor. The outline of what Winstanley thought would constitute a true commonwealth he sketched out for Cromwell, hoping as so many utopians in the seventeenth century hoped, that that hard-headed man of God would use his limitless power to bring the millennium into existence.

WINSTANLEY'S COMMUNIST COMMONWEALTH

Some eighteen months after the final failure of the communist venture at Cobham, Winstanley was moved, as he says, "to pick together" as many of his scattered papers as he could find, in one more effort to realize his idea of a true commonwealth. What had happened to him in the interval is unknown. If the authorities had thought it worth while to press the indictment returned against the Diggers, he may have served a jail sentence. When he reopened the question of communism by publishing *The Law of Freedom*, he evidently thought it wise to divorce the national project which he now offered to Cromwell from the unfortunate experiment that had failed in Surrey, for he nowhere referred to the latter. He speaks of his book as "intended for your view above two years ago", which is hard to credit, since he would scarcely have written and laid aside an elaborate appeal to Cromwell at the very time when he was issuing a continuous series of less elaborate appeals to Fairfax, to the army, and to Parliament. It is likely enough that Winstanley had long planned a more complete exposition of his ideas about a true commonwealth, separating them from the controversies connected with his attempt to cultivate the commons. In the winter of 1651 it was an obvious expedient to address the work to Cromwell, but I doubt whether this step would have been indicated until after the Battle of Worcester.

The outcome of the digging at Cobham had demonstrated the impossibility of cultivating the common land by communistic groups, so long as the legal power of the landlords over the unenclosed land remained intact, and it was obvious also that a fundamental change in the law could be made only by a national government free from the forces that had dominated Parliament. Accordingly Winstanley was led to add another to the list of national utopias of which Harrington's *Oceana*, published four years later, was the most famous. The immediate occasion of the work, he says, was a suggestion of Hugh Peters, that government and law ought to be accommodated to Scripture.[1] The general purport of the book is identical with that of the controversial tracts that Winstanley had published in 1649 and 1650. The kingly oppressor, he says, has been cast out but his powers and the abuses inherent in them are still intact: the clergy and their tithes, the lawyers and the Norman law, the monopoly of the land by the lords of manors. By creation-right the land belongs to all, and no man becomes rich by his own labors but only by being able to appropriate the labor of other men. Winstanley now undertakes to show, by experience, by Scripture, and by history, that all war and all civil disturbances arise from the struggle to gain possession and control of the land. He therefore appeals to Cromwell to cast out oppression and to realize true commonwealth-government by making England a communistic society. He still professes to confine the program of communist tillage to the common and the nationalized land, and he still rejects the idea of expropriating the landlords, but it is very hard to see how he thought the two systems could have persisted side by side. Whatever interest his "platform" possesses lies in its being the outline for a wholly communist society.

Though the general purpose is the same, there is a change of emphasis in *The Law of Freedom*. Winstanley seems to rely less upon a millenarian hope that the spirit will move men to bring in true commonwealth, and more upon the possibility that changing the organization of society will affect their motives and conduct. In one rather surprising passage he avows this kind of change.

> I speak now in relation between the oppressor and the oppressed; the inward bondages I meddle not with in this place, though I am assured that if it be rightly searched into, the inward bondages of the mind, as covetousness, pride, hypocrisy, envy, sorrow, fears, desperation, and madness are all occasioned by the outward bondage that one sort of people lay upon another.[2]

In his desire to see progress made Winstanley even says that some parts of his platform might be put into effect though communism were not

[1] Presumably in the Committee appointed January 20, 1651, to suggest to Parliament revisions of the laws. Peters appears to have been the *enfant terrible* of the Committee. See Bulstrode Whitelocke's *Memorials*, pp. 520, 521, 523, 528.

[2] P. 18 (bracketed paging).

adopted.[3] It is not likely that these passages imply any real change in Winstanley's convictions but he had clearly undergone a change of mood, induced by experience and by the failure of his year's agitation for the communal tilling of the common land. The millenarian expectations appropriate to the first stage of his revolutionary activity had given place to a soberer consideration of ways and means and a greater willingness to rely on changes in law and institutions.

In the opening three chapters of his book Winstanley undertakes to set forth the principles upon which he conceives the government of a true commonwealth to rest. This is evidently the result of an attempt to develop more affirmatively ideas that had remained implicit in his controversial tracts. In these his condemnation of the "kingly power" had been clearer than the idea of a commonwealth to which the kingly power stood opposed. In *The Law of Freedom* Winstanley developed the contrast more systematically. Government is a way of "ordering the earth and the manners of mankind" by law, and its purpose ought to be to enable men to live peaceably in freedom and plenty. There are, however, two different ways of ordering the earth—by private ownership and "the cheating art of buying and selling" and by communal ownership without buying and selling. There are therefore two kinds of government, kingly government and commonwealth, and two kinds of law. Kingly government, because it depends on private ownership, depends also on war and conquest, upon the dominion of some men over others through force and fraud, and upon lawyers and the clergy as the twin agencies of covetousness and subtlety necessary for that kind of government. Commonwealth, because it does away with buying and selling, is able to abolish the abuses and oppressions that go with them; it gives a lawful livelihood to the poor as well as to the rich, and its law arises from equity, reason, and righteousness.

In his third chapter Winstanley traces the two forms of government back to two antagonistic principles in human nature. These he calls common preservation—the tendency in a man to seek the good of others as well as himself—and self-preservation. True magistracy, as distinguished from the false magistracy of force, springs from the impulse to common preservation. In origin it begins with the family, in which the superior experience and wisdom of the father are applied to the protection and nourishment of his dependents. Adam, Winstanley says,

[3] P. 72 (bracketed paging).

was the first ruler, and the necessity of planting the earth to gain a common livelihood was his law. The fundamental law of a commonwealth, governed with a view to the common preservation, is that the strong should help and protect the weak and the foolish. The false magistrate is one who favors the rich and the strong; the true magistrate is one who casts out "self-ended" interests and protects the peace and liberties of the common people. The first is the root of all civil wars and revolutions; the second is the root of right government and peace. Essentially, therefore, Winstanley's contrast of kingly government and commonwealth is the contrast between acquisitiveness and competition on the one hand and cooperation and mutual aid on the other, the opposition upon which all communistic utopias have depended.

Having thus set forth the underlying principle of a commonwealth, Winstanley goes on to specify what might be called its chief political device. Like most of the early theorists of democracy he has been captivated by the idea of popular elections and short terms of office. In a commonwealth, he says, all officers are elected and hold office for a single year. He gives the familiar arguments to show that power long and continuously held corrupts the officials who have it, while frequent change keeps them faithful to the public interest and gives political experience to more persons. This part of Winstanley's argument probably shows an affinity with the political ideas of the Levellers. Like the Levellers also, and in contrast with what might have been expected of a person with millenarian tendencies, he shows no inclination to restrict political power to the saints. No one is excluded from the suffrage by his plan except persons whose interests attach them obviously to the Royalist side in the Civil Wars. He expresses himself as against even a moral qualification for voting, and against a religious qualification for officeholding, though "uncivil livers" ought not to be elected to office. For obvious reasons those who have profited by buying confiscated estates are to be excluded from a plan of government that aims at nationalizing this land for the use of the poor.

The fourth chapter of *The Law of Freedom*, which is the longest section of Winstanley's platform of government, is an elaborate effort to outline the officers required in a communistic commonwealth. True to the ideas that commonwealth begins with and grows from the family, he enumerates the father of a family as the first officer in the plan, each such person being responsible for the education of his dependents, for directing their labor, and for seeing that they are brought up in a useful trade. Beyond the family there are local officers—those responsible for each town, city, or parish—county officers, and national officers. The local officers in Winstanley's plan are of two kinds: the peacemakers, whose duty is mainly to keep the peace, and the overseers, whose duties are mainly industrial. The peacemakers appear to be modeled on the justices of the peace, except that they are arbitrators rather than judges. The settlement of local disputes by arbitration was a part of the Levellers' plan for the reform of local government, designed of course to circumvent the delays, costs, and technicalities of proceedings in the regular courts. The overseers are of four types, (1) those whose duty it is to protect the private property that in Winstanley's communistic scheme still belongs to each family; (2) those who oversee the practice of each trade and the system of apprenticeship by which the youth are to be educated in the trades; (3) those who oversee the common storehouses into which all goods are brought except those produced for immediate consumption; and (4) men over sixty years of age, who have a kind of roving commission to oversee everybody and everything. It is clear that Winstanley based the idea of his overseers upon a guild-system of production; he speaks with high commendation of the London companies and the oversight of production which they were supposed to exercise. The local officers include also a soldier, who is a kind of marshal to execute and enforce the orders of officers and courts, an executioner, and a task-master. The last has the custody and supervision of those who refuse to conform to the general plan, for like all communistic schemes, Winstanley's platform has to provide that those who do not work at the recognized occupations not only shall not eat, but also shall not have their freedom or the custody of their persons.

The essential institution of county government in Winstanley's plan is the county court, held four times a year like the Quarter Sessions, and consisting of a judge and of the peacemakers and overseers from the towns and parishes of the county. Here again Winstanley took a leaf from the Levellers' book. The judges are to be rigidly interdicted from interpreting the law but are to pronounce only its bare letter. This has been a perennial ideal of radicals whose purpose is to simplify the law and its procedure, and who see in judicial legislation a chief cause of

legal formality and technicality.[4] Above the county courts in Winstanley's plan is Parliament, which he describes as the highest court, having supervision of all other courts and officers, with power to remedy
all grievances. Nothing is said on the subject, but I assume that Winstanley would abolish the courts at Westminster, as the extreme Levellers proposed to do. Parliament is to be composed of representatives
chosen annually from the cities, towns, and counties. Winstanley shows,
however, no great confidence in parliaments: he proposes that legislation, after it is passed, shall not take effect for a month, in order that
the people may have a chance to register their objections. He did not
adopt the Leveller plan of limiting the legislative power with a written
constitution. The most positive duty of Parliament in Winstanley's
plan is very naturally to direct the planting of the "commonwealth
land", which consists of the common and of all the land recovered
from the church, the king, and the royalists. This land is to be permanently nationalized, but he does not undertake to frame rules by which
it is to be administered.

The same applies generally to Winstanley's account of the economic
organization of a society that has abolished buying and selling, which
he deals with in the latter part of his fifth chapter. Apart from the
overseers in his roster of officers, there is not much that can properly be
called an outline of a communistic economy. His plan is that all crops
when harvested, and all goods when manufactured, are to go into
public storehouses, some wholesale and some retail, and are to be
dispensed without price, upon the request of anyone who needs them,
either for his own consumption or as raw material for further processing. Winstanley had not reflected on the fact that the price-system which
results from buying and selling goods does regulate production and
that there would still have to be some kind of regulation, even in an
economy that was purely cooperative. Buying and selling seemed to
him nothing but a "cheating art", that gives an iniquitous advantage to

---

[4] John Lilburne proposed the following on judicial reform, as a petition to the
first Parliament to be elected pursuant to the adoption of the Agreement of the People: "That the next Representative be most earnestly pressed for the ridding of this
kingdom of those vermin and caterpillars, the lawyers, the chief bane of this poor
nation; to erect a court of justice in every hundred in the nation, for the ending of
all differences arising in that hundred, by twelve men of the same hundred annually
chosen by freemen of that hundred, with express and plain rules in English, made by
the Representative or supreme authority of the nation, for them to guide their judgments by." Reprinted by A. S. P. Woodhouse, *Puritanism and Liberty*, p. 366.

the cunning and unscrupulous, an estimate which may very well have had its roots in the personal humiliation of his bankruptcy.[5] By its abolition he expected that it would be possible to uproot covetousness and oppression. For the regulation of the system he relied upon criminal penalties against idleness, waste, and the failure to practice a useful trade. For its direction he depended upon the overseers, who are supposed not only to know the best processes for producing goods but also what goods are needed and in what quantities. Winstanley emphasized the duty of the overseers to encourage the discovery of new knowledge and its application to the arts and crafts. Inventors, he says, ought to be signally honored, and all useful discoveries ought to be made known at once to the whole country. Nevertheless, as was perhaps natural for a small tradesman in the seventeenth century, he still thought of industry as dominated by custom and as controlled by self-regulating crafts. For this reason his plan for a communistic society contained little in the way of economic analysis.

The most interesting parts of Winstanley's plan of government are those in which he sketches his ideas of public education. The first part of his fifth chapter is devoted to this subject. Both heads of families and the overseers of arts and trades are required to see that all children are instructed in morals and in useful trades, in languages and in the arts and sciences. It appears clear that Winstanley intends education to be extended to all citizens of the commonwealth. This is not, however, the point which he mainly stresses. What he thinks chiefly desirable is to avoid the creation of a class of professional scholars, educated only in book-learning, in reading and lazy contemplation, like his ancient enemies, the lawyers and the clergy. Every member of a commonwealth, therefore, ought to learn a useful trade or art and ought also to know something of languages, sciences, and history. The arts Winstanley describes as knowledge in practice, laborious and not traditional knowledge. He divides them into five classes: husbandry, with all the supplemental and derivative arts which have to do with the growing and utilization of crops that come from the soil; the arts that have to do with the production and processing of minerals; the arts that concern the care of domestic animals and the use of all the products derived from

---

[5] There is possibly a note of bitterness in Winstanley's occasional references to his reduction to the status of a day-laborer, "which I was never brought up to". See p. 67 (bracketed paging).

them; the arts that concern the growth and utilization of timber; and, finally, arts that depend upon the stars, among which he mentions astronomy, astrology, and navigation. Winstanley's commonwealth has a completely secularized education centered in the practical applications of knowledge.

He proposes also that popular education in secular subjects shall altogether replace the religious teaching of the church. In his outline of officers for the commonwealth the two whose work is most carefully described are the parish minister and the postmaster. The minister is a parish officer elected, like all other officers, for a single year. One day in seven is to be free from labor, but this has no religious significance. On this day the people meet in their parishes, partly that they may become acquainted with one another but chiefly for purposes of general public education. The minister has the direction of this but he has no monopoly of teaching, such as has been claimed by the ordained clergy. The teaching consists largely of reading from the laws of the commonwealth, but not expounding or interpreting them, and of lectures on public affairs. To supply material for the latter Winstanley provides another group of officers, the postmasters. The postmasters in each parish gather the local news and report it to the capital, where the reports are compiled and printed and a copy sent to each parish for publication at the weekly meetings. In addition to this kind of reading and lectures, Winstanley would have lectures on the arts and sciences, sometimes in English and sometimes in foreign languages, and also on moral subjects like the nature of man and the benefits of liberty. In all this, however, there is nothing that can be called religious instruction of a doctrinal sort. In Winstanley's commonwealth there is literally no church and no clergy, since he identified the practice of that profession with witchcraft.

> He who professes the service of a righteous God by preaching and prayer, and makes a trade to get the possessions of the earth, shall be put to death for a witch and a cheater.[6]

So far as his own views were concerned, Winstanley had clearly reached the conclusion that no sort of public worship was necessary. It does not appear what rights he would have extended to those who did not agree with him, which is curious, in view of his very emphatic endorsement

---

[6] P. 86 (bracketed paging).

of religious toleration in his earlier works. I suppose, though I am not certain, that he would have permitted churches whose membership was voluntary, so long as they relinquished any form of compulsory public maintenance.

Winstanley's secularizing of education was derived directly from his ideas about religion. By making religion exclusively an inner revelation and worship exclusively communion with God, he had divorced it from any relationship to learning, and had abolished any distinction between different branches of knowledge in respect of their relation to religion. This had a twofold effect: on the one hand it destroyed the study of divinity as a branch of learning and on the other it raised all the arts and sciences to the dignity formerly claimed by theology. To know the secrets of nature, he says, is to know the works of God. This is a knowledge by experience as much as that "experimental" knowledge of the spirit upon which he had insisted in his religious tracts. Hence the pursuit of useful knowledge in the arts and sciences is itself almost an act of worship. The very omnipresence of God in nature and of the inner light in human experience brought Winstanley to a completely secular idea of education and scholarship. In this he went squarely against all the prevailing ideas of Puritan education, though his conclusion was the culmination of ideas inherent in Puritanism itself. Again and again throughout the first half of the seventeenth century the Puritan clergy had attacked the remnants of medievalism in the English universities. Their object was to displace the ancient curriculum, based on scholastic metaphysics and dialectic, and to replace it with studies more suitable for the training of pulpit orators and pastors.[7] Thus rhetoric, moral philosophy, and the ancient languages became the essential parts of the course of study. Always, however, there was the assumption that the clergy formed a learned profession, with a body of demonstrated truth (usually thought to be Calvinist theology) at their back. All classes of Puritan clergy, Presbyterian and Independent, poured contempt on the "mechanick preachers" who leaped into notoriety with the spread of the Baptist and other sects.

The small group of Puritan mystics to whom Winstanley was allied, when they broke with the prevailing idea of the clergy, had necessarily to abandon the idea that education ought to be directed to training

---

[7] The subject is discussed with special reference to Milton in William Haller's *The Rise of Puritanism*, New York, 1938, pp. 297 ff.

clergymen. If a religious teacher required before everything else an intuition of spiritual truth, he could hardly be expected to get this from a study of Greek and Hebrew. In almost identical words John Saltmarsh and George Fox denied that university teaching could make a clergyman.[8] William Dell, who as Master of Caius College, Cambridge, had an educational position of some importance, went on to propose the secularizing of university studies:

> If the Universities will stand upon an human and civil account, as schools of good learning for the instructing and educating youth in the knowledge of the tongues, and of the liberal arts and sciences, thereby to make them useful and serviceable to the commonwealth . . . and will be content to shake hands with their ecclesiastical and anti-Christian interest, then let them stand during the good pleasure of God; but if they will still exalt themselves above themselves, and place themselves on Christ's very throne, as if they had ascended upon high to lead captivity captive and to give gifts to men for the work of the ministry . . . then let them in the name of Christ descend into that darkness out of which they first sprang.[9]

In his *Right Reformation of Learning, Schools, and Universities* [10] Dell outlined a system of publicly supported elementary schools for England, with high schools for teaching the languages, arts, and sciences in all the larger cities. Like Winstanley he favored the teaching of a trade with the study of books.

Winstanley's ideas about education, therefore, were not peculiar to him but were shared by those whom he most resembled in his religious ideas. Like Dell he looked toward an education open to the generality of the population, an education in subjects useful to the commonwealth and closer to experience and the practice of the useful arts. But with these men the high value that they set on knowledge at first hand grew

[8] "It is not a University, a Cambridge or Oxford, a pulpit or a black gown or cloak, that makes one a true minister of Jesus Christ." Saltmarsh's *Divine Right of Presbytery*, 1646. "The Lord opened unto me that being bred at Oxford or Cambridge was not enough to fit and qualify men to be ministers of Christ, and I wondered at it because it was the common belief of people." Fox's *Journal*, Vol. I, p. 75.

[9] *The Stumbling-Stone, wherein the University is Reproved*, 1653; cited from a reprint entitled *Christ's Spirit*, Germantown, Penna., 1760, pp. 155 f.

[10] *Select Works*, p. 578.

not from any usual kind of empirical philosophy but from the peculiar
form of mysticism embodied in their religious experience. It was the
knowledge of the inner light which, in the first instance, they contrasted
with verbal learning and the building up of vast systems of unverifiable
inferences. The very type and model of this kind of hair-splitting was
for them the attempts of literal-minded Puritans to spin out a whole
body of belief and practice from the texts of Scripture. In the case of
Winstanley that which cuts off clericalism at its root is the fact that the
divinity in which the clergy are trained and which they are supposed to
practice is an "imaginary" science. It is false in its learned pretensions
and, what is worse, it is pernicious in its social consequences. In the end
Winstanley became convinced that it was unwholesome both mentally
and morally, a result of semi-pathological fears and a cause of hysteria.
The passage in his *Law of Freedom* in which he condemns the "divining doctrine" is certainly the most remarkable he ever wrote. It must
have grown from much observation of the darker side of religious fa-
naticism, and it must constitute one of the most extraordinary indictments of Puritanism that was written in the seventeenth century.

There is a threefold discovery of falsehood in this doctrine.

For, first, it is a doctrine of a sickly and weak spirit, who hath
lost his understanding in the knowledge of the creation, and of the
temper of his own heart and nature, and so runs into fancies,
either of joy or sorrow.

And if the passion of joy predominate, then he fancies to himself a personal God, personal angels, and a local place of glory
which he saith he and all who believe what he saith shall go to,
after they are dead.

And if sorrow predominate, then he fancies to himself a personal devil and a local place of torment that he shall go to after
he is dead, and this he speaks with great confidence.

Or, secondly, this is the doctrine of a subtle running spirit, to
make an ungrounded wise man mad, that he might be called the
more excellent man in knowledge, for many times when a wise
understanding heart is assaulted with this doctrine of a God, a
devil, a heaven, and a hell, salvation and damnation after a man is
dead, his spirit being not strongly grounded in the knowledge of

the creation nor in the temper of his own heart, he strives and stretches his brains to find out the depth of that doctrine and cannot attain to it. For indeed it is not knowledge but imagination. And so, by poring and puzzling himself in it, loses that wisdom he had, and becomes distracted and mad. And if the passion of joy predominate, then he is merry and sings and laughs, and is ripe in the expressions of his words, and will speak strange things, but all by imagination. But if the passion of sorrow predominate, then he is heavy and sad, crying out, He is damned, God hath forsaken him, and he must go to hell when he die, he cannot make his calling and election sure. And in that distemper many times a man doth hang, kill, or drown himself. So that this divining doctrine, which you call spiritual and heavenly things, torments people always when they are weak, sickly, and under any distemper. Therefore it cannot be the doctrine of Christ the Savior.

For my own part, my spirit hath waded deep to find the bottom of this divining spiritual doctrine; and the more I searched, the more I was at a loss; and I never came to quiet rest, and to know God in my spirit, till I came to the knowledge of the things in this book. And let me tell you, They who preach this divining doctrine are the murderers of many a poor heart who is bashful and simple and that cannot speak for himself but that keeps his thoughts to himself.

Or, thirdly, This doctrine is made a cloak of policy by the subtle elder brother to cheat his simple younger brother of the freedoms of the earth. . . . So that this divining spiritual doctrine is a cheat. For while men are gazing up into heaven, imagining after a happiness, or fearing a hell after they are dead, their eyes are put out, that they see not what is their birthright, and what is to be done by them here on earth while they are living. This is the filthy dreamer and the cloud without rain.

And indeed the subtle clergy do know that, if they can but charm the people by this their divining doctrine to look after riches, heaven, and glory when they are dead, then they shall easily be the inheritors of the earth and have the deceived people to be their servants.[11]

---

[11] Pp. 60 ff. (bracketed paging).

Here was a new note in the secularism which spread over political thought and indeed over all thought after the Restoration. It grew not from philosophic rationalism, or from a skeptical indifference to religion, or from the repugnance of political-minded men to clericalism. On the contrary it sprang from an unusually intense and sincere form of religious experience and from the very essence of Protestantism. It was as genuinely a part of the Pauline tradition in Christianity as those elements which Calvinist Puritans liked better to emphasize. It was, as William James said of Quakerism, "a religion of veracity", the creation of men who had faced the fundamental unreasonableness of the world and of their own natures and, without benefit of clergy, had found serenity and the power to work, the widest scope possible for the exercise of intelligence, and a sense of human brotherhood that lifts the non-rational above the brutalities of irrationalism.

WINSTANLEY'S WORKS. A Transcription of the Title Pages

An appeale to all Englishmen, to judge between bondage and freedome, sent from those that began to digge upon George Hill in
Surrey; but now are carrying on, that publick work upon the little
heath in the parish of Cobham, neare unto George Hill, wherein
it appeares, that the work of digging upon the commons, is not
onely warranted by Scripture, but by the law of the commonwealth of England likewise . . . March 26, 1650.
Signed: Jerard Winstanley, Richard Maidley, Thomas James . . .
and divers others that were not present when this went to the
presse.
(A broadside)

An appeal to the House of Commons, desiring their answer: whether
the common-people shall have the quiet enjoyment of the commons and waste land; or whether they shall be under the will of
lords of mannors still. Occasioned by an arrest, made by Thomas
Lord Wenman, Ralph Verny knight, and Richard Winwood,
esq.; upon the author hereof, for a trespass, in digging upon the
common-land at Georges Hill in Surrey. By Gerrard Winstanly,
Iohn Barker, and Thomas Star, in the name of all the poor oppressed in the land of England . . . Printed in the year, 1649.
19 (i.e. 16) p.

The breaking of the day of God. Wherein, four things are manifested.
I. That the two witnesses are not in killing: but in rising from
death. II. The three daies and half: or 42 months of the saints
captivity under the beast, very near expired. III. Christ hath begun to reign in his saints, and to tread their corrupt flesh under
his feet. IIII. Christs dominion over the nations of the world,

near the approach. By Gerrard Winstanley. London, Printed by H. for Giles Calvert, at the black spread-Eagle at the west end of Pauls, 1648.

[16], 128 p.

The breaking of the day of God. Wherein, four things are manifested. I. That the two witnesses are not in killing: but in rising from death. II. The three dayes and half: or 42 months of the saints captivity under the beast, very near expired. III. Christ hath begun to reign in his saints, and to tread their corrupt flesh under his feet. IIII. Christ's dominion over the nations of the world, near the approach. By Gerrard Winstanley. London, Printed by I. C. for Giles Calvert at the Black-spread-Eagle, at the West end of Pauls, 1649.

[14], 137 p.

A declaration from the poor oppressed people of England, directed to all that call themselves, or are called lords of manors, through this nation; that have begun to cut, or that through fear and covetousness, do intend to cut down the woods and trees that grow upon the commons and waste land. Printed in the yeer, 1649.

"Signed for and in behalf of all the poor oppressed people of England, and the whole world." Forty-five signatures headed by Gerrard Winstanly.

[8] p.

A declaration of the bloudie and unchristian acting of William Star and John Taylor of Walton, with divers men in womens apparell, in opposition to those that dig upon George-hill in Surrey. London, Printed for Giles Calvert at the black Spread-Eagle at the West end of Pauls. 1649.

5 p.

Fire in the bush. The spirit bvrning, not consuming, but purging mankinde. Or, The great battell of God Almighty, between Michaell the seed of life, and the great red dragon, the curse fought within the spirit of man. With severall other declarations, and testimonies of the power of life. By Jerrard Winstanly . . . London, Printed for Giles Calvert, and are to be sold at the Black-Spread-Eagle, at the West end of Pauls. 1650.

[14], 77 p.

An humble request, to the ministers of both universities, and to all lawyers in every Inns-a-court. To consider of the Scriptures and points of law herein mentioned, and to give a rational and Christian answer, whereby the difference may be composed in peace, between the poor men of England, who have begun to digge, plow, and build upon the common land, claiming it their own, by right of creation. And the lords of mannours that trouble them, who have no other claiming to commons, then the kings will, or from the power of the conquest . . . By Gerard Winstanley . . . London, Printed by J. C. And are to be sold at the three Bibles, at the West end of Pauls church-yard, 1650.

[4], 16 p.

The law of freedom in a platform: or, True magistracy restored. Humbly presented to Oliver Cromwel . . . And to all Englishmen my brethren whether in church-fellowship, or not in church-fellowship, both sorts walking as they conceive according to the order of the Gospel: and from them to all the nations in the world. Wherein is declared, what is kingly government, and what is commonwealths government. By Jerrard Winstanley . . . London, Printed for the author, and are to be sold by Giles Calvert at the black Spred-Eagle at the West end of Pauls. 1652.

89, [3] p.

A Letter taken at Wellingborough. Signed by Jacob Heard and twenty-one others, including Gerrard Winstanley.
(From *A Perfect Diurnal*, April 1–8, 1650)

A letter to the Lord Fairfax, and his councell of war, with divers questions to the lawyers, and ministers: proving it an undeniable equity, that the common people ought to dig, plow, plant and dwell upon the commons, without hiring them, or paying rent to any. Delivered to the Generall and the chief officers on Saturday June 9. By Jerrard Winstanley, in the behalf of those who have begun to dig upon George-Hill in Surrey. London: Printed for Giles Calvert, at the black Spread-Eagle at the West end of Pauls. 1649.

13 p.

The mysterie of God, concerning the whole creation, mankinde. To be made known to every man and woman, after seven dispensations and seasons of time are passed over. According to the counsell of God, revealed to his servants. By Ierrard Winstanley . . . Printed in the yeere 164 [rest of date torn off]

[8], 67, [3] p.

The mysterie of God, concerning the whole creation, mankinde. To be made known to every man and woman, after seaven dispensations and seasons of time are passed over. According to the councell of God, revealed to his servants. By Gerrard Winstanley . . . London, Printed by I. C. For Giles Calvert, at the Black-spread-Eagle, at the West end of Pauls, 1649.

[8], 60 p.

The new law of righteousnes budding forth, in restoring the whole creation from the bondage of the curse. Or a glimpse of the new heaven, and new earth, wherein dwels righteousnes. Giving an alarm to silence all that preach or speak from hear-say, or imagination. By Gerrard Winstanley . . . London, Printed for Giles Calvert, at the black spread-Eagle at the west end of Pauls. 1649.

[12], 120 p.

A new-yeers gift for the Parliament and armie: shewing, what the kingly power is; and that the cause of those they call Diggers is the life and marrow of that cause the Parliament hath declared for, and the army fought for: the perfecting of which work, will prove England to be the first of nations, or the tenth part of the city Babylon, that fals off from the beast first, and that sets the crown upon Christs head, to govern the world in righteousness: by Jerrard Winstanley a lover of Englands freedom and peace . . . London, Printed for Giles Calvert, 1650.

49 p.

The saints paradice: or, The fathers teaching the only satisfaction to waiting soules. Wherein many experiences are recorded, for the comfort of such as are under spirituall burning . . . By Jerrard Winstanly . . . London, Printed for G. Calvert, and are to be sold at the black-spread-Eagle at the West end of Pauls.

[8], 85 p.

The saints paradise: or, The fathers teaching the only satisfaction to waiting souls. Wherein many experiences are recorded, for the comfort of such as are under spirituall burning . . . By Jerrard Winstanley . . . London, Printed for G. Calvert, and are to be sold at the black spred-Eagle at the West end of Pauls.

[8], 134 p.

Several pieces gathered into one volume: set forth in five books: viz. I. The breaking of the day of God, or Prophesies fulfilled. II. The mystery of God concerning the whole creation, mankind. III. The saints paradise, set forth for the comfort of such as are under spirituall burning. IV. Truth lifting up its head above scandals. V. The new law of righteousnesse. Written in the light of inward experience, by Gerrard Winstanly . . . London, Printed for Giles Calvert, and are to be sold at the Black-Spread-Eagle at the west end of Pauls. 1649.

There is a short preface dated December 20, 1649. Each book has its own title page. I, II, and V are dated 1649; III is undated; IV is dated 1650. Each is paged separately.

To his Excellency the Lord Fairfax and the Counsell of Warre the Brotherly Request of those that are called Diggers sheweth . . . Signed by John Heyman and six others.

(From the *Clarke Papers*, Vol. II, pp. 215 ff.)

To my Lord Generall and his Councell of Warr. December 8, 1649. Signed by Gerrard Winstanley.
>   (From the *Clarke Papers*, Vol. II, pp. 217 ff.)

The true levellers standard advanced: or, The state of community opened, and presented to the sons of men. By William Everard, Iohn Palmer, Iohn South, Iohn Courton, William Taylor, Christopher Clifford, Iohn Barker, Ferrard [*sic*] Winstanley, Richard Goodgroome, Thomas Starre, William Hoggrill, Robert Sawyer, Thomas Eder, Henry Bickerstaffe, Iohn Taylor, &c. Beginning to plant and manure the waste land upon George-Hill, in the parish of Walton, in the County of Surrey. London, Printed in the yeer, MDCXLIX.
>   22, [1] p.

Truth lifting up its head above scandals. Wherein is declared

What	{	God, Christ, Father, Son, Holy Ghost,	{	Scriptures, Gospel, Prayer, Ordinances of God	}	are.

>   By Gerrard Winstanly . . . London, Printed in the year 1649.
>   [16], 77 p.

Truth lifting up his head above scandals. Wherein is declared

What	{	God, Christ, Father, Sonne, Holy Ghost,	{	Scriptures, Gospel, Prayer Ordinances of God	}	are.

>   By Gerrard Winstanly . . . London, Printed for Giles Calvert at the Black-Spread-Eagle at the West end of Pauls near Ludgate. 1650.
>   [12], 45, [2] p.

A vindication of those, whose endeavors is only to make the earth a common treasury, called Diggers. Or, Some reasons given by them against the immoderate use of creatures, or the excessive community of women, called ranting; or rather renting . . .

[7] p.

A watch-word to the City of London, and the armie: wherein you
may see that Englands freedome, which should be the result of
all our victories, is sinking deeper under the Norman power, as
appears by this relation of the unrighteous proceedings of King-
stone-Court against some of the Diggers at George-Hill, under
colour of law; but yet thereby the cause of the Diggers is more
brightened and strengthened: so that every one singly may truly
say what his freedome is, and where it lies. By Jerrard Winstanly
. . . London, Printed for Giles Calvert at the Sign of the black
Spread-Eagle, at the West end of Pauls, 1649.

[4], 16 p.

THE MYSTERIE OF GOD CONCERN-
ING THE WHOLE CREATION,
MANKINDE (*Abstract*)

T HE title page is dated 1648; there was a second edition in 1649. Winstanley's name appears both on the title page and at the end of the
address to "my beloved countrymen of the County
of Lancaster". Since this address begins with an
apology for publishing, I infer that the pamphlet
was Winstanley's first work.

Copies of the edition of 1648 are to be found
in the British Museum; of the edition of 1649 in
the Harvard College Library and the Seligman
Library at Columbia University. It is included in
Several Pieces Gathered into one Volume, which
is in the Manchester Free Reference Library.

This abstract was made from the copy in the
Seligman Library.

THE MYSTERIE OF GOD

(*Abstract*)

T O MY BELOVED COUNTRYMEN OF THE COUNTY OF LANCASTER:
Do not be surprised to see my name here, for God does not
always choose the learned in whom to manifest himself. If
anything in this book seems strange, do not brand it as error, for I myself could not at first bear many truths of God in which I now see
beauty. As you desire that God should show love to you, be not offended to hear that He will show love even to those who have been
lost. It is for the glory of God that he shall redeem not part but all
mankind from death, for Christ gave himself a ransom for all.

The first fruit that the created being, Adam, brought forth was the
spirit of self-love aspiring to be equal with God, for every being has
a disposition to promote itself. When Adam ate the fruit of the tree,
he gave himself up to aspiring selfishness and delight in his new knowledge of good and evil, and he began to reject God. This selfishness in
the heart of Adam is the Serpent, by which he brings forth nothing
but pride, envy, discontent, and disobedience. This is the mystery of
iniquity, the aspiring of the creature to be an absolute being like God.
But if the creature were utterly lost, God would suffer dishonor because his work is spoiled. The mystery of God is this: that he will
destroy the power of darkness, and when his work is completed, he
will dwell in the whole creation, in every man and woman without exception, as he dwelt in Christ, the first manifestation of this mystery.
When Adam broke the covenant, God did not denounce an utter destruction upon mankind, but only upon the Serpent, or man's work
of rebellion against God. The curse against Adam was temporary;
God will destroy death and quicken mankind again and deliver whole
mankind from bondage.

This I know, first, by my own experience. Though I lay under bondage to the Serpent, I saw no bondage until God caused me to see that I was dead in sin. I was a stranger to God, though as I thought I was a professor of God. And though I was troubled at the power of darkness in me, I could not deny self until God pulled me out of selfish striving and gave me peace. And as God is pleased thus to deal with me, he made me see that he will become the life and liberty of his whole creation.

The same is known, second, by the testimony of Scripture. In the end every man shall be saved, though some at the last hour, and when this work is finished, other creatures, which were made only for man's use, will be dissolved into nothing, for there will then be no need for cattle, corn, meat or drink, or for sun, moon, and stars. First the curse of the law must be lifted and God appear as absolutely a God of love, as he does in being made flesh in Christ. This work of redemption is to be completed in seven dispensations, of which the present age is the sixth. In this age God begins to manifest himself in the flesh of the Saints; it will end with the perfect gathering of the Elect at the Resurrection. In this age the church is at a stand, some resting in the bare letter, some acknowledging God by the anointing of Christ within them. He that preaches from the book and not from the anointing is no true minister but a hireling that preaches only to get a temporal living. Some old professors, and book-hirelings especially, are offended and brand the Saints as men full of errors. But you must be dead to your customs before you can run into the sea of truth. At present some walk still according to example, and some walk more in spirit and in truth. In this age also the rage of the Serpent increases. To me it appears very plain that the great bitterness and reproaches now heaped on those called sectaries is the beginning of the beast's sorrow.

In the sixth dispensation God saves whom he will, but he gives the Serpent freedom still to fight against the Saints and overcome them. At the day of judgment, when the seventh dispensation will begin, both believers and disbelievers will be raised from the dead and rewarded or punished according to their works. The Serpent and all the disobedient ones in whom he dwelt will be cast into everlasting fire. But this is not the end. For even the lost, who were cast into the fire, shall receive mercy and the whole of mankind shall be delivered from the curse. The word everlasting in the Scriptures means only until the end of the dispensation during which the condemned lie under the wrath of God. There is no authority for the belief that sinners cannot be redeemed out of Hell. What is called the day of judgment is not a day but a long period. Only the Serpent remains at the end in eternal punishment. It quiets the heart to know that, whatsoever befalls, it is God's dispensation and that in his own time he will bring it to a good issue.

THE BREAKING OF THE DAY OF GOD (*Abstract*)

THE title page is dated 1648, and the address to "the despised sons and daughters of Zion" is dated May 20, 1648. There was a second edition dated 1649. Winstanley's name appears on the title page and at the end of the address.

The edition of 1648 is to be found in the British Museum and the Haverford College Library. That of 1649 is to be found in the Harvard College Library and the Seligman Library at Columbia University. It is included in *Several Pieces Gathered into one Volume*, which is to be found in the Manchester Free Reference Library.

This abstract was made from the copy in the British Museum.

THE BREAKING OF THE DAY OF GOD

(*Abstract*)

TO THE DESPISED SONS AND DAUGHTERS OF ZION: You are the objects of the world's hatred and reproach, and in these uproar risings you are condemned to death under the name of roundheads. You are the men they would chain up by an ecclesiastical power and would give no liberty to practice what God teaches you. You are despised because you are not of the world. But your redemption is near, for the Lord is burning up the dross of our flesh and shaking down corruption in kingdoms and churches. In the meantime the Serpent stirs up the world to maintain that corrupt power as long as it can. But if England is the tenth part of Babylon that shall fall off first from the beast, you shall see these divisions swallowed up in love, so that magistrates shall love the people and the people shall cheerfully obey magistrates. God is working out an inward and an outward peace and liberty for all.

Chapter I. The mystery of God is this, that He shall cast the Serpent out of man and dwell in him. The law and ceremonies of the Old Testament were types, making known how Christ should come in the flesh, but they were only a schoolmaster to lead to Christ. The sin of the Jews was to keep to Moses after Christ came, and it may well be the sin of the gentiles to keep to the letter of the Apostles after God has taken up his saints into spiritual enjoyment of Himself. The prophets failed to understand their own prophecies, but Christ now shows the right understanding of visions that were sealed up to the prophets. The book is a commentary on *Revelation*, xi, 3. It will explain what is the testimony of the witnesses there mentioned, who the witnesses were, the meaning of the 1260 days, how the two witnesses were slain, why they are unburied, and what shall follow their resurrection.

Chapter II. The testimony of the two witnesses is that Jesus and his Saints make one perfect man. The strength of God, in Jesus and the Saints, shall bruise the Serpent's head. God has need of witnesses that can prove their testimony not from books but from their own experienced knowledge. But the corrupt world makes laws to prevent the anointed from working upon whom he pleases and would restrain him to its own scanty measure.

Chapter III. The two witnesses are Christ in the flesh and Christ in the spirit or the mystical body of the Saints in whom the spirit of Christ dwells, including both learned and unlearned, rich and poor. Those who will not worship without the establishment of a human power are none of his witnesses. These witnesses are they who must prophesy in sackcloth for 1260 days; they are typified by the two candlesticks and the two olive trees. Zerubabel, who was the chief of the fathers of Israel, was the type of Christ; Joshua, clothed in filthy garments, was the type of the mystical body of Saints before God caused their iniquity to pass away. The battle of Christ against the beast typifies the struggle of the Saints against the wisdom of the flesh, strengthened by human authority. The remnant that were slain typifies the common people deceived by the learned wisdom of the beast. When Christ manifestly rules in the Saints, many call it a delusion, but he that believes in the whole Christ has the witness in himself. Heaven typifies either God or the Church. The stopping of the rain by the witnesses typifies either the withholding of God's justice on the beast, or the withholding of discoveries from the church, until the time is fulfilled.

Chapter IV. The days during which the witnesses shall prophesy in sackcloth signifies the time when the Saints see the truth of Christ blasphemed. The number, 1260 days, typifies the time from Christ's baptism until his death. This time typifies the battle of Christ against the dragon, and also the struggle between spirit and flesh in every believer. When men have a good conceit of their own learning, they call Christ a deceiver; and when a man is dead to his own wisdom, he cannot understand until God come into him. The writings of the prophets are dry shells until God gives experience of his love such as the prophets had. The 1260 days also typify the three ages and a half in which the church shall be in captivity to the anti-Christian power. These are (1) the time of magistracy out of joint, as in the

days of Nero; (2) the time of the universal bishop; (3) the time of
the reformed episcopacy. In the following half-age Christ is not allowed to choose his own church out of the world or to send forth his
own ministers. The unlearned are not allowed to preach, but only
such as are ordained. Anyone who attempts to set up the worship of
God by human law speaks like the beast, and any likewise who, without enforcing religion, refuses to accept as brethren those who are not
of their own way. But this half-age is now nearly finished, and the day
of Christ begins to shine.

Chapter V. The slaying of the two witnesses when they have finished testifying signifies the struggle of the beast against the Saints,
after they have made manifest that the seed of woman has broken the
serpent's head. The bottomless pit from which the beast rises is the
corrupt heart. of man. Corrupt wisdom is forcibly pressed upon the
Saints instead of the free grace of God. Men will not believe that
God will now give his spirit to tradesmen, as formerly He gave it to
fishermen, but believe that only those who have human ordination may
teach. Thus the flesh labors to kill God's witnesses by getting an authority from magistrates to make ecclesiastical laws, compelling all
men to conformity with forms of worship agreed upon. Ecclesiastical
power is not ordained of God but is got by crafty men from kings, to
kill the truth and persecute the Saints. The slaying of the witnesses
is not only a slaying of their bodies but also of their testimony, as the
Jews first killed the body of Christ and the ecclesiastical power then
killed his teaching. Thus against salvation by faith this power set up
a legal, ceremonial way of worship. It set up (1) the teaching of men
against the teaching of the spirit; (2) teaching according to books and
authorities against the teaching of the indwelling God; (3) oppression
against love; (4) a universal or national church against a church
called out of the world; (5) persecution of the Saints against honor-
ing them; (6) forms and customs against the communion of Saints;
(7) observance of days against the indwelling of Christ in the soul;
(8) corrupt forms of baptism, communion, and the maintenance of
ministers against Christ's clear teaching about these matters.

Chapter VI. The witnesses have lain dead nearly three and a half
days, and are now about to rise again. The troubles of the world at this
day are the cloud upon which they ascend to God. I have persuasions
in me, from experimental grounds of God's own working, that within

a few years God will make this manifest to the world, and this is confirmed by John's vision. The present is the time of the second woe described in *Revelation,* ix, 12 ff. Already the kingdom of Christ begins to appear, among the Saints that are scattered abroad. But by the angels of darkness in men they are branded as sectaries, schismatics, Anabaptists, and roundheads. The present is called the dividing of time because it is neither absolutely in bondage to ecclesiastical law nor absolutely free, but it may be hoped that England is the tenth part of the city of Babylon that shall fall off first from the beast. Though the two witnesses yet be dead under the power of discontent in outside professing Presbyterians and Independents, this will not last long. Men fancy that present troubles would disappear, if the worshiping of God in spirit could be beaten down and if all men could be forced to practice one outward, lazy, formal, customary, and tithe-oppressing way of pretended divine worship, but the time for this has gone by. The earthquake signifies God shaking down the false forms of pretended divine worship, and also kings, parliaments, universities, and human learning—all that stands in the way of His work. Then will come plentiful manifestations of God in his Saints, and the great will be filled with anger at seeing inferior people raised up to speak the deep things of God. Tradesmen will speak by experience the things they have seen in God, and the learned clergy will be slighted. This does not mean that there will be no laws or government, but that magistrates will delight in doing justice for the good of the commonwealth. It is the misery of this age that men try to uphold a usurped ecclesiastical power. They are even so mad that they deny magistracy, contrary to God's ordinance, unless it is upheld by ecclesiastical power. But this power has always been the great troubler of magistracy, enforcing uniformity in religion out of a desire for temporal livings. If magistrates would take back their power and would let the government of the church lie only on the shoulders of Christ, the pure reformation of civil magistracy would soon appear. The main cause of national troubles is the discontent of men that wander after ecclesiastical power. If magistrates will leave the work of the church alone, they will govern the commonwealth in justice and righteousness. Already the sun of righteousness has risen in some, and the bright shining of it will be England's liberty.

THE SAINTS PARADICE (*Abstract*)

THE title page is undated. According to the catalogue of the Thomason Library, Thomason
dated his copy July, 1658, but this cannot be correct for the first printing, since the pamphlet was
included in *Several Pieces Gathered into one Volume*, London, 1649. The book clearly preceded the
revelation that occasioned *The New Law of Righteousnes* and seems to be referred to in *Truth Lifting up its Head* (below, p. 107). Hence I infer that
it was written during the summer of 1648.

There were two editions. The copy in the Seligman Library at Columbia University has [8] + 85
pp. Copies of an edition having [8] + 134 pp. are
to be found in the Congregational Library (London), the Harvard College Library, the Library of
Princeton Theological Seminary, the Thomason Library at the British Museum. It is included in *Several Pieces Gathered into one Volume* in the Manchester Free Reference Library.

This abstract has been made from the copy in
the Seligman Library.

THE SAINTS PARADICE

(*Abstract*)

T O MY BELOVED FRIENDS WHOSE SOULS HUNGER AFTER SINCERE milk: The earth has been covered with darkness and the knowledge of God has been manifested only to a few scattered ones. I myself have known nothing but what I received from tradition, and I worshiped God, not knowing who He was or where He was. But at last it was showed to me that, while I builded upon any words or writings of other men, I builded upon sand. Man has a teacher within him and this is the spirit that made the globe and lives in every creature. The flesh leads men to imagine God in a place of glory beyond the skies, and it also leads men to kill those that differ from them, but righteousness is meek and full of love and sincerity. Souls have no peace until they have community with the spirit within them, but when they feel the spirit of righteousness governing their flesh, they begin to know God and they will be brought into community with the whole globe. Now the time approaches when the spirit will begin to appear in the flesh, when the poor shall receive the Gospel, when wise men after the flesh shall become fools and scholars become ignorant, and when the ignorant become learned in the experimental knowledge of Christ. Thus men will knit together in one body and will cease to teach, for everyone will be taught of the Father.

Chapter I. The Father's teaching is the only satisfaction to waiting souls. Some men teach from books and hearsay, and not from zeal for God but from desire for a living. Others speak from their own experience, and this is true ministry, but even this must cease, for the anointing which the Saints receive from the Father teaches them all things. God's teaching shall never cease, for it gives a feeling experience to the heart which can never be forgot. This alone overcomes the self-conceit and evil inclinations of the flesh. Not the Apostles' writings but the spirit that dwelt in them and inspired their hearts gives life and peace. Though men speak the very words of Scripture, but speak not with the mind of Him that gives life, they may be strangers or even enemies to the God of the Scriptures. But if the same anointing dwell in you as in the Apostles, you can see into the mystery of Scripture, though you should never hear the Scripture from men. If your comfort in God remain with you only while you read the Scriptures, there is a strangeness between you and the God of the Scriptures. When God sets you free from your bondage, you shall find the spirit in you, and in the midst of these national hurly-burlies, though you lack riches and food and clothing and even the communion of good people, you can rest quiet in God.

Chapter II. In these days the corruption of the flesh appears in unbelief, hypocrisy, cruelty, and slavish fear of men. Though some of the Saints give up their lives and liberties into the hands of wicked men, it will not be for long. For God will not suffer the scoffers to destroy God's people, whom they reproach as roundheads, Anabaptists, and Independents. When the counties rose against the Parliament's army some were not ashamed to say that they would destroy men, women, and children of the Independent party. God can make an outside professing service-book man kill an outside professing Presbyterian, or he can permit the latter to kill a hypocritical Independent, while the sincere hearted ones, scattered abroad in the kingdom, look on and are preserved. God will work the deliverance of the Saints and their number will increase, for the wicked fight not against the Saints but against God. The devil of unrighteous flesh has no power but what God gives him, and the time draws near when God will kill the Serpent.

Chapter III. God's righteous law is not the letter of the Commandments but the spirit in man that discovers to him his uncleanness and hypocrisy. The flesh seeks to swallow up the law of God, but the law shall swallow up the flesh. This enmity of natures between God and man is the devil, and its misery is hell. But the power of the devil is not a power distinct from God; the flesh and darkness within man are the devil, and it is the righteous law that makes this appear as enmity against God. The great mystery of God is this, that he will remove the mountain that lies between Him and His creature and will swallow up the enmity of our natures. Though the Saints are persecuted, God permits this that He may condemn the devil by the work of his own hands.

Chapter III (*sic*). The devil is not a power distinct from God but a dispensation of God, laying hold of the corruption in the creature to destroy it. The fear of the devil is the shining forth of the righteous law that burns up the enmity in human nature. When this enmity vanishes, the devil disappears; the creature lives in God and God in him, and this is liberty. Then the creature looks on God not as an angry God but as a God of love. When God permits you to see that it is He who shakes kingdoms, families, and estates, through the power of His righteous law, you will see that what you call the devil is within you, and you will see that, by the power of the anointing, you will be set free from the devil in a short time.

Chapter IV. At first men are troubled by the shining forth of the righteous law upon the proud heart, but when they are set free, they see that, whatever befalls, it is by the will of the Father, for burning up the pride of the flesh. Perhaps England is now cast into the fire to be purged of dross and set free, so that the spirit of love, truth, and oneness is near at hand. Neither a bitter nor a hypocritical spirit can be brought to God. Every Saint is a true Heaven, because God dwells in him and he in God, and the communion of Saints is a true Heaven. Similarly, Angel is used in a twofold sense, as the sparks of glory or heavenly principles set in men, and as men who have been wholly taken up into God so that God dwells bodily in them; such men, being made perfect, can never fall from God. When men harken to the whisperings of selfishness, these sparks become spirits of darkness. Salvation is the restoring of the creature to the liberty and peace of the king of righteousness. Pride, covetousness, anger, and self-love are angels of darkness in man that are destroyed by the restoration. Every man is a perfect created world. The spirit of right understanding has taken up his dwelling in this flesh, and from hence man is called a reasonable creature, which is a name given to no other creature but man, because the spirit of reason acts in him, and if men would submit themselves thereto, they would act righteously continually. If men would cleanse themselves of the wicked powers in them, there would speedily be love between all creatures; it is the powers of the heart that will not submit to the light of reason that has come into it.

Chapter V. The powers of Parliament and the Army must learn to worship the Lord in righteousness, for all unrighteous powers will be destroyed at the resurrection of Christ. This resurrection means that the spirit in mankind shall triumph over the flesh. For Christ is the life of every man and woman, and His rising from one to many persons shall enlighten all mankind and cover the earth with knowledge. You are not to be saved by believing that a man lived and died long ago at Jerusalem, but by the power of the spirit within you treading down all unrighteousness of the flesh. Neither are you to look for God in a place of glory beyond the sun, but within yourself and in every man. You are not saved until you experience the power of the spirit ruling your own evil inclinations. He that looks for a God outside himself, and worships a God at a distance, worships he knows not what, but he that submits to the spirit of righteousness within him, has community with the spirit in all creatures. What I hear another man speak is nothing to me until I find the same experience in myself; the testimony of others is known to be true by the testimony of the same experience within myself. The Spirit or Father is pure reason; Christ is the anointing that shall end the quarrel between the two natures in man; and the devil that troubles man is no third power, but the power of reason showing man his wickedness and filling him with shame. The spirit that knits all creatures together in love is reason, but the power that makes one creature tyrant over another, and even divides the creature against himself, is flesh or the devil. But this devil is the four evil angels within you: subtlety, hypocrisy, envy, and cruelty. None can free you but Christ, who is not a man at a distance but is the wisdom of the Father, who spirits the whole creation and dwells as king of righteousness in your very flesh. Now righteousness and peace have begun to reign, and their dominion shall have no end. When flesh becomes subject to the reason within it, it can never act unrighteously or trespass against others, but it does as it would be done by.

Chapter VI. An interpretation of three passages of Scripture. Only man's evil qualities are tormented. God's wrath is against sin but not against the sinner, and while He can never be reconciled to sin, He will make His creature one with Him.

TRUTH LIFTING UP ITS HEAD
ABOVE SCANDALS

T HE TITLE PAGE is dated 1649, but the address to "the Scholars of Oxford and Cambridge" is dated October 16, 1648. A second edition, dated 1650, is nearly identical with the first, the corrections apparently having been made by the printer rather than by Winstanley, since some of the most serious errors were not corrected. Winstanley's name appears on the title page and also at the end of the address. The pamphlet was occasioned by the imprisonment of William Everard at Kingston.

A copy of the edition of 1649 is in the British Museum; that of 1650 is in the Library of Princeton Theological Seminary and in the Seligman Library at Columbia University. It is included in *Several Pieces Gathered into one Volume*, in the Manchester Free Reference Library.

The text is reproduced from the copy in the British Museum.

TO THE SCHOLARS OF OXFORD AND CAM-
BRIDGE, AND TO ALL THAT CALL THEM-
SELVES MINISTERS OF THE GOSPEL IN
CITY AND COUNTRY

SIRS,

Y ou are the men that stand up, assuming the power to your
selves to teach the People the mystery of the Spirit; and that
you are the onely men sent of him for that office: therefore you
are called spirituall men, or men that are all spirit.

Many differences you see about spirituall things, arises up daily
amongst the people; it doth not belong to you to make parties; but to
judge of these differences, with a moderate and meek || spirit between
people and people; you are not to suffer flesh or selfish distemper to
breake forth from you; a hasty rash spirit cannot judge anything.

There are onely these two roots, from whence these differences spring
up, that is, either from the Spirit that made all things, or from humane
flesh, which is the Creature that is gone astray; and he that walks after
the flesh, denies the Spirit.

Now if you be spirituall, as you say, you are to judge of these differences, and declare what is of the Spirit, that it may stand; and what
is of the flesh that it may be trod under foot; that so the Lord alone,
that made flesh, may be exalted above *flesh*, in the day of his power, that
doth begin to shine forth. The rule that you judge by, you say are the
Scriptures of Prophets, Apostles and ancient writers; if so, then you
are not spirituall, or all spirit; neither have you the alone priviledge to
judge; for the || People having the Scriptures, may judge by them as
well as you.

If you say no, the People cannot judge, because they know not the
originall: I answer, neither doe you know the originall; though by
your learning you may be able to translate a writing out of *Hebrew*

or *Greek* into our mother tongue, *English*; but to say this is the originall Scripture you cannot: for those very Copies which the Prophets and Apostles writ, are not to be seen in your Universities.

You say you have the just Copies of their writings; you doe not know that but as your Fathers have told you; which may be as well false as true, if you have no better ground then tradition. You say that the interpretation of Scripture into our mother tongue is according to the mind of the *spirit*; you cannot tell that neither, unlesse you were able to say, that those who did interpret those writings, had had || the same testimony of Spirit, as the pen-men of Scriptures had; for it is the Spirit within that must prove those copies to be true: now you know that there are many translations and interpretations, which differ much one from another; which of them must the People take to be truest; seeing you your selves are at [a] losse?

One company of you sayes, this translation is the truth; and then the People must be forced to follow you: loe, here is Christ, saith the Prelats; another company of yours saies, such a translation is the truest; and then the People must be forced to follow them: as this halfe day of the Beast, cry, loe here is Christ,

First, here in the Presbytery; then there in the Independency: and thus you leade the People like horses by the noses; & ride upon them at your pleasure from one forme and custome to another, and so quite from the Spirit. ||

You presse the People with much violence, to maintain the Gospel: the People demands, What is the Gospel? You say, it is the Scriptures. The People replies again; *How can these Scriptures be called the ever-lasting Gospel, seeing it is torne in peeces daily amongst your selves, by various translations, inferences and conclusions; one pressing this, another that; and the People are lost in the midst of your waters?*

If you say, you can judge by the Spirit, why, then you have not the alone priviledge to judge neither; for the Spirit is not confined to your Universities; but it spreads from East to West, and enlightens sons and daughters in all parts.

If you say, that visions and revelations are ceased, and that the Spirit and Scriptures are still together; then you erre mightily in spending constructions upon the Scriptures, which is a revelation; and doth not rather leave the || Scriptures to their own genuine language, that People may read the very letter without alteration.

Two things, as you are Scripture men, you must judge of. First, what is the Gospel. Secondly, what is the report or declaration of the Gospel. I declare positively what I know; doe you take the Scriptures and disprove me if you can. First, The *Gospel* is the *Spirit* that ruled in the *Prophets* and *Apostles*, which testified to them, that in the later daies the same *Spirit* should be poured out upon all *flesh*. Secondly, then their writings is not the *Spirit*; but a report or declaration of that law and testimony which was within them.

Now the Spirit spreading it selfe from East to West, from North to South in sonnes and daughters, is everlasting, and never dies; but is still everlasting, and rising higher and higher in manifesting himselfe in and to mankinde. ||

But now the declaration of the *Spirit*, being but words gon out of the mouth, may be, and daily are corrupted by the subtilty of imaginary flesh; it is the *Spirit* within every man that tries all things: words cannot try all things: he that speakes from the flesh; shall of the *flesh* reap corruption; shall tast of misery that *flesh* brings upon himselfe: but he that speaks from the Spirit, shall of the Spirit reap life: or he that preaches the *Gospel*, *shall live of the Gospel*; that is, he that speakes from the *Spirit*, shall have inward peace, life, and liberty from the Spirit, in the midst of all worldly straights, he shall not want life and peace within.

You will say, what of all this?

I answer, it is matter of the greatest concernment; your Pulpit wrings against Errors: The People cries what are those errors? You answere, || that there are a company of men rose up that denies God and Christ, and the Scriptures, and the Gospel, and prayer, and all Ordinances; and yet you have not considered with a meek spirit what these men say; but cry them down without tryall: is this spiritual judging?

Well, matters of this nature, are to be judged with a wary and moderate spirit; covetous rashnesse can judge of nothing. I my selfe being branded by some of your mouthes, as guilty of horrid *blasphemy*, for denying all these, as you say, though you cannot prove it, was drawn forth by the Spirit to write what here followes; which I leave to the spirituall men all the world over to judge.

Whether you your selves, be not the very men that doe deny God, Scriptures and Ordinances of God; and that turnes the truthes of the Spirit into a lye; by leaving the letter, and walking || in your own inferences; and so by holding forth spirituall things by that imagination of the flesh, and not by the law and testimony of the Spirit within; and let them likewise judge whether those men you count such blasphemers; be not those men that doth advance God, Christ, Scriptures and Ordinances, in the spirituality of them.

When the Apostolicall gifts ceased, which was to speak from an inward testimony of what they heard and saw; as the Father did will it should cease for a time, times and halfe time; or fourty two moneths; then began the false Christs and false Prophets to arise, that speak from tradition of what they had read in Books; expounding those writings from their imaginary thoughts; getting a power from the Magistrate to protect them; and to punish such as speak from the testimony of Christ within them, which flesh is willing to oppose. ||

And then the flesh began to be advanced above the Spirit, from the time that the universall Bishop was raised, to this very hour; and so in every government; which imagination hath set up since that time false Christs, and false Prophets have arose from your Schools, and have filled the Earth with darknesse; so that now when the King of righteousnesse begins to arise, and fill the earth with his light; the Earth growes mad & full of rage: but though flesh be angry; assure your selves Christ will take the Kingdome, and rule in *flesh*. And here I rest,

A servant to

the Father;

Gerrard Winstanly.||

Oct. 16. 1648.

TO THE GENTLE READER

D EAR FRIEND *it is slanderously reported (by reason whereof some of you may be troubled to hear) that Chamberlain the* Redding *man, called after the flesh,* William Everard [1]; *doth hold blasphemous opinions: as to deny God, and Christ, and Scriptures, and prayer; and they call him a deceiver, and many filthy names; and upon this report of the raging multitude (some that call themselves Ministers, and some common people) the Bayliffs of* Kingston *have put him in prison, as he came through their Towne and took a nights lodging; and hath kept him there this weeke, upon these supposed scandals.*

Now I was moved to write what here followes, as a vindication of the man and my selfe, being slandered as well as he (by some of the Ministers) having been in his company; that all the world may judge of his and my innocency in these particular scandals; and that it may appear, as it will upon tryall, that the parish Ministers themselves, and every one that followes their way of worship; doth turn the Scriptures into a lye, by leaving the old || letter that the Apostles writ; and new

---

[1] When the Diggers began work at St. George's Hill, in April, 1649, William Everard, rather than Winstanley, was described as their leader. In the information lodged with the Council of State, he is said to call himself a prophet and to have been dismissed from the army; the officer whom Fairfax sent to investigate reported that he was "no better than a madman". See the *Clarke Papers*, Vol. II, pp. 210 ff. When Everard and Winstanley visited Fairfax, Everard seems to have been the chief speaker; he described himself as "of the race of the Jews", meaning presumably that he was of the chosen people, and, like the Quakers, he refused to remove his hat in the General's presence. The interview was reported in a news-sheet, *The Declaration and Standard of the Levellers of England delivered in a Speech . . . by Mr. Everard* (London, April 23, 1649), and this report was copied at length by Bulstrode Whitelock in his *Memorials*, under date of April 20. Apparently Everard's connection with the Diggers did not continue; he signed their first manifesto, *The True Levellers Standard Advanced*, but his name does not appear later. In the contemporary news-

moulding those Scriptures into their own language; walking according to their owne inferences and conjectures thereupon; and by holding forth God and Christ to be at a distance from men; they are the only men that deny God and Christ and Scriptures, and Ordinances, walking in the practise of their own invention, to which ignorant flesh closeth without examination: and so the greatest theeves cry, stop theefe first.

And here I shall adde one word as an accompt wherefore I use the word Reason, instead of the word God, in my writings, as you shall meet withall: If I demand of you, who made all things? And you answer God. If I demand what is God? You answer the spirituall power; that as he made; so he governs and preserves all things; so that the sum of all is this, God is the chief Maker or Governor, & this maker & governor is God: Now I am lost in this wheel that runs round, and lies under darkness.

But if you demand of mee, why I say Reason did make, and doth governe and preserve all things: I answer, Reason is that living power of light that is in all things; it is the salt that savours all things; it is the fire that burns up drosse, and so restores what is corrupted; and preserves what is pure; he is the Lord our righteousnesse.

It lies in the bottom of love, of justice, of wisdome; for if the Spirit Reason did not uphold and moderate these, they would be madnesse;

sheets he was commonly reported to have joined the Leveller rebellion in the army, which was terminated at Burford in May; for example, in *The Kingdom's Faithfull and Impartiall Scout,* under date of May 10, and *Mercurius Brittanicus,* May 8–15.

Unfortunately, Everard was not an uncommon name. Richard Baxter had known two men of that name, both sectaries, in Cromwell's army; *Reliquiae* (1696), p. 78. A certain William Everard, who may have been the Digger, had been implicated in the mutiny that occurred in the regiments at Ware in November, 1647, and had been put under arrest for saying it was lawful to kill the King; see the *Clarke Papers,* Vol. I, p. 419. There was an Everard also who was associated about 1649 with John Pordage, and Pordage was known to Baxter as the chief representative in England of Jakob Boehme's mysticism; see the *Reliquiae, loc. cit.* This conjunction is suggestive, since Pordage had been a curate in Reading, whence William Everard came. Everard had lived in Pordage's household, and in his trial for heresy in 1654 Pordage described him as a "conjurer"; Howell's *State Trials,* Vol. V, cols. 550–553, 556, 568. Like Winstanley, Pordage believed in the inner light, as a source both of revelation and of salvation, and Baxter implies that he was a source of subversive ideas about both property and magistracy. It is credible that William Everard may have been the man of that name who lived with Pordage and that he may have made Winstanley acquainted with Pordage's mysticism.

nay, they || could not be called by them names; for Reason guids them in order, and leads them to their right end, which is not to preserve a part, but the whole creation.

But is mans reason that which you cal God? I answer, mans reasoning is a creature which flows from that Spirit to this end, to draw up man into himselfe: it is but a candle lighted by that soul, and this light shining through flesh, is darkened by the imagination of flesh; so that many times men act contrary to reason, though they thinke they act according to reason.

By that light of Reason that is in man, he may see a sutablenesse in many things, but not in all things; for the reason that acts in another man, may see a weakenesse of reason that acts in me: but now the Spirit Reason, which I call God, the Maker and Ruler of all things, is that spirituall power, that guids all mens reasoning in right order, and to a right end: for the Spirit Reason, doth not preserve one creature and destroy onother; as many times mens reasoning doth, being blind by the imagination of the flesh: but it hath a regard to the whole creation; and knits every creature together into a onenesse; making every creature to be an upholder of his fellow; and so every one is an assistant to preserve the whole: and the neerer that mans reasoning comes to this, the more spirituall they are; the farther off they be, the more selfish and fleshy they be. ||

Now this word Reason is not the alone name of this spirituall power: but every one may give him a name according to that spirituall Power that they feel and see rules in them, carrying them forth in actions to preserve their fellow creatures as well as themselves.

Therefore some may call him King of righteousnesse and Prince of peace: some may call him Love, and the like: but I can, and I doe call him Reason; because I see him to be that living powerfull light that is in righteousnesse, making righteousnesse to be righteousnesse; or justice to be justice; or love to be love: for without this moderater and ruler, they would be madnesse; nay, the selfewilledliness of the flesh; and not that which we call them.

Lastly, I am made to change the name from God to Reason; because I have been held under darknesse by that word, as I see many people are; and likewise that people may rest no longer upon words without knowledge; but hereafter may look after that spirituall power; and know what it is that rules them, and which doth rule in and over all, and which they call their God and Governour or preserver. And this I hope will be a sufficient accompt why I alter the word: what here followes may give more light into the thing.

Gerrard Winstanly.

Reade and judg; let flesh be silent; let the Spirit be honored. ||

[1] TRUTH LIFTING UP HIS HEAD ABOVE SCANDALS

I HAVE said[2], That whosoever worships God by hear-say, as others tels them, knowes not what God is from light within himselfe; or that thinks God is in the heavens above the skyes; and so prayes to that God which he imagines to be there and every where: but from any testimony within, he knowes not how, nor where; this man worships his owne imagination, which is the Devill.

But he that is a true worshipper, must know who God is, and how he is to be worshipped, from the power of light shining in him, if ever he have true peace.

[2] And from hence a report is raised and is frequent in the mouthes of the teachers; That I deny God; And therefore First, I shall give account what I see and know is to be; and let the understanding in heart judge me.

Qu. *What is God?*

Ans. I answer, He is the incomprehensible spirit, Reason; who as he willed that the Creation should flow out of him: so he governes the whole Creation in righteousnesse, peace and moderation: And from hence he is called, The Lord, because there is none above him: And he is called, The Father, because as the whole creation came out of him, so he is the life of the whole creation, by whom every creature doth subsist.

Qu. *When can a man call the Father his God?*

Ans. When he feels and sees, by experience, that the spirit which made the flesh, doth governe and rule King in his flesh: And so can say, I rejoyce to feele and see my flesh made subject to the spirit of righteousnesse.

Qu. *But may not a man call him God, till hee have this experience?*

[2] Probably a reference to *The Saints Paradice.*

Ans. No: For if he doe, he lyes, and there is no truth in him; for whatsoever rules as [3] King in his flesh, that is his God. As for example; If pride, envy, frowardnesse, hypocrisy, uncleanesse, feare of men more then feare of God, or covetousnesse; If all, or any one of these, rule and governe thee, either all, or any one of these is thy God, and so thou worships the flesh, and that Devill is thy God. And the spirit of righteousnesse is not thy God, for thou dost not yet submit unto him.

Qu. But I hope that the Father is my Governor: and therefore may I not call him God?

Ans. Hope without ground is the hope of the hypocrite; thou canst not call him God, till thou be able in pure experience to say, Thy flesh is subject to him; for if thy knowledge be no more but Imagination or thoughts, it is of the Devill, and not of the Father: or if thy knowledge be meerly from what thou hast read or heard from others, it is of the flesh, not of the spirit.

Qu. When then may I call him God, or the mighty Governour, and doe not descend [deceive] my selfe?

Ans. When thou art, by that spirit, made to see him, rule and governe, not onely in thee, but in the whole creation: so that thou feels and sees, that the spirituall power that governes in thee, hath a community in thee with the whole globe; and thou art made [4] subject to that spirit of righteousnesse, peace, meeknesse and love, who doth subject all things to himselfe, and brings all things into a onenesse. Now thou mayst call him God warrantably, for thou knowest him to be the mighty governour: And that the government of the whole creation is upon the shoulders of that spirit, to which thou art made experimentally subject.

Waite upon him till he teach thee. All that reade doe not understand: the spirit only sees truth, and lives in it.

Qu. But how shall I know the spirit of the Father, so that I may call him God?

Ans. The spirit of the Father is pure Reason: which as he made, so he knits the whole creation together into a one-nesse of life and moderation; every creature sweetly in love lending their hands to preserve each other, and so upholds the whole fabrique.

Qu. Where doth this Reason dwell, which you call Father and Lord of all?

Ans. He dwels in every creature, according to the nature and being of the creature, but supreamely in man. Therefore man is called a Rationall creature, and the well-beloved son of the Father, because by his creation, he is to live in the light of Reason. [5] But when he acts unrighteously, he lives without Reason; and so contrary to his creation as a man. But when he acts righteously, then he lives in Reason, and Reason in him; and so according to his creation, to the honour of his Maker.

Qu. Give some example, how Reason made and governes the creation?

Ans. Take these among many; and yet you shall finde, that the further you dive into Reason, the more incomprehensible hee will appeare; for he is infinite in wisdome, and mighty in power, past finding out by flesh, till the flesh be made to see light in his light.

The clouds send downe raine, and there is great undeniable reason in it, for otherwise the earth could not bring forth grasse and fruit. The earth sends forth grasse, or else cattle could not be preserved. The cattle feed upon the grasse, and there is Reason in it, for else man could not be preserved. The Sunne gives his light and heate, or else the creation could not subsist. So that the mighty power, Reason, hath made these to give life and preservation one to another.

Reason makes a man to live moderately and peaceably with all; he makes a man just and righteous in all his actings; he kils frowardnesse, [6] envy and pride in a man: and why? where lyes the Reason? Because this man stands in need of others, and others stand in need of him; and therefore makes a man to doe as he would be done unto. Indeed Reason is of such a mighty power, that when he rules King in the flesh, he governes all things in righteousnesse, and there is no complainings or cryings out against oppression.

There is nothing but unreasonablenesse in all the powers of the flesh; as in coveteousnesse, pride, envy, and the like; and hereby the flesh brings misery and ruine upon it self. But pure and perfect Reason makes every thing to sing and rejoice in righteousnesse: When this King reignes the City is glad.

Qu. What Reason is there that I should have such temptations within, and afflictions without?

Ans. Reason sees it fit you should be befitted [buffeted] by your owne lusts, which you have chose to delight in; that hereby you being inwardly tormented and shamed, you may be drawne to owne and submit to the spirit, that gives peace and liberty; and so for ever after hate the motions of the flesh.

Qu. But what reason is there, that other men should oppresse me?

Ans. Still to let you see your owne unrighteousnesse [7] to others; therefore other unrighteous men are suffered to deale unrighteously with you, to let you see, that the wayes of unrighteousnesse brings nothing but paine; and when you are brought to this, the spirit which hath beene sleighted by you, is now owned and honoured.

Secondly, Reason suffers the flesh of other men to tyrannize over you for a time; that in the day, when he will sit upon the throne, all flesh may be silent before him, and confesse his Justice to be righteous upon them, for their unrighteousnesse one to another.

Now Reason suffers all these things to be, that the flesh may forsake himselfe; he seeing in Reasons light, that he being nothing but envy and misery to himselfe; and so may returne to the spirit, and submit thereunto; in whom his life and peace lyes.

Qu. And what is the end that Reason hath in all this?

Ans. To destroy the powers of the flesh; which leades creatures into divers waies of opposition one against another, and to bring all into pure experience of that sweet rest and peace that is in the unity of himselfe, the one spirit.

Qu. Is Reason to be seene in every creature?

Ans. Yes.

[8] *Qu. What Reason is to be seene in a Horse?*

Ans. Reason carries him along to eate his meat, that he may doe worke for the use of man.

Qu. But the horse doth not know this Reason that rules him?

Ans. No: Neither hath any creature that priviledge to see and know that Reason rules him, but man. Therefore he is said to be the Lord of creatures, because he knowes how to govern them by reason that is within himselfe.

Qu. But all men doe not see and know Reason to rule in them?

Ans. No: Therefore some are called unreasonable men; and though they are in the shape of men, yet their actings are like their horses, and they know the spirit that rules them, no more then their horses.

But now when a man knowes, that this King of righteousnesse, Reason, doth dwell in him, and rule in him; to which all the powers of his flesh are made subject, which indeed is Christ dwelling in the flesh. Now he may be said to be a perfect man, for he acts like a man, righteously: and so as the Father lives in him, he lives in the Father.

Qu. *Who is he that cals men to an account for their unrighteousnesse?*

[9] *Ans.* It is the mighty spirit, Reason, who is King of righteousnesse and King of peace; wherefore art thou proud, saith Reason? Wherefore art thou covetous? Wherefore art thou envious and bitter spirited against thy fellow creatures? Wherefore art thou unclean?

Ans. The Flesh answers, *It is to please my selfe.*

Qu. Reason answers, Didst thou make thy selfe, that thou shouldst live to thy selfe? Or did not I the Lord make thee to live unto me? I tell you, when Reason puts these questions to the heart, the heart will be struck dead.

Qu. *What is it to walke righteously, or in the sight of Reason?*

Ans. First, When a man lives in all acts of love to his fellow creatures; feeding the hungry; cloathing the naked; relieving the oppressed; seeking the preservation of others as well as himselfe; looking upon himselfe as a fellow creature (though he be Lord of all creatures) to all other creatures of all kinds; and so doing to them, as he would have them doe to him; to this end, that the Creation may be upheld and kept together by the spirit of love, tendernes and onenesse, and that no creature may complaine of any [10] act of unrighteousnesse and oppression from him.

Secondly, when a man lives in the knowledge and love of the Father, seeing the Father in every creature, and so loves, delights, obeyes, and honours the Spirit which he sees in the creature, and so acts rightly towards that creature in whom hee sees the spirit of the Father for to rest, according to its measure.

And whereas before he exercised outward senses to follow creatures; now he lives in the exercise of his spirituall senses, and hee doth rightly, and he knowes wherefore; for his soul now sees, feels, tasts, smels and hears the Father spiritually in all things, and so doth all things in love and cheerfull obedience to the Spirit, that discovers all things to him inwardly; whereby he is made able to doe acts of righteousnesse outwardly.

This man that is thus drawn up, knowes what it is to live in community with the Globe; and to live in community with the Spirit of the Globe.

In the next place, I said that Jesus Christ at a distance from thee, will not save thee; and that it is not the humane flesh, but the Spirit in that body, that is the Saviour, and the Seed, that must bruise the Serpents head [11] in mankind. And hence they say I deny Christ. Therefore I shall give accompt here unto by these questions.

Qu. *What is Jesus Christ?*

I answer, He is a man taken up to live wholly in the Father; or a meek spirit drawn up to live in the light of Reason. And here note two things.

1. That Jesus Christ that dyed at Jerusalem by the hands of the Jewes, he was the first in whom the Father did appeare bodily to dwell in; and that humane body was the Lambe that answered all the types of *Moses* Law: But that body tooke its name from the spirit that dwelt within it.

Qu. *What was that Spirit?*

Ans. He was the spirit of meeknesse and humility, which saved humane flesh from all distempers that ariseth from pride or covetousnesse, and this is the Child Jesus, a Saviour; for he destroyes the covetousnesse and pride in flesh, & frees the creature from all distempring fears and passions; and rules King, in meeknesse and quiet humility.

2. He was the spirit of the Father; that lived in the exercise and use of all the spirituall senses: and therefore as the Father was said to live in him, so he was said to live in the Father.

[12] Qu. *But shall not that humane body of Christ save me by his death?*

Ans. The Spirit in that humane body is the Saviour: *The flesh profits nothing:* the patient death of that humane body, declares the excellent power of the Spirit within it to be the alone Saviour of humane flesh from the curse and power of darknesse, that workes and rules in it, and so hath taken it prisoner.

And therefore when the same Anointing or Spirit that was sent downe into that body; is sent down into yours, *changing your vile bodies and making them like that glorious body,* killing all the cursed powers in the flesh; making your flesh subject to the Spirit; now you are become one with Christ, and with the Father, which is your salvation.

Qu. *But shall I not looke upon that body, which was called Iesus Christ, and expect salvation from him?*

Ans. Jesus Christ at a distance from thee, will never save thee; but a Christ within is thy Saviour: and therefore *Paul* after he had looked upon the Lambe a long time; that is looked upon Christ at a distance from himselfe, he saw that would bring him no peace; therefore saith he, *Though I have known Christ after the flesh, yet henceforth know I him no more:* [13] for now the mystery of God, that hath been kept secret from ages and generations past, is in these last daies revealed, *which is, Christ in you the hope of glory.*

Qu. *But was not that body killed, laid in the earth, and raised again from the dead, and ascended up to the Father into Heaven?*

Ans. He was killed by the curse that ruled in the Jewes, and was laid in the earth; here was the wisdome and power of the Father seen, that though all the powers of hell, or covetous, proud flesh did combine together, to oppresse, and then to kill a body, wherein he himselfe dwelt bodily; yet they could not distemper him, for he was still patient, and he was not heard to complain.

Qu. *Wherein was his wisdome and power seene in this?*

Ans. Hereby hee gives testimony to the World, that it is he himself that is the Seed that bruises the *Serpents* head, that is, in mankinde: for his spirit being so powerfull in flesh; kils the spirit of venome that is in flesh; and that body being laid in the earth purifieth the earth and purges it from that curse that man had filled it with by his unrighteousnesse; and so his spirit doth spirit the Earth in righteousnesse.

[14] Qu. *Did man fill the Earth with poyson and the curse?*

Ans. Yea, after he refused to live after the Spirit, his Maker; and made choyce to live upon the objects of the Creation, he then dyed and corrupted, and fell into all venimous and stinking unrighteousnesse: and as his body went to the earth, he did still poyson and corrupt the earth, and caused it to bring forth poysonous Vipers, Todes and Serpents, and Thornes and Bryars.

For the curse being first falen upon mankinde, through man it fell upon the other creatures, and the Earth was cursed for his sake; and the poyson of mans unrighteous body, dunging the Earth, filled the grasse and herbs with strong unsavory spirits, that flowed from him, whereby the cattell feeding, comes to be made bitter spirited, and mad one against another.

For the Ayre and Earth is all poysoned, and the curse dwels in both, through mans unrighteousnesse; he that should have kept within order, being made Lord of creatures, he put the Creation out of order, by forsaking his Maker, and by acting according to the flesh. Now this mighty spirituall man of *righteousnes*, Jesus Christ, doth purify humane flesh again; and so, restoring the head [15] first, doth new-spirit the Creation, and brings all into order again; taking away the bitternesse and curse, and making the whole Creation to be of one heart and one Spirit.

Qu. But it is said that his body rose again and ascended up through the cloudes into the skies, which is called Heaven, or place of Glory, where the Father dwels?

Ans. This speech hath blinded the understandings of many; for the Father is not confined to any one particular place; for he is in every place, and in every creature; and where Hee dwels in cleare manifestations, there is Heaven; and the higher manifestations the higher Heavens.

Now the body of Christ is where the Father is, in the earth, purifying the Earth; and his Spirit is entred into the whole creation, which is the heavenly glory, where the Father dwels; which is a glory above the flesh, and where he rules King and Lord, in and over all the Creation, purging out all strong spirited powers that cause sorrow; and bringing all into the unity of that one Spirit, himself. So that this Jesus Christ or mighty man that saves us, is not in one particular place: but every where.

And this certainly to me is very cleare, [16] That whereas the Apostles saw Christ arise and ascend, and were witnesses of his Resurrection, it was onely a declaration in vision to them, of the Spirits rising up: for death, and hel, and darknesse, and sorrow, could not hold him under; he saw no corruption; for as soon as that one body, in which he was confined for a time, was laid low; he rose presently up again in the bodies of the Apostles, & so began to spread in the Earth; and when his set time is expired, that the Beast, or flesh shall reign no more: Then he will spread himselfe in sons and daughters from East to West, from North to South; and never cease encreasing till this vine hath filled the Earth.

And truly this is great comfort to me, that envy could not kill that Spirit; but though it killed that body, through an appointed permission; yet the spirit rose up, and shewed himself, and went to his Father; that is, entred into the Creation, to purge it from the curse; and to spread himselfe in sons and daughters of the Earth; that by him their flesh being made subject, and saved from the curse, might by him become one with him and with his Father; that is, become one in spirit with him, and enjoy communion with the Spirit that is in the whole Globe.

[17] Qu. *But how shall I know that Christ dwels in me?*

Ans. It is the testimony of the Spirit it selfe that must give you satisfaction: for that which is a testimony within me, is not yours till the same Spirit make it yours: therefore you are to waite with a quiet and humble spirit, till the Father be pleased to teach you, and manifest himselfe to you, and then you shall know, what I speake, I speake not of my selfe; but what I have received from the Father.

Qu. *You seem to say, that the body of Christ was laid in the earth and remains there*: but *the Scriptures say, that he saw no corruption; how doth this agree?*

Ans. His body was laid in the Earth, as other dead bodies of men are; but it lay not in the Earth as other dead bodies doe; for other dead bodies lay there corrupting the Creation: but he rose up and purified the Creation; death or curse could not hold his body under its power.

Qu. *What doe you mean by Creation in this sence?*

Ans. I mean fire, water, earth and aire, of which four elements the whole creation [18] is made, and mankind is made up of them all. Now when the first man fell, he corrupted the whole creation, fire, water, earth and aire, and still as the branches of his body went to the earth, the creation was more and more corrupted, by the multiplicities of bodies, that stil saw corruption, for none rose up above the curse, but all lay under it. Now when the body of Jesus Christ went to the earth, that body likewise being made of fire, water, earth and ayre, he purified the whole creation, and rose up, and saw no corruption as others did.

Qu. *But how can he be said to be laid in the earth and remaine there, and yet rise up out of it purifying the creation?*

Ans. As his body was laid, by the hands of his enemies, in the earth as dead carrion, as they thought, like one of themselves, when they die: but his body corrupted not the creation, but rose up above corruption, purging it out.

Qu. *Explaine your meaning.*

Ans. His body; being made of the four Elements, which were corrupted by man in whom they all dwelt: they are restored again, from that bondage of corruption by the body of Christ, in whom they all dwelt [19] likewise: As thus; his breath rose up above the corruption of the Ayre, purifying the Ayre; his moysture rose up above the corruption of the waters, purifying the water; his heat and warmth rose up above the corruption of the fire, cleansing the fire: and his flesh and bones, rose up above the corruption of the earth and stones, purifying of them; and so he spreading himselfe in the body of the Creation took of the curse: so that the foundation of restoration of all things was laid in and by him; which when it is manifested then man kinde shall see the glory of it; and till that time, the whole Creation groaneth and travelleth in paine, *waiting for the manifestation of the Sons of God.*

Qu. *I but the Apostles saw him after he was risen, and touched him, and saw him ascend upwards?*

Ans. The declaration of Scripture, doth point out the mystery of Christs spirituall rising, and the exaltation of his spirituall power over the flesh, and over the corruption that is in the Creation: for the whole Scriptures are but a report of spirituall mysteries, held forth to the eye of flesh in words; but to be seene in the substantiall matter of them by the eye of the Spirit; and therefore the Apostle might well say, they [20] saw & touched Christ; for their very bodies and mindes were changed, *and made like to his glorious body*, for they were made new creatures, and were raised up above corruption; which was no other, but Christ rising up in them, and lifting up himselfe in their sight and feeling above the flesh.

Qu. *Why then I perceive that as the body of the first man was a representation of the whole Creation, and did corrupt it; so the body of Christ was a representation of the whole Creation, and restores it from corruption, and brings all into the unity of the Father again?*

Ans. This is very true; for in this particular lies the mystery of the Fall, and the restoration of all things again.

Qu. *But whither went the Spirit of Christ?*

Ans. To his Father; that is, entred into the spirit of the whole Creation; into that Spirit that breathed all forth of himselfe, and that governs all by himselfe; which is Reason; and so is become one with him; and being lifted up will draw the whole Creation to the spirit of onenes with himselfe, and with his Father. As a bucket of water first taken out of the Sea, and standing alone for a time, is afterwards powred into the Sea again, and becomes one with the Sea. And this is the Seed that comes to [21] bruise the Serpents head; and when his work was done in that one particular person, hee returned backe again to his Father, from whence he came; and now sends down his Spirit, and drawes up Sonnes and daughters; yea, the whole Creation into himselfe.

And truly this is great comfort to me, that whereas formerly there was not a man found that could remove the curse; but every one still increased the curse: now there is a man found that hath killed the curse in part; and the virtue of that sweet oyntment shall cleanse the whole; and this worke is now breaking out; for the Father will make the Creation to know it by experience, and it shall be hid no longer. And this points out the mystery of the first *Adam* and the second *Adam*; or the first Man and second Man, which the Father, Reason, was pleased should spring up in mankinde.

Qu. *What doe you mean by the first Adam, or first man?*

Ans. He is a *preparer*, to hold forth three names or titles of the one perfect power of darknesse, and yet a son that Reason hath brought forth: But this son is said to be of the earth, earthy; for he is a son that feeds, lives and delights himselfe altogether in and upon the objects of the earth; endeavouring [22] to make himself a Lord over his fellow creatures; in unrighteousnesse seeking to advance himselfe, though it be to others ruine; and this man hath lift up his heel against his Maker, and knowes him not.

Qu. *Is this Adam one single person or branch of humane flesh?*

Ans. Every particular branch of mankind, living upon the objects of the creation, and rejecting their maker, are the linage or generation of the first man: yea, being bound up all together, they make up but the one first *Adam*.

Qu. *Declare more plaine what this first man is?*

Ans. He is that mighty power of flesh, that leades flesh to live upon it selfe, and not to live upon its maker: it followes the way of the flesh with greedinesse, and jeeres and ejects the spirit. And this is called a mighty man, because he being to act his part in the great world first, as Father Reason will have it. He hath drawne all flesh into disobedience to the spirit. And this *Adam* hath beene very fruit-full; he hath filled the earth with himself, and covered all with his darknesse. For looke upon every man and woman in the world, that lives upon the objects of the creation, and not upon the spirit in the [23] creation, and they are but branches of the first man; and then put them all together into one lumpe, and they make up still, but the first man perfect; an earthy man, that knowes not the spirit: and there-fore when you see a man wholly delighting himselfe in the enjoy-ment of fellow creatures, you may call him truly *Adam*, or the first man.

Qu. *What is the spirit in the Creation?*

Ans. It is a meeke and loving spirit, liveing in the light and strength of reason, holding up the whole creation in a onenesse of sweet com-pliency in every creature, according to its place and office.

Qu. *What are those three names of one perfect power of darknesse, that the first man Adam was a preparer of?*

Ans. First, The King of darknesse, or aspiring power of the flesh, that lifts up his heele against his Maker, but yet lies within, and acts not.

Secondly, The beastly son that arises up from that rebelling power, and that is, Man, that holds forth this rebellion to fellow creatures; for now rebellion is broke out, and Reasons law is violated; the crea-tures flesh seekes to honour it selfe, and hath forsaken his Maker: here is the Father and the Son of darknesse.

[24] Thirdly, When the whole earth is filled with this disobedi-ence, so that you cannot meet with a branch of mankinde; but hee lives upon the objects of the creation, and not upon the spirit. This makes the first man perfect in darknesse, and the whole world is filled with uncleane breathing. Here is Father, Son, and uncleane spirit, or King, and Beast, and bottomlesse pit: Three names, but one power of darknesse, filling the earth, and corrupting the creation more and

more. All this is but the first man, that Reason would have to governe the earth.

Qu. *Why doth the Father suffer this first man to fill the earth so abundantly with unrighteousnesse?*

Ans. For two reasons; First, That mankinde may see, that though it spring up to an innumerable multitude of sonnes and daughters, all living upon creature objects, not upon the spirit, [these] are but still the one first man, that wearied out himselfe in vaine, and finds no true peace thereby.

Secondly, That the second man may have the more glory, when in the fulnesse of time he shall come, and pull the Kingdome out of the first mans hand, and tread him under foot, and rule righteously in flesh himselfe. Yea, and to begin this great worke, when all [25] the nations of the earth are filled with the wit and strength of the first man, who fights against the rising up of the Second man with violence: and therefore is it said, when the Son of man comes; shall he finde faith on earth? No: he must bring it along with him, and new-spirit the creation.

Qu. *What? Are all troubles, sinnes and sorrowes, the worke of the first man?*

Ans. Two things are to be observed in the first man; First, his revolt from the spirit, in making choyce to live upon the creation, and not upon the spirit: and hereby now the law of Reason is broke. And this is one thing, that such as are of the generation of the first mans flesh doth doe.

Secondly, Note the misery that this first man flesh doth bring upon himselfe: by so doing, he puls crosses and sorrowes within upon himselfe, and troubles without: for his unrighteous breath corrupts the aire, and raises hurtfull winds and weather; and his unrighteous flesh corrupts the earth, and causes it to send forth hurtfull crops, and poysonous Vipers: these are the fruits of his earthy choyce and labours; and therefore when you see misery in the world, then say, this is the fruit of living upon the creatures, and not upon the spirit.

[26] Well, From the beginning to this day, Reason hath suffered the first man to reigne, and to fill the earth: therefore is it said, *The first man is of the earth, earthy*; and he fils the earth, as one beane,

multiplying every yeare, fils the earth with that graine; which is but the multiplication of it selfe.

Adam, or first man, is looked upon in a three-fold sense.

First, *Adam*, or first man, that went astray from his Maker, which lived upon earth many thousand yeares agoe, which the eyes of every man is upon.

Secondly, Every man and woman that lives upon the objects of the creation, and not in and upon the spirit that made the creation, is a sonne and daughter of the first man; and being put altogether, make up but the one first man: so that we may see *Adam* every day before our eyes walking up and downe the street.

But Thirdly, I see the two *Adams* in every man: The first *Adam* hath his time to rule first in me; when the chiefe powers in me, lead me forth to looke after objects, and to delight in them, more then in the spirit. And this first man must act his part in me, till the fulnesse of time come, that the Father is pleased, that the second *Adam*, [27] Christ, shall come and take the Kingdome out of his hand, and deliver me from his bondage, and so rule King of righteousnesse for ever after in mee.

Qu. *What is the second man, or second Adam?*

Ans. He is a preparer likewise, to hold forth three clear names in one perfect power of life; who is called, the well-beloved Son; for this Son is said to be the Lord from heaven; or a mighty man, governing the earth in righteousnesse from the strength of pure Reason; not placing his delight upon the objects of the creation, as the first man did: But upon the enjoyment of that mighty power that made the creation, and that upheld it by himselfe.

Qu. *Is this second man one single person?*

Ans. First, This second man is a meek spirit, drawn up to live in the light and strength of pure Reason.

Now as the first man, ruling in flesh, drew mankinde from his maker, so this second man, ruling in flesh, drawes mankinde back againe to his maker. And this second man is called a man anointed, or mankind living in the light and strength of pure Reason, the essentiall Father. And so the whole bulke of mankinde, when they shall be drawne up to live in the unity of the one spirit, is the second [28] man, & every son and daughter of this spirit, is of the lynage of the second man.

Qu. *But shall this second man fill the earth, as the first man did?*

Ans. Yes, Reason hath so determined that as the first man filled the earth with unrighteousnesse, and corrupted all: So this second shall take the Kingdom in the latter dayes, and raign King of righteousnesse in flesh, and spread as far in restoring al things, as the first man corrupted all things.

Qu. *But hath this second man never ruled the earth?*

Ans. He hath appeared in the earth, but the first man having a limited time given him by the Father, would never let him rise up to rule, but still pressed him downe by persecution or death; he did never generally rule over the earth, as the first man hath done, but hath still been as a servant.

Qu. *But is his time now to come to rule the earth and fill it with himself?*

Ans. Yes: and shall have as large a priviledge to fill the earth, as the first man had surely; and he wil change times and customs, & fil the earth with a new law, wherin dwels righteousnes and peace. And justice, and judgment shal be the upholders of his kingdom. And he shal fill the earth with himself, as a corn of wheat multiplying every yeare, fils [29] the earth with that graine, so all that live in the light, and strength of pure Reason, in righteousnes are but the sons & daughters of the second man: And being looked upon in the bulke, they being made to be all of one heart and one spirit, they are but the second man still, that fils all, and is in all; though they overspread the earth. And this is the generation of the second man, or second Adam: mankinde living in and upon his maker from the power within himself.

Qu. *What are these three names, which this second man declares to be one perfect power of life?*

[*Ans.*] First, the Father Reason, that made all things; before the creation was brought forth he was not known. Secondly, the Son, and this is that part of the creation that holds him purely forth to the view of others. Now truth begins to shine, and Reason begins to be honoured by an humane body; so that here is Father and Son. Thirdly, when the whole earth is filled with the one spirit; this makes the second man perfect, for corruption and curse is removed; and the whole earth is filled with holy breathing; all acting and living in righteousnesse. And this is Jesus Christ the second man.

They say I deny the Gospell, and the doctrine of it; & hereunto I give this accompt.

[30] Qu. *What is the Gospel?*

Ans. It is the Father himselfe, that is, the Word, and glad tydings, that speaks peace inwardly to poore soules.

Qu. *But are not the writings of the Apostles and Prophets, the Gospell?*

Ans. These writings are the report or declaration of the Gospell; which are to cease, when the Lord himselfe, who is the everlasting Gospell, doth manifest himselfe to rule in the flesh of sonnes and daughters.

Qu. But did not *Paul* say, *This is the word of the Gospell, which we preach*; and so left those words in writing?

Ans. It is true, his writings are the word of it, or the report of it; but it is not the thing it selfe: for when it was reported, that the Father would dwell in the flesh, and destroy the Serpent: this report savoured sweet: But when man comes to see, and feel, and know, that the Father dwels and rules in him; This is farre more sweet: This is to enjoy the Gospell himselfe: The word of life within, and this shall never cease, but endures for ever.

Qu. *But how doe you know, that this is the Gospell?*

Ans. I know it by the testimony that is within my selfe, and by the sweet, peaceable [31] and soule-satisfying rest, that I have, through communion, with the spirit; The Lord our righteousnesse; In the midst of the mad rage of the world.

Secondly, For satisfaction to the world, I desire all men to take the Record, and search those Scriptures, for they are they that doe testifie of the truth hereof, as well as they testified of Christ, after the flesh, to be the Lambe. And this is the mystery and testimony of the Scriptures: The spirit dwelling and ruling in flesh.

The declaration or report of words out of the mouth or pen of men, shall cease; but the spirit endures for ever; from whence those words were breathed: as when I have the thing promised, the word of the promise ceases.

Qu. *What is the lively testimony or appearance of the everlasting Gospell to dwell in flesh?*

Ans. I answer; Justice and Judgement are the two witnesses, or the manifest appearance of the spirit; or the pure light of Reason,

teaching a man both to know what is righteous, and to doe righteously: And when these two rule in man, then is flesh subject to the
spirit.

Qu. *But I have heard men say, That the Scriptures are not onely
the word of God, but God himselfe:* [32] *for the word and spirit goe
together; as, In the beginning was the Word; and, The Word was
God.*

Ans. If that very written word were God himselfe, truly God then
would mightily be torne in pieces every day, by the bad interpretations of imaginary flesh.

But I answer; The spirit himselfe is the Word; This is the power
that tooke flesh and dwelt amongst us. And the Scriptures are the
testimony of those men, to whom this secret was revealed: by which
testimony within, they were made able to give,

First, A report, that such a mystery, as God manifest in the flesh,
should break forth and appeare in the world, in a child that should
be borne of a Virgin; and so all the writings of the Prophets fore-
told the coming of the man-child, the *Messiah*, The Lambe of God.
And so when the Pharisees told Christ he was a deceiver,

He answered, I am he; and unlesse that you believe that I am he,
you shall dye in your sinnes: and search the Scriptures of the Prophets, and you shall see, that they testifie of mee, that I am the *Messiah*; the Man-child; the Lamb, that am to answer all *Moses* types;
and the Prophet, whom the Father hath sent; For I came not to doe
my owne will, [33] but the will of him that sent me.

Secondly, The writings of the Apostles doe justifie the Prophets,
and declare positively, this is the Christ; the Son of the Father, well-
beloved: we ate and dranke with him; we saw him and heard him,
and were eye-witnesses, that the Rulers of the Jewes slew him, and
that the spirit raised him from the death.

Qu. *But doe the Apostles writings report no more but this?*

Ans. Yes; As they declared, when they saw and heard how the
spirit dwelt bodily in that humane flesh, or single man, Jesus Christ:
So they have declared, by the same testimony, that the same spirit
that ruled in him, should in the latter dayes be poured out upon
sonnes and daughters; and shall spread in the earth like the shining
of the Sun from East to West.

And this is that which this mouth and pen of mine doe testifie of to all that heare mee: that the same spirit that hath layne hid under flesh, like a corne of wheat for an appointed time, under the clods of earth, is now sprung out, and begins to grow up a fruitfull vine, which shall never decay, but it shall encrease, till he hath filled the earth. This is the Kingdome of God within man. [34] This is the graine of mustard seed, which is little in the beginning, but shall become a mighty tree. This is the fire, that shall dry and burne up all the drosse of mans worke, and turne all things into his owne nature. This is that spirit which is broke out, that will bring mankinde into one heart, and one minde: For, assure your selves, I know what I speake. The Thorne bush is burning; but the Vine is flourishing. The Ashes of the Thorne bush is laid at the root and feet of the Vine, and it growes abundantly.

Now search the Scriptures for this likewise, for they doe testifie of the sending of the spirit into the flesh of sons and daughters: and they testifie of the utter destruction of the man of sinne, the flesh, with all his curse, power inwardly and outwardly. Now he that doth jeere the spirit, or denies that the spirit shall come and rule in flesh in sons and daughters, as he did in that one man, Jesus Christ, is an Antichrist, and a Traitor to the Father, let him be whom he will.

Therefore learne to put a difference betweene the Report, and the thing Reported of. The spirit that made flesh is he that is reported of. The writings and words of Saints is the report. These reports being taken hold of, by corrupt flesh that would rule, are blemished [35] by various translations, interpretations and constructions, that King flesh makes; but those sons and daughters in whom the spirit rests, cannot be deceived, but judge all things.

They say, I deny the doctrine of the Gospell: I shall give this account to that.

Qu. *What is the doctrine of the Gospel of Jesus Christ?*

Ans. What Jesus Christ is, I have shewed before: The doctrine or report of him is this: That mankinde shall be by him reconciled to his Maker, and be made one in spirit with him: that is, that the curse shall be removed, and the power of it killed and consumed. And that created flesh, by that mighty power, the man of truth, should be made subject to the spirit that made it; so that the spirit, which is the Father, may become all in all, the chiefe ruler in flesh.

And truly this is but according to the current of the whole Scrip-

ture; that in the day of Christ, every one shall be made of one heart
and one spirit; that is, all shall bee brought in, to acknowledge the
Father, to obey him, walke humbly before him, and live in peace
and love in him. This is the doctrine of Christ and the Gospell. This
is glad tydings to heare of. But when you are made to enjoy this
doctrine as yours, then [36] you shall know what it is to know the
Son; and what it is to be set free by the Sonne; therfore wait upon
the Father, till he make forth himself in you.

Qu. *I waite, that's true, but I must use the meanes.*

Ans. That which you call meanes doth harden your hearts, and
blind your eyes, it shuts you out from sweet enjoyment; that is, to
run after men for teachings. I speake not rashly, I speak what I know,
and you shall finde before your soules taste of true peace, that whosoever takes those Scriptures, and makes exposition upon them, from
their imagination, and tels you that is the word of God, and hath seen
nothing: That they are the false Christs and false Prophets, and their
way of teaching is meer deceit both to your soules, and to your purses;
for now in this day of Christ which is begun, and which will have a
greater appearance ere long in the great world; Men must speak their
own experienced words, and must not speake thoughts.

For thoughts, and studies, and imagination of flesh, are the men
that are found gathering sticks upon this sabbath day, and these are
stoned to death by the Power that is arising in some already; and
shall be stoned to [37] death in all; that the Lord alone may be exalted in this day of his Power.

Qu. *Must I use no meanes at all, or what meanes must I use?*

Ans. These 3: first, let your chief endeavour be to act according to
your creation: that is, to doe as you would be done unto, by all creatures, as I have shewed; and Ile tell you, this is as needfull a gospell
doctrine to be practised as any I know for the present; for Ile assure
you, the world is at such a passe, yea, and among imaginary professors especially, that I know not who I can say is a sincere hearted
friend; so that I am sure the sonne of man at his coming finds no faith
in earth, neither in my flesh, nor in the flesh of others; he brings it
with him, and gives it to us.

Secondly, waite upon the Father with a meek spirit for his teaching.
And you shall find it a very hard thing to performe these two meanes:
for the flesh is both very unrighteous to seek it self, and it is very

hasty to have all knowledge, peace, and experience on a sudden; it's so proud and hasty, it will not wait.

Thirdly, if you would hear other men speak, you may doe two things; First, read the record, and there see what the testimony [38] of the Apostles and Prophets, your fellow servants, was; but do not alter their words, by forceing a meaning, till the Father teach you.

Secondly, if you would hear, then acquaint yourselves with such, as can speake from a testimony within: for as they received what they have from the pure teachings of the Father: so this second hand teaching will be pure teaching to you; but be sure you do not prefer this second hand teaching before the first: for now the everlasting word and gospel must reveale himself to you, or else you cannot be satisfied.

I have now discharged my service to the Father, in this declaration: remember what is tould you, despise not the Fathers meanes, by preferring the way and meanes of the flesh, above the wayes of the Father.

They say, I deny the Scriptures, because I say, that the Scriptures were not appointed for a rule to the world to walke by, without the spirit; but were the testimony of the Father in those men that writ them, for the comfort and benefit of those that are drawn up into communion with the same spirit: And to this I shall give this accompt.

Qu. *What is the Law and Testimony which if* [39] *a man speak not according to it, it is because there is no light in him?*

Ans. This Law and Testimony to which I must have recourse for my comfort, is not the words or writings of other men without me; But the spirit of the Father in me, teaching me to know him by experience; and when I can speake purely what I doe see and heare from the Father; this is the Law and Testimony within me, from which I speake, and if I speak not from this Law within, I have no knowledge in me.

Qu. *But are not the Scriptures, the Law and Testimony of the Father?*

Ans. It was the Law and Testimony of the spirit which rested in and upon the Prophets and Apostles, for they writ what they saw in vision, and they spake what they heard by voice, speaking to them spiritually.

Qu. *But are not those Scriptures the Law and Testimony for people to walk by in these dayes?*

Ans. No: For this is to walke by the eyes of other men, and the spirit is not so scanty, that a dozen or 20 pair of eyes shall serve the whole world; but every sonne and daughter as they are called children of light, have light within themselves: The same spirit that fils one, fils all; and makes the whole number of them, according to their severall [40] measures, to be of one heart and one mind.

Qu. *But may not men take these Scriptures, and spend construction upon them; and hold forth those constructions to others, as perfect light, by way of office?*

Ans. I answer no: neither reason nor Scripture allowes any man to speake any words, but what he knowes positively to be truth. And he that spends constructions thereupon, speaking from his imagination, he speaks from the flesh and devill, and so he makes himself to be a traytor to the father, in holding forth that to be truth which is no truth. And a thief, robber, and unrighteous dealer with the Prophets and Apostles: First, in taking their words as his own: and secondly, in expounding their meaning, and so putting his own meaning upon their words.

But yet he that hath the same spirit, may speak the same word, where the Father hath given him the same sight and experience: for no man can safely tell another, this is a positive truth of God, till he have the same testimoniall experience within himself as the penmen of Scripture had: and this I am sure all that stand up to teach by way of office have not; therefore it is clear, that the power that sets up such teachers [41] is not from the Father commanding, but from the flesh; being suffered by the Father for a time, that when he comes to throw downe his enemies, flesh may be shamed, and he honoured.

That man that cannot speak the testimony of the Father, no other way, but from his book as he reads, or from the mouth of another what he heares: as the publike teachers doe, speakes by hearsay and not from experience, and so declares himself to be a false Christ, a false prophet, that runs to teach others, before he have any discovery of God within himself.

Qu. *But are not the Scriptures the truths of God?*

Ans. Yes, for they declare, that the spirit was the mighty governour of the flesh of those that writ them, and so the truths of God the great governour in the pure experience of those penmen.

And I shall demand of you how you know that these Scriptures are the word of God, in the sense you call them, but [by] the testimony of the spirit within your selves; I say, there is no way to know but by the spirit himself; seeing there are so many expositions upon them, which without doubt hath varied the copies: if it were possible to [42] see those very writings from the prophets and Apostles own pen: which is not to be seen.

But when the spirit comes in he must, nay he doth and will declare his own meaning. And so the spirituall man judges all things, and he himself is judged of no man: he can judge the flesh, and passe righteous judgement, because he sees and knowes what the flesh is. The flesh cannot judge him, for if he doe, it is not righteous judging, but rash censure.

Qu. *What use is to be made of the Scriptures?*

Ans. First, they are, or may be kept as a record of such truths as were writ not from imagination of flesh, but from pure experience, and teachings of the Father. Secondly, we are taught thereby to waite upon the Father with a meek and obedient spirit, till he teach us, and feed us with sincere milk, as he taught them, that wrote these Scriptures.

Thirdly, when I look into that record of experimentall testimony, and finde a sutable agreement betweene them, and the feeling of light within my own soule, now my joy is fulfilled. And every man and woman may declare what they have received, and so become preachers one to another.

For the Scriptures doth but declare the [43] sending down of the spirit and how he shall rule in the earth in the latter dayes: but they doe not declare every particular measure and beame of the spirits ruling, for this the sons and daughters are to declare, by their particular experiences, as they are drawn up.

Qu. *But when I read the Scriptures and finde a perswasion in my heart, that they are true, may I not owne them as a truth, and speak them as a truth; and speak them to others?*

Ans. You may deliver the same words you reade which you are perswaded of, but to passe construction [upon] the meaning, by way of office, teaching others; this you cannot do. There is an imaginary perswasion grounded upon thoughts, or as he conceives; but this is a sandy foundation, and deceiveth all the world. Secondly, there is an experimental perswasion, grounded upon sight and feeling of the spirit of truth, ruling king within him; and this is the rock that will never fayl.

Qu. But did not the Apostles and Christ take texts of Scripture, and expound them, as Philip *did to the* Eunuch, *and* Christ *from the* 61 Esay?

Ans. They did not preach and expound any text customarily, as the parish gods do: but such particular Scriptures as the oportune time and occasion served, to declare [44] Christ to be the lambe of God, or the great prophet which the Father promised to send.

So that all the Scriptures of the ancient prophets, which they spake from, were only to make it appear that the Messias was come: but they did not preach in setled parishes, forcing the people by the hand of the magistrate, to come and hear them, and give them a maintenance for so doing, under pain of punishment; the Scriptures know no such custome or way to be used: therefore whosoever lives in such a practise, denies the Scripture, and are enemies to Jesus Christ.

But now if any one take Scriptures, that speak of the spirits ruling in flesh, and so proves the truth of the Scripture by his own testimony or witnesse within himselfe; this may be done, but for any other way of expounding Scripture I know none, neither will, nor doth the Scripture warrant any other, but what advances the spirit and throws down the flesh, by the speakers own experience.

Qu. But may not the powers of a land compell their people, some to preach, and others to hear Scriptures expounded as the manner is in England?

Ans. I answer, That power that compels is the little horne, or dragon, wheresoever [45] it sits; and that expounding is a flat denial of those Scriptures, and treason against the spirit; liberty is to be given to every one in the case, for the kingdome of Christ hath an interest herein.

Lands and Kingdoms are most commonly governed more by the wisdome of the flesh, then of the spirit: and why? because the spirit gave that power into the hand of flesh for a certain time, and when the flesh is judged for his action, the Lord wil condemn him for his unrighteous, cruell self-seeking and oppressing government over his lambs and sheep.

The Powers of the Land punished Christ and his Apostles for holding forth their testimony of the Father which was within them; but they did not compell any to hear them, or to follow them: it is an easyer thing for magistrates to be breaking forth against such as speak from a pure testimony, then against such as speak from imaginary studies of the flesh, both in regard of the powers of the flesh within them, blinding their eyes, and because of so many envious spirits against truth, that will be flattering the magistrate, and telling him tales of slander on purpose to incense him against the sincere hearted in the land, because they hate them, [46] through ignorance that is in them; not knowing the Majesty of the Lord that is in his servants, whom they despise.

Qu. What must the powers of a Land doe then in the matters of Religion, as they call it?

Ans. First, they must suffer every one that will, quietly to keepe the record in their houses, or to read it, or speak of it one to another, and they that find their own experience to suite therewith, speaking from a pure testimony, and walkes in all acts of righteousnesse towards his fellow creatures; It is the charge which the Father hath put into the hand of the Magistrate, to protect these from their oppression of unreasonable men.

Secondly, if any man walk unrighteously towards his fellow creature in civil matters: the Powers of a land must punish him, according to the nature of his offence, and so to be a terror to all unrighteousnesse.

Qu. But what if the Powers of a Land command some of their people to hold forth the Scriptures to the rest, and they be willing to obey?

Ans. If they doe, they can command their servants only to read them, and to such people as are willing to hear them read, but they cannot command their servants to spend constructions thereupon, neither can they [47] force the people to come to hear those constructions; but must leave both parties at liberty: neither can they force the people to give the tenths of their increase, for a yearly maintenance to those servants: neither can those servants say, we speake truthes, and what differs from our constructions are errors; and so call upon the Magistrate their master, to punish such, whom they brand for hereticks; for all these things denie the Scriptures: and is contrary to the spirit of the Father: and doe tie his hands, and hinder the setting up of pure service, and sow enmity to the Fathers own way of teaching.

They say, I deny Father, Son and Holy Ghost, but wherefore they raise such a scandall, I cannot tell; yet hereof I shall give this accompt.

Qu. *What is Father, Son and Holy-Ghost?*

Ans. These are three names given to the one Spirit; As first, the Father, he is the spirit Reason; out of whom the creation of heaven and earth, with every branch of it proceeded. The Spirit, in whom all things lay before there was any manifestation, appeared visible: and this is called the fiery orbe, or spirit of burning, that will trie all mens works, of what nature they be.

Secondly, the Son is the light and declaration [48] of the Father, to the creation, after it was come forth: and here first note, that every creature in its place, and stature, is a son to the Father; because every single creature doe demonstrate his maker to the view of his fellow creature, every one as a candlestick, holding forth the Father by the light that is in it self, for indeed the light that is in it, is the Father himself, and the Father shewes forth himself to the creation: by every particular parcell of the creation, but these are but darke or weake shining Suns, Suns over which the clouds are much spread.

But now perfect man, is the Son of the Father, in perfect glory, for when the Father rules and shines in him bodily, then he can declare the Father by all his senses, to the creation, which no other creature can doe but he.

Therfore man is called the supream creature, and he can call the spirit, Lord; because he sees and heares, feels, smels and tastes, that he who is the spirit of gentlenesse, uniting all together in love, and sweet compliancie, doth governe the whole creation, and subjects all the flesh under him, and makes it serviceable. Now that man that is not humble and subject to the spirit his maker, he is a Sun under a dark eclipse; he hath [49] the forme of the Son indeed that hath no brightnesse in him, he is not the well beloved Son. So you see here is the Father and the Son both in one person and spirit.

Now thirdly, the Holy Ghost is a man in whom the Father dwels bodily, which is, Emanuel, God with us, and in and by whom the Father doth manifest his power in doing great works. And he is said to be holy, because the darknesse of the flesh is subdued under the feet of the spirit, and the spirit rules in flesh over all his enemies.

And he is called the Go-host, or the strength of heaven; living and walking in flesh, as an host or army of men are called the strength of the land, and going up and down for the defence of the land, against all enemies; so I say, perfect man hath the strength of the Father dwelling bodily in him. And one man thus drawne up, is as an hoste of men, or a strong army, or a Go-host, going or travelling among enemies, and subduing them under his feet, by the power of the spirit that is in him.

And thus did the man Jesus Christ, tread all enemies powerfully under foot, and shranke not, he was a Go-host, or a travelling army of mighty strength, which way soever he went; the spirit dwelt in him without [50] measure. And the particular Saints likewise, as they are drawn up into the Father, they have this tearme given them, that one shall chase a hundred, and a hundred put ten thousand to flight; this declares they are go-hosts, or armies of mighty strength.

Now he that sins against the Father or the Son, in the former sense of Son-ship as I said, shall be forgiven, and here he speakes of creatures one trespassing against another, and in so doing sins against the Father, that is, the light in them. And here flesh may possibly walke in wayes of opposition to the Father, as he shines forth in creatures, or as he shines forth out of man weakly; but he that sins against that body in whom the Father dwels bodily, shall not be forgiven.

A man may sin against other sons and be forgiven; but he that sins against this beloved son, this holy Ghost, this strength of the Father, shall never be forgiven.

By the word, He, or whosoever doth sinne is not meant here the creature man, but the man of sin, or powerfull serpent within the flesh: for this strong wicked man fights against the strength of heaven, this would not have the *spirit* to dwel in flesh bodily; & why? because he *himself* would dwel there, & would have the spirit to be under his proud feet; [51] therefore there is an irreconcilable difference between the man of sin, the serpent, and the man of righteousnes, the Spirit, both striving to dwell in man, but the spirit will prove the stronger.

Qu. *But if it must only be the cursed one in me that shalbe destroyed, Ile live as I list; I shalbe saved?*

Ans. Know this, that this body of sin and the flesh is so nearly wrapped each in other, that before the spirit hath parted them, thou shalt roar in bitternesse and wish thou hadst never been borne; and the more familiarity thou hast had with thy cursed lust, the sharper will thy torments be; the founder cannot burn away the drosse, but must burn the gold too in the fire.

Qu. But if you take it Spirit; Father, Son and holy Spirit, and leave the word Ghost out, as to be a declaration of the Father, as some say?

Ans. Then the Spirit doth declare holy breathing, as when man was first made, his maker breathed into him the breath of life, and man became a living soul: so that the spirit in the man is, the life and breath of God in the man, and so a holy spirit.

And in this sense likewise the man of sin, the powers of the curse in man, seeke to destroy the light, life and breathing of God in man; but he must be destroyed under the feet [52] of the spirit, who will dwell himself in his own house, which house is man.

Qu. But how came in that distinction of holy Spirit, and of uncleane spirit; which are phrases often used?

Ans. Before man rejected the spirit his maker, the spirit was his breath and life. And he lived in the spirit treading the objects of the creation under his feet in comparison, but after that man began to look after the objects of the earth, delighting himself to live upon or among fellow creatures more then the spirit; and so chose to himself another livelihood and protection, then his master; then his breath or power that guided him, became mixed and turned uncleane.

Qu. Unfold your meaning in this a little more?

Ans. The spirit made the flesh to be his house to dwell in, and set man in the midst of the creation, as a lord to govern the creature, which while he governed according to the light of his maker within him, he did al in righteousnesse; but when he fell off, and delighted to follow the lusts of his eye, the lusts of his heart, and guidance of the flesh, then he governed al in unrighteousnesse, and so pulling death and curse upon himself, and upon the earth.

[53] For the spirit that made all creatures, did know that man as he was flesh, would be looking after fellow creatures, and take delight in the creation more then in the spirit of the creation; who was his maker that dwelt within, and lay covered from the eyes of flesh.

Therefore Reason the essentiall Father, gave this Law, that in that day, that man left off to own his maker that dwelt within him, and [began] to suck delight from the creation, he should then die, or be cast into a condition to live below the spirit, that is, to live upon the creature, and not upon the spirit; And the spirit would suffer himself thus for a time to be trod under foot, til the fulnesse of time came, that he would rise up like seed of wheat, from under those darke and heavy clods of fleshy earth, and so himself, the seed out of whom all things came, would bruise the serpents head, that powerfull proves [?] that was in flesh to looke after objects without him, rather then into the spirit within him.

Qu. *Why then you seeme to say, that the Law which Reason gives occasioned man to fall?*

Ans. Very true, for if there had been no Law, there had been no transgression, if there had beene no binding law of reason to require [54] him to cleave only to his maker, and to eye and own him principally; then he had not done evill though he had placed his delight in the objects of the earth, his fellow creatures.

For note here, it is one thing to live in and upon the spirit, and another thing to sleight the spirit, and to live in and upon the creation, that came out or forth of the spirit.

Qu. *I intreat you to tell me what you meane by the Spirit?*

Ans. The Spirit is the alone being of himself, that gave a being to whatsoever we see and hear, for whatsoever you see or hear, is but the breathings forth or declaration of an infinite being that was before them; as the words of a mans mouth are the declaration of the spirit or power within; and are created by the spirit, and so hold forth as a creature to the creation.

And therefore the Spirit is called, the Father, the King, the mighty God or Governor, *Jehovah, Elohim*, the Lord, and the like. Now he is called the Lord, because he is the power that rules in and over the whole globe of heaven and earth, for they are all governed by this one spirit.

Qu. *But is death and darknesse made by this one Spirit likewise?*

[55] *Ans.* The one spirit made light and darknesse, as in the great body of night and day, so in the litle body man; for that power of darknesse that dwels in humane flesh, and which leads the creature captive into complainings and sorrow, was made by the Spirit; by these words, *In the day that thou eatest thereof, thou shalt die.* As well as he made that power of light, liberty, and life; by those words, *Live*; yea, I say, *Live.*

Qu. *I pray explaine this a little more?*

Ans. After the Spirit had made the creation, and mankinde to governe it: Now Reason would manifest himself to this creation by the works of his own hands, therefore let any man stand alone to the Law of Reason his Maker, to see whether he would stick to the one spirit, and live in him, or cleave to the creatures, and live in them; and man rejected the spirit, and cleaved to the creature; and so by virtue of the Law, cast himself under the power of death and darknesse, which was the curse, that Reason inflicted.

And thereupon the spirit within man being a prisoner to the flesh, or divell: As Reason would have it so for a time, that when he comes to arise up in flesh, like a corne of wheat from under the clods of the [56] earth: the creation may then come to know the spirit that is within it, is the mighty Power, and that al the creation being rested upon, is still but weaknesse, and cannot give true Rest, that so the Father alone may be all in all.

Qu. *What is the devill?*

Ans. The flesh of man within, and the objects of the creation without, is the divel; under which the spirit within is for a time buried and lies silent; and while man is subject to his flesh, or to the objects before him, he is carried away prisoner under the power of darknesse; for let him goe from creature to creature, all are too weake to worke his peace, or let him have all the desires of his flesh satisfied, even that delight brings pain and sorrow, no true peace.

Qu. *And why is the flesh of man within, and objects without, called the devill?*

Ans. Because when it is King it leads the spirit of man into darknesse; yea, into utter darknesse and sorrow far from light, life, and true peace; for it drawes men to live upon the creation, and to reject the spirit. This is that you call the serpent which tempted *Adam.*

Qu. *How doe you mean, make it more clear?*

Ans. The flesh of man having lifted up [57] his heele against the Spirit within, which was his Maker, seeks life and contentment, from objects without in the globe, not from the Spirit Reason that dwels within, and that holds al together by the Power. As for example; covetous flesh delights in the enjoyment of riches or creatures; pride of the flesh delights in the enjoyment of the sight of the eye, or inward delights placed upon visible objects.

Now the man lives in, and upon the creation, not in and upon the Spirit in the creation; and though he say that the Father is his God, yet he lies, for he is led and ruled by the flesh, which is the devil, or father of lies which throwes the man into vexation and sorrow every foot, for if his covetousnesse, pride, and lusts be satisfied, he hath peace; but this is the peace of the flesh, or devil; and let his covetousnesse or pride be crost, and then he is filled with vexation; which is hel or darknesse, even the torments of the flesh or devil.

And the Law of Reason suffered the flesh thus to fall and to weary out himself in his own folly, that when the Spirit is pleased to breake forth and manifest himself to rule in flesh, then man may see his wise flesh hath nothing that is good in al his selfish actings; [58] but that the spirit that brought it forth, is the mighty Power.

And when the Fathers time is come to manifest himself to any one, he will then dispell the darknesse, which by his Law he made, and will set the creature free from the bondage of that darknes, burne up all those thornes and briars that flesh hath brought to terrifie it self; and will take up the creature into his own liberty and life; And then the Spirit shall be all in all: whereas the flesh generally living up on objects is all in all, or chiefe ruler in every man.

Qu. *What is it to live in the Spirit?*

Ans. When flesh is made to see, and to be subject to the spirit that brought it forth, and is guided by the light of Reason and righteousnesse, that mightie power ruling it; And not led away like a bear by the nose, by every object before his eyes, which the flesh lusts after to enjoy, and places contentment in.

They slander me, And say, I deny Prayer: And to this I shall give this accompt.

Qu. *What is Prayer?*

Ans. Prayer is of a threefold nature; First, it is to pay the king of righteousnesse his due; and that is for every man to act according to the creation of a man, which is to do [59] righteously to all fellow creatures, he being the lord of the creatures.

As first, to doe righteously to his own body, in taking food moderately, for the preservation of the health of it, and not to be excessive in drunkennesse and gluttony; and not to give away to the unclean lusts of the flesh, which tends to the destruction of himself; for if the Spirit, Reason, within a man let the flesh alone, and doth not govern and moderate it in righteousnesse, it will destroy it selfe in a short time: let the flesh walke in Reasons law of moderation and righteousnesse, and it shall be preserved from heart breaking sorrows.

Secondly, act righteousnesse to all fellow creatures; till the ground according to Reason; use the labour of your cattell with Reason; follow your course of trading in righteousnesse, as Reason requires; doe to men and women, as you would have them doe to you; and by so doing you shall live as Reasonable creatures, you shall act according to the creation of a man, and so pay the King of Righteousnesse his due; for when you hold forth him in your conversation, to the view of others, you honour him, you glorifie his name, and give him thanks: and this is one part of prayer.

[60] *Qu. Thus the heathen walked according to the light of nature, but Christians must live above nature?*

Ans. Then English Christians are in a lower and worser condition, then the heathens, for they doe not so much. Men that are guided by principles of fair dealing void of deceit, knowe not this day how to live, but they will be cheated and cosoned; and is this life of Christians (for all England is so called) above the life of the heathens? Surely the life of the heathens shall rise up in judgement against you, from the greatest to the least. But let me tell you, that that man whosoever he be, that is not carefull to look into the light of his nature, and follow the rules of that light, to do as he would be don unto, shall never come to see the Spirit, that made and that dwels in nature, which is the Father of the whole creation. And if you know not him, then I pray tell me what God you worship or pray to?

But secondly, Prayer lies in the Reasonings of the heart, as thus: Ask this question within thy selfe; Is covetousnesse the name of the Lord, or the name of the flesh? the answer within thee will be, it is the name of the flesh, not the name of the Lord; now if thou walke in covetousnesse, how can thou [61] be said to honor the Lord by thy words in prayer, when thou honorest the name of the flesh, in thy practise.

And so is pride, is envy, is rash anger, is hypocrisie, is self-will, is unmercifull cruelty, is zeale without knowledge, is uncleannesse; the name of the flesh, or the name of the Lord; thy owne heart will give answer, they be the name of the flesh, not the name of the Lord, and thou livest in the practise and power of those lusts; and givest the Lord a few customary words, and thinkest his service lies in them. I will have thee to know that the time is now breaking forth; yea, it is begun, that they that worship the Father shall worship him in spirit and truth, and not in lip labor and custome, according to the imagination of flesh.

Qu. *What is the name of the Lord, then? I propound this question within my heart.*

Ans. The name of the Lord, is Love, joy, peace, meeknesse, obedience, self-denial, chastasie [charity?], humility, mercifulnesse, Reason.

Now he that is drawne up thus to Reason within himself, and to see himself, this man is praying continually, and calling upon the name of the Lord continually, whatsoever he doth, whatsoever he thinkes, which way soever he goes, he shall have [62] still fresh occasions thus to be reasoning within himself; and this reasoning will do two things.

First, it will strike the heart dead; when thou comest to see that for all thy praying in words, yet thou art at a losse, for thou honorest the name of the flesh in practise, and only worshipest the Lord with wind, like the way of the world; your servant Sir; when he could kill him in his heart: when these things comes home to thee, thou wilt be struck dead, and thy mouth be stopped; and this is a great power that stops the rage of flesh.

Secondly, this way of prayer or calling upon the name of the Lord will kill thy distempers as they arise, and wil keep thy heart in peace, this I know, if thou wilt beleeve anothers testimony, for now the name of the flesh is spied out, and the poyson of it killed; for when once Reason begins to enlighten thee, he will be thy keeper. The name of the Lord likewise is hereby advanced; first, within thy selfe, thou fearest and tremblest before him. Secondly, outwardly thou art moved to act righteousnesse to others, from the savour of this sweet oyntment.

Now that man doth not live lesse or more in the practise of those two rules laid down; [63] did never pray in all his life, though he use the words of prayer every day.

Words and actions going together are the declaration of a sincere heart; but words in prayer, without acting according to creation, as the generall practise is, are declarations of hypocriticall and deceived flesh: let his profession be what it will be.

Therefore professors look to your selves, both priests and people, there is light broke out that will lay open the hipocrisie of your private actings to the view of the whole creation, and you shall not cover your shame, doe all you can. Thus much for the second part in prayer.

Thirdly, prayer lies in words or utterance, but this is the remotest part of prayer. Now words among men should be the declaration of the heart among men, but oftentimes they are not; for men have good words many times in prayer, which they have got by tradition, which their hearts are strangers to; and so they draw nigh God with their lips, but their hearts are removed: and this hypocriticall darknesse hath at this day overspread pulpit worship, and almost all family worship. But our God hath left us a remnant on earth, whose hearts wait upon him, or else we had been as *Sodom,* here in England before this day.

[64] Qu. *But when shall I use or speak words in prayer?*

Ans. When the power of the Spirit within doth give words to the mouth to utter; for he that speakes words before the Lord, and not from his power, speakes he knowes not what, and his prayer is the vain babling of the heathen, that think to be heard, for their much speaking.

Qu. *We all know that without the heart words of prayer are nothing, and there is no man that makes conscience of his wayes, dares speake, unlesse he feel his heart upright.*

Ans. This is the language in professors mouths, but they neither know nor practise their own words; for let me tell you, and your heart shall bear witnesse, that I speake truly, that many times when you are put upon it to pray, as you call it, you find your self empty of words, now you will not wait upon the Father till he give words of knowledge; but the pride of the flesh will put you on, and force words out of your mouth though they appear ful of confusion to your selves, and likewise to the standers by: and tels you, what will others thinke of thee, if thou neglect to pray or preach as thou hast been accustomed; and so shame of men within thee, puts thee upon speaking a multitude [65] of confused words before the Lord. But Reason tels thee, when thou comes before the Lord, let thy words be few and faithfull.

Qu. *But must I use no words at all in prayer?*

Ans. I tell thee when the power within thee gives words to thy mouth to utter, then speak, and thou canst not but speak; but he that speakes before the Lord, whatsoever he be, learned, or unlearned, before he hath received power from on high, that man offers the sacrifice of a fool, not considering what he doth.

Well, thou hast now heard what prayer is, both in the heart, and in the mouth, and in the hand. These words shall not die, they are sincere milke which once a wearied soul did suck from the Fathers owne breasts of love, and wherein he now walks, and finds true rest in the Father; they are words of truth and sobernesse.

Therfore though thou go on in thy customary way of praying words in the pulpit, and in families, yet know, that thou art left without excuse, and thou shalt be brought before the King, and condemned for thy hypocrisie, to the shame and torment of thy whole man.

[96, i. e., 66] Lastly, they say, I deny the ordinances of God, and that I live above all Ordinances, which is my pride: Hereunto I shall give this accompt.

First, that I doe walke in the dayly practise of such Ordinances of God, as Reason and Scriptures doe warrant.

Secondly, that the Clergie and professors of *England*, in their publike worships doe practise their own inventions, which neither Reason, nor Scripture, doth warrant; and yet they call them Gods Ordinances; by which practise they are the men that deny God and Christ, and turne the Scriptures into a lie.

First, then the Ordinances of God, which Reason and Scripture doth warrant, and which I dayly walke in, are these.

First, I pray continually, calling upon the name of the Lord, in the manner I declared before; and for that search these Scriptures, and let Reason be judge. *Eccl.* 5.1, 2. 1. *Cor.* 14.15. *Esay.* 29.13. *Psa.* 66.18. *Mat.* 6.5, 6.2. *Cor.* 13.5. *Psal.* 4.5. *Act.* 1.4, 8. *Psal.* 52.9. *Gal.* 5.19, 22.

Secondly, I speak to others as occasion is tendered, from the testimony within my selfe, of what I have heard and seene and received from the Father, and let Reason be [67] judge. *Act.* 4.20. 1. *Cor.* 11.23. *Act.* 8.30. *Ps.* 51.12, 13. *Act.* 2.14. *Mat.* 5.1, *&c. Luke* 4.21. *Ioh.* 3.11.

Thirdly, It is my endeavour and practise, to doe to others as I would have them do to me; for this is to act according to the creation of a man, the chief Ordinance; let Reason be judge. *Mat.* 7.12. *Rom.* 12.20. *Mat.* 25.35. *Esay.* 1.16, 17, *&c.* 1. *Joh.* 3.17. *Rom.* 14.10. *Deut.* 1.16. *Esay.* 33.15, 16.

Fourthly, if I have knowledge, peace, or any good, I rejoyce to see the Father breathing forth love, in the strength I receive there from: I am ready as occasion is tendred, to put forth my hand to refresh others, and hereby I give the Father thanks. And if I want any of those refreshments my self, my heart frets not, but is quiet, and made to wait upon the Father patiently, till he give me such things I want, in his own time. *Psa.* 9.14. *Act.* 15.31. *Luke* 22.32. *Psal.* 123.2. *Zeph.* 3.8. *Gal.* 5.5. *Esay.* 8.17

Fiftly, I can, without grudging, suffer others to walk to that measure of knowledge they have received, though it differ from mine; yet holding forth my light with tendernesse to such as I see of meek spirits; and can without rashnesse (for I know what I speak) condemne, where I see a heart lifted [68] up in pride, waiting upon the Father, til he destroy the Serpent, and then make us all of one heart, and one spirit. *Rom.* 12.10. 1. *Peter* 4.10. *Psal.* 37.7. *John* 7.34. 1. *Cor.* 6.2. *Rom.* 14.5, 12.

Sixtly, I doe and can breake bread, with any in whom I see but the least measure of the Father rising up; that is, I can eate and drinke with them in any house, where I meet with them, speaking of the things of the Father to them, and hearing them speak to me; for this is to break bread, from house to house, in singlenesse of heart; this is the communion of Saints in that particular; let Reason judge. *Act.* 2.46. *Judg.* 13.15. *Gen.* 18.4, 5. *Joh.* 21.5, &c. *Act.* 16.34.

Seventhly, for Baptism, I have gon through the ordinance of dipping, which the letter of the Scripture doth warrant, yet I doe not presse any one thereunto; but bid every one to waite upon the Father, till he teach and perswade, and then their submitting will be sound; for I see now that it is not the materiall water, but the water of life; that is the spirit, in which soules are to be dipped, and so drawn up into the one spirit, and all these outward customes and formes are to cease, and passe away. *Mat.* 3.15, 16. *Act.* 8.38. *Joh.* 3.22, 23. 1. *Cor.* 12.13. *Joh.* 4.21, &c. 1. *Cor.* 13.1.

[66, i.e., 69] Eightly, that Sabbath which I observe, is the day of Christ, wherein he is manifesting his power to save me from the curse; & so my soul is continually breathing forth, what I receive from him. I feel his power, in this day of his power, subduing the powers of my flesh more and more under me, and filling me with himself. In whom I rest, and find sweet contentment; and this is the Antitipe of Moses seventh day. *Heb.* 4.3. *Esay.* 2.11. *Psal.* 110.3. *John* 8.56. *Revel.* 19.6. *Mat.* 11.28.

They that will observe Gods Ordinances, must walk in the light of pure Reason, or according to the command or example of Reasons

Scripturs, in the very letter of them, without making inferences or constructions; for he that gives liberty to do so, gives liberty to alter the Scriptures.

But what I have declared here, and what I practise, to me is the light of pure Reason, who is the judge of all; and according to example and command of Scriptures in the letter; therefore I owne the Scripture and Ordinances of God in the spiritual power of them, letting them shine in their own luster not mixing my own conjectures with them.

Now observe those Ordinances, which neither [70] Reason, nor Scripture doth warrant, and which you walke in, calling them Gods Ordinances.

First, you use words of prayer by custom, observing dayes, and times, and seasons, and places, whether ye have the power of prayer in you; yea, or no; witnesse your set formes, or the confusion that is in your *ex tempore* prayers; read these Scriptures, and let Reason judge whether this be a service with the whole heart. *Gal.* 4.10, 11. *Mat.* 6.5. *Lu.* 18.10. *John* 4.21, &c. *Esay.* 29.13.

Secondly, you preach not occasionally from the testimony within your selves, but customarily from your imaginary studies, of what you have heard and read from others; and make a trade of it, to get a living by; but you say, you are commanded to preach, because *Paul* bid *Timothy* to preach in season, and out of season; this doth not concern you to take up preaching to make it a trade: prove your command within your self, or else you have no warrant from the Spirit so to do, though you be learned in all the languages under the Sun, if you run before you be sent. *Eze.* 13.3. *Jer.* 23.21, 30, &c. *John* 10.12. *Dan.* 8.23, &c, *John* 3.11. *Micah.* 3.11, 12.

Thirdly, you use words of prayer, before [71] and after sermon, a custome the Scriptures ownes not; read the Record, and let Reason judge, whether you finde the power of prayer so customarily in you, or whether it be not covetousnes in you to get a temporal living that stirs you up to use this trade; and grosse ignorance in the people to consent with you, and the vain babling of the heathens. *Mat.* 5.1. *Acts* 2.14. *Iohn* 8, &c. *Acts* 13.9.

Fourthly, your preaching is exposition of words and texts, a custome that Christ and his Apostles never used nor commanded; indeed Christ did expound the 61 of *Esay*, but it was upon occasion, to give forth his testimony, that he was the Messias, he made not a trade of it customarily to get a living by. *Mica.* 3.5. *Zacha.* 13. 4, 5. *Act.* 13. 9. *Act.* 7. 2. *Acts.* 21.40.

Fifthly, you petition the magistrate to compel the people to come to hear you pray and preach, or if you doe not petition, yet your ancestors have done it: And you allow of such a compulsion, and never tell the magistrate of his evill in so doing. A forcing power, which Christ and his Apostles never practised; indeed they did foretell the rising up of his power, which *Daniel* calls the little horne. *Dan.* 8. 23, 24, 25. *Luke* 11. 47, 48. [72] *Mat.* 15.6. *Luke* 9.50, 53, *&c. Rev.* 13.6. *Rev.* 17.2. *Mat.* 24.26, 27. *Rom.* 14.5, 12.

Sixtly, you call a parish (which is so called and made for civil good sake) a Church, and all that lives within the bound of that parish, you say, are bound to maintain one of you, that stands up to teach them, what you have read and heard from others; telling them, you speak from God, when your own soules know you lie; for you speak other mens words not your own experience; but your lyes now shall be covered no longer. Nay, you say, if the people refuse to give you tithes, you tell the Magistrate, it is his duty to force them, all which is not warrantable, neither from Reason nor Scripture. *Mica.* 3.5. *Ier.* 23.21. *Ezek.* 13.7. *Luke* 9.54, *&c. Heb.* 7.12.

Seventhly, you say and practise, that the first day of the week is the Sabbath day, and so making use of the Magistrates power, endeavour to compell the people to keep that day after the manner of the Jewish tipe, meerly to uphold your own trade; a practise which the writings of the New Testament warrant not; for the keeping of that first day, was not a forced businesse, but a voluntary act of love among themselves, having a tast of the day of Christ, the Antitipe of [73] *Moses* seventh day. *Iohn* 20.19. *Psal.* 110.3. *Esay.* 2.11.

Eightly, you say and practise, that breaking bread and drinking wine in a mixed company, if they be al parishioners, al sitting either afraid or ashamed one of another in a slavish bondage, none to speake, but one of you, is the breaking of bread which the Apostles did practise: But neither Reason nor Scripture doth warrant your practise, for it is a meer table gesture, eating and drinking in love and sweet communion one with another from house to house: Read *Act.* 2.46. *Ier.* 18.4, 5.

Ninthly, you sprinkle children, and call that the baptisme of Christ, a practise which there is not the least command or example in Scripture to warrant; yet you doe it, for it mightily deceives the people, and moves them to uphold your trade. *Acts* 8.13. 1. *Cor.* 12.13.

Tenthly, you assume the office of preaching the Gospel, because you are bred up in humane learning, which the Scriptures doth not countenance in the least; and while you doe it, you persecute the Gospell it selfe, which is the Lord, or Spirit within; and you teare in peeces the declarations of the Gospel, which is the Scriptures, by your various [74] expositions, and so all you doe, is but to trouble the children, and to throw durt upon their food. *Moses* a shepheard; *Amos* a fruit gatherer; *Apostles* fisher-men; *Christ* a carpenter; such as the Lord made preachers, not such as made themselves preachers, that had biggest purses.

Thus I have given a tast of my own practise, and if the priests, who say they own the Scriptures, and they say, I deny the Scriptures and Gods Ordinances; therefore let all men judge between us, whether is in the fault, and let truth hereafter be owned and practised.

They that practise any way of worship which neither Reason nor Scripture warrants, do deny the Scriptures.

But the Ministers of England, and such as follow them in the practise of praying, preaching; sprinkling children, breaking bread, sabbaths, Church societies, & Ministers maintenance, as they practise in their customary way of performances, which they call Gods ordinances; hath neither Reason nor Scripture to warrant them.

Therefore you that call your selves Ministers, are the men that deny the Scriptures and Gods ordinances, setting up your owne inferences and constructions above the Scriptures, [75] leaving the antient letter which the Apostles and Prophets writ, and set up a new moulded way of Ordinances of your own framing, by inferences and conjectures. And by thus new moulding the Scriptures, you deny God, and Christ, the one Spirit, from whence the Scriptures were breathed.

Let the Record be searched without drawing inferences from it, and let all judge. Let us speak the Scripture words, not force a meaning, least we speake contrary to the mind or spirit of them.

Well, all that I shall say, is this; let all men cease spending constructions upon the Scriptures, and leave the pure Scriptures to shine in their own luster, not mixing imaginary inferences with them; they were the declarations of truth in the Prophets and Apostles.

And let us leave the pure teachings of the Father in every man, to conjoyn themselves with those Scriptures, and then there will be no jarring, but a sweet harmony of peace and love, betweene the experience of every man and those Scriptures.

FINIS.

[76] *Leave of your trade, yee proud Priests then,*
*   and trouble not the Spirit:*
By forcing sense, from the Saints words,
*   if ye would life inherit.*
Let every one speak what he knowes,
*   and utter what's received:*
And let not any soul by you,
*   hereafter be deceived.*
For you as traytors to our God,
*   have stood to justify:*
That your constructions are all truths,
*   and other lights a lie.*
Your fleshly learning yee have own'd,
*   as sound, divine, and good:*
Though you by that in ages still,
*   have shed the childrens blood.*
But know yee now, the time is come,
*   for truth to spread all over:*
And he will tread you down apace,
*   and all your lies discover.*
Leave off therefore I say, betimes,
*   and stoope unto our God:*
If yee would life, and peace enjoy,
*   with them that know the Lord.*

[77] *Postscript*

If Reason, King, doe rule in thee,
*   There's truth, and peace, and clemency:*
No rash distemper will there be,
*   No filthy lusts, but chastitie.*
In all thy actions to behold,
*   Just dealing, love, as pure as gold.*

When Reason rules in whole mankinde,
    Nothing but peace, will all men finde:
Their hearts he makes both meeke, and kinde,
    And troublesome thoughts he throws behinde.
For he is truth, and love, and peace,
    Makes wars and lewdnesse for to cease.
He makes no prisons for the poor,
    He doth condemne and judge the whore:
He makes all men to sin no more,
    As they have done in times before;
But restores all to what hath beene,
    And heales the creature of his sin.
    And why doe men so clamor then,
    Against this powerfull King in men?

FINIS.

THE NEW LAW OF RIGHTEOUSNES

T HE title page is dated 1649, and the address to "the Twelve Tribes of Israel" is dated January 26, 1648 (n.s. 1649). The pamphlet is mentioned in *A Watch-word to the Parliament* as the first statement of Winstanley's communism, revealed to him in a trance (below, p. 315). The title page bears Winstanley's name, which appears also at the end of the address.

Copies are to be found in the following collections: The Library of Jesus College (Oxford), The Library of the Princeton Theological Seminary, and The Seligman Library at Columbia University. It is included in *Several Pieces Gathered into one Volume*, in the Manchester Free Reference Library.

The text is reproduced from the copy in the Library of the Princeton Theological Seminary.

TO THE TWELVE TRIBES OF ISRAEL THAT ARE CIRCUMCISED IN HEART, AND SCATTERED THROUGH ALL THE NATIONS OF THE EARTH

DEAR BRETHREN,

THOUGH *you have been, and yet are the despised ones of the world, yet the blessing of the most High (your King of Righteousnesse) is in you, and shall spread forth of you to fill the earth. You are the field wherein the treasure hath lien hide; all the dark and cloudy dayes of the Beasts time, times and dividing of time now expiring.*

Though dark clouds of inward bondage, and outward persecution have over-spread you; yet you are the firmament, in whom the Son of righteousnesse will rise up, and from you will declare himself to the whole Creation; for you are Sion || *whom no man regards, out of whom salvation shall come.*

That blessing (which is the seed of Abraham) lies hid in you, that is and must be the alone Saviour and joy of all men, from inward and outward bondage, and the restorer of the whole Creation from the curse it groans under.

He lies hid in you, he is hated, persecuted and despised in you, he is Jacob *in you, that is and hath been a servant to* Esau *a long time; but though this* Jacob *be very low, yet his time is now come, that he must rise, and he will rise up in you that are trod under foot like dust of the earth; he will glorifie himself both in you and from you, to the shame and downfall of* Esau.

The report of this blessed promised *seed, shall go through the Earth in this ministration of the Spirit that is now rising up, as well as that ministration of the flesh and letter, that now begins to draw back, and his* dominion, *when he begins to rule the* Nations, *shall*

149

reach from one end of heaven to the other; *the* whole earth shall be filled with the knowledge of the Lord, and of his Dominion there shall be no end. *This is the consolation of Israel, it draws near to be made manifest, wait for it with patience.*

You whom I writ to are the seed of Abraham, *and the blessing of* Isaac and Jacob; *but let me tell you, not the* seed of *Abraham* after || the flesh: *for* Ishmael *and* Esau, *are not to share in this* portion; *Their portions was of the earth, and they have received them, and spent them already by their* unrighteousnesse; *your portion is the Lord himself which endures for ever.*

The powers of the flesh are to be made servants unto the promised seed; *and now comes the time that the elder sons, that are born after the flesh, shall serve the younger sons, in whom the* blessing *lies; this is the fall of* Esau, *and the rising of* Jacob, *and shall be really done in the sight of the whole Creation as the other was.*

You are the Abrahamites *in whom the* blessing *remaines, that lives not now in the* type, *but enjoyes the* substance *of circumcision*; For he is not a Jew, that is one outward in the flesh; but he is a Jew, that is one inward, whose circumcision is of the heart: *Whether he be born of the Nation of the* Jews *extant in the world, or whether he be one born of other Nations in whom the* blessing *remaines*; *it is* Abrahams *promised seed that makes a* Jew; *and these are they of whom it is said,* Salvation is of the Jews.

What was that seed of Abraham, that is called the blessing?

It is the Law and power of righteousnesse, which made Abraham to forsake his Isaac, his dearest relations in the flesh, rather then he would || *refuse the way of his Maker; and herein Abraham found peace: So that this King of righteousnesse, and this Prince of peace that ruled in Abraham, is the blessing of all Nations, for this shall save his people from their sins, and free them from all distempers of the unrighteous flesh. This is the one spreading power that shall remove the curse, and restore all things from the bondage every thing groans under.*

This is called Abrahams *seed, because* Abraham *sprang from him, as a tree grows from the seed, which gave the tree its being and its name: And the Law of righteousnesse and peace, dwelling and ruling in any one is the seed of* Abraham, *and the severall branches of men and women in whom that power rests, are children and of the family of* Abraham.

For it was not the man of the flesh that was called Abraham, *but the Law of righteousnesse and peace, that did rule and govern in that body, he was the* Abraham; *the flesh is honoured with such a name by him that dwelt therein; the name of the flesh before this righteous power was manifest in it, was Abram.*

As the humane body called Christ, *was not the anointing, but the Spirit in that body, was the* Christ, *or the spreading power of righteousnesse, which was to fill the earth with himself. That body was but a house or temple for the present work, which was to draw down* Moses *Law* || *and become the substance of his types, and lambs, and sacrifices; for that body was the lamb, that did fulfill the righteous will, by his voluntary and free-will offering up of himself, without forcing.*

So then: This Law of righteousnesse and peace, is Abrahams *seed; nay that manifestation in that humane body, was* Abraham *himself; for* Abraham *is known to the Creation, by acting in or from that power that ruled the flesh. And every man or woman, born of* Jew *or* Gentile, *in whom this power rules and breaks forth, are the children of* Abraham, *and the man* Abraham *in whom the spirit dwelt in a lesse measure; for he hath failings, was a type of the Man* Christ Jesus, *in whom the Law of righteousnesse and peace dwelt bodily, for there was no sin or unrighteousnesse in that body.*

Therefore Christ *hath the honour above his brethren, to be called the spreading power, because he fils all with himself; And because this power did appear to the Creation first in* Abraham *of all men we hear of, therefore every one that follows after him, and that are ruled by the same Law, are called children of* Abraham, *or children of that seed.*

But Christ *the anointing he hath the preheminence, for* Abraham *sprang from him, and all* Abrahamits *are but a tree or vine that did spring from that one seed: for indeed the spirit* || *of life, lies in the bottom, which lifted up both* Abraham *and his children, and is the one seed of righteousnesse and life, from which every one springs, what name soever any righteous body is called.*

Now this seed doth promise himself to be the blessing of all Na-

tions, and the restorer of all things from bondage; but the Nations of the earth, since that report was made, never yet enjoyed the benefit of it; for the curse hath still rested upon the Creation, and hath been rather multiplied from year to year; so that at this very day, those in whom the first fruits of restauration appears, do see darknesse, nay thick darknesse do cover man-kind: And the curse doth rest mightily in the fire, water, earth and air; all places stinks with the abomination of the curse; So that a man can go into no place, but he shall see the curse and enmity is that power that rules the creatures, that makes them jar one against another.

Likewise misery breaks forth upon man-kind, from these four Elements of which his body is made, and the curse rests within him, and the curse dwels round about him; But Abrahams *seed, is and must be the blessing of all Nations, and shall spread as far as the curse hath spread, to take it off.*

And this seed (Dear Brethren) hath lien hid in you, all the time appointed, and now is breaking forth. And the Nations shall know, That ‖ salvation or restauration rather, is of the Jews, *that King of righteousnesse and Prince of peace, that removes the curse, and becomes himself the blessing, arises up in you, and from you, and fils, and will fill the earth, both man-kind, and the whole Creation, Fire, Water, Earth and Air, for the blessing shall be every where.*

And though the seed of the flesh have cast you out for evil, and you have been the despised ones of the earth, and the children of the flesh refuses to buy and sell with you, yet now your glory is rising. And the ancient prophesie of Zecharie *shall be fulfilled,* That ten men shall take hold of the skirt of him that is a Jew, saying, Let us go with you, for we have heard that God is with you.

This new Law of righteousnesse and peace, which is rising up, is David *your King, which you have been seeking a long time, and now shall find him coming again the second time in the personall appearance of sons and daughters; he will be a true* Davider *indeed, between flesh and spirit, between bondage and libertie, between oppressours and the oppressed; he is and will be the righteous Judge; he will lead your captivitie captive, and set you down in peace.*

He is now coming to raign, and the Isles and Nations of the earth shall all come in unto him; he will rest every where, for this blessing will fill all places: All parts of the Creation in whom ‖ the curse remains shall be shaken and moved, and the seed of the flesh shall find peace no where: He will throw down the mountaines of the flesh, fill up the low valleys of the spirit, he will make rough wayes smooth, and crooked wayes strait, he will make the earth fruitfull, and the winds and the weather seasonable; he will throw all the powers of the earth at your feet, and himself will be your governour and teacher, and your habitations on earth shall be in peace, that so you that are the Citie of the Lord, New Jerusalem, *the place of his rest, may be the praise of the whole earth.*

If any one say: The glory of Jerusalem *is to be seen hereafter, after the body is laid in the dust; it matters not to me what they say, they speak their imagination, they know not what.*

I know that the glory of the Lord shall be seen and known within the Creation, and the blessing shall spread in all Nations; and Jerusalem *indeed which is* Abrahams *children, spirituall* Israel *gathered together, shall be the praise and glory of the whole earth; and the restauration of all things is to be seen within the Creation of Fire, Water, Earth and Air. And all bodies that are made of the compound of these four Elements, are to be purged and delivered from the curse; and all shall know that this almighty King* || *of righteousnesse is our Saviour, and besides him there is none.*

The swords and counsels of flesh shall not be seen in this work, the arm of the Lord onely shall bring these mighty things to passe, in this day of his power; and the hearts of men shall tremble and fail them with fear to see the misery that is coming upon the world, for the glory and riches of men shall be brought low, and the Lord alone shall be exalted. Therefore all that I shall say is this; Though the world, even the seed of the flesh despise you, and call you by reprochfull names at their pleasure; yet wait patiently upon your King, he is coming, he is rising, the Son is up, and his glory will fill the earth.

And when you see the Doves flock to the windows (not to your Church-windows) but to the teachings of the Father, for his discoveries are the windows that lets the light of the Father shine into the soul: and these are dreams, voices and revelations *immediately from the Father himself, his own inward teaching, without which the soul is* hungry, *and* flocks *unto* the inward discoveries *and* teaching of the Father for satisfaction, *forsaking all other in point of inward rest.*

When you see or hear of the risings up of Israel, *like* the noise of mighty waters, *carrying* || *all before them, then rejoyce and say,* Your redemption draws near, *and the* reports *from the Lord are true: wait with a meek and quiet spirit for the consolation of* Israel, *even the coming forth of the deliverer, That shall* turn ungodlinesse from *Jacob.* Then shall Jacob rejoyce, and Israel shall be glad. *So I rest.*

January 26.
1648.

> *A waiter for the consolation*
> *of Israel*
> JERRARD WINSTANLEY.

[1] THE NEW LAW OF RIGHTEOUSNES BUD-DING FORTH, TO RESTORE THE WHOLE CREATION FROM BONDAGE OF THE CURSE

CHAP. I.

THERE is nothing more sweet and satisfactory to a man, then this: to know and feel that spirituall power of righteousnesse to rule in him, which he cals God. For while the flesh through hasty and violent lusts, doth rebell against the spirit, it hath no true peace, but is still pulling misery upon himself. But when the created flesh is made subject to the law of righteousnesse, and walks uprightly in the Creation, in the light of that spirit, then it lies down in rest.

[2] In other writings [1] I have declared what I know, That Almighty power & ever living Spirit is, which rules and preserves the whole Creation; fire, water, earth and air, and of every creature in these elements; or that is made up of all these in a compound matter as all flesh is. And something I shall here add to the rest, which I only hold forth to my fellow creature, man; not customarily to make a trade of it, for fleshly ends, but occasionally as the Light is pleased to manifest himself in me; that others from me, and I from them may be witnesses each to other, of our Maker how he shines forth in his own light, through each other to the profit of the Creation. 1 *Joh.* 1. 3, 4.

In the beginning of time the whole Creation lived in man, and man lived in his Maker, the spirit of Righteousnesse and peace, for every creature walked evenly with man, and delighted in man, and was ruled by him; there was no opposition between him and the beast, fowls, fishes, or any creature in the earth: so that it is truely said, The whole Creation was in man, one within, and walked even with

---

[1] The reference seems to be especially to *Truth Lifting up its Head.*

him; for no creature appeared to be a visible enemy to him: for every creature gave forth it self, either for pleasure or profit of man, who was Lord of all: And man lived in his Maker the Spirit, and delighted in no other; there was an evennes between man and all creatures, and an evennesse between man and his Maker the Lord, the Spirit.

But when man began to fall out of his Maker, and to leave his joy and rest which he had in the spirit of Righteousnesse, and sought content from creatures and outward objects, then he lost his dominion, and the creature fell out of him, and became enemies and apposers of him, and then rise up mountaines, and valleys, and hils, and all unevennesse, both in mans heart, and in mans actions. And as the man is become selfish; so are all the beasts [3] and creatures become selfish; and man and beast act like each other, by pushing with their horns of power, and devouring one another to preserve self.

And truly as man might see all creatures lived at rest in him in the beginning, so he may see all creatures in him now, but in a rest-lesse condition, groaning under bondage, waiting for a restauration. The covetousnesse, the subtilty, the cruelty, the pride, the envy, the devouring power that is in the flesh of man are the very distempers that are in such and such beasts and fowls: So that while man is ruled by such powers, and declares no other actions but what is in the beast; he indeed goes in the shape of a man, but properly he is a beast of such and such a ravenous principle. And this now is the curse, Man is gone out of his Maker, to live upon objects; and the creatures are gone out of man, to seek delight in pushing and devouring one another, and the whole Creation of fire, and water, earth and air; and all bodies made of these are put out of order, through mans rejecting the Spirit to live upon objects.

But now the time is come, that the Spirit will draw all things into man againe, to live and be at rest in him, as their Governour, as their Lord, and man and the Creation shall become even againe, and so man returning to his Maker, to rest in peace in none but him. The whole Creation shall be governed, preserved & comforted by the one spirit, the King of Righteousnesse, and all bondage, curse and tears shall be done away: And this is that I wait for, being assured it shall be accomplished, having received a taste.

But as the state of the world is, in the generality, I am made to see,

That in times past and times present, the branches of man-kind have acted like the beast or swine; And though they have called one [4] another, men and women, yet they have been but the shadows of men and women. As the Moone is the shadow of the Sun, in regard they have been led by the powers of the curse in flesh, which is the *Feminine* part; not by the power of the righteous Spirit which is Christ, the *Masculine* power. *Rom.* 8. 13. *Ephes.* 2. 2.

But when they come to see the spirituall Light that is in every creature, and in that power and light do walk righteously towards other creatures, as well beasts as man-kinde, that the creation as much as in them lies one by one, may be upheld and preserved in its glory; then they begin to appear and act like men; and rise up from the low earth of a beastly and swinish nature, to acknowledge and honour their Maker in the light of himself. *Psal.* 36. 9.

Experience shews us That every beast doth act in oppression and cruelty, towards such creatures, as he can master at advantage. And thus doth the flesh of man, which is the King of beasts: For when the wisdome and power of the flesh raigns, which in deed is *Adam*, that man that appeared first to rule the earth, man-kinde, and by his un-righteousnesse makes it a land of barrennesse: For this first *Adam* is such a selfish power, that he seeks to compasse all the creatures of the earth into his own covetous hands, to make himself a Lord, and all other his slaves. *Rev.* 13.4.

And though he gets lands, moneys, honours, government into his hands, yet he gives the King of righteousnesse, but a company of fawning words of love and obedience; for he makes unrighteousnesse to dwell in heaven and earth, that is, in the whole Creation, by his unrighteous government, and so he becomes the chief Rebell, the Serpent, the Devil, the Murderer, oppressing the Creation, setting himself above all in tyranny: And this power is the curse which the whole Creation groans under, [5] waiting for a restoration by Christ the King and law of righteousnesse, who is the restorer of all things. *Rom.* 8.21, 22.

And here first I shall declare what *Adam* the first man is, who to me appears to be the wisdome and power of the flesh, carrying along the Creation, man, to live upon creature objects, and to loath and despise the Spirit that made all, and that dwels in all things according to the capacity of every single creature: and all that *Adam* doth is to advance himself to be, The one power; he gets riches and government into his hands, that he may lift up himself, and suppresse the universall liberty, which is Christ. And if he preach, or pray, or performe any service relating to the Spirit, it is for this end, that he may get peace thereby, and so seeks to honour flesh by procuring his own peace, by his own wit and pollicy if that would doe.

So that this *Adam* appears first in every man and woman; but he sits down in the chair of Magistracy, in some above others; for though this climbing power of self-love be in all, yet it rises not to its height in all; but every one that gets an authority into his hands, tyrannizes over others; as many husbands, parents, masters, magistrates, that lives after the flesh, doe carry themselves like oppressing Lords over such as are under them; not knowing that their wives, children, servants, subjects are their fellow creatures, and hath an equall priviledge to share with them in the blessing of liberty.

And this first *Adam* is to be seen and known in a two fold sense.

First, He is the wisdome and power of the flesh in every man, who indeed is the beast, and he spreads himself within the Creation, man, into divers branches; As into ignorance of the Creatour of all things, into covetousnesse after objects, into pride and envy, lifting up himself above others, and [6] seeking revenge upon all that crosses his selfish honours; and into hypocrisie, subtilty, lying imagination, self-love; from whence proceeds all unrighteous outward acting. This is the first *Adam* lying, ruling and dwelling within man-kinde. And this is he within every man and woman, which makes whole man-kinde, being a prisoner to him, to wonder after the beast, which is no other but self, or upon every thing whereupon self is stamped.

Secondly, The first *Adam* is the wisdome and power of flesh broke out and sate down in the chair of rule and dominion, in one part of man-kind over another. And this is the beginner of particular interest, buying and selling the earth from one particular hand to another, saying, *This is mine*, upholding this particular propriety by a law of government of his own making, and thereby restraining other fellow creatures from seeking nourishment from their mother earth. So that though a man was bred up in a Land, yet he must not worke for himself where he would sit down. But from *Adam*; that is, for such a one that had bought part of the Land, or came to it by inheritance of his deceased parents, and called it his own Land: So that he that had no

Land, was to work for those for small wages, that called the Land theirs; and thereby some are lifted up into the chair of tyranny, and others trod under the foot-stool of misery, as if the earth were made for a few, not for all men.

For truly the common-people by their labours, from the first rise of *Adam*, this particular interest upheld by the fleshes law to this day, they have lifted up their Land-lords and others to rule in tyranny and oppression over them. And let all men say what they will, so long as such are Rulers as cals the Land theirs, upholding this particular propriety of *Mine and Thine*; the common-people shall never have [7] their liberty, nor the Land ever freed from troubles, oppressions and complainings; by reason whereof the Creatour of all things is continually provoked. O thou proud selfish governing *Adam*, in this Land called *England*! Know that the cries of the poor, whom thou laieth heavy oppressions upon, is heard.

This is unrighteous *Adam*, that dammed up the water springs of universall liberty, and brought the Creation under the curse of bond-age, sorrow and tears: But when the earth becomes a common treasury as it was in the beginning, and the King of Righteousnesse comes to rule in every ones heart, then he kils the first *Adam*; for covetous-nesse thereby is killed. A man shall have meat, and drinke and clothes by his labour in freedome, and what can be desired more in earth. Pride and envy likewise is killed thereby, for every one shall look upon each other as equall in the Creation; every man indeed being a parfect Creation of himself. And so this second *Adam* Christ, the restorer, stops or dammes up the runnings of those stinking waters of self-interest, and causes the waters of life and liberty to run plentifully in and through the Creation, making the earth one store-house, and every man and woman to live in the law of Righteousnesse and peace as members of one houshold.

And in the next place I shall declare the mystery of the Spirit in a two-fold way:

First, he makes the Creation, man-kinde, to see, loath and forsake this *Adam*, this fleshly man: This devil or power of darknesse that rules in the creatures, and leads them into waies that brings misery, pain and death, which is hell, a condition of uncomfortable darknesse of the curse.

Secondly, He makes man-kinde to see, to love and delight in the

Spirit Reason, which is the law of Righteousnesse, that made them, and settles them [8] in peace; when in the light and power thereof, they are made to forsake the flesh with all his wayes of bondage; for truly when the flesh is made subject to Reason, that light that inlightens every thing, then it hath peace and liberty, and is freed from those heart-aking pressures and sorrows, which the flesh puls upon himself by his violent, rash, unrighteous, and unreasonable actings.

The Almighty hath declared three methods in discovering this mystery in the compasse of six dayes, or 6000 years near hand expired; in every one of which he draws man-kind higher and higher into himself, out of the power of the Serpent or bondage. And when he alone is advanced, he draws all men after him, which is the finishing up of the mystery.

The first Method is this: He was pleased to call forth *Moses* to be his servant, and in, by and through him, he reveals himself to lie under types, shadows, sacrifices; that man-kind by them might be led to see his Maker; And this was the Covenant of an outward testimony, which *Moses*, a man that was mixed with flesh and spirit, was Mediatour of. And this

Secondly did point out the Apostolical testimony which was to be manifested in aftertimes; and that was to acknowledge honour, and bear witnesse of the Lamb Jesus Christ, that was the substance of *Moses*. For the Apostles declare themselves to be witnesses of Christ, the great Prophet, that *Moses* said should come after him, to whom every man should hearken, and then leave the teachings of shadows, which they receive from him. *Act.* 3.22.

Therefore say they, *We eat and drank in his presence, we heard him speak, and saw his miracles, and bear testimony to the world, that the Rulers of the Jews slew him, and that he was raised from the dead by the Almighty power.* And this single appearance of the [9] man Christ Jesus (for herein the righteous Law dwelt bodily) was a more spirituall declaration then the former. And this types out

The third Method of Divine discovery, which indeed doth finish the mystery; and herein the Lord takes up all into himself, even into that Spirit that governs the Creation; for he is in all, and acts through all. And all power of righteousnesse that appears in any subject is still but the Lord, in such or such a discovery; for as the man Christ Jesus swallowed up *Moses*; and so the Spirit dwelt bodily in that Lamb, which was spread abroad in the types; And man-kind is to behold the Law of Righteousnesse, in none, but in that his wel-beloved Son. *Eph. 4. 6. Rom.* 8.22, 23.

Even so that single body is a type: That the same Spirit that filled every member of that one body, should in these last dayes be sent into whole mankind, and every branch shall be a joint or member of the mysticall body, or severall spreadings forth of the vine, being all filled with the one Spirit, Christ the anointing, who fils all with himself, and so he becomes the alone King of Righteousnesse and peace that rules in man. And the powers of the flesh which is the Serpent or curse, shall be subdued under him, and man-kind shall be made onely subject to this one Spirit, which shall dwell bodily in every one, as he dwelt bodily in the man Christ Jesus, who was the Son of man. 1 *Cor.* 12. 13. *Act.* 2. 17. *Jer.* 31.34.

Now as *Moses* declared, That the Lamb Jesus Christ should be that great Prophet to whom every one should give ear, & delivered it in general termes, leaving the particular discoveries of his new doctrine to the Lamb himself when he came; and so did not go about to imagine matters that was above his circle; and we see the Doctrine of Jesus Christ, when he came, far exceeded the Doctrine of *Moses*; the [10] one being the substance of the other, and so more spiritual makings forth then the other.

Even so, the man Christ Jesus, the great Prophet, declared in general termes what should be in later times; leaving it to every son and daughter, to declare their particular experiences, when the Spirit doth rise up in them, and manifests himself to them. *For they that believe* (saith he) *out of their bellies shall flow rivers* (or plentifull discoveries) *of the water of life. Joh.* 7.38.

Therefore as *Moses* gave way to Christ; for when Christ appeared in flesh, *Moses* administration began to be silent and drew back, and set Jesus Christ in the chair to be the great Prophet that should be the teacher in types after him. And the ministration of these discoveries were to raign in the world, their appointed times. *Luke* 9.33, 36.

Even so the Lamb Christ Jesus, or that single body, gives way to the holy Ghost, or spreading Spirit; *If I go not away, the Comforter cannot come to you*; *for he that dwels bodily in me, is to spread him-*

self in you, that as the Father in me, and I in him are one: even so I in you, and you in me, may become one with the Father. Joh. 16.7. Joh. 17.21

And the testimony of the Apostles declares as much: *Though we have known Christ after the flesh,* (in one single body) *yet now henceforth know we him no more so;* but we look after that mystery, which hath been kept secret from ages and generations past, which is *Christ in you, the hope of glory.* And therefore I must tell you that yet live in dipping, in water and observation of Gospel-forms and types, you live yet under the ministration of Jesus Christ after the flesh, declaring the Lamb Christ to remain as yet in one single person. 2 *Cor.* 16. *Col.* 1.27.

But know you, that as the ministration of *Moses* gave way to this; so this ministration is to give way [11] to the inward teachings of Christ, and the spreading of the Spirit, in sons and daughters, which will more excellently declare the glory of the mystery. The man Christ Jesus himself, told the woman of *Samaria; Woman the time is coming that neither in Jerusalem, nor in this mountain shall men worship the Father, but they that worship him shall worship him in Spirit and in Truth,* for the Father seeks such to worship him. Joh. 14: [4.21.]

By these words, The Son of man declares, that both outward forms, customs and types of *Moses* worship under that ministration at *Jerusalem,* likewise all forms and customs, and types of this ministration of himself, as the Lamb held forth at a distance to be our Mediatour, should all cease and give way to the spirituall worship of the Father in the latter dayes; or to the spreading of the Divine power in men, the one Law of Righteousnesse, being the teacher of all. *Luke* 17.21. Joh. 6.45.

So that upon the rising up of Christ in sons and daughters, which is his second comming, the ministration of Christ in one single person is to be silent and draw back, and set the spreading power of Righteousnesse and wisdom in the chair, of whose Kingdom there shall be no end. So as all things were gone out from the Spirit, and were gone astray and corrupted. The Spirit in this great mystery of truth being manifested in flesh, burns up that drosse out of the Creation, and draws in all things back again into himself, and declares himself to be the alone wisdom and power of Righteousnesse, that rules, dwels, that governs and preserves both in and over the whole Creation. And now the Son delivers up the Kingdom unto the Father; And he that is the spreading power, not one single person, become all in all in every person; that is, the one King of Righteousnesse in every one. *Joh.* 16.7. *Dan.* 3.44. 2. *Cor.* 5.19. 1. *Cor.* 5.24.

[12] Here we may see what the dividing of time is, which is the last period in which the Beast is to reign; for now every ministration pleads his priviledge, till the Law of Righteousnesse draws up all in himself. *Moses* yet pleads a priviledge in the practice of the Jews after the flesh. The Son of man, or Christ in one single person pleads a priviledge, and not onely the true ministration of the Son of man according to the Apostles declaration; But likewise many false forms, customs and observations of Divine worship are raised up, through a wrong understanding of those Scriptures, all plead a priviledge. *Dan.* 7.25.

And lastly, the ministration of the Spirit, forsaking all types and formes, worshipping the Father in the substance of truth. This now pleads his priviledge, as his due right by course. So that you see here is the dividing of time. But this last ministration is the sufferer for the present, as being denied his right by the former, that ought to give way. *Ioh.* 4. 23.

And as the worshippers in *Moses* ministration, envied and killed such as worshipped the Son of man, the Lamb: So now, those that worship Christ at a distance in their severall Congregations and forms, and are most zealous therein, are in these dayes the most bitterest enemies to the ministration of Christ in Spirit and in truth.

But when this ministration of the Spirit spreads himself, he will make the greatest separation that ever was. For though Israels separation out of Egypt amazed the world, and the separation of gathered Congregations out of Parish Churches (so called) did trouble the earth, though it is no more but going out of one form into another, not into the unitie of the one Spirit. Yet this ministration of the Spirit now rising up by right of inheritance, will take peace from the world much more: for he hath begun, and he will and shall go on, to gather the scattered [13] of Israel together, out of all Ægyptian bondages, and self-seeking oppressing government, and out of all forms and customes of the Beast, to worship the Father in spirit and truth, being made to be all of one heart and one minde: And this shall more and more appear, as the earth grows up to be a common treasury for all.

Therefore let me tell you, That all your enmity will not uphold your forms, your imprisoning, and reviving, and making law to suppresse such as are contrary to you, will never work your will, but pull miseries and shame upon your selves; as the zealous Scribes and Pharisees did in killing of Christ the Sonne of man: Therefore be patient, look up for teaching in this dividing of time, when the Law of Righteousnesse arises up; and makes himself more manifest, he will reconcile all, make every one to be of one heart and one minde; and no other power must be the restorer, but this King of Righteousnesse and Peace: for this is he that makes men doe as they would be done unto, And then envie and bitternes dies. *Acts* 4. 32. *Isa.* 60. 16.

Now search the Scriptures, you that stand up to be Teachers, that say I deny the Scriptures, and let them judge me, whether I deny them or no; but one thing you shall finde to your shame, that those Scriptures of the Prophets and Apostles, which you seeme to preserve with such love and zealous tendernesse, shall cast the first stone at you, to stone you out of your Pulpits; for you doe not professe those Scriptures in love to them, but in zealous covetousnesse to uphold your trade. *Joh.* 5. 45. *Joh.* 2. 15.

For now when Christ begins to arise up in sons and daughters, whereby the Scriptures are honoured and proved true Prophecies, Promises, Visions, and Revelations; you deny their testimony, and cry out Visions and Revelations are ceased; and so [14] you will ever have people to be hearing you speak the declaration, because you live by it; but if any receive the power from on high, you cry out upon it, It is self-conceit, errour and blasphemy: Well, he is at worke that will discover your shame; *Wickedness shall slay the wicked, though no mans hand be upon him.*

CHAP. II.

THERE are three more discoveries of Christ, to make the mystery of the Spirit shine in its excellency. As

First, The great world, wherein are variety of creatures, a Sunne, Moon, Stars, Earth, Grasse, Plants, Cattle, Fish, Fowl, and Man, the Lord over the lower Creatures, all sweetly conjoyned to preserve each other, is no other but Christ spread forth in the Creation; and so upholding the Creation by his own wisdome and power; for he is the maker, the preserver and restoring Spirit.

Therefore his name is called, *I, and I am, The Lord, and besides me there is no Saviour*; But this is Christ very remote; for though he rule in the whole Creation, yet no single creature could discern or spie him out; he is in every one, and yet that single one knew him not.

And therefore this one Almighty power began to make forth himself in visible descriptions before the creatures, causing every creature to hold forth the light and power that is in them, that so the mighty Creatour may at length be known, in the clear sighted experience of one single creature, man, by seeing, hearing, tasting, smelling, feeling. This one power of Righteousnesse, as he rests in the [15] Creation, that man may be the mouth that shall make a clear discovery of Christ to others from the testimony that is in himself; for hee is to see Christ within himself, before hee can see him in other creatures. *Ioh.* 14.17. And therefore,

Secondly, The Scripture in their severall declaration, types, prophecies, visions, voyces, revelations, actings of men, in patient doing and suffering in righteousnesse, is no other but Christ in the letter, lying under the experimentall words of those Pen-men, setting forth the one Almighty, in his severall actings, and his severall conditions, wherein he hath appeared to the view of the whole Creation; but seen and known only, by the one creature, man, in whom hee is purposed to dwell bodily. *Col.* 2.9.

But still here is a large distance between Christ and the bulk of man-kinde; for though some few particular ones have seen him, and could declare him, yet others are ignorant of him: So that the universalitie of man-kinde may see these two discriptions of Christ, that is in the Creation, and in the Scriptures, both without themselves.

And when any attains to see Christ in these outward discoveries, it is full of sweet delight, but this settles no true peace; for that delight that is fetching in from things at a distance from us, may be lost againe, and return into its proper seat againe: As the pleasant beames is of the Sun, which refreshes the outward man, may be lost, for when the Clouds come between, the beames returne into the Sun again, which is their proper seat, and men loseth, the refreshing, warmth and heat. And therefore,

Thirdly, Christ or the spreading power of light, is drawing the knowledge of himself, as he lies in all things, into the clear experience of man, into whole man, yea, into every branch of man-kinde and he the Sonne of Righteousnesse will not only [16] shine into, but fix himself in every one. So that perfect man shall be no other but *God manifest in flesh*: for every manifestation of this power in any creature, shall be seen, known, rejoyced in, and be declared of by man. *Ier*. 31.34. *Ioh*. 8.22. *Rom*. 8.22

The light, and heat, and Spirit of the Sunne, shall be declared by the Sonne of Righteousnesse in man: The sweet compliance of love in one creature towards another; as the clouds to water the earth, the earth to send forth the fruits to preserve the living creatures, that feeds thereupon, shall be declared by that living power, Love and Righteousnesse, that is seated in man towards any creature.

So that, though this one Almighty power be spread in the whole Creation, yet it will appear to have his chief residence in man, that in, by and through man, that one spirit may rule and govern the works of his own hands in Righteousnesse. *Eph*. 1.23. 1. *Joh*. 2.12.

Every declaration of Christ in the Scriptures, shal be seen and known in the clear experience of every sonne and daughter (when this mystery is finished) for Christ, who indeed is the anointing, shall fill all, and all shall be the fulnesse of the anointing: So that whatsoever a condition a man is in, it is one or other condition that the childe Jesus was in, growing upwards towards man-hood; there is child-hood, youth and old-age in the anointing. *Isa*. 21.13.

For the wisdome and power of truth, that was poured upon the head of the Son of man, grows upwards towards perfection in sons and daughters: Even as wee see any tree, corn or cattell, grows up in the eye of man by degrees; for as these creatures doe not attaine to perfection on a sudden; neither doth the spirit of Righteousnesse rise up on a sudden perfection, but by degrees.

And therefore, *He that beleeves makes not hast*; The hastie flesh would have all content on a sudden, [17] but the spirit is moderate and rises up patiently, its powerfull and quick, and yet slow; its slow, but yet sure; it will sit down in peace in a man, though it run thorow many thorns and briars first.

Yea, I say, whatsoever condition you are in Christ or the anointing being in you, appears in that condition in you. If you be in a condition of poverty, so was Christ the Son of man, he had *not whereon to lay his head.* If you be hated for *Righteousnesse sake,* so was he, nay it is the anointing in you that is hated. If angry, proud and tyrant-ruling flesh seek to imprison you and kill you, so they dealt with him, and it is still the righteous man in you that is opposed. *Isa.* 53.3.

If you be made to joy in the Father, the Spirit of truth; it is he within you that rejoyces in himself; if you feel a waiting, meek spirit in you, it is still Christ in you, *who is meek and lowly.* If you feel the power of love dwell within you, leading you to love enimies, and to do as you would be done unto, it is Christ in you, who is the law of love and Righteousnesse. *Ioh.* 14.

And in every condition you are in, this law of the Spirit meets with the powers of your own flesh fretting and fighting against him: For envy, frowardnesse, self-love, covetousnesse are the power of darknesse in you, that fights against the Spirit, that sweetly seeks the preservation and peace of all. But that opposing power in you is the devil, serpent and power of darknesse, which Christ the power of light, rising up in you; will destroy; and so *mortality shall be swallowed up of life.*

And Christ will not sit down in peace, rejoycing in you, till he hath subdued all these inward and outward enemies under his feet, and himself become the alone King of Righteousnesse in you; for he is that *mighty King, that shall be established upon the* [18] *holy hill of Sion;* that is, He shall be only King, *unto whom every man & woman shal be made a subject; This King shall raigne for ever and ever:* And this is he you would call God; but indeed the *power of darknesse* is the god that rules in most men and women, both professours and others: and they will subject to this their god of darknesse, till the power of light Christ take him away. *Ier.* 23.5, 6. 2. *Thes.* 2.7.

So that whatsoever estate a son or daughter is in, it is still but Christ combating with his enemies, in that estate, drawing all into himself, and destroying all opposing powers, that himself may remain to be the one alone Almighty power, spread forth every where, and so doing the will of the Father, brusing the Sarpents head in you; and that he himself, who is the divine, may grow up, flourish, remaine and bring forth aboundance of fruit in you, when your created flesh is purged from bondage, and made subject to him. 1. *Co.* 15.27.

But if Christ and the Father be all one power and wisdome, why do you make a distinction, as if they were two?

I answer, The Father is the universall power, that hath spread himself in the whole globe; The Sonne is the same power drawn into, and appearing in one single person, making that person subject to the one Spirit, and to know him that dwels every where.

There is not a person or creature within the compasse of the globe, but he is a sonne of the Father; or the breakings forth of that power in one body; now every small creature is the light of the Father, though it be a dark one; but man living in the light of the Father, is called *The wel-beloved Sonne*, because that one power of Righteousnesse dwels bodily in him, and the whole Creation is drawn up into that one centre, man.

[19] And now the Lord alone is exalted in this day of his power; for now the Serpent is cast out of heaven, all powers of darknesse are subdued, and the Spirit remaines conquerour in man, yet in single man; and so filling the living earth, man-kinde in all his branches with himself, the one Spirit.

This spreading power is the Fathers house, in which there are many mansions, or dwelling places; every creature lives herein: for *in and by him every one lives, and moves, and hath his being*: This is to speak truth as it is in Jesus. This is *Sion* that is above, where the Father dwels in his glory. *Sinai* is the mountaine of flesh, that is to be burned with fire, that is, the Spirit of Righteousnesse is the fire, that will burn up all unrighteous powers in the flesh. *Ephes.* 1.6.

And to see this power of Righteousnesse spreading himself every where, destroying death, and preserving the Creation, is to see him you would call God, with open face; and you can never see him plainly and nakedly, till you come thus to see him; therefore you Priests and zealous professors, learne hereafter to know what power it is you call God: for the word God, signifies a Governour, and it may as well be attributed to the devil, as to the law of Righteousnesse; for assure your selves, if covetousnesse, pride and bitter envy doe rule you, as it is apparent this dark power rules most of you, then the devil is that god you worship; and you are strangers and enemies to the Spirit of Truth that dwels every where, which you seem to call your God or Ruler.

[20] CHAP. III.

AND this is no new Gospel, but the old one; It is the same report that the Pen-men of Scriptures gave for the everlasting Gospel, *God with us*, or God *manifest in flesh*. The Father exalted above all, and in all; for the Prophets and Apostles declare these two things.

First, the Spirit spreads himself abroad in sacrifices and types, as in *Moses* time, and then takes all into himself againe; the Spirit manifest in one person, as in the son of man; For all the writings of old and new Testament, are all centered in Christ, and are swallowed up into him: And this Christ is not only confined to the Lamb Jesus anointed, but is the enlarging of the same anointing, in the particular persons of sonnes and daughters, in whom the same spirit of truth the comforter, is to be manifest in after times. *Ioh.* 16.7.

And this power shall not only fill man-kinde, and be all in all therein, but all other creatures, of all kinde according to their severall degrees, shall be filled with this one spirit, anointing: As *Pauls* testimony reports, that the whole Creation of all kindes of creatures, in whom the curse is spread through mans unrighteousnesse, doth all groan and travell, waiting for the manifestation of the sonnes of God. *Rom.* 3.22.

When man-kinde shall be restored, and delivered from the curse, and all spirited with this one power, then other creatures shall be restored likewise, and freed from their burdens: as the Earth, from thorns, and briars, and barrennesse; the Air and winds from unseasonable storms and distempers; the Cattle from bitternesse and rage one against another. And the law of righteousnesse [21] and love shall be seated in the whole Creation; from the lowest to the highest creature. And this is the work of restoration.

So that all the glory and content that man takes in other creatures of the earth, it is but a rejoycing in himself; or that spirit that is within him being more and more filled with peace to see, feel, taste, smell and hear, the power of the whole Creation, to have a sweet complyancy of love in him, and with him.

For now all jarring, rashnesse, violent storms, barrennesse of the earth, corruption in fire and water, enmity in battles, oppressing principles in one man over another, are all kept and swept away like locusts, by this strong East winde, the Lord himself at his coming. And every creature in his kinde sings in Righteousnesse, and man lives and rules in the strength of that Law, by reason whereof all teares are wiped away. And when this glory is finished, as it must be; for it is begun to be made manifest, for the *poor they doe receive the Gospel*: and it is yet hid from the *learned ones*, the teachers and rulers of the world.

Then those writings are made good, *That all enemies are subdued under the feet of the anointing*, who is this spreading power of Right-eousnesse, and there is no opposite power remaining. For the power that shall now appear, is no other but the Lord himself, dwelling every where: And the whole Creation is his garden wherein he walks and delights himself, And now the Kingdome is delivered up into the Fathers hand, the *one Spirit* that fils *all*, and *is in all*. *Psa.* 110.1. 1 *Cor.* 15.24.

And the distinction of dominion in one single person over all, shall cease, and no distinction shall be owned, but *King of Righteousnesse, dwelling in every one, and in the whole body of the Creation*; [22] all being sweetly and quietly subject to him, and he sweetly and quietly ruling in them: And *this shall be that City Sion, of which glorious things are spoken.* 1. *Cor.* 12.13.

And now in this new heaven and new earth, he himself who is the King of Righteousnesse doth dwel and rule; and this is the excellency of the work; when a man shall be made to see *Christ* in other crea-tures, as well as in himself; every one rejoycing each in other, and all rejoycing in their King. *Rev.* 5.13.

O ye hear-say Preachers, deceive not the people any longer, by telling them that this glory shal not be known and seen, til the body is laid in the dust. I tel you, this great mystery is begun to appear, and it must be seen by the material eyes of the flesh: And those five senses that is in man, shall partake of this glory.

This is Christ rising up and drawing al things into himself. This is the *Spirits* entrance into the Father; which is heavenly glory which rises, and shal rise higher and higher in *Israel, He that hath part in the first Resurrection, the second death*, of the bodies laying down in the dust, *shal have no power*, to break their peace, or hinder their glory, but shall further the increase of it.

But now that power of unrighteousnesse, that rules and fights in man-kinde against this, shall be destroyed, subdued, and shall never be reconciled to, nor partake of this glory.

My meaning is this, The power of pride, and the power of humility, shal never dwel quietly in one heart together.

The power of love, tendernesse and righteousnesse, and the power of envy, hardnesse of heart and covetous unrighteousnesse, shall never dwel quietly in one heart together.

Uncleannesse and chastity shal not dwel in peace together: The son of the bond-woman, rebellious [23] flesh, shal not be heir with the son of the free-woman, flesh made subject to the Law of Righteousnesse within himself.

There is no quiet peace in a man, til the Kingdome of darknesse be conquered, and the Serpent be cast out and so the heart made *a fit temple or house for the Spirit to dwel bodily in.*

A man is not counted a man from the bulk of his body of flesh, but the power that dwels in that body of flesh, is the man, either the righteous man or the wicked: And if the wicked power rule in the body of the flesh, this is he that must be burned up, subdued, destroyed, and never enter into rest. This is Christs enemy. *Mat.* 12. 29.

But if the righteous power doe rule, or being weak, and so is kept under by the other dark power doth hunger and thirst after righteousnesse, that he might be King. This power is to be redeemed from bondage, and set at liberty, and sit down in rest and peace. This is Christ rising out of the dust, and hee shall wholly be raised up to live and dwel in the Father, and the Father in him, and all opposite powers of bondage, that now afflicts, shal be trod under his feet. *Isa.* 6. 10.

Therefore now you zealous Preachers and Professors in al forms, if you have eyes look within your selves, and see what power rules within the bodies of your flesh; If you finde that the inward power is envy, rash anger, covetousnesse, self-honouring, secret pride, uncleannesse of flesh, close dissimulation, and the like; know you, that that power is your self, your very self, a devil, the serpent, the subtil, and yet strong power of darknesse, that would fain be counted an Angel of Light. 1. *Cor.* 4.4.

And though you be called by the name of such a man, or such a woman, yet you are but *the father of lies*, and of the power of bondage that must be [24] destroyed and perish: And that humane flesh, that you dwell in, being part of the Creation, shall be cleansed off you, by the spirit of burning, till it be freed from you, that are the curse, the bondage of it under whom it groans. And when you are cast out, who is the serpent, it shall be a temple for the Father himself to dwell in, a garden wherein he himself will take delight. For it is thou, O thou wicked power that is the curse, I say, The thorns and briars that troubles the Creation, and thou must be rooted out, and sorrow, and everlasting weeping shall be thy portion, for thou shalt never find the prince of peace.

Well, I know you that would be Angels of light and are not, will count this which I speak madnesse, but you shall find these words true. For all powers that are opposite to the power of Righteousnesse must, and shall be destroyed, *and the Lord alone shall be exalted in this day of his power*, and this power of Righteousnesse shall be exalted in flesh, as well as over flesh. *Jerem.* 23. 6.

Who was it that put the Son of man to death? Was it the humane flesh? or the power of darkness, that ruled in flesh?

Surely that power of darknesse in the flesh did it; and that cursed power, was the *Scribes* and *Pharisees*: And so now that power of enmity, that rules in those bodies of yours, making your bodies of the flesh slaves to its lusts and will, is still the *Scribes* and *Pharisees*, or devil, that fights against Christ, and would not suffer him to rise up in flesh; but cals his power blasphemy, because he crosses you; for if he rise in flesh, you must fall in flesh; If he be King, as he must be, you must be his foot-stool.

Well, mind what power rules in you, whether it be a particular, confining, selfish power, which is the Devil, the *Scribes* and *Pharisees*.

[25] Or whether it be a universall spreading power, that delights in the liberty of the whole Creation, which is Christ in you.

The particular selfish power, when it is either crossed or shamed, it grows mad and bitter spirited, and endeavours either to kill that body it dwels in, or some others that angers it.

But the Power of Christ, the Law of Righteousnesse ruling within, is not moved to any such rashnesse, it is patient, meek and loving; and doth act righteously both to his own body, and to others, though they be his enemies.

CHAP. IV.

AND truly here lies the chiefest knowledge of a man, to know these two powers which strives for government in him, and to see and know them distinctly one from the other, that he may be able to say, This is the name and power of the flesh: and this is the name and power of the Lord.

For these two powers are the two *Adams* in mankind; they are *Jacob* and *Esau*, striving who shall rule in the Kingdom, the flesh first.

Or these are the Son of the bond-woman, *viz.* The powers of the flesh, which is the serpent, Devil, or power of darknesse.

Or the Son of the free woman, which is Christ, the wisdom and power of Righteousnesse, ruling in flesh, and making it free from the others bondage.

And here I shall declare, what I know the first *Adam* or son of bondage is. And secondly, What the second *Adam*, or son of the free-woman is; both which Powers I have seen and felt manifested in this body of my flesh.

[26] First, I shall shew, how the first *Adam* in his time of rule, hath suppressed and kept under the second man, the anointing.

And then secondly, how this second man in the time appointed of his rising, doth kill and crucifie the first *Adam* daily, with all his lusts, and freeth me from that slavery.

The first *Adam* kils and crucifies Christ in me, when I consent and make provision to satisfie my pride over humility, covetousnesse over contentednesse, envy over love, lust before chastity, esteeming the power of an humble, loving and righteous spirit, towards the poorest creature, but a low and contemptible thing, or the like. Now Christ is crucified in me, he rules not, he acts not in a lively power; but the first man of the flesh he governs the Kingdom, my body in unright-eousnesse. And Christ lies buried in this earthly tabernacle, under those cursed powers in my enslaved body.

But then secondly, When the fulnesse of time comes, that it is the Fathers will, that Christ the spirit of truth shal arise above the power of unrighteousnesse in me; that is, humility arises above pride, love above envy, a meek and quiet spirit above hasty rash anger, chastity above unclean lusts, and light above darknesse. Now the second *Adam*

Christ, hath taken the Kingdom my body, and rules in it; *He makes it a new heaven, and a new earth, wherein dwels Righteousnesse. Isa. 65. 17.*

I shall explain these two *Adams* a little more:

First then, The first *Adam*, or man of the flesh, branches himself forth into divers particulars, to fetch peace into himself, from objects without himself.

As for example, covetousnesse is a branch of the flesh or first man, that seeks after creature enjoyment or riches; to have peace from them.

[27] Pride looks abroad for honour; Envy seeks the revenge of such as crosses his fleshy ends, by reproch, oppression, or murder. Unclean lusts seeks to embrace strange flesh.

Imagination flies abroad, to devise wayes to satisfie the flesh in these desires: Hypocrisie turns himself into divers shapes; yea, sometimes into an Angel of light, a zealous Professour to compasse these ends.

And self-love (which is ignorant of the universal power) lies couching in the bottom, sending those six several powers of darknesse abroad to fetch in peace to delight self, that lies at home in the fleshy heart.

And all these powers make up but one perfect body of sin and death, one Devil, or one compleat power of darknesse; or that whorish power, called the Beast with seven heads.

And it is called the Beast, because all those seven discoveries are of the flesh; and flesh is no other, but a beast; and the wise flesh of man, is said to be the beast, the King of beasts, that *was to raign fourty two months, or for a time, times, and dividing of time, and then he should be destroyed by the man of Righteousnesse, Christ. Rev.* 13. 1.

And truly upon every head there is ten horns, that is, there are many branchings forth of powers from every head to satisfie self; which are Kings indeed. *Revel.* 12. 14.

And they are called *ten horns every head*, encountering against the five senses of the left hand man, and against the five senses of the right hand man of righteousnesse, and so fights against every particular spreading forth of Christ.

So that these Kings are not to be restrained to the *Kings of the Nations*; though that is true, such powers are enemies to Christ, and *they must yield up their Kingdoms unto him,* and those that are angry against Christ are to be destroyed. *Revel.* 11. 18.

[28] But these ten horns are Kingly powers of the flesh, that rules within every man, leading him captive under the body of the power of darknesse; for there is not the branching forth of evil in any kind to delight self, but it springs forth from one or other of those seven heads, all joyning to honour and advance the Beast.

The man of Righteousnesse Christ, he is the second *Adam,* and he spreads himself as far as the other, to undermine him, and to take the Kingdom (that is, the created flesh, or the living earth man-kind) out of that Devils hand.

For Christ is the spreading power of Righteousnesse; and therefore he is called, *The anointing,* which was poured upon that humane body, called by the name *Iesus, the Son of man, and dwelt bodily* there for a time; but afterward was to spread in sons and daughters, many bodies. 1. *Ioh.* 2. 27.

As the *oyl* upon *Aarons* head, *ranne down to the skirts of his garments;* if any one find rest and peace in this precious Alabaster, which is the wisdome and power of the spirit, he finds it not by looking upon him at a distance from him, but by seeing and feeling that power, ruling within the body of his flesh. *Luke* 17. 21.

As thus contentednesse in all straits or poverty, to live upon providence, is this second *Adam* in thee, killing thy discontented covetousnesse.

Humility and meeknesse is the same anointing which kils pride and loftines.

Love to enemies; yea, the law of love flowing forth to every creature, is Christ in you, which kils envy and rash anger.

Chastitie in the flesh, kils uncleannesse; wisdom that is pure and plain down right, kils a subtil over-reaching imagination.

Sincerity and singlenesse of heart (the same anointing) kils hypocrisie; and love to others, doing as a [29] man would be done unto; and so respecting the publick preservation of all creatures, doth kill self-love.

And all these seven branchings forth of the pure spirit, makes but one body Christ, or one Almighty power of Mercie and Justice, the holy breathing, or *Emanuel, God in us.*

And every one of these seven eyes, or seven attributes of the Divine, branches themselves forth into several horns of power, to destroy the man of the flesh, and to deliver man-kind from his bondage. For let the first *Adam* run out in what shape he will; the second *Adam* follows after to trip up his heels; to subdue him, and to take the Kingdom from him; that so, when all enemies are subdued, the Almighty power of righteousnesse, which is the Father, may become all in all. *Rev. 5. 6.*

And this now declares the meaning of that speech, *That Christ saves his people from their sins;* not only in pardoning evil Actions, and removing the evil of sorrow from them, but principally to kill and subdue the powers of the flesh, and to make a man subject to the spirit; and now a man is saved from his sins, and not till now. And this is to be made a new creature, in whom old corrupt lusts are passed away, and every power in him is a new power.

Now there is no man or woman needs go to *Rome*, nor hell below ground, as some talke, to find the Pope, Devil, Beast or Power of darknesse; neither to go up into heaven above the skies to find Christ the word of life. For both these powers are to be felt within a man, fighting against each other. And in that soul wherein Christ prevails, they know that this is truth, for they find peace in the salvation that comes out of *Sion.*

[30] CHAP. V.

THIS first man is he, *by whose disobedience many are made sinners,* or by whom the whole Creation is corrupted; Therefore you Preachers, do not you tell the people any more, That a man called *Adam,* that disobeyed about 6000 years ago, was the man that filled every man with sin and filth, by eating an apple. *Rom. 5. 19.*

For assure your selves, this *Adam* is within every man and woman; and it is the first power that appears to act and rule in every man. It is the Lord *Esau* that stepped before *Iacob,* and got the birthright, by the Law of equity was more properly *Iacobs.*

Though *Iacob,* who is the power and wisdom that made flesh did draw back, and gave way, that the wisdom and power of flesh should possesse the Kingdom, and rule first; till *Esau,* by delighting in unrighteous pleasures, lost both birth-right and blessing; and left both in the hand of *Iacob* the King, that rules in righteousnesse, that is to rise up next.

The Apple that the first man eats, is not a single fruit called an Apple, or such like fruit; but it is the objects of the Creation; which is the fruit that came out of the Seed, which is the Spirit himself that made all things: As riches, honours, pleasures, upon which the powers of the flesh feeds to delight himself.

And this is the messe of pottage which he prefers before righteousnesse, or before righteous walking in the Creation towards every creature, which is Christ, that power that appears in the fulnesse of time to take the Kingdom and rule next.

Therefore when a man fals, let him not blame a man that died 6000 years ago, but blame himself, even the powers of his own flesh, which lead him astray; [31] for this is *Adam* that brings a man to misery, which is the man flesh, or the strong man within that keeps the house, till the man of Righteousnesse arise and cast him out, who is the second *Adam*.

And this second man is he, *By whose obedience many are made righteous*; that is, by the power of Christ, man-kind is purged from its drosse; and this second man, I say, which is the righteous power, doth cast the other man (which is the unrighteous power) out of the house, even the heart, and makes it a temple for himself to dwell in. *Isa.* 43. 11.

Now these two powers did the Father ordain should have their course to rule in the earth man-kinde: And this is that day and night, the light and darknesse, Winter and Summer, heat and cold, Moon and Sun, that is typed out by the Fabrick of the great world; for within these two powers is the mystery of all divine workings wrapped up.

The first power, that is of darknesse, or the Chaos of confusion, proves selfish and hurtfull to others, tearing its own and the other mans children, especially to pieces, by cruelty, covetousnesse and oppression; *For he that is after the flesh, persecutes him that is born after the spirit. Gal.* 4. 29.

And in the fulnesse of time; that is, When the first man hath filled the Creation full of his filthinesse, and all places stinks with unrighteousnesse, as it doth at this day; then it pleaseth the Father, that his own wisdome and power should arise up next to rule in man-kind in righteousnesse, and take the Kingdome out of the others hand, and restore all things, and establish the Creation in peace, and declare himself to be the alone Saviour of the world, and to be the most excellent, nay the almighty power. *Rom.* 8. 22.

The first man *Adam*, is called, *The Son of God*, a power that the Almighty was pleased should be manifest; but this is the *son of disobedience*, the son [32] that goes astray, a son causing sorrow and shame, and so becomes the serpent, the Devil, the power of darknesse, the Beast, the Whore, the father of lies, the murder of man-kind, and the bottomlese pit, out of which all unrighteousnesse and misery rises up. *Rev.* 19. 2.

But the second *Adam* is called, *His wel-beloved Son*; the Son of his delight, the Son bringing honour and peace; Why? Because by him the opposing power is cast out, and the wisdome and power of Righteousnesse, which is the Lord, is that wisdom and power that rules in and over man-kind, and the flesh is made subject hereunto without grumbling; and so all things becomes the Lords. 1. *Cor.* 1.24

And this Son or second *Adam* is called, *The Lord, The King of righteousnesse, The Prince of Peace, The Saviour, The mighty God, The Restorer of all things, The Salvation, The Consolation of Israel, The Blessing of all Nations of the Earth, The Powers of Light or Reason.*

And thus we see the Father hath ordained, that the powers of dark flesh should rule over him that made him for a time, and he who is the Father of all things would be a servant, and that dark flesh should be the *mystery of iniquity*, or *Antichrist*, that should oppose and *exalt himself above all that is called God*, till by the other greater power, the Father himself arising up in the Creation, he be taken out of the way. *Phil.* 2.7. 2. *Thes.* 2.4.

This teaches every son and daughter, to wait with patience and quietnesse of spirit under all temptations, till the Fathers turn come, according to his own appointment to rule in flesh; And *then their sorrows shall be turned into joy, and their mourning into laughter: All tears shall be wiped away, and they shall be delivered from the bondage, and live in freedom and peace. Ephes.* 1.5. *Joh.* 16.20. *Rev.* 21. 23.

[33] These two powers, I say, are typed out by *Iacob* and *Esau*;

Iacob put forth his arm first, and it is marked by the midwife, and then he draws it in again: then *Esau* comes fully forth, and is called the elder brother.

Iacob is Christ, the *elect or chosen one*, or the *Almighty power and wisdome*, that first put forth his arm of strength in making man-kind; but the *powers of the flesh*, which is *Esau*, or the *rejected one*, the reprobate, steps before (by permission) and gets the government of the Kingdom (man-kind) first; and he is suffered to raign, till Christ supplant him, and takes both birth-right and blessing from him. *Isa.* 44. 1, *and Chap.* 42. 1.

Or rather takes possession of his own Right and Kingdom, man-kind; for he appeared first; and so by the law of equity and reason, he is the elder brother; though *Esau* or the powers of the flesh got the dominion to rule in the Creation, by a violence, which the wisdom and power of the spirit, suffered and ordained to be.

This second man is the spirituall man, that judges all things according to the law of equity and reason, in moderation and love to all, he is not a talker, but an actour of Righteousnesse. *Cor.* 2. 15.

But the man of the flesh, which would be counted an Angel of light, cannot judge any thing in righteousnesse; for all his judgement and justice is selfish, and confined to particular ends, not to the publick safety and preservation; he is a great Preacher and talker of righteous things, but no actour of righteousnesse, or if he do, it is very slowly, it is when *Iacob* over powers him, his judgement is hasty, unadvised rashnesse, at randome, hap hazard, right or wrong, he knows not. And sometime he is moderate, for by ends to himself; and sometimes full of bitter censures to hurt others.

[34] CHAP. VI.

THE man of the flesh, judges it a righteous thing, That some men that are cloathed with the objects of the earth, and so called rich men, whether it be got by right or wrong, should be Magistrates to rule over the poor; and that the poor should be servants nay rather slaves to the rich.

But the spiritual man, which is Christ, doth judge according to the light of equity and reason, That al man-kinde ought to have a quiet substance and freedome, to live upon earth; and that there shal be no bond-man nor begger in all his holy mountaine.

Man-kinde was made to live in the freedome of the spirit, not under the bondage of the flesh, though the lordly flesh hath got a power for a time, as I said before; for every one was made to be a Lord over the Creation of the Earth, Cattle, Fish, Fowl, Grasse, Trees, not any one to be a bond-slave and a beggar under the Creation of his own kinde. *Gen.* 1. 28.

That so every one living in freedome and love in the strength of the Law of Righteousnesse in him; not under straits of poverty, nor bondage of tyranny one to another, might al rejoyce together in Righteousnesse, and so glorifie their Maker; for surely this much dishonoured the Maker of all men, that some men should be oppressing tyrants, imprisoning, whipping, hanging their fellow creatures, men, for those very things which those very men themselves are guilty of; let mens eyes be opened, and it appears clear enough, That the punishers have and doe break the law of equity and reason, more, or as much as those that are punished by them.

[35] None will be offended at this, but the children of Lord *Esau*, the first man flesh, which must perish for his unrighteous government, for thereby he hath lost himself, sold or passed over his birthright and blessing unto *Iacob*, the King of Righteousnesse that is now rising up, to rule according to the pure law of equity and reason.

And when this King raigns, the city that is, the heart of every one in whom truth dwels, wil rejoyce; but while the man of unrighteousnesse raigns in and over man-kinde, truly every body wee see is filled with sorrow and complainings, and it is not without cause.

As the powers and wisdome of the flesh hath filled the earth with injustice, oppression and complainings, by mowing the earth into the hands of a few covetous, unrighteous men, who assumes a lordship over others, declaring themselves thereby to be men of the basest spirits. *Dan.* 4. 17.

Even so, when the spreading power of wisdome and truth, fils the earth man-kinde, hee wil take off that bondage, and give a universall liberty, and there shal be no more complainings against oppression, poverty, or injustice.

When every son and daughter shall be made comfortable to that one body, of Jesus the anointed, and the same power rules in them, as in him, every one according to their measure, the oppression shall cease, and the rising up of this universal power, shal destroy and sub-due the selfish power. *Phil.* 3. 21.

But this is not done by the hands of a few, or by unrighteous men, that would pul the tyrannical government out of other mens hands, and keep it in their own heart [hands], as we feel this to be a burden of our age. But it is done by the universall spreading of the divine power, which is Christ in mankind making them all to act in one spirit, and in and after [36] one law of reason and equity.

And when this universall power of Righteousnesse is spread in the earth, it shall destroy *Babylon the great City* of fleshy confusion in one hour; that is he will pull the Kingdome and Government of the world out of the hands of tyrannicall, unseasonable acting flesh, and give the lands and riches that covetous, unrighteous men hath hoarded up within their own selfish power, into the hands of spirituall *Israel*; that so there may be no complainings, no burdens, nor no poor in *Canaan*, but that it may be a *Land flowing with milke and honey*, plenty of all things, every one walking righteously in the Creation one to another, according to the law of equity and reason, as it was in the beginning, And as *Babylon* measured out to others, so that it shall be, measured to him again. *Rev.* 18. 8. *Ps.* 105. 45.

And surely as the Scriptures threaten misery to rich men, bidding them *Howl and weep, for their gold and silver is cankered, and the rust thereof cries unto heaven for vengeance against them,* and the like. Surely all those threatnings shal be materially fullfiled, for they shall be turned out of all, and their riches given to a people that wil bring forth better fruit, and such as they have oppressed shall inherit the Land.

The rich man tels the poor, that they ofend Reasons law, if they take from the rich; I am sure it is a breach in that Law in the rich to have plenty by them, and yet wil see their fellow creatures men and women to starve for want; Reason requires that every man should live upon the increase of the earth comfortably; though covetousnesse fights against Reasons law.

The rich doth lock up the treasures of the earth; and hardens their hearts against the poor. The poor are those in whom the blessing lies, for they first *receive* [37] *the Gospel*, and their gifts of love and tendernesse one to preserve another, shall be the condemnation of the rich: And secondly, the inheritances of the rich shall be given to those poor, and there shall be no beggar in *Israel*.

And there is equity and Reason in it, for the King of Righteousnesse, did not make some men to be tyrants, and others to be slaves, at the beginning, for this burden riseth up afterwards. *Esau* stepped into the birth-right before *Iacob*, till the time come that he shall be taken away again.

In the first enterance into the Creation, every man had an equall freedom given him of his Maker to till the earth, and to have dominion over the beasts of the field, the fowls of heaven, and fish in the Seas. But this freedom is broke to pieces by the power of covetousnesse, and pride, and self-love, not by the law of Righteousnesse. And this freedom will not be restored, till the spreading power of Righteousnesse and peace rise up in the earth, making all men and women to be of *one heart, and one mind*, which must come to passe, for that Scripture was never fulfilled yet. *Gen*. 1. 28. *Rom*. 8. 22, &c.

The powers of flesh shall never partake of this priviledge, for he is the curse that must be removed; Selfish Councellours, Selfish Governours, Selfish Souldiers, shall never be honoured in setling this restoration; The Lord himself will do this great work, without either sword or weapon; weapons and swords shall destroy, and cut the powers of the earth asunder, but they shall never build up.

For the *Law-giver in righteousnesse shall come out of Sion, that shall turn covetous oppressing ungodliness from Jacob.*

For surely the Father will give as large a liberty to his children to inherit the earth, as he gives to the beast of the field; though they break over hedges, [38] and eat in any pasture, they do not imprison and hang one another, the earth is a common livelyhood for them, the restraint ariseth from selfish covetousnesse, and lordly proud flesh, that hath got the government, and saith, *The spirit hath given it him*. Indeed thou hast it for a time, not by right of blessing, but by permission, that through thy unrighteousness thou maist fall and never rise again: And that righteous *Jacob* may arise, who hath been thy servant, and never fall again; and then *the elder shall serve the younger.*

I do not speak that any particular men shall go and take their neighbours goods by violence, or robbery (I abhor it) as the condition of the men of the Nations are ready to do in this fleshly setled government of the world, but every one is to wait, till the Lord Christ do spread himself in multiplicities of bodies, making them all of one heart and one mind, acting in the righteousnesse one to another. It must be one power in all, making all to give their consent to confirm this law of righteousnesse and reason.

For when the work is made manifest, it shall be a universall Power that shall rise up in the earth (mankind) to pull the Kingdom and outward government of the world out of the hands of the tenant *Esau,* king-flesh; and this shall be made manifest in all the Nations of the earth; *For the Kingdoms of this world shall become the Kingdoms of the Lord Christ. Revel.* 11. 15.

And this universall power of a righteous law, shall be so plainly writ in every ones heart, that none shall desire to have more then another, or to be Lord over other, or to lay claim to any thing as his; this phrase of *Mine and Thine* shall be swallowed up in the law of righteous actions one to another, for they shall all live as brethren, every one doing as they would be done by; and he that sees his brother in wants, and doth not help, shall smart for his iniquity, [39] from the hand of the Lord, the righteous Judge that will sit upon the throne in every mans heart. There shall be no need of Lawyers, prisons, or engines of punishment one over another, for all shall walk and act righteously in the Creation, and there shall be no beggar, nor cause of complaining in all this holy Mountain. *Heb.* 8. 10. *Act.* 4. 32. *Jam.* 2. 13. 1 *Ioh.* 3. 17. *Hos.* 3. 18.

Therefore I say to all, wait, be patient in your present bondage, till our brethren be brought in likewise; *Forsake the way of Babylon, and commit your cause to him that judgeth righteously;* The work of freedom is in the hand of Christ, and he is the righteous freedom; he hath begun to spread himself, and he goes on mightily, and will go on. *The poor receives the Gospel* daily; Christ is drawing all men after him, he is calling in the Isles and Nations of the world, to come to this great Battell, even to deliver the oppressed, and to destroy the oppressour, to spoil him that spoiled, and yet was never spoiled himself; *And so to lead captivity captive, and let the prisoners of hope go free. Rev.* 6. 11.

CHAP. VII.

WHEN this universall law of equity rises up in every man and woman, then none shall lay claim to any creature, and say, *This is mine, and that is yours, This is my work, that is yours*; but every one shall put to their hands to till the earth, and bring up cattle, and the blessing of the earth shall be common to all; when a man hath need of any corn for cattle, take from the next storehouse he meets with. *Act.* 4. 32.

There shall be no buying nor selling, no fairs nor markets, but the whole earth shall be a common treasury [40] for every man, for the earth is the Lords. And man kind thus drawn up to live and act in the Law of love, equity and onenesse, is but the great house wherein the Lord himself dwels, and every particular one a severall mansion: and as one spirit of righteousnesse is common to all, so the earth and the blessings of the earth shall be common to all; for now all is but the Lord, and the Lord is all in all. *Eph.* 4. 5, 6.

When a man hath meat, and drink, and cloathes he hath enough, and all shall cheerfully put to their hands to make these things that are needfull, one helping another; there shall be none Lord over others, but every one shall be a Lord of him self, subject to the law of righteousnesse, reason and equity, which shall dwell and rule in him, which is the Lord; *For now the Lord is one, and his name and power one, in all and among all. Zech.* 14. 9.

Their rejoycings and glory shall be continually in eying and speaking of what breakings forth of love they receive from the Father, singing *Sions* songs one to another; to the glory of him that sits upon the throne, for evermore.

This universall freedom hath never filled the earth though it hath been fore-told by most of the Prophets. This is the glory of *Jerusalem*, which never yet hath been the praise of the whole earth. And this will be no troublesome businesse, when covetousnesse, and the selfish power is killed and cast out of heaven, and every one is made willing to honour the King of Righteousnesse in action, being all of one heart and one mind: Truly we may well call this a new heaven, and a new earth, wherein dwells righteousnesse. And that prophesie will not generally be fulfilled till this time. *Rev.* 12. 9.

If it be thus, then saith the scoffer, mens wives shall be common too? or a man may have as many wives as he please?

[41] I answer, The Law of Righteousnesse and Reason saith no: For when man was made, he was made male and female, one man and one woman conjoyned together by the law of love, makes the Creation of humane flesh perfect in that particular; *Therefore a man shall forsake father and mother, and cleave only to his wife, for they twain are but one flesh.* Reason did not make one man and many women, or one woman and many men to joyn together, to make the Creation perfect, but male and female in the singular number, this is enough to encrease seed. And he or she that requires more wives, or more husbands then one, walks contrary to the Law of Righteousnesse, and shall bear their shame: Though this immoderate lust after strange flesh, rule in the bodies of men now, while the first *Adam* is King, yet it shall not be so when the second man rises to raign, for then chastitie is one glory of the Kingdom.

But what if a man break that law of Righteousnes, as many do under this fleshly government which is yet extant?

I answer, He shall then become servant to others, and be as a fool in *Israel*; the wrath of the Lord shall be upon him, and lose the priviledge of Sonship, till the law of righteousnesse in him become his King. And those that loses that priviledge, shall know they have lost a blessing. The proud, covetous and unrighteous men, ere many years wheel about, will tell the world by their lamentation and torment, what it is to lose the blessing of son-ship.

The manifestation of a righteous heart shall be known, not by his words, but by his actions; for this multitude of talk, and heaping up of words amongst professours shall die and cease, this way of preaching shall cease, and verbal worship shall cease, and they that do worship the Father, shall worship him by walking righteously in the Creation, in the [42] strength of the Law of Love and equity one to another. And the time is now coming on, that men shall not talk of righteousnesse, but act righteousnesse. *Ier.* 31. 34. *Joh.* 4. 23.

And they that in these times, will not observe this Rule, to walk righteously in the Creation, waiting quietly till Christ come to restore all things, he shall have sorrows, troubles and discontents of heart within, vexing, grudging, rash passions, he shall have no true peace, but be filled with confusion, and be a slave to his lusts.

The Father now is raising up a people to himself out of the dust, that is, out of the lowest and despised sort of people, that are counted the dust of the earth, man-kind, that are trod under foot. In these, and from these shall the Law of Righteousnesse break forth first, for the poor they begin to receive the Gospel, and plentifull discoveries of the Fathers love flows from them, and the waters of the learned and great men of the world, begins to dry up like the brooks in Summer. *Matth.* 11. 25. 1 *Cor.* 1. 27.

When this restoration breaks forth in righteous action, the curse then shall be removed from the Creation, Fire, Water, Earth and Air. And Christ the spreading forth of Righteousnesse, shall be the onely Saviour, that *shall make Jacob to rejoyce, and Israel to be glad.*

There shall be no barrennesse in the earth or cattle, *for they shall bring forth fruit abundantly.* Unseasonable storms of weather shall cease, for all the curse shall be removed from all, and every creature shall rejoyce in Righteousnesse one in another throughout the whole Creation. *Zach.* 3. 4, &c.

Thomas Dydimus, that is, the unbelief of your hearts cries out, When will these things be? not in our time? I cannot believe such things till I see them?

[43] Well, lay aside your doubtfull questioning, and let every one set himself to walk righteously in the Law of love one towards another, and wait the Lords time; this work is to be done upon flesh, not by flesh. The Lord will have none of your flesh wit, policy or strength to setle this work, for he alone will be honoured in this day of his power, it must be his own handy work, that must bring this restoration to passe, yea, and he will hasten this work, as speedily, as the *Midianites* Army was destroyed, and *Sodom* and *Gomorrah* burned, and as speedily, and as unlooked for, as plenty came into *Samaria*; mens unbelief cannot hinder this work of Righteousnesse. *Isa.* 60. 22.

The Lord will do this work speedily, *Babylon* shall fall in one hour, *Israel* shall rise in one hour; O when this righteous Law shall rule in every one, there will be springings up of joy and peace, and the blessing of the Lord shall rest every where. *Joh.* 7. 38.

The whole earth we see is corrupt, and it cannot be purged by the hand of creatures, for all creatures lies under the curse, and groans to be delivered, and the more they strive, the more they entangle themselves in the mud; therefore it must be the hand of the Lord alone that must do it.

None can remove the curse from fire, water, earth and air, but the Almighty power himself. And this work is called, the Restoration of all things; for all things groan and travel in pain under bondage, waiting for this manifestation.

And seeing every creature that is burdened waits for the coming in of the blessing, then surely no flesh can settle this work, for all flesh is corrupt; this work shall not be done by sword, or weapon, or wit of the flesh, but by the power of the Lord, killing covetousnesse, and making man-kind generally to be of one heart and one mind. *Gen.* 18. 18.

[44] But why hath not the Lord done this all this time that is past?

I answer, Covetous, wise and lordly flesh would raign in the Kingdom, man-kind first, and would be counted the onely power to govern the Creation, in an excellent order. And the Lord gave this dominion into his hand, but withall told him, that if he governed the Creation unrighteously, he and all the Creation should die and fall under the curse.

Well, the powers of the flesh, Lord *Esau* was advanced, and hath ruled with such self-seeking ends, that he hath made all creatures weary of his government, and the whole earth to stink and to groan under the burden of it, longing to be delivered. *Rom.* 8. 21, Etc.

For first, they that stand up to teach others, they teach for gain, and preach for hire, and fils people with division and confusion, through their pride and envy, and they do this by the Authority of the governing power, by which they have ingrossed the earth into their hands. A man must not take a wife, but the Priest must give her him. If he have a child, the Priest must give the name. If any die, the Priest must see it laid in the earth. If any man want knowledge or comfort, they teach him to go to the Priest for it; and what is the end of all this, but to get money: if a man labour in the earth to eat his bread, the Priests must have the tenths of his encrease, or else some oppressing impropriatour, that shares the tithes between himself and the Priest; which Law was brought in by the Pope, and still upheld by such as call themselves, the Christian Protestants.

All which is high treason and mighty dishonourable to Christ the great Prophet, whom they seem to shew love to; here the earth stinks, because this hath been established by a compulsive binding power, whereby the Creation is held under bondage: this is the fruit of imagination.

[45] Secondly, For matter of buying and selling, the earth stinks with such unrighteousnesse, that for my part, though I was bred a tradesmen, yet it is so hard a thing to pick out a poor living, that a man shall sooner be cheated of his bread, then get bread by trading among men, if by plain dealing he put trust in any.

And truly the whole earth of trading, is generally become the neat art of thieving and oppressing fellow-creatures, and so laies burdens, upon the Creation, but when the earth becomes a common treasury this burden will be taken off.

Thirdly, For Justices and Officers of State, that should relieve people in their wrongs, and preserve peace, they multiply wrongs, and many, if not most times oppresses the poor, and lets the offending rich go free, by laying aside the letter of their laws, as the Priests doth the Scriptures; and acts by subtil covetousnesse and smooth words to get money, or else ruling by their own wills, through envy to imprison and oppresse others, letting poor people lie in prison half a year many times, and never bring them to trial at all.

And thus the people have been and are oppressed by false imprisonments and punishments, not for the breach of any known law, but to satisfie the will of the Justice, Bailiffs or Officer, against all reason and equity, as if the people made Officers to be their Ægyptian taskmasters: Nay, let all men speak openly as they find, and I am sure they will say that the Justices and most state Officers, doth more oppresse, then deliver from oppression.

And thus I see that the whole earth stinks, by the first *Adams* corrupt Government; therefore it is the fulness of time, for *Jacob* to arise, extream necessity cals for the great work of restoration, and when the restorer of the earth hath a little more manifested [36, i. e., 46] himself, he wil make the earth a common treasury, and sweep away all the refuge of lies, and all oppressions, by making all people to be of one heart and one minde, and then the Law of Righteousnesse and peace, shal be the King that shal rule in every man, and over every man, who indeed is the Lord himself, who is and wil be all, and in all.

And now seeing there is nothing found but complainings and tears under his oppressions, it is the fulnesse or fittest time now for *Iacob* to arise, & restore all things, who indeed is Christ: And for *David* to raigne, who indeed is Christ the great devider between flesh and spirit, & the great law-giver of peace and truth, *For besides him there is no Saviour; He indeed is the blessing of all Nations, and the joy of the whole earth.*

Therefore tremble, thou Lord *Esau*, thou proud and covetous flesh, thou art condemned to die, the sentence is begun to be put in execution, for *the poor begins to receive the Gospel*; thou shalt wast, decay and grow weaker and weaker, til thy place be no where found in earth, and Christ the blessing of the Creation, shal rise up and spread, and fil the earth, and all creatures shall rejoyce under his shadow.

Therefore you *Tribes of Israel*, that are now in sackcloth, every man with his hands upon his loins, like a woman in travel, stand stil and see the salvation of *David* your King; this is called the *time of Iacobs trouble*; for indeed the Spirit that is in you, is oppressed under the burden of cursed flesh, But he shall be delivered, the time of his resurrection is come, and his rising shal be your glory; his light shal desperse your darknesse, and cover the earth with the knowledge of himself, for the blessing shal be every where. *Ier.* 30. 6.

Iacobs troubles formerly was two-fold,

[37, i. e., 47] First, His Kindred and friends endeavoured to hinder him of his temporal lively-hood, and to make the earth to become a burden to him, by changing his cattell, and taking those earthly blessings from him, which the Lord had given him.

Secondly, when *Iacob* had a liberty to take wives, children, and cattell, and to goe live free of himself; his kindred runs after him, and tels him, he had stolen away their gods; and for that, begins afresh to trouble him.

And the same troubles are the portion of those in whom *Iacobs* spirit rests. For,

First, Their kindred and neighbours endeavours to make them poor in the world, and to oppresse them with the burden of poverty and straits.

Secondly, Now the Father is drawing *Iacob* out of *Babylon*, and makes his children to forsake the forms and customs of the National worship, to *worship the Father in Spirit and Truth*. Now kindred and neighbours in the flesh cries out, O these men steals away our gods, and by reproaches, imprisonments or wrong dealing, seeks to oppresse and suppresse them. Wel this is but stil the time of *Iacobs* troubles, but he shall be delivered out.

Well let the lordly flesh scoffe and laugh and cry, O when shal this be! and say with the Lord of *Samaria, it is impossible,* for it is madnesse thus to speak; wel, such may live to see it, but shal not enjoye the blessing; for when *Iacob* arises, that is now very low, and he must rise, then *Esau* shal be his servant, *The elder shall serve the younger,* and thy portion shal be wraped up in *Jacobs* lap, for all is his.

For now the Father is raissing up a people to himself out of the dust, and of the stones, that is, poor despised people, that are trod upon like dust and [48] stones, shal be now raised up, and be made the blessing of the earth, *and the high mountaines shall be laid low, the lofty looks of men shal be pulled down, and the Lord alone shall be exalted in this day of his power.*

CHAP. VIII.

As I was in a trance not long since, divers matters were present to my sight, which here must not be related. Likewise I heard these words, *Worke together. Eat bread together;* declare this all abroad. Likewise I heard these words. *Whosoever it is that labours in the earth, for any person or persons, that lifts up themselves as Lords & Rulers over others, and that doth not look upon themselves equal to others in the Creation, The hand of the Lord shall be upon that labourer: I the Lord have spoke it and I will do it;* Declare this all abroad.

After I was raised up, I was made to remember very fresh what I had seen and heard, & did declare al things to them that were with me, and I was filled with abundance of quiet peace and secret joy. And since that time those words have been like very fruitfull seed, that have brought forth increase in my heart, which I am much prest in spirit to declare all abroad.

The poor people by their labours in this time of the first *Adams* government, have made the buyers and sellers of land, or rich men, to become tyrants and oppressours over them.

But in the time of *Israels* restoration, now begining, when the King of Righteousnesse himself shall be Governor in every man; none then shall work for hire, neither shal any give hire, but every one shal work in love: one with, and for another; and [49] eat bread together, as being members of one houshold; the Creation in whom Reason rules King in perfect glory. *Ier*. 23. 5, 6.

He that cals any part of the Creation his own in particular, in this time of *Israels* return from the mistery of *Ægyptian* bondage, is a destroyer of the Creation, a lifter up of the proud covetous flesh againe, a bringer in of the curse againe, and a mortal enemy, to the Spirit. *Act*. 4. 32.

For upon *Israels* returne from captivity, the Lord himself wil burn up the curse, and restore the Creation, fire, water, earth and air from that slavery, and make the earth to be a common treasury to them all; for they are but one house of Israel still, though twelve Tribes; And they have but one King, one Law-giver, one teacher amongst them all, even the Lord himself, who is Reason, The King of Righteousnesse; they are all filled with one spirit, and they shall all live comfortably upon one earth; and so the whole earth is the Lords. *Ier*. 35. 38. *Isa*. 29. 20, 21. *Rom*. 8. 21. *Ioh*. 6. 45.

And this is the inward and outward liberty, which the Lord wil give to *Sion*. And this work is begun, the foundation of this spiritual building is laid, and the spreading of this one spirit in every sonne and daughter, and the lifting up the earth to be a common treasury, wil make *Jerusalem a praise in the whole earth*, and the glory of the earth indeed, and so the Father of all things shall be honoured in the works of his own hands. *Zech*. 8. 3. *Isa*. 62. 17.

No man shal have any more land, then he can labour himself, or have others to labour with him in love, working together, and eating bread together, as one of the Tribes or families of Israel, neither giving hire, nor taking hire.

He that is now a possessour of lands and riches, and cannot labour, if he say to others, you are my fellow creatures, and the Lord is now making the [40, i. e., 50] earth common amongst us; therefore take my land only let me eat bread with you, that man shall be preserved by the labours of others.

But if any man have Land, and neither can work nor wil work, but wil strive to rule as a tyrant, burdening the Creation, the hand of the Lord shall fal upon him, either to destruction or torment; and if his life be given for a prey, he shall be made to work and eat his bread with the sweat of his own brows, not of others, til he know himself to be a member, not a Lord over the Creation; and thus he shall be dealt with, that hath lost the benefit of Sonship. 2 *Thes.* 3. 10. *Gen.* 3. 19.

All the punishment that any one shall receive for any unrighteous act, whereby he begins to bring the curse againe upon the Creation, he shall only be made a *Gibeonite* to work in the earth, not in a prison, and the eyes of all shall be upon him; and the greatest offence will be this; for any to endeavour to raise up some few to rule over others, & so to set up particular interest againe, and to bring in buying and selling of land againe, the sore displeasure of the Lord shall be such a peoples portion.

Israel is not to imprison or torment any by death or smaller punishments, but only to cause them to work and eat their own bread, for he or they that inflicts any other punishment, upon fellow creatures, is an unrighteous actour in the Creation, and shall himself be made a servant to all, till he by the spirit in him, is made to know himself to be equal to every man, not a Lord over any, for all men looked upon in the bulk are but the Creation, the living earth.

This imprisoning, punishing and killing, which is the practice of the first *Adam*, yet visible to the world, is the curse. And it is a mighty dishonour to our maker, that one part of the Creation should [41, i. e., 51] destroy another, it was not so from the beginning; but it is an honour to our maker that every part of the Creation should lend a mutual help of love in action to preserve the whole. *Mat.* 7. 12.

But is not this the old rule, *He that sheds mans bloud by man shall his bloud be shed?*

I answer, it is true, but not as usually it is observed; for first know, That the Spirit is the man who hath determined to suffer himself to be killed, and lie dead in the streets or under the several forms of *Babylon* government, three daies or times and a half. The serpent is he, or the wicked man that kils the man of Righteousnesse, or sheds his bloud, for that space of time, which is indeed the wisdome and power of the flesh, killing the wisdom and power of the Spirit, and ruling in the Spirits own house, the heart, for a time. *Rev.* 11. 8. *Dan.* 7. 25. 2. *Cor.* 4. 4.

Therefore now it is declared, that the Serpent or beastly power of flesh, that kils the Spirit, shall himself be killed by the Spirit, when the Spirit begins to rise; and I can tell you that the resurrection is begun, for all the great fightings is between flesh and Spirit; *The seea of the woman shall bruise the Serpents head. Gen. 3. 15.*

It is not for one creature called man to kill another, for this is abominable to the Spirit, and it is the curse which hath made the Creation to groan under bondage; for if I kill you I am a murderer, if a third come, and hang or kill me for murdering you, he is a murderer of me; and so by the government of the first *Adam,* murder hath been called Justice when it is but the curse. *Exo. 20. 13.*

Besides none can call himself a man, till the man Christ or Spirit rule in him, for til then; the greatest Lord of all, is but a Beast and one Beast kils another; for a man wil never kill a man; therefore said the man Christ Jesus *I came not to destroy but to* [52] *save*; therefore such as kill are farr from being Saints or children of Christ, for they are the children of the Serpent, whose delight and work is to kill the man-child; but he that sheds this mans bloud, by the *same man shall his bloud be shed,* in the resurrection: Therefore O thou proud flesh, that dares hang and kil thy fellow creatures, that is equall to thee in the Creation, Know this, that none hath the power of life and death, but the Spirit, and al punishments that are to be inflicted amongst creatures called men, are only such as to make the offender to know his maker, and to live in the community of the righteous Law of love one with another. *Luk. 6. 56. Rev. 12. 4.*

For talking of love is no love, it is acting of love in righteousnesse, which the Spirit Reason, our Father delights in. And this is to relieve the oppressed, to let goe the prisoner, to open bags and barns that the earth may be a common treasury to preserve all without complainings; for the earth was not made for a few to live at ease upon, and to kil such as did not observe the Law of their own making, but it was made for all to live comfortably upon, and the power of life and death is reserved in the hand of the Spirit, not in the hand of flesh: None ought to kil, but such as can make alive; therefore let every one walk righteously in the Creation, and trust the Spirit for protection. *Mat. 7. 12.*

He that makes a zealous profession of the Spirit, as all professours doe, and yet doth not act this universall power of Righteousnesse, in labouring the earth for a common treasury, is a meer self-lover, and he professes but himself, and is a complementing enemy to Reason the King of Righteousnesse: and if stil thou saist, it is the Spirit, whom thou doest worship, then make it manifest to the world, what spirit this is that rules everywhere besids Reason.

[53] And further he that denies this community, denies the Scriptures Likewise, whether the Preachers, professours, or rich men, that upholds this unrighteous power of particular propriety. *Act.* 4. 32.

Therefore you dust of the earth, that are trod under foot, you poor people, that makes both schollars and rich men your oppressours by your labours, Take notice of your priviledge, the Law of Righteousnesse is now declared.

If you labour the earth, and work for others that lives at ease, and follows the waies of the flesh by your labours, eating the bread which you get by the sweat of your brows, not their own: Know this, that the hand of the Lord shal break out upon every such hireling labourer, and you shal perish with the covetous rich men, that have held, and yet doth hold the Creation under the bondage of the curse.

This voice of the Lord, work together and eat bread together, doth advance the law of Reason and Righteousnesse; the rising of this is the fall of mistical *Babylon,* the oppressing flesh: the living in the practice of this Law of love, declares the Scriptures of the Prophets and Apostles, to be a true declaration of the Spirit, and no lie. He that denies the practice of this, lives in a continual denial of those Scriptures.

Therefore you selfish tyth-taking Preachers, and all others that preaches for hire, with all covetous professours, take notice that you are the *Judahs* that betraid Christ, and the *Pharisees* that put him to death, and you stil persue the murder, by standing up to hinder Christ from rising and coming in sons and daughters, his second time in flesh.

I have now obeyed the command of the Spirit that bid me declare this all abroad, I have declared [54] it, and I wil declare it by word of mouth, I have now declared it by my pen. And when the Lord doth shew unto me the place and manner, how he wil have us that are called common people, to manure and work upon the common Lands, I wil then go forth and declare it in my action, to eat my bread with the sweat of my brows, without either giving or taking hire, looking upon the Land as freely mine as anothers; I have now peace in the Spirit, and I have an inward perswasion that the spirit

THE NEW LAW OF RIGHTEOUSNES 195

of the poor, shal be drawn forth ere long, to act materially this Law of Righteousnesse.

If man-kinde knew their liberty, which their Creatour Reason, hath given us; none would be offended at this new Law, that is to be writ in every mans heart, and acted by every mans hand.

They that submit in love, and offers what they have freely to further this work, shal prosper and finde peace, for they honour our Maker, by lifting up the Creation in Righteousnesse. They that wil not submit freely, the hand of the Lord shal be as sure upon them as it was upon *Pharaoh*, who is their type.

O you great *Adams* of the earth, that cals the earth yours, and looks upon others as servants and slaves to you, as if the earth were made only for you to live at ease and honour upon it, while others starved for want of bread at your feet, and under your oppressing government. Behold the King the Lord of Hosts hath sent his servants, to bid you let Israel goe free, that they may serve him together, in community of spirit, and in community of the earthly treasure.

Be not you more proud and hardhearted, then *Pharaoh* your type, if you be, as it is like you wil, for the anti-type oft times is more powerfull then the type; then assure your selves, plagues shall [55] multyply, and Israel shal be pulled from under your burdens with a strong hand, and stretched out arm, and you, and all your company shal perish together. The Lord hath spoke it, and he will doe it. *Heb.* 2. 7, 8, &c.

All the men and women in *England*, are al children of this Land, and the earth is the Lords, not particular mens that claims a proper interest in it above others, which is the devils power.

But be it so, that some wil say, This is my Land, and cal such and such a parcel of Land his own interest; Then saith the Lord, let such an one labour that parcel of Land by his own hands, none helping him: for whosoever shal help that man to labour his proper earth, as he cals it for wages, the hand of the Lord shal be upon such labourers; for they lift up flesh above the spirit, by their labours, and so hold the Creation stil under bondage.

Therefore if the rich wil stil hold fast this propriety of *Mine and thine*, let them labour their own Land with their own hands. And let the common-People, that are the gatherings together of Israel from under that bondage, and that say the earth is ours, not mine, let them labour together, and eat bread together upon the Commons, Mountains, and Hils.

For as the inclosures are called such a mans Land, and such a mans Land; so the Commons and Heath, are called the common-peoples, and let the world see who labours the earth in righteousnesse, and those to whom the Lord gives the blessing, let them be the people that shal inherit the earth. Whether they that hold a civil propriety, saying, *This is mine*, which is selfish, devilish and destructive to the Creation, or those that hold a common right, saying, *The earth is ours*, which lifts up the Creation from bondage. *Isa.* 62. 8, 9.

[56] Was the earth made for to preserve a few covetous, proud men, to live at ease, and for them to bag and barn up the treasures of the earth from others, that they might beg or starve in a fruitful Land, or was it made to preserve all her children, Let Reason, and the Prophets and Apostles writings be Judge, the earth is the Lords, it is not to be confined to particular interest.

None can say, Their right is taken from them; for let the rich work alone by themselves, and let the poor work together by themselves; the rich in their inclosures, saying, *This is mine*; The poor upon their Commons, saying *This is ours*, the earth and fruits are common.

And who can be offended at the poor for doing this? None but covetous, proud, lazy, pamper'd flesh, that would have the poor stil to work for that devil (particular interest) to maintain his greatnesse, that he may live at ease.

What doe we get by our labour in the earth, but that we may eat bread and live together in love and community of righteousnesse, *This shall be the blessing of* Israel. *Isa.* 62. 8.

But as *Esau* hath setled his Kingdome, they that work live in straits; *They that live idle surfet with fulnesse, and makes all places stink with unrighteous envious oppression.*

Wel, when the Lord cals forth Israel to live in tents, which I believe wil be within a short time, he wil protect them; This Trumpet is stil sounding in me, *Work together, Eat bread together, declare this all abroad. Ier.* 25. 37, 38.

Surely the Lord hath not revealed this in vain; for I shal see the fruit of righteousnesse follow after it, which wil be the beginning of the great day of veangence to the Oppessour, that hath held the earth [57] under the bondage of civil propriety: ruling a Tyrant over others: forcing the poor to work for hire: But in the day of restoration of *Israel* is not to eat the bread of a hireling in no kind; he is neither to give hire, nor take hire.

Did the light of Reason make the earth for some men to ingrosse up into bags and barns, that others might be opprest with poverty? Did the light of Reason make this law, that if one man have not such abundance of the earth as to give to others he borrowed of; that he that did lend should imprison the other, and starve his body in a close room? Did the light of Reason make this law, that some part of man kinde should kil and hang another part of man-kinde, that could not walk in their steps?

Surely Reason was not the God that made that law; for this is to make one part of the Creation alwaies to be quarrelling against another part; which is mighty dishonour to our Maker.

But covetousnesse, that murdering God of the world, was that Lawmaker, And that is the God, or ruling power, which all men that claim a particular interest in the earth, do worship. 2 *Cor.* 4. 4.

For the Earth is the Lords; that is, the spreading power of righteousnes, not the Inheritance of covetous, proud flesh that dies. If any man can say that he makes Corn or Cattle, he may say, That is mine: But if the Lord make these for the use of his Creation, surely then the earth was made by the Lord, to be a common Treasury for all, not a particular Treasury for some.

If any man can say, he can give life, then he hath power to take away life: But if the power of life and death be only in the hand of the Lord; then surely he is a murderer of the Creation, that takes away the life of his fellow Creature man, by any law whatsoever: For all laws that are made by any man [58] to take away the life of man, is the upholder of the curse. *Ex.* 20. 13.

But what if some steal or whore, or become idle, and wil not work, but live upon others labours, as rich men do, that cal the land theirs?

I answer; If any manifest such a Achanish or Serpents power, as to endeavour to bring in the curse againe upon the Creation, he shal not be imprisoned, hanged or killed; for that is the worke of the *Midianites* to kil one another; to preserve themselves, and self interest, But the punishment of such shal be this, he shal be set to work, and have land appointed him to work upon, and none shal help him:

he shal have a mark set upon him al this time, that every ones eie may be upon him, as upon a fool in *Israel*: he shal be a servant to every one; til such time as the spirit in him, make him know himself to be equal to others in the Creation.

If any do steal, what wil they do with it? None shal buy or sel, and al the while that every one shal have meat, and drink, and cloaths, what need have they to steal? Their stealing shal get them nothing, but to lose the benefit of Sonship; And that is to be set alone, to eat his own bread, none having communion with him.

For every one shal know the Law, and every one shal obey the Law; for it shal be writ in every ones heart; and every one that is subject to Reasons law, shal enjoy the benefit of Sonship. And that is in respect of outward community, to work together, and eat bread together; and by so doing, lift up the creation from the bondage of self interest, or particular propriety of mine and thine; which is the Devil and Satan, even the God of this world, that hath blinded the eies of covetous, proud flesh, and hath bound them up in chains of darknesse. *Act.* 4. 32.

The universal spirit of righteousnesse hath been [59] slain by covetous, proud flesh; this 1649 years ago: But now that spirit begins to arise againe from the dead, and the same Beast seeks to hinder his rising; or else watches to kil the Manchild after he is brought forth. Covetous proud flesh wil kil a Tyrant, but hold fast the same Tyrannie and slaverie over others in his own hand; he wil kil the Traitor, but liks wel the Treason, when he may be honoured or lifted up by it. *Rev.* 12. 4. 2. *King.* 20. 16.

Look upon the mountaines and little hils of the earth, and see if these prickling thorns and briars, the bitter curse, does not grow there: Truly Tyrannie is Tyrannie in one as wel as in another; in a poor man lifted up by his valour, as in a rich man lifted up by his lands: And where Tyrannie sits, he is an enemy to Christ, the spreading spirit of righteousnesse: He wil use the bare name, Christ, that he may the more secretly persecute, and kil his power.

Tyrannie is a subtile, proud and envious Beast; his nature is selfish, and ful of murder; he promises fair things for the publique; but all must be made to center within self, or self interest not the universal libertie.

Wel, to be short, Let every one know, if they wait upon their

Maker they wil know, That the universal power of righteous Communitie, as I have declared, is *Canaan*, the land of rest and libertie, which flows with milk and honey, with abundance of joy and peace in our Maker, and one in another. *Zach.* 8. 3. *to* 12.

But the condition of the world, that upholds civill interests of mine and thine: Is *Egypt* the house of bondage; and truly *Pharoahs* taskmasters are very many, both Teachers and Rulers.

Therefore thus said the voyce of the spirit in me, guiding my eie to the powers of the earth three times, Let Israel go free: Let Israel go free: Let [60] Israel go free: Work all together, Eat bread altogether: Whosoever labours the earth for any one, that wil be a burdning Ruler over others, and does not look upon himself as equal to others in the Creation, the hand of the Lord shal be upon that labourer: I the Lord have spoken it, and I wil doe it: Declare this all abroad, Israel shal neither give hire, nor take hire.

Surely this is both ful of reason and equity; for the earth was not made for some, but for al to live comfortably upon the fruits of it: And there cannot be a universal libertie, til this universal communitie be established.

All tears, occasioned through bondage, cannot be wiped away, til the earth become in use to all a common Treasurie: And then *Jerusalem* wil become a praise to the whole earth, and not til then.

At this time the barren land shal be made fruitfull; for the Lord wil take off the curse: And if any grumble and say, The Heaths and Commons are barren, and the like, and so draw against the work: All that I say, let them go their way; their portion is not here; they live in the low flesh, not in the height of the spirit: And they know not the mysterie of the Lord, who is now restoring Israel from bondage, and fetching them out of all lands where they were scattered, into one place, where they shal live and feed together in peace. *Zach.* 8. 11, 13.

And then there shal be no more pricking briar in all the holy Mountain, This shal be the glory of all, they shal lie down in rest: This is the Branch; This is Israel; This is Christ spread in sons and daughters; This is Jerusalem the glory of the whole earth: Where then wil be the railing, persecuting Priest, or the Tyrant Professour, that sucks after the bloud and miserie of those, that wil not joyn in his forms? *Hos.* 2. 15. *Isa.* 60. 21.

[61] But indeed as yet, as the state of the world is while the first *Adam* yet sits in the Chair, and corrupts the Creation by his unrighteous wisdom and power; I say at this time, the feirce wrath of the King of Righteousnesse is threatned over this Land called *England*, and indeed over all the whole earth, where particular interest bears rule, and enslaves the Creation.

And if covetous, proud flesh stil uphold this self-propriety, which is the curse and burden which the Creation groans under: Then O thou covetous earth, expect the multyplying of plagues, and the fulfilling of all threatning prophesies and visions for thy downfal in miserie.

But if thou wouldst find mercie, then open thy barns and treasuries of the earth, which thou hast heaped together, and detains from the poor, thy fellow creatures: This is the only remedy to escape wrath: and the door of acceptance to mercie is yet open, if thou do this: The Judge of Truth and Right waits yet upon thy comming into him.

Therefore, O thou first *Adam*, take notice, that the Lord hath set before thee life and death, now chuse whether thou wilt, for the time is near at hand that buying and selling of land shall cease, and every son of the land shal live of it.

Divide *England* into three parts, scarce one part is manured: So that here is land enough to maintain all her children, and many die for want, or live under a heavy burden of povertie all their daies: And this miserie the poor people have brought upon themselves, by lifting up particular interest, by their labours.

There are yet three doors of hope for *England* to escape destroying plagues:

First, let every one leave off running after others for knowledge and comfort, and wait upon [62] the spirit Reason, til he break forth out of the Clouds of your heart, and manifest himself within you. This is to cast off the shadow of Learning, and to reject covetous, subtile proud flesh that deceives all the world by their hearsay, and traditional preaching of words, letters and sillables, without the spirit: And to make choyce of the Lord, the true Teacher of every one in their own inward experience; The mysterie of the spirit, and the mysterie of *Babylon. Luke. 24. 49. Mat. 15. 14.*

Secondly, Let every one open his bags and barns, that al may feed upon the crops of the earth, that the burden of povertie may be removed: Leave of this buying and selling of Land, or of the fruits of the earth; and as it was in the light of Reason first made, so let it be in action, amongst all a common Treasurie; none inclosing or hedging in any part of earth, saying, this is mine; which is rebellion and high treason against the King of Righteousnesse: And let this word of the Lord be acted amongst all; work together, eat bread together. *Act.* 4. 32.

Thirdly. Leave off dominion and Lordship one over another, for the whole bulk of man-kinde are but one living earth. Leave off imprisoning, whiping and killing; which are but the actings of the curse: And let those that hitherto have had no Land and have been forced to rob and steal through povertie; hereafter let them quietly enjoy Land to work upon, that every one may enjoy the benefit of his Creation, and eat his own bread with the sweat of his own brows: For surely this particular propriety of mine and thine, hath brought in all miserie upon people. For first, it hath occasioned people to steal one from another. Secondly, it hath made Laws to hang those that did steal: It tempts people to doe an evil action, and then kils them for doing of it: Let all judge if this be not a great devil.

[63] Well: If every one would speedily set about the doing of these three particulars I have mentioned, the Creation would thereby be lift up out of bondage, and our Maker would have the glory of the works of his own hands.

They that offer themselves, and what treasure they have, freely, to further this work, shal find mercy, and the blessing of all Nations shal be his Comfortor: They that hinder this common interest of earthly community, and wil keep up the tyrannical government of old Adam stil, the hand of the Lord shal be upon that person, whosoever he be. 1. *P.* 5. 3. *Iudge.* 5. 2, 9.

Thus saith the Lord to all the great ones, that are cloathed with objects, and are lifted up flesh with honours in the government of the world: Let Israel go quietly out of your bondage that they may serve me: If you wil not let him go, I wil not come with 10 plagues, as upon Egyptian Pharoah of old, but I wil multiply my plagues upon thee, thou stout-hearted Pharaoh, that makes shew of love to me, and yet all is but like Jehu, to lift up thy self over the remnant in the Land.

Adam is the commer in of bondage, and is the curse that hath taken hold of the Creation: And he may wel be called A-dam, for indeed he does dam and stop up the streams of the waters of life and libertie.

When slaverie began to creep in upon the Creation, the Spirit might wel cry out in Lamentation, Ah-dam, A-dam, which draws together; a head of corrupted waters, of covetous, proud and imaginary flesh, to stop the streams of the waters of life and libertie.

But saith the Spirit our Maker, The seed from whence the Creation sprang, shall bruise that Serpents head, and open the dam againe, and cause the waters of the Spirit which is Life and Libertie [64] to run free againe without any stoppage.

This A-dam stops up the waters of Life and Libertie in a two-fold way.

First, he ties up the Creation, man, in chains of darknesse within it self: For there is not a man and woman found, since Adam's rise (but the man Christ Jesus, in whom the seed ruled in power) but they were bound up in bondage to covetousnesse, pride, imagination, and to all the powers of the flesh: So that the free running streams of the Spirit of life were stopped, that they could not run; which hath made every one cry, O wretched man that I am, who shal deliver me from this body of sin or death? Here you see that knowledge, libertie and comfort hath been stopped or dammed up within the Creation, man.

Secondly, this A-dam, being the power of covetous, proud flesh, he sets up one part of the Creation, man, to rule over another, and makes Laws to kil and hang that part of the Creation, that wil not submit to the ruling part. And so he is become a God, ruling in the spirits own house, not preserving the Creation, but does set the Creation together by the ears, to kil it self, to the mighty dishonour of our Maker: Therefore when the people would have *Saul* to rule them; the Spirit declared, that that outward ruling power was the curse; and he set him up in his wrath to be a scourge, not a blessing.

Now whereas the Creation, man, should live in equalitie one towards another; this A-dam hath lifted up mountaines and hils of oppressing powers, and there by that, dammed and stopped up that universal communitie: Therefore at the first rising up of this serpentine power to enslave the Creation, he might wel be declared by way of Lamentation, A-dam Adam.

[65] Covetousnesse, or self-love; is the dam; the letter A: before,

declares, that he is a preparer to miserie, and is delivered by way of Lamentation, Ah: or A-dam.

Covetousnesse, or self-love, is the man of sin, that appears first. The imagination arising from that covetous power is the woman, or Eve, which like the Ivie, clings about the tree; and so covetousnesse and imagination, does beget between them a supposed joy, pleasure and delight; but it proves a lie.

These two, Covetousnesse and Imagination, the man and the woman of sin, or A-dam, and his Eve, or Ivie, does beget fruit or children, like both Father and Mother; as pride, and envy, hypocrisie, crueltie, and all unclean lusts pleasing the flesh. And now the dam-head is made up strong, to stop the streams of waters of life and universal libertie: But in the fulnesse of time, the Spirit wil break down this dam-head againe, and cause the waters of the Spirit of life to flow again plentifully.

And herein you may see, how the publique Preachers have cheated the whole world, by telling us of a single man, called Adam, that kiled us al by eating a single fruit, called an Apple.

Alas, this Adam is the dam that hath stopped up the freedome of the Spirit within and without; so that while he rules, a man can have no community with the spirit within himself, nor community of love with fellow creatures, he does so puff them up with covetousnesse, and pride, and desire of Lordly rule one over another.

Do but look into every man and woman, and into al the actions of the world, and tel me whether that first Adam be one single man, as the publique Preachers tel you; or is not more truly that covetous, proud and imaginary power in flesh, that hath [66] dammed and stopped up the way of the spirit of life, and universal libertie; and so he is that Father of lies, and Satan, that holds the Creation under bondage, til the Son, which is the light in the Creation, shine forth, and sets us at libertie: And if the Son set you free, you are free indeed.

This Son is the second Adam, which is A-dam indeed, that stops the streams of bondage from running, and sets the Creation at libertie again.

CHAP. IX.

WHAT I have spoken, I have not received from books, nor study, but freely I have received, and freely I have declared what I have received: And the Declarations of the Lord through his servant shal not be in vain.

The beholding and feeling of the Law of righteousnesse within me, fils my whole soul with precious peace, the savour of the sweet ointment; and I know as this power of love spreads in al mens hearts, as it wil spread, for Jacob must rise: Then there shall be no begger, no tears, no complaining, no oppression: but the blessing of the Lord shal fil the earth: *Then our swords shall be beaten into plow irons, and our spears into pruning hooks, and then shall the Lord be known to be the salvation of Israel, and the restoration of the whole Creation. Amos. 7. 2. Mic. 4. 3.*

If any man be offended here, let him know, I have obeyed my Maker herein, and I have peace in him.

When the Man, Jesus Christ, was on earth, there was a sweet communitie of love between all the members of that humane body: For the spirit that was within, made every member a servant to the [67] other, and so preserved the whole body in peace; one member did not raign over another in tyrannie.

Even so, when the humane body was laid in the earth, the Spirit, which indeed is Christ, came again the second time upon the Apostles and Brethren, while they were waiting for that promise at Jerusalem. *Luke* 24. 49.

And as Christ then began to spread himself in sons and daughters, which are members of his mystical body, they did not rule in slavery one over another; neither did the rich suffer the poor to beg and starve, and imprison them as now they do: But the rich sold their possessions, and gave equality to the poor, and no man said, that any thing that he possessed was his own, for they had all things common. *Act.* 4. 32.

But this community was a vexation to *Esau,* the covetous proud flesh, and he strove to suppresse this community: And the Lord he gives this Beast a toleration to rule 42 months, or a time, times, and dividing of time; and in that time to kil the two Witnesses, that is, Christ in one body, and Christ in many bodies; or Christ in his first and second comming in flesh, which is Justice and Jugement ruling in man. *Rev.* 11. 2, 9. *Rev.* 12. 14.

I, but now the 42 months are expiring, we are under the half day of the Beast, or the dividing of time, and Christ, or the two Witnesses, are arising and spreading himself again in the earth: And when he hath spread himself abroad amongst his Sons and daughters, the members of his mystical body, then this community of love and righteousnesse, making all to use the blessings of the earth as a common Treasurie amongst them, shal break forth again in his glory, and fil the earth, and shal be no more supprest: And none shal say, this is mine, [68] but every one shal preserve each other in love.

As Christ does thus rise and spread, those that have riches, gold and silver, and the like, and are taken into the onenesse of this Spirit, they shall come, and offer up their treasures willingly, not daring to keep it: That those that have nothing may have part, and enjoy the blessing of the earth with themselves, being all members of that one body, unto whom the Kings of the East, called the Wise men, offered gifts, gold frankinsense and myrrhe while he was the Child Jesus. *Exo.* 25. 2. *Ezra* 7. 16. *Mat.* 2. 11.

But those that do not come in and offer what they have, willingly, to the work of the Lord, they shal be stripped naked of all, and shal either be destroyed by the plagues that shal come upon the earth; or at best if their lives be given them, they shal be servants, and not enjoy the benefit of Sonship, til the Spirit of the Son rise up in them, and make them free. *Ioh.* 8. 32.

So that this work is not done by wars, councels, or hands of men, for I abhor it; though by those the government of Esau shal be beaten down, and the enemy shal destroy one another. *Dan.* 8. 25.

But the Lord alone wil be the healer, the restorer, & the giver of the new law of righteousnes, by spreading himself every where and so drawing al things up into himself.

And the declaration of this law of righteousnesse shal rise out of the dust, out of the poor people that are trod under foot: For, as the declaration of the Son of man was first declared by Fisher-men, & men that the learned, covetous Scholars despised: so the declaration of the righteous law shal spring up from the poor, the base and despised ones, and fools of the world; and humane learning, and such as love the oppression of exacting Tyths, shal not be honoured in his businesse: For they that stand up [69] to be publique Teachers are *Iudas*, that come to the Magistrates, and covenants with them for the tenths of every mans encrease, and they wil hinder Christ from rising, and betray him into their hands; that so the covetous and proud flesh may rule in oppression over their fellow Creature quietly. *Mat.* 23. 16.

And assure your selves it wil appear, that the publique Preachers, that stand up customarily to make a living by their teaching others, as they cal it: these are the curse, and the spreaders of that curse, and the hinderers of Christ from rising; and the bitter Scribes and Pharisees to suppresse Christ where he rises, calling him a Blasphemer. 1. *Ioh.* 2. 27. *Ioh.* 6. 45.

For the Father wil have all men to look up to him for teaching, and to acknowledge no other teacher and ruler but himself: but these men wil have al people to look for knowledge to come through them; and that none can have knowledge but such as are taught by such Preachers as they: But covetousnesse after a temporal living, and secret pride sets them to work, and they shal be ashamed; for the Lord alone now shal be exalted, and he himself wil draw up al things into himself. *Ioh.* 10. 13.

And al this great change, or seting up of this new law of righteousnesse, ruling in every one, and making every one to consent and act thus in love, is but the fullfilling of Prophesies, and Visions, and Reports of the Scriptures: Let the Record be searched, and let the publique Preachers deny it if they can.

Wel: this wil be a great day of Judgment; the Righteous Judge wil sit upon the Throne in every man and woman: And that saying of the prophet, that he saw every man with his hands upon his loyns, like a woman in travel, is now fulfiling; every covetous, unrighteous heart shal smart with sorrow and shal be ready to fail them to see the miserie that is comming upon the earth: This day of Judgment [70] wil be sharp and short, shortned for the Elects sake.

The man of the flesh, or King *Esau*, wil struggle hard, before he give up the body of his Army; he wil put forth all the subtil wit, and oppressing unrighteousnesse that he hath, before he deliver up the Kingdom to *Iacob*: But truly, Gaffer Dragon, you had better yield at first; for the longer thou stand it out, the sorer shal thy torment be; for down thou must, and Christ must rise.

Do what thou wilt, speak what thou wilt against Christ the Anointing, thou shalt come off a loser: threaten, reproach, imprison, whip, work hypocritically, oppresse, kil and slay, fawn and frown, do things out of fear, or do things out of heavy rashnesse, or out of a watchful moderation, as thou thinks, stil thou shalt lose ground; for all thou doest, is to advance self, and thou must perish, the Judgment is sealed, the things that are determined against thee, are comming upon thee. *Dan.* 11. 36.

Thou shalt find it shal not be as it hath been; while the forty two months were in being, thou prospered and encreased in strength. But now it is done, it is done, it is done, time shal be no more to thee; for now the man of righteousnesse shal take the Kingdom, and rule for ever and ever, and of his dominion shal be no end; he hath made himself manifest, he is in the head of his Army already, *gathering in the Isles and Nations of the earth to himself.* Justice and Judgment are his witnesses, and that *Standard,* which he wil maintain, and wil tread al proud *flesh under his feet, For the poor receives the Gospel. Rev.* 11. 2.

He hath opened the salt-mines already, the streams thereof runs apace, and begins to over-run the banks of rotten stinking oppressing injustice, they wil purge out corruption and bring the earth (mankind) into a pleasant savour. *Mat.* 5. 13.

[71] The windows of heaven are opening, and the light of the Son of Righteousnes, sends forth of himself delightful beams, and sweet discoveries of truth that wil quite put out the covetous traditional blear-eyes; but wil mightily refresh the single eyed *Nathaneels*: Light must put out darknesse; the warm Sun wil thaw the frost, and make the sap to bud out of every tender plant, that hath been hid within, and lain like dead trees all the dark cold cloudy daies of the Beast that are past, and silence every imaginary speaker, and declare their hypocrisie, and deceit openly.

Now the tender grasse wil cover the earth, the Spirit wil cover al places *with the abundance of fruit,* that flows from himself, young and old shal al honour the Lord, and be taught of no other but him; the wheat fields which is the best grain (the Fathers own people) shal flourish abundantly; the bondage of beastly Ceremonies, forms, customs, abominable actings in unrighteousnesse shal cease, there shal be lesse talking, preaching and prating, and more righteous acting; *The voice of mourning shall be heard no more, the birds shall sing merrily on every bough.*

O rejoyce, rejoyce, for the time that the Lord God omnipotent wil raign in al the earth is beginning, and he wil be servant to the Dragon, Beast, and man of the flesh no longer, but wil tread down that murdering power, and make him his footstool.

This is the work of the Lord, that wil stop the mouths of all hearsay and imaginary Preachers; *All mouths shall be silent, and not dare to speak, till the power of the Lord within give words to the mouth to utter.* And when men that are ful of wast words, are made to see, they speak they know not what; when they shal see they speak other mens words [72] (like Parots) not their own, and sometimes they speak words from their imagination, which may be false as wel as true for ought they know, for they have had neither voice, vision, nor revelation to warrant their words, when they see this, Then they shal be ashamed and confounded in themselves. *Rev.* 12. 9, *&c.*

For now lip service is to be judged to death, and every one shal be fetched in to worship the Father in Spirit and in truth, or else they shal perish; for mens words shal grow fewer and fewer, their actions of Righteousness one to another more and more, and there shal no love be esteemed of, but what is manifest in righteous actions.

And this shal be the rule that every one shal observe, to walk righteously in the Creation, towards all Creatures, according to the Law of equity and Reason; and this Law shal be writ in every ones heart; and he that hath this law in his heart is marked for a son or daughter: they that have it not are marked for enemies and rebels to the Father, And such a one is a *Cain. Rev.* 11. 15, 18.

The Kingdoms of the whole world must become the Kingdoms of the Lord Christ; and this the Nations are angry at; Therefore count it no strange thing to see wars and rumours of wars, to see men that are put in trust to act for publike good, to prove fals, to see commotions of people every where like flouds of water stirred up, ready to devour and overflow one another; To see Kings storm against the people; To see rich men and gentry most violent against the poor, oppressing them and treading them like mire in the street, Why is all this anger?

But because the man of the flesh is to die, his day of judgment is come, he must give up the Kingdom and Government of the earth (man-kind) into the hand of his neighbour that is more righteous then he, For *Jacob* now must have the blessing, he is [73] blessed, yea and shal be blessed, and *Esau* shal become his servant; *The poor shal inherit the earth.*

CHAP. X.

AND here now is made plain, That *the first shall be last, and the last first*; The powers of the flesh or *Adam* in me, he appeared first, and trampled the man-child, the power of righteousnesse and peace under foot.

I, but when the man-child begins to rise up to rule, the other fals and becomes the tail, the last, nay must be destroyed.

Two Kings that claimes interest in one Kingdom, can never live quietly together, *Light and darknesse will be fighting,* till the one be conquered. And surely the man of Righteousnesse, or that last man that appears, shal be the first, that shal be honoured, and become the preserving and restoring power the great Law-giver, that *shall rule in the new heaven and in the new earth in righteousnesse.*

Or further, The first, that is, the worshipping of God in types, ceremonies, formes and customs, in set times and places, which are the invention of the first man, which doth slight and loath the way of inward Righteousnesse; for they that live in established forms, are filled with dislike, and willingly would neither buy nor sell, with those whom the Lord hath drawn up to live in him, they cannot indure the way of the Spirit, let them say and professe what they wil; for he that is strict in a formal customary way of worship, knows not what it is to worship in spirit and truth, or to walk righteously in the Creation, but is bitter spirited and meerly selfish. *Gen.* 4. 5. *Rev.* 13. 17. *Rom.* 9. 31, 32.

[74] And this power appears first in a man, and makes people very zealous professours of God and Christ, in preaching, praying and hearing. But without knowledge, what God and Christ is, and they know not what they do, nor the end wherefore they do so. *Rom.* 10. 2.

And their teachers in the same forms are blind guides and poor hearts; both shall fall into the ditch, and be mired in their own inventions most pittifully. And when you come to see your selves stick in confusion, and disorder, and knowing that your teachers have deceived you,

Then you will remember these words, *That the first must be last.* *Moses* though he was a good man, yet he was not to enter into the land of *Canaan*, which types out this to me, *That the first man of the flesh shall never enter into the Fathers rest. Deu. 34. 4.*

Then likewise you shall see, that your zeal was but zeal without knowledge, and that heat in you did but carry you along to advance self, not to advance the Lord. And that covetousness was the Lord, chief Ruler in you, which being crossed grew impatient, and that impatiency you called it, *The zeal of the Lord*; when experience teacheth you silence, you will not be offended at these words, but ashamed of your self.

And here likewise you may see, what it is to make a Sermon; for a Sermon is a speech made from the man-seer; which is Christ within; for this anointing sees the Father in every thing.

And therefore Christ in that one body, The Lamb, was called a great Prophet or Seer, Now that man or woman that sees the Spirit, within themselves, how he enlightens, how he kils the motions of the flesh, and makes the flesh subject to Righteousnesse, and so can see *light in his light*; this man or woman is able to make a Sermon, because they can speak by experience of the light and power of Christ within [77, i. e., 75] them, who is indeed the man-Seer. *Joh.* 1. 9. *Joh.* 3. 11.

But now he that speaks from imagination, or from tradition (and not from experience of what he sees) cannot make a Sermon, as the publike Preachers generally do, and so he is a deceiver, or false Christ, and false Prophet, that runs before he be sent, put forward by secret pride and covetousnes, to get a temporal living.

Therfore let none speak so discontentedly against *Adam*, the first man by Creation, that they say lived on earth about 6000 years ago, as though he brought in the misery upon all; for the Scriptures seem to declare, that there were men in the world before that time.

For when *Cain* had killed his brother *Abel*, which in one verse *Moses* seemes to say, was the third man in the world, yet in a few verses following, writing of *Cains* punishment, declares *Cains* own words, *Thou hast set a mark upon me, and every one that sees me, wil kil me*: And yet by the story before, there were no more men in the world, but his Father *Adam* and he, now *Abel* being dead. *Gen.* 4. 14.

Therefore certainly this *Adam*, or first man that is spoken of, is he that is within, as I have spoke of, which kils or surpresses *Abel*, who is the anointing; I am sure I have found him the cause of my misery, and I can lay the blame on no man, but my self. The first power that appears and draws my body into disobedience.

And this is he that is the causer of all your sorrow and tears, he is *Adam* within, it is your self, your very fleshly self, be angry at none but your self. The Self is the first *Adam* that fals from the Spirit; he is those branching powers in created flesh that leads you from your maker; therfore blame not *Adam* without you, but blame *Adam* the first man within you; he within hath disobeyed, and forsaken Reasons Law of Righteousnesse.

[76] You are the man and woman that hath eaten the *forbidden fruit*, by delighting your self more in the objects of the Creation, then in the Spirit; for the Spirit is the seed, the Creation is the fruit.

As the Apple is the fruit from the root of the Apple-tree, so selfishnesse is the fruit of the fruit; it arises up (not from the Spirit) but from the Creation. And this is the Serpent whose head must be bruised, that so the great maker of all things, may delight in the worke of his own hands; when all the branchings forth of selfishnesse is destroyed, and the Creation made subject only to the will of the Creatour. *Gen.* 3. 15.

And this wil be the winding up of the great mystery spoken of, *God manifest in the flesh* (not selfishnesse manifested in flesh) for this I say is the *Serpent whose head must be bruised*.

Now if you delight more in the objects of the earth, to please selfe, then in the *spirit that made all things*, then you eat of the forbidden fruit, you take the Apple, and become naked and ashamed, and are made afraid to own the spirit, least you despise fellow-creatures.

And likewise being ashamed and afraid of the law of righteousnesse, because it doth testifie of you, that your *deeds are evil*; and so begets sorrow and trouble in your heart; you presently run and hide your self from him amongst the creatures, & run preaching, and praying, and sheltering your self in a Congregation, as a member, and so doth sow the figge-leaves of your own observing forms, and customary invented Righteousnesse together, to hide your soul from the face of displeasure, that you may not see your self; for the sight of your self is your hell.

Whereas indeed you should flie to the Law of Righteousnesse, and act righteously within the Creation, and so honour the Spirit by owning of him, and [77] wait upon him til he speak peace.

For nothing wil hide you from his presence: Reasons Law wil shine forth & torment your unrighteous self-seeking power, and *bruise that Serpents head*, all his hidings wil not save himself, for you must come to the fire, and that drosse must be burned up, before a Reconciliation can be wrought between him and his Creation.

Adams innocency is the time of child-hood; and there is a time in the entering in of the understanding age, wherein every branch of man-kinde is put to his choice, whether he wil follow the Law of Righteous-nesse, according to the Creation, to honour the Spirit.

Or whether he wil delight self, in glorying in the objects of the earth unrighteously. Now if he chuse to satisfie his lusts and his self-wil, and forsake Reasons Law, he shal fal downwards into bondage, and lie under the powers of darknesse, and live no higher then within the circle of dark flesh, that hath no peace within it self, but what he fetches from creatures without him.

But if he chuse the way of Righteousnesse, and follow the light of Reasons Law, then he shal partake of rest, peace and libertie of the Spirit, as if there were no creature objects at all; for he that hath peace within, *uses the world as though he used it not*, and hath content and joy, though he have no creature to have communion with.

But seeing that the man of the flesh wil and must appear to rule in the Kingdome of man-kinde first; *All men are gone astray, and all flesh have corrupted their waies*, and the curse is spread abroad thorow the Creation: And therefore the whole Creation waits for a Restoration, or for the rising up of Christ the second man, the blessing, who must bruise the head of bondage, and reconcile al men to peace and [78] liberty. And as the curse is seen and felt within, so the blessing of free-dom and life, must rise up, and be seen and felt within. *Gen.* 18. 18.

Therefore let not your blind guides deceive you any longer; Doe not look beyond your selves to *Adam*, a man that died 6000 years agoe, though they bid you; but look upon *Adam* within your self, who hath wrought your woe. And for the time to come, wait upon the rising of the second *Adam*, the Law of Righteousnesse within you, to deliver you from the bondage of the first power.

And here you may see the deceit of imagination and fleshly wisdom and learning; it teaches you to look altogether upon a history without you, of things that were done 6000 years agoe, and of things that were done 1649 years agoe, of the carriage of the *Scribes* and *Pharisees* then against the son of man.

And so carrying you first to one age of the world, then to another age of the world, travelling Sea and Land to find rest; and the more that human learning and his professours travels abroad, the further off from rest they are, for they meet with nothing but confusion and straits, and no true peace: And why?

Because that which a man seeks for, whereby he might have peace, is within the heart, not without. The word of life, Christ the restoring spirit, is to be found within you, even in your mouth, and in your heart: *The Kingdome of heaven* (which is) Christ *is within you*, and disobedient *Adam* is within you; for this is *Esau* that strives with *Jacob* in the womb of your heart to come forth first.

And this let me tel you, and you shal find it true, Goe read all the books in your Universitie, that tels you what hath been formerly, and though you can make speeches of a day long from those readings yet you shall have no peace, but your hearts still [79] shal be a barren wildernesse, and encrease in sorrow till your eyes return into your selves, and the spirit come from on high to make you read in your own book your heart. *Isa.* 32. 9. to 16.

Wherein you shall find the *mystery of iniquity*, *The man of sinne*, that first *Adam*, that made you a sinner. And the mystery of godlinesse, the second *Adam* Christ, who, when he arises up therein, he makes you righteous and restores you again to life.

And hence it is, that many a poor despised man and woman, that are counted blasphemers, by the understanding Pharisees of our age, as the learned Pharisees of old called Christ, and people are afraid to buy and sell [with] them, but casts out their names for evil; yet these have more sweet peace, more true experience of the Father, and walks more righteously in the Creation, in spirit and truth, then those that cal themselves teachers and zealous Professours. *Phil.* 3. 10, 11.

And why? Because these single hearted ones are made to look into themselves, wherein they can read the work of the whole Creation, and see that History seated within themselves; they can see the mystery of Righteousnesse, and are acquainted every one according to his measure, with that spirit of truth that is to be *the blessing of the whole earth*, and that enlightens al that come into the world; these are the dust and stones of the earth, that are trod under foot: *But out of this Sion whom no man regards, shal the Deliverer come.*

But now those that are called Preachers, and great professours that runs a hearing, seeks for knowledge abroad in Sermons, in books and Universities, and buyes it for money, as *Simon Magus* would have done, and then delivers it out again for money, for a 100 l. or 200 l. a year. And those men that speak from an inward testimony of what they have seen [89, i. e., 80] and heard from the Lord, are called by these buyers and sellers, Locusts, factious, blasphemers, and what not, as the language of Pulpits runs, but the Lord wil whip such traders out of his Temple.

And truly the whole world wanders after the Beast, and though the people many of them, doe see that their Preachers are blinde guides, bitter spirited: proud and covetous, yet they are ashamed and afraid to disown them, O great bondage under the devils.

And hence it is that they think they are wise and learned, and the only men sent of God to preach the Gospel, til the power of Righteousnesse come and declare before all the world, that they are enemies to the Gospel, and knows him not, for the anointing is the glad tidings, which are manifest within the heart, not [at] a distance from men.

And so Christ takes these wise and learned in their own crafty covetousnes and pride, and declares them to be very silly men, the most ignorant of all, blinde guides, painted sepulchers, Prophets that run before they be sent, and the great fooles of the world, and troublers of *Israel*, and the *Scribes* and *Pharisees* that stand up to hinder Christ from rising, or to cast reproachfull dirt upon him, where he rises, as much as they can to keep him down, and hold him under as a servant still; and this they will doe till they be swept away amongst the refuse of lies, as part of that treasure, for that must be your portion.

Nay let me tel you, That the poorest man, that sees his maker, and lives in the light, though he could never read a letter in the book, dares throw the glove to al the humane learning in the world, and declare the deceit of it, how it doth bewitch & delude man-kinde in spiritual things, yet it is that great Dragon, that hath deceived all the world, for it draws [81] men from knowing the Spirit, to own bare letters, words and histories for spirit: The light and life of Christ within the heart, discovers all darknesse, and delivers mankind from bondage; *And besides him there is no Saviour.*

CHAP. XI.

WELL, in the next place, I must declare to you, that all that which you call the history, and have doted upon it, and made it your idol, is all to be seen and felt within you, before you cast off true peace.

Adam and Christ you have heard are both to be seen within the heart, *Cain* and *Abel* is to be seen within: *Abraham* (a power that prefers the honour of Righteousnesse, before a beloved *Isaac*) is to be seen within. Meek spirited *Moses*, that rules your bodies by an outward Law of Righteousnesse, is to be seen within you; killing of Sacrifices, and offering them up, is to be seen within you. *Israel*, or one that is a wrestler is to be seen within you. And this is Christ the elect one that fights against your lusts. *Col.* 1. 27.

The *Canaanites, Amalekites, Philistines*, and all those armies of the Nations, even troops of unrighteous powers, one following another, are to be seen within you, making war with *Israel*, Christ within you.

The Land of *Canaan*, the habitation of rest, is to be seen within you, travelling and drudging in the wildernesse, and then comming to rest upon the seventh day, is to be seen within you.

Judas, a treacherous self-loving and covetous spirit, The Commanders of the *Jews* (the chief powers that are within the flesh) first condemning, [82] then killing, then buying Christ, is to be seen within you.

Christ lieing in the grave, like a corn of wheat buried under the clods of the earth for a time, and Christ rising up from the powers of your flesh, above that corruption and above those clouds, treading the curse under his feet, is to be seen within.

The stone that lies at the mouth of the sepulcher, your unbelief, the removing of that stone, setting you at libertie, is to be seen within you.

Heaven and hell, light and darknesse, sorrow and comforts is all to be seen within, the power of darknesse, and the power of light and life is to be seen within you. Good Angels (which are divine discoveries or sparks of that glory) And bad Angels (which are the powers of the flesh let loose out of the bottomlesse pit selfishnesse, and so working its own miserie) are to be seen within.

For man-kind is that Creation, in which the great Creatour of all things wil declare and manifest himself; Therefore it was said, That

God was in Christ, That one anointed humane body, reconciling or drawing all things into himself, and so making peace.

For while al things are out of that one power of Righteousnesse, jarring and flashing against him; there is no peace in the Creation, but sorrow, tears and vexation; but when all things are made to lie down quiet in him, and acknowledge him in all, and are subject to him, the alone King of Righteousnesse, now there is rest and peace every where.

Therefore if you look for heaven, or for manifestation of the Fathers love in you in any place, but within your selves, you are deceived; for what glory soever you shal be capable of to see with your eyes or hear with your ears, it is but the breakings forth of that glorious power that is seated within for [83] the glory of the Father is not without him, but it is all within himself, or rises up from within, & is manifested abroad; *The Kings daughter is all glorious within:* All that glory which declares heaven, is seen within that spirit, that rules within the Creation man-kind.

And further, if you look for any other hell or sorrows in any other place, then what shall be made manifest within the bottomlesse pit, your very fleshly self, you are deceived, and you shall find that when this bottomlesse pit is opened to your view, it will be a torment sufficient, for from hence, doth the curse spread, and all that misery you are or may be capable of, it is but the breakings forth of that stinking dunghill, that is seated within you, & is that power of darkness, that rules within the Creation, your body.

If the power of Righteousnesse & peace take possession and rule in you, then you shall live in rest, and be free from hell and sorrow, death and bondage. If the Lamb be the light of your heart, *all tears shall be wiped away*, and you shall be in peace. *Rev.* 21. 23.

But if the selfish power rule your heart; then as you live now upon uncertainties, in confusion and vexation: so this manifestation of hell, darknesse and sorrows, shall multiply within you; and when your body goes to the Earth, you multiply the curse upon the Creation, and so you enter into the body of the Serpent, that must be burned and consumed by the power of the Lord.

Hell and the curse doth rule within created flesh in every family of the earth, and will rule till the seed of *Abraham* (the blessing of the

Lord come) and burn up that serpent, and deliver the Creation from that burden.

And let me tell you, That this seed, This blessing of the Lord is rising up in every family that lives after [84] the flesh; Whether Parents, brethren or sisters, they do hate, grudge and persecute those in whom the blessing begins to rise up, and tramples upon them like dust; but out of that dust of the earth (man-kind) shall the deliverer come *that shall turn ungodlinesse from Jacob.* A few years now will discover more, and then that prophecy shall be materially fulfilled, *Then ten men shall take hold of him that is a Jew, saying, we will go with you, for we have heard that God is with you. Zech. 8. 23.*

The heart of man is the place wherein heaven and hell, for nature and kind, are both to be seen, that is, when the Law of Righteousnesse rules, there is Christ or the Kingdom of heaven within, even the manifestations of the Father appears in glory to the sweet rest and peace of that soul.

But when the power of unrighteousnesse rules in the heart, which is the Serpent, Dragon or God of this world; this is hell or kingdom of darknesse; for first the man sees and feels himself in bondage to his lusts, and to the powers of his flesh. This is death, and the curse that he lies under.

And then secondly, The man sees himself under bondage of sorrows and torment, and the increase of this sensiblenesse, is, & will be an intolerable misery.

As it is said, That the King of Righteousnes takes delight in nothing, but what is within himself, and what proceeds out of himself: So the Heaven of an enlivened heart is not a local place of glory at a distance from him, but the seeing and feeling the Father within, dwelling and ruling there; and to behold the glory of that power proceeding forth of himself, to which he is made subject, through which he walks righteously in the Creation, and in which he rests in peace.

Even so, the souls that are lost and ashamed in their work, are not tormented by any terrour without [85] them in any local place, but their hell or place of torment is within themselves, seeing and feeling themselves chained up in bondage, to fears, terrours, sorrows, afrightments, intolerable vexations, and powers of lust, and under all that cursed darknesse, untill the judgement of the great day.

And what misery or torment doth or shall appear from outward objects, it is but the breakings forth of their own cursednesse, that creates misery to himself, and so goes forth to fetch in torment from without.

For he that hath a troubled conscience, turns every thing into gall and worm-wood to terrifie himself, thinking every bush to be a devil to torment him, he saies, he sees fearfull shapes without; but they arise from the anguish of his tormenting conscience within, for they be the shapes and apparitions of his own cursed flesh that is presented to him, which comes not from any other but out of the bottomlesse pit, the Serpents power, but rules and dwels within him, and the sight of this is like the misery of tender flesh burning in the fire.

Let a man lie upon his sick bed, and to the view of others the chamber is quiet, yet he saith, he seeth devils, and flames, and misery, and torments. Well, this is but the risings up of his own unrighteous heart, the flames of the bottomlesse pit that appear to himself.

For certainly unrighteous flesh is hell, the appearance or risings up of unrighteous flesh to its own view, is the torments of hell. Pride, lust, envy, covetousnesse, hypocrisie, self-love, and the like, being crossed by the spirit of Light, are the particular devils that torment the soul in hell, or in that dark condition.

Or if so be a man be tormented by visible bodies of fury, and ugly shapes, as he apprehends, they be [86] all the creatures of his own making, and rods which the flesh hath made to whip and punish himself withall; for a man suffers by no other but by the work of his own hands.

And as he hath acted envy, venome and poison in strange wayes of oppression, walking unrighteously in the Creation: Even so, when his soul comes to be judged, he shall apprehend snakes, scorpions, toads, devils in bodily shapes, and flames of fire and direfull noises, and pits of darknesse, which are creatures of his own making, or the shapes and fashion of those unrighteous turnings, and windings, and actings of his unrighteous soul, that now appear in their own colours to his own torment, and this is hell.

For if the flesh be righteous within, there is nothing without can trouble it. When the bodies of men are laid in the grave, we have a word, That he is either in heaven or hell: Now the senses of the body are not sensible of either such. But now the power that ruled in that body righteously or unrighteously, is fully manifested to it self. If the power of Righteousnesse did rule, now it enters into the Spirit, the great Ocean of glory, the Father himself: If the power of unrighteousnesse did rule, now it enters into the curse, & encreases the body of death, corruption and enmity, and becomes the bondage and Burden of the Creation, that must be purged out by fire.

If there be a local place of hell, as the Preachers say there is, besides this I speak of, time will make it manifest but as yet none ever came from the dead to tell men on earth, and till then, men ought to speak no more then they know; what I speak, I speak from what I have in some measure seen within me, and as I have received from the Lord in clear light within my self.

But is not hell the execution of Justice? And is [87] not God the Authour of that wrath? As it is said, *Is there any evil in the Citie, and the Lord hath not done it?*

I answer, This is warily to be understood, lest we dishonour the Lord, in making him the Authour of the creatures misery, as one of late in his Pulpit, an Universitie man in my hearing did relate, and by his multitude of words, darkened knowledge mightily; therefore I shall deliver what I have received concerning this.

First know, that there is mention of three Gods in the Scriptures.

1. The Magistrate, *I said ye are gods.*

2. The Devil, *The god of this world hath blinded your eyes.*

3. The King of Righteousnesse is called God, *The Lord God omnipotent reigns.*

Now the Magistracie is a ruling power, called God; by their righteous Government a Kingdom may be kept in peace, but by their unrighteous Government, they trouble every body, and the people may say, Thou, O our God, hast destroyed us.

Secondly, The devil or the powers of the flesh in every man and woman is a ruling power, called god, that brings misery to every body, and corrupts the whole Creation, fire, water, earth and air.

1. By drawing the Creature into unreasonable wayes: which wayes and works,

2. Becomes the creatures own tormentours, when by the light of the Sun of Righteousnesse, man is made to see himself; for all mens sorrows are but the risings up of their own works against themselves. Therefore people may say to the devil, or their unrighteous flesh, O

thou, our God, thou hast destroyed us, thou hast deceived us, O God, thou promisedst peace, and afterwards writest bitter things against us. Our own works are our tormenting devils.

[88] Then thirdly, The King of Righteousnesse is the ruling power, called God; but he is not the Authour of the creatures misery, for his dealing with unrighteous flesh is two-fold, which is the righteous Justice and Judgement of the King.

First, he suffers man to take his own course and to act his own will, and to follow his own lusts, letting him alone, and permitting him a time to do what he will, for wise, proud and covetous flesh thinks himself to be a god, or an Angel of light, and that his wisdom and power is the onely power. And now if the righteous King should not give him this libertie, he would say he had wrong done him, therefore Reason lets him have his will to act his principles, that when the time comes that he shall be made to see himself and his works, he may be left without excuse.

This declares the Almighty power of patience, love and meekness in the King towards his creature, that he can suffer himself to be a servant to that cursed power in the flesh to this end, that he may take that fleshly wisdom in his craft, destroy that curse, and save his creature, man, from that bondage; That after that man hath had trial of his own wisdom and power of his flesh and finds it a devil, and that there is no blessing in it; he may then come to lie down in the wisdom and power of the King of Righteousnesse in rest and peace.

Secondly, In the fulnesse of time; that is, when all flesh hath corrupted his wayes; then the King or Sun of Righteousnesse arises up, and lets man in his light to see himself to be a devil. The King layes no hand upon him, but lets him see himself; and the mans own works become the devils that torment him. If a man have sore eyes, and look in the Sun, his eyes smart; now that smart comes not from the Sun, but the venome of the eyes rises up & torments [89] it self, when the Sun causes it to see or feel it self.

This declares the wisdom, power, Justice and holinesse of the King, that when he rises he can make flesh to see it self, and needs do no more, but shine forth and burn in his brightnesse, by whom that curse or drosse in the flesh is consumed and cannot stand; therefore if flesh were righteous it would stand before the righteous Law; but seeing it cannot stand, it appears unrighteous, to be a devil and no Angel of light.

And this method of the Father brings glory to his own name, that he alone is the one almighty power and wisdom.

This is Justice in the righteous Judge, and shews him to be the pure Law, and flesh kils and torments it self.

I, but when the waters drowned the world, and the fire burned *Sodom*, this was a Judgement more then letting flesh see his own unrighteousnesse. I answer, The overflowings of the water in that manner to drown, and the breakings forth of the fire in that manner to burn, waste and consume, were the rising up of the curse that was in the water and fire, to destroy the unrighteous flesh of man, that caused it.

For when the Father made the Creation, he made all Elements to uphold one another in Righteousnesse, and one creature to preserve another; therefore it was all very good. But this rising up of creatures to destroy one another is the curse, which unrighteous man, that is, the Lord of the creatures, hath brought upon the Creation.

I, but how comes the fire and water to break forth to destroy at some times more then another?

I answer, When the fulnesse of time comes, that earth begins to stink with the abominations of man, then the Father arises up and shews himself within the Creation of fire, water, earth and air. And [90] the curse that is brought upon this by man cannot abide the presence of the Lord, but rises up and runs together into a head to oppose the Lord; but indeed it destroyes man that was the cause of it. So that the risings up of waters, and the breakings forth of fire to waste and destroy, are but that curse, or the works of mans own hands, that rise up and run together to destroy their Maker, and torment him that brought the curse forth.

While water and fire are useful, the blessing of the Creation lies in them, and comes from them to preserve the Creation for the glory of the Maker.

But when they break forth to waste and destroy, this is the curse, the burden of the Creation, that breaks forth to destroy unrighteous man that caused it.

And it doth break forth when the Lord appears in the Creation; as I said, when the Sun shines the venome in sore eyes rises up and smarts: So when righteous power begins to move in the fire, and upon the water, the curse that is in these Elements arises up and disturbs the Creation, to the destruction of man whose work it is.

I, but one man kils another by wars, and such like, Is not this the wrath of God upon them?

I answer in the same manner as I did before; for as the cursed flesh in one body torments it self, when he sees himself a devil,

So multitudes of bodies of men are still but one flesh, or one earth: And when the Sun of Righteousnesse begins to shine into this earth, the venimous parts rise up to kill and destroy light, but in the end the flesh destroyes it self.

Let the power of humility and Righteousnesse appear to a proud, unrighteous, covetous man, and shew him his evil, as in these dayes it doth, he swels [91] presently, and rises up to make war to maintain himself to be an Angel of light; and pride being dispersed into divers bodies, cannot yield one to another, to preserve one another, but rise up to destroy each other in the light of the Sun: The Sun shines, and the dunghill casts up his stinking smell: The Lord he shines, and proud flesh kils one another; flesh kils but it self.

And truly I must tell you, That all these wars, and killing one another are but the rising up of the curse: destroying Armies of men are but the curse, the burden which the Creation groans under: For in the beginning, all was very good, and the Creation at first was made to preserve it self; and this rising up to destroy the Creation, is the curse.

And the Spirit of the Father, that dwels in any humane body that is killed, doth run into the Ocean of life, and purifies the Creation from the curse.

But did not God send the *Chaldeans* and *Sabeans* to punish *Job?* Yes, the god Devil did; but not the God of Righteousnesse: For the Devil desired a libertie to try *Iob*, and the righteous power, Reason, gave him leave; onely told him, he should not touch his life; and then the Devil sends these enemies, and burns his house, and kils his children; give but libertie to the curse, and he doth much mischief.

Who was it that the god Devil did afflict? Not an enemy to the King of Righteousnesse, but a body in whom he dwelt: Yea, the Father did but suffer himself to be persecuted by the Devil, in that humane body *Iob:* That at last, that power of darknesse, which is the Accuser of the Brethren, and the bondage of the Creation, might be made manifest in the light of the Sun, and so be cast out justly.

Now the end of all is this, that unrighteous flesh that thinks himself an Angel of light, and the onely [92] power, may be proved to be a

Devil, and so be cast out of the Creation and perish: That Jacob, the King of Righteousnesse, the blessing of peace, might arise up and reign for ever in the Creation, when all enemies are subdued under his feet.

There is a time appointed of the righteous Judge, that all flesh shall see it self in its own colours; and when the flesh doth see it self in his own beastly shapes, he will appear so deformed, so piteous a confused Chaos of miserie and shame, that the sight thereof shall be a great torment to himself.

Therefore take notice of this, you proud, envious, covetous, bitter-spirited, and unrighteous men and women; this self-satisfying glory in which you live, and seem to have rest, shall become your hell-torment, when you are made to see your unrighteous, treacherous self, as you must when the Judge sits upon the Throne.

You that are now ashamed to own the righteous spirit, and fear to offend men, lest they should either reproch you, or injure you: And so will do any thing, though unrighteous, to preserve the good words of devilish men; you shall then see you are not men, not Saints, but Devils and cursed enemies, even the Serpents power, that must be burned.

CHAP. XII.

ALL these declare the half hours silence, that is to be in Heaven; for all mouths are to be stopped by the power of Reasons Law shining within the heart: And this abundance of talk that is amongst people, by Arguments, by disputes, by declaring expositions upon others word and writing, by long discourse, called preaching, shall all cease. *Rev.* 8. 1. *Ier.* 31. 34.

[93] Some shal not be able to speak, they shal be struck silent with shame, by seeing themselves in a losse, and in confusion: Neither shal they dare to speak, til they know by experience within themselves what to speak; but wait with a quiet silence upon the Lord, til he break forth within their hearts, and give them words and power to speak.

And this shal be a mark of a covetous, proud and close Hypocrite, to be ful of words, preaching by arguments and expositions, putting a meaning upon other mens words and writings, telling stories by hear-say of what they have read and heard from men, as the fashion is now in publique work.

For none shal dare to speak (unlesse it be those that are sealed to destruction) but what they understand in pure experience; every one speaking his own words, not another mans, as the Preachers do, to make a trade of it; for he that speaks from tradition and imagination, and makes a trade of his preaching to others, to get a living by, is a child of the curse, and covetousnesse is his Lord.

Men must leave off teaching one another, and the eies of all shal look upwards to the Father, to be taught of him: And at this time, silence shal be a mans rest and libertie, it is the gathering time, the souls receiving time, it is the forerunner of pure language. 1. *Ioh.* 2. 27.

None shal be offended at this, but the covetous and proud Serpent; and he wil vex and fret, if the people wil not heare him preach; and think he hath much wrong done him, if he be slighted. Wel Judas, thou must be slighted, thy preaching stinks before the Father, and he wil draw his people out of thy confusion, and leave thee naked and bare, and thy shame shall be made manifest to the whole Creation, for indeed thou art the curse.

While a man is busying his head in studying what [94] hath been done in *Moses* time, in the Prophets time, in the Apostles, and in the Son of mans time, called Jesus the Anointed, and doth not wait to find light and power of righteousnesse to arise up within his heart,

This man is a piteous, barren creature, though he have all the learning of Arts and Sciences under the Sun; for the knowledge of Arts is but to speak methodically of what hath been; and conjecture what shal be; both which are uncertain to the Speaker: But he that speaks from the original light within, can truly say, I know what I say and I know whom I worship.

This silence shal be both particular in every son and daughter, and general in the practice of all before their eies; and looking upwards and waiting for teaching from the great and only Teacher, Christ, the great Prophet; for truly the time is come, that all flesh shal be made silent, and leave off multiplying of words without knowledge before the Lord, both in preaching and praying.

And your Preachers shal be all the objects of the Creation through which the Father wil convey himself into you, and manifest himself before you: these shal be your outward Preachers.

And the same word of power speaking in, and to your hearts, causing your hearts to open to his voyce, shall be your Teacher within: And that mouth that stands up to teach others, and doth not declare the Lord in a pure language, shall bear his shame, whosoever he be.

None shall need to turn over books and writings (for indeed all these shal cease too) to get knowledge; but every one shal be taken off from seeking knowledge from without, and with an humble, quiet heart, wait upon the Lord, til he manifest himself; for he is a great King, and worthy to be waited upon.

[95] His testimony within, fils the soul with joy and singing; he gives first experience: and then power to speak forth those experiences. And hence you shal speak to the rejoycing one of another, and to the praise of him that declares his power in you; he that speaks his thoughts, studies and imagination, and stands up to be a Teacher of others, shal be judged for his unrighteousnesse, because he seeks to honour flesh, and does not honour the Lord. 2. *Cor.* 12. 13.

Behold the Anointing that is to teach all things, is comming to create new Heavens, and new Earth, wherein Righteousness dwels; and there shal not be a vessel of humane earth, but it shal be filled with Christ.

If you were possible to have so many buckets as would contain the whole Ocean, every one is filled with the Ocean, and perfect water is in all; and being put all together, make up the perfect Ocean, which filled them all.

Even so, Christ, who is the spreading power, is now beginning to fil every man and woman with himself; he wil dwel and rule in every one, and the law of reason & equitie shal be Christ in them; every single body is a star shining forth of him, or rather a body in and out of whom he shines; and he is the Ocean of power that fils all. *Eph.* 1. 23. *Ch.* 4. 5. 6. *Ro.* 8. 23.

And so the words are true, the Creation man-kinde, shal be the fulnesse of him that fils all in all: This is the Church, the great Congregation, that when the mysterie is compleated, shal be the mystical body of Christ all set at libertie from inward and outward straits and bondage: And this is called the holy breathing, that hath made all new by himself, and for himself.

Before this truth be believed in by mankinde, you shal see much troubles in the great world; the first *Adam* wil strive mightily before he loose his [96] Kingdom; he can pretty quietly hear, that Christ will rule in sons and daughters that are scattered abroad.

But to hear that the Kingdoms of the world shal be Christ's Dominions likewise, and that the material earth shall be his possession, as well as the earth mankind; O this cuts *Adam* to the heart; all the world will storm and be angry, when this is made known. *Rev.* 11. 15, 18.

Wars and rumours of wars will multiply; Father will be against Son, and Son against Father, the love of many shall wax cold; and zealous professours, that live without the spirit, shall become the most bitter enemies to Christ, and prove very treacherous, self-seeking, self-loving, ful of subtil policy to waste and wear out every one that seeks to advance Christ, by their bitternesse and oppression: But all in vain, for Christ must rise, and the powers of the flesh must fall.

CHAP. XIII.

FROM what hath been hitherto spoken, if there were no experience to prove it, it appears, that the first *Adam* or fleshly man, seeks life, peace and glory to himself, from creatures and things that are without him. As first, he seeks content and peace from wife, children, friends, riches, places of dominion over others, and from such like: But that peace that is built upon such hay and stubble-foundations, will fall and come to nothing. 1. *Cor.* 3. 12.

Secondly, the fleshly man seeks content and peace from Sermons, Prayers, Studies, Books, Church-fellowship, and from outward Forms and Customs [97] in Divine Worship: But that peace that is built upon this foundation of gold, silver and pretious stones, will fall and come to nothing likewise. *Ro.* 9. 31. *Isa.* 28. 9.

All creatures teats are to be dried up, that the soul can suck no refreshing milk from them, before the Lord teach it knowledge.

Some there are, nay almost every one, wonders after the Beast, or fleshly man; they seek for new *Jerusalem*, the City of *Sion*, or Heaven, to be above the skies, in a locall place, wherein there is all glory, and the beholding of all excellent beauty, like the seeing of a show or a mask before a man: And this not to be seen neither by the eies of the body till the body be dead: A strange conceit.

But, poor Creatures, you are deceived; this expectation of glory without you, will vanish, you shall never see it; this outward heaven is not the durable Heaven; this is a fancy which your false Teachers put into your heads to please you with, while they pick your purses, and betray your Christ into the hands of flesh, and hold *Jacob* under to be a servant still to Lord *Esau.*

Wel, what a man sees or hears to day, may be gone to morrow; all outward glory that is at a distance from the five senses, and taken in by a representation, is of a transient nature; and so is the Heaven that your Preachers tell you of.

But when the second *Adam* rises up in the heart, he makes a man to see Heaven within himself, and to judge all things that are below him: He makes many bodies to be the declarers of him, who is the one power of righteousnesse that rules therein: And this is Heaven that will not fail us, endurable riches, treasures that shall not wax old, and where moth and rust cannot corrupt, nor thieves break through and steal: This Christ is within you, your everlasting rest and glory.

[98] And as the man of the flesh fetches in comforts from without, seeking content in and from Creatures, and Creature-objects; so he envies every one that crosses his desires; crosse him in his pride, covetousnesse and uncleannesse, and he grows extream angry at every body; tell him that his formall and customary preaching and praying, is but self-seeking, not setting up the Lord, and he is filled with rage against those that tel him so.

But he never looks within to check himself, he takes no remedy there at all, and lets those Devils lie quiet within; and if any be sent, I say, from the Lord, to disturb those his lusts, he will disturb that messenger, if he can; but he will cherish himself within: He thinks that whatsoever he doth is good, and that whatsoever crosses that power that is in his heart, doth crosse the Lord.

But truly it is no other but the Serpents power, which must be destroyed; he fetches in content from the Creatures that are without him; and his envy and discontent runs after things and Creatures that are without, which crosses his fleshly desires.

But now the man of righteousnesse, Christ, when he rises up in the heart, he loves all that are without him; and he envies none but the Serpent within, which troubles the Creation; and so is quite different to the other.

For as soon as Christ is rose up in a man, the first thing he doth, he takes revenge of the pride, lust, envy, covetousnesse, which ruled within the flesh, and casts that Serpent and Dragon out of Heaven: That is, out of that part of the Creation; and makes a man to cry out upon himself, and to hate and abhor his cursed lusts, which lead him captive.

He makes a man to look abroad with the eie of pitty and compassion to fellow-Creatures; but to look with the eie of hatred and loathing upon the [99] Serpent, his unclean lusts, desiring nothing so much as the death of the body of sin within. So that the law of righteousnesse may reigne in peace in his soul: O thou cursed envy, cursed rash anger, cursed uncleannesse: O cursed Devil, cursed Father of lies, that will not suffer Christ to rise up and reign: O thou enemy of all righteousnesse, thou wicked one, thou curse, thou power of darknesse, thou fleshly power, thou shalt be destroyed and subdued under Christ's feet, whom thou fightest against. *Zach*. 4. 7.

The greatest combate is within a man, when the King sits upon the Throne, judging unrighteous flesh, and bruising that Serpents head. And though this be trouble and torment for a time to the Creature, yet Christ at last will sit down in him, who is Prince of peace, and King of righteousnesse. *Rev*. 4. 2.

The created flesh of man is the Beast, the King of Beasts; the same principles as are in other Creatures, are in humane flesh: The difference between man and other beasts, is this, The flesh of man is made an understanding Soul, capable to know Reason, and to walk in his light: Other beasts cannot.

Now the wise flesh is meerly selfish, he seeks himself in every thing he doth, and would be a Lord and Ruler, not only over the Beasts of the field, but over creatures of his own kind, whom his Maker made equall to himself; and so strives to fetch in all other Creatures, to advance his content, though it be to the losse and misery of other men.

This is the Beast, Lord *Esau*, the wise and covetous, self-seeking flesh, that hath sold his birth-right and blessing to *Jacob*, for the pleasure of unrighteousnesse a small time: And now he must be turned out, and deliver all up to *Jacob*, and he is extreamly vext, and will not yield quiet possession, but stand out stifly, till he be cast out, by the universall power of Reasons law.

[100] Now the rule and dominion of Jacob doth not bring losse and misery to any; his law is so established in love, that the whole Creation finds peace under it, sorrow and tears, beggary and oppression shall be done away, and the blessing of the Lord Jacob shall fill the earth. *Gen*. 18. 18.

So then we see, that the great battell of God Almighty, is between this selfish power, the Beast and fleshy man; and the universall power, Christ, the man of righteousnesse; for the flesh would be wiser then its Maker: for though his Maker would have the whole Creation, and every creature to enjoy the benefit of their Creation, and to live free from straits comfortably: Yet the wise and covetous flesh seeks to live free in honour and quiet in himself, & makes laws to imprison, kill and waste every one, that will not conforme to his selfish Government. *Rev.* 19. 19.

Now the Father wil destroy the Beast in the open field by fair play, and hath given him all advantages as may be; for he hath given the Beast the dominion, and himself is a Servant under his dominion, and will undermine the wise and covetous Beast, by righteous sufferings, and acting as a Servant: And the Father encounters with the Beast or Dragon, in a three-fold posture of war.

As First, by the Sacrifices under the Law, the Spirit thereby declared the destruction of the Beast; and the Spirit lay hid under those types and shadows, fighting against the Beast; and the wise flesh in those daies fought against his Maker: This is a distance of Cannon-shot.

Secondly, In the prison of Jesus Christ, the Lamb, the Father fought against the Beast: and killed him; for the Dragon was cast out of that Heaven or Creation, in whom the Father dwelt bodily; for that flesh was wholly made subject to the Spirit; this was at a closer distance closing in the Front: But [101] the wise flesh hath many strong holds, even the multitudes of men and women, which he fortifies against the Spirit.

And therefore in the third posture, which is now begun, the Father encounters, and wil encounter with the Beast every where: that is, with the wise but covetous, unrighteous flesh, in every son and daughter; and so bruise that Serpents head in the whole body of his Army.

And before he hath done, he wil fire all the strong-holds of this murderer, so that he shall not have a place to keep garrison in; for the Father will subdue the whole bulk of man-kind, and make all that living earth subject to himself, and fil all with holy breathing: This is the spreading of the Anointing: This is the glory of the Elect One; glorious things are spoken of thee, O thou City of God.

This holy breathing is the Kingdom of Heaven within you, when he rules within you, and the Kingdom of Heaven without you likewise, when you see the same glory rule in others, in which you rejoyce: And this is the last encounter the Father wil have with the Dragon.

This is the great day of Judgment (judging and condemning, and putting the Serpent to death every where). This is the day of Christs power, in which he wil subdue all his enemies under his feet, & deliver up the Kingdom to his Father.

Therefore marvel not to see the people turn from one way of worship to another; for the Father is driving this people through al the waies, and forms, and customs, and reformation, and governments of the Beast, to weary them out in all; that so they may find rest for the soles of their feet no where, in no outward form of worship; til they come to lye down in him (forsaking all forms) to worship the Father in spirit and truth; that is, to walk righteously in the Creation.

[102] And this restlesnesse of people, running from one form and custome to another, meeting with confusion and curse every where, is no other but the dividing of time, the half day or image of the Beast, which is the last period of his time: Then saith the Angel, It is done; time to the Beast shall be no more.

And while it is thus, poor Creatures they are in bondage within, for they know not what to do; the way to Sion is not yet cleare, and they are filled with sighings and secret mournings, to see themselves in confusion and losse, to stick in the mire, but cannot come out: This is inward slaverie, under which they lie. *Psa.* 40. 2.

Then, poor Creatures, they are under an outward bondage, under the hand of Tyrant flesh, that rules the Kingdom, and that divises the several fleshy forms and waies of government, to which if any refuse to conform, then they must be imprisoned, reproached or tortured by punishments in what kind or other, by the hands of fellow Creatures, that are the oppressing Task-masters under the Tyrant flesh; so that weak spirits are kept under in awe, either by fear or shame: And thus *Iacob* hath been very low, but he must rise.

For the Antichristian Captivitie is expiring, many have attained to inward freedom already, they wait upon the Lord for outward freedom, that the yoke may be taken off their backs: *Israel's* Captivitie in the 70 years in *Babylon*, was but a type of this Antichristian slavery under L. *Esau*, the powers of the flesh, that compasses mankind about with many straits & dangers, for acknowledging his Maker.

But as every thing hath his growth, his raign, and end, so must this slavery have an end; The proud and covetous hearts cry, what slavery is this? we know not what he speaks: It is true you do not know; [103]

but they who have lesse or more attained to the resurrection of the dead know what I say; and shall rejoyce in the declaration of this power, waiting the Lords leisure with a calm silence, til he hath gathered together our brethren that must partake of the blessing with us.

CHAP. XIV.

To see the Divine power in the Creation-objects is sweet; but to see him ruling in the heart is sweeter: The first sight is at a distance far off, as to see him in meat, drink, cloaths, friends, victories, riches, prosperity, to see him in the Sun, Moon, Stars, Clouds, Grasse, Trees, Cattle, and all the Earth, how he hath sweetly caused every one of these to give in assistance to preserve each other Creature: Or rather how he himself in these gives forth preservation and protection from one another, and so unites the whole Creation together, by the unity of himself.

Or further, to see the Divine power in prayer, in Discourse, in Communion of Saints, in Reading, in every sweet and refreshing that a man meets within, all these, is the Almighty Comforter: But this is to behold that glory abroad, to see and meet him from home, to behold him in Creatures without us: which sight and enjoyment is often, and may be totally lost and the soul left alone again, and so filled with mourning in his absence, O when shal I see my beloved, whom my soul loves.

The Spouse had seen Christ in the manner aforesaid, but she had lost him again; for if she had never seen him, she could not have called him her Beloved, and mourn in his absence. Let a man [104] eat never so hearty a dinner, yet within a few hours he wil be empty again and ready to languish; and thus all comforts that are taken in from any creature without us, may be, nay wil be, must be lost, that so a man may come to know the Lord.

But now to see the King sitting in his banqueting-house, to see the Law of Righteousnesse and peace ruling and dwelling in the heart, and to be refreshed with those sweet-smelling spices, the discoveries of the Fathers love within; This is the Word of God; This is sweeter then the honey or the honey-comb, for this is to see him near at hand, even within the heart ruling and resting there.

This is the Kingdome of heaven within you; This is the city of

refuge that wil not fail a man; This is the Rock of defence and offence; This the power that makes a man bold as a Lion; If a man be
cast into any straits, his heart dies not like *Nabals* the man of the flesh;
but he feels peace and content within, and so is at rest.

Let come what wil come, the man knows it is the wil of the Father
it shal be so, and he feels a quiet peace compasse his heart, so that he
seeth and feeleth peace within; and rejoyceth in the excellency of it,
he seeth and feeleth love and patience within, and rejoyceth in the
glory of that sweet ointment, that doth cast a delightful savour all
his soul over.

Now though this man be in prison, be in straits, be forsaken of all
his friends in the flesh, none wil buy nor sell with him, because they
count him a man of strange opinions and blasphemies, call him an
Atheist, a sot, a Papist, a blasphemer that hath forsaken God and
goodnesse, because he wil neither preach nor pray, nor say grace when
he sitteth down to meat, as the custome of Professours are,

Yet this man is not alone, for his Father is with [105] him, The
Father lives in him, and he lives in the Father.

The Father wil have his people, whom he draws up to worship
him in spirit and truth, to be secret and silent; to be slow of speech
for a little season, yet quick-sighted and Eagle-eyed, though they be
silent, they are not sottish drones, they shall discern and judge others
righteously, though others shall not discern and judge them, but by
rash censure, which is not righteous.

The righteous actions and patient silence, of those that are drawn
up to wait upon the Lord, shall be the greatest shame and condemnation to the ignorant professours and talking people, that ever broke
out. The wise flesh that would be an Angel of light, is full of words,
but dead to the Law of Righteousnesse. The Saints must die to waste
words, but be made alive to Righteousnesse, walking uprightly in the
Creation, to the glory of the Maker of all things; hereby Lord *Esau*
will be under-mined, and his house and Kingdom wil fall about his
ears.

For though the man of the flesh be altogether for outward preaching, praying, observation of forms and customs, and knows not how
to worship, if these be taken away: he hath no peace if these be gone.

But now the man of Righteousnesse sees death in all outward forms,
if the inward power be wanting; therfore his eye is stil inward, to see

the Law of Righteousnesse ruling there, and guiding the body to be a profitable member in the Creation. And this is the most excellent sight, to see the divine power in ones self, ruling, dwelling and living within; which if it doe, that body wherein it dwels, shal be wholly subject in al his [acts?] to that Law of Righteousnesse.

They that know what the power of love and the Law of Righteousnesse is, they know what I say, and [106] can understand me; but to others these reports sound strangely, and may draw words of reproach and slander from them; but it matters not, they cannot hurt.

They that live in the light, they see the Lord abroad, and they see him at home, they see him in other creatures, and they see and feel him in their own hearts, in patient and quiet submitting, to what is his will; so that there is a sweet agreement between the disposing hand of God without, and his power within.

He that thus sees the Lord, the antient of daies, the one Almighty power, doth mightily honour him; when nothing can be done abroad, either in adversity or prosperity, but the divine power that rules in the heart, consents, rejoyces and grudges not. And now the Lord is one, and his name or power one, every where.

The sight of the King of Glory within, lies not in the strength of memory, calling to mind what a man hath read and heard, being able by a humane capacity to joyn things together into a method; & through the power of free utterance, to hold it forth before others, as the fashion of Students is in their Sermon work; which a plough man that was never bred in their Universities may do as much; nay, they do more in this kind (as experience shews us) then they that take Tythes to tell a story.

But the sight of the King within, lies in the beholding of light arising up from an inward power of feeling experience, filling the soul with the glory of the Law of Righteousnesse, which doth not vanish like the taking in of words and comfort from the mouth of a hearsay Preacher, or strength of memory.

But it continues like the Sunne in the firmament shining forth, from that established power [107] of the divine within, and the enlivened heart shall as soon be seperated from glorying in the Law of Righteousnesse that dwels in him; as the heat and light of the Sunne, can be seperated from the Sunne.

And truly let me tell you, That as a man finds abundance of sweet peace in his heart, when he is made to live in the Kingdome of heaven: So the words that this man speaks from this power within, are very profitable to others, & are good seed; wheresoever they are sown, they will spring up and bring forth fruit, for words spoken from the light of experience, have a two-fold operation upon the heart of the hearers.

For first, if I lie under straits and bondage in my spirit, by reason of some inward and outward troubles, but especially by reason of the enthraldome to my own lusts that over-powers me, so that I cannot do what I would,

Then the words of experience from the mouth of one that hath been in that condition, and is passed thorow it, sounds liberty and life to my weary soul; I speak what I have felt in this particular.

Secondly, If I delight in any way of the flesh, as to seek peace in creatures abroad without me, or to seek satisfaction to my envy, self-will and lust; and in the midst of this my folly I do occasionally hear the words of experience from some other, declaring such actions and motions to be the powers of the flesh and devil, and not of the spirit of righteousnesse,

Presently those words take peace from the earth; that is, from proud flesh; and fill the whole soul with anger, distemper, grudging, and torment. And this is another operation that pure language produces, which is a launcing of the dead flesh that the disease may be cured.

[108] For this wounding is not to the ruine of the creature, but it is a medicine sent from the Lord to heal him; to take away the evil peace from the flesh, that so the created part may lie down in rest, and be at peace in Christ, which cannot be moved.

For every comfort that is of the flesh shall be shaken and removed, but Christ the one power of Righteousnesse and peace, shall not be shaken nor moved, but stand firm for ever. And by this you may see the difference between the kingdom of the flesh and devil, which must be shaken to pieces and fall: And the kingdom of heaven or of God, that endures for ever, and is that Rock that cannot be moved.

CHAP. XV.

W HAT do you mean by the kingdom of devil or flesh?

I answer, Covetousnesse, the selfish power ruling in a man, is the kingdome of darknesse in that man: And as this power hath corrupted the Creation (mankind) so it rules, or hath ruled in every single one more or lesse; but is the curse. And every one that hath lain under the bondage of this selfish power, and is in any measure delivered, he can from that experience declare, what the power of darknesse is in whole mankind, as I have shewed how secretly and closely this selfish power branches himself forth in every one, till by the light of Reasons Law shining within, he is discovered and cast out.

But what is it for a man to live in the kingdom of hell, devil or darknesse?

I answer, when a man takes delight in nothing but in satisfying of the lusts of his own heart; when [109] the way of the flesh is pleasing, and the way of the spirit of Righteousnesse is a burden to him; when he glories in himself, and feeds with delight upon his covetousnesse, pride, envy, lust, self-will, and in every thing that pleaseth flesh.

And if he can but overcome that power that checks or crosses his will, O then this man is in his Kingdome, he rejoyces and is very well pleased, but it is the kingdome of the flesh, that must be shaken and removed; This is no other but the glorying in that which is a mans shame.

What is the kingdom of Heaven, or of Christ?

Ans. The Law of Righteousnesse and peace, ruling and dwelling in mankind, is the kingdom of heaven, this is the universall power bearing rule, treading the flesh-power under his feet.

What is it for a man to live in the kingdom of heaven?

Ans. When mankind or any single person is so made subject to the King of righteousnesse, that all his delight is to walk according to that law towards every creature in the Creation, through love to the Fathers honour that made al. He glories in that law of righteousness, which he finds seated in his heart, & finds content no where else; and when the Spirit is honoured, this man is in his kingdom, he hath what he would have.

While the kingdom of darknesse rules in a man, if he knows it not, his sin is the lesse, but when he comes to know the lusts of his flesh, and delight therein, in opposition to the righteous Law which he sees some light in also; this makes the man exceeding sinfull, for now he sins against the law of light shining in him, and causing him to see himself.

Even so when the divine power rules in a man, and he knows it not, as it may be in some measure, this mans joy is but small; for a man may act [110] from the power of love and righteousnesse, and yet not see nor know the excellency of that power which guides him.

But when a man is made to see and know the law of love and right-eousnesse within him, and delights to act from that power of life and liberty, which he seeth and feeleth seated in him, Now this man is carried on with much joy and sweet calmness, meeknesse and modera-tion, and is full of glory. This is the excellency of the work of Christ, not onely to make flesh subject to righteousnesse, but to know himself made subject, & to rejoyce in the sweet enjoyment of that prince of peace to make a man rejoyce, & to know the ground of his joy is un-moveable.

What do you mean by divine, and divine power?

I answer, The divine is the spreading power of righteousnesse, which is Christ that filleth the whole Creation with himself.

And he is called a tree or a vine, because he doth not lie in one single person, but spreads himself in mankind, and every single body in whom he breaths, is but a bough or bud of the vine.

So that look upon all together in whom Christ is spread, and they make up but one vine, knit together by that one spirit, into one body; whether they be poor or rich; learned or unlearned; and therefore those rich men that despise the poor; and those learned University men that despise the unlearned, are pricks of the thorn-bush, not branches of the vine; they be the curse that is now near to burning.

And every single one alone in whom Christ breaths, is but a parcel of the vine, in whom the divine power dwels and rests: Even as every branch of an Apple-tree, is filled with the sap, which is the life of the whole tree.

Christ is said to be the divine, because he grows [111] and flour-ishes in the time of light; he is the Sonne himself; he is a vine or tree that grows by day in the heat of light, and so brings forth abundance of fruit to the glory of the Father; Trees that grow in the heat of the Sun bring forth pleasant fruit.

So those that are branches of this vine, that grows in the heat and life of one spirit the King of Righteousnesse, bring forth abundance of the fruit of Righteousnesse, according to the nature of the vine they grow from.

Therefore the Saints are called, Children of the day, not of the night; for they speak what they know in experience, and what they have received feelingly from the Lord; and their actions and words are not at random, for they act Righteousness within the Creation, from the law of Reason and Righteousnesse, which they feel seated within.

Every one that doth act or speak from the light and power of the day-vine within himself, can give an account of his words and actions: But this is the glory, that *Adam*, the man of the flesh hides himself from: This is the Law of Righteousnesse, which fleshly Israel could not behold: This is the new Covenant which our Clergie is unacquainted with.

Now opposite to this Divine, which is Christ, there is a night-vine, which is the power of selfishnesse, or the bottomlesse pit spread abroad in mankind; And every man and woman that is guided by this selfish power of darknesse, are but branches of the night-vine.

And this night-vine which I called Lord *Esau*, or fleshly man, hath filled the whole earth with darknesse (under pretence of his learning and fleshly Government) so that he is a spread tree. But he is called by the Spirit, the Thorn-bush.

The fruit that he brings forth is sour and bitter, and good for nothing but the dunghill; for trees that [112] grow alwayes in the shade or place of darknesse, where the heat and light of the Sun doth not cooperate, brings forth unpleasant fruit.

Now this night-vine (but rather Thorn-bush) is the branchings forth of the wisdom and power of selfish flesh: every bud from it, is a sharp prickle: treacherous & covetous *Judas*, is one branch from that root, and he hath risen up to a mighty great tree; for every treacherous and covetous heart, is but the buddings forth of *Judas*.

So envious Scribes & Pharisees, are other branches from the same root, & these have risen up into mighty spreading trees; for every one that is zealous without knowledge, making a profession of the spirit of righteousnesse, & yet grudging and hating the way of the spirit, are but the buddings forth of the Scribes & Pharisees, that killed Christ after the flesh, and now is spread in every Land and Family, to hinder Christ from rising, or else to suppresse and kill him againe if they could after he is risen up in sons and daughters.

So covetous *Demas*, proud *Simon Magus*, froward *Nabal*, unrighteous *Elimas*, and such like, are all the buddings forth of the thornbush, and have covered the earth with their branches, to keep it in darknesse, and to hide the Sun of Righteousnesse from it.

And all these are centred in the Clergy, the Universities are the standing ponds of stinking waters, that make those trees grow, the curse of ignorance, confusion and bondage spreads from hence all the Nations over.

The paying of tythes, the greatest sin of oppression, is upheld by them; pride, covetousnesse, idlenesse, bitternesse of spirit, despising and treading all under-foot; in whom the spirit of the Lamb appears, is upheld by them; these are the standing enemies against Christ.

[113] Their Churches are the successours of the *Jews* Synagogues, and are houses of bondage; their Universities are successours of the *Scribes* and *Pharisees* houses of learning. And though they persecuted Christ and the Apostles, and would own none of their Doctrines; yet when they found that Christs Doctrines began to fill the earth, and to make the way of the Law odious, and their trade began to fail,

Then did those houses of learning begin to take in and own the writings of the Apostles, and to own that doctrine, prevailing with the Magistracy through the deceit of their subtilety, to establish tythes in their hands still for their maintainance (though Christs doctrine threw down that oppression). And then from legall Sacrificers, they became hearsay-Preachers of the Gospel, not from any testimony of light within themselves, but from the writings of the Apostles, which they professe great love to, and keep charily, for their tythes sake; and by the one they deceive the souls of people, for they preach the letter for the Spirit, and by the other they pick their purses.

And this is very manifest by their carriage; for though those writings which they live by, were not writings that proceeded from any Schollars, according to humane art, but from Fishermen, Shepherds, Husbandmen, and the Carpenters son, who spake and writ as the Spirit gave them utterance, from an inward testimony,

Yet now these learned schollars have got the writings of these inferior men of the world so called, do now slight, despise and trample
them under feet, pressing upon the powers of the earth, to make laws
to hold them under bondage, and that lay-people, trades-men, and
such as are not bred in schools, may have no liberty to speak or write
of the Spirit.

And why so? Because out of these despised ones, [114] doth the
spirit rise up more and more to clearer light, making them to speak
from experience; and every fresh discovery of the Father, shines
more glorious then the old, till at last the creature is made to see the
Father face to face in his own light.

But now the learned schollars having no inward testimony of their
own to uphold their trade by a customary practice, they hold fast the
old letter, getting their living by telling the people the meanings of
those trades-mens words and writings; but alas, they mightily corrupt
their meaning, by their multitude of false expositions and interpretations; for no man knows the meaning of the spirit, but he that hath
the spirit.

And if the Father send forth any of these tradesmen, to declare
the testimony which is in them: as in these dayes he sends forth many.
And these true labourers shall encrease, let the Universitie men do
the worst they can; yet the Schollars seek to suppresse them, calling
them new-lights, factious, erroneous, blasphemers, and the like.

And why do they all this? Because the light of truth that springs
up out of this earth, which the schollars tread under feet, will shine so
clear, as it will put out the candle of those wicked learned deceivers.

And therefore many of them that are more ingenious or subtile
then the rest, seeing light arises much amongst the people, begin to
comply with the people, and give people their liberty to speak as well
as they, and denie the tithes upon this condition, the people will give
them a free contribution, and own them as the chief Preachers and
Prophets sent of God, and to look upon themselves as underlings to
the schollars.

And therefore stir up people to gather into Congregations, and to
make choice of one man to be [115] their Preacher, though they shall
have a liberty to speak in the Congregation as well as he. But all this
is but deceit of the flesh, to draw people under a new bondage, and
to uphold the hearsay-preaching, that in time matters may be wheeled

about again, to advance the schollars, and give them the supremacy in teaching.

And what is the end of all this; but onely to hinder Christ the great Prophet from rising, and whereas people should all look up to him for teaching, and acknowledge no other teacher and ruler but Christ, the Law of Righteousnesse dwelling in every mans heart; the schollars would have the people to look up to them for teaching; and truly let me speak what I find, the more that you look upon them, or any men for teaching, the more you shall be wrapped up in confusion and bondage.

And therefore the upshot of all your Universities and publick Preachers, and men-teachers, is onely to hinder Christ from rising, and to keep *Jacob* under, and make him a servant and a slave to the man of the flesh.

So that all this [to] do in the world about hear-say preaching and setled forms of worship, is no other but the spreadings forth of the thorn-bush, the fleshly man, to hinder the worship of the Father in spirit and truth: And all those strict and zealous Preachers and Professours of other mens words and writings, and upholders of forms and customs, are no other but the Scribes, Pharisees and *Judas*, that still pursue Christ in enmity.

And this is the Reason, why man-kind are so ignorant, and cold-spirited, in the acknowledgment of the Father; because the night-Vine, or branches of the Thorn-bush, are so mighty great and thick, that they hide the light and heat of the Sun of Righteousnesse from it.

[116] This is the man of sin, the mysterie of iniquity, that lets and must let, till he be taken out of the way: Indeed this Thorn-bush doth so prick, that none dares meddle with it, unlesse he be well cloathed with Christ.

This Thorn-bush or night-Vine, grows in the cold time of the night, while the Sun of Righteousnesse is under the Clouds; and the fruit it brings forth is unpleasant, as pride, covetousnesse, envy, self-love, hypocrisie, confusion, bondage, and all the misery under the power of darknesse, to make Lord *Esau* a compleat Tyrant; and they that act from this Vine, are called children of the night.

Now from hence it appears, what horrible proud men the Clergie are, that call themselves Divines; or Christ that grows in the light of the Father, when alas their light is but a candle stoln from the Apostles and Prophets writings, it is not their own light, it is but hear-say in them.

Surely their pride and covetousnesse declares them to be the false Christs and false Prophets, and that they are branches of the Thorn-bush, that are full of sharp pricks, in regard they endeavour to uphold a forced maintenance from the people, whether they will or no; and force the people to be silent, to hear them preach hear-say: and not to gainsay or question what they say under pain of punishment, or being counted factious, or sowers of sedition.

This is the bondage the people are under, by these publique Preach-ers: First, they are filled with confusion, by their saying and un-saying, for they know not what they say; they darken knowledge by their words. Secondly, they are like to be crushed in their estates, by the power of corrupt Magistrates, if they oppose these Preachers.

Doth not their shame almost appear to all men? If it do not, it will do ere long; assure your selves, [117] you Priests, you must fall, and be turned out as *Iudas, Simon Magus*, and the Scribes and Pharisees, that are the greatest enemies to Christ, the spreading power of right-eousnesse.

The Father doth not send hear-say men, to be Labourers in his Vineyard, but such as he first fils with the Divine power, and then sends them to work in his Vineyard: So that still it is but Christ in them, that is, the one man that is sent of the Father; for the Father sends none but his beloved Son, who is the law of righteousnesse and peace, the spreading power.

And you shall find, you proud and covetous Priests, ere long, that poor despised ones of the world, that have this law in their hearts, are the labourers that are sent forth; and you that call your selves Divines, and Labourers, you are Traitors and Enemies to the spirit; you have had warning enough, you are left without excuse; you are the men whose mouths must be stopped; not by the hand of Tyranni-call, humane power, as you have stopped the mouths of others, I abhor it; for the Lord himself, whom you dishonour by your hypocrisie, will stop your mouth with shame and sorrow, when he makes you to see your selves to be Devils, Deceivers, Scribes and Pharisees *Simon Magus's, Demas's,* and *Judas's,* that are Traitors to the spirit.

But if you say, you do not assume the name of Day-vines, but of

Divines, as you write your selves, you are as bad under this description, of Divines, or Diviners, witches, sorcerers, deceivers, as *Balaam* was; and as the maid that got her Masters much gain by divination.

Surely you are no other but Witches and Deceivers, for you hold forth letter for spirit, make people believe that your words of hear-say are [118] the testimony and experience of the spirit within you; and you pick their purses extremly by this divination and sorcerie.

Well, your word Divinity darkens knowledge; you talk of a body of Divinity, and of Anatomyzing Divinity: O fine language! But when it comes to triall, it is but a husk without the kernall; words without life; the spirit is in the hearts of the people whom you despise and tread under foot: You go on selling words for money to the blind people whom you have deceived; and the spirit is not in your service, for your publique service stinks before him; your preaching, praying, and yours and the peoples joyning in your publique Worship, is abomination to the Lord: For you are the men and people that draw nigh God with your lips; but your hearts are removed: Love and righteous acting within the Creation, is not to be found in your hands.

And therefore to conclude; seeing the alone peace of the heart lies in seeing and feeling Christ the Divine power, to arise up and rule within; and every soul is in confusion, bondage and sorrow, till he have true light and feeling hereof, as I have declared my own experience,

Then surely it commands all mouths to be silent, that speak from hear-say, and to wait for the resurrection of Christ within; for he that speaks from hear-say, and yet saith, Thus saith the Lord, he lies, and he dishonours the Lord: And Secondly, he wrongs the soul of the hearer, by deceiving them, and so walks unprofitably in the Creation, by making them believe, that his divination are words of knowledge spoke from a pure testimony.

Surely if the Lord himself did not become the Teacher of his poor despised people, we should have been overspread with the Egyptian darkness, as [119] the Universitie men are by whom the earth is corrupted, and overspread with thick darknesse.

Well, you have prophesies and promises in the writings of Prophets and Apostles, wait upon the Lord till you see the fulfilling of them within your selves, or to your clear experience: And leave off your much talk about words and sillables for by this multitude of waste discourse, people are blinded, that they neither mind the Prophesies of Scriptures, nor wait for their fulfilling.

Truly I can speak in experience, that while I was a blind Professour and a strict goer to Church, as they call it, and a hearer of Sermons, and never questioned what they spake, but believed as the learned Clergy (the Church) believed; and still forgot what I heard; though the words they spake were like a pleasant song to me, while I was hearing: And this I know is the condition of all your publique zealous Professours, let them say what they will, for they live in confusion, ignorance and bondage to the fleshly man;

While I was such a one, I say, I was counted by some of the Priests a good Christian, and a godly man, though all that was in me was but zealous ignorance: But since it pleased the Father to reveal his Son in me, and cause me to speak what I know from an inward light and power of life within,

Now both the same Priests, and the Professours, whom they have deceived; my former acquaintance now begin to be afraid of me, and call me a blasphemer, and a man of errors, and look upon me as a man of another world; for my own particular, my portion is fallen to me in a good ground; I have the Lord, I have enough.

I look upon them with the eye of pitty and love, seeing them as yet to lie under those strong delusions, and powers of darknesse, which I my self did lie [120] under, waiting upon the great restorer of all things, till he manifest himself in them, and then we shall become one againe, and never be divided.

O my dear friends in the flesh, despise not this word I speak; wait upon the Lord for teaching; you will never have rest in your souls, till he speak in you: run after men for teaching, follow your forms with strictnesse, as you know I have done, you shall still be at losse, and be more and more wrapped up in confusion and sorrow of heart: I speak what I have found.

But when once your heart is made subject to Christ, the law of righteousnesse, looking up to him for instruction, waiting with a meek and quiet spirit, till he appear in you: then you shall have peace, then you shall know the truth, and the truth shall make you free; then you shall know that I speake truth.

Well, I wil conclude, and leave this writing in the hand of the world: Some may be offended at it, if they be, I care not: Some may have their joy fullfilled in seeing a conjuncture of experience between me and them: Though my words may seem sharp to some, yet I do not write them out of any envy to any man, but out of love to all; and so doing to my fellow creatures, as I would they should do to me; walking (in this particular, as my endeavour is in all other) uprightly and righteously in the Creation; speaking the truth as it is in Jesus; that is, speaking my own words, what I see and feel in my own experience, from that light of Christ within, and not by hear-say or imagination, whereby humane learning in matters of Divine things, deceives all the world, and laps every man up in darknesse: So I rest.

FINIS.

THE TRUE LEVELLERS STANDARD
ADVANCED

THE title page is dated 1649, and Thomason dated his copy April 26. The address to the reader is signed by John Taylor and is dated April 20, 1649. The title page bears the names of Winstanley and fourteen others. The same names are printed at the end.

Copies are to be found in the following collections: The Baker Library at the Harvard Graduate School of Business Administration, The John Rylands Library (Manchester), The Newberry Library, The Seligman Library at Columbia University, The Thomason Library at the British Museum, The Library of the University of Cincinnati, and The Library of Yale University. The text is reprinted in part by A. S. P. Woodhouse, in *Puritanism and Liberty* (London, 1938), p. 379.

The text is reproduced from the copy in the Library of the University of Cincinnati.

TO ALL MY FELLOW CREATURES THAT
SHALL VIEW THESE ENSUING LINES

THE God of this world blinding the eyes of the men of the world, has taken possession of them and their Lives, Rules and Raigns, and in a high measure opposeth the everlasting spirit, the King of Righteousness; both in them, and in the whole Creation, bending all its wit and power to destroy this spirit, and the persons in whom it lives, rules and governs; making Lawes under specious pretences, yea and penalties too, that all Nations, Tongues, and Languages, shall fall down and worship this god, become subject, yea in slavery to it, and to the men in whom it dwels: But the god of this world is Pride and Covetousness, the rootes of all Evil, from whence flowes all the wickedness that is acted under the Sun, as Malice, Tyranny, Lording over, and despising their fellow Creatures, killing and destroying those that will not, or cannot become subject to their Tyranny, to uphold their Lordly Power, Pride, and Covetousness.

I have had some Conversation with the Authour of this ensuing Declaration, and the Persons Subscribing, and by experience find them sweetly acted and guided by the everlasting spirit, the Prince of Peace, to walk in the paths of Righteousness, not daring to venture upon any acts of injustice; but endeavouring to do unto all, as they would have done to them, having Peace and Joy in themselves, knit together and united in one Spirit of Glory and Truth, Love to their fellow Creatures, Contentation with Food || and Rayment, shewing much Humility and Meekness of spirit; such as these shall be partakers of the Promise.

Blessed are the Meek, for they shall inherit the Earth.

Secondly, For this action of theirs, in labouring to Manure the wast places of the Earth, it is an action full of Iustice and Righteousnesse, full of Love and Charity to their fellow Creatures; nothing of *the god of this world, Pride and Covetousnesse seen in it, no self-seeking, or glorying in the Flesh.*

Vouchsafe to reade, or view over these ensuing Lines yee Powers of the Earth; Oh that Reason might sit upon the throne of your hearts as Iudge; I am confident there is nothing written in anger or hatred to your persons, but in love to them as fellow Creatures; but against that which have bound up your own Spirits in slavery; if you could speak impartially, your own Consciences can bear me witnesse, and only bears sway in your forcing you to exercise Tyranny, scourging and trampling under foot your fellow Creatures, especially those whose eyes are opened and can cleerly discover the great Devil, Tyranny, Pride, and Covetousnesse working to and fro upon your Spirits, and raigning in you, which will prove your own destruction: The Angels that kept not their first Estate, are reserved under Chains of darknesse unto the Iudgment of the great day.

The whole Creation are the Angels of the everlasting Spirit of Righteousnesse, they are all ministring spirits, speaking every Creature in its kind the Will of the Father. The Chariots of God are 20000 thousands of Angels, *Psal. &c.*

But yee the great ones of the Earth, the Powers of this world, yee are the Angels that kept not your first estate, and now remain under Chains of darknesse: Your first Estate was Innocency and Equallity with your fellow Creatures, but your Lordly power over them, both Persons and Consciences, your proud fleshly imaginations, lofty thoughts of your selves, are the fruits of darknesse which you are kept under: The whole Creation groaneth and is in bondage, even until now, waiting for deliverance, and must wait till he that with-holdeth be taken away, that man of sin, that Antichrist which sits in the throne, in the hearts of the men of this world, the Powers of the Earth, above all that is called God. ‖

I know you have high thoughts of your selves, think you know much, and see much, but the Light that is in you is Darknesse; and how great is that darknesse? They that live in the light of the Spirit can discover that to be the blacknesse of darknesse which you count light. And truly, a great Light, a bright Morning Star which will flourish and spread it self, shining in Darknesse, and darknesse shall not be able to comprehend it, though you Spurn never so much against it.

I expect nothing but opposition, mockings, deridings from Lord Esau *the man of Flesh: I know it will be counted in the eye of Flesh, a foolish undertaking, an object of scorn and laughter; but in this is their Comfort and incouragement, That the power of Life and Light, the Spirit by whom they are commanded, will carry them on, strengthen and support them, rescuing them from the Jaw of the Lyon and Paw of the Bear; For great is the work which will shortly be done upon the Earth. Despise not Visions, Voyces and Revelations; examine the Scriptures, Prophesies are now fulfilling; be not like* Josephs Brethren, *speak not evil of things you know not: For whatsoever is of God will stand, do what you can, though you may crush it for a time, the time is neer expired; it will spring up again and flourish like a green Bay tree: What is not of the Father will fall to the ground, though you bend all your wit, power and policy to keep it up; but of that will be no Resurrection. That the eternal Spirit may enlighten you, that Reason may dwel in you, and act accordingly, is the desire of your Loving Friend, and Fellow Creature,*

April 20,
1649.

JOHN TAYLOR. ||

[6] A DECLARATION TO THE POWERS OF ENGLAND, AND TO ALL THE POWERS OF THE WORLD, shewing the cause why the common people of England have begun, and gives consent to digge up, manure, and sowe corn upon George-Hill in Surrey; by those that have subscribed, and thousands more that gives consent

I n the beginning of Time, the great Creator Reason, made the Earth to be a Common Treasury, to preserve Beasts, Birds, Fishes, and Man, the lord that was to govern this Creation; for Man had Domination given to him, over the Beasts, Birds, and Fishes; but not one word was spoken in the beginning, That one branch of mankind should rule over another.

And the Reason is this, Every single man, Male and Female, is a perfect Creature of himself; and the same Spirit that made the Globe, dwels in man to govern the Globe; so that the flesh of man being subject to Reason, his Maker, hath him to be his Teacher and Ruler within himself, therefore needs not run abroad after any Teacher and Ruler without him, for he needs not that any man should teach him, for the same Anoynting that ruled in the Son of man, teacheth him all things.

But since humane flesh (that king of Beasts) began to delight himself in the objects of the Creation, more then in the Spirit Reason and Righteousness, who manifests himself to be the indweller in the Five Sences, of Hearing, Seeing, Tasting, Smelling, Feeling; then he fell into blindness of mind and weakness of heart, and runs abroad for a

Teacher and Ruler: And so selfish imagination taking possession of the Five Sences, and ruling as King in the room of Reason therein, and working with Covetousnesse, [7] did set up one man to teach and rule over another; and thereby the Spirit was killed, and man was brought into bondage, and became a greater Slave to such of his own kind, then the Beasts of the field were to him.

And hereupon, The Earth (which was made to be a Common Treasury of relief for all, both Beasts and Men) was hedged in to In-closures by the teachers and rulers, and the others were made Servants and Slaves: And that Earth that is within this Creation, made a Common Store-house for all, is bought and sold, and kept in the hands of a few, whereby the great Creator is mightily dishonored, as if he were a respecter of persons, delighting in the comfortable Livelihood of some, and rejoycing in the miserable povertie and straits of others. From the beginning it was not so.

But this coming in of Bondage, is called *A-dam*, because this ruling and teaching power without, doth *dam* up the Spirit of Peace and Liberty; First within the heart, by filling it with slavish fears of others. Secondly without, by giving the bodies of one to be imprisoned, punished and oppressed by the outward power of another. And this evil was brought upon us through his own Covetousnesse, whereby he is blinded and made weak, and sees not the Law of Righteousnesse in his heart, which is the pure light of Reason, but looks abroad for it, and thereby the Creation is cast under bondage and curse, and the Creator is sleighted; First by the Teachers and Rulers that sets themselves down in the Spirits room, to teach and rule, where he himself is only King. Secondly by the other, that refuses the Spirit, to be taught and governed by fellow Creatures, and this was called Israels Sin, in casting off the Lord, and chusing *Saul*, one like themselves to be their King, when as they had the same Spirit of Reason and government in themselves, as he had, if they were but subject. And Israels rejecting of outward teachers and rulers to embrace the Lord, and to be all taught and ruled by that righteous King, that *Jeremiah* Prophesied shall rule in the new Heavens and new Earth in the latter dayes, will be their Restauration from bondage. *Ier.* 23.5,6.

But for the present state of the old World that is running up like parchment in the fire, and wearing away, we see proud Imaginary [8] flesh, which is the wise Serpent, rises up in flesh and gets dominion in some to rule over others, and so forces one part of the Creation man, to be a slave to another; and thereby the Spirit is killed in both. The one looks upon himself as a teacher and ruler, and so is lifted up in pride over his fellow Creature: The other looks upon himself as imperfect, and so is dejected in his Spirit, and looks upon his fellow Creature of his own Image, as a Lord above him.

And thus *Esau,* the man of flesh, which is Covetousness and Pride, hath killed *Jacob,* the Spirit of meeknesse, and righteous government in the light of Reason, and rules over him: And so the Earth that was made a common Treasury for all to live comfortably upon, is become through mans unrighteous actions one over another, to be a place, wherein one torments another.

Now the great Creator, who is the Spirit Reason, suffered himself thus to be rejected, and troden under foot by the covetous proud flesh, for a certain time limited; therefore saith he, *The Seed out of whom the Creation did proceed, which is my Self, shall bruise this Serpents head, and restore my Creation again from this curse and bondage; and when I the King of Righteousnesse raigns in every man, I will be the blessing of the Earth, and the joy of all Nations.*

And since the coming in of the stoppage, or the *A-dam,* the Earth hath been inclosed and given to the Elder brother *Esau,* or man of flesh, and hath been bought and sold from one to another; and *Iacob,* or the yonger brother, that is to succeed or come forth next, who is the universal spreading power of righteousnesse that gives liberty to the whole Creation, is made a servant.

And this Elder Son, or man of bondage, hath held the Earth in bondage to himself, not by a meek Law of Righteousnesse, But by subtle selfish Councels, and by open and violent force; for wherefore is it that there is such Wars and rumours of Wars in the Nations of the Earth? and wherefore are men so mad to destroy one another? But only to uphold Civil propriety of Honor, Dominion and Riches one over another, which is the curse the Creation groans under, waiting for deliverance.

[9] But when once the Earth becomes a Common Treasury again, as it must, for all the Prophesies of Scriptures and Reason are Circled here in this Community, and mankind must have the Law of Righteousnesse once more writ in his heart, and all must be made of one heart, and one mind,

Then this Enmity in all Lands will cease, for none shall dare to seek a Dominion over others, neither shall any dare to kill another, nor desire more of the Earth then another; for he that will rule over, imprison, oppresse, and kill his fellow Creatures, under what pretence soever, is a destroyer of the Creation, and an actor of the Curse, and walks contrary to the rule of righteousnesse: (*Do, as you would have others do to you; and love your Enemies, not in words, but in actions*).

Therefore you powers of the Earth, or Lord *Esau*, the Elder brother, because you have appeared to rule the Creation, first take notice, That the power that sets you to work, is selvish Covetousnes, and an aspiring Pride, to live in glory and ease over *Iacob*, the meek Spirit; that is, the Seed that lies hid, in & among the poor Common People, or yonger Brother, out of whom the blessing of Deliverance is to rise and spring up to all Nations.

And Reason, the living king of righteousnesse, doth only look on, and lets thee alone, That whereas thou counts thy self an Angel of Light, thou shalt appear in the light of the Sun, to be a Devil, *A-dam*, and the Curse that the Creation groans under; and the time is now come for thy downfal, and *Iacob* must rise, who is the universal Spirit of love and righteousnesse, that fils, and will fill all the Earth.

Thou teaching and ruling power of flesh, thou hast had three periods of time, to vaunt thy self over thy Brother; the first was from the time of thy coming in, called *A-dam*, or a stoppage, till *Moses* came; and there thou that wast a self-lover in *Cain*, killed thy brother *Abel*, a plain-hearted man that loved righteousnesse: And thou by thy wisdom and beastly government, made the whole Earth to stinck, till *Noah* came, which was a time of the world, like the coming in of the watery Seed into the womb, towards the bringing forth of the man child.

And from *Noah* till *Moses* came, thou still hast ruled in vaunting, pride, and cruel oppression; *Ishmael* against *Isaac*, [10] *Esau* against *Iacob*; for thou hast still been the man of flesh that hath ever persecuted the man of righteousnesse, the Spirit Reason.

And Secondly, From *Moses* till the *Son of Man* came, which was a time of the world, that the man child could not speak like a man, but lisping, making signs to shew his meaning; as we see many Creatures that cannot speak do. For *Moses* Law was a Language lapped up in Types, Sacrifices, Forms, and Customs, which was a weak time.

And in this time likewise, O thou teaching and ruling power, thou wast an oppressor; for look into Scriptures and see if *Aaron* and the Priests were not the first that deceived the people; and the Rulers, as Kings and Governors, were continually the Ocean-head, out of whose power, Burdens, Oppressions, and Poverty did flow out upon the Earth: and these two Powers still hath been the Curse, that hath led the Earth, mankind, into confusion and death by their imaginary and selvish teaching and ruling, and it could be no otherwise; for while man looks upon himself, as an imperfect Creation, and seeks and runs abroad for a teacher and a ruler, he is all this time a stranger to the Spirit that is within himself.

But though the Earth hath been generally thus in darknesse, since the *A-dam* rise up, and hath owned a Light, and a Law without them to walk by, yet some have been found as watchmen, in this night time of the world, that have been taught by the Spirit within them, and not by any flesh without them, as *Abraham, Isaac, Iacob,* and the Prophets: And these, and such as these, have still been the Butt, at whom, the powers of the Earth in all ages of the world, by their selvish Laws, have shot their fury.

And then Thirdly from the time of the *Son of man,* which was a time that the man-child began to speak like a child growing upward to manhood, till now, that the Spirit is rising up in strength. O thou teaching and ruling power of the earthy man, thou hast been an oppressor, by imprisonment, impoverishing, and martyrdom; and all thy power and wit, hath been to make Laws, and execute them against such as stand for universal Liberty, which is the rising up of *Iacob*; as by those ancient enslaving Laws not yet blotted out, but held up as weapons against the man-child.

[11] O thou Powers of *England,* though thou hast promised to make this People a Free People, yet thou hast so handled the matter, through thy self-seeking humour, That thou hast wrapped us up more in bondage, and oppression lies heavier upon us; not only bringing thy fellow Creatures, the Commoners, to a morsel of Bread, but by confounding all sorts of people by thy Government, of doing and undoing.

First, Thou hast made the people to take a Covenant and Oaths to endeavour a Reformation, and to bring in Liberty every man in his place; and yet while a man is in pursuing of that Covenant, he is imprisoned and oppressed by thy Officers, Courts, and Justices, so called.

Thou hast made Ordinances to cast down Oppressing, Popish, Episcopal, Self-willed and Prerogative Laws; yet we see, That Self-wil and Prerogative power, is the great standing Law, that rules all in action, and others in words.

Thou hast made many promises and protestations to make the Land a Free Nation: And yet at this very day, the same people, to whom thou hast made such Protestations of Liberty, are oppressed by thy Courts, Sizes, Sessions, by thy Justices and Clarks of the Peace, so called, Bayliffs, Committees, are imprisoned, and forced to spend that bread, that should save their lives from Famine.

And all this, Because they stand to maintain an universal Liberty and Freedom, which not only is our Birthright, which our Maker gave us, but which thou hast promised to restore unto us, from under the former oppressing Powers that are gone before, and which likewise we have bought with our Money, in Taxes, Free-quarter, and Bloud-shed; all which Sums thou hast received at our hands, and yet thou hast not given us our bargain.

O thou *A-dam*, thou *Esau*, thou *Cain*, thou Hypocritical man of flesh, when wilt thou cease to kill thy yonger Brother? Surely thou must not do this great Work of advancing the Creation out of Bondage; for thou art lost extremely, and drowned in the Sea of Covetousnesse, Pride, and hardness of heart. *The blessing shall rise out of the dust which thou treadest under foot, Even the poor despised People, and they shall hold up* [12] *Salvation to this Land, and to all Lands, and thou shalt be ashamed.*

Our Bodies as yet are in thy hand, our Spirit waits in quiet and peace, upon our Father for Deliverance; and if he give our Bloud into thy hand, for thee to spill, know this, That he is our Almighty Captain: And if some of you will not dare to shed your bloud, to maintain Tyranny and Oppression upon the Creation, know this, That our Bloud and Life shall not be unwilling to be delivered up in meekness to maintain universal Liberty, that so the Curse on our part may be taken off the Creation.

And we shall not do this by force of Arms, we abhorre it, For that is the work of the *Midianites* to kill one another; But by obeying the Lord of Hosts, who hath Revealed himself in us, and to us, by labouring the Earth in righteousness together, to eate our bread with the sweat of our brows, neither giving hire, nor taking hire, but working together, and eating together, as one man, or as one house of Israel restored from Bondage; and so by the power of Reason, the Law of righteousness in us, we endeavour to lift up the Creation from that bondage of Civil Propriety, which it groans under.

We are made to hold forth this Declaration to you that are the Great Councel, and to you the Great Army of the Land of *England*, that you may know what we would have, and what you are bound to give us by your Covenants and Promises; and that you may joyn with us in this Work, and so find Peace. Or else, if you do oppose us, we have peace in our Work, and in declaring this Report: And you shall be left without excuse.

The Work we are going about is this, To dig up *Georges-Hill* and the waste Ground thereabouts, and to Sow Corn, and to eat our bread together by the sweat of our brows.

And the First Reason is this, That we may work in righteousness, and lay the Foundation of making the Earth a Common Treasury for All, both Rich and Poor, That every one that is born in the Land, may be fed by the Earth his Mother that brought him forth, according to the Reason that rules in the Creation. Not Inclosing any part into any particular hand, but all as one man, working together, and feeding together as Sons [13] of one Father, members of one Family; not one Lording over another, but all looking upon each other, as equals in the Creation; so that our Maker may be glorified in the work of his own hands, and that every one may see, he is no respecter of Persons, but equally loves his whole Creation, and hates nothing but the Serpent, which is Covetousness, branching forth into selvish Imagination, Pride, Envie, Hypocrisie, Vncleanness; all seeking the ease and honor of flesh, and fighting against the Spirit Reason that made the Creation; for that is the Corruption, the Curse, the Devil, the Father of Lies; Death and Bondage that Serpent and Dragon that the Creation is to be delivered from.

And we are moved hereunto for that Reason, and others which hath been shewed us, both by Vision, Voyce, and Revelation.

For it is shewed us, That so long as we, or any other, doth own the Earth to be the peculier Interest of Lords and Landlords, and not common to others as well as them, we own the Curse, and hold the Creation under bondage; and so long as we or any other doth own

Landlords and Tennants, for one to call the Land his, or another to hire it of him, or for one to give hire, and for another to work for hire; this is to dishonour the work of Creation; as if the righteous Creator should have respect to persons, and therefore made the Earth for some, and not for all: And so long as we, or any other, maintain this Civil Propriety, we consent still to hold the Creation down under that bondage it groans under, and so we should hinder the work of Restoration, and sin against Light, that is given into us, and so through the fear of the flesh man, lose our peace.

And that this Civil Propriety is the Curse, is manifest thus, Those that Buy and Sell Land, and are landlords, have got it either by Oppression, or Murther, or Theft; and all landlords live in the breach of the Seventh and Eighth Commandements, *Thou shalt not steal, nor kill.*

First by their Oppression. They have by their subtle imaginary and covetous wit, got the plain-hearted poor, or yonger Brethren, to work for them, for small wages, and by their work have got a great increase; for the poor by their labour lift up Tyrants to rule over them; or else by their covetous wit, they [14] have out-reached the plain-hearted in Buying and Selling, and thereby inriched themselves, but impoverished others: or else by their subtile wit, having been a lifter up into places of Trust, have inforced people to pay Money for a Publick use, but have divided much of it into their private purses; and so have got it by Oppression.

Then Secondly for Murther; They have by subtile wit and power, pretended to preserve a people in safety by the power of the Sword; and what by large Pay, much Free-quarter, and other Booties, which they call their own, they get much Monies, and with this they buy Land, and become landlords; and if once Landlords, then they rise to be Justices, Rulers, and State Governours, as experience shewes: But all this is but a bloudy and subtile Theevery, countenanced by a Law that Covetousness made; and is a breach of the Seventh Commandement, *Thou shalt not kill.*

And likewise Thirdly a breach of the Eighth Commandement, *Thou shalt not steal*; but these landlords have thus stoln the Earth from their fellow Creatures, that have an equal share with them, by the Law of Reason and Creation, as well as they.

And such as these rise up to be rich in the objects of the Earth; then by their plausible words of flattery to the plain-hearted people, whom they deceive, and that lies under confusion and blindness: They are lifted up to be Teachers, Rulers, and Law makers over them that lifted them up; as if the Earth were made peculiarly for them, and not for others weal: If you cast your eye a little backward, you shall see, That this outward Teaching and Ruling power, is the Babylonish yoke laid upon Israel of old, under *Nebuchadnezzar*; and so Successively from that time, the Conquering Enemy, have still laid these yokes upon Israel to keep *Jacob* down: And the last enslaving Conquest which the Enemy got over Israel, was the *Norman* over *England*; and from that time, Kings, Lords, Judges, Justices, Bayliffs, and the violent bitter people that are Free-holders, are and have been Successively: The *Norman* Bastard *William* himself, his Colonels, Captains, inferiour Officers, and Common Souldiers, who still are from that time to this day in pursuite of that victory, Imprisoning, Robbing, and killing the poor enslaved *English* Israelites.

[15] And this appears cleer, For when any Trustee or State Officer is to be Chosen, The Free-holders or Landlords must be the Chusers, who are the *Norman* Common Souldiers, spred abroad in the Land; And who must be Chosen? but some very rich man, who is the Successor of the *Norman* Colonels or high Officers. And to what end have they been thus Chosen? but to Establish that *Norman* power the more forcibly over the enslaved *English*, and to beat them down again, when as they gather heart to seek for Liberty.

For what are all those Binding and Restraining Laws that have been made from one Age to another since that Conquest, and are still upheld by Furie over the People? I say, What are they? but the Cords, Bands, Manacles, and Yokes that the enslaved *English*, like *Newgate* Prisoners, wears upon their hands and legs as they walk the streets; by which those *Norman* Oppressors, and these their Successors from Age to Age have enslaved the poor People by, killed their yonger Brother, and would not suffer *Iacob* to arise.

O what mighty Delusion, do you, who are the powers of *England*, live in! That while you pretend to throw down that *Norman* yoke, and *Babylonish* power, and have promised to make the groaning people of *England* a Free People; yet you still lift up that *Norman* yoke, and slavish Tyranny, and hold the People as much in bondage, as the Bastard Conquerour himself, and his Councel of War.

Take notice, That *England* is not a Free People, till the Poor that have no Land, have a free allowance to dig and labour the Commons, and so live as Comfortably as the Landlords that live in their Inclosures. For the People have not laid out their Monies, and shed their Bloud, that their Landlords, the *Norman* power, should still have its liberty and freedom to rule in Tyranny in his Lords, landlords, Judges, Justices, Bayliffs, and State Servants; but that the Oppressed might be set Free, Prison doors opened, and the Poor peoples hearts comforted by an universal Consent of making the Earth a Common Treasury, that they may live together as one House of Israel, united in brotherly love into one Spirit; and having a comfortable livelihood in the Community of one Earth their Mother.

[16] If you look through the Earth, you shall see, That the landlords, Teachers and Rulers, are Oppressors, Murtherers, and Theeves in this manner; But it was not thus from the Beginning. And this is one Reason of our digging and labouring the Earth one with another, That we might work in righteousness, and lift up the Creation from bondage: For so long as we own Landlords in this Corrupt Settlement, we cannot work in righteousness; for we should still lift up the Curse, and tread down the Creation, dishonour the Spirit of universal Liberty, and hinder the work of Restauration.

Secondly, In that we begin to Digge upon *George-Hill*, to eate our Bread together by righteous labour, and sweat of our browes; It was shewed us by Vision in Dreams, and out of Dreams, That that should be the Place we should begin upon; And though that Earth in view of Flesh, be very barren, yet we should trust the Spirit for a blessing. And that not only this Common, or Heath should be taken in and Manured by the People, but all the Commons and waste Ground in *England,* and in the whole World, shall be taken in by the People in righteousness, not owning any Propriety; but taking the Earth to be a Common Treasury, as it was first made for all.

Thirdly, It is shewed us, That all the Prophecies, Visions, and Revelations of Scriptures, of Prophets, and Apostles, concerning the calling of the Jews, the Restauration of Israel; and making of that People, the Inheritors of the whole Earth; doth all seat themselves in this Work of making the Earth a Common Treasury; as you may read, *Ezek.* 24. 26, 27, *&c. Jer.* 33. 7. to 12. *Esay.* 49. 17, 18, *&c. Zach.* 8. from 4. to 12. *Dan.* 2. 44, 45. *Dan.* 7. 27. *Hos.* 14. 5, 6, 7. *Joel* 2. 26, 27.

Amos 9. from 8. to the end. *Obad.* 17. 18. 21. *Mic.* 5. from 7. to the end. *Hab.* 2. 6, 7, 8, 13, 14. *Gen.* 18. 18. *Rom.* 11. 15. *Zeph.* 3. *&c.* *Zach.* 14. 9.

And when the Son of man, was gone from the Apostles, his Spirit descended upon the Apostles and Brethren, as they were waiting at *Ierusalem*; and the Rich men sold their Possessions, and gave part to the Poor; and no man said, That ought that he possessed was his own, for they had all things Common, *Act.* 4. 32.

[17] Now this Community was supprest by covetous proud flesh, which was the powers that ruled the world; and the righteous Father suffered himself thus to be suppressed for a time, times and dividing of time, or for 42 months, or for three dayes and half, which are all but one and the same term of time: And the world is now come to the half day; and the Spirit of Christ, which is the Spirit of universal Community and Freedom is risen, and is rising, and will rise higher and higher, till those pure waters of *Shiloe*, the Well Springs of Life and Liberty to the whole Creation, do over-run *A-dam*, and drown those banks of Bondage, Curse, and Slavery.

Fourthly, This work to make the Earth a Common Treasury, was shewed us by Voice in Trance, and out of Trance, which words were these,

Work together, Eate Bread together, Declare this all abroad.

Which Voice, was heard Three times: And in Obedience to the Spirit, Wee have Declared this by Word of mouth, as occasion was offered. Secondly, We have declared it by writing[1], which others may reade. Thirdly, We have now begun to declare it by Action, in Diging up the Common Land, and casting in Seed, that we may eat our Bread together in righteousness. And every one that comes to work, shall eate the Fruit of their own labours, one having as much Freedom in the Fruit of the Earth as another. Another Voice that was heard was this,

Israel shall neither take Hire, nor give Hire.

And if so, then certainly none shall say, This is my Land, work for me, and I'le give you Wages: For, The Earth is the Lords, that is, Mans, who is Lord of the Creation, in every branch of mankind; for as divers members of our human bodies, make but one body perfect; so every particular man is but a member or branch of mankind; and mankind living in the light and obedience to Reason, the King of righteous-

---

[1] In *The New Law of Righteousnes.*

ness, is thereby made a fit and compleat Lord of the Creation. And the whole Earth is this Lords Man, subject to the Spirit. And not the Inheritance of covetous proud Flesh, that is selvish, and enmity to the Spirit.

[18] And if the Earth be not peculiar to any one branch, or branches of mankind, but the Inheritance of all; Then it is Free and Common for all, to work together, and eate together.

And truly, you Counsellors and Powers of the Earth, know this, That wheresoever there is a People, thus united by Common Community of livelihood into Oneness, it will become the strongest Land in the World, for then they will be as one man to defend their Inheritance; and Salvation (which is Liberty and Peace) is the Walls and Bulwarks of that Land or City.

Wheras on the other side, pleading for Propriety and single Interest, divides the People of a land, and the whole world into Parties, and is the cause of all Wars and Bloud-shed, and Contention every where.

Another Voice that was heard in a Trance, was this,

> *Whosoever labours the Earth for any Person or Persons, that are lifted up to rule over others, and doth not look upon themselves, as Equal to others in the Creation: The hand of the Lord shall be upon that Laborer: I the Lord have spoke it, and I will do it.*

This Declares likewise to all Laborers, or such as are called Poor people, that they shall not dare to work for Hire, for any Landlord, or for any that is lifted up above others; for by their labours, they have lifted up Tyrants and Tyranny; and by denying to labor for Hire, they shall pull them down again. He that works for another, either for Wages, or to pay him Rent, works unrighteously, and still lifts up the Curse; but they that are resolved to work and eat together, making the Earth a Common Treasury, doth joyn hands with Christ, to lift up the Creation from Bondage, and restores all things from the Curse.

Fifthly, That which does incourage us to go on in this work, is this; We find the streaming out of Love in our hearts towards all; to enemies as well as friends; we would have none live in Beggery, Poverty, or Sorrow, but that every one might enjoy the benefit of his creation: we have peace in our hearts, and quiet rejoycing in our work, and filled with sweet content, though we have but a dish of roots and bread for our food.

[19] And we are assured, that in the strength of this Spirit that hath manifested himself to us, we shall not be startled, neither at Prison nor Death, while we are about his work; and we have bin made to sit down and count what it may cost us in undertaking such a work, and we know the full sum, and are resolved to give all that we have to buy this Pearl which we see in the Field.

For by this work we are assured, and Reason makes it appear to others, that Bondage shall be removed, Tears wiped away, and all poor People by their righteous Labours shall be relieved, and freed from Poverty and Straits; For in this work of Restoration, there will be no begger in Israel: For surely, if there was no Begger in literal Israel, there shall be no Begger in Spiritual Israel the Anti-type, much more.

Sixthly, We have another encouragement that this work shall prosper, Because we see it to be the fulness of Time: For whereas the Son of Man, the *Lamb,* came in the Fulness of Time, that is, when the Powers of the World made the Earth stink every where, by oppressing others, under pretense of worshiping the Spirit rightly, by the Types and Sacrifices of *Moses* law; the Priests were grown so abominably Covetous and Proud, that they made the People to loath the Sacrifices, and to groan under the Burden of their Oppressing Pride.

Even so now in this Age of the World, that the Spirit is upon his Resurrection, it is likewise the Fulness of Time in a higher measure. For whereas the People generally in former times did rest upon the very observation of the Sacrifices and Types, but persecuted the very name of the Spirit; Even so now, Professors do rest upon the bare observation of Forms and Customs, and pretend to the Spirit, and yet persecutes, grudges, and hates the power of the Spirit; and as it was then, so it is now: All places stink with the abomination of Self-seeking Teachers and Rulers: For do not I see that every one Preacheth for money, Counsels for money, and fights for money to maintain particular Interests? And none of these three that pretend to give liberty to the Creation, do give liberty to the Creation; neither can they, for they are enemies to universal liberty; So that the earth stinks with their Hypocrisie, Covetousness, Envie, sottish Ignorance, and Pride.

[20] The common People are filled with good words from Pulpits and Councel Tables, but no good Deeds; For they wait and wait for good, and for deliverances, but none comes; While they wait for liberty, behold greater bondage comes instead of it, and burdens, oppres-

sions, taskmasters, from Sessions, Lawyers, Bayliffs of Hundreds, Committees, Impropriators, Clerks of Peace, and Courts of Justice, so called, does whip the People by old Popish weather-beaten Laws, that were excommunicate long ago by Covenants, Oaths, and Ordinances; but as yet are not cast out, but rather taken in again, to be standing pricks in our eys, and thorns in our side; Beside Free-quartering, Plundering by some rude Souldiers, and the abounding of Taxes; which if they were equally divided among the Souldiery, and not too much bagd up in the hands of particular Officers and Trustees, there would be less complaining: Besides the horrible cheating that is in Buying and Selling, and the cruel Oppression of Landlords, and lords of Mannours, and quarter Sessions; Many that have bin good House-keepers (as we say) cannot live, but are forced to turn Souldiers, and so to fight to uphold the Curse, or else live in great straits and beggery: O you *A-dams* of the Earth, you have rich Clothing, full Bellies, have your Honors and Ease, and you puffe at this; But know thou stout-hearted *Pharaoh*, that the day of Judgement is begun, and it will reach to thee ere long; *Jacob* hath bin very low, but he is rising, and will rise, do the worst thou canst; and the poor people whom thou oppresses, shall be the Saviours of the land; For the blessing is rising up in them, and thou shalt be ashamed.

And thus you Powers of England, and of the whole World, we have declared our Reasons, why we have begun to dig upon *George* hill in Surrey. One thing I must tell you more, in the close, which I received *in voce* likewise at another time; and when I received it, my ey was set towards you. The words were these:

Let Israel go free.

Surely, as Israel lay 430. yeers under *Pharaohs* bondage, before *Moses* was sent to fetch them out: Even so Israel (the Elect Spirit spread in Sons and Daughters) hath lain three times so long already, which is the Anti-type, under your Bondage, and cruel Task-masters: But now the time of Deliverance is come, [21] and thou proud *Esau*, and stout-hearted Covetousness, thou must come down, and be lord of the Creation no longer: For *now the King of Righteousness is rising to Rule In, and Over the Earth.*

Therefore, if thou wilt find Mercy, *Let Israel go Free*; break in pieces quickly the Band of particular Propriety, dis-own this oppressing Murder, Oppression and Thievery of Buying and Selling of Land, owning of landlords, and paying of Rents, and give thy Free Consent to make the Earth a Common Treasury, without grumbling; That the yonger Brethren may live comfortably upon Earth, as well as the Elder: That all may enjoy the benefit of their Creation.

And hereby thou wilt *Honour thy Father, and thy Mother:* Thy Father, which is the Spirit of Community, that made all, and that dwels in all. Thy Mother, which is the Earth, that brought us all forth: That as a true Mother, loves all her Children. Therefore do not thou hinder the Mother Earth, from giving all her Children suck, by thy Inclosing it into particular hands, and holding up that cursed Bondage of Inclosure by thy Power.

And then thou wilt repent of thy *Theft*, in maintaining the breach of the eighth Commandment, by *Stealing* the Land as I say from thy fellow-creatures, or yonger Brothers: which thou and all thy landlords have, and do live in the breach of that Commandment.

Then thou wilt *Own no other God*, or Ruling Power, *but One*, which is the King of Righteousness, ruling and dwelling in every one, and in the whole; whereas now thou hast many gods: For Covetousness is thy God, Pride, and an Envious murdering Humor (to kill one by Prison or Gallows, that crosses thee, though their cause be pure, sound, and good reason) is thy God, Self-love, and slavish Fear (lest others serve thee as thou hast served them) is thy god, Hypocrisie, Fleshly Imagination, that keeps no Promise, Covenant, nor Protestation, is thy God: love of Money, Honor, and Ease, is thy God: And all these, and the like Ruling Powers, makes thee Blind, and hard-hearted, that thou does not, nor cannot lay to heart the affliction of others, though they dy for want of bread, in that rich City, undone under your eys.

[22] Therefore once more, *Let Israel go Free*, that the poor may labour the Waste land, and suck the Brests of their mother *Earth*, that they starve not: And in so doing, thou wilt keep the *Sabbath day*, which is a day of *Rest*; sweetly enjoying the Peace of the Spirit of Righteousness; and find Peace, by living among a people that live in peace; this will be a day of *Rest* which thou never knew yet.

But I do not entreat thee, for thou art not to be intreated, but in the *Name of the Lord*, that hath drawn me forth to speak to thee; I, yea I say, I Command thee, To *let Israel go Free*, and quietly *to gather together into the place where I shall appoint; and hold them no longer in bondage.*

And thou *A-dam* that holds the Earth in slavery under the Curse: If thou wilt not *let Israel go Free*; for thou being the Antitype, will be more stout and lusty then the *Egyptian Pharaoh* of old, who was thy Type; Then know, That whereas I brought *Ten* Plagues upon him, I will *Multiply* my Plagues upon thee, till I make thee weary, and miserably ashamed: And *I will bring out my People with a strong hand, and stretched out arme.*

Thus we have discharged our Souls in declaring the Cause of our Digging upon *George-Hill* in *Surrey*, that the Great Councel and Army of the Land may take notice of it, That there is no intent of Tumult or Fighting, but only to get Bread to eat, with the sweat of our brows; working together in righteousness, and eating the blessings of the Earth in peace.

And if any of you that are the great Ones of the Earth, that have been bred tenderly, and cannot work, do bring in your Stock into this Common Treasury, as an Offering to the work of Righteousness; we will work for you, and you shall receive as we receive. But if you will not, but *Pharaoh* like, cry, *Who is the Lord that we should obey him?* and endeavour to Oppose, then know, That he that delivered Israel from *Pharaoh* of old, is the same Power still, in whom we trust, and whom we serve; for this Conquest over thee shall be got, *not by Sword or Weapon, but by my Spirit saith the Lord of Hosts.*

[23]

William Everard,	*Ferrard Winstanley,*
Iohn Palmer,	*Richard Goodgroome,*
Iohn South,	*Thomas Starre,*
Iohn Courton.	*William Hoggrill,*
William Taylor,	*Robert Sawyer,*
Christopher Clifford,	*Thomas Eder,*
Iohn Barker.	*Henry Bickerstaffe,*
	Iohn Taylor, &c.

FINIS.

A DECLARATION FROM THE POOR OPPRESSED PEOPLE OF ENGLAND

THE title page is dated 1649, and Thomason dated his copy June 1. The pamphlet has Winstanley's name, with forty-four others, at the end. On stylistic grounds, and also because the tone is in places more belligerent than usual, I think it likely that others beside Winstanley had a hand in the writing. The pages are not numbered.

Copies are to be found in the following collections: The Baker Library at the Harvard Graduate School of Business Administration, Bibliotheca Lindesiana, The Huntington Library, The Newberry Library, The Seligman Library at Columbia University, The Thomason Library at the British Museum; another copy in the British Museum.

The text is reproduced from the copy in the Seligman Library.

A DECLARATION FROM THE POOR OP-PRESSED PEOPLE OF ENGLAND

W E whose names are subscribed, do in the name of all the poor oppressed people in *England*, declare unto you, that call your selves Lords of Manors, and Lords of the Land, That in regard the King of Righteousness, our Maker, hath inlightened our hearts so far, as to see, That the earth was not made purposely for you, to be Lords of it, and we to be your Slaves, Servants, and Beggers; but it was made to be a common Livelihood to all, without respect of persons: And that your buying and selling of Land, and the Fruits of it, one to another, is *The cursed thing*, and was brought in by War; which hath, and still does establish murder, and theft, in the hands of some branches of Mankinde over others, which is the greatest outward burden, and unrighteous power, that the Creation groans under: For the power of inclosing Land, and owning Propriety, was brought into the Creation by your Ancestors by the Sword; which first did murther their fellow Creatures, Men, and after plunder or steal away their Land, and left this Land successively to you, their Children. And therefore, though you did not kill or theeve, yet you hold that cursed thing in your hand, by the power of the Sword; and so you justifie the wicked deeds of your Fathers; and that sin of your Fathers, shall be visited upon the Head of you, and your Children, to the third and fourth Generation, and longer too, tell your bloody and theeving power be rooted out of the Land.

And further, in regard the King of Righteousness hath made us sensible of our burthens, and the cryes and groanings of our hearts are come before him: We take it as a testimony of love from him, that our hearts begin to be freed from slavish fear of men, such as you are; and that we finde Resolutions in us, grounded upon the inward law of Love, one towards another, To Dig and Plough up the Commons, and waste Lands through *England*; and that our conversation shall be so unblameable, That your Laws shall not reach to oppress us any longer, unless you by your Laws will shed the innocent blood that runs in our veins.

For though you and your Ancestors got your Propriety by murther and theft, and you keep it by the same power from us, that have an equal right to the Land with you, by the righteous Law of Creation, yet we shall have no occasion of quarreling (as you do) about that disturbing devil, called *Particular Propriety:* For the Earth, with all her Fruits of Corn, Cattle, and such like, was made to be a common Storehouse of Livelihood to all Mankinde, friend and foe, without exception.

And to prevent all your scrupulous Objections, know this, That we must neither || buy nor sell; Money must not any longer (after our work of the Earths community is advanced) be the great god, that hedges in some, and hedges out others; for Money is but part of the Earth: And surely, the Righteous Creator, who is King, did never ordain, That unless some of Mankinde, do bring that Mineral (Silver and Gold) in their hands, to others of their own kinde, that they should neither be fed, nor be clothed; no surely, For this was the project of Tyrant-flesh (which Land-lords are branches of) to set his Image upon Money. And they make this unrighteous Law, That none should buy or sell, eat, or be clothed, or have any comfortable Livelihood among men, unless they did bring his Image stamped upon Gold or Silver in their hands.

And whereas the Scriptures speak, That the mark of the Beast is 666, the number of a man; and that those that do not bring that mark in their hands, or in their foreheads, they should neither buy nor sell, *Revel.* 13. 16. And seeing the numbering Letters round about the English money make 666[1], which is the number of that Kingly Power and Glory (called a *Man*), And seeing the age of the Creation is now come to the Image of the Beast, or Half day, And seeing 666 is his mark, we expect this to be the last Tyrannical power that shall raign; and that people shall live freely in the enjoyment of the Earth, without bringing the mark of the Beast in their hands, or in their promise;

---

[1] I can explain this only on the supposition that the letter M was overlooked. The lettering, with somewhat differing abbreviations on different coins, was as follows: Carolus D. G. Mag. Br. Fr. et Hi. Rex. The significant letters are MDCLXVI = 1666.

and that they shall buy Wine and Milk, without Money, or without price, as *Isaiah* speaks.

For after our work of the Earthly community is advanced, we must make use of Gold and Silver, as we do of other mettals, but not to buy and sell withal; for buying and selling is the great cheat, that robs and steals the Earth one from another: It is that which makes some Lords, others Beggers, some Rulers, others to be ruled; and makes great Murderers and Theeves to be imprisoners, and hangers of little ones, or of sincere-hearted men.

And while we are made to labor the Earth together, with one consent and willing minde; and while we are made free, that every one, friend and foe, shall enjoy the benefit of their Creation, that is, To have food and rayment from the Earth, their Mother; and every one subiect to give accompt of this thoughts, words and actions to none, but to the one onely righteous Judg, and Prince of Peace, the Spirit of Righteousness that dwells, and that is now rising up to rule in every Creature, and in the whole Globe. We say, while we are made to hinder no man of his Priviledges given him in his Creation, equal to one, as to another; what Law then can you make, to take hold upon us, but Laws of Oppression and Tyranny, that shall enslave or spill the blood of the Innocent? And so your Selves, your Judges, Lawyers, and Justices, shall be found to be the greatest Transgressors, in and over Mankinde.

But to draw neerer to declare our meaning, what we would have, and what we shall endevor to the uttermost to obtain, as moderate and righteous Reason directs us; seeing we are made to see our Priviledges, given us in our Creation, which have hitherto been denied to us, and our Fathers, since the power of the Sword began to rule, And the secrets of the Creation have been locked up under the traditional, Parrat-like speaking, from the Universities, and Colledges for Scholars, And since the power of the murdering, and theeving Sword, formerly, as well as now of late yeers, hath set up a Government, and maintains that Government; for what are prisons, and putting others to death, but the power of the Sword; to enforce people to that Government which was got by Conquest and Sword, and || cannot stand of it self, but by the same murdering power? That Government that is got over people by the Sword, and kept by the Sword, is not set up by the King of Righteousness to be his Law, but by Coveteousness, the great god of the world; who hath been permitted to raign for a time, times, and dividing of time, and his government draws to the period of the last term of his allotted time; and then the Nations shall see the glory of that Government that shall rule in Righteousness, without either Sword or Spear,

And seeing further, the power of Righteousness in our hearts, seeking the Livelihood of others, as well as our selves, hath drawn forth our bodies to begin to dig, and plough, in the Commons and waste Land, for the Reasons already declared,

And seeing and finding our selves poor, wanting Food to feed upon, while we labor the Earth, to cast in Seed, and to wait tell the first Crop comes up; and wanting Ploughs, Carts, Corn, and such materials to plant the Commons withal, we are willing to declare our condition to you, and to all, that have the Treasury of the Earth, locked up in your Bags, Chests, and Barns, and will offer up nothing to this publike Treasury; but will rather see your fellow-Creatures starve for want of Bread, that have an equal right to it with your selves, by the Law of Creation: But this by the way we onely declare to you, and to all that follow the subtle art of buying and selling the Earth, with her Fruits, meerly to get the Treasury thereof into their hands, to lock it up from them, to whom it belongs; that so, such coveteous, proud, unrighteous, selfish flesh, may be left without excuse in the day of Judgment.

And therefore, the main thing we aym at, and for which we declare our Resolutions to go forth, and act, is this, To lay hold upon, and as we stand in need, to cut and fell, and make the best advantage we can of the Woods and Trees, that grow upon the Commons, To be a stock for our selves, and our poor Brethren, through the Land of *England*, to plant the Commons withal; and to provide us bread to eat, till the Fruit of our labors in the Earth bring forth increase; and we shall meddle with none of your Proprieties (but what is called Commonage) till the Spirit in you, make you cast up your Lands and Goods, which were got, and still is kept in your hands by murder, and theft; and then we shall take it from the Spirit, that hath conquered you, and not from our Swords, which is an abominable, and unrighteous power, and a destroyer of the Creation: But the Son of man comes not to destroy, but to save.

And we are moved to send forth this Declaration abroad, to give notice to every one, whom it concerns, in regard we hear and see, that some of you, that have been Lords of Manors, do cause the Trees and Woods that grow upon the Commons, which you pretend a Royalty unto, to be cut down and sold; for your own private use, whereby the Common Land, which your own mouths doe say belongs to the poor, is impoverished, and the poor oppressed people robbed of their Rights, while you give them cheating words, by telling some of our poor oppressed Brethren, That those of us that have begun to Dig and Plough up the Commons, will hinder the poor; and so blinde their eyes, that they see not their Priviledge, while you, and the rich Free-holders, make the most profit of the Commons, by your over-stocking of them with Sheep and Cattle; and the poor that have the name to own the Commons have the least share therein; nay, they are checked by you, if they cut Wood, Heath, Turf, or Furseys, in places about the Common, where you disallow. ||

Therefore we are resolved to be cheated no longer, nor be held under the slavish fear of you no longer, seing the Earth was made for us, as well as for you: And if the Common Land belongs to us who are the poor oppressed, surely the woods that grow upon the Commons belong to us likewise: therefore we are resolved to try the uttermost in the light of reason, to know whether we shall be free men, or slaves. If we lie still, and let you steale away our birthrights, we perish; and if we Petition we perish also, though we have paid taxes, given free quarter, and ventured our lives to preserve the Nation's freedom as much as you, and therefore by the law of contract with you, freedom in the land is our portion as well as yours, equal with you: And if we strive for freedom, and your murdering, governing Laws destroy us, we can but perish.

Therefore we require, and we resolve to take both Common Land, and Common woods to be a livelihood for us, and look upon you as equal with us, not above us, knowing very well, that *England*, the land of our Nativity, is to be a common Treasury of livelihood to all, without respect of persons.

So then, we declare unto you, that do intend to cut our Common Woods and Trees, that you shall not do it; unless it be for a stock for us, as aforesaid, and we to know of it, by a publick declaration abroad, that the poor oppressed, that live thereabouts, may take it, and employ it, for their publike use, therefore take notice we have demanded it in the name of the Commons of *England,* and of all the Nations of the world, it being the righteous freedom of the Creation.

Likewise we declare to you that have begun to cut down our Common Woods and Trees, and to fell and carry away the same for your private use, that you shall forbear, and go no farther, hoping, that none that are friends to the Commonwealth of England, will endeavour to buy any of those Common Trees and Woods of any of those Lords of Mannors, so called, who have, by the murdering and cheating law of the sword, stoln the Land from yonger brothers, who have by the law of Creation, a standing portion in the Land, as well, and equall with others. Therefore we hope all Wood-mongers will disown all such private merchandize, as being a robbing of the poor oppressed, and take notice, that they have been told our resolution: But if any of you that are Wood-mongers, will buy it of the poor, and for their use, to stock the Commons, from such as may be appointed by us to sell it, you shall have it quietly, without diminution; but if you will slight us in this thing, blame us not, if we make stop of the Carts you send and convert the Woods to our own use, as need requires, it being our own, equal with him that calls himself the Lord of the Mannor, and not his peculiar right, shutting us out, but he shall share with us as a fellow-creature.

For we say our purpose is, to take those Common Woods to sell them, now at first to be a stock for our selves, and our children after us, to plant and manure the Common land withall; for we shall endeavour by our righteous acting not to leave the earth any longer intangled unto our children, by self-seeking proprietors; But to leave it a free store-house, and common treasury to all, without respect of persons. And this we count is our dutie, to endeavour to the uttermost, every man in his place (according to the nationall Covenant which the Parliament set forth) a Reformation, to preserve the peoples liberties, one as well as another: As well those as have paid taxes, and given free quarter, as those that have either born the sword, or taken our moneys to dispose of them for publike use: for if the Reformation must be according to the word of God, then every one is to have the || benefit and freedom of his creation, without respect of persons; we count this our duty, we say, to endeavour to the uttermost, and so shall leave those that rise up to oppose us without excuse, in their day of Judgment; and our precious blood, we hope, shall not be dear to us, to be willingly laid down at the door of a prison, or foot of a gallows, to justifie this righteous cause; if those that have taken our money from us, and promised to give us freedom for it, should turn Tyrants against us: for we must not fight, but suffer.

And further we intend, that not one, two, or a few men of us shall sell or exchange the said woods, but it shall be known publikly in Print or writing to all, how much every such, and such parcell of wood is sold for, and how it is laid out, either in victualls, corn, ploughs, or other materialls necessary.

And we hope we may not doubt (at least we expect) that they that are called the great Councel and powers of *England*, who so often have declared themselves, by promises and Covenants, and confirmed them by multitude of fasting daies, and devout Protestations, to make *England* a free people, upon condition they would pay moneys, and adventure their lives against the successor of the *Norman* Conqueror; under whose oppressing power *England* was enslaved; And we look upon that freedom promised to be the inheritance of all, without respect of persons; And this cannot be, unless the Land of *England* be freely set at liberty from proprietors, and become a common Treasury to all her children, as every portion of the Land of *Canaan* was the Common livelihood of such and such a Tribe, and of every member in that Tribe, without exception, neither hedging in any, nor hedging out.

We say we hope we need not doubt of their sincerity to us herein, and that they will not gainsay our determinate course; howsoever, their actions will prove to the view of all, either their sinceritie, or hypocrisie: We know what we speak is our priviledge, and our cause is righteous, and if they doubt of it, let them but send a childe for us to come before them, and we shall make it manifest four wayes.

First, by the National Covenant[2], which yet stands in force to bind Parliament and people to be faithful and sincere, before the Lord God Almighty, wherein every one in his several place hath covenanted to preserve and seek the liberty each of other, without respect of persons.

---

[2] The Solemn League and Covenant pledging Parliament and the nation to a "real reformation" was adopted on September 25, 1643.

Secondly, by the late Victory over King *Charls*, we do claime this our priviledge, to be quietly given us, out of the hands of Tyrant-Government, as our bargain and contract with them; for the Parliament promised, if we would pay taxes, and give free quarter, and adventure our lives against *Charls* and his party, whom they called the Common enemy, they would make us a free people; These three being all done by us, as well as by themselves, we claim this our bargain, by the law of contract from them, to be a free people with them, and to have an equall priviledge of Common livelihood with them, they being chosen by us, but for a peculiar worke, and for an appointed time, from among us, not to be our oppressing Lords, but servants to succour us. But these two are our weakest proofs. And yet by them (in the light of reason and equity that dwells in mens hearts) we shall with ease cast down, all those former enslaving, *Norman* reiterated laws, in every Kings raigne since the Conquest, which are as thornes in our eyes, and pricks in our sides, and which are called the Ancient Government of *England*.

Thirdly, we shall prove, that we have a free right to the land of *England*, being borne therein as well as elder brothers, and that it is our right equal with them, and they with us, to have a comfortable livelihood in the earth, without owning any || of our owne kinde, to be either Lords, or Land-Lords over us: And this we shall prove by plain Text of Scripture, without exposition upon them, which the Scholars and great ones generally say, is their rule to walk by.

Fourthly, we shall prove it by the Righteous Law of our Creation, That mankinde in all his branches, is the Lord of the Earth, and ought not to be in subjection to any of his own kinde without him, but to live in the light of the law of righteousness, and peace established in his heart.

And thus in love we have declared the purpose of our hearts plainly, without flatterie, expecting love, and the same sincerity from you, without grumbling, or quarreling, being Creatures of your own Image and mould, intending no other matter herein, but to observe the Law of righteous action, endeavouring to shut out of the Creation, the cursed thing, called *Particular Propriety*, which is the cause of all wars, bloud-shed, theft, and enslaving Laws, that hold the people under miserie.

Signed for and in the behalf of all the poor oppressed people of *England*, and the whole world.

Gerrard Winstanly	James Manley	Iohn Ash
Iohn Coulton	Thomas Barnard	Ralph Ayer
Iohn Palmer	Iohn South	Iohn Pra
Thomas Star	Robert Sayer	Iohn Wilkinson
Samuel Webb	Christopher Clifford	Anthony Spire
Iohn Hayman	Iohn Beechee	Thomas East
Thomas Edcer	William Coomes	Allen Brown
William Hogrill	Christopher Boncher	Edward Parret
Daniel Weeden	Richard Taylor	Richard Gray
Richard Wheeler	Urian Worthington	Iohn Mordy
Nathaniel Yates	Nathaniel Holcombe	Iohn Bachilor
William Clifford	Giles Childe, senior	William Childe
Iohn Harrison	Iohn Webb	William Hatham
Thomas Hayden	Thomas Yarwel	Edward Wicher
James Hall	William Bennigton	William Tench

FINIS.

A LETTER TO THE LORD FAIRFAX
AND HIS COUNCELL OF WAR

THE title page is dated 1649 and states that the letter was delivered on June 9. Winstanley's name appears both on the title page and at the end.

Copies are to be found in the following collections: The Bodleian, New College (Edinburgh), The Seligman Library at Columbia University, The Thomason Library at the British Museum, Trinity College (Dublin), Yale University Library. It is reprinted in the *Harleian Miscellany* (1808–1811), Vol. XI, pp. 485 ff.; (1808–1813), Vol. VIII, pp. 586 ff.

The text is reproduced from the copy in the Seligman Library.

TO THE LORD FAIRFAX, GENERALL OF THE ENGLISH FORCES, AND HIS COUNCELL OF WAR

SIR,

OUR digging and ploughing upon *George*-hill in Surrey is not unknown to you, since you have seen some of our persons, and heard us speak in defence thereof: and we did receive mildnesse and moderation from you and your Councell of Warre, both when some of us were at White-hall before you, and when you came in person to *George*-hill [1] to view our works; we indeavour to lay open the bottome and intent of our businesse, as much as can be, that none may be troubled with doubtfull imaginations about us, but may be satisfied in the sincerity and universall righteousnesse of the work.

We understand, that our digging upon that Common, is the talk of the whole Land; some approving, some disowning; some are friends, filled with love, and sees the worke intends good to the Nation, the peace whereof is that which we seeke after; others are enemies filled with fury, and falsely report of us, that we have intent to fortifie our selves, and afterwards to fight against others, and take away their goods from them, which is a thing we abhor: and many other slanders we rejoyce over, because we know ourselves cleare, our endeavour being no otherwise, but to improve the Commons, and to cast off that oppression and outward bondage which the Creation groans under, as much as in us lies, and to lift up and preserve the purity thereof.

And the truth is, experience shews us, that in this work of Community in the earth, and in the fruits of the earth, is seen plainly a pitched battaile between the Lamb and the Dragon, between the Spirit of love, humility and righteousnesse, which is the Lamb appearing in

---

[1] Winstanley and Everard went to Whitehall to present the Diggers' case to Fairfax on April 20, 1649, and Fairfax visited St. George's Hill on May 26.

flesh; and the power of envy, pride, and unrighteousnesse, which is the Dragon appearing in flesh, the latter power striving to hold the Creation under slavery, and [2] to lock and hide the glory thereof from man: the former power labouring to deliver the Creation from slavery, to unfold the secrets of it to the Sons of Men, and so to manifest himselfe to be the great restorer of all things.

And these two powers strive in the heart of every single man, & make single men to strive in opposition one against the other, and these strivings will be till the Dragon be cast out, and his judgement and downfall hastens apace, therefore let the righteous hearts wait with patience upon the Lord, to see what end he makes of all the confused hurley burleys of the world.

When you were at our Works upon the Hill, we told you, many of the Countrey-people that were offended at first, begin now to be moderate, and to see righteousnesse in our work, and to own it, excepting one or two covetous Free-holders, that would have all the Commons to themselves, and that would uphold the Norman Tyranny over us, which by the victorie that you have got over the Norman Successor, is plucked up by the roots, therefore ought to be cast away. And we expect, that these our angry neighbours, whom we never wronged, nor will not wrong, will in time see their furious rashnesse to be their folly, and become moderate, to speak and carry themselves like men rationally, and leave off pushing with their hornes like beasts; they shall have no cause to say wee wrong them, unlesse they count us wrongers of them for seeking a livelihood out of the common Land of England by our righteous labour, which is our freedome, as we are Englishmen equall with them, and rather our freedome then theirs, because they are elder brothers and Freeholders, and call the Inclosures their own land, and we are younger brothers, and the poore oppressed, and the Common Lands are called ours, by their owne confession.

We told you (upon a question you put to us) that we were not against any that would have Magistrates and Laws to govern, as the Nations of the world are governed, but as for our parts we shall need neither the one nor the other in that nature of Government; for as our Land is common, so our Cattell is to be common, and our corn and fruits of the earth common, and are not to be bought and sold among us, but to remaine a [3] standing portion of livelihood to us and our children, without that cheating intanglement of buying and selling, and we shall not arrest one another.

And then, what need have we of imprisoning, whipping or hanging Laws, to bring one another into bondage? and we know that none of those that are subject to this righteous law dares arrest or inslave his brother for, or about the objects of the earth, because the earth is made by our Creator to be a common Treasury of livelihood to one equall with another, *without respect of persons*.

But now if you that are elder brothers, and that call the Inclosures your own land, hedging out others, if you will have Magistrates and Laws in this outward manner of the Nations, we are not against it, but freely without disturbance shall let you alone; and if any of we Commoners, or younger Brothers, shall steal your corne, or cattell, or pull down your hedges, let your laws take hold upon any of us that so offends.

But while we keep within the bounds of our Commons, and none of us shall be found guilty of medling with your goods, or inclosed proprieties, unlesse the Spirit in you freely give it up, your laws then shall not reach to us, unlesse you will oppresse or shed the blood of the innocent: and yet our corn and cattell shall not be locked up, as though we would be propriators in the middle of the Nation: no, no, we freely declare, that our corn and cattell, or what we have, shall be freely laid open, for the safety and preservation of the Nation, and we as younger brothers, living in love with you our elder brothers, for we shall endeavour to do, as we would be done unto; that is, to let every one injoy the benefit of his Creation, to have food and rayment free by the labour of his hands from the earth.

And as for spirituall teachings, we leave every man to stand and fall to his own Master: if the power of covetousnesse be his Master or King that rules in his heart, let him stand and fall to him; if the power of love and righteousnesse be his Master or King that rules in his heart, let him stand and fall to him; let the bodies of men act love, humility, and righteousnesse one towards another, and let the Spirit of righteousnesse be the Teacher, Ruler and Judge both in us and over us; and by thus doing, [4] we shall honor our Father, the Spirit that gave us our being. And we shall honor our Mother the earth, by labouring her in righteousnesse, and leaving her free from oppression and bondage.

We shall then honor the higher powers of the left hand man, which is our hearing, seeing, tasting, smelling, feeling, and walk in the light of reason and righteousnesse, that is, the King and Judge that sits upon this five cornered Throne, and we shall be strengthened by those five well springs of life, of the right hand man, which is, understanding, will, affections, joy and peace, and so live like men, in the light and power of the Son of righteousnesse within our selves feelingly. What need then have we of any outward, selfish, confused Laws made, to uphold the power of covetousnesse, whenas we have the righteous Law written in our hearts, teaching us to walk purely in the Creation.

Sir, The intent of our writing to you, is not to request your protection, though we have received an unchristian-like abuse from some of your souldiers; for truly we dare not cast off the Lord, and make choice of a man or men to rule us. For the Creation hath smarted deeply for such a thing, since Israel chose *Saul* to be their King; therefore we acknowledge before you in plain English, That we have chosen the Lord God Almighty to be our King and Protector.

Yet in regard you are our brethren (as an English Tribe) and for the present are owned to be the outward Governors, Protectors and Saviours of this Land, and whose hearts we question not, but that you endeavour to advance the same King of righteousnesse with us, therefore we are free to write to you, and to open the sincerity of our hearts freely to you, and to all the world.

And if after this report of ours, either you, or your Forces called souldiers, or any that owns your Laws of propriety, called freeholders, do abuse or kill our persons, we declare to you that we die, doing our duty to our Creator, by endeavouring from that power he hath put into our hearts to lift up his Creation out of bondage, and you and they shall be left without excuse in the day of Judgement, because you have been spoken to sufficiently.

And therefore our reason of writing to you is this, in regard [5] some of your foot souldiers of the Generalls Regiment, under Captain *Stravie* that were quartered in our Town, we bearing part therein as well as our neighbours, giving them sufficient quarter, so that there was no complaining, did notwithstanding, go up to George-hill, where was onely one man and one boy of our company of the diggers. And at their first coming, divers of your souldiers, before any word of provocation was spoken to them, fell upon those two, beating the boy, and took away his coat off his back, and some linnen and victualls that they had, beating and wounding the man very dangerously, and fired our house.

Which we count a strange and Heathenish practise, that the soulderie should meddle with naked men, peaceable men, Countrymen, that meddled not with the souldiers businesse, nor offered any wrong to them in word or deed, unlesse, because we improve that victory which you have gotten in the name of the Commons over King *Charles*, do offend the soulderie. In doing whereof, we rather expect protection from you then destruction. But for your own particular, we are assured of your moderation and friendship to us, who have ever been your friends in times of straits; and that you would not give Commission to strike us, or fire or pull down our houses, but you would prove us an enemy first.

Yet we do not write this, that you should lay any punishment upon them, for that we leave to your discretion, only we desire (in the request of brethren) that you would send forth admonition to your souldiers, not to abuse us hereafter; unlesse they have a Commission from you; and truly if our offences should prove so great, you shall not need to send souldiers for us, or to beat us, for we shall freely come to you upon a bare letter.

Therefore that the ignorant, covetous, free-holders, and such of your ignorant souldiers, that know not what freedom is, may not abuse those that are true friends to Englands freedom, and faithfull servants to the Creation, we desire, that our businesse may be taken notice of by you, and the highest Councell the Parliament, and if our work appear righteous to you, as it does to us, and wherein our souls have sweet peace, in the midst of scandalls and abuses;

[6] Then in the request of brethren, we desire we may injoy our freedom, according to the Law of contract between you and us, That we that are younger brothers, may live comfortably in the Land of our Nativity, with you the elder brothers, enjoying the benefit of our Creation, which is food and rayment freely by our labours; and that we may receive love, and the protection of brethren from you, seeing we have adventured estate and persons with you, to settle the Land in peace, and that we may not be abused by your Laws, nor by your souldiers, unlesse we break over into your inclosures as aforesaid, and

take away your proprieties, before you are willing to deliver it up. And if this you do, we shall live in quietnesse, and the Nation will be brought into peace, while you that are the soulderie, are a wall of fire round about the Nation to keep out a forraign enemy, and are succourers of your brethren that live within the Land, who indeavour to hold forth the Sun of righteousnesse in their actions, to the glory of our Creator.

And you and the Parliament hereby, will be faithfull in your Covenants, Oaths and promises to us, as we have been faithfull to you and them, in paying taxes, giving free-quarter, and affording other assistance in the publike work, whereby we that are the Common People, are brought almost to a morsell of bread, therefore we demand our bargain, which is freedom, with you in this Land of our Nativity.

But if you do sleight us and our cause, then know we shall not strive with sword and speare, but with spade and plow and such like instruments to make the barren and common Lands fruitful, and we have, and still shall, commit our selves and our cause unto our righteous King, whom we obey, even the Prince of peace to be our Protector; and unto whom you likewise professe much love, by your preaching, praying, fastings, and in whose name you have made all your Covenants, Oaths, and promises to us: I say unto him we appeal, who is and will be our righteous Judge, who never yet failed those that waited upon him, but ever did judge the cause of the oppressed righteously.

We desire that your Lawyers may consider these questions (which we affirm to be truths) and which gives good assurance by the Law of the Land, that we that are the younger brothers [7] or common people, have a true right to dig, plow up and dwell upon the Commons, as we have declared.

1. Whether *William the Conqueror* became not to be King of England by conquest, turned the English out of their birthrights, burned divers townes, whereof thirty towns were burned by him in Windsore Forrest; by reason whereof all sorts of people suffered, and compelled the conquered English for necessity of livelihood to be servants to him and his Norman souldiers?

2. Whether King *Charles* was not successor to the Crown of England from *William the Conqueror*, and whether all Laws that have

been made in every Kings Reign, did not confirm and strengthen the power of the Norman Conquest, and so did, and does still hold the Commons of England under slavery to the Kingly power, his Gentry and Clergie?

3. Whether Lords of Mannours were not the successors of the Colonells and chief Officers of *William the Conqueror*, and held their Royalty to the Commons by Lease, Grant and Patentee from the King, and the power of the sword was and is the seale to their Title?

4. Whether Lords of Mannours have not lost their Royalty to the common land, since the common People of England, as well as some of the Gentry, have conquered King *Charles*, and recovered themselves from under the Norman Conquest?

5. Whether the Norman Conqueror took the land of England to himself, out of the hands of a few men, called a Parliament, or from the whole body of the English People? Surely he took freedom from every one, and became the disposer both of inclosures and commons; therefore every one, upon the recovery of the conquest, ought to return into freedom again, without respecting persons, or els what benefit shall the common people have (that have suffered most in these wars) by the victory that is got over the King? It had been better for the common people there had been no such conquest; for they are impoverished in their estates by Free-quarter and Taxes, and made worse to live then they were before. But seeing they have paid Taxes, and given Free-quarter according to their estates, as much as the Gentry to theirs, it is both reason and equity that they should have the freedom of the land for their livelihood, which is the [8] benefit of the commons, as the Gentry hath the benefit of their inclosures.

6. Whether the freedom which the common people have got, by casting out the Kingly power, lie not herein principally, to have the land of their nativity for their livelihood, freed from intanglement of Lords, Lords of Mannours, and Landlords, which are our taskmasters. As when the enemy conquered England, he took the land for his own, and called that his freedom; even so, seeing all sorts of people have given assistance to recover England from under the Norman yoke, surely all sorts, both Gentry in their inclosures, Commonalty in their Commons, ought to have their freedom, not compelling one to work for wages for another.

7. Whether any Lawes since the coming in of Kings, have been

made in the light of the righteous law of our creation, respecting all alike, or have not been grounded upon selfish principles, in fear or flattery of their King, to uphold freedom in the Gentry and Clergie, and to hold the common people under bondage still, and so respecting persons?

8. Whether all Lawes that are not grounded upon equity and reason, not giving a universal freedom to all, but respecting persons, ought not to be cut off with the Kings head? We affirm they ought.

If all lawes be grounded upon equity and reason, then the whole land of England is to be a common treasury to every one that is born in the land: But if they be grounded upon selfish principles, giving freedom to some, laying burdens upon others, such lawes are to be cut off with the Kings head; or els the neglecters are Covenant, Oaths and Promise-breakers, and open hypocrites to the whole world.

9. Whether every one without exception, by the law of contract, ought not to have liberty to enjoy the earth for his livelihood, and to settle his dwelling in any part of the Commons of England, without buying or renting Land of any; seeing every one by Agreement and Covenant among themselves, have paid taxes, given free-quarter, and adventured their lives to recover England out of bondage? We affirm, they ought.

10. Whether the Laws that were made in the daies of the [9] Kings, does give freedom to any other people, but to the gentry and Clergy, all the rest are left servants and bondmen to those task-masters; none have freedom by the Laws, but those two sorts of people, all the common people have been, and still are burdened under them.

And surely if the common people have no more freedom in England, but only to live among their elder brothers, and work for them for hire; what freedom then have they in England, more then we can have in Turkie or France? For there, if any man will work for wages, he may live among them, otherwise no: therefore consider, whether this be righteous, and for the peace of the Nation, that Laws shall be made to give freedom to impropriators and Free-holders, when as the poor that have no land, are left still in the straights of beggery, and are shut out of all livelihood, but what they shall pick out of sore bondage, by working for others, as Masters over them, and if this be not the burthen of the Norman yoke, let rationall men judge: therefore take not away men, but take away the power of tyranny and bad government, the price is in your hand, and let no part of the Nation be wronged for want of a Representative.

And here now we desire your publike Preachers, that say they preach the righteous law, to consider these questions, which confirms us in the peace of our hearts, that we that are the common people born in England, ought to improve the Commons, as we have declared, for a publike Treasury and livelihood, and that those that hinder us are rebells to their Maker, and enemies to the Creation.

First, we demand I or No, whether the earth with her fruits, was made to be bought and sold from one to another? and whether one part of mankind was made a Lord of the land, and another part a servant, by the law of Creation before the fall?

I affirme, (and I challenge you to disprove) that the earth was made to be a common Treasury of livelihood for all, *without respect of persons*, and was not made to be bought and sold: And that mankind in all his branches is the lord over the Beasts, Birds, Fishes, and the Earth, and was not made to acknowledge any of his owne kind to be his teacher and ruler, but the spirit of righteousnesse only his Maker, and to walk in his light, and so to [10] live in peace, and this being a truth, as it is, then none ought to be Lords or Landlords over another, but the earth is free for every son and daughter of mankind, to live free upon.

This question is not to be answered by any text of Scripture, or example since the fall, but the answer is to be given in the light of it self, which is the law of righteousnesse, or that Word of God that was in the beginning, which dwells in mans heart, and by which he was made, even the pure law of creation, unto which the creation is to be restored.

Before the fall, *Adam*, or the Man did dresse the garden, or the earth, in love, freedom, and righteousnesse, which was his rest and peace: But when covetousnesse began to rise up in him, to kill the power of love and freedom in him, and so made him (mankind) to set himself one man above another, as *Cain* lifted up himself above *Abel*, which was but the outward declaration of the two powers that strive in the man *Adams* heart; and when he consented to that serpent covetousnesse, then he fell from righteousnesse, was cursed, and was sent into the earth to eat his bread in sorrow: And from that time began particular propriety to grow in one man over another; and the sword brought in propriety, and holds it up, which is no other but the power of angry covetousness: For, *Cain* killed *Abel*, because *Abels* principles, or religion, was contrary to his. And the power of the sword is still *Cain* killing *Abel*, lifting up one man still above another. But *Abel* shall not alwaies be slain, nor alwaies lie under the bondage of *Cains* cursed propriety, for he must rise: And that *Abel* of old was but a type of *Christ*, that is now rising up to restore all things from bondage.

2. I demand, whether all wars, blood-shed, and misery came not upon the Creation, when one man indeavoured to be a lord over another, and to claime propriety in the earth one above another? Your Scripture will prove this sufficiently to be true. And whether this misery shall not remove (and not till then) when all the branches of mankind shall look upon themselves as one man, and upon the earth as a common Treasury to all, without respecting persons, every one acknowledging the law of righteousnesse in them and over them, and walking in his light purely? then cast away your buying and selling the earth, with [11] her fruits, it is unrighteous, it lifts up one above another, it makes one man oppresse another, and it is the burthen of the Creation.

3. Whether the work of restoration lies not in removing covetousnesse, casting that Serpent out of heaven, (mankind) and making man to live in the light of righteousnesse, not in words only, as Preachers do, but in action, whereby the Creation shines in glory? I affirm it.

4. Whether is the King of righteousnesse a *respecter of persons*, yea, or no? If you say no, then who makes this difference, that the elder brother shall be lord of the land, and the younger brother a slave and beggar? I affirm, it was and is covetousnesse, since the fall, not the King of righteousnesse before the fall, that made that difference; therefore if you will be Preachers, hold forth the law of righteousnesse purely, and not the confused law of covetousnesse, which is the murtherer: the law of righteousnesse would have every one to injoy the benefit of his creation, that is, to have food and rayment by his labour freely in the land of his nativity, but covetousnesse will have none to live free, but he that hath the strongest arme of flesh; all others must be servants.

5. Whether a man can have true peace by walking in the Law of

covetousnesse and self, as generally all do, or by walking in the Law
of universall righteousnesse; doing as he would be done by? I affirm
there is no true peace, till men talk lesse, and live more actually in
the power of universall righteousnesse. Then you Preachers, lay aside
your multitude of words, and your selfish doctrines, for you confound
and delude the people.

6. Whether does the King of righteousnesse bid you love or hate
your enemies, if you say love them, then I demand of you, why do
some of you in your Pulpits, and elswhere, stir up the people to beat,
to imprison, put to death or banish, or not to buy and sell with those
that endeavour to restore the earth to a common treasury again?
surely at the worst, you can make them but your enemies; therefore
love them, win them by love, do not hate them, they do not hate you.

7. Whether it be not a great breach of the Nationall Covenant, to
give two sorts of people their freedom, that is, Gentry and Clergy,
and deny it to the rest? I affirm it is a high breach, for [12] mans
Laws makes these two sorts of people, the Antichristian task-masters
over the common people. The one forcing the people to give them
rent for the earth, and to work for hire for them. The other which is
the Clergy, that force a maintenance of tithes from the people; a
practise which Christ, the Apostles and Prophets never walked in;
therefore surely you are the false Christs, and false Prophets, that
are risen up in these latter daies.

Thus I have declared to you, and to all in the whole world, what
that power of life is, that is in me. And knowing that the Spirit of
righteousnesse does appear in many in this Land, I desire all of you
seriously in love and humility, to consider of this businesse of publike
community, which I am carried forth in the power of love, and clear
light of universall righteousnesse, to advance as much as I can; and
I can do no other, the Law of love in my heart does so constrain me,
by reason whereof I am called fool, mad man, and have many slan-
derous reports cast upon me, and meet with much fury from some
covetous people, under all which my spirit is made patient, & is
guarded with joy and peace. I hate none, I love all, I delight to see
every one live comfortably. I would have none live in poverty, straits
or sorrows; therefore if you find any selfishnesse in this work, or discover any thing that is destructive to the whole Creation, that you
would open your hearts as freely to me in declaring my weaknesse to

me, as I have been open-hearted in declaring that which I find and feel much life and strength in. But if you see righteousnesse in it, and that it holds forth the strength of universall love to all without respect to persons, so that our Creator is honored in the work of his hand, then own it, and justifie it, and let the power of love have his freedom and glory.

Jerrard Winstanly.

[13] The Reformation that England now is to endeavour, is not to remove the Norman *Yoke* only, and to bring us back to be governed by those Laws that were before *William the Conqueror* came in, as if that were the rule or mark we aime at: No, that is not it; but the Reformation is according to the Word of God, and that is the pure Law of righteousnesse before the fall, which made all things, unto which all things are to be restored: and he that endeavours not that, is a Covenant-breaker.

This Letter with the Questions were delivered by the Authors own hand to the Generall, and the chief Officers, and they very mildly promised they would read it, and consider of it.

FINIS.

A DECLARATION OF THE BLOUDIE AND UNCHRISTIAN ACTING OF WILLIAM STAR AND JOHN TAYLOR OF WALTON

THE title page is dated 1649, and the attack complained of is said to have occurred on June 11. The pamphlet is anonymous but was almost certainly written by Winstanley.

Copies are to be found in the following collections: The Seligman Library at Columbia University, The Thomason Library at the British Museum.

The text is reproduced from the copy in the Seligman Library.

[1] A DECLARATION OF THE BLOODY AND UNCHRISTIAN ACTING OF WILLIAM STAR, AND JOHN TAYLOR OF WALTON,

With divers men in womens apparell, in opposition to those that dig upon George-hill in Surrey, &c.

UPON the 11. day of June 1649, foure men only being fitting and preparing the ground for a winter season, upon that Common called George-hill, there came to them, *William Starr* of *Walton,* and *Iohn Taylor,* two free-holders, being on horseback, having at their heels some men in womens apparell on foot, with every one a staffe or club, and as soon as they came to the diggers, would not speak like men, but like bruit beasts that have no understanding, they fell furiously upon them, beating and striking those foure naked men, beating them to the ground, breaking [2] their heads, and sore bruising their bodies, whereof one is so sore bruised, that it is feared he will not escape with life.

These foure men all the time were quiet and patient, willing and resolving to deliver up their lives unto their Creator at that time, knowing no other, but that the others purpose was to murder; and it is believed, when those furious divells *Taylor* and *Starr* went from them, they thought they had been dead, in regard they left them feeble, and weak, and sore wounded, lying upon the ground, yet after some time recovering strength, three were able to rise and walk, the fourth that is in danger of his life was brought home in a cart, being not able to move: yet very cheerfull all of them in spirit, not willing to seek revenge, but have committed their cause to him that judges righteously, to whom vengeance belongs, resolving as soon as their bodies are well, to go on in that righteous work: and if the Father have purposed that the life of their bodies must be sacrificed, to justifie this cause, they find a quiet and contented willingnesse to submit to his will. One thing may be observed to set forth the malicious wickednesse in *Taylor* and *Star*, which is this:

These foure men desired that they would bring them before their Law to answer in justification of the work, yet those divells, with the men in womens apparell, would not agree to that, but fell on, beating with their long staves upon their bodies without mercie, a testimony sufficient that this cause of digging is just and good, in regard of the furious and bloudy actings of men against such as carrie on the work with love and patience, which is a strange thing in a Christian Land, [3] and done by such men as are professing Christians; considering withall, that these diggers do only make use of the Commons, seeing they have paid taxes, and given free-quarter; and therefore by the Law of contract, ought to have freedom therein, as well as the free-holders have freedom in their Inclosures; the diggers declaring, they will neither meddle with Corn, Cattell, nor inclosure Land, but only in the Commons; and that they are ready to answer to all the Laws of the Land as Defendents, but not as Plaintiffs. Surely this fury in the free-holders declares plainly, that they got their Lands, both they and their Fathers, by murder, violence, and theft, and they keep it by the same power in regard they will not speak like men, but fight and devoure like beasts. Well let the world take notice, that we that do justifie this cause of digging, have obeyed the Lord, in setting forward this work of endeavouring to bring the earth into a Community, and we have peace and purposes to go on, and we are lively witnesses, and shall be at the day of Judgement, against these and all others that have and may so furiously oppose us; and rebelliously fight against the Prince of Peace, the great Saviour that is now spreading himself in the earth to bring all things into a onenesse, and to deliver the Creation from bondage.

Right understanding and peace among brethren, is the strength of a Land, ignorance and fury brings shame and destruction. England is a Land, wherein the Power of the most High hath greatly declared his Power, both in casting down the pride of many mens hearts, and making them subject to righteousnesse, and in casting down the bodies of some that were proud oppressors [4] to be as dung to the earth, dashing one power against another, changing times and customes, and therein trying the sincerity of many that make a great shew of love to him.

Every one that seems to prevaile over another, saies, God gave him the victory, though his conquest be tyranny over his brother, making the King of Righteousnesse the Author of sorrowes, and comfort, not knowing the distinction between the power of darknesse and the power of light: Victories that are got by the sword, are but victories of the Murtherer, and the joy of those victories is but the joy of *Caine,* when he had killed his brother *Abel;* the Dragon hath fought against the Dragon, and one part conquered another, and great joy hath been amongst the Midianites for those victories, and the King of Righteousnesse hath been a looker on, and suffered them to breake each other to pieces, that his power at last might come in.

But now O England know this, that thy striving now is not only Dragon against Dragon, Beast against Beast, Covetousnesse and Pride against Covetousnesse and Pride, but thou now begin'st to fight against the Lamb, the Dove, the meek Spirit, the power of love, and wilt not willingly suffer that Prince of Peace to have a house to dwell in upon earth (which is humane bodies), but seekst to imprison, beat, kill, or else to withdraw all assistance of favour from them: Well, thou hast rejoyced in thy former victories one beast over another, and thou hast had, and may have seeming victories over the Lamb, and may rejoyce; but know, that this stone (which is alone) against whom thou hast [5] begun to lift up thy heel, shall grind thee to powder. Love suffers under thy furie, love suffers under thy hypocrisie, under thy pride, carelesse, covetous, hard-hearted, self-seeking children. Love bears all things patiently, he suffers thee to reproach, to fight, to oppose, and to rejoyce in doing those things. Love secretly seeks thy preservation, but thou openly seekest his destruction, and glories like a man that hath put off his armour at every seeming shew of victory: but the battell between the Dragon and the Lamb is begun in the midst of thee, and a few years now will let all the world see who is strongest, love or hatred, freedom or bondage.

Therefore thy battells now are not as they were, for now the Lord, the Prince of Peace comes to save thee, and thou fight'st against him as an enemy, and wilt not be saved by him, he calls for Peace, thou cal'st for war, he calls to Freedome, thou cal'st still for bondage, he saith put up thy Sword and live in love, thou saist draw the Sword against all that will live in love. Well, England take thy course, but know for all this thou shalt come to Judgement.

FINIS.

AN APPEAL TO THE HOUSE OF COMMONS

THE title page is dated 1649, and Thomason dated his copy July 11. Several news sheets say that it was presented to the House on July 24: *The Kingdom's Faithfull Scout*, July 20–27; *The Moderate Messenger*, July 23–30; *The Moderate Intelligencer*, July 19–26; *The Perfect Weekly Account*, July 18–25.

Copies are to be found in the following collections: Bibliotheca Lindesiana, The Bodleian, The Guildhall Library, The Huntington Library, Lincoln's Inn Library, The Seligman Library at Columbia University, The Thomason Library at the British Museum.

The text is reproduced from the copy in the Seligman Library.

[3] AN APPEAL TO THE HOUSE OF COMMONS,

Desiring their Answer; Whether the Common-People shall have the quiet enjoyment of the Commons and Waste Lands: Or whether they shall be under the will of Lords of Mannors still

SIRS,

THE cause of this our Presentment before you, is, An Appeal to you, desiring you to demonstrate to us, and the whole Land, the equity, or not equity, of our cause; And that you would either cast us by just reason under the feet of those we call Task-Masters, or Lords of Mannors, or else to deliver us out of their Tyrannical hands: In whose hands, by way of Arrest, we are for the present, for a Trespass to them, as they say, In digging upon the Common-Land. The setling whereof, according to Equity and Reason, wil quiet the mindes of the oppressed people; it will be a keeping of our Nationall [4] Covenant; it will be peace to your selves, and make *England* the most flourishing, and strongest Land in the world; and the first of Nations that shall begin to give up their Crown and Scepter, their Dominion and Government into the hands of Jesus Christ.

The cause is this, we, amongst others of the common people, that have been ever friends to the Parliament, as we are assured our enemies wil witness to it, have plowed and dig'd upon *Georges-Hill* in *Surrey,* to sow corn for the succour of man, offering no offence to any, but do carry our selves in love and peace towards all, having no intent to meddle with any mans inclosures, or propriety, til it be freely given to us by themselves, but only to improve the Commons and waste Lands to our best advantage, for the relief of our selves and others, being moved thereunto by the Reason hereafter following, not expecting any to be much offended, in regard the cause is so just and upright.

Yet notwithstanding, there be three men [1] (called by the people *Lords of Manors*) viz. *Thomas* Lord *Wenman, Ralph Verny* Knight, and *Richard Winwood* Esquire, have arrested us [2] for a trespass in digging upon the Commons, and upon the Arrest we made our appearance in *Kingstone* Court[3], where we understood we were arrested for medling with other mens Rights; and secondly, they were incouraged to arrest us upon your Act of Parliament (as they tell us) to maintain the old Laws [4]; we desired to plead our own cause, the Court denied us and to fee a Lawyer we cannot, for divers reasons, as we may shew hereafter.

Now Sirs, our case is this, for we appeal to you, for you are the only men that we are to deal withall in this business; Whether the common people, after all their taxes, free-quarter, and loss of blood to recover *England* from under the *Norman* yoak, shal have the freedom to improve the Comons, and waste Lands free to themselves, as freely their own, as the Inclosures are the propriety of the elder brothers? Or whether the Lords of Manors shall have them, according to their old Custom from the Kings Will and Grant, and so remain [5] Task-Masters still over us, which was the peoples slavery under Conquest.

We have made our appeal to you, to settle this matter in the Equity and Reason of it, and to pass the sentence of freedom to us, you being the men with whom we have to do in this business, in whose hands there is power to settle it, for no Court can end this controversie but your Court of Parliament, as the case of this Nation now stands.

Therefore we intreat you to read over this following Declaration, wherein we have declared our Reason, that the Commons and waste

[1] The property belonged to Francis Drake of Walton-upon-Thames. See the fuller account of the matter in *A Watch-word to the City of London*, below, p. 319, n. 5. See the account of this trial in the Introduction, pp. 17 f.

[2] The names on the title page are Winstanley, John Barker, and Thomas Star. In *A Watch-word to the City of London* the name of Henry Bickerstaffe appears in place of John Barker's.

[3] See below, p. 319, n. 4.

[4] On February 17, 1649, Parliament passed two acts authorizing justices of the peace and other officers of courts to continue until new commissions were issued, and permitting actions, etc., in the name of the Keepers of the Liberty of England, in place of the King.

lands is the common peoples, and that in equity you ought to let them quietly enjoy them, as the elder brothers quietly enjoy their inclosures. The profit of this business to the Nation, the quietting of the hearts of the poor oppressed that are groaning under burthens and straights, and the peace of your own hearts, to see the peace of the Nation setled in his plat-form, will much countervail the spending of so much time.

Sirs, you know, that the Land of *England* is the land of our Nativity, both yours and ours, and all of us by the righteous Law of our Creation, ought to have food and rayment freely by our righteous labouring of the earth, without working for hire, or paying rent one to another.

But since the fall of man from that righteous Law, The Nations of the world have rise up in variance one against another, and fought against, murdered, and stoln the land of their Nativity one from another, and by their power of their conquests, have stil set up some to rule in tyranny over others, and thereby have enslaved the conquered, which is a burden the whole Creation hath, and yet does groane under. The teeth of all Nations hath been set on edge by this sour grape, the covetous murdering sword.

England, you know, hath been conquered and enslaved divers times, and the best Laws that *England* hath, (viz. *Magna Charta*) were got by our Forefathers importunate petitioning unto the Kings, that stil were their Task-masters; and yet these best laws are yoaks and manicles, tying one sort of [6] people to be slaves to another; Clergy and Gentry have got their freedom, but the common people stil are, and have been left servants to work for them, like the *Israelites* under the *Egyptian* Task-masters.

The last enslaving yoak that *England* groaned under, (and yet is not freed from) was the *Norman*, as you know; and since *William* the Conqueror came in, about six hundred years ago, all the Kings that stil succeeded, did confirm the old laws, or else make new ones, to uphold that *Norman* conquest over us; and the most favouring laws that we have, doth stil binde the hands of the enslaved *English* from enjoying the freedom of their creation.

You of the Gentry, as wel as we of the Comonalty, all groaned under the burden of the bad Government, and burdening laws under the late King *Charls*, who was the last successor of *William* the Conqueror: you and we cried for a Parliament, and a Parliament was called, and wars, you know, presently begun, between the King, that represented *William* the Conqueror, and the body of the *English* people that were enslaved.

We looked upon you to be our chief Councel, to agitate business for us, though you were summoned by the Kings Writ, and chosen by the Free holders, that are the successors of *William* the Conquerors souldiers; you saw the danger so great, that without a war *England* was like to be more enslaved, therefore you called upon us to assist you with plate, taxes, freequarter, and our persons; and you promised us, in the name of the Almighty, to make us a free people; thereupon you and we took the National Covenant with joynt consent, to endeavour the freedom, peace and safety of the people of *England*.

And you and we joyned purse and person together in this common cause; and *Wil.* the Conquerors successor, which was *Charls*, was cast out; and thereby we have recovered our selves from under that *Norman* yoak; and now unless you and we be meerly besotted with covetousness, pride, and slavish fear of men, it is, and will be our wisdom to cast out all those [7] enslaving laws, which was the Tyrannical power that the Kings prest us down by: O shut not your eyes against the light, darken not knowledg, by dispute about particular mens priviledges, when universal freedom is brought to be tried before you, dispute no further when truth appears, but be silent, and practise it.

Stop not your ears against the secret mourning of the oppressed, under these expressions, lest the Lord see it, and be offended, and shut his ears against your cries, and work a deliverance for his waiting people some other way then by you.

The maine thing that you should look upon is the Land, which calls upon her children to be freed from the entanglement of the *Norman* Task-masters, for one third part lies waste and barren, and her children starve for want, in regard the Lords of Manors will not suffer the poor to manure it.

When *William* the Conqueror came in, he took the land from the *English*, both the Enclosures from the Gentry, and the Commons and waste lands from the common people, and gave our land to his *Norman* souldiers.

Therefore seeing we have with joynt consent of purse and person conquered his successor, *Charls*, and the power now is in your hand, the Nations Representative; O let the first thing you do, be this, to set the land free. Let the Gentry have their inclosures free from all *Norman* enslaving intanglements whatsoever, and let the common people have their Commons and waste lands set free to them, from all *Norman* enslaving Lords of Mannors, that so both elder and younger brother, as we spring successively one from another, may live free and quiet one by, and with another, not burthening one another in this land of our Nativity.

And this thing you are bound to see done, or at least to endevor it, before another Representative succeed you; otherwise you cannot discharge your trust to God and man, for these Reasons,

First, if you free not the Land from entanglement of all [8] *Norman* yoaks, or rather bondages, so that the people, one as well as another may enjoy the benefit of their creation, that is, to have the land free to work upon, that they may eate their bread in righteousness; that is to say, let the Freeholders have their freedom to work quietly in their Inclosures, and let the common people have their Commons and waste lands quiet to themselves. If you establish not this, seeing power now is in your hand, you will be the first that break Covenant with Almighty God.

For you swore in your National Covenant to endevour a Reformation according to the Word of God, which Reformation is to restore us to that Primative freedom in the earth, in which the earth was first made and given to the sons of men, and that is to be a common treasury of livelihood to all, without working for hire, or paying rent to any, for this is the Reformation according to the Word of God before the fall of man, in which there is no respect of persons.

And seeing in particular you swore to endeavour the freedom, peace and safety of this people of *England*, shutting out no sort from freedom; therefore you cannot say that the Gentry and Clergy were only comprehended, but without exception, all sorts of people in the land are to have freedom, seeing all sorts have assisted you in person and purse, and the common people more especially, seeing their estates were weakest, and their misery in the wars the greatest.

Therefore let the Gentry and Freeholders have their inclosures freed from all entanglements of Fines, Heriots, and other burdens, and let the common people have their Commons and waste lands freed from entanglements of the *Norman* Lords of Mannors, and pluck up all *Norman* Tyranny by the roots, and so keep your Covenant, that you, and all sorts of people may live in peace one among another.

Secondly, if this freedom be not granted quietly, you will pull the blood and cries of the poor oppressed upon your heads; First, because you have taken their money in taxes, and freequarter from them, whereby they are made worse able to live then before the wars. Secondly, because in your low [9] estate, when you called upon us to come and help a bleeding dying Nation, and we did come with purse and person, and under-went great hardship, and you stil promised us freedom in the end, if in case you and we prevailed over the *Norman* successor, and we have prevailed.

And if now, while the price is in your hand, you should stil leave us under the *Norman* Lords of Manors, and will not quietly suffer us to plant our selves upon the Commons, and waste land, which is ours by the law of our Creation, and which is ours now by conquest from under our oppressor, for which we have paid taxes, given free-quarter, and adventured our lives; the Common-land now is as freely the common peoples, as you can say the Inclosures are your propriety.

If you deny this freedom, then you justly pull the blood and cries of the poor oppressed upon you, and are Covenant-breakers, and wil be proved double hypocrites; First, to Almighty God, in breaking Covenant with him, for in his Name you made the Covenant. Secondly, to men, in breaking Covenant with them, for the matter of the Covenant was the freedom, peace, and safety of the people of *England*, taking in all sorts of people.

Thirdly, if you do not set us free from the *Norman* yoake, now after you have taken our Taxes and Free-quarter from us, whereby we have dearly bought our Freedom, and you thereupon promised freedom, and you have power now to give it, for if you speak the word the *Norman* yoaks will be broke, and all sorts will rejoyce in freedom and righteousness; but if you will not, you give a just occasion to the common people of *England*, never to trust the fair words of a Parliament any more, as you were alwayes very slow in trusting the King, when he swore by the word of a King, because you found that subtilty and Self lay under, and no reality.

And truly the hearts of people are much falling from you, for your breach of Promises when you have power to keep them, and for your neglect of giving them their freedom, and removing burthens; and what danger may ensue by that to [10] your selves, and the Nations, you know how to judg; and for our parts we are sorry to hear the muttering of the people against you.

O that there were a heart in you to consider of these things, and act righteousnesse, how sweetly might you and the people live together: If you grant this freedom we speak of, you gain the hearts of the Nation; if you neglect this, you will fall as fast in their affections as ever you rise: I speak what I see, and do you observe; slight not that love that speaks feelingly, from the sence of the Nations burdens.

Fourthly, If still you should establish the old *Norman* laws, and confirm Lords of Manors in their ancient Custom, and oppressing power over the Common-people, you would now at length, after the wars with King *Charls* are over, take part with such (as is known very well) as have been either flat enemies, or ambidexters all along the wars, and will cast such as have been your true friends, at the feet of the Nations enemies, to be still oppressed by their cruelty. Surely if these Lords and Free-holders have their Inclosures established to them in peace, is not that freedom enough? Must they needs have the Common-land likewise? As *Ahab*, that was restlesse till he had *Naboths* Vineyard, and so in the midst of their abundance, yet will eat the bread out of the poores mouthes. O, the land mourns in her children, under the hard hearted covetousnesse of these men.

Fifthly, If you establish the old *Norman* laws, That Lords of Manors shall still have the Commons and waste lands, then you are the maintainers of the old *Norman* Murder and Theft still; for Lords of Manors came to be Tyrants over the poor enslaved English, by the Murder and Theft of *William* the Conquerour, and downwards to this day they have held title to their Royalties therefrom, and from the will of the King; for when he had conquered, he turned the English out, and gave their land to his *Norman* souldiers.

Sixthly, If you establish the old *Norman* laws, and this especially, That the Lords of Manors shall still be Lords of the [11] Common land, and the Common people be still enslaved to them, then you pull the guilt of King *Charles* his blood upon your own heads; for then it will appear to the view of all men, That you cut off the Kings head, that you might establish your selves in his Chair of Government, and that your aym was not to throw down Tyranny, but the Tyrant.

But alas, the Kings blood was not our burthen, it was those oppressing *Norman* laws, whereby he enslaved us, that we groaned under.

Let it not be said in the ears of posterity, That the Gentry of England assembled in Parliament, proved Covenant-breakers, Oaths, Protestations, and promise-breakers to God, and the Common people, after their own turn was served; and killed the King for his power and government, as a thief kils a true man for his money. I do not say you have done so, but for shame dally no longer, but cut off the bad laws, with the Kings head, and let the poor oppressed go free, as well as the Gentry and Clergy, and you will finde more peace. Let the Common land be set free, break the *Norman* yoak of Lords of Manors, and pull not the cryes and blood of the poor oppressed upon you.

Seventhly, Know this, That if ever you, or any Parliament of England, do England good, you must make all your laws in the light of equity and reason, respecting the freedom of all sorts of people; but if you respect some sort of people, to wit, the Gentry, and Clergy, and give freedom to them; for they, by vertue of your Act of Parliament, establishing the old *Norman* laws, do arrest and trouble me and others, for digging upon the Commons, whereas by vertue of the Victory over the King, in regard I have of my estate given free quarter and taxes for Englands liberty, as they have done, I have as much right to the Common land as they; therefore I say, if the Gentry and Clergy must have their *Norman* power established to them, and the Common people, that are more considerable for number and necessities, be left still under the yoak, you will be proved the foolish builders.

Surely if you found out the Court of Wards [5] to be a burden, [12] and freed Lords of Mannors, and Gentry from paying Fines to the King; and freed their children from the slavery of falling Ward; Let the common People be set free too from paying homage to Lords of Mannors; and let all sorts have freedome by vertue of this Conquest over the *Norman* successor. And seeing you took away the will of the King from enslaving Lords of Mannors, Take away the will of Lords of Mannors from enslaving the Common People.

Thus sirs, we have made our Appeal to you, as the only men that must, and can give sentence of freedome in this controversie, and that you will not leave us in the cruell hands of Lords of Mannors, the

[5] The Court of Wards and Liveries had been abolished on February 24, 1646.

successors of the *Norman* Task-masters; For there are but three wayes
that Lords of Manors can lay claime to the Common land, and yet all
three are too weak to build a just title upon:

First, if they can prove, that the Earth was made by Almighty God
peculiarly for them, and not for others equall with them; then we
have trespassed in digging upon their rights; but the Earth was made
as free for us as for them; therefore they have trespassed against us
their fellow-creatures, in troubling us by their tyrannicall Arrest, and
hindering us from our righteous labor.

Secondly, if they say, that others sold or gave them the title to the
Commons, by way of Inheritance; They are to prove by what Authority
any other had from the pure Law of our Creation, to give away or sell
the Earth from the use of any of their fellow creatures, it being the
common storehouse of livelihood for all, without respect of persons.

He that sels the Earth, and he that buyes, doth remove the land
mark from the third person, because the land that is bought and sold,
belongs to the third man, as well as to the other two that buys and
sels; and they two persons that buys and sels, and leaves the land that
is bought for an inheritance to their children, excluding others, they
murder the third man, because they steal away his livelihood from
him; for after a man hath bought the land, and paid money for it to
another, [13] he saith, this is my land, I have paid for it; But the
third man comes in, and saith, the land is mine, equall with you by
the law of Creation; And so he that is the buyer, he begins to draw
his sword, and to fight; and if he conquer, he rejoyces, and says, the
land is now mine indeed, I have bought, and I have conquered. But
thou covetous person, so long as there is another man in the world
besides thee, and him whom thou hast killed, the Earth belongs to
him as well as to thee; And this is the case of the Nations of the
world, and thus propriety came in, and hath been left as an Inheritance to Children; which is the burden the Creation groans under.

Here we see who are thieves and murderers; even the buyers and
sellers of land, with her fruits, these are they that take away another
mans right from him; and that overthrowes righteous propriety, to
uphold particular propriety, which covetousnes the God of this world
hath set up.

But thirdly, if Lords of Manors say, as it is truth, that they hold
title to the Commons by custome, from the Kings will, as they do,

this is as bad as the other; for we know the King came in by conquest, and gave the land to these forefathers, to be task-masters over the conquered *English*. But if you say, that these later Kings were chosen by the people, it is possible it might be so, but surely it was when his greatness over-awed them, or else they would never have chosen him to enslave them, and to set task-masters over them.

But seeing the Common People have joyned person and purse with you, to recover your selves from under the tyranny of Kings, and have prevailed; the Common people now have more truer title to the common lands, then the Lords of Manors, for they held title by Conquest and sword of the King (we now the common people have recovered the land again by conquest and sword in casting out the King) so that the title of Lords of Manors is broke.

[14] Therefore now the Common people have more true title to the Common land, then Lords of Manors have, in regard they have recovered themselves out of slavery by taxes, free quarter, and conquest, yet we shut them not out, but let them take part with us as fellow creatures, and we with them, and so honour our Creator in the work of his own hands.

Thus we have declared our Cause without flattery to you; if you leave us in the hands of oppression, and under the power of the old tyrannicall laws, know this, that we suffer in pursute of our Nationall Covenant, endeavouring a Reformation in our place and calling, according to the word of God, and you shall be left without excuse.

Set the Land free from Oppression, And righteousnesse will be the Laws, Government, and strength of that People.

[15] THESE ARE SOME OF THE NORMAN LAWS WHICH WILLIAM THE CONQUEROR BROUGHT INTO ENGLAND

FIRST, he turned the *English* out of their Lands, and placed his *Norman* Souldiers therein, and made those that had the greatest portion, Lords, and Barons, and gave them a Royalty to the Commons, to hold from his Will, as a custome, whereby the common people should not plant themselves any where in the Land, upon any Common-land, but some Lord of Manor or other should know of it, and hinder them, as these three that have arrested us, *viz. Wenman, Verny,* and *Winwood,* Lord, Knight, and Esquire, the three Estates of the *Norman* Gentry, will not suffer us to dig quietly upon *Georges* Hill, but seek to drive us off, having no more claim thereunto but an ancient Custom, which they hold from the Kings Will, whereby they have, and stil would tyrannize over the people: And this is the rise and standing of Lords of Manors.

[19; i. e., 16] Secondly, another *Norman* Law is this, *William* the Conqueror caused the Laws to be written in the *Norman* and *French* tongue, and then appointed his own *Norman* people to expound and interpret those Laws, and appointed the *English* people to pay them a Fee for their paines, and from hence came in the trade of Lawyers; he commanded likewise that no man should plead his own cause, but those Lawyers should do it for them.

Thirdly, *William* the Conqueror broke that good and quiet course of ending controversies in a neighbourhood, and commanded the people to come up to *Westminster* to the four Terms every year to have their Causes tried.

Fourthly, *William* the Conqueror brought in the paying of Tithes to the Clergy, in thankfulness to the Pope, and Clergies good services in preaching for him, and so to perswade the people to embrace him.

These are some of the *Norman* Laws and Burthens, which if removed, it would be much ease and quiet to this Nation.

FINIS.

A WATCH-WORD TO THE CITY OF
LONDON AND THE ARMIE

THE title page is dated 1649 and the address, August 26, 1649. Thomason dated his copy September 10. Winstanley's name occurs both on the title page and at the end of the address.

Copies are to be found in the following collections: The Baker Library at the Harvard Graduate School of Business Administration, The Guildhall Library, The Seligman Library at Columbia University, and the Thomason Library at the British Museum.

The text is reproduced from the copy in the Seligman Library.

TO THE CITY OF LONDON, FREEDOME AND
PEACE DESIRED

THOU City of London, I am one of thy sons by freedome, and I do truly love thy peace; while I had an estate in thee, I was free to offer my Mite into thy publike Treasury Guild-hall, for a preservation to thee, and the whole Land; but by thy cheating sons in the theeving art of buying and selling, and by the burdens of, and for the Souldiery in the beginning of the war, I was beaten out both of estate and trade, and forced to accept of the good will of friends crediting of me, to live a Countrey-life, and there likewise by the burthen of Taxes and much Free-quarter, my weak back found the burthen heavier then I could bear; yet in all the passages of these eight yeers troubles I have been willing to lay out what my Talent was, to procure Englands peace inward and outward, and yet all along I have found such as in words have professed the same cause, to be enemies to me. Not a full yeere since, being quiet at my work, my heart was filled with sweet thoughts, and many things were revealed to me which I never read in books, nor heard from the mouth of any flesh, and when I began to speak of them, some people could not bear my words, and amongst those revelations this was one, *That the earth shall be made a common Treasury of livelihood to whole mankind, without respect of persons*; and I had a voice within me bad me declare it all abroad, which I did obey, for I declared it by word of mouth wheresoever I came, then I was made to write a little book called, *The new Law of righteousnesse*, and therein I declared it; yet my mind was not at rest, because nothing was acted, and thoughts run in me, that words and writings were all nothing, and must die, for action is the life of all, and if thou dost not act, thou dost nothing. Within a little time I was made obedient to the word in that particular likewise; for I tooke my spade and went and broke the ground upon

George-hill in Surrey, thereby declaring freedome to the Creation, and that the earth must be set free from intanglements of Lords and Landlords, and that it shall become a common Treasury to all, as it was first made and given to the sonnes of men: For which doing the Dragon presently casts a flood of water to drown the manchild, even that freedom that now is declared, for the old Norman Prerogative Lord of that Mannour Mr. *Drake* [1], caused me to be arrested for a trespasse against him, in digging upon that barren Heath, and the unrighteous proceedings of Kingstone Court in this businesse I have here declared to thee, and to the whole land, that you may consider the case that England is in; all men have stood for freedom, thou hast kept fasting daies, and prayed in morning exercises for freedom; thou hast given thanks for victories, because hopes of freedome; plentie of Petitions and || promises thereupon have been made for freedome, and now the common enemy is gone, you are all like men in a mist, seeking for freedom, and know not where, nor what it is: and those of the richer sort of you that see it, are ashamed and afraid to owne it, because it comes clothed in a clownish garment, and open to the best language that scoffing *Ishmael* can afford, or that railing *Rabsheka* can speak, or furious *Pharaoh* can act against him; for freedom is the man that will turn the world upside downe, therefore no wonder he hath enemies.

And assure your selves, if you pitch not right now upon the right point of freedome in action, as your Covenant hath it in words, you will wrap up your children in greater slavery then ever you were in; the Word of God is Love, and when all thy actions are done in love to the whole Creation, then thou advancest freedome, and freedome is Christ in you, and Christ among you; bondage is Satan in you, and Satan among you: no true freedom can be established for Englands peace, or prove you faithfull in Covenant, but such a one as hath respect to the poor, as well as the rich; for if thou consent to freedom to the rich in the City, and givest freedome to the Free-holders in the Countrey, and to Priests and Lawyers, and Lords of Mannours, and Impropriators, and yet allowest the poor no freedome, thou art then a declared hypocrite, and all thy prayers, fasts, and thanksgivings are, and will be proved an abomination to the Lord, and freedome him-

[1] See below, p. 319, n. 5.

selfe will be the poors portion, when thou shalt lie groaning in bondage.

I have declared this truth to the Army and Parliament [2], and now I have declared it to thee likewise, that none of you that are the fleshly strength of this Land may be left without excuse, for now you have been all spoken to, and because I have obeyed the voice of the Lord in this thing, therefore doe the Free-holders and Lords of Mannours seek to oppresse me in the outward livelihood of the world, but I am in peace. And London, nay England, look to thy freedom; I'le assure thee, thou art very neere to be cheated of it, and if thou lose it now after all thy boasting, truly thy posterity will curse thee, for thy unfaithfulnesse to them: every one talks of freedome, but there are but few that act for freedome, and the actors for freedome are oppressed by the talkers and verball professors of freedome; if thou wouldst know what true freedome is, read over this and other my writings, and thou shalt see it lies in the community in spirit, and community in the earthly treasury, and this is Christ the true manchild spread abroad in the Creation, restoring all things into himselfe; and so I leave thee,

August 26. 1649.

> Being a free Denizen of thee, and a true
> lover of thy peace,
> *Jerrard Winstanly.*

[2] In *A Letter to the Lord Fairfax* and *An Appeal to the House of Commons.*

[1] A WATCH-WORD TO THE CITY OF LON-
DON, AND THE ARMY

WHEREAS we *Henry Bickerstaffe* [3], *Thomas Star*, and *Jerrard Winstanly*, were arrested into Kingstone Court [4], by *Thomas Wenman, Ralph Verny*, and *Richard Winwood*, for a trespasse in digging upon George-hill in Surrey, being the rights of Mr. *Drake* [5] the Lord of that Mannour, as they say, we all three did appear the first Court day of our arrest, and demanded of the Court, what was laid to our Charge, and to give answer thereunto

[3] On the title page of *An Appeal to the House of Commons* the name of John Barker appears in place of Henry Bickerstaffe. See the account of the trials at Kingston in the Introduction, pp. 17 f.

[4] By a charter of Charles I, granted in 1628, the court of record for the Borough of Kingston-upon-Thames had cognizance of pleas, actions, suits, trespasses, etc., in the Hundreds of Kingston, Elmbridge, Copthorne, and Effingham. The court consisted of two bailiffs and the recorder, "one skilled in the laws". The Parish of Walton was in Elmbridge.

[5] Sir Ralph Verney (1613–1696) of Claydon (Bucks.) was the eldest son of Sir Edmund Verney, the King's standard bearer, who was killed at Edgehill, and brother of Edmund Verney who was killed at Drogheda. Ralph sat in the Long Parliament for Aylesbury. He took the parliamentary side against his father and brother, but was exiled for refusing to take the Covenant in 1643 and expelled from the House in 1645. He lived in France until 1653. His estates were sequestered in 1646, but the sequestration was taken off in 1648 through the efforts of his wife. See the *Memoirs of the Verney Family during the Civil War*, by Frances Parthenope Verney, London, 1892; S. R. Gardiner's *History of the Great Civil War*, Vol. III (1891), pp. 14 ff.

Thomas Wenman, Second Viscount Wenman (1596–1665) of Thame Park (Oxon.) sat for Oxfordshire in the Long Parliament. He was one of the commissioners who met the King at Colnbrook in 1642, and one of the commission appointed to treat with the King in 1644. Like Francis Drake he was excluded from the House in Pride's Purge and retired to Thame in 1649. He was connected by marriage with the family of Sir Alexander Denton, whose daughter Elizabeth was the wife of Francis Drake.

Richard Winwood (1608–1688) of Ditton Park (Bucks.) was the son of Ralph Winwood, who was secretary of state to James I. He sat for New Windsor in the Long Parliament. He was a member of the Parliamentary Committee that met the King at Oxford in January, 1642, and also of the committee to present the petition after our selves: But the answer of your [6] Court was this, that you would not tell us what the Trespasse was, unlesse we would fee an Attorney to speak for us; we told them we were to plead our own cause, for we knew no Lawyer that we could trust with this businesse; we desired a copie of the Declaration, and profered to pay for it; and still you denied us, unlesse we would fee an Attorney[7]. But in conclusion, the Recorder of your Court told us, the cause was not entred; we appeared two Court daies after this, and desired to see the Declaration, and still you denied us, unlesse we will fee an Attorney; so greedy are these Attorneys after money, more then to justifie a righteous cause: we told them we could not fee any, unlesse we would willfully break our Nationall Covenant, which both Parliament and people have taken joyntly together to endeavour a Reformation. And unlesse we would be professed Traytors to this Nation and Common-wealth of England, by upholding the old Norman tyrannicall and destructive Lawes, when they are to be cast out of equity, and reason be the Moderator.

Then seeing you would not suffer us to speak, one of us brought this following writing into your Court, that you might read our answer; because we would acknowledge all righteous proceedings in Law, though some slander us, and say we deny all Law, because we

the King's attempt to arrest the five members. He was a relative and close friend of the Verney family; see the *Memoirs, passim.*

Francis Drake of Walton-upon-Thames, a younger brother of Sir William Drake of Shardeloes, sat in the Long Parliament for Amersham (Bucks.) and for Surrey in Cromwell's Parliament in 1655. See *The Victoria History of the Counties: Buckinghamshire*, Vol. III, pp. 145, 147, 149; *ibid., Surrey*, Vol. III, p. 470; *Surrey Archeological Collections*, Vol. VII, pp. 211 ff. He was an intimate friend of the Verney family and a relative by reason of his marriage to Elizabeth Denton, Ralph Verney's cousin. I do not know why his suit against Winstanley was brought in the name of Verney, Wenman, and Winwood; possibly these men were trustees for the property under a marriage settlement. See the *Memoirs of the Verney Family, passim.*

[6] Though the pamphlet as a whole was addressed to the City of London, it included (pp. 2–7) a document addressed to his local opponents, which Winstanley tried to place before the court at Kingston.

[7] The bar admitted to practice in borough courts was often limited by agreement between the court and the local lawyers. Cf. *Reading Records: Diary of the Corporation*, Ed. J. M. Guilding, Vol. IV, p. 218, where there is a protest against the admission of a fourth practitioner in addition to the customary three. Note the reference (below, p. 333) to Mr. Gilder, "the atturney of Kingstone Court". Winstanley's argument in the following pages, which he offered to the court, is obviously no proper legal pleading in a suit for trespass, so that he was technically in default for non-appearance.

deny the corruption in Law, and endeavour a Reformation in our place and calling, according to that Nationall Covenant: and we know if your Lawes be built upon equity and reason, you ought both to have heard us speak, and read our answer; for that is no righteous Law, whereby to keep a Common-wealth in peace, when one sort shall be suffered to speak, and not another, as you deal with us, to passe sentence and execution upon us, before both sides be heard to speak.

[2] This principle in the forehead of your Laws, foretells destruction to this Common-wealth: for it declares that the Laws that follow such refusall, are selfish and theevish, and full of murder, protecting all that get money by their Laws, and crushing all others.

The writer hereof does require Mr. *Drake*, as he is a Parliament man, therefore a man counted able to speak rationally, to plead this cause of digging with me, and if he shew a just and rationall title, that Lords of Mannours have to the Commons, and that they have a just power from God, to call it their right, shutting out others; then I will write as much against it, as ever I writ for this cause. But if I shew by the Law of Righteousnesse, that the poorest man hath as true a title and just right to the Land, as the richest man, and that undeniably the earth ought to be a common treasury of livelihood for all, without respecting persons: Then I shall require no more of Mr. *Drake*, but that he would justifie our cause of digging, and declare abroad, that the Commons ought to be free to all sorts, and that it is a great trespasse before the Lord God Almighty, for one to hinder another of his liberty to dig the earth, that he might feed and cloath himself with the fruits of his labor therefrom freely, without owning any Landlord, or paying any rent to any person of his own kind.

I sent this following answer to the Arrest, in writing into Kingstone Court: In foure passages, your Court hath gone contrary to the righteousnesse of your own Statute Laws: for first it is mentioned in 36. *Ed.* 3. 15. that no Processe, Warrant, or Arrest should be served, till after the cause was recorded and entred; but your Bailiffe either could not, or would not tell us the cause when he arrested us, and Mr. *Rogers* your Recorder told us the first Court day we appeared, that our cause was not entred.

Secondly, we appeared two other Court daies, and desired a copy of the Declaration, and profered to pay for it, and you denied us. This is contrary to equity and reason, which is the foundation your Lawes are, or should be built upon, if you would have England to be a Common-wealth, and stand in peace.

Thirdly, we desired to plead our own cause, and you denied us, but told us we must fee an Attorney to speak for us, or els you would mark us for default in not appearance. This is contrary to your own Laws likewise, for in 28. *Ed.* 1. 11. chap. there is freedome given to a man to speak for himself, or els he may choose his father, friend or neighbor to plead for him, without the help of any other Lawyer.

[3] Fourthly, you have granted a judgement against us, and are proceeding to an execution, and this is contrary likewise to your own Laws, which say, that no plaint ought to be received, or judgement passed, till the cause be heard, and witnesses present, to testifie the plaint to be true, as Sir *Edward Cook*, 2. *part of Institutes* upon the 29. chap. of *Magna Charta*, fol. 51. 52. 53. The *Mirror of Justice*.

But that all men may see, we are neither ashamed nor afraid, to justifie that cause we are arrested for, neither to refuse to answer to it in a righteous way, therefore we have here delivered this up in writing, and we leave it in your hands, disavowing the proceedings of your Court, because you uphold Prerogative oppression, though the Kingly office be taken away, and the Parliament hath declared England a Common-Wealth; so that Prerogative Laws cannot be in force, unlesse you be besotted by your covetousnesse and envy.

We deny that we have trespassed against those three men, or Mr. *Drake* either, or that we should trespasse against any, if we should dig up, or plow for a livelihood, upon any the wast Land in England, for thereby we break no particular Law made by any Act of Parliament, but only an ancient custome, bred in the strength of Kingly Prerogative, which is that old Law or custome, by which Lords of Mannours lay claime to the Commons, which is of no force now to bind the people of England, since the Kingly power and office was cast out; and the common people, who have cast out the oppressor, by their purse and person, have not authorized any as yet, to give away from them their purchased freedome; and if any assume a power to give away, or withhold this purchased freedome, they are Traytors to this Common-Wealth of England: and if they imprison, oppresse, or put to death any for standing to maintain the purchased freedome, they are murderers and thieves, and no just rulers.

Therefore in the light of reason and equity, and in the light of the

Nationall Covenant, which Parliament and people have taken, with joynt consent: all such Prerogative customes, which by experience we have found to burden the Nation, ought to be cast out, with the Kingly office, and the Land of England now ought to be a free Land, and a common treasury to all her children, otherwise it cannot properly be called a Common-Wealth.

Therefore we justifie our act of digging upon that hill, to make the earth a common treasurie. First, because the earth was made by Almighty God to be a common treasury of livelihood for whole mankind in all his branches, without respect of persons; and that not any one [6, i. e., 4] according to the Word of God (which is love) the pure Law of righteousnesse, ought to be Lord or landlord over another, but whole mankind was made equall, and knit into one body by one spirit of love, which is Christ in you, the hope of glory, even [as] all the members of mans body, called the little world, are united into equality of love, to preserve the whole body.

But since the fall of man there from, which came in by the rising up of covetousnesse in the heart of mankind (to which Serpent the man consented) and from thence mankind was called *A-dam*: for this covetousnesse makes mankind to be a stoppage of freedome in the creation, and by this covetous power, one branch of mankind began to lift up himself above another, as *Cain* lifted up himself, and killed his brother *Abel*: and so one branch did kill and steal away the comfortable use of the earth from another, as it is now: the elder brother lives in a continuall theevery, stealing the Land from the younger brother. And the plain truth is, theeves and murderers, upheld by preaching witches and deceivers, rule the Nations: and for the present, the Laws and Government of the world, are Laws of darknesse, and the divells Kingdome, for covetousnesse rules all. And the power of the sword over brethren in Armies, in Arrests, in Prisons, in gallows, and in other inferiour torments, inflicted by some upon others, as the oppression of Lords of Mannours, hindring the poore from the use of the common Land, is *Adam* fallen, or *Cain* killing *Abel* to this very day.

And these Prerogative oppressors are the Adamites & Cainites that walk contrary to the Word of God (which is love) by upholding murder and theft, by Laws which their Fathers made, and which they now justifie; for in the conquests that Kings got, their Ancestors did murder and kill, and steal away the earth, and removed the Land mark from the conquered, and made Laws to imprison, torment, or put to death, all that would adventure to take the Land from them againe, and left both that stoln Land, and murdering Laws to their children, the Lords of Mannours, and Freeholders, who now with violence, do justifie their Fathers wickednesse, by holding fast that which was left them by succession.

For what are all the Laws of the Nations, in this corrupt covetous Government, lifting up one branch of *Adam* mankind above another, the Conqueror above the conquered, or those that have power above them that are weak, I say what are they, but Laws of murder and theft, yea enmity it self, against the Law of righteousnesse, which is love, which makes people do, as they would be done unto?

[5] And so all Kingly power (in one or many mens hands), raigning by the sword, giving the use of the earth to some of mankind (called by him his Gentry) and denying the free use of the Earth to others, called the younger brothers, or common people, is no other but *Cain* lifted up above *Abel*; the Prerogative Lawes is *Belzebub*, for they are the strength of covetousnesse and bondage in the creation, lifting up one, and casting down another: the Atturneys, and Priests, and Lawyers, and Bayliffs are servants to *Belzebub*, and are Devils; their Prisons, Whips, and Gallows are the torments of this Hell, or government of darknesse; for mind it all along, and you shall see, that covetousnesse and bitter envie gets freedome by these Lawes; But the sincere and meek in spirit, is trod under foot.

And this is that power, that hath made such havock in the Creation, it is that murderer and Devill that is to be cast out: this power of covetousnesse, is he that does countenance murder and theft in them that maintaines his Kingdom by the sword of Iron, and punishes it in others: and so that which is called a sin in the Common people, if they act such things, is counted no sin in the action of Kings, because they have the power of the sword in their hands, the fear whereof makes people to feare them.

But since this Kingly Office, by the Parliament, is cast out of *England*, and *England* by them is declared to be a free State or Commonwealth, we are in the first place thereby set free from those bonds and ties that the Kings laid upon us: Therefore this Tyranny of one over another, as of Lords of Mannors over the Common people, and for people to be forced to hire Lawyers to plead their causes for them, when they are able to plead themselves, ought to be taken away with the Kingly Office, because they are the strength of the Antient Prerogative custom.

Secondly we justifie our digging upon *George's* hill to make the Earth a common Treasury, because all sorts of people have lent assistance of purse and person to cast out the Kingly Office, as being a burden *England* groaned under; therefore those from whom money and blood was received, ought to obtain freedom in the Land to themselves and Posterity, by the Law of contract between Parliament and People.

But all sorts, poor as well as rich, Tenant as well as Landlord, have paid Taxes, Free-quarter, Excise, or adventured their lives, to cast out that Kingly Office.

Therefore, all sorts of people ought to have freedom in the Land of this their nativity, without respecting persons, now the Kingly Office is cast out, by their joynt assistance. And those that doe imprison, oppresse and take away the livelihood of those that rise up to take Possession of this purchased freedome, are Traitors to this Nation, and Enemies to righteousnesse: [6] And of this number are those men that have arrested, or that may arrest the Diggers, that endeavour to advance freedom; therefore I say all sorts ought to have their freedom.

And that in regard they have not only joyned persons and purses together, but in regard likewise, they took the Nationall Covenant, with joynt consent together, which the Parliament did make, of whom Mr. *Drake* that caused us to be arrested was one; which Covenant likewise, the Ministers in their Sermons, most vehemently prest upon the people to take, the intent whereof was this, That every one in his severall place and calling, should endeavor the peace, safety and freedom of *England,* and that the Parliament should assist the people, and the people the Parliament, and every one that had taken it, should assist those that had taken it, while they were in persuit thereof, as in the sixth Article of the Nationall Covenant.

But now Mr. *Drake* that was one that made this Covenant, and the *Surrey* Ministers that took it with great zeal at *Kingstone,* which I was eye witnesse to, and shall be of their hypocrisie therein, have set up a Lecturer [8] at *Cobham* on purpose to drive off the Diggers to forsake the persuit of their Covenant, are the most vehement to break Covenant, and to hinder them that would keep it, neither entring into peace themselves, nor suffering them that are entring in to enter.

But in regard some of us did dig upon *George's* Hill, thereby to take Possession of that freedom we have recovered, out of the hands of the Kingly Office, and thereby endeavour a Reformation in our place and calling according to the Word of God (which is Love): And while we are in persuit of this our Covenant, we expect both Parliament that made the Covenant, and the Officers of this Court, and Parish Ministers, and Lords of Mannors themselves, and especially Mr. *Drake,* to assist us herein, against all that shall oppose us in this righteous work of making the Earth a common Treasury; and not to beat us, imprison us, or take away our estates or lives, unlesse they will wilfully break Covenant with God and man, to please their own covetous froward heart, and thereby declare themselves to be the worst of Devils.

Therefore, in that we doe dig upon that Hill, we do not thereby take away other mens rights, neither do we demand of this Court, or from the Parliament, what is theirs and not ours: But we demand our own to be set free to us and them out of the Tyrannicall oppression of antient custome of Kingly Prerogative; and let us have no more gods to rule over us, but the King of righteousnesse only.

Therefore as the Free-holders claime a quietnesse and freedom in their inclosures, as it is fit they should have, so we that are younger brothers, or [7] the poore oppressed, we claime our freedome in the Commons, that so elder and younger brother may live quietly and in peace, together freed from the straits of poverty and oppression, in this Land of our nativitie.

Thus we have in writing declared in effect, what we should say, if we had liberty to speak before you, declaring withall, that your Court cannot end this Controversie in that equity and reason of it, which wee stand to maintaine: Therefore we have appealed to the Parliament[9], who have received our Appeal and promised an Answer, and we wait for it; And we leave this with you, and let Reason and

---

[8] A lecturer was a clergyman appointed to preach, but not having charge of the parish.
[9] In *An Appeal to the House of Commons,* which was presented on July 24, 1649.

righteousnesse be our Iudge; therefore we hope you will do nothing rashly, but seriously consider of this cause before you proceed to execution upon us.

You say God will blast our work, and you say, you are in the right, and we are in the wrong: Now if you be Christians, as you say you are; Then doe you act love to us, as we doe to you; and let both sides waite with patience on the Lord, to see who he blesses; but if you oppose by violence, arrest us, judge, condemn and execute us, and yet will not suffer us to speak for our selves, but you will force us to give money to our Enemies to speak for us, surely you cannot say your cause is right; but hereby you justifie our cause to be right, because you are the Persecutors of a loving meek-spirited people, and so declare that the God you say that will blast us, is covetousnesse, whom you serve by your persecuting power.

Covetous might may overcome rationall right for a time,
But rationall right must conquer covetous might, and that's the
life of mine.

The Law is righteous, just and good, when Reason is the rule,
But who so rules by the fleshly will, declares himself a foole.

Well, this same writing was delivered into their Court, but they cast it away and would not read it, and all was because I would not fee an Atturney; and then the next Court day following, before there was any tryall of our cause, for there was none suffered to speak but the Plaintiffe, they passed a Iudgement, and after that an Execution.

Now their Iury was made of rich Free-holders, and such as stand strongly for the Norman power: And though our digging upon that barren Common hath done the Common good, yet this Iury brings in damages of ten pounds a man, and the charges of the Plaintiffe in their Court, twenty nine shillings and a peny; and this was their sentence and the passing of the Execution upon us.

[8] And 2 dayes after (for in this case they can end a cause speedily in their Court; but when the Atturney and Lawyers get money they keep a cause depending seven yeares, to the utter undoing of the parties, so unrighteous is the Law, and Lawyers) I say, two dayes after they sent to execute the execution, and they put *Henry Beckerstaffe* in prison, but after three dayes, Mr. *Drake* released him again, *Beckerstaffe* not knowing of it till the release came; They seek after

Thomas Star to imprison his body, who is a poore man not worth ten pounds.

Then they came privately by day to *Gerrard Winstanleys* house, and drove away foure Cowes; I not knowing of it and some of the Lords Tenants rode to the next Town shouting the diggers were conquered, the diggers were conquered. Truly it is an easie thing to beat a man, and cry conquest over him after his hands are tied, as they tyed ours. But if their cause be so good, why will they not suffer us to speak, and let reason and equity, the foundation of righteous Lawes, judge them and us. But strangers made rescue of those Cowes, and drove them astray out of the Bailiffes hands, so that the Bailiffes lost them; but before the Bailiffes had lost the Cowes, I hearing of it went to them and said here is my body, take me that I may come to speak to those *Normans* that have stolne our land from us; and let the Cowes go, for they are none of mine; and after some time, they telling me that they had nothing against my body, it was my goods they were to have; then said I: take my goods, for the Cowes are not mine; and so I went away and left them, being quiet in my heart, and filled with comfort within my self, that the King of righteousnesse would cause this to work for the advancing of his own Cause, which I prefer above estate or livelyhood,

Saying within my heart as I went along, that if I could not get meat to eat, I would feed upon bread, milk and cheese; and if they take the Cowes, that I cannot feed on this, or hereby make a breach between me and him that owns the Cowes, then I'le feed upon bread and beere, till the King of righteousnesse clear up my innocency, and the justice of his own cause; and if this be taken from me for maintaining his Cause, I'le stand still and see what he will doe with me, for as yet I know not.

Saying likewise within my heart as I was walking along, O thou King of righteousnesse shew thy power, and do thy work thy self, and free thy people now from under this heavy bondage of miserie, *Pharaoh* the covetous power. And the answer in my heart was satisfactory, and full of sweet joy and peace: and so I said, Father, do what thou wilt, this cause is thine, and thou knowest that the love to righteousnesse makes me do what I do.

I was made to appeal to the Father of life in the speakings of my heart [9] likewise thus: Father thou knowest that what I have writ or spoken, concerning this light, that the earth should be restored and become a common Treasurie for all mankind, without respect of persons, was thy free revelation to me, I never read it in any book, I heard it from no mouth of flesh till I understood it from thy teaching first within me. I did not study nor imagine the conceit of it; self-love to my own particular body does not carry me along in the mannaging of this businesse; but the power of love flowing forth to the liberty and peace of thy whole Creation, to enemies as well as friends: nay towards those that oppresse me, endeavouring to make me a beggar to them. And since I did obey thy voice, to speak and act this truth, I am hated, reproached, and oppressed on every side. Such as make profession of thee, yet revile me. And though they see I cannot fight with fleshly weapons, yet they will strive with me by that power. And so I see, Father, that *England* yet does choose rather to fight with the Sword of Iron, and covetousnesse, then by the Sword of the Spirit which is love: and what thy purpose is with this land, or with my body, I know not; but establish thy power in me, and then do what pleases thee.

These and such like sweet thoughts dwelt upon my heart as I went along, and I feel my self now like a man in a storm, standing under shelter upon a hill in peace, waiting till the storm be over to see the end of it, and of many other things that my eye is fixed upon: But I will let this passe,

And return again to the Dragons Den, or Hornets nest, the selfish murdering fleshly Lawes of this Nation, which hangs some for stealing, and protects others in stealing; Lords of Mannours stole the land from their fellow creatures formerly in the conquests of Kings, and now they have made Lawes to imprison and hang all those that seek to recover the land again out of their thieving murdering hands.

They took away the Cowes which were my livelyhood, and beat them with their clubs, that the Cowes heads and sides did swell, which grieved tender hearts to see: and yet these Cowes never were upon *George* Hill, nor never digged upon that ground, and yet the poore beasts must suffer because they gave milk to feed me, but they were driven away out of those Devills hands the Bailiffes, and were delivered out of hell at that time.

And thus Lords of Mannours, their Bailiffes the true upholders of the *Norman* power, and some Freeholders that doe oppose this publick work, are such as the countrey knowes have beene no friends to that Cause the Parliament declared for, but to the Kingly power; and now if they get the foot fast in the stirrup, they will lift themselves again into the *Norman* saddle; and they do it secretly; for they keep up the *Norman* Lawes and thereby Traytours to freedome get into places of Law and power, and by [10] that will enslave *England* more then it was under the Kingly power.

Therefore *England* beware; thou art in danger of being brought under the *Norman* power more than ever. The King *Charles* that was successour to *William* the Conquerour thou hast cast out: and though thy Parliament have declared against the Kingly office, and cast it out, and proclaimed *England* a Common-wealth [10], that is to be a free land for the liberty and livelyhood of all her children;

Yet *William* the Conquerours Army begins to gather into head againe, and the old *Norman* Prerogative Law is the place of their rendezvous: for though their chief Captain *Charles* be gone, yet his Colonells, which are Lords of Mannours, his Councellours and Divines, which are our Lawyers and Priests, his inferiour officers and Souldiers, which are the Freeholders, and Land-lords, all which did steal away our Land from us when they killed and murdered our Fathers in that *Norman* conquest: And the Bailiffes that are slaves to their covetous lusts and all the ignorant bawling women against our digging for freedome, are the snapsack boyes and the ammunition sluts that follow the *Norman* Camp.

These are all striving to get into a body againe, that they may set up a new *Norman* slaverie over us; and the place of their rendezvous, Prerogative power is fenced already about, with a Line of Communication. An act made by a piece of the Parliament to maintain the old Lawes[11]; which if once this Camp be fortified in his full strength, it

[10] On February 7, 1649, the House of Commons adopted a resolution asserting "that it had been found by experience . . . that the office of King in this nation . . . is unnecessary, burdensome, and dangerous to the liberty, safety, and public interest of the people of this nation, and therefore ought to be abolished". The act making this resolution effective was passed on March 19 and proclaimed in the City by the Lord Mayor on May 30. An Act declaring and constituting England a Free Commonwealth, to be governed by "the representatives of the people in Parliament . . . without any King or House of Lords", was passed on May 19, 1649.

[11] The Act of February 17, 1649, permitting actions, etc., in the name of the Keepers of the Liberty of England, in place of the King.

will cost many a sighing heart, and burdened spirit before it be taken.

And this *Norman* Camp are got into so numerous a body already, that they have appointed their Sutlers to drive away the Cowes which were my livelyhood, and some of them they would sell to make money of to pay the Atturney, *Gilder,* and Lawyers their fees, for denying the diggers our priviledge to plead our own cause; for as it is clearly seen that if we be suffered to speak we shall batter to pieces all the old Lawes, and prove the maintainers of them hypocrites and Traitours to this Common-wealth of *England,* and then the Atturneys and Lawyers Trade goes down, and Lords of Mannours must be reckoned equall to other men. And this covetous flesh and blood cannot endure.

And other of the Cows were to be killed to victuall the Camp, that is, to feed those *Normans, Wil Star* & *Ned Sutton,* both Freeholders & others the snapsack boyes, and ammunition drabs that helped to drive away the Cows, that they might be encouraged by a belly full of stoln goods to stick the closer to the businesse another time. Or else the price of these Cowes was to pay for the sack and Tobacco which the *Norman* officers of Knights, Gentlemen, and rich Freeholders did spend at the White Lion at *Cobham,* [11] when they met the 24. of *August,* 1649, to advise together what course they should take to subdue the diggers; for say they, if the cause of the diggers stand, we shall lose all our honour and titles, and we that have had the glory of the earth shall be of no more account then those slaves our servants and yonger brothers that have been footstools to us and our Fathers ever since the *Norman William* our beloved Generall took this land (not by love) but by a sharp sword, the power by which we stand: and though we own Christ by name, yet we will not do as he did to save enemies, but by our sword we will destroy our enemies, and do we not deserve the price of some of the diggers Cows to pay us for this our good service? And doe not our reverend Ministers tell us that *William* the Conquerour and the succeeding Kings were Gods annointed? And do not they say that our inclosures which were got by that murdering sword, and given by *William* the Conquerour to our Fathers, and so successivly from them, the land is our inheritance, and that God gave it us, and shall these broken fellows, and beggarly rogues take our rights from us, and have the use of the land equall with us? Thus do these *Norman* Gentlemen comfort their hearts, and support themselves with broken reeds, when they meet together in their Counsels.

But stay you *Norman* Gentlemen, let me put in a word amongst you, doth the murderers sword make any man to be Gods anointed? Surely, Iesus Christ was called Gods annointed not because he conquered with a Sword of iron, but because he conquered by love, and the spirit of patience: therefore your Generall was not Gods annointed, as Christ was.

And then the Earth was not made to be the successive inheritance of children of murderers, that had the strongest arm of flesh, and the best sword, that can tread others under foot with a bold brasen forehead under colour of the Law of justice as the *Norman* power does; But it was made for all by the Law of righteousnesse, and he gives the whole Earth to be the inheritance of every single branch of mankind without respect of persons, and he that is filled with the love of this righteous King, doing as he would be done by is a true annointed one.

Therfore, that god whom you serve, and which did intitle you Lords, Knights, Gentlemen, and Landlords, is covetousnesse, the god of this world, which alwayes was a murderer, a devil and father of lies, under whose dark governing power, both you and all the nations of the world for the present are under. But the King of righteousnesse or God of love whom I serve, did not call the earth your inheritance, shutting out others, but gave the earth to be a common treasurie to whole mankind (who is the Lord of it) without respect of person.

[12] This power of love, is the King of righteousnesse, the Lord God Almighty that rules the whole Creation in peace, that is the Seed that breaks covetousnesse the Serpents head; he is the restoring power, that is now rising up to change all things into his own nature, he will be your Iudge, for vengance is his; and for any wrong you have done me, as I can tell you of many, yet I have given all matters of judgment and vengance into his hand, and I am sure he will doe right, and discover him that is the true Trespasser, that takes away my rights from me.

And take notice of this, you Lords of Mannors, and Norman Gentry, though you should kill my body or starve me in prison, yet know, that the more you strive, the more troubles your hearts shall be filled with; and doe the worst you can to hinder publick freedom, you shall come off losers in the later end. I meane you shall lose your Kingdom of darknesse, though I lose my livelihood, the poor Cowes that is my living, and should be imprisoned; you have been told this 12 Months agoe, that you should lose ground by striving, and will you not take warning, will you needs shame your selves, to let the poore Diggers take away your Kingdome from you? Surely, the power that is in them, will take the rule and government from you, and give it a people that will make better use of it.

Alas! you poor blind earth mouls, you strive to take away my livelihood, and the liberty of this poor weak frame my body of flesh, which is my house I dwell in for a time; but I strive to cast down your kingdom of darknesse, and to open Hell gates, and to break the Devils bands asunder, wherewith you are tied, that you my Enemies may live in peace, and that is all the harm I would have you to have.

Therefore you Lords of Mannors, you Free-holders, you Norman-Clergy, oppressing Tith-mungers, and you of the Parliament men, that have plaid fast and loose with this poor Nation, for what is past let it goe; hereafter advance freedom and liberty, and pluck up bondage; and sinne no more by Lording it over your Lords and Masters, that set you upon those Parliament Seats, lest worse things befall you then yet hath.

But to return again to Mr. *Gilders* advice, the Atturney of *Kingstone* Court, and the proceeding of that Court with the Cowes; you heare how they did judge, condemn and execute me, not suffering me to speak; and though those four Cowes were rescued out of their hands by strangers, not by me; and so by their own Law, they should have looked after the Rescuers, yet contrary to their own Law, they came againe to *Winstanleys* dwelling a fortnight after, and drove away seven Cowes and a Bull in the night time, some of the Cowes being Neighbour's that had hired pasture; and yet the damage which their Norman Iury, and their covetous besotted, [13] ignorant Atturney Mr. *Gilder*, had judged me to pay for a Trespasse in digging upon that barren *George's* Hill, was but eleven pound nine shillings and a penney charges & all, which they are like never to have of me, for an empty carrier will dance and sing before these Norman theeves and pick-purses: And thus you see they judged and passed sentence upon me but once at their prerogative pleasure, which they call *Englands* Law: but they executed me twice, that they might be sure to kill me. But yet these Cowes likewise are brought home againe, and the heart of my Enemies is put into the pound of vexation because the Cowes are set free. Surely, these Lords of Mannors and the Atturney Mr. *Gilder*, that gave advice to Arrest us for digging, have burned their Bibles long agoe, because they have so quite and clean forgotten that Petition in the Lords prayer, *forgive us our trespasses as we forgive them*; for they make this a trespasse against them, for digging upon the wast land of our mother the Land of *England* for a livelihood, when as their Law it self saith, *That the Commons and wasts belong to the poore.*

So that you see the Norman Camp is grown very numerous and big, that they want much beeffe to vituall them, and they are such hungry ones, that they will eat poor lean Cowes that are little better then skin & bone; and poor Cowes if I keep them in the winter, they are like to be poorer for want of Hay; for before the report of our digging was much known, I bought three Acres of grasse of a Lord of a Mannor, whom I will not here name, because I know the councel of others made him prove fals to me; for when the time came to Mow, I brought mony to pay him before hand; but he answered me, I should not have it, but sold it to another before my face; this was because his Parish Priest, and the *Surrey* Ministers, and sorry ones too they are that have set up a Lecturer at *Cobham* for a little time, to preach down the Diggers, have bid the people neither to buy nor sell with us, but to beat us, imprison us, or banish us; and thereby they prove themselves to be members of the Beast that had two horns, like a Lamb, and yet spake like a Dragon, & so they fulfill that Scripture in *Rev.* 13. 16. *that no man might buy and sell, save he that had the mark of the Beast.* Or else surely, they do it on purpose to quicken us to our work, and to drive us to Plant the Commons with all speed as may be.

But though the Cowes were poor, yet they care not, so the skins will but pay the Lawyers and Atturney *Gilder* his Fees, and the flesh to feed the snapsack boyes, either to eat and make merry with, or else to sell to make money of, to pay those that drive away the Cowes for their paines or charges they have been at, in this 18 weeks striving to beat the Diggers off their work: But the bones will serve the Bailiffs to pick, because their action will be both proved thievery in stealing another mans cattell, and their [14] trespasse very great against the same man, in opening all the Gates round about the ground, where *Winstanley* dwels, and let Hogs and common Cattell into the standing barly and other corn, which the right owner will seek satisfaction for.

So that the fury of this Norman Camp against the Diggers is so great, that they would not only drive away all the Cowes upon the ground, but spoyl the corn too, and when they had done this mischief, the Bayliffs, & the other Norman snapsack boyes went hollowing and shouting, as if they were dancing at a whitson Ale; so glad they are to do mischief to the Diggers, that they might hinder the work of freedome.

And why are they so furious against us? but because we endeavour to dig up their Tythes, their Lawyers Fees, their Prisons, and all that Art and Trade of darknesse, whereby they get money under couller of Law; and to plant the plesant fruit trees of freedom, in the room of that cursed thornbush, the power of the murdering sword; for they say, they doe all they do by the Law of the Land which the Parliament hath confirmed to them by an Act: And if so, Then Souldiers where is the price of your bloud? and Countrey-men, and Citizens Where is the price of your Taxes and Free quarter? If this be the freedom you are like to have, to be beaten and not be suffered to say why doe you so, and shall have no remedy, unlesse you will Fee a Lawyer (an Enemy) to plead for you, when you are able to plead your own cause better your self, and save that charge, and have your cause ended sooner and with more peace and quietnesse.

And you zealous Preachers, and professors of the City of *London* and you great Officers and Souldiery of the Army, Where are all your Victories over the Cavaliers, that you made such a blaze in the Land, in giving God thanks for, and which you begged in your Fasting dayes, and morning Exercises; Are they all sunck into the Norman power again, and must the old Prerogative Laws stand; what freedom then did you give thanks for? Surely, that you had killed him that rid upon you, that you may get up into his saddle to ride upon others; O thou City, thou Hypocriticall City! thou blindfold drowsie *England*, that sleps and snorts in the bed of covetousnesse, awake, awake, the Enemie is upon thy back, he is ready to scale the walls and enter Possession, and wilt thou not look out.

Does not the streames of bondage run in the same river that it did, and with a bigger stream of Norman power; so that if you awaken not betimes, the flood of the Norman Prerogative power, will drown you all; here's more rivers comes into the maine stream, since the storm fell and the waters of fury rises very high, banked in by Laws; and while you are talking and disputing about words, the Norman Souldiers are secretly working among you to advance their power again; and so will take away [15] the benefit of all your victories by a subtile act of intricate Lawes, which the sword in the field could not do against you: and when you have lost that freedom, which you boasted of that you will leave to your posterity, then who must give thanks, you that vapoured in words, or they that lay close in action, waiting to trip up your heels by pollicy, when the sword could not do it.

I tell thee thou *England*, thy battells now are all spirituall. Dragon against the Lamb, and the power of love against the power of covetousnesse; therefore all that will be Souldiers for Christ, the Law of righteousnesse, joyn to the Lamb. He that takes the iron sword now shall perish with it, and would you be a strong Land and flourish in beauty, then fight the Lambs battels, and his strength shall be thy walls and bulwarks.

You Knights, Gentlemen, and Freeholders, that sat in councell at the White Lion in *Cobham* to find out who are our backers, and who stirs us up to dig the Commons, Ile tel you plainly who it is, it is love, the King of righteousnes ruling in our hearts, that makes us thus to act that the creation may be set at liberty, and now I have answered your inquirie, do what you can to him and us his servants: And we require you in his name, to let our cause have a publick triall, and do not work any longer in darknesse, set not your Bailiffes and slaves to come by night to steal away the Cowes of poore men under colour of justice, when as the cause was never yet heard in open Court.

He that backs you, and that sets you to work, to deny to us your younger brother the use of the common land, is covetousnesse, which is Beelzebub, the greatest devil, so that there is the 2 generalls known, which you & we fight under, the 2 great Princes of light and darknes, bondage and freedom, that does Act all flesh in the great controversies of the world. These are the 2 men that stir in this busines, that is, the wicked man that councels & backs you to be so envious and furious against us, and the righteous man Christ, that backs and councells us to love you our enemies. And do we not see that *Gebal, Ammon* and *Amaleck,* and all the rabble of the nations, Lords, Knights, Gentlemen, Lawyers, Bailiffes, Priests, and all the *Norman* snapsack boyes, and ammunition women to the old *Norman* Camp do all combine together in the art of unrighteous fury, to drive the poore diggers off from their work, that the name of community and freedome which is Christ, may not be known in earth. Thus I have dealt plainly with you all, and I have not flattered Parliament, Army, City, nor Countrey, but have declared in this and other writings the whole light of that truth revealed to me by the word of the Lord: and I shall now wait to see his hand, to do his own work in what time, and by what instruments he pleases. And I see the poore must first be picked out, and honoured in this work, for they begin to receive the word of righteousnesse, but the rich generally are enemies to true freedome.

The work of digging still goes on, and stops not for a rest:
The Cowes were gone, but are return'd, and we are all at rest.
[16] *No money's paid, nor never shall, to a Lawyer or his man*
To plead our cause, for therein wee'll do the best we can.
In Cobham *on the little Heath our digging there goes on.*
And all our friends they live in love, as if they were but one.

Thus you Gentlemen, that will have no Law to rule over you, but your Prerogative will must be above Law, and above us that are the yonger brothers in the Land; but if you say, no, your wil shal be subject to Law: then I demand of you Mr. *Drake,* Mr. *Gilder,* and other the Bailiffes and Officers of *Kingston* Court, why will you arrest us, and trouble us, and say we trespasse against you, and though we came to answer to your arrest, and to plead our own cause, yet contrary to the equity, nay contrary to the bare letter of the Law, as I shewed you before, you denyed me that priviledge, but went on and did condemne and execute a forceable power upon body and goods, is not your will here above Law? Do you not hereby uphold the *Norman* conquest?

Mr. *Drake,* you are a Parliament man, and was not the beginning of the quarrel between King *Charles* and your House? This the King pleaded to uphold Prerogative, and you were against it, and yet must a Parliament man be the first man to uphold Prerogative, who are but servants to the Nation for the peace and liberty of every one, not conquering Kings to make their wil a Law? Did you not promise liberty to the whole Nation, in case the Cavalier party were cast out? And why now wil you seek liberty to your self and Gentry, with the deniall of just liberty and freedome to the common people, that have born the greatest burden?

You have arrested us for digging upon the common Land, you have executed your unrighteous power, in distraining cattel, imprisoning our bodies, and yet our cause was never publickly heard, neither can it be proved that we have broke any Law, that is built upon equity and reason, therfore we wonder where you had your power to rule over us by will, more then we to rule over you by our will. We request you before you go too far, not to let covetousnesse be your Master, trample not others under your feet, under colour of Law, as if none knew equity of Law but you; for we and our estates shall be thorns in your eyes, and pricks in your sides, and you may curse that Councell bid you beg our estates, or imprison our persons. But this we request that you would let us have a fair open triall, and do not carry on the course of Law in secret, like *Nicodemus* that is afraid to have his businesse come to light; therefore I challenge you once more, seeing you professe your selves Christians, to let us be brought to a trial of our cause; let your ministers plead with us in the Scriptures, & let your Lawyers plead with us in the equity & reason of your own Law; and if you prove us transgressours, then we shal lay down our work and acknowledge we have trespassed against you in digging upon the Commons, & then punish us. But if we prove by Scripture & reason, that undeniably the land belongs to one as well as another, then you shal own our work, justifie our cause, & declare that you have done wrong to Christ, who you say is your Lord and master, in abusing us his servants, & your fellow creatures, while we are doing his work. Therefore I knowing you to be men of moderation in outward shew, I desire that your actions towards your fellow creatures may not be like one beast to another, but carry your selves like man to man; for your proceeding in your pretence of law hitherto against us is both unrighteous, beastly & divelish, and nothing of the spirit of man seen in it. You Atturnies and Lawyers, you say you are ministers of justice,

& we know that equity and reason is, or ought to be the foundation of Law; if so, then plead not for mony altogether but stand for universall justice & equity; then you will have peace; otherwise both you with the corrupt Clergy will be cast out as unsavoury salt.

FINIS.

TWO LETTERS TO LORD FAIRFAX

THESE letters were written in December, 1649. They are reprinted, by permission of the Royal Historical Society, from the *Clarke Papers*, Vol. II, pp. 215 ff. They were probably sent also to the Council of State, since an abstract of Winstanley's letter occurs in the *Calendar of State Papers, Domestic*, 1653–1654, p. 338; the document is misplaced and belongs in the volume for 1649.

TO HIS EXCELLENCY THE LORD FAIRFAX AND THE COUNSELL OF WARRE THE BROTHERLY REQUEST OF THOSE THAT ARE CALLED DIGGERS SHEWETH

THAT whereas wee have begun to digg upon the Commons for a livelihood, and have declared to your Excellency and the whole world our reasons, which are four. First, from the righteous law of Creation that gives the earth freely to one as well as to another without respect of persons. Secondly, by vertue of yours and our victory over the King, whereby the enslaved people of England have recovered themselves from under the Norman Conquest; though wee doe not as yet enjoy the benefitt of our victories, nor cannot soe long as the use of the Common land is held from the younger bretheren by the Lords of Mannours, that as yet sitte in the Norman chaire, and upholde that tyranny as if the kingly power were in force still; and a third reason that moved us to digg was the perswasion of our hartes that the Parliament and Army would make good their bargaine with us; for you promised that if wee would adventure person and purse to recover England from under that Norman oppression you would make us a free people, and you have obtained the victory by your owne and our assistance, and there is nothing wanting from you to us but makeing good your bargaine to us, for by the law of reason and contract wee have bought our freedom of the Parliament and Army, who have the power of the sword in your hands, by our blood, taxes, and free quarter. And wee are perswaded of your faithfullness to us for two reasons. First, your promises, which as you are Gospell professours wee expect you will make good, and soe give us our freedome, which wee have dearely paid for, and you have received our moneys the fruits of our labours. Secondly, your Covenant to God, unto whome first wee kept fasting dayes, and praied him to help and deliver this oppressed Nation, and then after any victory over our oppressour Charles you apointed daies of thanks-giving unto God. Now in the third place, God expects from you and the Parliament to performe your Covenant in deede and worke as well as in words, and let the oppressed goe free unto whom you promised freedome; and though you have fought for it, yet wee have paid for it, and soe have purchased that same freedome with you, that is that wee may live in the earth without poverty; for (fourthly) wee digg upon the Common to make the earth a common treasury, because our necessity for food and rayment require it.

Now Sirs, divers repulses wee have had from some of the Lords of Mannours and their servants, with whome wee are patient and love-ing, not doubting but at last they will grant liberty quietly to live by them; and though your tenderness have moved us to bee requesting your protection against them, yet wee have forborne, and rather waited upon God with patience till hee quell their unruely spirits, and of prosecuting Sauls to make them righteous Pauls; and in regard likewise the souldiers did not molest us, for that you tould us when some of us were before you, that you had given command to your souldiers not to meddle with us, but resolved to leave us to the Gentlemen of the Cuntry and to the law of the Land to deale with us; which wee were satisfied with, and for this halfe year past your souldiers have not meddled with us.

But now Sirs, this last weeke upon the 28th of November, there came a party of souldiers commanded by a cornet, and some of them of your owne Regiment, and by their threatneing words forced 3 labouring men to helpe them to pull downe our 2 houses, and carried away the wood in a cart to a Gentleman's house who hath bin a Cavaleer all our tyme of warrs, and cast 2 or 3 old people out who lived in those houses to lye in the open feild this cold weather, (an action more becomeing the Turks to deale with Christians then for one Christian to deale with another); but if you inquire into the business you will finde that the Gentlemen that sette the souldyers on are enemyes to you, for some of the cheife had hands in the Kentish riseing against the Parliament, and wee know, and you will finde it true if you trust them so farr, that [they] love you but from the teeth outward.

Therefore our request to you is this, that you would call your souldiers to accompt for attempting to abuse us without your commission, that the Cuntry may know that you had noe hand in such an unrighteous and cruell act. Likewise wee desire that you would continue your former kindnesse and promise to give commission to your souldiers not to meddle with us without your order, and wee shalbee very thankfull to you and remayne

Yours and England true borne sonnes and frends.

John Heyman	
An: Wrenn	
Hen: Barton	*in the behalfe of*
Jo^n Coulton	*others called the*
Robert Cosler	*Diggers.*
John Palmer	
Jacob Heard	

TO MY LORD GENERALL AND HIS COUN-
CELL OF WARR

SIR,

I UNDERSTAND that Mr. Parson Platt [1] with some other Gentlemen, have made report to you, and the Councell of State, that
wee that are called Diggers are a riotous people, and that wee will
not bee ruled by the Justices, and that wee hold a mans house by violence from him, and that wee have 4 guns in it, to secure ourselves,
and that wee are drunkards, and Cavaleers waiteing an opportunity to
helpe to bringe in the Prince, and such like.

Truely Sir, these are all untrue reports, and as false as those which
Haman of old raised against sincere harted Mordecay to incense
Kinge Ahasuerus against him. The conversacion of the diggers is not
such as they report, wee are peaceable men, and walke in the light
of righteousness to the utmost of our power. Our enemies have sent
divers tymes to beate us, and to pull downe our houses, yet wee never
gave them bad language, nor resisted againe, but tooke all their abuses
patiently, waiteing upon God till hee make their harts quiett, that wee
may live in peace by them; but truely the same things which they
falsely report of us, wee and all the people round about us, can and
would prove to their faces, if yow should call us face to face, some
of them were alwayes Cavaleers, and had a hand in the Kentish riseing, and were cheife promoters of the offensive Surry petition; but
wee doe not speake this to ripp up old quarrells, neither doe I desire
to mencion their names, least yow should thinke wee were enemies;
for truely it is our desire to conquer them with love, though they

---

[1] John Platt became rector of West Horsley in 1643 when the incumbent was ejected
by the Presbyterians. He was a member, in 1647, of the Guildford Classis and a "trier"
for Surrey. He was ejected from the living by the Act of Conformity in 1662, and
died at Westbrook in 1670. As Winstanley says, he was lord of the manor at Cobham
"by marriage"; i e., to Margaret, the daughter of Sir Humphrey Lynde. There is a
biographical note on Platt in *Calamy Revised*, by A. G. Matthews (1934), p. 391.

much abuse us that have alwayes bin your friends, as the enemy themselves, if they were face to face, can say not otherwise.

Now Sir, the end of our digging and ploughing upon the common land is this, that wee and all the impoverisht poore in the land may gett a comfortable livelyhood by our righteous labours thereupon; which wee conceive wee have a right unto, (I speake in the name of all the poore commoners) by vertue of the conquest over the King, for while hee was in power hee was the successour over [i. e., of] William the Conquerour, and held the land as a conquerour from us, and all Lords of Mannours held tytle to the common Lands from him; but seeing the common people of England by ioynt consent of person and purse, have caste out Charles our Norman oppressour, wee have by this victory recovered ourselves from under his Norman yoake, and the lande now is to returne into the ioynt hands of those who have conquered, that is the commonours, and the land is to be held noe longer from the use of them by the hand of anye who⟨se those⟩ will uphold the Norman and Kingly power still; and if soe, then wee that are impoverished by sticking to the Parliament and you, shall loose the benefitt of all our taxes, free quarter, and blood, and remayne slaves still to the kingly power in the hands of Lords of Mannours, which wee have cast out of the hands of Charles.

Therefore wee poore oppressed Commoners claime freedome in the common land, by vertue of the Parliaments promises and ingagement, and of the armies actinge; for wee did beleive and rely thereupon, being as wee conceive it a firme bargaine between you and us; for you and the Parliament in effect said to us, 'Give us your taxes, free quarter, excise, and adventure your lives with us to cast out the oppressour Charles, and wee will make yow a free people', therefore by the law of contract as wee expected was firmly made and confirmed on our part by performance, wee claime this freedome to enioy the common land for our livelihood, for wee have bought it by our bloud and money.

Secondly, wee claime this freedome by equality in the conquest over the Kinge, for the Parliament told us what they did they did it for the safety and peace of the whole nation, the army told us they fought not for themselves, but for the safety and peace of the whole Nation, and yow and wee ioyned our forces togeather to procure our freedome, and have obteyned it; therefore if there bee a spoyle of the common land to be gathered, as there is, it is to bee equally devided betweene yow that went to warr, and wee that stay'd at home and paid you, that is, as the Gentry have their inclosure free to themselves, soe wee the poore impoverisht commoners claime freedome in the common land by vertue of this conquest over the Kinge, which is gotten by our ioynt consent.

Thirdly, wee know that England cannot bee a free Commonwealth, unless all the poore commoners have a free use and benefitt of the land; for if this freedome bee not granted, wee that are the poore commoners are in a worse case then we were in the King's dayes, for then wee had some estate about us, though we were under oppression, but now our estates are spent to purchase freedome, and wee are under oppression still of Lords of Mannours tyranny; therefore [unless] wee that are poore commoners have some part of the land to live upon freely, as well as the Gentry it cannott bee a common wealth, neither can the kingly power bee removed soe longe as this kingly power in the hands of Lords of Mannours rules over us.

Now Sir, if you and the Counsell will quietly grant us this freedome, which is our owne right, and sett us free from the kingly power of Lords of Mannours, that violently now as in the Kings dayes holde the commons from us, (as if wee had obteyned noe conquest at all over the kingly power), then the poore that ly under the great burden of poverty, and are alwayes complayning for want, and their miseries increased because they see noe meanes of releife found out, and therefore cry out continually to you and the Parliament for releife and to make good your promises, wilbe quietted.

Wee desire noe more of yow then freedome to worke, and to enioy the benefitt of our labours—for here is wast land enough and to spare to supply all our wants—but if yow deny this freedome, then in righteousness wee must raise collections for the poore out of the estates, and a mass of money will not supply their wants; because many are in want that are ashamed to take collection money, and therefore they are desperate, and will rather robb and steale, and disturb the land, and others that are ashamed to beg would doe any worke for to live, as it is the case of many of our diggers that have bin good housekeepers; but if this freedome were granted to improve the common lands then there would bee a supply to answer everyones inquire, and the murmurings of the people against yow and the

Parliament would cease, and within a few yeares wee should have noe beggers nor idle persons in the land.

Secondly, hereby England would bee enriched with all commodity with in it selfe which they each would afford; and truely this is a stayne to Christian religion in England, that wee have soe much land ly wast, and soe many starve for want; and further, if this freedome bee granted, the whole land wilbee united in love and strength, that if a forraigne enemy like an army of ratts and mice come to take our inheritance from us, wee shall all rise as one man to defend it.

Then lastly, if you will grant the poore commoners this quiett freedome to improve the common land for our livelyhood, wee shall reioyce in yow and the army in protecting our worke, and wee and our worke wilbee ready to secure that, and wee hope there will not bee any kingly power over us, to rule at will and wee to bee slaves, as the power has bin, but that you will rule in love as Moses and Joshua did the Children of Israell before any kingly power came in, and that the Parliament wilbee as the Elders of Israell, chosen freely by the people to advise for and assist both yow and us.

And thus in the name of the rest of these called Diggers and Commonours through the land, I have in short declared our mynde and cause to you in the light of righteousness, which will prove all these reports made against us to bee false and distructive to the uniteing of England into peace.

Per me Gerrard Winstanley for my selfe and in the behalfe of my Fellow Commoners.

December the 8th, 1649.

A NEW-YEERS GIFT FOR THE PAR-LIAMENT AND ARMIE

THE title page is dated 1650, and Thomason dated his copy January 1. Winstanley's name appears on the title page.

Copies are to be found in the following collections: Bibliotheca Lindesiana, The Bodleian, and The Thomason Library at the British Museum; there is another copy in the British Museum.

The text is reproduced from the copy in the Thomason Library.

[1] A NEW-YEERS GIFT SENT TO THE PAR-
LIAMENT AND ARMIE

G ENTLEMEN of the Parliament and Armie; you and the Common people have assisted each other, to cast out the Head of oppression which was Kingly power, seated in one mans hand, and that work is now done, and till that work was done you called upon the people to assist you to deliver this distressed bleeding dying nation out of bondage; And the people came and failed you not, counting neither purse nor blood too dear to part with to effect this work.

The Parliament after this have made an Act to cast out Kingly power, and to make *England* a free Common-wealth.[1] These Acts the People are much rejoyced with, as being words forerunning their freedome, and they wait for their accomplishment that their joy may be full; for as words without action are a cheat, and kills the comfort of a righteous [2] spirit, so words performed in action does comfort and nourish the life thereof.

Now Sirs, wheresoever we spie out Kingly power, no man I hope shall be troubled to declare it, nor afraid to cast it out, having both Act of Parliament, the Souldiers Oath, and the common peoples consent on his side; for Kingly power is like a great spread tree, if you lop the head or top-bow, and let the other Branches and root stand, it will grow again and recover fresher strength.

If any ask me, What Kingly power is? I Answer, there is a twofold Kingly power. The one is, The Kingly power of righteousnesse, and

---

[1] On February 7, 1649, the House of Commons adopted a resolution declaring that "the office of king in this nation . . . is unnecessary, burdensome, and dangerous to the liberty, safety, and public interests of the people of this nation, and therefore ought to be abolished". An Act giving effect to this resolution was passed on March 19 and proclaimed on May 30. An Act declaring England to be a free commonwealth was passed on May 19, 1649.

this is the power of Almightie God, ruling the whole creation in peace, and keeping it together. And this is the power of universall love, leading people into all truth, teaching every one to doe as he would be done unto, now once more striving with flesh and blood, shaking down every thing that cannot stand, and bringing every one into the Unitie of himself, the one Spirit of love and righteousnesse, and so will work a thorough restauration. But this Kingly power is above all, and will tread all covetousness, pride, envy, and self-love, and all other enemies whatsoever, under his feet, and take the kingdom and government of the Creation out of the hand of self-seeking and self-honouring Flesh, and rule the alone King of Righteousness in the earth; and this indeed is Christ himself, who will cast out the curse; But this is not that Kingly power intended by that Act of Parliament to be cast out, but pretended to be set up, though this Kingly power be much fought against both by Parliament, Armie, Clergie, and people; but when they are made to see him, then they shall mourn, because they have persecuted him.

But the other Kingly power, is the power of unrighteousness, which indeed is the Devil; And O that there were such a heart in Parliament and Army, as to perform your own Act; then People would never complain of you for breach of Covenant, for your Covetousness, Pride, and too much Self-seeking that is in you. And you on the other-side would never have cause to complain of the Peoples murmurings against [3] you. Truly this jarring that is between you and the People is The Kingly Power; yea that very Kingly power which you have made an Act to cast out; therefore see it be fulfilled on your part; for the Kingly power of Righteousness expects it, or else he will cast you out for Hypocrites and unsavory Salt; for he looks upon all your Actions, and truly there is abundance of Rust about your Actings, which makes them that they do not shine bright.

This Kingly power is covetousness in his branches, or the power of self-love, ruling in one or in many men over others, and enslaving those who in the Creation are their equals; nay, who are in the strictness of equity rather their Masters: And this Kingly power is usually set in the Chair of Government, under the name of Prerogative, when he rules in one over other: And under the name of State Priviledge of Parliament, when he rules in many over others: and this Kingly power, is alwayes raised up, and established by the Sword, and therefore he is called the Murderer, or the great red Dragon, which fights against *Michael*, for he enslaves the weakness of the People under him, denying an equal freedom in the Earth to every one, which the Law of Righteousness gave every man in his creation. This I say is Kingly power under darkness, and as he rules in men, so he makes men jar one against another, and is the cause of all Wars and Complainings; he is known by his outward actions, and his action at this very day fills all places; for this power of darkness rules, and would rule, and is that only Enemy that fights against Creation and National Freedom: And this Kingly power is he, which you have made an Act of Parliament to cast out. And now you Rulers of *England*, play the men, and be valiant for the Truth, which is Christ: for assure your selves God will not be mocked, nor the Devil will not be mocked; for First you say and profess you own the Scriptures of Prophets and Apostles, and God looks that you should perform that Word in action: Secondly you have Declared against the Devil, and if you do not now go through with your work, but slack your hand by hypocritical self-love, and so suffer this dark Kingly power to rise higher and Rule, you shall find [4] he will maule both you and yours to purpose.

The life of this dark Kingly power, which you have made an Act of Parliament and Oath to cast out, if you search it to the bottom, you shall see it lies within the iron chest of cursed Covetousness, who gives the Earth to some part of mankind, and denies it to another part of mankind: and that part that hath the Earth, hath no right from the Law of creation to take it to himself, and shut out others; but he took it away violently by Theft and Murder in Conquest: As when our Norman *William* came into *England* and conquered, he turned the English out, and gave the Land unto his Norman Souldiers every man his parcel to inclose, and hence rose up Propriety; for this is the fruit of War from the beginning, for it removes Propriety out of a weaker into a stronger hand, but still upholds the curse of Bondage; and hereby the Kingly power which you have made an Act, and Sworn to cast out, does remove himself from one chair to another; and so long as the Sword rules over brethren, (mind what I say) so long the Kingly power of darkness Rules, and so large as yet is his Kingdom; which spreds from Sea to Sea, and fills the Earth; but Christ is rising who will take the Dominion and Kingdom out of his hand, and his power of Righteousness shall rise and spred from East to West, from North to South, and fill the Earth with himself, and cast the other cursed power out; when Coveteousness sheaths his Sword, and ceases to rage in the field, he first makes sharp Laws of Bondage, That those that are conquered, and that by him are appointed not to enjoy the Earth, but are turned out, shall be Servants, Slaves, and Vassals to the Conquerers party: so those Laws that upholds Whips, Prisons, Gallows is but the same power of the Sword that raged, and that was drunk with Blood in the field.

King *Charles*, it is true, was the Head of this Kingly power in *England*, and he Reigned as he was a Successor of the last Norman Conquerer: and whosoever you be, that hath Propriety of Land, hath your Titles and Evidences made to you in his or his Ancestors Name, and from his and their Will and Kingly power; I am sure, he was not our Creator, [5] and therefore parcelled out the Earth to some, and denied it to others, therefore he must needs stand as a Conquerer, and was the Head of this Kingly power, that burdens and oppresses the People, and that is the cause of all our Wars and Divisions; for if this Kingly power of Covetousness, which is the unrighteous Divider, did not yet Rule: both Parliament, Army, and rich People, would cheerfully give consent that those we call Poor should Dig and freely Plant the Waste and Common Land for a livelihood, seing there is Land enough, and more by half then is made use of, and not be suffered to perish for want. And yet O ye Rulers of *England*, you make a blazing profession, That you know, and that you own God, Christ, and the Scriptures: but did Christ ever declare such hardness of heart? did not he bid the rich man go and sell all that he hath and give to the Poor? and does not the Scripture say, If thou makest a Covenant, keep it, though it be to thy loss: But truly it will not be to your loss, to let your fellow Creatures, your equals in the Creation, nay those that have been faithful in your Cause, and so your Friends; I say it will not be to your loss to let them quietly improve the Waste and Common Land, that they may live in peace, freed from the heavie burdens of Poverty; for hereby our own Land will be increased with all sorts of Commodities, and the People will be knit together in love, to keep out a forreign Enemy that endeavours, and that will endeavour as yet, to come like an Army of cursed Ratts and Mice to destroy our inheritance; so that if this Freedom be quietly granted to us, you grant it but to your selves, to English-men, to your own flesh and blood: and you do but give us our own neither, which Covetousness, in the Kingly power hath, and yet does hold from us; for the Earth in the first Creation of it, was freely given to whole mankind, without respect of Persons; therefore you Lords of Mannors, and you Rulers of *England*, if you own God, Christ and Scripture, now make Restitution, and deliver us quiet possession of our Land, which the Kingly power as yet holds from us.

While this Kingly power raigned in one man called *Charls*, all sorts of people complained of oppression, both Gentrie and [6] Common people, because their lands, Inclosures, and Copieholds were intangled, and because their Trades were destroyed by Monopolizing Patentees, and your troubles were that you could not live free from oppression in the earth: Thereupon you that were the Gentrie, when you were assembled in Parliament, you called upon the poor Common-People to come and help you, and cast out oppression; and you that complained are helped and freed, and that top-bow is lopped off the tree of Tyrannie, and Kingly power in that one particular is cast out; but alas oppression is a great tree still, and keeps off the sun of freedome from the poor Commons still, he hath many branches and great roots which must be grub'd up, before every one can sing Sions songs in peace.

As we spie out Kinglie power we must declare it, and cast it out, or else we shall deny the Parliament of *England* and their Acts, and so prove Traitors to the Land, by denying obedience thereunto. Now there are Three Branches more of Kinglie power greater then the former that oppresses this Land wonderfully; and these are the power of the Tithing Priests over the Tenths of our labours; and the power of Lords of Mannors, holding the free use of the Commons, and wast Land from the poor, and the intolerable oppression either of bad Laws, or of bad Judges corrupting good Laws; these are branches of the Norman conquest and Kingly power still, and wants a Reformation.

For as for the first, *William* the Couqueror promised, That if the Clergie would preach him up, so that the people might be bewitched, so as to receive him to be Gods Anointed over them, he would give them the Tenths of the Lands increase yeerly; and they did it, and he made good his Promise; and do we not yet see, That if the Clergie can get Tithes or Money, they will turn as the Ruling power turns, any way; to Popery, to Protestanisme; for a King, against a King, for Monarchy, for State-Government; they cry who bids most wages, they will be on the strongest side, for an Earthly maintenance; yea, and when they are lifted up, they would Rule too, because they are called Spiritual men: It is true indeed, [7] they are spiritual; but it is of the spiritual power of Coveteousness and Pride; for the spiritual power of Love and Righteousness they know not; for if they knew it, they would not persecute and raile against him as they do.

The Clergie will serve on any side, like our ancient Laws, that will serve any Master: They will serve the Papists, they will serve the Protestants, they will serve the King, they will serve the States; they are one and the same Tools for Lawyers to work with under any Government. O you Parliament-men of *England,* cast those whorish Laws out of doors, that are so Common, that pretend love to every one, and is faithful to none; for truly, he that goes to Law, as the Proverb is, shall die a Beggar: so that old Whores, and old Laws, picks men pockets, and undoes them: If the fault lie in the Laws, and much does, burn all your old Law-Books in *Cheapside,* & set up a Government upon your own Foundation: do not put new Wine into old Bottles; but as your Government must be new, so let the Laws be new, or else you will run farther into the Mud, where you stick already, as though you were fast in an *Irish* Bogge; for you are so far sunke, that he must have good eyes that can see where you are: but yet all are not blind, there are eyes that sees you: but if the fault lies in the Judges of the Law, surely such men deserve no power in a Reforming Common-wealth, that burdens all sorts of People.

And truly Ile tell you plain, your Two Acts of Parliament are excellent and Righteous: The One to cast out Kingly power; The Other to make *England* a Free Common-wealth: build upon these Two, it is a firm Foundation, and your House will be the glory of the World; and I am confident, the righteous Spirit will love you: do not stick in the Bogge of covetousness; Let not self-love so be-muddy your brain, that you should lose your selves in the thicket of bramblebush-words, and set never a strong Oak of some stable Action for the Freedome of the poor, Oppressed that helped you when you complained of Oppression. Let not Pride blind your eyes, that you should forget you are the Nations Servants, and so prove *Solomons* words good in your selves, That Servants ride on [8] Horse-back and Coaches, when as Princes, such as Chose you, and set you there, go on foot: and many of them, through their love to the Nation, have so wasted themselves, that now they can hardly get Bread, but with great difficulty. I tell you this is a sore Evil, and this is truth; therefore think upon it, it is a poor mans Advice, and you shall finde weight in it, if you Do as well as Say.

Then Secondly for Lords of Mannors, They were *William* the Conquerors Colonels and Favourites, and he gave a large circuit of Land to every one, called A Lord-ship, that they might have a watchful eye, that if any of the conquered English should begin to Plant themselves upon any Common or waste Land, to live out of sight or out of slavery, that then some Lord of Mannor or other might see and know of it, and drive them off, as these Lords of Mannors now a dayes, endeavours to drive off the Diggers from Digging upon the Commons; but we expect the Rulers of the Land will grant unto us their Friends, the benefit of their own Acts against Kingly power, and not suffer that Norman power to crush the poor Oppressed, who helped them in their straits, nor suffer that Norman power to bud fresher out, & so in time may come to over-top our deer bought Freedom more then ever.

Search all your Laws, and Ile adventure my life, for I have little else to lose, That all Lords of Mannors hold Title to the Commons by no stronger hold then the Kings Will, whose Head is cut off; and the King held Title as he was a Conqueror; now if you cast off the King who was the Head of that power, surely the power of Lords of Mannors is the same; therefore performe your own Act of Parliament, and cast out that part of the Kinglie power likewise, that the People may see you understand what you Say and Do, and that you are faithful.

For truly the Kinglie power reigns strongly in the Lords of Mannors over the Poor; for my own particular, I have in other Writings as well as in this, Declared my Reasons, That the common Land is the poor Peoples Proprietie; and I have Digged upon the Commons, and I hope in time to obtain the Freedom, to get Food and Raiment therefrom by righteous [9] labour, which is all I desire; and for so doing, the supposed Lord of that Mannor hath Arrested me twice; First, in an Action of 20.l.[2] Trespass for Plowing upon the Commons, which I never did; and because they would not suffer me to Plead my own Cause, they made shift to pass a Sentence of Execution against some Cows I kept, supposing they had been mine, and took them away; but the right Owner reprieved them, & fetched the Cowes back; so greedy are these Theeves and Murderers after my life for speaking the truth, and for maintaining the Life and Marrow of the Parliaments Cause in my Actions.

And now they have Arrested me again [3] in an Action of 4.l. trespas for digging upon the Comons, which I did, & own the work to be righteous, & no trespas to any: This was the Attorney of *Kingstone's* Advice, either to get Money on both sides, for they love Mony as deerly as a poor mans dog do his breakfast in a cold morning (but regard not justice) or else, That I should not remove it to a higher Court, but that the cause might be tryed there, and then they know how to please the Lords of Mannors, that have resolved to spend hundreds of pounds but they will hinder the poor from enjoying the Commons; for they will not suffer me to plead my own Cause, but I must Fee an enemie, or else be condemned and executed without mercy or Justice as I was before, and so to put me in Prison till I pay their unrighteous Sentence; for truly Attourneys are such neat work-men, that they can turn a Cause which way those that have the big-gest purse will have them: and the Countrie knows very well, That *Kingstone* court is so full of the Kinglie power; that some will rather lose their Rights, then have their causes tryed there: one of the Of-ficers of that court, told a friend of mine, That if the Diggers cause was good, he would pick out such a Jurie as should overthrow him: And upon my former Arrest, they picked out such a Jurie as Sen-tenced me to pay 10.l. damages for plowing upon the commons, which I did not do, neither did any witness prove it before them: So that from *Kingstone* Juries, Lords of Mannors, and Kinglie power, *Good Lord deliver us.*

Do these men obey the Parliaments Acts, to throw down [10] Kinglie power? O no: The same unrighteous doing that was com-

---

[2] The plaintiffs asked for £20 but the jury gave them £10.

[3] The record of the court at Kingston does not show that Winstanley was named in the suit for which damages of £4 were assessed. See the Introduction, p. 17, n. ·

plained of in King *Charles* dayes, the same doings is among them still:
Monies will buy and sell Justice still: and is our 8 yeers Wars come
round about to lay us down again in the kennel of injustice as much or
more then before? are we no farther learned yet? O ye Rulers of
England, when must we turn over a new leaf? will you alwayes hold
us in one Lesson? surely you will make Dunces of us; then all the
Boyes in other Lands will laugh at us: come, I pray let us take forth,
and go forward in our learning.

You blame us who are the Common people as though we would
have no government; truly Gentlemen, We desire a righteous government with all our hearts, but the government we have gives freedom
and livelihood to the Gentrie, to have abundance, and to lock up
Treasures of the Earth from the poor, so that rich men may have
chests full of Gold and Silver, and houses full of Corn and Goods
to look upon; and the poor that works to get it, can hardly live, and
if they cannot work like Slaves, then they must starve. And thus the
Law gives all the Land to some part of mankind whose Predecessors
got it by conquest, and denies it to others, who by the righteous Law
of Creation may claim an equall portion; and yet you say this is a
righteous government, but surely it is no other but selfishnes, which
is the great Red Dragon, the Murtherer.

England is a Prison; the variety of subtilties in the Laws preserved
by the Sword, are bolts, bars, and doors of the prison; the Lawyers
are the Jaylors, and poor men are the prisoners; for let a man fall
into the hands of any from the Bailiffe to the Judge, and he is either
undone, or wearie of his life.

Surely this power [of] the Laws, which is the great Idoll that
people dote upon, is the burden of the Creation, a Nurserie of Idleness, luxurie, and cheating, the only enemie of Christ the King of
righteousness; for though it pretend Justice, yet the Judges and Law-
Officers, buy and sell Justice for money, and wipes their mouths like
Solomons whore, and says it is my calling, and never are troubled
at it.

[11] Two things must cast out this Idoll: First, Let not people send
their children to those Nurseries of Covetousness, *The Innes of Court.*
Secondly, let not people live in contention, but fulfill Christs last commandment, *Love;* and endeavour to practice that full point of the
Law and the Prophets, *Doe as you would be done by,* and so cast out

envie and discontent. Woe to you Lawyers, for your trade is the bane and miserie of the world; your power is the only power that hinders Christ from rising; the destruction of your power will be the life of the World; it is full of confusion, it is Babylon, and surely its fall is neer, in regard the light of truth is rising, who will consume your power, but save your persons by the words of his mouth, and brightnesse of his coming.

The Lawyers trade is one of the false Prophets, that says, Lo here is Christ, Ile save you in this Court, and lo there is Christ, Ile save you in that Court: but when we have tried all, we are lost, and not saved, for we are either utterly made Beggars by this Saviour, the Law, or else we are nursed up in hardnesse of heart and cruelty against our fellow creature whom we ought to love and preserve, and not destroy: This Saviour jeeres righteousnes, and bids every man save himself, and never regard what becomes of another, and so is a plain destroyer of the Creation; Surely that Wo pronounced against Lawyers by the Man Christ must be fulfilled, delay is no payment: Therefore you Parliament and Army that have power in your hands, reform the Law; and suffer none to be called to practice Law but reformed ones; nay suffer every man to plead his own cause, and choose his own Lawyer, where he finds the most ingenuous man: Wel, every mans burthen in this Age fills their mouths with words of Lamentation against Law and Lawyers sufficiently; therefore you that have an opportunitie to ease the cry of the oppressed, shut not your eies and eares, but cast out this covetous corruption whereby corrupt Lawyers doe oppress the People; it is another Branch of the Kingly power.

You Gentlemen of *Surrey*, and Lords of Mannors, and you Mr. Parson *Platt* [4] especially, that lay almost a fortnight [12] waiting and tempting the Lord *Fairfax* to send Souldiers to drive off the Diggers; when he granted your Desire, it was but to secure the Shereiff, for he did not give them commission to beat us, which we thank him for; and we thank the Souldiers for their moderation, that they would not strike poor wormes, *Englands* and the creations faithful friends, though you would have moved them thereunto. My Advice to you Gentlemen is this, Hereafter to lie still and cherish the Diggers, for they love you, and would not have your finger ake if they could help

---

[4] For John Platt, rector at West Horsley, see above, p. 346.

it; and why should you be so bitter against them? O let them live by you; some of them have been Souldiers, and some countrie-men that were alwayes friends to the Parliaments cause, by whose hardship and meanes you enjoy the creatures about you in peace; and will you now destroy part of them that have preserved your lives? O do not do so; be not so besotted with the Kinglie power; hereafter let not the Attourneyes or Lawyers neatly councel your Money out of your purses, and stir you up to beat and abuse the Diggers, to make all rational men laugh at your folly, and condemn you for your bitterness: If you have yet so much Money, give it not away to destroy men, but give it to some poor or other to be a Stock, and bid them go and Plant the common; this will be your honour, and your comfort; assure your selves you never must have true comfort tell you be friends with the poor; therefore come, come, love the Diggers, and make restitution of their Land you hold from them; for what would you do if you had not such labouring men to work for you?

And you great Officers of the Army and Parliament, love your common Souldiers, (I plead for Equity and Reason) and do not force them by long delay of Payment to sell you their deer bought Debenters for a thing of naught, and then to go and buy our common Land, and crown Land, and other Land that is the spoil one of another, therewith: Remember you are Servants to the commons of *England,* and you were Volunteers in the Wars, and the common people have paid you for your pains so largely, that some of us have not left our selves hardly bread to eate; and therefore if there be a spoil [13] to be gathered of crown Lands, Deans, Bishops, Forrests Lands and commons, that is to come to the poor commons freely; and you ought to be content with your wages, unless you will denie Christ and the Scriptures; and you ought not to go and buy one of another that which is common to all the Nation; for you ought neither to buy nor sell other mens Proprietie by the Law of creation; for Christ gives you no such Warrant. As soon as you have freed the Earth from one intanglement of Kinglie power, will you intangle it more, and worse by another degree of Kinglie power? I pray consider what you do, and do righteously: We that are the poor commons, that paid our Money, and gave you free Quarter, have as much Right in those crown Lands and Lands of the spoil as you; therefore we give no consent That you should buy and sell our crown Lands and waste

Lands, for it is our purchased inheritance from under Oppression, it is our own, even the poor common peoples of *England*: It was taken from us, and hath been held from us by former conquests, whereof the Norman conquest was the last, which is cast out by yours and our joynt Assistance; therefore you cannot in Equity take it from us, nor we cannot in Equity take it from you, for it is our joynt purchased inheritance; we paid you your wages to help us to recover it, but not to take it to your selves, and turn us out, and buy and sell it among your selves; for this is a cheat of the Kinglie swordlie power which you hold up; and we profess to all the world, in so doing you denie God, Christ, and the Scriptures whom ye professed you own: for God, Christ, and Scriptures owne no such practice: Likewise we profess to all the Creation, That in so doing, you rob us of our Rights; & you kill us, by denying to give us our livelihood in our own inheritance freely, which is the crown Land and Comon Land and waste Lands, Bishops & Deans, which some of you begin to say you are not satisfied in your conscience to let us have: I, well spoke, tender hearted Covetousness; if you do so, you will uphold the Kinglie power, and so disobey both Acts of Parliament, and break your Oath, and you will live in the breach of those Two Commandements, *Thou shalt not kill: Thou shalt not steal*; by denying us the Earth which is our [14] Livelyhood, and thereby killing us by a lingring death.

Well, the end of all my Speech is to point out the Kingly power, where I spie it out, and you see it remains strongly in the hands of Lords of Mannors, who have delt discourteously with some who are sincere in heart, though there have some come among the Diggers that have caused scandall, but we dis-own their wayes.[5]

The Lords of Mannors have sent to beat us, to pull down our houses, spoil our labours; yet we are patient, and never offered any violence to them again, this 40 weeks past, but wait upon God with love till their hearts thereby be softned; and all that we desire is, but to live quietly in the land of our nativity, by our righteous labour, upon the common Land which is our own, but as yet the Lords of the Mannor so formerly called, will not suffer us, but abuse us. Is not that part of the Kingly power? In that which follows I shall cleerly prove it is, for it appears so cleer that the understanding of a child does say, It is Tyranny, it is the Kingly power of darkness, therefore

---

[5] Cf. Winstanley's *Vindication*, below, p. 399.

we expect that you will grant us the benefit of your Act of Parliament that we may say, Truly *England* is a Common-wealth, and a free people indeed.

Sirs, Though your Tithing Priests and others tell you, That we Diggers do deny God, Christ, and the Scripture, to make us odious, and themselves better thought of; yet you will see in time when the King of Righteousness whom we serve does cleer our innocencie, That our actions and conversation is the very life of the Scripture, and holds forth the true power of God and Christ. For is not the end of all preaching, praying, and profession wrapped up in this action, namely, *Love your enemies, and doe to all men, as you would they should do to you, for this is the very Law and the Prophets.* This is the New Commandement that Christ left behind him. Now if any seem to say this, and does not do this, but acts contrary, for my part I owne not their wayes, they are members that uphold the curse.

[15] Bare talking of righteousnesse, and not acting, hath ruled, and yet does rule king of darkness in the creation; and it is the cause of all this immoderate confusion and ignorance that is in men.

But the actings of righteousnesse from the inward power of love, shall rule King of righteousnesse in the creation now in these later dayes, and cast the other Serpent and fiery scorpion out; for this is Christ the restoring power: and as he rises up, so multitude of words without action (which is hypocrisie) is to die, his judgment hastens apace.

If any sort of people hold the earth to themselves by the dark Kingly power, and shut out others from that freedom, they deny God, Christ, and Scriptures, and they overthrow all their preaching, praying, and profession; for the Scriptures declare them to be Hypocrites, Scribes and Pharisees, *that say, and do not*; they have words, and no deeds: Like Parson *Platt* the Preacher at *Horsley* in *Surrey,* a Lord of Mannor (by marriage) of the place where we digg, who caused a poor old mans house that stood upon the Common, to be pulled down in the evening of a cold day, and turned the old man, and his wife, and daughter to lie in the open field, because he was a Digger: and he, and other Lords of Mannors, and Gentlemen sent their servants up and down the Town, to bid their Tenants and neighbours, neither to give the Diggers lodging nor victuals, on pain of their displeasure. Though this Parson *Platt* preach the Scriptures, yet

I'll affirm, he denyes God, Christ, and Scriptures, and knowes nothing of them; for covetousness, pride, and envie hath blinded his eyes. A man knowes no more of righteousness than he hath power to act; and surely, this cruelty of preaching *Platt* is an unrighteous act.

If the Diggers were enemies, (oh you Lords of Mannors) as they are not, you ought to love them: I am sure, they love you; and if you doubt it, put them to the tryall; you shall find them more faithfull than many of those pick-thank slaves, and belly-god servants to whom your ears are open, when they bring tales full of envie to you against us.

We are told likewise, That to make us who are called Diggers, odious, and to incense you against us, there came to the [16] Generall and Councell of State, divers Justices, and others, and told you, that we Diggers were Cavaliers, and that we waited an opportunity, and gathered together to stand up for the Prince.

But all that know us can prove that to be a false report, to the dishonour of those Justices; for we have been friends to the Parliaments cause, and so do continue, and will continue; for this work of digging, to make *England* a free Common-wealth, is the life and marrow of the Parliaments cause. And the two Acts of Parliament, the One, to cast out Kingly power, the Other, to make *England* a free Commonwealth, declares it: and we do obey those Acts, and will obey them, for they hold forth righteousnesse.

But for our rising in arms for the Prince, or any other, let any come and see our strength and work, and they will say, It is a meer envious slander cast upon us, to incense you against us.

Besides, You shall see by and by, That our principles are wholly against Kingly power in every one, as well as in one. Likewise we hear, that they told you, that the Diggers do steal and rob from others. This likewise is a slander: we have things stollen from us; but if any can prove that any of us do steal any mans proper goods, as Sheep, Geese, Pigs, as they say, let such be made a spectacle to all the world: For my part, I own no such doing, neither do I know any such thing by any of the Diggers. Likewise they report, that we Diggers hold women to be common, and live in that bestialnesse: For my part, I declare against it; I own this to be a truth, That the earth ought to be a common Treasury to all; but as for women, *Let every man have his own wife, and every woman her own husband*; and I know none of

the Diggers that act in such an unrationall excesse of female communitie: If any should, I professe to have nothing to do with such
people, but leave them to their own Master, who will pay them with
torment of minde, and diseases in their bodies.

These and such-like tales, we hear, are brought to you, to incense
you against us: but we desire you to mark them that bring them, for
we partly know who they be, and we can tell [17] them to their faces,
they were Cavaliers, and had hands in the Kentish Rising, and in
stirring up that offensive *Surrey* Petition [6], which was the occasion of
bloodshed in *Westminster*-yard, and they would rejoyce to see the
Prince come in with an Armie to over-top you: for we know, they love
you not but from the teeth outwards, for their own ends: And these
are the proud *Hamans*, that would incense you against the *Mordecaies*
of the Land, even your true-hearted friends, the Diggers. Well, in
the midst of our slanders we rejoyce in the uprightness of our hearts,
and we do *commit our cause to him that judgeth righteously.*

Upon these lying reports, and importunitie to the General, it seems
the General granted the Lords of Mannor to have some souldiers to
go along with the Sheriff, to pull down the Diggers houses; and so
the souldiers did come: but they were very moderate and rationall
men, and as they were sent to secure the Sheriff, so they did: but there
was no cause; for, though the Gentlemen possess'd the General, that
they feared opposition from the Diggers, yet the souldiers saw they
lifted not up a finger in discontent, but fought against those dragons,
the Lords of Manors, with the spirit of love and patience: for when
the two Lords of Manor sat among the souldiers on horsback and
coach, and commanded their fearfull tenants to pull down one of the
Diggers houses before their faces, and rejoyced with shouting at the
fall; yet some of the Diggers stood by, and were very chearfull, and
preached the Gospel to those Turkish *Bashaws*, which are words of
life, and in time will prove words of terrour, to torment their awak-
ened consciences.

And the poor tenants that pulled down the house, durst do no
other, because their Land-lords and Lords looked on, for fear they
should be turned out of service, or their livings; as a poor honest

---

[6] The Surrey Petition, presented to Parliament on May 16, 1648, asked that the
King be "restored to his due honor and just right". Its presentation occasioned a riot
in which some eight or ten persons were killed and a hundred injured.

man, because he looked with a cheerfull countenance upon the Diggers (though he was affraid to come neer, or affraid to speak openly, lest his Landlords setting-dogs should smell the sound of his words, and carry a pick-thank tale, which his Lords ears are much open to) a Baily was sent presently to him, to warn him out of his house.

[17, i. e., 18] Can the Turkish Bashaws hold their slaves in more bondage than these Gospel-professing Lords of Manors do their poor tenants? and is not this the Kingly power? O you Rulers of *England*, I pray see that your own acts be obeyed, and let the oppressed go free.

And when the poor enforced slaves had pulled down the house, then their Lords gave them ten shillings to drink, and there they smiled one upon another; being fearfull, like a dog that is kept in awe, when his Master gives him a bone, and stands over him with a whip; he will eat, and look up, and twinch his tail; for they durst not laugh out, lest their Lords should hear they jeer'd them openly; for in their hearts they are Diggers. Therefore, you Lords of Manors, if you have none to stand for you but whom you force by threatning, then leave off striving against the spirit, and say you are fallen, and come in and embrace righteousnesse, that you may finde mercy betimes.

The next day after this, there came two souldiers and three Country-men to another house which the Diggers had set up, (which the Sheriff the day before had let alone, for, as some say, he was grieved to see what was done,) one of these souldiers was very civill, and walked lovingly with the Diggers round their corn which they had planted, and commended the work, and would do no harm (as divers others were of the same minde) and when he went his way, gave the Diggers 12*d.* to drink: but the other souldier was so rude, that he forced those three Country-men to help him to pull down the house, and railed bitterly: the men were unwilling to pull it down; but for fear of their Landlords, and the threatning souldier, they did put their hands to pull it down.

And seeing Parson *Platt* (the Lord of that Manor) will not suffer the Diggers to have a house, (wherein he forgets his Master Christ, that is persecuted in naked, hungry, and houselesse members) yet the Diggers were mighty cheerfull, and their spirits resolve to wait upon God, to see what he will do, and they have built them some few little hutches like calf-cribs, and there they lie anights, and follow their work adayes still with wonderfull joy of heart, taking the spoyling of their goods [18, i. e., 19] cheerfully, counting it a great happinesse to be persecuted for righteousnesse sake, by the Priests and Professors, that are the successors of *Judas,* and the bitter-spirited Pharisees that put the man Christ *Jesus* to death. And they have planted divers Acres of Wheat and Rye, which is come up, and promises a very hopefull crop, committing their cause to God, and wait upon him, saying, O thou King of righteousnesse, do thine own work.

O that you would search and try our wayes narrowly, and see whether we deny God, Christ, Scriptures, as the Priests slander us we do; and you shall finde, that the Scriptures warrant our action, and God in Christ is the life of our souls, and the support of our spirits in the midst of this our sharp persecution from the hands of unreasonable men, who have not faith in Christ, but uphold the Kingly power, which you have Voted down.

Likewise, you shall see, that we live in the performance of that work which is the very life and marrow of the Parliaments Cause, whereby we honour the Parliament and their Cause: as you shall see by this following Declaration, unfolding the foundation whereupon *Englands* Laws are, or the Freedom of a Common-wealth ought to be built, which is Equity and Reason.

In the time of the Kings, who came in as Conquerors, and ruled by the power of the Sword, not only the Common land, but the Inclosures also were captivated under the will of those Kings, till now of late that our later Kings granted more freedom to the Gentry than they had presently after the Conquest; yet under bondage still: for what are prisons, whips and gallows in the times of peace; but the laws and power of the sword, forcing and compelling obedience, and so enslaving, as if the sword raged in the open field?

England was in such a slavery under the Kingly power, that both Gentry and Commonaltie groaned under bondage; and to ease themselves, they endeavoured to call a Parliament, that by their counsels and decrees they might find some freedom.

But *Charles* the then King perceiving that the Freedom [20] they strove for, would derogate from his Prerogative-tyranny, therupon he goes into the North, to raise a War against the Parliament, and took WILLIAM *the Conqueror's* Sword into his hand again, thereby to keep under the former conquered English, and to uphold his Kingly power

of self-will and Prerogative, which was the power got by former
Conquests; that is, to rule over the lives and estates of all men at his
will, and so to make us pure slaves and vassals.

Well, This Parliament, that did consist of the chief Lords, Lords
of Manors, and Gentry, and they seeing that the King, by raising an
Army, did thereby declare his intent to enslave all sorts to him by the
sword; and being in distresse, and in a low ebb, they call upon the
common people to bring in their Plate, Moneys, Taxes, Free-quarter,
Excise, and to adventure their lives with them, and they would endeavour to recover *England* from that *Norman* yoak, and make us a
free people: and the common people assent hereunto, and call this the
Parliaments Cause, and own it, and adventure person and purse to
preserve it; and by the joynt assistance of Parliament and People, the
King was beaten in the field, his head taken off, and his Kingly power
voted down; and we the Commons thereby virtually have recovered
our selves from the Norman Conquest, we want nothing but possession of the spoyl, which is a free use of the Land for our livelyhood.

And from hence we the common people, or younger brothers, plead
our propriety in the Common land, as truly our own by vertue of this
victory over the King; as our elder brothers can plead proprietie in
their Inclosures; and that for three reasons in *Englands* law.

First, By a lawfull purchase or contract between the Parliament and
us; for they were our Landlords and Lords of Mannors that held the
freedom of the Commons from us, while the King was in his power;
for they held title thereunto from him, he being the head, and they
branches of the Kingly power, that enslaved the people by that ancient Conquerors Sword, that was the ruling power: For they said,
Come and help us against the King that enslaves us, that we may be
[21] delivered from his Tyranny, and we will make you a free
People.

Now they cannot make us free, unlesse they deliver us from the
bondage which they themselves held us under; and that is, they held
the freedom of the Earth from us: for we in part with them have
delivered our selves from the King: now we claim freedom from
that bondage you have, and yet do hold us under, by the bargain and
contract between Parliament and us, who (I say) did consist of
Lords of Manors, and Landlords, whereof Mr. *Drake*, who hath
arrested me for digging upon the Common, was one at that time:

Therefore by the law of Bargain and Sale, we claim of them our freedom, to live comfortably with them in this Land of our Nativity; and this we cannot do, so long as we lie under poverty, and must not be suffered to plant the commons and waste land for our livelihood: for, take away the land from any people, and those people are in a way of continuall death and misery; and better not to have had a body, than not to have food and rayment for it. But (I say) they have sold us our freedom in the common, and have been largely paid for it; for by means of our bloods and money, they sit in peace: for if the King had prevailed, they had lost all, and been in slavery to the meanest Cavalier, if the King would. Therfore we the Commons say, Give us our bargain: if you deny us our bargain, you deny God, Christ, and Scriptures; and all your profession then is and hath been hypocrisie.

Secondly, The Commons and Crown land is our propriety by equall conquest over the Kingly power: for the Parl. did never stir up the people by promises and covenant to assist them to cast out the King, and to establish them in the Kings place and prerogative power: No, but all their Declarations were for the safety and peace of the whole Nation.

Therefore the common-people being part of the Nation, and especially they that bore the greatest heat of the day in casting out the oppressor: and the Nation cannot be in peace, so long as the poor oppressed are in want, and the land is intangled and held from them by bondage.

[22] But the Victory being obtained over the King, the spoyl which is properly the Land, ought in equity to be divided now between the two Parties, that is, Parliament and Common-people. The Parliament, consisting of Lords of Manors, and Gentry, ought to have their inclosure Lands free to them without molestation, as they are freed from the Court of Wards.

And the Common-people, consisting of Souldiers, and such as paid Taxes and Free-quarter, ought to have the freedom of all waste and common land, and Crown-land equally among them; the Souldiery ought not in equity to have all, nor the other people that paid them to have all; but the spoyle ought to be divided between them that stay'd at home, and them that went to Warr; for the Victory is for the whole Nation.

And as the Parliament declared, they did all for the Nation, and not for themselves onely; so we plead with the Armie, they did not fight for themselves, but for the freedom of the Nation: and I say, we have bought our Freedom of them likewise by Taxes and Free-quarter: therefore we claim an equall Freedom with them in this Conquest over the King.

Thirdly, We claim an equall portion in the Victory over the King, by vertue of the two Acts of Parliament, the One to make *England* a Free Common-wealth; the Other to take away Kingly power. Now the Kingly power (you have heard) is a power that rules by the Sword in covetousnesse and self, giving the earth to some, and deny-ing it to others: and this Kingly power was not in the hand of the King alone; but Lords, and Lords of Manors, and corrupt Judges, and Lawyers especially, held it up likewise; for he was the head, and they, with the Tything-priests are the branches of that Tyrannical Kingly power; and all the several limbs and members must be cast out, before Kingly power can be pulled up root and branch. Mistake me not, I do not say, Cast out the persons of men: No, I do not desire their fingers to ake: but I say, Cast out their power, whereby they hold the people in bondage, as the King held them in bondage. And I say, it is our own Freedom we claim, both by bargain, and by equality in the Conquest; [23] as well as by the Law of righteous Creation, which gives the Earth to all equally.

And the power of Lords of Mannors lies in this: They deny the Common people the use and free benefit of the Earth, unless they give them leave, and pay them for it, either in Rent, in Fines, in Homages, or Heriots. Surely the Earth was never made by God, that the Younger brother should not live in the Earth, unless he would work for, and pay his Elder brother Rent for the Earth: No; this Slavery came in by Conquest, and it is part of the Kingly power; and *England* cannot be a Free Common-wealth, till this Bondage be taken away. You have taken away the King; you have taken away the House of Lords [7]: Now step two steps further, and take away the power of Lords of Mannors, and of Tything Priests, and the intolera-

---

[7] On February 5, 1649, the House of Commons adopted a resolution asserting "that the House of Peers in Parliament is useless and dangerous and ought to be abolished". An Act giving effect to the resolution was passed on March 17.

ble oppressions of Judges, by whom Laws are corrupted; and your work will be honourable.

Fourthly, if this Freedom be denied the Common people, To enjoy the Common Land; then Parliament, Army and Judges will deny Equity and Reason, whereupon the Laws of a well-governed Common-wealth ought to be built: And if this Equity be denied, then there can be no Law, but Club-Law, among the people: and if the Sword must raign, then every Party will be striving to bear the Sword; and then farewel Peace; nay, farewel Religion and Gospel, unless it be made use of to intrap one another, as we plainly see some Priests and others make it a Cloke for their Knavery. If I adventure my life, and fruit of my labour, equal with you, and obtain what we strive for; it is both Equity and Reason, that I should equally divide the Spoil with you, and not you to have all, and I none: And if you deny us this, you take away our Propriety from us, our Moneys and Blood, and give us nothing for it.

Therefore, I say, the Common Land is my own Land, equal with my fellow-Commoners; and our true Propriety, by the Law of Creation: it is every ones, but not one single ones: Yea, the Commons are as truely ours by the last excellent two Acts of Parliament, the Foundation of *Englands* new righteous [24] Government aimed at, as the Elder brothers can say the Inclosures are theirs: for they adventured their Lives, and covenanted with us to help them to preserve their Freedom: And we adventured our lives, and they covenanted with us, to purchase and to give us our Freedom, that hath been hundreds of yeers kept from us.

Dæmona non Armis, sed Morte subegit Iesus.

By patient Sufferings, not by Death,
Christ did the Devil kill;
And by the same, still to this day,
his Foes he conquers still.

True Religion, and undefiled, is this, To make restitution of the Earth, which hath been taken and held from the Common people, by the power of Conquests formerly, and so *set the oppressed free.* Do not All strive to enjoy the Land? The Gentry strive for Land, the Clergie strive for Land, the Common people strive for Land; and

Buying and Selling is an Art, whereby people endeavour to cheat one another of the Land. Now if any can prove, from the Law of Righteousness, that the Land was made peculiar to him and his successively, shutting others out, he shall enjoy it freely, for my part: But I affirm, It was made for all; and true Religion is, To let every one enjoy it. Therefore, you Rulers of *England*, make restitution of the Lands which the Kingly power holds from us: *Set the oppressed free*; and come in, and honour Christ, who is the Restoring Power, and you shall finde rest.

[25] THE CURSE AND BLESSING THAT IS IN MANKINDE

In the beginning of Time, the Spirit of Universal Love appeared to be the father of all things: The Creation of Fire, Water, Earth, and Air, came out of him, and is his clothing. *Love* is the *Word*.

The Creation is the House or Garden, in which this one Spirit hath taken up his seat, and in which he manifests himself: For if ever Love be seen or known, he appears either in the inward feeling within your hearts, loving All with tender love; or else appears towards you, from outward objects, as from other Men, or other creatures.

There are two Earths, in which the Spirit of Love declares himself. First, the Living Earth, called *Mankinde:* this is the Creation, or the living soul. And when this Spirit of universal Love rules King therein, this Earth is then in peace, and is grown up to the perfection of a man anointed. But when Self or Particular love rules, which is called the sin Covetousness, then this Earth is brought into Bondage, and Sorrow fills all places. This is the dark side of the Cloud, in which there is no true peace.

Secondly, in the great Body of Earth in which all creatures subsist, the Spirit of Universal Love appears, to preserve his Creation in peace: for Universal Love unites not onely Mankinde into an oneness, but unites all other creatures into a sweet harmony of willingness to preserve Mankinde. And this Spirit of Love spread abroad, is the same Spirit of Love that is supreme in Man: and this is the Righteous man.

But when Covetousness or Particular love began to work, then not onely Mankinde was divided amongst themselves, but all creatures were divided, and enmity rose up amongst them, [26] setting one against another; and this power is the wicked man: mark him where you see him, which is the Murderer, and must be cast out.

Wel, In the begining, universal love appeared to be the father of al things, (though self-love in our experience rules in man first) and as he made mankinde to be the Lord of the Earth, so he made the Earth to be a common Treasury of livelihood to whole mankind without respect of persons; and for all other creatures likewise that were to proceed from the Earth.

Mankind is the cheif creature, and the Spirit of universal Love in his branches, is the Lord of all the Earth; and this Spirit in man unfolds himself in Light and Darkness: his face is called the universal power of Love: his back parts is called the selfish power: or thus, the one is called the Son of Bondage which causes shame, the other is called the Son of Freedom, which brings peace and honour: these Two strive in the womb of the Earth which shal come forth first; and which shall rule; the fleshy man hath got the start; but the other will prove the stronger, and cast him out with honour.

While this Spirit of Lordship in the last day time of mankind, was universal Love and Righteousness leading every single branch of mankind to do to another as he would be done unto; then every thing was in peace, and there was a sweet communion of Love in the creation: and as the Spirit was a common Treasurie of Unitie and Peace within, so the Earth was a common Treasurie of delight for the preservation of their bodies without, so that there was nothing but peace upon the face of the whole Earth.

This was mans estate, before the fall or the day time of mankind; for since the time that our Bibles speak of *Adam* to this day, is about 6000 yeers; and this time hath been the night time of mankind: and *Esays* time was about midnight when in one of his words he cries, *Watchman, What of the night? Watchman, What of the night?* the seventh thousand yeer which is now dawning, will be the rising of the Son of universal Love again, and of the dispersing of the night or darkness; for as the night and day, Sun and Moon, hath their exchanges, [27] so hath these Two powers, called Sons of God in mankind; and in this age wherein we now live, is the expiring of the selfish power, and the rising up of the Blessing which hath been spoke of in al ages, but now appearing like lightning from east to west, casting out the Mysterie of Iniquitie, or self power, by the word of his mouth, and by the brightness of his comming, and so bringing peace.

So that, as there is the power of Light, which is universal Love, called the Blessing which brings Peace; so there is the power of Darkness, which is particular or self love, and this is called the Curse, for it brings sorrow: and while this rules King in the Earth, as it doth at this day visibly through the whole Earth, few are saved, that is, few enter into rest and peace; for this power hath filled all places, with his stinking self seeking Government, and troubles every body.

As there is light and darkness, day and night, clouds and cleerness moving upon the face of the great Earth; and as there is Earth and Waters in the great World which runs round; so mankind is called sometimes Earth, sometimes Waters; and as the Sun in the skies moves upon the great Earth and makes that fruitful which seemed dead, while the Sun is under the dark cloudy winter quarter:

Even so the Son of universal Love, who is the Spirit and power of universal Freedom, he moves upon the living waters mankind, and makes him, who all the dark time past was a Chaos of confusion, lying under Types, Shadows, Ceremonies, Forms, Customes, Ordinances, and heaps of waste words, under which the Spirit of Truth lay buried, now to enlighten, to worship in Spirit and Truth, and to bring forth fruit of Righteousness in action.

In our present experience, The darkness or self-love goeth before; and light or universal love follows after; the flesh runs hasty and quick, and loses himself in unrational excessive action; the true Spirit comes slowly after, and takes the Crown.

Darkness and Bondage, doth oppress Liberty and Light; and the power of universal Love appears most sweet and full [28] of glory, when the power of self Love or Covetousness hath tortured the Creation (mankind) with bitter Tyranny: for this is the Dragon or Murderer that must be cast out; before the Creation (man) can sing *Halelujah* in peace.

So then you may see, That the innocency, light, and purity of mankind is this, when the Spirit of universal Love lives in him, and he lives in Love, enjoying the sweet Union and communion of Spirit, each with other.

When they enjoy the sweet delight of the Unitie of one Spirit, and the free content of the fruits and crops of this outward Earth, upon which their bodies stand: this was called The mans innocency, or pleasure in the Garden before his fall, or the day time of mankind; and day is more glorious then night; and greater honour to be a child of the day, then of the night.

The fall of mankind, or his darkness is this, When that Son of universal Love, which was the seed, out of which the creation sprung forth, did begin to go behind the cloud of flesh, and to let self-seeking flesh which would needs be a God, stand alone by his imaginary light, as we see, while the Sun is in the skies, a man sees and knows his footsteps, but when the Sun is set under the cloud of the dark night, then he imagins his way, and oft times stumbles and falls:

Even so, when universal Love shines in his glory in mankind, he stumbles not, he walks in the light, because the light is in him; but when the light within withdrawes and lets flesh stand alone, Flesh, that is, The selfish power will not wait in peace, and acknowledge himself in a loss and in darkness, till the Sun rise again:

But will fain be a God, and calls his weakness strength; and though there appears nothing but deformity, yet he would have it called beauty; and because his inward power is not sutable to his outward profession, he is tormented: he is a Saint without, but a Devil within: but if thou wouldest have peace, act as thou art, shew thy self abroad in action what thou art secretly; but when thou beginst to imagine a content and happiness to thy self, by thy hypocritical self invention, [29] then thou art tormented, or shalt be.

And by this imagination, mankind tears himself in pieces; as one of your Colonels of the Army said to me, *That the Diggers did work upon* George Hill *for no other end but to draw a company of People into Arms*; and sayes *our knavery is found out, because it takes not that effect.*

Truly thou Colonel, I tell thee, Thy knavish imagination is thereby discovered, which hinders the effecting of that Freedom which by Oath and Covenant thou hast Engaged to maintain: for my part, and the rest, we had no such thought; we abhor fighting for Freedom, it is acting of the Curse and lifting him up higher; and do thou uphold it by the Sword, we will not; we will conquer by Love and Patience, or else we count it no Freedom: Freedom gotten by the Sword is an established Bondage to some part or other of the Creation; and this we have Declared publickly enough; therefore thy imagination told thee a lye, and will deceive thee in a greater matter, if Love doth not kill him: Victory that is gotten by the Sword, is a Victory that slaves gets one over another; and hereby *men of the basest Spirit* (saith *Daniel*) *are set to Rule:* but Victory obtained by Love, is a Victory for a King.

But by this you may see what a liar imagination is, and how he makes hate, and tears the Creation in pieces; for after that self Love hath subdued others under him, then imagination studies how to keep himself up and keep others down.

This is your very inward Principle, O ye present powers of *England*, you do not study how to advance universal Love; if you did, it would appear in action: but imagination and self-love mightily disquiets your mind, and makes you call up all the powers of darknesse to come forth and help to set the Crown upon the head of Self, which is that Kinglie power you have Oathed and Vowed against, and yet uphold it in your hands.

Imagination begets Covetousnesse after pleasure, honour, and riches: Covetousnesse begets Fear, least others should crosse them in their Design; or else begets a Fear of want, [30] and this makes a man to draw the creatures to him by hook or crook, and to please the strongest side, looking what others do, not minding what himself doth.

Like some of your great Officers, that told me, *That we Diggers took away other mens Propriety from them, by Digging upon the Common;* yet they have taken mine and other mens proprietie of money (got by honest labour) in Taxes and free-quarter to advance themselves and not allow us that they promised us; for it [is] this beam in their own eies they cannot see.

This Fear begets hypocrisie, subtlety, envie, and hardness of heart, which makes a man to break all promises and engagements, and to seek to save himself in others ruine, and to suppresse and oppresse every one that does not say as he sayes, and do as he does.

And this hardness of heart begets pride and security, and this begets luxurie and lust of the flesh, and this runs into all excess with greedines, and being in discontent against any that crosses his pleasure, till his heart become fully like the heart of a Beast, as it is apparent in some at this day.

And thus by the power of self-love being advanced by the covetous sword against universall love, that power of darkness rises up to perfection in mankind, and so he makes one branch to tear and devour another by divisions, evill surmisings, envious fightings, and killing, and by oppressing the meek in Spirit, by unrighteous Laws, or by his self will managing good Laws unrighteously, as corrupt Judges know how to do it, and think none sees them, whereby part of mankind hath freedom, and another part is cast out and thrown under bondage.

And all this falling out or quarrelling among mankind, is about the earth who shall, and who shall not enjoy it, when indeed it is the portion of every one, and ought not to be striven for, nor bought, nor sold, whereby some are hedged in, and others hedged out; for better not to have had a body, then to be debarred the fruit of the Earth to feed and cloth it; and if every one did but quietly enjoy the earth for food [31] and raiment, there would be no wars, prisons, nor gallows, and this action which man calls theft would be no sin, for universall love never made it a sin, but the power of covetousness made that a sin, and made Laws to punish it, though he himself live in that sin in a higher manner, then he hangs or punisheth. Those very men that punish others for theft do theeve and rob, as Judges and Lawyers that take Bribes, or that takes their Clients money, and through neglect lose their cause: Parliament and Army lives in Theft, when as they take the Commoners money, and free-quarter, and tell them what they do is to make *England* a free Common-Wealth, and yet all they doe is to make the Gentry free, and leaves the Commoners under bondage still; or else why do you send your Souldiers to beat a few naked Spademen off from digging the Commons for a livelihood, why do you not let the oppressed go free? have they not bought it of you by their monies and blood as well as the Gentrie, and will not you make good your Contract: Well, he that made the earth for us as well as for you will set us free though you will not: when will the Vail of darknes be drawn off your faces? will you not be wise O yee Rulers?

Well, this power of darknes is mans fall, or the night time of mankind.

But Universall love hath declared that he will rise again, and he himself who is the Seed, will bruise that Serpents head, and reconcile mankind to himself again, and restore him to that Innocencie and Peace which he is fallen from. When this Son arises in more strength, and appears to be the Saviour indeed, he will then make mankind to be all of one heart and one mind, and make the Earth to be a common treasurie, though for the present in outward view there is nothing but darkness and confusion upon the face of the earth, mankind.

When self love began to arise in the earth, then man began to fall, this is *Adam* or the power of darkness that stops up the waters and wel-springs of life, or the clouds that hide the Son of righteousness from man.

[32] This *Adam* or dark power was small at the first, but he is risen to great strength, and the whole Earth is now filled with him, as *Isaiah* saith, *Darknes hath covered the Earth,* mankind. For let any that hath eyes look either to them above or them below, and they see darknes or the Devil rule, and this curse destroys the Earth. The Creation sits like *Rachel* sighing, mourning, and groaning under his oppressing power, and will not be comforted because they see no saviour to appear for their deliverance.

Indeed there are many saviours in word, but none in deed, and these great false Christs and false Prophets, does destroy the Creation under the colour of saving it, and the people sees them not, but looks upon them as saviours, calling others false Christs and false Prophets that speak against them.

The first false Christ that promises to save the Creation, is covetous Kingly power, resting in the hand of one man, or in the hand of many, but this power saves but part, and holds another part of the creation in bondage, and any government that rules by swordly power doth so throughout all lands; therefore he is a false Christ, and no true saviour.

The Preaching Clergie or universative power, promises to save the Creation declaratively, but he is a false Christ, he saith and doth not, Pharisee-like, but will force people to maintain him from the Earth by their labours, for his sayings, by the Laws of the Kingly power; he saith, some are elected to salvation, and others are reprobated; he puts some into heaven, thrusts others into hell never to come out, and so he is not a universall Saviour; that is no salvation to the creation, mankind, while any part groans for the true Saviour, when he comes he will wipe away all teares, he comes not to destroy any but to save all.

Then the power of the Lawyers, he saith he will save the Creation, and this false Christ proves the greatest devourer and tearer of the creation of any other, for while he carries burthened men from one court to another promising to save them, he at last saves himself and destroyes others, and laughs at others losse, and throwes men further from peace then he [33] found them before he medled with them: Well, From the Bailiffe to the Judge, these are the creations of this Egyptian Taskmaster, and no burthen of cheating like to it, for he promises Justice, but behold nothing but oppression is in his hands.

Then next, The Art of buying and selling promises to save the Creation, and bring it into peace, but this is a hypocriticall false cheating Christ too, for hereby covetous self-love with his flattering tongue cheats honest hearted ones, and casts them under tyranny, and gets the fulness of the Earth into his hands, and locks it up in chests and barns from others, and saith this is righteous, and God gave it him, but thou cheater, thou liest; God the King of righteousness gave it thee not, he bids thee sell all that thou hast and give to the poor, he doth not bid thee lock it up from the poor, therefore thou trading art, thou art no true saviour neither, but a Devil, thou savest part, and destroyest another part, yea and afterwards destroyest that part which at first thou seemedst to save.

Now all these saviours are linked together, if one truly fall all must fall, they all promise to save the Creation, but destruction is in their hands and actions, they all seek to set up self and particular power, and so to save but part of the creation, for every one are destroyers of universall love: They that sit in these seats would be called men of publike Spirits, but truly you are all selfish, you are afraid to own publike spirited men, nay you are ashamed some of you to be seen walking or talking with true publike spirited men, called *Levellers*.

But well, yet there is a promise of restoration and salvation to the whole creation, and this must be wrought by a power contrary to darkness, for all those former saviours lie under darkness, nay are branches of the power of darkness it self, and darkness can never kill darkness; but now the true Saviour must be a power quite opposite to darkness: And this is,

The power of Universall Love, light and righteousness and if ever the creation be wholly saved, this power must be the [34] saviour, for this is the blessing, and he will declare himself the true Saviour indeed, the other is but the curse, this is the true restorer, the true seed with us, as he arises and spreads, he will bruise the Serpents head in every one, and bring peace to all, and wipe away all tears from the creation, and make a thorough salvation of it through the whole earth, and leave none under bondage.

This is the Sun of righteousness. When he ariseth, he disperseth darkness, and will make all ashamed that had hands in promoting of the other false saviours power; but I must leave this, and speak a little more of the present condition mankind lies under, and this is darknes or the fall, and in this estate ignorant inslaved flesh would ever run round in it, and never come out, but counts it freedom, but they that know the burthen of this estate hunger after freedom.

This darknes is twofold, first inward, and that is the power of darkness in his branchs, as covetousness, envy, pride, hypocrisie, self-love, this is the curse in man, and this darkness hath and yet doth cover the earth; this power would be as God, and makes one to rule over another, and he is so proud that he will hasten to rule though he kill others for honour, and this is he that stirs up wars and dissention, and thereby he destroyes himself.

Secondly this inward power sets one against another, and so fills the earth with dark actions, and causeth some part of mankind to tread others under foot and puts them into bondage, and they that act this power calls it, The power and Ordinance of God, which is true: It is God indeed, but it is the god of the world, the prince of darknes, not the King of Righteousnesse; it is the power of the Beast who is limited to rule for a time, times, and dividing of time, and *England* is under that dividing of time, therefore I hope, *England* shall be the tenth part of the Citie confusion that shall fall from the Beast first:

And this dark power or imaginarie covetousnesse hath raised a platform of oppression in the creation, under which the creation groans, and waits to be delivered; and it is raised thus,

[35] First this dark power within makes every one to love himself with others loss, just like Beasts of the Field; and this made mankind to begin to loath or envie each others Freedom and peace, and hereby the Union and Communion of Love within is broke, and mankind is faln from it: then this inward Covetousnesse makes mankind to fight one against another for the Earth, and breaks Communion in that, and falls from content therein likewise, and every one seeks to save himself to take the Earth to himself, but none or few seeks the things of Christ, or of universal Love.

Nay Covetousnesse is such a god, that where he Rules he would have all the Earth to himself, and he would have all to be his servants, and his heart swels most against Communitie; calling Communitie a thief, that takes other mens Rights and Proprietie from them, but communitie will force nothing from any one, but take what is given in love, of that which others have wrought for; but no man yet hath bestowed any labour upon the Commons that lies waste; therefore the Diggers doth take no mans proper goods from them in so doing, but those that by force spoyls their labours, takes their proper goods from them, which is the fruit of their own labours.

Well, you see how Covetousnesse would have all the Earth to himself, though he let it lie waste: he stirs up Divisions among men, and makes parties fight against parties; and all is but for this, Who shall enjoy the Earth, and live in honour and ease and rule over others: and the stronger party alwayes rules over the weaker party.

And hence came in Kingly power to rule outwardly, dividing between members of that one body mankind, giving the Earth to that party called Gentry, who are the Successors of some late Conquests, and denying the Earth to the poor Commoners who are the Successors of some that were last Conquered.

So that by Kingly power the Earth is divided as it is now at this day: but as the Scriptures say, *Kings were given for a plague to the people, not a blessing:* And I beleeve the Nations [36] have found this very true to their great sorrow: and the way to cast out Kingly power again, is not to cast them out by the Sword, for this doth but set him in more power, and removes him from a weaker to a stronger hand: but the only way to cast him out, is, For the People to leave him to himself, to forsake fighting and all oppression, and to live in love one towards another: This power of Love is the true Saviour.

The party that is called a King was but the head of an Army, and he and his Army having Conquered, shuts the conquered out of the Earth, and will not suffer them to enjoy it, but as a servant and slave to him; and by this power the creation is divided, and part are cast into bondage; so that the best you can say of Kingly power that Rules by the Sword is this, He is a murderer and a theif.

And by this power the Earth is thus divided.

The several Nations of the Earth where Kings rule, are the several situation of such grand Theeves and Murderers, that will rule over others by the Sword, upholding a forced Propriety, which is the

Curse; and persecuting the community of Love, which is Christ the blessing.

And under them they have their cheif Favourits or neerest Souldiers in Office to himself, and to these he allows the greatest portion of the Earth, every one his part, called a Lordship: and next to them the inferior Officers or Souldiers, are appointed out lesser parcels of the Earth, called free-Holders, paying no slavish Rent or Homage to any: but only acknowledgment, That the King is their General or Head still.

And these Lords of Mannors and Free holders having thus seated themselves in the Earth, by taking other mens proper labours from them by the Sword, are appointed by the King as Watchmen, That if any of the conquered slaves seek to Plant the Common waste Earth without their leave, they may be known and beaten off: So that the god from whom they claim Title to the Land as proper to them, shutting out others, was Covetousnesse the Murderer, the swordly power, [37] that great red Dragon, who is called, The god of the World.

But the King of Righteousnesse, who is universal Love, who is the Lord God Almighty, bidding every one *do as they would be done by*; made the Earth for All, without respect of person, and shuts out none from enjoying a peaceable livelihood that hath a body; therefore they that build upon the power of the Sword, upholding covetous Propriety, are enemies to the law of Righteousnesse, which is, *Love your enemies, do as you would be done by.*

But one of your Officers told me, *What?* (saith he) *If we grant to every one to have the Land of England in Common, we do not only destroy Propriety, but we do that which is not practised in any Nation in the world.*

I Answered, It was true; Propriety came in you see by the Sword, therefore the Curse; for the murderer brought it in, and upholds him by his power, and it makes a division in the Creation, casting many under bondage; therefore it is not the blessing, or the promised seed.

And what other Lands do, *England* is not to take pattern; for *England* (as well as other Lands) hath lyen under the power of that Beast, Kingly propriety: But now *England* is the first of Nations that is upon the point of Reforming: and if *England* must be the tenth part of the City *Babylon* that fals off from the Beast first, and would have that honour, he must cheerfully (and dally no longer) cast out

Kingly covetous Propriety, and set the Crown upon Christs head, who is the universal Love or Free community, and so be the leader of that happy Restoration to all the Nations of the world: And if *England* refuse, some other Nation may be chosen before him, and *England* then shall lose his Crown, for if ever the Creation be Restored, this is the way which lies in this Two fold power:

First *Community of Mankind,* which is comprised in the unity of spirit of Love, which is called Christ in you, or the Law writen in the heart, leading mankind into all truth, and to be of one heart and one mind.

[38] The Second is *Community of the Earth,* for the quiet livelihood in food and raiment without using force, or restraining one another: These two Communities, or rather one in two branches, is that true Levelling which Christ will work at his more glorious appearance; for Jesus Christ the Saviour of all men, is the greatest, first, and truest Leveller that ever was spoke of in the world.

Therefore you Rulers of *England,* be not ashamed nor afraid of Levellers, hate them not, Christ comes to you riding upon these clouds; look not upon other Lands to be your pattern, all Lands in the world lie under darkness, so doth *England* yet, though the neerest to Light and Freedom of any other; therefore let no other Land take your Crown.

You have set Christ upon his throne in *England* by your Promises, Engagements, Oathes, and Two Acts of Parliament, the One to cast out Kingly power; the Other to make *England* a Free Common wealth: Put all these into sincere Action, and you shall see the work is done, and you with others shall sing *Halelujah* to him that sits upon the Throne, and to the Lamb for evermore.

But if you do not, the Lamb shall shew himself a Lion, and tear you in pieces for your most abominable dissembling Hypocrisie, and give your Land to a People who better deserves it: I have varied a little, therefore I will return to what I was speaking.

I told you, *That the Murdering and Theeving Sword hath found out a Platform of Tyrannical Government, called Kingly Power.*

First here is the King, the Head of the murdering power, or great red Dragon.

Then there are Lords of Mannors, who have the greatest circuit of Land, because the next in Power to the Head.

Then there are Free-holders, that took the particular Inclosures which they found in a Land when they Conquered it, and had turned out those that had bestowed labour upon it, [39] by force of the Sword, in the field, or else by sequestring afterwards: These several parcels of Land are called Free-hold-Land, because the Enjoyers or their Ancestors were Souldiers, and helped the King to conquer; and if any of latter yeers came to buy these Free-holds with Money got by Trading, it doth not alter the Title of the Conquest; for Evidences are made in the Kings Name, to remove the Free-holds so bought from one mans hand to another.

But now Copy-hold lands are parcels hedged in, and taken out of the common waste land since the conquest, acknowledging Homage, Fines, and Heriots to the Lord of that Mannor or circuit in which that Inclosure by his leave is made: this Homage still confirmes the power of the conquests.

The Lords of Mannors acknowledged Homage to the King in that Court of Wards, which you have taken away to ease your selves.

But the Copy-holders you will have to acknowledge Homage to Lords of Mannors still; and is not this partiality? O you Rulers, make the poor as free to the Earth as your selves, and honour Righteousnesse.

Now for the drawing in of the People to yeeld Obedience to this Platform of Kingly tyrannical power, to which People are made subject through fear,

The Kingly power sets up a Preaching Clergy to draw the People by insinuating words to conform hereunto, and for their pains Kingly power gives them the Tithes: And when the Kingly power hath any Design to lift up himself higher, then the Clergy is to Preach up that Design, as of late in our Wars the Preachers most commonly in their Sermons medled with little but State matters: and then if People seeme to deny Tythes, then the Kingly power by his Lawes doth force the people to pay them: so that there is a confederacie between the Clergy and the great red Dragon: the Sheep of Christ shall never fare well so long as the wolf or red Dragon payes the Shepherd their wages.

Then next after this, the Kingly power sets up a Law and Rule of Government to walk by: and here Justice is pretended, [40] but the full strength of the Law is to uphold the conquering Sword, and to preserve his son Propriety: therefore if any one steal, this Law will hang them, and this they say is of God; and so this Kingly power hath power over the lives and labours of men at his pleasure; for though they say the Law doth punish, yet indeed, that Law is but the strength, life and marrow of the Kingly power, upholding the conquest still, hedging some into the Earth, hedging out others; giving the Earth to some, and denying the Earth to others, which is contrary to the Law of Righteousnesse, who made the Earth at first as free for one as for another.

Yea that Kingly power in the Lawes appointed the conquered poor to work for them that possesse the Land, for three pence and four pence a day, and if any refused, they were to be imprisoned; and if any walked a begging and had no dwelling, he was to be whipt; and all was to force the slaves to work for them that had taken their Propriety of their labours from them by the Sword, as the Laws of *England* are yet extant, and truly most Lawes are but to enslave the Poor to the Rich, and so they uphold the conquest, and are Lawes of the great red Dragon.

And at this very day poor people are forced to work in some places for 4, 5, and 6 pence a day; in other places for 8, 10, and 12 pence a day, for such small prizes, now Corn being deer, that their earnings cannot find them bread for their Family; and yet if they steal for maintenance, the murdering Law will hang them; when as Lawyers, Judges, and Court Officers can take Bribes by whole sale to remove one mans Propriety by that Law into another mans hands: and is not this worse theevery then the poor mans that steals for want? Well, this shewes, that if this be Law, it is not the Law of Righteousnesse; it is a Murderer, it is the Law of Covetousnesse and self-love; and this Law that frights people and forces people to obey it by Prisons, Whips, and Gallows, is the very kingdom of the Devil, and Darknesse, which the Creation groans under at this day.

And if any poor enslaved man that dares not steal, begins [41] to mourn under that bondage and saith, We that work most have least comfort in the earth, and they that work not at all, enjoy all; contrary to the Scripture which saith, *The poor and the meek shall inherit the earth;*

Presently the tithing Priest stops his mouth with a slam and tels him that is meant of the inward satisfaction of mind which the poor shall have, though they enjoy nothing at all, and so poor creatures, it is true, they have some ease thereby, and made to wait with patience, while the Kingly power swims in fulness, and laughs at the others miserie; as a poor Cavalier Gentlewoman presented a Paper to the Generall in my sight, who looked upon the woman with a tender countenance; but a brisk little man and two or three more Colonels puld back the Paper not suffering the Generall to receive it, and laught at the woman who answered them again, I thought said she, you had not sate in the seat of the scornfull; this was done in *White-hall* upon the 12. of *December,* 1649.

Well, all that I shall say to these men that will enjoy the earth in realitie, and tell others they must enjoy it in conceit, surely your judgement from the most High sleepeth not; the Law of Retaliation, like for like, laughing for laughing, may be your portion; for my part I was alwayes against the Cavaleers cause; yet their persons are part of the Creation as well as you, and many of them may enter into peace before some of you scoffing *Ishmaelites;* I am sure you act contrary to the Scripture which bids you *Love your enemies, and doe as you would be done by,* and this Scripture you say you own; why then do you not practice it, and doe to the Cavaliers as the Prophet *Eliah* bid the King of *Israel* do to his enemies whom he had taken prisoners, *Set bread and water* (saith he) *before them, and send them to their master in peace.*

Come, make peace with the Cavaliers your enemies, and let the oppressed go free, and let them have a livelihood, and love your enemies, and doe to them, as you would have had them do unto you if they had conquered you: Well, let them go in peace, and let love wear the Crown.

[42] For I tell you, and your Preachers, that Scripture which saith, *The poor shall inherit the earth,* is really and materially to be fullfilled, for the Earth is to be restored from the bondage of sword proprietie, and it is to become a common Treasurie in reallitie to whole mankind, for this is the work of the true Saviour to doe, who is the true and faithfull Leveller, even the Spirit and power of universall love, that is now rising to spread himself in the whole creation, who is the blessing, and will spread as far as the curse had spred to take it of, and cast him out, and who will set the creation in peace.

This powerfull Saviour will not set up his Kingdom nor rule his

Creation with sword and fighting, as some think and fear, for he hath declared to you long since, that they that take the sword to save themselves shall perish with the sword.

But this shall be the way of his conquest, even as in the daies of the Beast, the whole world wondred after him, set him up, and was subject to him, and did persecute universall love, and made War against him and his Saints, and overcame them for a time.

Even so the Spirit of love and blessing shall arise and spread in mankind like the Sun from East to West, and by his inward power of love, light, and righteousnes, shall let mankind see the abomination of the swordly Kingly power, and shall loath themselves in dust and ashes, in that they have owned and upheld him so long, and shall fall off from him, loath him and leave him.

And this shall be your miserie O you covetous oppressing Tyrants of the Earth, not only you great self-seeking powers of *England*, but you powers of all the World. The people shall all fall off from you, and you shall fall on a sudden like a great tree that is undermined at the root. And you powers of *England* you cannot say another day but you had warning, this falling off is begun already, divisions shall tear and torter you, till you submit to Communitie; O come in, come in to righteousness that you may find peace.

You or some of you hate the name *Leveller*, and the chiefest [43] of you are afraid and ashamed to own a *Leveller*, and you laugh and jeer at them; Well, laugh out poor blind souls, the people and common Souldiers both lets you alone, but they laugh in their hearts at you, and yet desire that you did know the things that concern your peace.

The time is very neer that the people generally shall loath and be ashamed of your Kingly power, in your preaching, in your Laws, in your Councels, as now you are ashamed of the *Levellers*; I tell you Jesus Christ who is that powerfull Spirit of Love is the head *Leveller*, and *as he is lifted up, hee will draw all men after him,* and leave you naked and bare, and make you ashamed in your selves, his appearance will be with power; therefore Kisse the Son O ye Rulers of the earth, least his anger fall upon you. The wounds of Conscience within you from him shall be sharper then the wounds made by your sword, he shook heaven and earth when *Moses* Law was cast out, but he will shake heaven and earth now to purpose much more, and nothing shall stand but what is lovely; be wise, scorn not the Councell of the poor, least you be whipt with your own rod.

This great Leveller, Christ our King of righteousness in us, shall cause men to beat their swords into plowshares, and spears into pruning hooks, and nations shall learn war no more, and every one shall delight to let each other enjoy the pleasures of the earth, and shall hold each other no more in bondage; then what will become of your power? truly he must be cast out for a murtherer; and I pittie you for the torment your spirit must go through, if you be not fore-armed, as you are abundantly forewarned from all places; but I look upon you as part of the creation who must be restored, and the Spirit may give you wisedom to foresee a danger, as he hath admonished divers of your rank already to leave those high places, and to lie quiet and wait for the breakings forth of the powerfull day of the Lord. Farewel, once more. Let *Israel* go free.

[44] A BILL OF ACCOUNT OF THE MOST RE-MARKABLE SUFFERINGS THAT THE DIGGERS HAVE MET WITH FROM THE GREAT RED DRAGONS POWER SINCE APRIL 1. 1649. Which was the first day that they began to digge, and to take possession of the commons for the poor on George-Hill in Surrey

THE *first time, divers of the Diggers were carried Prisoners into* Walton *Church, where some of them were struck in the Church by the bitter Professors and rude Multitude; but after some time freed by a Justice.*

2 *They were fetched by above a hundred rude people, whereof* John Taylor *was the Leader, who took away their Spades, and some of them they never had again: and carried them first to Prison at* Walton, *and then to a Justice at* Kingstone, *who presently dismissed them.*

3 *The Dragonly enemy pulled down a House which the Diggers had built upon* George-Hill, *and cut their Spades and Howes to pieces.*

[45] 4 *Two Troops of Horse were sent from the General to fetch us before the Councel of War, to give Account of our Digging.*

5 *We had another House pulled down, and our Spades cut to pieces.*

6 *One of the Diggers had his head sore wounded, and a Boy beaten, and his Cloathes taken from him: divers being by.*

7 *We had a Cart and Wheels cut in pieces, and a Mare cut over the back with a Bill when we went to fetch a Load of Wood from* Stoak-Common, *to build a House upon* George-Hill.

8 *Divers of the Diggers were beaten upon the* Hill, *by* William Star *and* John Taylor, *and by men in womens apparel, and so sore wounded, that some of them were fetched home in a Cart.*

9 *We had another House pulled down, and the Wood they carried to* Walton *in a Cart.*

10 *They Arrested some of us, and some they cast into Prison; and from others they went about to take away their Goods, but that the Goods proved another mans, which one of the Diggers was Servant to.*

11 *And indeed at divers times besides we had all our Corn spoyled; for the Enemy was so mad, that they tumbled the Earth up and down, and would suffer no Corn to grow.*

12 *Another Cart and Wheels was cut to pieces, and some of our Tooles taken by force from us, which we never had again.*

13 *Some of the Diggers were beaten by the Gentlemen, the Sheriff looking on, and afterwards Five of them were carried to* White-Lion *Prison, and kept there about 5 weeks, and then let out.*

14 *The Sheriff with the Lords of Mannors and Souldiers standing by, caused two or three poor men to pull down another House: and divers things were stoln from them.*

15 *The next day two Souldiers and two or three Countrymen sent by Parson* Platt, *pulled down another House, and* [46] *turned a poor old man and his wife out of doors to lie in the field in a cold night.*

And this is the last hitherto; and so you Priests as you were the last that had a hand in our persecution, so it may be that Misery may rest in your hand; for assure your selves, God in Christ will not be mocked by such Hypocrites that pretend to be his neerest and deerest Servants as you do, and yet will not suffer his hungry, naked, and house-less members to live quiet by you in the Earth, by whose Blood and Monies in these Wars, you are in peace.

And now those Diggers that remain, have made little Hutches to lie in like Calf-cribs, and are cheerful; taking the spoyling of their Goods patiently, and rejoycing that they are counted worthy to suffer persecution for Righteousnesse sake: and they follow their work close, and have Planted divers Acres of Wheat and Rie, which is come up and promises a very fruitful crop, and Resolves to preserve it by all the diligence they can, and nothing shall make them slack but want of Food, which is not much now, they being all poor People, and having suffered so much in one expence or other since they began; for Poverty is their greatest burthen; and if any thing do break them from the Work, it will be that.

> *You Lordly Foes, you will rejoyce*
> *this newes to hear and see;*
> *Do so, go on; but wee'l rejoyce*
> *much more the Truth to see:*
> *For by our hands truth is declar'd,*
> *and nothing is kept back;*
> *Our faithfulness much joy doth bring,*
> *though victuals we may lack.*
> *This tryal may our God see good,*
> *to try, not us, but you;*
> *That your profession of the Truth,*
> *may prove either false or true.*

[47] And these are the Troubles and Persecutions that the Diggers have gone through since they began, besides many particular abuses from rude Spirits, and multitudes of slanders, lyes, and bad names, that the mouths of the scoffing *Ishmaelites* are filled with, and the secret enmity that hath come from close Hypocrites, that goe for great Professors.

> *But now Profession, thou art tryed*
> *to purpose, all shall see,*
> *And verbal talk it will appear*
> *a Devil for to be:*
> *For actions pure, holds forth the life*
> *of God and Christ most dear:*
> *And false Dissembling now must die,*
> *if Scriptures you will hear;*
> *You preaching men if Truth you'l own,*
> *see Truth be acted to,*
> *Or else to Christ you will appear*
> *to be his mortal foe.*
> *Scribes, Pharisees, and the Theif,*
> *that* Judas *was by name,*
> *Great preachers were, but for no deeds,*

the Truth they much did stain:
No deeds you'l say! Yes, that they had:
  its true they had indeed;
But what deeds were they you can see?
  no herb, but stinking weed:
For Persecution ever was
  the Work that came from them,
And deadly foes they ever were,
  to Christ, and righteous men.

And here I end, having put my Arm as far as my strength will go to advance Righteousness: I have Writ, I have Acted, I have Peace: and now I must wait to see the Spirit do his own work in the hearts of others, and whether *England* shall be the first Land, or some other, wherein Truth shall sit down in triumph.

[48] But O *England, England,* would God thou didst know the things that belong to thy peace before they be hid from thine eyes: The Spirit of Righteousness hath striven with thee, and doth yet strive with thee, and yet there is hope. Come in thou *England,* submit to Righteousness before the voice go out, my Spirit shall strive no longer with Flesh; and let not Covetousnesse make thee oppresse the poor.

We have Declared our Reasons for our Digging plentifully enough; and you Rulers of *England,* will you alwayes be like deaf Adders, &c? We have received many affronts from Lords of Mannors and their Servants divers times; yet nothing makes us be at a stand, Whether *England* shall be the first Land that shall fall off from the Beast, and set Righteousnesse upon the Throne, or no, but the late Action of the head of the Souldiery, in granting a party of Horse to come and weaken us.

Gentlemen of the Souldiery, be not offended, for you promised me in *Whitehal* Gallerie, that you would not meddle with us, but leave us to the Law of the Land, and the Country Gentlemen to deal with us, and so you did a long time, and we hope in time that love and patience will conquer our furious enemies.

Yet we understand, which a little troubles us, yet content That the Generall gave his consent that the Souldiers should come to help to beat of the Diggers, and to pull down their Houses; it is true, the Souldiers with the Gentlemen our enemies came, and caused others to pull down our houses, but the Souldiers did not meddle, none but one, but expressed sorrow to see the Passages.

But though they were modest, and expressed tenderness, yet the Generals grant and the Soulders presence was a great crush to our business; Gentlemen of the Army, we have spoke to you, we have appealed to the Parliament, we have declared our cause with all humilitie to you all, and we are Englishmen, and your friends that stuck to you in your miseries, and these Lords of Mannors that oppose us were wavering on both sides, yet you have heard them, and answered their request [49] to beat us off, and yet you would not afford us an Answer.

Yet love and patience shall lie down and suffer; Let pride and covetousness stretch themselves upon their beds of ease, and forget the afflictions of *Joseph,* and persecute us for righteousness sake, yet we will wait to see the issue, the power of righteousness is our God; the globe runs round, the longest Sun-shine day ends in a dark night; and therefore to thee O thou King of righteousness we doe commit our cause; Judge thou between us and them that strive against us, and those that deal treacherously with thee and us, and doe thine own work, and help weak flesh in whom the Spirit is willing.

FINIS.

A VINDICATION OF THOSE WHOSE ENDEAVORS IS ONLY TO MAKE THE EARTH A COMMON TREASURY, CALLED DIGGERS

THE text is dated February 20, 1649 (n.s. 1650), and an addition on the last page is dated March 4, 1649 (n.s. 1650). Winstanley's name appears at the end of the text and on the last page.

Copies are to be found in the following collections: The Bodleian, The Haverford College Library, and The Thomason Library at the British Museum.

The text is reproduced from the copy in the Thomason Library.

A VINDICATION OF THOSE, WHOSE EN-DEAVORS IS ONLY TO MAKE THE EARTH A COMMON TREASURY, CALLED DIG-GERS or, Some Reasons given by them against the immoderate use of creatures, or the excessive community of women, called Ranting; or rather Renting

IRST, those that are called Diggers; doe looke upon the Ranting Practise, to be a Kingdome without the man; which moth and rust doe, may, and will corrupt; and which thieves may break through and steale away; It is Kingdome that lies in objects; As in the outward enjoyment of meat, drinke, pleasures, and women; so that the man within can have || no quiet rest, unlesse he enjoy those outward objects in excesse; all which are vanishable. Therefore it is the Devills Kingdome of darknesse, and not the Kingdome of heaven nor true peace within.

Secondly, this outward life, in the abundant eating and drinking, and actuall community with variety of women is the onely life of the five sences, which is the life of the Beast, or living flesh; And fights against reason, who is the seed or tree of life, or the righteous man that is within. For when the sensitive power, which is the sonne of bondage rules, the Reason which is the sonne of freedome, is trod under foot, and in the absence thereof the whole body, whole Families, nay, whole Nations are distempered; But when Reason rules in the house or heart not suffering the sences to runne into excesse in any action: then the whole body enjoyes quiet rest and peace. Therefore that immoderate ranting practise of the Sences is not the true life of peace.

Thirdly, the Ranting practise is the proper Kingdome of Covetousnesse, or King Lust of the flesh, which is the Kingdome of darknesse, full of unreasonablenesse, madnesse and confusion; it is the land of darknesse, bringing forth nothing but miserie to the Inhabitants thereof, for,

Fourthly, it is destructive to the body, house, or Temple, wherein Reason or the spirituall power dwells; it brings diseases, infirmenesse, weaknesses and rottennesse upon the body, and so ruines the house about the mans eares, that he cannot live in quiet peace; for diseases of body causes sorrow of || mind. And as moderation in any action brings peace, so excesse brings diseases and death. Therefore the unrationall ranting practise is not the life of rightnesse nor peace.

Fifthly it brings vexation to the mind or man within, for when you want your delight in the excessive copolation with Women, and in the superabundant eating and drinking, which is the wastfull spending of the Treasures of the Earth, As the Ranting practise is, Then Anger, rage and varietie of vexations possesses the mind, and inflames their harts to quarrelling, killing, burning houses or Corne, or to such like distructivenesse.

Sixthly, The Ranting practise is a peace breaker; it breaks the peace in Families, and rents in peeces mankind, For where true Love hath united a man and woman to be Husband and Wife, and they live in peace, when this Ranting power or king lust of the flesh comes in, he seperates those very friends, causing both sides to run into the Sea of confusion, madnesse and distruction, to leave each other, to leave their Children, and to live in discontent each with other.

It pretends love to all men and women. But yet he is a beast that respects persons; for the richest and fairest must be his associate.

Seventhly, This excesse of Feminine society, hinders the pure and naturall Generation of man, and spills the seed in vaine, and instead of a healthfull groth of mankind it produces weaknesse and much infirmnesse, through immoderate heat; so || that either the Mother hath much more paine in child bearing, or els the child is fild with such infirmnesse, that it proves a burden to the Mother or nurse or through deseases he brings with him into the world he proves either not long lived, or a foole, or else a sickly weakly thing that is a burden to himselfe: So that this [im]moderat Ranting, is not a healthfull builder up of the creation man, but a violent waster and destroyer of the health and strength of man. This false generating fire is the foundation of much lamentation, for children begotten through this forced immoderat heat of lust proves furious and full of rage; it is a breeder of much distemper, Warres, and quarrells; It is one cause if not the chief of the rising up of the hairie man, which is a destroyer of himselfe and others. And the mother and child begotten in this manner is like to have the worst of it, for the man will be gone and leave them; and regard them no more then other women, like a Bull that begets a Calfe, that never takes care neither for Cow nor Calfe, after he hath had his pleasure. Therefore you women beware, for this ranting practise is not the restoring, but the destroying, power of the creation.

Eighthly, The Ranting practise, is the support of Idlenesse, for they that are the Sons and Daughters of that unrationall power neither can nor will work, but live idle, like wandring bussy bodies, expressing and cheating others, that are simple and of a civill flexible nature, so that by seeking their owne freedom they imbondage others which is the selfish, but not ‖ the universall Love, for true Love seeks the preservation of others as of one selfe, or else for want of food and rayment, through an inward proud sullennesse, either sterves their owne bodies, or else through an inward rage endeavours the ruine of others.

Ninthly, This Ranting power, or god, is full of sutletie to deceive others of what they earn, and is a nurse of hardnesse of heart against others, when he hath deceived them, for this is his nature: to get what he can from others labours, to eat up others and made them poore, and then to laugh and rejoyce in others poverty.

Tenthly, The Ranting power, would make this Covenant with all men, to put out their eyes, or suffer him quietly to put them out, and to see by his eyes, and to walk by his legges, and then he calls them high lighted creatures, otherwise he tells them they live belowe them, and is in the dark, and rather then proud civility would be counted ignorant, it will yeeld, and first stands looking and saying, I can say nothing against this ranting practise, and then afterwards yeelds and then is ensnared and taken by the suttle devouring ranting Beast. But now he that obeys reasons law of righteousnesse within, shall escape that snare.

Eleventhly, This Ranting power, is the resurrection of the uncleane doggish beastly nature, it is the resurrection of the filthy, unrighteouse power in all his branches, and it is high now, || but will rise higher, for it must rise to the hight to shew himselfe a compleat man of darknesse, that he may come to judgement, and so be cast out of heaven, That is, out of mankinde.

For as he is upon his resurrection, so the man of pure life, reason, and righteousnesse, is upon his resurrection too, Who is rising to purge and to restore the creation, and to set it downe in peace. And these two men, one of Light, and the other of darknesse, now strives with great vehemencie; the sonnes of darknesse may live in their vanishable peace and tread the sonnes of light under feet but the sonnes of peace shall rise up, and take peace from the Earth.

There is only two things, I must speak as an Advice in Love

First, let every one that intends to live in peace, set themselves with dilligent labour to Till, Digge, and Plow, the Common and barren Land, to get their bread with righteous moderat working, among all moderat minded people; this prevents the evill of Idlenesse, and the danger of the Ranting power.

Secondly, Let none goe about to suppresse that ranting power by their punishing hand, for it is the work of the Righteous and rational spirit within, not thy hand without that must suppresse it; But if thou wilt needs be punishing: Then see thou be without sinne thy selfe, and then cast the first Stone at the Ranter; Let not sinners punish others for sin, but let the power of thy Reason and righteous action, shame and so beat downe their unrationall actings. ||

Would thou live in peace; Then look to thy own wayes, mind thy owne Kingdome within, trouble not at the unrational government of other mens kingdomes without; Let every one alone, to stand and fall to their owne Master for thou being a sinner, and strives to suppresse sinners by force, thou wilt thereby but increase their rage, and thy owne trouble: but do thou keep close to the Law of righteous reason, and thou shalt presently see a returne of the Ranters: for that spirit within must shame them, and turne them, and pull them out of darknesse.

This I was moved to write as a Vindication of the Diggers, who are slandered with the Ranting action: And my end is only to Advance the Kingdome of peace in and among mankinde, which is and will be torne in peeces by the Ranting power, if reason do not kill this five headed, or sencitive Beast.

All you that are meerly civill, and that are of a loving and flexible disposition wanting the strength of reason: and the life of universall love, leading you forth to seeke the peace and preservation of every single body as of one's selfe; You are the People that are like to be tempted, and set upon and torne into peeces by this devouring Beast; the Ranting power.

Febr. this 20. 1649.

Gerrard Winstanley. ||

Therefore know all yee Lasivious feedars, Sarvers of your own bellies, that ye are breeders of all foule filthy beastly and Abominable Children, which come into the world to preach to the Nation, where they appeare, what the first signe of filthy Sinne or lasivious feeding heat begot, for lasivious feeding causeth lacivious acting, which if they knew the resurrection or eternall Iudgement, they durst not act.

I am told there are some people goes up and downe in the Country among such as are friends to the Diggers gathering Monyes in their name. And they have a note wherein my name and divers others are subscribed. This is to certifie that I never subscribed my name to any such note. Neither have we that are called Diggers received any money by any such Collections, therefore to prevent this Cheat: we desire if any are willing to cast a gift in, to further our work of Digging upon the Commons, that they would send it to our owne hands by some trustie friend of their owne.

March this 4th. 1649.

Your friend
Gerrard Winstanley.

FINIS.

AN APPEALE TO ALL ENGLISHMEN

A BROADSIDE dated March 26, 650. The only copy that I know is in the Thomason Library at the British Museum. The text is reproduced from that copy.

AN APPEALE TO ALL ENGLISHMEN, to judge between Bondage and Freedome, sent from those that began to digge upon *George* Hill in *Surrey;* but now are carrying on, that publick work upon the little Heath in the Parish of COBHAM, neare unto GEORGE Hill, wherein it appeares, that the work of digging upon the Commons, is not onely warranted by Scripture, but by the Law of the *Common-wealth* of *England* likewise.

BEHOLD, behold, all *Englishmen,* The Land of *England* now is your free Inheritance: all *Kingly* and Lordly entanglements are declared against, by our *Army* and *Parliament.* The *Norman* power is beaten in the field, and his head is cut off: And that oppressing *Conquest* that hath raigned over you by *King* and *House of Lords,* for about 600. yeares past, is now cast out, by the *Armies* Swords, the *Parliaments* Acts and Lawes, and the *Common-wealths* Engagement.

Therefore let not *Sottish* covetousnesse in the *Gentrey,* deny the poore or younger Brethren, their just Freedom to build and plant Corne upon the common wast Land: nor let slavish fear, possesse the hearts of the poor, to stand in awe of the *Norman* Yoake any longer, seeing it is broke. Come, those that are free within, turn your Swords into Plough-shares, and Speares into pruning-hookes, and take *Plow* and *Spade,* and break up the Common Land, build you Houses, sow Corne, and take possession of your own Land, which you have recov-

NOW these few Considerations, we offer to all *England,* and we appeale to the judgement of all rational and righteous men; whether

ered out of the hands of the *Norman* oppressour.

The common Land hath lain unmanured all the dayes of his *Kingly* and *Lordly* power over you, by reason whereof, both you and your Fathers, (many of you) have been burthened with poverty, And that Land which would have been fruitfull with Corne, hath brought forth nothing but heath, mosse, furseys, and the curse, according to the words of the Scriptures: *A fruitful Land is made barren, because of the unrighteousnesse of the People that ruled therein, and would not suffer it to be planted, because they would keep the Poor under bondage, to maintain their own Lordly Power, and conquering covetousnesse.*

But what hinders you now? will you be slaves and beggers still, when you may be Freemen? will you live in straits, and die in poverty, when you may live comfortably? will you allwayes make a profession of the words of *Christ* and *Scripture:* the sum whereof is this. *Do as you would be done unto, and live in love?* And now it is come to the point of fulfilling that righteous Law: wil you not rise up & act, I do not mean act by the sword, for that must be left? But come, take *Plow* & *Spade*, build & plant, & make the wast Land fruitfull, that there may be no begger nor idle person among us; for if the wast Land of *England* were manured by her Children, it would become in a few yeares the richest, the strongest, and flourishing Land in the World, and all *Englishmen* would live in peace and comfort; And this freedom is hindered by such as yet are full of the *Norman* base blood, who would be Free men themselves, but would have all others bond-men and Servants, nay slaves to them.

The Law of the *Scriptures* gives you a full freedom to the Earth, and makes Man-kind free in all his Members; *for God, or the creating spirit, is no respector of persons.*

this we speak be not that substantiall Truth brought forth into action, which Ministers have preached up, and all religious men have made profession of; for certainly, God who is the King of righteousness, is not a

The *Ministers* who preache up the Law of the
Scriptures, plead for their Freedom in the Earth,
and say, *The Labourer is worthy of his hire*. But
these *Ministers*, are faulty in two things. First, They
will set themselves to work, in that they will run before they be sent, and then force the People by the
power of the Sword-Law, to give them wages, or
Labourers hire. And they will not take 12 *d*. a day as
other Labourers have, but they will compell 100 *l*.
or more to be paid them yearly. Secondly, They lay
claime to Heaven after they are dead, and yet they
require their Heaven in this World too, and grumble
mightily against the People that will not give them
a large temporal maintenance. And yet they tell the
poor People, that they must be content with their
Poverty, and they shall have their Heaven hereafter. But why may we not have our Heaven here
(that is, a comfortable livelihood in the Earth) And
Heaven hereafter too, as well as you, *God is no respector of Persons?*

Therefore say we, while we have bodies that must
be fed and cloathed, let us have Earth to plant, to
raise food and rayment by our labours, according to
the Law of our Creation, and let us live like men of
your own Image and forme.

But if you say, that this is onely old *Adams* condition to look after the Earth; but the new *Adam
Christ*, lookes after Heaven above, and mindes not
the Earth, As one publick Minister told us, why truly
then we say, you make old *Adam* who brings in the
curse to be more rational and tender over our bodies;
then the second *Adam Christ* who brings in the blessing to all Nations.

But if it be old *Adams* condition to desire a Livelihood as we are men, and to live free from straits:
Then I would have all those *Ministers* to cast aside
their 100 *l*. or 200 *l*. a yeare, and go and beg their
food and rayment of others, and expect their Heaven

God of words
only, but of
deedes; for it is
the badge of hy-
pocrisie, for a
man to say, and
not to do.
Therefore we
leave this with
you all, having
peace in our
hearts, by de-
claring faithful-
ly to you, this
light that is in

hereafter, as they bid the poor men do.

But you covetous blind deceivers, know this, that as old *Adam* brings *Man-kind* into bondage and straits, so the second *Adam* brings *Man-kind* into Freedom, plenty and peace, here in this Earth while bodies are living upon earth: therefore he is said to be the joy of all Nations here on Earth, and the restorer of the whole Creation, that groanes under bondage here on Earth.

Well *Englishmen,* The Law of the *Scriptures,* gives you a free and full Warrant to plant the Earth, and to live comfortably and in love, doing as you would be done by: And condemns that covetous *Kingly* and *Lordly* power of darkness in men, that makes some men seeke their freedom in the Earth, and to deny others that freedom. And the *Scriptures* do establish this Law, to cast out *Kingly* and *Lordly* self-willed and oppressing power, and to make every Nation in the World a free *Common-wealth.* So that you have the *Scriptures* to protect you, in making the Earth a common Treasury, for the comfortable Livelihood of your bodies, while you live upon Earth.

Secondly, You have both what the *Army* and *Parliament* have done to protect you, as it will appeare by this graduall consideration.

First, *King Charles* was the successour of the *Norman* Conquest, and raigned as a Conquerour over *England,* for his Power held the Land from us, and would rather see us die in poverty, or hang us up, then suffer us to plant the *Commons* for our livelihood. And *Lords* of *Mannours* hold claiming to their *Copy-holds,* and to the *Commons,* under or from the *King:* so that *Kings* and *Lordly* power, is the power of the *Conquest* over the people.

Secondly, *Our Common-wealths Army* have fought against the *Norman* Conquest, and have cast him out, and keepes the field. By vertue of which victory, both the Title of the *King,* and the Title of

us, and which we do not onely speake and write, but which we do easily act & practise. Likewise we write it, as a Letter of congratulation, and encouragement to our dear fellow *Englishmen,* that have begun to digge upon

Lords of *Mannors* to the Land as *Conquerors* is lost. And the Land now is as free to others as to them; yea, according to *Davids* Law, to them that staid at home with the stuffe, as to them that went out to warre: And by this victory, *England* is made a free *Common-wealth*. And the common Land belongs to the younger Brother, as the Enclosures to the elder Brother, without restraint.

Then Thirdly, The *Parliament*, since this victory, have made an *Act* or *Law*, to make *England* a free *Common-wealth*. And by this *Act* they have set the People free, from *King* and *House of Lords* that ruled as *Conquerors* over them, and have abolished their self will and murdering Lawes, with them that made them.

Likewise they have made another *Act* or *Law*, to cast out *Kingly* Power, wherein they free the People from yielding obedience to the *King*, or to any that holds claiming under the *King*. Now all *Lords* of *Mannours*, Tything Priests and impropriators, hold claiming or Title under the *King*, but by this Act of *Parliament* we are freed from their Power.

Then lastly, The *Parliament* have made an *Engagement*, to maintain this present *Common-wealths* Government, comprised within those 2. *Acts* or *Lawes* against *King* and *House of Lords*. And calles upon all Officers, Tenants, and all sort of People to subscribe to it, declaring that those that refuse to subscribe, shall have no priviledge in the *Common-wealth* of *England*, nor protection from the Law.

Now behold all *Englishmen*, that by vertue of these 2. Lawes, and the *Engagement*, the Tenants of Copyholds, are freed from obedience to their Lords of *Mannors*, and all poor People may build upon,

the Commons, thereby taking possession of their freedom in *Willinborow* [1] in *Northamptonshire:* And at *Cox Hall* in *Kent*, waiting to see the chains of slavish fear to break and fall off from the hearts of others

---

[1] For the cultivation of the commons at Wellingborough see *A Declaration of the Grounds and Reasons,* below, Appendix, p. 649. Cox Hill is in Kent, about five miles northwest of Dover on the road toward Canterbury. I know of no record of cultivating the commons there.

and plant the *Commons*, and the *Lords* of *Mannours* break the Lawes of the Land & the *Engagement*, & still uphold the *Kingly* and *Lordly Norman* Power, if they hinder them, or seek to beat them of from planting the *Commons*.

Neither can the *Lords* of *Mannors* compell their Tenants of Copy-holds, to come to their *Court-Barons*, nor to be of their *Juries*, nor take an Oath to be true to them, nor to pay fines, Heriots, quit-rent, nor any homage, as formerly, while the King and Lords were in their power. And if the Tenants stand up to maintain their Freedom, against their *Lords* oppressing power, the Tenants forfeit nothing, but are protected by the *Laws* and *Engagement* of the Land.

And if so be, that any poor men build them houses, and sow Corne upon the *Commons*, the *Lords* of *Mannors* cannot compell their Tenants to beat them of: And if the Tenants refuse to beat them off they forfeit nothing, but are protected by the *Lawes* and *Engagement* of the Land. But if so be, that any fearfull or covetous Tenant, do obey their *Court-Barons*, and will be of their *Jury*, and will still pay Fines, Heriots, quit-Rents, or any homage as formerly, or take new Oaths, to be true to their *Lords*, or at the Command of their *Lords*, do beat the poor men off from planting the *Commons*; then they have broke the *Engagement*, and the Law of the Land, and both Lords and Tenants are conspiring to uphold or bring in the *Kingly* and *Lordly* Power again, and declare themselves enemies to the Army, and to the Parliament, and are traytors to the *Commonwealth* of *England*. And if so be they are to have no protection of the Lawes, that refused to tak the *Engagement*, surely they have lost their protection by breaking their *Engagement*, and stand lyable to answer for this their offence, to their great charge and trouble, if any will prosecute against them. Therefore you

in other Countries, till at last the whole Land is filled with the knowledge & righteousness of the restoring power, which is *Christ* himself, *Abrahams* seed, who will spread himself til he become the joy of all Nations.

Englishmen, whether Tenants or labouring men, do not enter into a new bond of slavery, now you are come to the point that you may be free, if you will stand up for freedom; for the Army hath purchased your freedom. The Parliament hath declared for your freedom, and all the Lawes of the *Commonwealth* are your protection, so that nothing is wanting on your part, but courage and faithfulness, to put those Lawes in execution, and to take possession of your own Land, which the *Norman* Power took from you, and hath kept from you about 600. yeares, which you have now recovered out of his hand. And if any say that the old Lawes and Customes of the Land, are against the Tenant and the poor, and intitle the Land onely to the *Lords* of *Mannours* still, I answer, all the old Lawes are of no force, for they are abolished, when the *King* and *House* of *Lords* were cast out. And if any say, I but the Parl: made an Act to establish the old Lawes, I answer, this was to prevent a sudden rising upon the cutting off the *Kings* head; but afterwards they made these 2. Lawes, to cast out *Kingly* Power, and to make *England* a *Commonwealth.* And they have confirmed these 2. by the *Engagement,* which the People now generally do own and subscribe: therefore by these Acts of freedom, they have abolished that Act that held up bondage. Well, by these you may see your freedom, and we hope the *Gentry* hereafter, wil cheat the poor no longer of their Land, and we hope, the *Ministers* hereafter will not tell the poor they have no right to the Land, for now the Land of *England,* is and ought to be a common Treasury to all *Englishmen,* as the severall portions of the Land of *Canaan,* were the common Livelihood to such and such a Tribe; both the elder and younger Brother, without respect of persons. If you deny this, you deny the Scriptures. And now we shall give you some few encouragements out of many, to move you to stand

Jerard Winstanley.

Richard Maidley.

Thomas James.

John Dickins.

John Palmer.

John South, Elder.

Nathaniel Holcomb.

Thomas Edcer.

Henry Barton.

John South.

Jacob Heard.

Thomas Barnat.

Anthony Wren.

up for your freedom in the Land, by acting with *John Hayman.*
Plow and *Spade* upon the *Commons.*

1. *By this meanes within a short time, there will be no begger nor idle person in* England, *which will be the glory of* England, *and the glory of that Gospel, which* England *seemes to professe in words.* *William Hitchcock.*

2. *The wast and common Land being improved, will bring in plenty of all Commodities, and prevent famine, and pull down the prizes of Corne, to 12 d. a Bushel, or lesse.* 3. *It will prove* England *to be the first of Nations, or the tenth part of the City* Babylon, *which falls off from the covetous beastly Government first; and that sets the Crown of freedom upon Christs head, to rule over the Nations of the world, and to declare him to be the joy and blessing of all Nations. This should move all Governours to strive, who shall be the first that shall cast down their Crownes, Scepters, and Government at Christs feete, and they that will not give Christ his own glory, shall be shamed.* 4. *This Commonwealths freedom will unite the hearts of* Englishmen *together in love so that if a forraign enemy endeavour to come in, we shall all with joynt consent rise up to defend our Inheritance, and shall be true one to another. Whereas now, the poor see, if they fight, and should conquer the Enemy, yet either they or their Children are like to be slaves still, for the Gentrey will have all. And this is the cause why many run away and faile our Armies in the time of need. And so through the Gentries hardness of heart against the poor: The Land may be left to a forraigne enemy, for want of the poorers love sticking to them; for say they, we can as well live under a forraign enemy working for day wages, as under our own brethren, with whom we ought to have equal freedom by the Law of righteousness.* 5. *This freedom in planting the common Land, will prevent robbing, stealling, and murdering, and Prisons will not so mightily be*

Henry Hancocke.

John Barry.

Thomas Starre.

Thomas Adams.

John Coulton.

Thomas South.

Robert Sayear.

Daniel Freland.

Robert Draper.

Robert Coster.

And divers

others that were

filled with Prisoners; and thereby we shall prevent that hart breaking spectacle of seeing so many hanged every Sessions as there are. And surely this imprisoning and hanging of men is the Norman *power still, and cannot stand with the freedom of the Commonwealth, nor warranted by the Engagement; for by the Lawes and Engagement of the Commonwealth, none ought to be hanged, nor put to death for other punishments may be found out. And those that do hang or put to death their fellow* Englishmen, *under colour of Lawes, do break the Lawes and the Engagement by so doing, and casts themselves from under the protection of the Commonwealth, and are traytors to* Englands *freedom, and upholders of the Kingly murdering power. 6. This freedom in the common earth, is the poorers right by the Law of Creation and equity of the Scriptures, for the earth was not made for a few, but for whole Mankind, for God is no respector of Persons.*

not present

when this went

to the Presse.

March,

26.

1650.

AN HUMBLE REQUEST TO THE MINISTERS OF BOTH UNIVER-SITIES AND TO ALL LAWYERS IN EVERY INNS-A-COURT

THE title page is dated 1650 and the address to the ministers, April 9, 1650. Winstanley's name appears on the title page and at the end of both addresses.

Copies are to be found in the following collections: The Forster Library at the Victoria and Albert Museum and The Seligman Library at Columbia University.

The text is reproduced from the copy in the Seligman Library.

TO THE READER,

THE *occasion of the publication of this Request to the Ministers and Lawyers was this: Upon a discourse between Parson* Plat [1], *Lord of the* mannor *of* Cobham, *and* Gerard Winstanley, *about the matter of digging upon the Commons in his Lordship.*

Mr. Plat *did promise and engage himself with loving expressions, and words savouring of much moderation, tenderness and reason, that if* Gerard Winstanley *could prove by Scriptures, the lawfulnesse of the work, that is, that the earth was made to be a common Treasury, and ought to remain so to whole Mankind, without respect of persons: That he would never hereafter molest the Diggers, but quietly suffer them to build and plant the Commons in his Lordship: And that he would bring in his Estate, and become one in that community.*

This which here followes is a Copy of those Scriptures I delivered to him, which he had not then time to read over; but upon discourse at the same time, upon the same Scriptures, he did not gain-say, but by his words of Gentleness declared a condescension, to the light of that universall freedom, held forth thereby to Mankind.

For the present I offer this to the consideration of all rational and Christian-spirited men, to judge in the case; And according as Mr. Plat *gives answer, I shall be as ready to declare and publish.*

For the present farewell.

per me, GERARD WINSTANLEY.

[1] For John Platt, rector at West Horsley, see above, p. 346, n. 1.

TO THE MINISTERS OF BOTH UNIVERSI-
TIES, AND THE LAWYERS OF EVERY
INNS-A-COURT

Gentlemen, Brethren, and Englishmen,

Yrou all heare of the difference between *Lords* of *Mannours,* and
the poor People of *England.* The poor people say, the common
Land is their due, by right of Creation, and by the Lawes of a
Common-wealth. And being encouraged herefrom, do build houses,
and plant them corn for their Livelihood, upon the Commons and
wast Land, that they may live like men, in their right of Creation; and
that they may enjoy the benefit of a free Common-wealth, as they are
Englishmen.

The *Lords of Mannours* say, it is not their Creation-right; thereupon beat them, pull down their houses, and much abuse them, pushing the poor with their hornes of power, like unrational Beasts.

And though the difference rise higher and higher between them,
both in point of Conscience, and point of Law yet hitherto, there does
not any appear to reconcile the difference

But Gentlemen, let it not be said hereafter among posterity but that
there were some wise men among you, that were not blinded by passion, covetousness, and self-interest; but that you would adventure to
speak for righteousness, and that took the cause of the poor into your
hands.

This difference between Lords of Mannours and the poor, about
the common Land, is the greatest controversie that hath rise up this
600. yeares past.

If reason and righteousness which is the foundation of Scriptures,
and just Lawes do give it us: let us have our freedom quietly; if
neither reason nor righteousness give us this freedom, we will lie
still, and never trouble you more.

Therefore I leave these following Scriptures and Considerations to you, and rest,

April 9th.
1650.

A fellow-Commoner of England, and true friend to Freedom,

GERARD WINSTANLEY.

[1] *The whole Earth: By the Law of Creation, is the Common treasury of free Livelyhood, to whole Mankind. And those Lords of Mannors, and others, that deny any part of mankind, this creation-freedome in the earth, are sinners in the highest degree, and are up-holders of the fall & curse of Mankind.*

To prove this by Scripture.

IT is plaine, that the Scriptures consists of Three Parts. First, they declare the righteous Law of Creation, wherein God gives to all Mankind, equall freedome, without respect of persons.

Secondly, they declare the fall of Mankind from this righteous Law; and the various unrighteous actings of Mankind, under his falne estate, or power of darknesse, by whom he is taken prisoner.

Thirdly, they declare the restoration of Mankind to his creation-righteousnesse: By whom he is restored: And the actings and conversation of Mankind upon his resurrection from under that dark, or faln estate.

Ile begin with the First, and take notice how the Scriptures gives an universal freedome in the Earth to whole Mankind.

In *Genesis*, God said, *Let us make Man*: By Man, in the singular number implies Mankind. *And let them have dominion*: By Them, in the plurall number implies, whole Mankind in all his branches. Gen. 1. 26.

Againe: he created Man; that is: Mankind. *Male and female, created he Them*. And bid them, in the plurall number: *increase, and multiply, and replenish the earth:* and after Mankind, in his varietie of branches, did increase and fill the earth. Then the creating Power, or God, gives 2 Commands more. Ver. 27. & Ver. 29.

First, *To subdue the Earth*. And this implies, plowing, digging, and all kind of manuring. So then observe. That bare and simple working in the Earth, according to the freedome of the Creation, though it be in the sweat of mans browes, is not the curse.

But for one part of Mankind to be a Task-master, and to live Idle; and by the Beast-like power of the sword, does force another [2] part of Mankind to worke as a servant and slave, This is the power of the curse, which makes mankind eat his bread in sorrow by the sweat of his browes.

The Second Command from God, was this, to Mankind. *That he should have dominion over the Fish, Fowle, Beasts, Hearbs, Plants.* And this implies that whole Mankind, spread abroad in variety of bodies, and yet but the unity of one Creation, Mankind is the Lord of the Earth: As *David* saith; *The earth is the Lords*: that is, Mankinds. Psal. 24. 1.

But there is not the least tittle spoken, that one part of Mankind should subdue, and rule in oppression over another, for this came in after the fall, and is the Beastly Power that hath beene suffered to reigne, for a time, times, and dividing of time. Dan. 7. 25.

When Mankind lives in the unity of the one Spirit of Righteousnesse, he lives in the light, and the light lives in him; which is Christ in him, the light of the Father, or the restoring Power.

But when Mankind lives in division, contention, and covetousnesse, one part of Mankind hedging themselves into the earth by force and sword, (as experience shewes, the strongest sword rules over the weakest) and thereby shutting out another part of Mankind, making them slaves. Jam. 4. 1.

Now Mankind lives under the power of the Fall, In darknesse, and darknesse lives in him. And this darknesse is the Devill, or sonne of bondage, which causes all division and sorrow. 2 Cor. 4. 4.

This same Creation-Right, or common freedome in the earth among Brethren, was confirmed by Covenant from God, to *Noah*, and his Seed, without limitation or respect of persons. Gen. 9. 9.

So that, we see when that Almighty power did work a restoration in the earth, he gave the earth still to be in common; shutting out none, from enjoying the benefit of his Creation: But when Mankind began to quarrell about the earth; and some would have all, and shut out others, forcing them to be servants; This was Mans fall, it is the ruling of the curse, and is the cause of all divisions, wars, and pluckings up. Jer. 45. 5.

This same Creation-Right, or Universall Freedome in the earth, was confirmed by Covenant to *Abraham*, and his Seed, not limiting, or restraining any part. Now in this Covenant to *Abraham*, [3] God points out the work of restoration by Christ, the restoring Power, who shall be the joy and blessing of all Nations. Gen. 17. 8.

So that in the work of restoration, God brings Mankind to this uni-versall freedome in the Earth, without respect of persons, according to the righteous Law of the first creation of all things.

In the next place, the Scriptures declare the Fall of Mankind from this righteous Law of Creation.

And the fall of Man, is declared in these words: Mankind being in honour, abideth not; that is: he being made the Lords of the Earth, and had dominion over the Fish, Fowle, and Beasts, and was free in himselfe; yet he abode not in that honour. Psal. 49. 12.

For one part of Mankind, seeking to enslave another part, setting up one to be a King, or Lord, casting another at his foot-stoole, the stronger part hedging himselfe into the Earth, by Armies and Selfe-will Lawes, and thereby hedged out others, did hereby become like the Beasts that perishe. Rev. 19. 19, 20.

And how is that? even as the beasts, that pushes one another with their hornes, so does Mankind; so that Mankind, in their Actings each to other, is become a Beast: And this Beastly Power was to reigne for a time, times, and dividing of times. Rev. 12. 14. Dan. 7. 25.

Therefore, whosoever upholds this Beastly Power, and yet saies they are the Sons of Christ, or restoring power, they lie, *they deceive themselves, and the truth is not in them.*

The Scriptures likewise declare the actings of Mankind under the fall, or in darknesse. *Cain* rose up in discontent, and killed his brother *Abel.* The quarrell rise about the Earth; for *Abels* industry made the earth more fruitfull than *Cain;* thereupon *Cain* would take away *Abels* labour from him by force. Gen. 4. 3.

These two Brothers did type out, or fore-run all the acting be-tweene man and man, from that time to this; being a plaine declara-tion of that darknesse, into which Mankind is falne.

Moses Law of equity, was but the moderation, or the curbing in of the Fall of Mankind: for his Law was not the restorer: but, saith he, *there is one comes after me, mightier then I, and him ye shall heare,* which is Christ, the restoring Spirit. Deut. 5. & Chap. 18. 18.

All the wars and divisions in Israels time, and since: and all [4] buying and selling of Land, and the fruits of the earth, which is the art of cheating one another, is but the actings of Mankind in dark-nesse, under the power of the fall; for, both Kings, Rulers, and all people, have had their checks from God, for their unrighteous walking, or cruelty against *Abels* plain-hearted Spirit. And all the great combustions that hath been, and yet is, in the world, is but politick, covetous, murdering *Cain*; holding *Abel*, or the honest plaine dealing heart under him; or the son of bondage, persecuting the son of freedome. Gen. 23. 4. Gal. 4. 29. Jam. 4. 1. Isa. 33. 1.

Now in the Third Particular. The Scriptures declares the restoration of Mankind, to his Creation-righteousnesse; or that the Sonne of Righteousnesse shall rise up, and expell the darknesse.

And there are 3 degrees of this: First the Scriptures declares promises of restoration; as in these words: *The Seed of the Woman shall bruise the Serpents head. Abraham's* Seed shall be the joy and blessing of all Nations. The bright appearing of Christ, the restoring Power, shall destroy Anti-Christ, or that darknesse in man, called the Mystery of iniquity, that rules in, and enslaves Mankind. *And in the latter dayes, they shall be all taught of God, and the Spirit of truth, shall lead them into all truth.* And such like. Gen. 3. 15. Gal. 3. 8. 2 Thes. 2. 8. Heb. 8. 10. 1 Joh. 2. 27. Joh. 6. 45. Mat. 7. 12.

Now these, and such like promises, declares the restoring of Mankind to his originall righteousnesse, and that they shall be brought to be of one heart, and of one mind; and that they shall be freely willing to let each other enjoy their Creation-rights, without restraining, or molesting one another; but every one doing as they would be done by.

Secondly, the Scriptures declares Prophecies, foretelling the restoration, in such words as these. *The Swords shall be beaten into Plowshares, and Spears into pruning-hooks, and Nations shal learn war no more; but the Lion and the Lamb shall feed together: the wast places shall be builded, and the desolate land shall be tilled, whereas it lay desolate in the sight of all that passed by.* Isa. 2. 4. & Chap. 11. Ezek. 36. 34, 35.

This shewes, that the Commons, Heaths, and waste land, that hath lain barren, by reason of the unrighteousnesse of Kings, and Lords of Mannors, that would not suffer the enslaved poore to till, and manure it, shall in the day of Christs Power, be manured, [5] and be made fruitfull, that there may be no beggery nor misery among Mankind, but that every body may freely enjoy their creation rights. Joel 2. 21. Psal. 107. 34. Zachar. 8.

Thirdly, the Scriptures declares the resurrection of the spirit of freedome within Man-kind. As in these words; *The whole creation groaneth and travelleth in pain, waiting for a restoration.* And *Oh wretched man that I am, who shall deliver me from this body of sinne*: That is, who will deliver mee from my covetousnesse, pride, envy, uncleannesse, self-love, and this great power of darkness in me, that hinders me, that I cannot doe to others, as I would have them doe to me: And that enslaves mee within, so that I cannot quietly suffer others to enjoy their creation rights in the earth. Rom. 8. 20. Rom. 7. 24.

The Apostles were hated, slandered, persecuted, and bore all patiently, rather then strive againe, that they might hold forth the righteous law of creation: This shewes the resurrection of the spirit of Love in them.

Jesus Christ was slandred, beaten, reviled, and at last put to death, for no cause; yet hee reviled not againe, but suffered all patiently, that he might honour his Father. The spirit of Righteousnesse; this shewes the resurrection of the spirit from under darknesse, and a growing up of freedome and light.

This spirit of Love, Patience, Humility, and Righteousnesse, is called the light of the world, and the salt of the earth, which brings mankind into a moderate, meeke, Loving, and seasonable condition: It is the restoring spirit, teaching all men to doe as they would be done by. He that hath this spirit, will never strive to be a Lord of Mannor, or a divider of Land; for he will quietly suffer every one to enjoy the freedome of his creation. This spirit destroyes all enmitie: This is the Gospel: This is Christ, appearing to be the joy of all Nations, which the Ministers of Christ must preach if they be faithfull to Christ. Math. 7. 12. Rev. 11. 15. Dan. 7. 27. Eph. 2. 15.

This is the spirit of poverty, that hath been a servant in the world a long time, but now is appearing and rising up to draw all men after him.

This poore man is hee, that saves Man-kinde from utter ruine, and yet he is despised by Ignorance. This poore man spread abroad [6] in sonnes and daughters, shall inherit the Earth: This is he that will give Man-kind a full freedome in the earth, and take off all bondages, therefore he is called the blessing of the earth. But the power of covetousnesse, which is the divider of land, is called the curse of the Earth, and murtherer. Psal. 37. 9, 10.

Jesus Christ bid the young man sell all that hee had, and give to the poore: This speech extends to all men, as well as to that selfe-conceited young man. Luk. 3. 5, 6.

When Christ appeares in glory, in the day of his power, hee will make crooked wayes streight, and ruffe wayes smooth, throw downe the Mountaines, and fill up the Valleyes.

This declares the universall restoration of Man-kind to the law of righteousnes, from whence he fell; for when once the Law of Love and truth is written in the heart of Man-kinde, they will never quarrell one with another about the earth, who shall have it, and who not, for it is the birth-right and Inheritance of all.

For saith Christ, though the Gentiles seeke Dominion and Lordship one over another, yet saith Christ, it shall not be so among you who are my followers. Matth. 20. 25.

Now these of the Parliament, Armie, Clergy, Lawyers, and people of *England* that professes to follow Christ: and yet exercises Lordship over their brethren, not suffering their brethren quietly to live by them on the Earth; they doe deceive themselves, and are hypocrites.

Therefore *woe, woe, woe, to you Rich men* (and Lords of Mannors) *howle and weepe. The oppressor shall fall: and he that takes the sword, and rules by it over brethren, shall perish by it.* He that hedges himselfe into the earth, and hedges out his brother, not suffering his brother to enjoy the benefit of his creation; That man is a Thiefe, and a Murtherer, and an Enemie to Christ. Jam. 5. 1. Isa. 16. 4. Matth. 26. 52. Exod. 20. 13, 15.

And here I conclude, that these fore-mentioned Scriptures being but a gleaning of the Bible, gives a full warrant to all poore men, to build them houses, and plant corne upon the Commons and unnurtured land, for their comfortable livelihood, as they are part of Man-kind, being the right of their creation.

[7] And whosoever denies or hinders them of this freedome, doth deny God, Christ, and Scriptures, and overthrows true and pure undefiled religion.

True Religion, and undefiled, is to let every one quietly have earth to manure, that they may live in freedome by their labours; for it is earth that every one seekes after, that they may live in peace, let them say what they will.

The practise of the Gentry is to have the Earth to themselves: It is that the Armie fights for: It is that the Clergy preaches for; for if you deny him Tithes, or a Maintenance, you shall not heare of him.

Nay, is it not the bottome of all National lawes, to dispose of the Earth: and does not this appear to be true, by the practise of Lords of Mannors and the Gentrie, that cannot be at rest for vexing and fretting, because poore men begins to see their creation-freedome, and begins to build upon, and plant the Commons.

And men that in other cases are mild and seemingly loving, are like Lions and Devils, ready to kill and destroy these poore diggers; and not only the Gentry, but the Clergy generally are mad against this worke: Well, the power of darknesse, and the fall, rules in these men; for if the restoring spirit, Christ, were in them, they would doe as they would be done by.

And seeing the Scriptures confirms this creation-Right to whole man-kind, then in the next place it followes,

That all the Title and Power, which Lords of Mannors have to the Common land, whereby they beate the people off from this their freedome, Is no other but the will of Kings, who were Conquerours, and ruled successively by swordly power, inslaving the creation Mankind in England.

First then consider, That King *C H A R L E S* and his Lawes was the Successor of the person and power of *William* the Conquerour; for he did not rule by the law of creation, suffering every one to enjoy their creation-right on the earth: But by the lawes of a Conquest, which intitles some to the earth, and shuts out others.

Secondly, That K. *Charles*, and that Kingly Lordly conquering government, is cast out of England, by the victory of the Armie over [8] him; and by words and Acts of Parliament. If they doe not againe lose this their honour and peace too, by their selfe-love and covetousnesse, suffering the enemie to cheate them by policy, and thereby being in Kingly power again, who could not overcome them in the Field.

And seeing Kingly and Lordly power is declared against both by Army and Parliament, the people wants nothing now but possession of the Common-wealths freedome; for our freedome must not lye within the clasps of a Booke, in words that may be read; nor in the bare title of a Victory: but it must be freedome really enjoyed, or else it will do us no good.

The first Parliament law, which encourages the poore Commoners of England, to plant the Commons and wast land, is this; wherein they declare England to be a free Common-wealth: This Law breakes in pieces the Kingly yoake, and the lawes of the Conquerour, and gives a common freedome to every English-man, to have a comfortable livelihood in this their own Land, or else it cannot be a common-wealth.

Secondly, The Parliament did make this law, presently after the Kings head was cut off; That they would establish all the old ancient fundamentall lawes, wherein the Lives, Liberties, persons and estates of the people of England without exception, were concerned.

By this they give a common freedome to every English man to have and enjoy the land for their comfortable livelihood by their labours, without restraint of any.

For the Ancient fundamentall Law is *Salus populi*, the safety, peace, and preservation of the whole body of the people, excepting none.

And this fundamentall law, called *Salus populi*, was that which gave life and strength to the Parliament and Army to take up Armes against the King; for they had not the least letter of any written law for their warrant at that time, all the lawes being for the King, and none against him.

Now if there be any Ancient Lawes of the Conquerour unrepealed, whereby the people are hindered of a quiet enjoyment of a Common-wealths freedome, they are all blotted out and abolished by this Act of Parliament, which hath declared

[One line seems to be missing. The omission occurs also in the copy in the Forster Library at the Victoria and Albert Museum.]

[9] Therefore the poor people, being part of our *Commonwealth*, and being impoverished by the *Kingly* and *Lordly* Power, which is now cast out, are freed from the oppressions of all those Lawes, whereby their lives, liberties, persons and creation-rights, were enslaved: And *Salus populi* is the fundamentall Law, that gives that life and strength and courage to build upon and plant the common Land, for their comfortable livelihood. This is the *Commonwealths* Law, and the *Commonwealths* Freedom.

3. Thirdly, The *Parliament* have made an act to free the People, from yielding obedience to the *King*, and to all that hold claiming under the *King*. This Law likewise throwes down the power of the Conquest, and makes *Englishmen* free in their Land, that they may live comfortably in their *English Commonwealth*, and quietly enjoy their Land now, which they could not, while the conquering *Kingly*, and *Lordly* Power ruled.

4. Fourthly, The *Parliament* hath made an *Engagement*, to maintain this present *Commonwealths* Government, against *King* and house of *Lords*. This likewise is but a confirmation of the first, to make *England* a free *Commonwealth*. And that all *Englishmen* may enjoy the comfortable livelihood in the Land, as Brethren, without restraint; for if I have not freedom to live in peace, and enjoy food and rayment by my Labors freely, it is no *Commonwealth* at all.

Now in the purchasing of this declared freedom, the common people of *England*, have spent their Estates, as well as the Gentry, partly by their free hearts in lending money to the *Parliament*, partly by Taxes, partly by free quarter, and partly by plunder in times of Warre. By all which our proprieties are wasted, and the fruit of our labours laid down and accepted of, both by *Parliament* and *Army*, to be a price to purchase *Salus populi*, the peoples creation-freedom, out of the oppressing power of *Kingly* power.

Therefore in reason and justice, I conceive, that if the poor people do build houses, and plant corne upon the Commons of *England*, for a livelihood, they are protected and warranted both by Scriptures, and the Lawes of the present *Commonwealth*: And we expect the Officers of the Law, will be as [10] faithful to us, to put us in possession, as our Law-books are to declare our common freedom.

And whereas some Justices do say, that for poor men to dig and plant upon the Commons, they do bring themselves within the statute, to be punished for vagrants, idle or wandring rogues: to this I answer.

1. That the Justice cannot call these men vagrants, or wandring rogues; for by the letter of the Law, it is no vagrancie to dig and work; but when men are idle, wanderers, begging up and down, these the Law lookes upon as punishable.

But the Diggers they set themselves to work, according to the Law of creation, as they are *Englishmen*, upon the Commons of *England*, claiming the priviledges of the *Common-wealth,* according to the Lawes of a *Common-wealth,* that they may not beg, nor be forced to steale through want, and so be hanged by the Kingly and Lordly Law.

2. Secondly, Their digging upon the Commons for a livelihood, is no Riot [2], though some Justices would make it; for they do not fight against any. And their meeting together, is no unlawfull or riotous meeting, unlesse the gathering together of many people in one field, to dig, plow, or reap, be a Riot, or an unlawfull meeting.

These Lawes against Riots, or unlawfull meetings, as they call it, was the Law of the fearfull Kingly Conqueror, lest the common people by their often meeting should understand their creation-freedom, and so should joyn together, to conquer and cast out him that had conquered them.

Yet the Gentry and Lords of Mannors, who are part of the *Kingly* and *Lordly* Power, they have met divers times in Troops, and have beaten and abused the Diggers, and pull'd down their houses. Yet we do not heare that the *Clergy, Lawyers,* or *Justices,* who would be counted the dispensers of righteous justice, do speak against them for Rioters, but against the poor labouring men still, checking the Labourers for idleness, and protecting the Gentry that never work at all: therefore if idle persons, who wander up and down idly, be punishable by the Statutes; Then judge whether it be not the idle Gentry, rather then the laborious poor man.

[11] These things I leave to the consideration of all rationall men to judge of, they being the foundation, whereupon our work of community in the earth, according to the Law of creation, being reason and justice, is builded. And I desire any rational man, *Minister* or *Lawyer,* to answer these, either to confirm us, or else to raise up this foundation of Scriptures and Law, not by take him *Jaylor,* which is the language of the Beast; but by reason which is the voice of the man.

Though this work of digging upon the Commons, have many enemies, yet I am assured of the righteousnesse of the work, and it shall take root in one place or other, before many yeares passe over *Englands* head, I can set no time, but I wait for the consolation of *Israel*

---

[2] This suggests that the indictment of the Diggers for riot and unlawful assembly was probably returned at the Quarter Sessions after Easter in 1650. See the Introduction, p. 20.

to arise up, and break forth in others, as I have a taste of him in my self.

The voice of the *Dragon* is, kill him, pull down his house, beat him, arrest him, take him *Jaylor,* imprison him, he is a rogue.

But the voice of the Lamb is, love your enemies, let him live, the earth is his creation-right as well as mine: therefore let us do as we would be done unto.

Ministers and *Lawyers,* will you all stand looking on, and see the *Lords* of *Mannors* exercise *Kingly* Power over the poor men that claime their creation-right in the earth, and be silent?

You would be called dispensers of Justice: here is a point of justice for you to decide: this is the point upon which you shall either stand or fall, be saved or damned; for you are put upon the tryal.

The week before *Easter,* Parson *Plat,* Minister of *Horsley,* being the Lord of the Mannor of *Cobham,* where the Diggers were at work, And *Thomas Sutton,* the impropriator [3] of *Cobham,* came in person, and brought divers men, whom they hired to pull down a poor mans house, that was built upon the Commons, and kikt and struck the poor mans wife, so that she miscarried of her Child, and by the blowes and abuses they gave her, she kept her bed a week.

[12] And at this time I went to Mr. *Plat,* and spoke with him, about our freedom in the Commons, he answered me, if I could make it good by Scriptures, he would never trouble us more, but let us build and plant: Nay he said, he would cast in all his estate, and become one with the diggers.

The next week after I carried him this writing afore printed, being *Munday* in *Easter* week, and upon our discourse, he seemed to consent to many things, and was very moderate, and promised me to read it over, and to give me an Answer: moreover he promised me, that if the diggers would not cut the wood upon the Common, he would not pull down their houses: And the diggers resolved for peace sake, to let the wood alone till people did understand their freedom a little more.

And upon *Fryday* in *Easter* week, he came and brought his answer, which was this. He came accompanied with about 50. men, and had hired 4. or 5. of them, to fire down the diggers houses: some that stood by said, do not fire them, the wood will do some good; his

---

[3] The advowson of the living belonged to the Sutton family of Heywood in Cobham.

answer was, no, no, fire them to the ground, that these Heathens, who know not God, may not build them again; for if you let the wood alone, they will build again.

Thereupon at the Command of this Parson *Plat*, they set fire to six houses, and burned them down, and burned likewise some of their housholdstuffe, and wearing Clothes, throwing their beds, stooles, and housholdstuffe, up and down the Common, not pittying the cries of many little Children, and their frighted Mothers, which are Parishioners borne in the Parish. And yet some of these hired men, lives not in the Parish, and some are strangers newly come into the Parish: and so were bewitched by the covetous make-bate Priests, to do this heathenish turkish act.

The poor diggers being thus suddainly cast out of their houses by fire, both they, their wives and Children were forced to lie upon the open Common all night: yet the rage of Parson *Plat* and his Company rested not here, but in the night time, some of them came again upon the Commons, while the diggers were quiet, and some of them in bed, and said, we have [13] Authority from our Master, that is Mr. *Plat*, to kill you, and burn the rest of your goods, if you will not be gone: thereupon Sir *Anthony Vincents* Servant, called *Davy*, struck at one, and cut some of their Chaires and other Goods to peeces, frighting the women and Children again. And some of the Diggers asked them, why they would do thus cruelly by them, they answered, because you do not know God, nor will not come to Church.

Surely if the God of these men, by their going to Church, teach both their preacher and they, to do such cruel deedes; we will neither come to Church, nor serve their God. Mr. *Plat* in his Sermons can say, *live in peace with all men, and love your Enemies*: therefore if the Diggers were enemies, he ought to love them in action; but it is a true badge of an hypocrite, to say, and not to do.

Let every Mans actions be tryed, and see who serves God, They or the Diggers. Mr. *Plat* and the Gentlemen (so would be called) that were with him, were full of rage, and gnashed their tongues with vexation; but the Diggers are patient, chearfull, quiet in spirit, loving to those that have burned their houses.

Therefore the poor Diggers have got the Crown, and weare it, and the Priests and Gentry have lost their Crown: The poor have striven with them 12. moneths, with love and patience: The Gentlemen have answered them all the time with fury; they would have the Earth and all freedom, but they will not suffer the poor to have either earth or freedom, but what they hire of them.

But though the Devill be let loose to swell against us, in these Gentry that rule over us, by *Kingly* Power, or Law of *Norman* Conquest, notwithstanding, they have taken the Engagement, to cast out *Kingly* Power: yet his time to be chained up drawes nigh: and then we are assured this righteous work of earthly community, shall have a most glorious resurrection out of his ashes.

Nay farther, if this satisfies not Mr. *Plat,* but he & *Tho: Sutton,* of *Cobham,* have hired three men, to attend both night and [14] day, to beat the Diggers, and to pull down their tents or houses, if they make any more; and if they make Caves in the earth, they threaten to murther them there, so that they will not suffer the poor Diggers to live, neither above nor below ground: if they beg, they whip them by their Law for vagrants, if they steal they hang them; and if they set themselves to plant the Common for a livelihood, that they may neither beg nor steale, and whereby *England* is inriched, yet they will not suffer them to do this neither: And so hereby these Gentlemen take away both creation-right, and Common-wealths right from the poor Diggers; for they command the poor enslaved Tenants and Neighbors likewise, not to suffer any of the Diggers to have any lodging in their houses, nor to sell them any meat for their money.

And thus the fury of Parson *Plat,* exceedes the fury of any other Lord of Mannor. The chief setters on to burn these houses, and to abuse the Diggers, was Parson *Plat,* Sir *Anthony Vincent* [4] his Tenants and Servants, were most of them there; likewise *Thomas Sutton* and *William Star,* these are they that say the Commons belong to the poor, and yet these rich men are agrieved to see the poor make use of the Commons: the actors in this *Turkish* designe, were furious beyond the fury of the Beasts; but many of those that came were

[4] I am not able to explain what seems to be a curious error on Winstanley's part. Sir Anthony Vincent was lord of the manor of Stoke d'Abernon, which adjoins Cobham. He had been sheriff of Surrey in 1637 and had died in 1642. He was succeeded by his son, Sir Francis Vincent, who was still living in 1653 and hence must have owned the property in 1650. If a different family is intended, I have not been able to identify it. See the *Victoria History of the Counties: Surrey,* Vol. III, pp. 286, 458.

threatned by *Vincent* his chief men, to be turned out of their Livings, if they came not, so that this is not an act of the tenants by free consent, but the Gentlemen hired others to do it.

These men do so powerfully act the Image of the Beast, that they will neither buy nor sell with any freely, nor let any have land, houses, or work under them, but such as have the mark of the Beast; that is, such as are filled with fear of them, and are obedient to their beastly Power. And some of them say, they do God good service, if they can destroy or kill the Diggers. Thus the Scriptures are fulfilled. Rev. 13. 17.

And now they cry out the Diggers are routed, and they rang bells for joy; but stay Gentlemen, your selves are routed, and you have lost your Crown, and the poor Diggers have won the Crown of glory.

[15] For first you have not routed them by Law, for you durst not suffer the Diggers plead their own cause, so that it never came to any tryal; and you have no Law to warrant your Lordly power in beating of the Diggers, but the will of Kingly swordly power, which is self-will, and Club-law.

Secondly, You have not routed the Diggers by dispute; for your impatient, covetous, and proud swelling heart, would not suffer you to plead rationally with them.

Neither thirdly, have you routed them by Scriptures; but the Diggers have routed you by your own Law; by reason, by Scriptures, and patient suffering all your abuses; and now your name shall rot, and your own power shall destroy you.

When the *Scribes* and *Pharisees* of old, (these Lords of Mannors Ancestors) had put *Jesus Christ* to death, they rejoyced, and sent gifts one to another, and made merry, and in such like words, said they had routed him. And so now these *English* Pharisees, because they have acted the power of the Beast, and to the eye of the Beast, seeme to stand uppermost for a time, they say they have routed the Diggers.

But they are mistaken, for the Diggers keep the field of patience, quietness, joy and sweet rest in their hearts, and are filled with love to their enemies; but the Gentlemen are so impatient, they cannot rest for fretting, jearing, rayling, and gnashing their tongues with vexation.

They wil not suffer the Diggers to look to the Corne which is planted upon the Commons, being about eleven Acres: neither will they look to it themselves, but let the Cattle spoile it, that they may say, see, their labor comes to nothing. Are not these men the curse of *England,* that wil not suffer others to live by them, and will rather spoile corne in these dear times, then let the poor enjoy their own righteous labors upon the Commons?

[16] This work of digging, being freedom, or the appearance of Christ in the earth, hath tried the Priests and professors to the uttermost, and hath ripped up the bottom of their Religion, and proves it meere witchcraft, and cosonage; for self love and covetousnesse is their God, or ruling power. They have chosen the sword, and they refuse love; when the Lamb turnes into the Lion, they will remember what they have done, and mourne.

And thus I have faithfully declared all the businesses, and though the power of their covetousnesse, self-loving flesh, hath for the present trod our weak flesh down; yet the strength of our inward man, hath overcome them; and is the Lord God Almighty, above that power that rules in them.

We have declared our Testimony, and now let freedom and bondage strive who shall rule in Mankind: the weapons of the Sonnes of bondage being carnall, as fire, club, and sword; the weapons of the Sonnes of freedom being spiritual, as love, patience, and righteousnesse.

FINIS.

A LETTER TAKEN AT WELLINGBOROUGH [1]

Thursday Aprill 4.
The true Copy of a letter taken at *Wellingborough* in Northamptonshire, with some men that were there apprehended for going about
to incite people to digging, and under that pretence gathered mony
of the Wel-affected for their assistance:

THESE are to certifie all that are Friends to universall freedome, and that looke upon the Digging and Planting the
Commons to be the first springing up of freedome, to make
the earth a common treasury that every one may enjoy food and rayment freely by his labour upon the earth, without paying rents or
homage to any fellow creature of his own kind, that every one may be
delivered from the tyranny of the conquering power; and so rise up
out of that bondage to enjoy the benefit of his Creation: This I say is
to certifie all such that those men that have begun to lay the first stone
in the foundation of this freedome; by digging upon Georges Hill,
and the Common called Little heath in *Cobham*, in regard of the
great opposition hitherto from the enemy, by Reason whereof they
lost the last summers work, yet through inward faithfullnesse to advance freedome they keep the field still and have planted divers Acres
of Corn and built 4. houses, and now this season time goes on digging,
endeavouring to plant as much as they can; but in regard of poverty
their work is like to flagge and droppe: Therefore if the hearts of
any be stirred up to cast any thing into this treasury, to buy Victualls
to keep the men alive, and to buy Corn to cast into the ground, it will
keep alive the beginning of publique Freedom to the whole Land,
which otherwise is ready to die again for want of help; And if you

---

[1] From *A Perfect Diurnal*, April 1–8, 1650. Reproduced from the copy in the Thomason Library at the British Museum.

hear hereafter that there was a people appeared to stand up to advance publique freedome, and strugled with the opposing power of the Land for that they begin to let them alone, and yet these men and their publique work was crushed, because they wanted assistance of food and Corne to keep them alive; I say if you heare this it will be trouble to you when it is too late, that you had monies in your hands, and would not part with any of it to purchase freedome, therefore you deservedly Grone under Tyranny and no Saviour appeares; but let your Reason weigh the excellency of this worke of digging the Commons, and I am sure you will cast in something.

And because there were some treacherous persons drew up a note and subscribed our names to it, and by that moved some freinds to give mony to this work of ours, when as we know of no such note, nor subscribed our hands to any, nor never received any money from such Collection,

Therefore to prevent such a Cheat, I have mentioned a word or two in the end of a Printed Book [2] against that treachery, that neither we nor our Friends may be cheated: And I desire, if any be willing to communicate of their substance unto our worke, that they would make a Collection among themselves, and send that mony to *Cobham* to the Diggers owne hands, by some trusty friend of your owne, and so neither you nor we shall be cheated.

The Bearers hereof *Thomas Heaydon*, and *Adam Knight*, can relate by word of mouth more largely the condition of the Diggers and their work and so we leave this to you to doe as you are moved.

Iacob Heard, Io: South junior, *Henry Barto, Tho: Barnard, Tho: Adams, Will. Hitchcoke, Anthony Wrea, Robert Draper, William Smith, Robert Coster, Gerrard Winstanley, Io: South, Tho: Heydon, Io. Palmer, Tho: South, Henry Handcocke, Io: Batt, Dan: Freland, Io: Hayman, Robert Sawyer, Tho: Starre, Tho: Edcer*, Besides their Wives and Children, and many more if there were food for them.

A Copy of their travels that were taken with the four men at Wellingborow. *Out of* Buckinghamshire *into* Surry, *from* Surry *to* Middlesex, *from thence to* Hartfordshire, *to* Bedfordshire, *again to* Buckinghamshire, *so to* Barkeshire, *and then to* Surry, *thence to* Middlesex,

---

[2] *A Vindication of those whose Endeavors is only to Make the Earth a Common Treasury*, above, p. 403.

and so to Hartfordshire, *and to* Bedforshire, *thence into* Huntingdon-
shire, *from thence to* Bedfordshire, *and so into* Northamptonshire,
and there they were Apprended.

They visited these towns to promote the Businesse. Colebrook,
Hanworth, Hounslow, Harrowhill, Watford, Redburn, Dunstable,
Barton, Amersley, Bedford, Kempson, North Crawly, Cranfield,
Newport, Stony-Stratford, Winslow, Wendover, Wickham, Windsor,
Cobham, London, Whetston, Mine, Wellin, Dunton, Putney, Roy-
ston, St. Needs, Godmanchester, Wetne, Stanton, Warbays, Kimol-
ton, *from* Kimolton *to* Wellingborow.

FIRE IN THE BUSH

THIS is the only pamphlet by Winstanley that cannot be readily assigned to a fairly definite date. On the one hand the doctrine of communism is asserted without qualification; the pamphlet must therefore follow *The New Law of Righteousnes,* which is dated January 26, 1649, and which first stated the revelation. There is, however, no reference in *Fire in the Bush* to any event connected with the attempt to cultivate the commons. It seems, therefore, that the pamphlet was written either in February or March, 1649, in the interval between the revelation and the beginning of work at St. George's Hill, or after the final collapse of the movement in the spring of 1650. In favor of the earlier date is the similarity of *Fire in the Bush* to Winstanley's early religious writings and its differences from *The Law of Freedom.* Nevertheless, the only known edition of the pamphlet is dated 1650 on the title page. It seems to me credible that, after the failure of his movement, Winstanley addressed to the churches a pamphlet dealing with the religious foundation of his communism and ignoring both his abortive effort to put it into practice and also the civil constitution of a communist society, which he outlined for Cromwell the next year. At least the probability is great enough so that I have not cared to place the pamphlet a year in advance of the earliest date at which it is known to have been printed. Winstanley's name appears both on the title page and at the end of the Address to the Reader.

Copies are to be found in the following collections: The Bodleian, The Haverford College Library, and The Seligman Library at Columbia University.

The text is reproduced from the copy in the Seligman Library.

TO ALL THE SEVERALL SOCIETIES OF PEOPLE, CALLED CHURCHES, IN THE PRESBYTERIAN, INDEPENDENT, OR ANY OTHER FORME OF PROFESSION, IN THE SERVICE OF GOD

BRETHREN, and fellow-members of Mankinde; This following declaration of the word of Life was a free gift to me from the Father himselfe; And I received it not from men; when I had writ it, I was moved to send it to you immediately; but I delayed it by almost a fortnight, and thought not of it; then one night as I waked out of sleep, the voyce was in my very heart and mouth, ready to come forth; goe send it to the Churches; Thereupon I was filled with great Love to you, my heart panting with love towards you, pittying your condition; in that there is a great striving, as || it were for life among you, and yet you lie under the power of death and bondage, and know not, or at least doth not actually hold forth that you know, that spirit which in words you seeme to professe.

You speake and preach of the life of Love; But you have not the power of it; your verball profession, without the pure righteous action, shews you generally to be outlandish men, of severall Nations, under the government of darknesse, and that you are not yet the true Inhabitants of the Land of Love. Before you live you must die, and before you be bound up into one universall body, all your particular bodies and societies must be torne to pieces; for the true Light is comming now once more, not onely to shake the Earth, that is, *Moses* worship, but Heaven also; That which you call Gospell-worship, and the Kingdome without shall fall, that so the Kingdome within may be established; for all your particular Churches are like || the inclosures of Land which hedges in some to be heires of Life, and hedges out others; one saying Christ is here with them; Another saying no: but he is there with them; but truly brethren, you shall see and finde, that Christ who is the universall power of Love is not confined to parties, or private chambers; but he is the power of Life, Light, and Truth, now rising up to fill the Earth, Mankinde with himselfe.

Well, I have obeyed the voyce; and I have sent this to you, with a heart free and full of love towards you; Some of you will receive this with gentlenesse; others will be offended; To some it will be refreshing, but others will storme, and prepare warre against it; And the *Ishmaelites* they will scoffe; but be it so: yet my Armour is tryed, I am sure it will keep off the blow.

You shall finde I speake of the Garden of *Eden*, which is the spirit of man, not the spirit of Beasts. And in || that Garden there are weeds and hearbs. The weeds are these. Selfe-Love, Pride, Envie; Covetousnesse after riches, honours, pleasures, Imagination, thinking he cannot live in peace, unlesse he enjoy this or that outward object; And sometimes the joy of envie when he obtaines his end; and sometime the sorrow of Covetousnesse when he is crost, rules as King in the Garden. And the stinking weeds over-spreads the sweet flowers and hearbs, which are the lights of the spirit of truth.

There is likewise the most venemous weed called Hypocrisie, attended with evill surmising, grudgings, speaking and promising, nay, swearing one thing, yet doing another, inventing much shew of holinesse to compasse his selfish ends; and while he rules King, as he doth rule at this day; he is assisted with vain glory, feare of being disthroned, oppressing others, unmercifull; carelesse of former promises and engagements; persecuting those who doth such things || as he promised and vowed to doe, whilst he was a servant, and such like.

And as you may call those by the name of weeds; so likewise you may call them outlandish men; for they are not the true native Inhabitants of the heart, but strangers to the righteous spirit. And all these with their fellowes make up but one power of darknesse, Devill, or Father of lies. And this power is the night time of mankinde, or the absence of the Sonne of righteousnesse from the heart. This power is the reprobate which the word of life hath rejected, this shall never enter into true rest; this is the wicked man, or Dragon in you, which causes all warres and sorrowes; and the sonne that causes shame; the sonne of bondage, which must not abide in the heart for ever, but must be cast out.

Therefore, so long as you labour under this selfish, darke, imaginary power, you are strangers to the Sonne of righteousnesse; If this darke power bear sway || in you; it is he whom you professe, and it is he whom you call God, and Christ; for that power that you hold forth in your actions, is the spirit you professe; If your actions be full of selfe love, as you may know it by your hastie anger, when your Religion is questioned, and by your snappish bitternesse against those that differs from you; then this darke power is he you worship.

There is likewise in the garden of *Eden* (mans heart) sweet flowers and hearbs; As Joy, Peace, Love, humility, selfe-denyall, patience, sincerity, truth, or equitie. These are the true inhabitants in the righteous Land; and all these make up but one power, or body, which is the seed or Tree of Life in you. And this power is the day-time of Mankinde, or the presence of the Sonne of righteousnesse in the heart; This power is the Elect, the Sonne of the Father in whom he delights; this Sonne shall live for ever in rest, peace, and in the power of eternall life; This is the righteous || man, this is *Michaell*, the Seed Christ, or blessing.

Therefore, consider what spirit you professe, and live not in darknesse any longer; Babes and sucklings doe see, and can say, that in your established formes you worship, and professe you know not what; you say one thing and doe another; you make God and Christ a very cheat to the world, as if he were all words and no deeds; Indeed your king Hypocrisie is so; But the King of righteousnesse, which your established formes hath and doe dishonour before the Nations, is not so; and you all must and shall be torne in pieces, and scattered, and shamed; for your excessive pride, covetousnesse, hardnesse of heart, selfe-love, and hypocrisie, and your verball profession shall be loathed by all, and be cast out, as stinking, imaginary dung of false-hearted ones, who professes Love in words, and in actions deny Love; but lifts up the Devill and covetousnesse and bondage. ||

If you truly owne Christ, you will cheerefully hold forth the restoring spirit in your actions; Christ the Anoynting spirit doth not enslave any, but comes to set all free; he comes not to destroy but to save; he comes not to put sackcloath and mourning weeds upon mankinde, but to pull them off and to wipe away all teares.

So long as the Earth is intangled, and appropriated into particular hands, and kept there by the power of the sword; as it is, and your profession holds it up, so long the Creation lies under bondage; And the Devill, who is the power of covetousnesse, or murderer, doth rule, and is the God, whom you generally professe; for you acknowledge Christ in words, and the Dragon in your actions; and so hypocrisie reignes King in the Earth at this very day.

But if any of you will truly acknowledge Christ, now in the end of your dayes, come joyne hands and hearts together, and set the Earth free; nothing || now stands in the way of *Englishmen*, but inward covetousnesse; Be not like the Rats and Mice, that drawes the treasures of the Earth into your holes to looke upon, whil'st your fellow-members, to whom it belongs as well as to you by the Law of Creation, doe starve for want; But you have no warrant from the Law of Righteousnesse so to doe; whensoever you lock up the treasure of the Earth, and desire more then food and rayment, you doe evill.

When you know the Sonne within, as you can talke much of him without, then the Sonne will set you free; and truly he is comming on a maine, to breake downe all your pinfoulds, and to lay all open to the Common; the rough wayes he will make smooth, and crooked wayes strait; and levell mountaines and valleys.

And covetous, proud selfe-Love, and ruling and teaching hypocrisie shall tye up, or restraine his spirit no longer; for the voyce is gone out, freedome, freedome, || freedome: he that hath eares to heare, let him heare, he that is filthie, let him be filthy still, till he be cast out as dung and unsavory salt; And so I leave this with you, as I was commanded, and bid you farewell.

Being a friend to Love, wading through
the bondage of the world

JERRARD WINSTANLY. ||

THE MATTERS CONTAINED IN THE FOL-LOWING DISCOURSE

* There are no chapters in the text with the starred titles.

[1] FIRE IN THE BUSH. The Spirit burning, not consuming, but purging Mankinde

CHAP. I. *What the Garden of* Eden *is.*

THE whole Creation of fire, water, Earth and Aire; and all the varieties of bodies made up thereof, is the cloathing of God: so that all things, that is A substantiall being, looked upon in the lump, is the fulnesse of him, that fills all with himselfe, he is in all things, and by him all things consist.

[2] And this God, or almighty Ruler, is universall Love, strength and life; And as he begets and brings forth every thing, in their degree and kinde: so he is the Restorer of all things, from that defilement, death and sorrow, which they fall into, and the alone deliverer from the oppressing power, preserving every one in peace; Therefore he is called the Lord God, Almighty; for he is the onely, and alone living spirit, which dwells every where, and can doe, what he will.

And of all those bodies, that are called Creatures; or the clothing of God, Mankinde is the chief. And because the Father or spirit of all things, manifests himselfe in mankinde, in life, strength, and wisdome more then in any other creature, therefore mankinde is made the Lord of all; And the whole Earth is this: The Lords.

For when all things were produced, and appeared very good in the liking, and content of the creating spirit: The word of Command, was to whole mankinde (not to one or a few single branches of mankinde) doe thou take possession, over the fish, fowle, Beast; and doe thou till the Earth; and doe thou multiplie and fill the Earth: And no part or branch of mankind is shut out by him from this imployment.

For as the great Earth, and the inferiour creatures therein are as the Commons, Forrests, and delights of God in the out Coasts of the Creation; Even so Mankind, The living Earth is the very Garden of *Eden,* wherein that spirit of Love, did walke, and [3] delight him-selfe principally, as being the Head and Lord of all the rest.

In this Garden are five Rivers. Hearing, Seeing, Tasting, Smelling, Feeling, which we in our age of the world, call five Senses; And these five water springs, doe refresh and preserve the whole Creation, both of the out coasts, and of the Garden.

In this Garden Mankind, and in every branch of him, there is a Tree of knowledge, of good and evill, called Imagination; and the Tree of Life, called universall Love, or pure knowledge in the power.

When Mankinde, or the living soule feeds upon, or delights himselfe in the fruit of that tree of good and evill, which is selfish, unwarranted, and unexperienced Imagination, which is his weaknesse and disease: then he looses his honour and strength, and falls from his dominion, Lordship, and becomes like the Beasts of the field, void of understanding; For the Lord of so great and vast a body as the Creation is, must know all things cleerely, as they be, and not by blinde Imagination, that leads mankind sometimes astray, as well as sometimes in the right way.

When mankind is guided by Imagination, he runs a great hazard upon life and death; This power is he, that calls good evill, and evill good. This knowes not the creating Spirit in inward feeling; but does fancie him to be sometimes one thing, sometimes another; and still dwells in the dark Chamber of uncertainty.

[4] And while Mankinde eates of this Tree, and delights himselfe here, he is driven out of the Garden, that is, out of himselfe, he enjoyes not himselfe, he knowes not himselfe; he lives without the true God, or ruler, and is like the Beasts of the field, who live upon objects without them; And does not enjoy the Kingdome within himselfe; but seekes after a Kingdome and peace without him: as the Beasts doe.

This Imagination is he that fills you with feares, doubts, troubles, evill surmisings and grudges, he it is that stirs up warres and divisions; he makes you lust after every thing you see, or heare of, and promises delight to you, in the enjoyment; as in riches, places of Government, pleasures, societie of strange women: and when you have all these, which you thinke or imagine to have content in, presently troubles follow the heeles thereof; and you see your selfe naked and are ashamed.

So that the selfish imaginary power within you, is the power of darknesse; The father of lies, the deceiver, the destroyer, and the

Serpent that twists about every thing within your selfe, and so leads you astray from the right way of life and peace. And the whole world of mankinde, generally at this day, through all the nations of the world, is eating of this Tree of knowledge, of good and evill, and are cast out of themselves, and knowe not the power that rules in them; and so are ignorant of their God; This is the fulnesse of the Beasts time, it is his last period; all places, persons, and things stinke [5] with his imaginary power of darknesse in teaching, and ruling: therefore it is that fulnesse of time, in which the Restorer of all things will come, to deliver the Creation from that bondage and curse, and draw up all things to live in him, who is the true life, rest, and Light of all things.

For in the midst of this Garden likewise, there is the Tree of Life, who is this blessing, or restoring power, called universall Love, or pure knowledge, which when mankinde by experience begins to eat thereof, or to delight himselfe therein, preferring this Kingdome and Law within, which is Christ, before the Kingdome and Law, that lies in objects without, which is the devill:

Then man is drawne up into himselfe againe; or new *Ierusalem*, which is the spirit of truth, comes downe to Earth, to fetch Earth up to live in that life, that is a life above objects; even to live in the enjoyment of Christ, the righteous spirit within himselfe, and to tread the earthly life, that lies in objects without, under foot; This is the life, that will bring in true community; and destroy murdering propriety. Now mankinde enters into the garden of Gods rest, and lives for ever; he enjoyes his Kingdome, and the word within himselfe; he knowes sinne and sorrow no more; for all teares now, which blind Imagination brought upon him, are wiped away; And man is in peace.

This Tree of Life I say, is universall Love, which our age calls righteous Conscience, or pure Reason; or the Seed of life that lies under the clods [6] of Earth, which in his time is now rising up to bruise the Serpents head, and to cast that imaginary murderer out of the Creation.

This Seed is he, that leads mankinde into Truth, making every one to seeke the preservation and peace of others, as of themselves; This teaches man inwardly to know the nature and necessity of every body, and to administer to every body accordingly. This was the Father in Jesus Christ, who let him see what was in man; This was that Godhead that dwelt bodily in Christ, reconciling the world to himselfe, and so making peace: when this almighty power of Life rules King of righteousnesse within; then Satan, or outward objects, shall finde nothing in you to close with him, when he tempts. This is the King-dome of Heaven within, and the white stone, with the new name written therein, which no man knowes the glory, beauty, life, peace, and largenesse of, but they which have it.

This power is not a selfe-Lover; But the universall Lover; This will have all saved, that is, will have all live in peace and rest. This Tree of life is full of humility, sincerity, patience, tendernesse, mod-eration, Reason, Wisdome, Truth, Righteousnesse, Chastitie, Joy, Peace, Liberty, yea full of the well springs of sweet life.

This is the blessing of *Abraham*, the promised Seed, that remaines within, as a servant for a time, times, and dividing of time; then he is to arise and cast out the Dragon, and to purge out that drossie, [7] imaginary power, that is crept in to defile the Creation; And so prop-erly he is called the restorer, Saviour, Redeemer, yea and the true and faithfull Leveller.

And when this tree of Life is fed upon and delighted in, (by the five Sences, which is the Creation, Mankind, or the living Soule) Then these five Rivers are called pure Rivers of the waters of life; for the life of truth and peace is in them, and they are the sweet con-veyers of the waters, or breathings of life, from one to another through the whole body: and so bringing all into a onenes, to be of one heart and one minde; And there is but one God and King in all, and among all, who is *Michael* our Prince of peace.

And the whole Creation now, will laugh in righteousnesse, for there will be no murmuring or complaining heard in all the moun-taine of the Lord.

For this I can say, when this tree of Life begins to rule within a particular heart; he casts out sorrow, feares, inward pressures; he sub-dues muttering, surmising, heart rising; he kills Envie, pride, vaine-glory, uncleane lust; in one word, he casts the wicked man out, and takes possession of his owne house and Temple himselfe, (The heart) and lets it downe in peace, so that the heart shall sit singing, where are all my enemies become? they are sunk, they are gone, as if I never had any. All bondage within is gone, sighing and sorrowing is done away; my heart now indeed is a Land of Righteousnesse, full of life, light, and fruit of peace and truth: Hallelujah: [8] praise, honour and glory to him that sits upon the throne, and to the Lambe for evermore.

And as there is this change and alteration wrought within a particular body; and all the power, Authority, and government of Imagination is plucked up, and cast out, and a New Kingdome wherein dwels righteousnesse is set up:

Even so, as this restoring spirit spreads himselfe in variety of bodies, and he will spread; for he is the vine, teaching, and ruling every one, till at length the whole creation is brought into the unity of himselfe; so that, That saying is fulfilled, you shall be all taught of God, and I will be your God, I the one spirit of Love; and you, the whole body of mankinde, shall be my people.

Then that great reformation, and restauration spoken of, shall be made manifest in the Nations of the world; then those pluckings up, shakings downe, tearing to pieces of all rule, power and Authority, shall be known [for] what it is; that so Christ alone may be exalted in that day of his power.

For now Mankinde every where, shall be made to speake and act purely according to the life and necessity of every body, and every businesse; and keep his dominion and Lordship; And all inferiour creatures shall stand in awe of, and reverence and love man. And the wisdome and Love in man, shall preserve all others in safety and peace.

[9] CHAP. II. *What the Tree of Knowledge of Good and evill is.*

BUT when Imagination is fed upon, and delighted in, as it is at this day amongst most people; This is he that puts all out of order, he corrupts the five Senses, and makes mankinde walke disorderly, and to teare and devoure members of his owne kinde, just like the Beast of the field, and to differ nothing from them: the Beasts, they prey and devoure one another; so does imaginary man, fights, makes wars, kills, robs, destroyes, and wasts one another. This is the reigne of the Beast, and yet he would be called a God, though he be the murderer; well, thou art and still shalt be called a God; But thou art the God of the world, that runs round, and when thou art brought to where thou beganst, then thy dayes are done, thou must dye. And the voyce is pronounced, it is done, time shall be to thee no more; And thou shalt be destroyed without hand, that is, without sword or weapons; which is the rocke of defence; for Christ will consume thee, by the word of his mouth, and by the brightnesse of his comming.

Well, this Imaginary power is the darke side of the cloude; This is the Sonne of the mother Earth mankinde, which causes shame; This is the curse, the Serpent, the Devill, and his power hath filled [10] the Creation, and is the burden it grones under; This is the power of darknes.

And he would be as God, knowing good and evill, therefore the Almighty power of Life, affords him a time, times, and dividing of time to rule in mankinde. And while he rules, he fills all creatures with sorrow and slavery, and so in the end of his appointed time, he is proved a Devill, and not the true God, the destroyer and murderer, and not the Saviour. The curse and not the blessing of the Creation, the power of darknesse, and not the power of Light.

This is the darknesse, that hath covered the Earth, and the curse that destroyes all things, this is he that calls light darknesse, and dark-nesse light, good evill, and evill good; and while this power rules in mankinde, mankinde is in prison and bondage within himselfe, and sees no Light.

And under this power of Imagination, the whole government of the world amongst the sonnes of men is built; all Nations are under this Kingdome of darknesse; the frame of this worldly government, is the Devills proper Kingdome; And the power of the sword fight-ing and killing, cannot throw downe his Kingdome, but set it up in more power; But that power that must destroy the dark Kingdome is a power contrary to him; And that is, Love and patience. Live in this life; and thou killst the Devill, and shakest his Kingdome about his eares. This power of Love and patience, acted with a cheerefull life, kills Imagination.

[11] Indeed Imagination is that God, which generally every one worships and ownes; and in the matter, they worship a lye, the Devill and meere nothing; This is he that makes everie one wise in his owne conceit; that makes men, Envie, censure, and destroy one another; and to take pleasure in none but what pleases selfe. This Imagination feares where no feare is: he rises up to destroy others, for feare, least

others destroy him: he will oppresse others, least others oppresse him; and feares he shall be in want hereafter; therefore he takes by violence, that which others have laboured for. And, so he beates the even ground before him, like a blinde man, that imagines that hill or block lies in his way.

And though this dark power be a God, or mighty ruler in man-kinde; yet as soone as he appeared to rule, the true Light appeares to breake his peace; as soone as Imagination began to sit upon the throne (Mans heart), The seed of Life began to cast him out, and to take his Kingdome from him; So that this is the great battaile of God Almighty; Light fights against darknesse, universall Love fights against selfish power; Life against death; True knowledge against imaginary thoughts.

These two powers are *Michaell* and the Dragon, and this battaile is fought in Heaven, (that is, in mankinde, in the garden of *Eden*) where God principally resolves to set up his throne of righteous government, it is not fought in the spirit of Beasts; but in Heaven in the spirit of Mankinde, [12] who is the Lord. And this battaile in our age of the world, growes hotter and sharper then formerly; for we are under the dividing of time, which is the last period of the Beasts raigne; And he will strive hardest now.

But it will be in vaine, he must loose his Kingdome; for the Lambe will cast the Dragon out, and bring all into Peace; then every thing shall appeare naked, and bare before the Lord of the whole Earth, and all Imaginary coverings shall be taken off every where.

Now the end of all societies of Churches, preaching, praying, Ordinances, should be to finde out this darknesse, and to cast it out; And to worship the Father in Spirit and truth; And so to advance the Blessing, or the Sonne in whom the Father is well pleased. That so mankinde might cease speaking and acting from thoughts and Imagination, and may come to speake and act purely, as the truth was in Jesus, he being the supreame Lord of the Earth.

This, you Preachers, and Professors, is, or at least should be the end of your profession; And if you come short of this, you loose all your paines, and will be ranked among imaginary Hypocrites, that worship they know not what, but as their fancie tells them; And that is neither better nor worse, but the Devill which you worship.

Therefore if man would live purely, to the honour of that spirit in him, which is called the Seed; he is then to know, what spirit is it, that rules in [13] him, and to act from it, for that spirit that rules is the God, whether it be Imagination, or whether it be the light of life, which is universall Love.

This is the shame and misery of our age, That every one professes Christ and the spirit, and they will preach of, and pray to the Spirit; And yet they know not inwardly, by what spirit or inward power they are ruled; Every one lookes upon a God and a ruler without him, as the Beast of the field does, few sees their Ruler within; These have lost their dominion and Lordship, and they live under the curse, and are blinde in their Imagination, and are ignorant of the wayes of truth.

These are cast out of the Garden, they live out of themselves upon the Earth; they live upon riches, honors, pleasures, Ministers, Lawyers, Armies, wife, children, Ordinances, customes, and all outward formes of worship, or in that beastly community with women; nowadayes cryed up by the lust of the flesh; yea upon any thing without them, which they imagine good: take away these and they dye, they know not how to governe themselves, nor others; these have lost their Dominion and Lordship; their Kingdome is without, and their peace is placed upon perishing things, and as they vanish, so doth their peace and their Kingdome.

For they have no peace nor Kingdome within; God and they have no sweet Communion together; the living soule and the creating Spirit are not one, but divided; the one looking after a Kingdome without him; the other drawing him to looke and [14] waite for a Kingdome within him, which moth and rust doth not corrupt, and theeves cannot breake through and steale; this is a Kingdome that will abide; the outward Kingdome must be taken from you.

They that live upon outward objects are filled with inward trouble, and pierced through with many sorrowes; slavish feare within them keepes the way of the tree of life; they dare not live in the life of free community, or universall Love; least others jeare, hate, and trouble them; or least they come to want food and rayment; for Imagination thinks, if they love and succour others, yet others will not love them againe; These know not the Spirit, they live without upon the Earth; upon objects, under that darke power, called unbeliefe.

But when man lives in the life of universall Love, then God walkes and delights himselfe in his garden mankinde; and man who is the living soule, consisting of hearing, seeing, tasting, smelling, feeling, hath sweet content and communion, with that ruling spirit of love, righteousnesse and peace within, and this is Christs Kingdome, or the day of the Lord within.

While mankinde lives out of himselfe, feeding his imaginary fancie upon outward perishing objects; then the creating Spirit, and the living soule are at variance, and opposition; the Spirit would have man live within himselfe, and take delight in Love, humility, patience, chastity, wisdome, Justice, and all such sweet smelling spices that rules in the heart, [15] leading forth the body to act accordingly; for this is the Anoynting in him, that teaches man all things, and leads him into all truth.

But Imaginary man, he cannot live within himselfe; this is madnesse and foolishnesse to him, he must run abroad for delight, and content his sences altogether in outward objects, and strives with greedinesse after outward contents: And jeeres, laughes, hates, and persecutes the Spirit, calling him madnesse, blasphemys confusion, and that will destroy all government and order; which Imagination hath set up in the world. And this now is the hot time of the day: God, or the creating Spirit takes no delight, to walke in his garden while it is so hot an opposition, betweene him and darke flesh.

But when Mankinde begins to look within himself, and sees his pride, Envie, Covetousnesse, Lust of the flesh, anger, hypocrisie, and nothing but darknesse and discontent; and begins to say with himselfe; oh what have I done, how am I falne? all outward content in objects flies away, and I am left naked, and want Light, life, and rest within.

Oh that I could see and feele Love, humility, chastity, sincerity, truth, wisdome, contentednesse, and peace live and rule in power in me: Then I should rejoyce abundantly, in the enjoyment of my selfe, within my selfe; though all other outward contentments in objects were taken away; though I were poore without, yet if I were rich within, I could rejoyce: if I were in prison, without, If I [16] were in freedome within, I could rejoyce; if all my outward friends and objects forsooke me; yet if I had familiar friendship, with that sweet Spirit within, I should have peace enough: No life like to the life within; This Kingdome within is excellent, and full of glory; the outward Kingdome and peace is a deceiver, it forsakes a man in his misery; but the inward Kingdome never failes a man, in life nor death: Oh that I did enjoy this Kingdome within.

This now is the coole of the day; And the heate of opposition betweene flesh and Spirit begins to decline; flesh sees his folly, and growes very weary thereof; the patience of the spirit is honoured by the flesh. And that righteous Ruler (God), The Seed and tree of Life, begins to walke in this coole of the day, with delight, in the middle of the garden (Mans heart); the sweet breathings of that pure spirit is now entertained, and falne Earth begins to see himselfe naked, and to acknowledge his nakednesse before the spirit, and is ashamed.

And declares how he came by his nakednesse; Even by embracing objects, and seeking a Kingdome without himselfe; his covetous heart closing with that imaginary conceit, promised him much delight; but like a subtill Serpent, he hath deceived him: And now the Seed begins to worke, to bruise the Serpents head, and man begins to looke upward, towards the life of the Spirit within, which he sees now is a life above the life of Earthly objects.

[17] Well, saith the Spirit, to this shattered Earth: Thou seest thy selfe naked, and thou seest the Serpent that deceived thee; and thou art now separated from me; thou lookedst for peace and rest without, and thou art deceived; Thou art afraid to look within, because thy conscience, the Light, that is within thee, which is my selfe, condemns thee; And this feare is the fruit of thy Imagination; thou fearst where there is no cause of feare; Thou lookedst for good to come from objects without, but behold sorrow; thou thoughtst, Oh that if thou hadst lost outward objects, thou couldst have had no inward joy; But thou seest now, how Imagination, that Serpent, hath deceived thee; oh thou living soule, how art thou falne?

But the seed of all things, which is my selfe, will bruise that Serpents head, and I will restore thee againe; I am thy Redeemer, and besides me there is none.

But yet the Battell between *Michaell*, that Seed, and the Dragon, that Imaginary power, is not ended, it begins againe to be fought in heaven, that is, within the garden mankinde; and the day growes hot againe, flesh and spirit does begin afresh to oppose each other sharply.

For Imagination begins to tell the soule; If thou enjoyst not fulnes of all objects, thou wilt want and starve for food, and so presently feare of poverty takes the throne and reignes; and feare bids thee goe, get what thou canst, by hooke or by crooke, least thou want, and perish, and die miserably.

[18] Thou seest how full of hardnesse of heart and deceit every man is; each one seeking to save himselfe; And if thou want food and rayment, Love and Life within, will not preserve thy body from misery.

Then thou seest the treachery of men beset thee, poverty threatning thee, thy body weake, thy mind distempered with feare and care what to doe, and how to live; Some laughs at thee, others cheats thee, yea, such as seeme to professe the same spirit thou strivest for, are most bitter against thee; and they looke after objects more then the inward life, for who more covetous, and hard then they; And wilt thou be alone? yea, thou art alone, where is any one that ownes, or tenders thee.

Well, saith the soule, this is an evill time; and then saith Imaginary feare, filling the soule with sorrow, oh that this body had never been borne, I would I had dyed in the wombe; If this be the happinesse of a man, I would I had been a Bird, a Beast, or some other creature. While I had no care of doing rightly, I could live, I had friends, I had peace; But since I began to doe as I would be done by: friends now stands a farre off; every body hates me, and I am open to all misery; does righteousnesse bring thee to this, oh miserable wretch?

This now is a battell of another nature, then the former was; for in the first battell, the Imaginary flesh was lofty and stout, and full of presumption, selfe-conceit, scoffes, jeeres, Envie, vaporing, and secret subtilty, laughing in his sleave as we say, at the wayes of the Spirit of Life.

[19] But now he is in another temper, he is furnished with the weapons of slavish feare, evill surmising, sense of misery, sometimes angry, sometimes ready to dispaire, and to curse the day of his birth, his soule takes pleasure in nothing without, and yet hath no peace within.

And in this battell likewise, God and man, flesh and spirit are separated, there is no sweet agreement; The selfish Imagination would be a God still, and fight strongly to keep the tottering kingdome, and will not leave off till the Spirit of burning, who is consuming fire, Even God himselfe; come and fire Imagination out of all his strong holds, and with a strong power redeeme the imprisoned Earth from his presumptuous and dispairing bondage.

Though there was a parley before, between flesh and spirit; the man and his righteous God; In the coole of the day, while the living Earth saw himselfe a little naked, and was under a little sence of trouble, and feare, yet the Serpent (Imagination) is not conquered by a sleight parley; but by a stronger contest; for after this parley within himselfe, man is cast out of himselfe, that is, out of the garden, to seeke content in outward objects; as in riches, friends, wife, children, and the like; and then the battell grows hot againe.

For if our true peace and rest, lie in objects and in a Law without, as Imagination would have it, then the Spirit is not within the Creation, but without; And if so, then there may be places found, where the Spirit is not, and then God is not every [20] where, and so, the words of Jesus Christ were not true, when he said, the Kingdome of Heaven is within you; and the word is nigh you, even in your mouth and in your heart; and as the Apostle said, *God the Father is above all, and through all, and in you all. Eph.* 4. 6.

But the Spirit is within; for the Creation is his clothing; God was in Christ, reconciling the world (or falne Earth) to himselfe, he was not without him in objects, offering peace; but he was within, drawing him from the deceitfulnesse of objects that fades away, to looke for rest and peace only within, therefore it is said, Christ is our rest, that is, the Anointing within, is our rest, who teacheth us all things, and leads us into all truth.

And by this Relation; you see here is the living soule, mankind; then here is the fall of mankinde; Then here is the rising or restoring of Mankinde.

And that which hath by Imagination, or *Judas* Ministry, been held forth to us, to be without us, as *Adam*; the Serpent, the Garden, the Tree of Knowledge, of Good and evill; and the Tree of Life; and the fall of Man, and promise of redemption, all to be without; yet all these are within the heart of man clearly.

And whether there was any such outward things or no, it matters not much, if thou seest all within, this will be thy life.

Therefore in this which followes, I shall write of these three particulars.

The Living Soule, which is pure nature, that was called very good.

[21] Then the Serpent, or curse, which is the Imaginary power of darknesse, or mans fall.

Then the Seed of life, the blessing, called the restoring power, delivering mankinde from that bondage, and setting him downe in rest and peace within himselfe.

CHAP. III. *What the Tree of Life is.*

AND when Mankinde begins to enter into himselfe againe, and to enjoy rest, and peace, and Life within, which is the resurrection of Christ; then woe, woe, woe, to the imaginary power, that rules the world, he shall be shaken with terror, and fall, and burst asunder, for this is *Iudas* and the Pharisees that have killed Christ all along.

But now Christ, or the Anoynting, is arising up in sonnes and daughters, they must dye: Therefore, whatsoever government is set up by Imagination, shall be throwne downe; *For every plant, which my heavenly Father hath not planted, shall be rooted out.*

Surely then there is a foure-fold power, much Idolized, and doted upon by covetous flesh, which must be shaken to pieces; And woe, woe, woe, to the Inhabitants of the Earth, to those that live in, or are the upholders of those powers.

The first is the Imaginary, teaching power, called [22] hear-say, booke-studying, University, Divinity, which indeed, is *Iudas* Ministry, for this cries *hayle Master*, to the Spirit, and seemes to kisse him in Love, in outward shew, by preaching of him, and by long prayers to him; But betrayes him into the hand of the selfish power.

This power or ministrie, must destroy himselfe, as *Iudas* did; and so he doth, for the divisions within the publick Ministry makes him burst asunder; and all his inward bowells, of Covetousnesse, Pride, selfe-seeking, evill surmisings, grudging, hypocrisie, seeking to please men more then the righteous power, and all their close envy; is discovered.

Then secondly, The Imaginary Kingly power, who by the power of the sword, and successive conquests doe set up one part of Mankinde, to rule over another; pretending to keep the Creation in peace, but yet proves a selfe-upholder; By murder and theft, treading others under foot; this power takes ease, honour, fulnesse of the Earth to himselfe by the sword, and rules over the labours and bodies of others at his will and prerogative.

This power must be shaken to pieces.

Therefore you Kings and Monarchs, and State rulers, that upholds kingly Authority in your hands; come in, and kisse the Sonne betimes; it is not long, before he will more gloriously appeare, to shake terribly the Nations, not *England* only, but all Nations; for the dominion of Christ is to reach from East to West, from North to South; and of [23] his Kingdome there shall be no end.

Thirdly, the imaginary Judicature, called the Law of Justice; which indeed is but the declarative will of Conquerours, how they will have their Subjects be ruled; And this pretends to keep all in peace, and yet it is the very support of Envie, hardnesse of heart, and unrighteous covetousnesse; Therefore woe to you, Lawyers, that bindes heavie burdens upon mens shoulders, which you yourselves will not touch with the least of your fingers.

Fourthly, buying and selling of the Earth, with the fruits of the Earth; This is an Imaginary Art, to fetch in content from without, and breeds discontent, and divides the creation, and makes mankinde to imprison, enslave, and destroy one another.

These foure imaginary selfish powers, are to be shaken to pieces at the resurrection of Christ; For these are they, that all the time, times, and dividing of time of the Beasts Raigne put Christ to death; And these are they which Christ will destroy, by the brightnesse of his comming, and by the word of his mouth.

Therefore woe, woe, woe, to the Inhabitants of the Earth whose delight, peace, and life lies in, and upon objects without them; and are strangers to the spirit within them.

These foure powers are the foure Beasts, which *Daniel* saw rise up out of the Sea. *Dan.* 7. 3, *&c.* And this Sea is the bulke and body of mankinde, which is that Sea, and waters, upon which the Spirit [24] of God is said sometimes to move; for out of Mankinde arises all that darknesse and Tyranny that oppresses it selfe; And though these Beasts appeare divers, one from another, yet they are all one in their power; for Imaginary-selfe ruling in mans heart, is the Father that created and bred them all.

The first Beast which *Daniell* saw rise up out of the deceived heart of mankinde, was like a Lion; and had Eagles wings: And this is

Kingly power, which takes the Sword, and makes way to rule over others thereby, dividing the Creation, one part from another; setting up the Conqueror to rule, making the conquered a slave; giving the Earth to some, denying the Earth to others; And his Eagles wings betokens his swiftnesse, to ride on horse back, or march on foot quick, from place to place, conquering, and to conquer.

The Imaginary selfishnesse created this power, to burden and oppresse the Creation, which was the worke of the righteous Spirit.

Yet-*Daniell* saw this Beast lifted up from the Earth, and made to stand upon the feet like a man, and a mans heart was given to it, that is, This Power should be the Image of true Magistracie, and while the Beastly power of self-Love rules in the hearts of mankinde; this Kingly power should be the preserver of the meeke in spirit, and so help the woman.

And when the time comes for Christ to reigne, this Beast shall deliver up his Crowne, Scepter, Authority, [25] and government unto Christ, and lay all downe at his feet. *Rev.* 4. 9, *&c.*

The second Beast was like a Beare; And this is the power of the selfish Lawes, which is full of covetousnesse, and of a Beare-like tearing and devouring nature; and he had three ribs in the mouth, which are these,

First, the power of Prisons, whereby he kills and devoures.

Secondly, the power of whiping, banishment, and confiscation of goods, whereby he kills.

Thirdly, the power of hanging, pressing, burning, martering; whereby he kills, and devoures much flesh, for take these three ribs out of the mouth of the Law, or Innes of Court trade, and that Beast hath no power, but dies.

The third Beast was like a Leopard, spotty; and this is the thieving Art of buying and selling the Earth with her fruits one to another. Imaginary selfish Covetousnesse created this Beast likewise; And this Beast had foure wings; Policy, Hypocrisie, Self-Love, and hardnesse of Heart; for this Beast is a true self-Lover, to get the Earth to himselfe, to lock it up in Chests and barnes, though others starve for want.

And this Beast had foure heads, that guides him, and upholds him in his wayes.

The first is the power of the sword fighting for it.

Secondly, the power of the Law, enslaving others to it.

Thirdly, the power of the covetous Imaginary [26] Clergie, preaching it up, and drawing the people to wander after him.

Fourthly, the power of a blinde deceived Heart, over-awed with feare of men, and a conceit that it is a righteous Art; And this Beast had dominion to rule.

The fourth Beast is the Imaginary Clergy-Power, which indeed is *Iudas*; and this is more terrible and dreadful then the rest; and though he come last, yet indeed he is the Father, that begot the other; All these Beasts, they differ in shape, and yet they agree all in one oppressing power, supporting one another; one cannot live without another; and yet they seeme to persecute one another; and if one truly die, all dies.

What is the reason? only this; they shew hereby, that either alone, or altogether, they are the curse and plague upon the Creation, and is the cause of all sorrowes and teares, amongst mankinde; for they devoure abundantly, and yet they rise out of the Sea, even from the body of deceived, covetous, darke, powered mankinde, in the night time of that world.

These foure Beasts are all very fruitfull; for from them, as from foure Fountaines, or Monarchs, springs up divers heads and hornes; that is, severall spreadings forth, of selfish tyrannicall Power, whereby the Creation is opprest and burdened; and these reigne in power, while propriety rules as King; but when righteous community rises, which is the [27] blessing, then they all fall, and are shaken to peeces.

The Creation will never be in quiet, peace, till these foure Beasts, with all their heads and hornes, the variety of their branching powers doe run into the Sea againe, and be swallowed up in those waters; that is, into Mankinde, who shall be abundantly inlightned; and Light, Life, and truth shall mightily overflow, as the waters of the Seas over the Earth; and all those Beasts with their selfe-will powers, shall sinke like mudd to the bottome, and their place shall be seene no more.

These are the heards of swine, that must perish in the waters.

This worke Christ will bring to passe, at his more glorious appearance, he will consume the mysterie of iniquity, by the brightnesse of his comming. You Angells of the Lord, who are the Lights of the Earth, speake aloud, roare out, and spare not, pour out the appointed plagues upon the Beast, in this her hypocriticall, dividing of time.

These are the foure Beasts, or selfish Beastly powers, that rise up out of the Sea, to oppresse, burden, and destroy universall Love, and their returne back into the Sea, will be the rising up of Love, who is the Sonne of righteousnesse, causing day-light.

The kingly Power, he tooke the sword to kill and conquer; and to lift up selfe, to be the Ruler; for all Lawes of the Nations are Lawes made by the will of this murderer, kingly power.

And this Beast shall be throwne downe by his [28] owne power; for out of the Serpents root shall come forth a Cocatrise, that shall devoure the body. I wonder not to see the *Midianites* destroy one another; He that takes the sword shall perish with the sword. This kingly power fighting, is the Army of the *Midianites*.

Therefore where you see Army against Army, It is but the kingly power divided, tearing, and devouring itselfe; for as he riseth by his owne sword, so he shall fall by his owne sword, as the *Midianites* did; they sheathed their swords one in anothers bowells, while *Israell* looked on, and at last tooke the spoyle:

So shall kingly power doe in his severall governments by the sword; they shall dash one against another; Time shall dash against times, and times shall dash against the dividing of time; and the divisions in the dividing of time shall destroy him; till the Creation be cleansed of these plagues; and that curse which hath destroyed the Earth, shall now in the period of time destroy himselfe.

And this makes way for Christ, the universall Love, to take the Kingdome, and the dominion of the whole Earth.

Therefore you souldiers, you may see the end of your trade; it is a destroyer, and shall be destroyed by it selfe, and surely you shall finde no true peace herein; No, no; there is no peace and rest but in Christ the Saviour; your trade upholds the murderer, or the Devill.

Now the other three Beasts; who are Clergy, [29] Law, and Buying and Selling; these rise up by craft; supported by the kingly power; And the chiefe Beast is the Clergy, he bred all the other; He is a King, understanding darke sayings, and he shall by craft deceive many; the other Beasts are this Beasts sons, he bred them.

For this teaching Art first bids mankinde to looke abroad for a teacher and a ruler, and to look abroad for Justice and content; and when he had deceived them so to doe, then he put mankinde upon buying and selling of the Earth and her fruits, and so by that meanes the Creation is divided and Mankinde is put upon an Art to cheat, and burden himselfe; for the Earth ought to remaine a standing portion to them, and their children successively, by the righteous Law of Creation.

Then this teaching Art found out the Law; calling it the Law of Justice; a very good name, to cover his knavery; for he is a mighty Beast with great teeth, and is a mighty devourer of men; he eates up all that comes within his power; for this Proverb is true, goe to Law, and none shall get but the Lawyer. The Law is the Fox, poore men are the geesse; he pulls of their feathers, and feeds upon them.

These foure Beasts are the Fountaines of Tyranny to the Creation; they are of a fruitfull generation; one begetting divers Beasts that are of mighty devouring natures; But the most dreadfull and terrible Beast, is the Clergy Power; for though the other three raised him up by action; yet this Imaginary [30] learned Beast raised them up by policie; for selfe ends.

For this stamped the other under foot, saith *Daniell;* And is not this true? hath not the Clergy ruled over kingly Power, Law, and buying and selling, and brought all under his Command? for at the first, he was onely a teaching Power, and then it was a Beast, differing from the rest, yet he stamped them under foot, and all the other had their strength and succour from him, by his teaching and imaginary instruction.

Out of this teaching Beast rise up ten hornes; or the branching forth of his strength in ten particulars; Five fighting against the powers of the Creation, Hearing, Seeing, Tasting, Smelling, Feeling, which is called the body of the living soule, that is, very good.

And five fighting against the powers of righteousnesse, which is Understanding, Will, Affection, Joy, and Peace; which is called the Seed, and making war against him; and so darkning Heaven and Earth.

This is he, that restraines the liberty of the outward man, not suffering him to have a free enjoyment of his portion in the Earth; making such actions to be sinne, which the righteous creating Spirit made not a sinne.

And he restraines thereby the liberty of the inward man; not suffering him to act in the liberty of himselfe; for he makes a man a sinner for a word, and so he sweeps the Stars of Heaven downe with [31] his tayle, he darkens Heaven and Earth, and defiles body and mind.

For so long as I must not act, according to the freedome of my owne spirit and power within me; but must be guided by others without me, and punished for such actions, which others in the ruling Chaire doe, in a higher nature then I doe; I am then in bondage, and my eyes are put out.

And this is the Covenant, that the outward teaching power makes with the branches of Mankinde, to put out their owne eyes, to see by others; telling them none can see, but schollars: so that this fourth Beast, is more dreadfull then the other three; for it stamps the other three under foot, and rules over all.

And out of the ten hornes of this Beast, rise up another little horne; and this is the dominion and rule which the teaching power takes up, called Ecclesiasticall power; and this little horne was raised, by a power that was not his owne; for the kingly power puts that dominion and rule into his hands; While he remained onely a teaching power, he stamped the other under him, and overawed others by his deceitfull words.

But now he hath got a power to rule, called Ecclesiasticall power, which is the extract of selfish righteousnesse, from the seeming righteousnesse of the foure Beasts into one ruling power, and by this, which was little in the beginning; There were three of the first hornes plucked up; that is:

Kingly Power, Law, and buying and selling; for [32] the Little horne, or ruling Clergie lifted up himselfe above all these, and made these uncover and fall to him; he had dominion and power over all these, and these were in subjection and afraid, and bowed to him; He by his teaching lifted up these, and these by their acting lifted up him to rule; and he by his ruling treads these under his proud covetous feet.

And this is he, who is said to be a King of a fierce countenance; understanding, darke saying, that is mighty, but not by his owne power, and he shall by craft and power destroy many; his rising was in the latter dayes, when transgressions were come to the full; when people were most blinde, by his outward teaching; then they easily receive him to be the outward ruler over their soules; for now the Sea being bemuddied, that is, mankinde being mightily deceived, he by his learned policy, riseth up out of that deceived Sea, for all the peeple wandered after him, though he sore oppressed them. *Dan.* 8. 23. *Rev.* 13. 3.

And as the sword, which is not his power, lifted him up and supports him, by forcing the people to pay him tithes; for the Law of the Magistrate forces the people to pay them.

And he being lifted up, he made war with the Saints, and overcame them, for a time, times, and dividing of time; But as he was lifted up by others power, through his owne craft; Even so he shall be destroyed againe, without hand; the Sword shall not destroy him, he shall be discovered in all his oppressing, hypocriticall, bewitching knavery, by the [33] light and wisdome of the Spirit of Truth, that shall rise up out of the Sea of mankinde likewise, appearing in sonnes and daughters of righteousnesse, in the latter dayes.

As *Paul* said, Christ shall destroy him by the word of his mouth, and by the brightnesse of his comming. *Dan.* 7. 26, *&c.* 2 *Thess.* 2. 8.

When Christ the Anoynting spirit rises up, and inlightens mankind, then in his light, they shall see the deceit and falshood of this Beast, that hath deceived all the world; and shall fall off from him, and leave him naked and bare; and if he will teach and rule, let him shew his power over the Beasts; for the people will all looke up to God, to be taught and governed by him.

The discovery of the fulnesse, and foulnesse of this Beast, throwes downe all the rest likewise; for when mankinde begins to fall off from one part of the beastly power, he will fall from all, for they all depend one upon another.

Kingly power depends upon the Law, and upon buying and selling; and these three depend upon the Clergy, to bewitch the people to conforme; and all of them depend upon Kingly power by his force, to compell subjection from those that will not be bewitched.

But when mankinde once sees, that his teacher and ruler is within him; then what need is there of a teacher and ruler without; they will easily cast off their burden.

Therefore woe, woe, woe, to the Inhabitants [34] of the Earth;

when Christ rises in power, and begins to come in glory with his Saints. This discovery is coming on apace.

Therefore you Souldiers, and you great Powers of the Earth, you need not feare that the Levellers will conquer you by the sword; I doe not meane the fighting Levellers, for they be your selves; but I meane Christ levelling; who fights against you, by the sword of Love, patience and truth; for whosoever takes the Iron sword to fight against you, are your owne sonnes, that fights against you; for Christ came not to destroy, but to save; But Antichrist, whose power you are, came not to save, but to destroy.

Therefore, if there be any amongst you, that count truth and peace precious, take the Spirits advice, and come out of Babylon, dwell no longer in the Courts and wayes of Imaginarie confusion; come into truth, Light, and Liberty, and be at peace.

When Christ comes, and is glorified with thousand thousands attending upon him, they shall not be cloathed with devouring instruments, like Dragons, but be cloathed with Love, Righteousnesse and Peace, like Lambs; And at his appearing, said *Daniell,* the Beast was slaine; and his body given to the burning flame; that is, all the Imaginary selfish Power, that made people run abroad for a Teacher, and a Ruler, was all cast into the fire of pure Light, and was consumed in that unquenchable flame; Even destroyed by [35] the brightnesse of Christs comming, as darknesse vanisheth when Light comes in. *Dan.* 7. 11.

He that hath Eares to heare, Let him heare what the Spirit speaks.

CHAP. IV. *What the Serpent is.*

IF this be true, It will destroy all government, and all our Ministry and religion?

I answer, it is very true; for all government and Ministry, that is lifted up by Imagination, is to be throwne downe, and plucked up: That Christ alone may be exalted in the day of his power. And you have Scripture for it; "Then cometh the end, when he shall have delivered up the Kingdome to God, even the Father, when he shall have put downe all rule, and all Authoritie, and all power; for he must reigne, till he hath put all enemies under his feet". 1 *Cor.* 15. 24.

Looke back into Ages past, and see what overturnings, and pluckings up there hath been of the Authority, power, and government of

Nations; Every government standing his period; for when it was universally proved a Devill, a destroyer, and waster: then it was throne downe.

And this casting downe, plucking up, and wars [36] in the Nations shall be till Christ, The Law of universall Love comes to reigne; and then he shall settle all in peace, and be the true restorer.

You oppressing powers of the world, who think God hath blessed you, because you sit downe in that Chaire of Government, out of which the former Tyrants are gone: Doe you remember this? your overturning, overturning, overturning, is come on to you, as well as to your fellow break-promises, that are gone before; You that pretend to be saviours of the people, and to seeke the peace of the whole Nation; and yet serve your selves upon the peoples ruines, not regarding the crie of the poore, surely you must have your overturnings too.

For such a Government, as preserves part, and destroyes another part of the Creation, is not the power of Christ, but of Antichrist; That Government that gives liberty to the Gentry to have all the Earth, and shuts out the poore Commoners from enjoying any part: ruling by the tyrannicall Law of Conquest over brethren; this is the Government of imaginarie, selfe-seeking Antichrist; And every plant which my heavenly Father hath not planted, shall be rooted out.

This man will have no government some will say.

I answer, you run too fast; True Government is that I long for to see, I waite till the power, Authority, and government of the King of righteousnesse [37] rule over all, for as yet the power and dominion of the Prince of darknesse rules every where, and that is the government, which must be throwne down.

But government is called Magistracy, and all Magistracie is of God.

I Answer, Magistracie is a good name, and the mystery of iniquity, hath not only got this name, but many other excellent names: to be set upon the head of his blacknes of darknesse, that under a good name he may goe undiscovered, and he puts bad names upon things that are excellent.

Therefore let us see, whether Imaginary government, that divides part of mankinde to enjoy the Earth, and the other part not to enjoy the Earth, is worthy of the name, Magistracie; No, no; such a dividing, selfe loving power is an enemie to Magistracie.

For Magistracie hath two excellent principles in his nature, which the darke selfish government is an enemy to.

First Magistracie signifies a great Light, as much as to say, greater Light of Love, greater Light of Humility, greater Light of Reason, greater Light of Truth, keeping promise and covenant; greater Light of Peace, and tendernesse of heart, greater Light of boldnesse, in a cause that is universally righteous.

And where this power, Authority and government rules, this is pure Magistracie, and it is the Life and power of Christ.

[38] Secondly, Magistracie signifies the greatest Band, that ties the Creation together in peace, and this band is universall Love; for this Love streames out to preserve all, and despises none; This is the unitie of the Spirit, and the band of peace; this is pure Majestie indeed, that ties people together in Love; And this is the power, Authoritie, and government of Christ; The love of Christ in us, constraines all men to doe his will.

Now looke and see, is the Magistracie of the Nations like this? Is it a light of pure excellency and universall Love above others? doth it tie the Creation together, in the unity of spirit, and band of peace? we cannot say it doth, or if any say it doth, then I'le answer.

What meanes then the lowing of the Oxen, and bleating of the Sheep? what meanes such complaints, that those that sit in the Chaire of Magistracie, are covenant, promise, and oathes-breakers, and are selfe-Lovers; Lovers of honour, money and ease, and regard not the cries of the oppressed? They favour the rich for reward, and despise and sleight the poore. They give the Earth to some, and denie the Earth others, by reason whereof murmurings, and divisions multiplie, and so uphold the slavish Law of conquests.

Now judge: Is such a Magistracie as this the greatest Light? doth this tye the Creation together in the unity of spirit and band of peace? surely as yet, the mysterie of iniquitie sports himselfe, [39] uncontrouled under this excellent name or covering, called Magistracie; but the babes and sucklings will draw off his vaile, and shew all his nakednesse and shame him.

If you would finde true Majestie indeed, goe among the poore despised ones of the Earth; for there Christ dwells, and there you shall see Light and Love shine in Majestie indeed, rising up to unite the

Creation indeed, into the unitie of spirit, and band of peace; the blessing of the Lord is amongst the poore, and the covetous, scoffing, covenant-breaking, thieves and murderers, that croud themselves under the name Magistracie, shall be sent emptie away.

These great ones are too stately houses for Christ to dwell in; he takes up his abode in a manger, Inne, and amongst the poore in spirit, and despised ones of the Earth.

Secondly, Imaginarie Ministrie and Religion is to be plucked up, as unsavorie salt; and this is the learned publick Ministrie of the world; for this Ministrie is set up by craft and covetousnesse, how to draw the Earth, and the labours of men into the Clergies hands; These men make themselves ministers, as a man teaches birds to speake; But they doe not stay till Christ make them, for that will be too long for them to wait, the rich Benefices will be all taken up.

This Ministrie having learned other mens words, by their long education in their Universitie Schooles, takes upon them to interpret [40] other mens words and writings, and this imaginary studie of theirs, they call pure Doctrine, and tells the people it is pure Religion to come and heare their Sermon, and to give them Tithes, or a large maintenance for so doing.

But this is a false Prophet, he runs before he be sent; Study and Imagination was never appointed, and sent of Christ to be a Minister for him, this is Antichrists Ministrie.

For when Christ sent out his Disciples to preach, he saith, that which you have heard and seen, goe preach; and saith *Paul*, we cannot but speake the things which we have heard and seen from the Father; But the Universitie publick Ministrie runs before he be sent; they take up another mans message, and carries abroad other mens words, or studies or imagines a meaning; and this is their ministrie; This is not to preach the truth, as it was in Jesus, purely and experimentally, as they received it of the Father, but as they receive it from man, and by man.

The Scriptures of the Bible were written by the experimentall hand of Shepherds, Husbandmen, Fishermen, and such inferiour men of the world; And the Universitie learned ones have got these mens writings; and flourishes their plaine language over with their darke interpretation, and glosses, as if it were too hard for ordinary men now to understand them; and thereby they deceive the simple, and makes a prey of the poore, and cosens them of the Earth, and of the tenth of their labors.

[41] And because those mens writings are taking with the world, therefore these learned ones shuts out the true Penmen in whom the Spirit dwells, and saith now, such Mecanicks must not meddle with spirituall things; and so by covetous policie, in opposition to the righteous spirit, they engrosse other mens experimentall spirituall teachings to themselves; as if it were their owne by University or Schoole learning succession. Pope like. Nay just the Pope.

And by their blacknesse of darknesse, in their Schoole-learning, they have drawne a veyle over the truth; And Light by them is hid from the world; for the plaine truth is, this Imaginary ministrie is neither better nor worse, but plaine unmasked *Iudas*. And the snappish bitter profession, that cries it up, is the unmasked murdering Scribes, and Pharisees.

The one betrayes Christ, the spirit of righteousnesse with a kisse, pretending a great deale of Love to the Spirit, by preaching and praying, to a God without, they know not where, nor what he is.

The other kills him, and will not suffer him to appeare in the world; for these snappish professors calls every thing blasphemie, unlesse they approve of it, still tying the Spirit to themselves; saying, Loe, here is Christ in this man, and loe, there is Christ in that man.

But Christ is the Light of Life, spread abroad, and he is now rising in Husbandmen, Shepherds, [42] Fishermen; And by these he first takes off the black interpretation, that the imaginary learned Scholars by their studies have defiled the Scriptures of old with, and restores them to their owne genuine and pure Light.

And then to discover his appearance in sonnes and daughters, in a fuller measure, the poore despised ones shall be honoured first in the worke; and from this dust, the blessing shall arise to cover the whole Earth with peace, and with the knowledge of the Lord.

For this is the vine that shall overspread the Earth, and shall be confined no longer within a Colledge, or private University Chamber, or under a covetous, proud, black gowne, that would alwayes be speaking words: but fall off when people begins to act their words.

When Jesus Christ the Sonne of man was upon Earth, in that one person, he could very seldome speake but the hypocriticall snappish Pharisees were either silent, and watched to trap him in his speech, to bring him into bondage; or else with open mouth they cryed out, he is a blasphemer, a Devill, and a friend of Publicans and sinners, condemning him, because he was no scholar. How knowes this man letters seeing he never learned.

And have not the Pharisees of our age, who are the imaginary bitter professors, the same subtlety and language? And as they of old sought to kill Christ; so these endeavour to suppresse him, and [43] will not suffer him to arise in sonnes and daughters; though the Scripture declare it, which they make such a strict profession of, as if they would not loose one letter.

These professors will still confine Christ to a private chamber, and to particular bodies, and restraine him, who is the universall power of Love and peace. They owne him in words, but they denie him in power; they worship God at a distance, not knowing where he is, nor what they worship; And they call this blasphemie, to say Christ is in you, though the Scriptures which they professe say the same. "Know you not that Christ is in you; And the Kingdom of Heaven is in you; And they that worship the Father, must worship him in spirit within, and in truth of action without, and fulfilling the Law and the Prophets." Love your enemies, and doe as you would be done by, in actions and not in words only.

CHAP. V. *What the living Soule (Man) is, that is called very good.*

IN the body of mankinde, and indeed, in every single body, there are three particulars necessary to be knowne, without which no man can know himselfe, let him say what he will.

The first is the Creature, or the living Soule, [44] which before the curse defiles it, is very good, and this was the Image of God (or of the righteous spirit) in flesh, or first *Adam*; And this living soule is the heaven, in which the battell is fought between the curse and the blessing: *Michaell* and the Dragon; And this living soule is the wax fitted to receive, either the impression of the curse, and so prove disobedient to righteousnesse, or the impression of the blessing, and so prove obedient to righteousnesse.

Secondly, there is the mysterie of iniquitie, or the power of deceit, and this is the God of the world, or Prince of darknesse; that deceives the living soule first, and takes possession, and this in one man is the

Image, or rather nature of that one power of darknesse, or Devill, that is spread abroad through the Creation, to cover over, or keep downe the blessing, or Seed of Life from rising.

Thirdly, the Life of God, or of the righteous spirit rising up in the living soule, and casting the curse or power of darknesse out, and bringing Mankinde into peace; and this is the second *Adam*, or the Lord from Heaven.

Now this living soule Mankinde is a Beast, and the King of Beasts; for the life of the five Sences onely is the life of the Beast; And this Beast in every one, as well as in the whole, is to raigne for a time, times, and dividing of time, before mankinde can be united to the life of the righteous God, and made one with that one spirit of [45] universall Love. As Jesus Christ prayd, Father, I pray that they may be one in us, as thou oh Father art one in me, and I in thee, they were not united yet.

The Image of God in flesh dyed, and was put out by darknesse; But the Seed, or spirit of true life rising up from under that darknesse, dies no more, but lives for ever; This spirit is the tree of Life.

Therefore, you that say you know but one power, be not deceived; for if this one power of righteousnesse, which is the tree of Life rule in you, then you are new creatures indeed, you are one with the Father and the Sonne; And then you shall know death no more: that is, you shall not live in opposition to the spirit of righteousnesse no more, neither in thought, word, nor deed; And then all sorrow and teares shall flie away likewise, and you shall be at rest, which is the day of the Lord, or the Light or day time of Mankinde. Darknesse is now swallowed up and gone.

But if selfish actions, and selfish Principles live in their strength in you still; if Imagination be Ruler, truly then, that one power is but the power of darknesse, to whom you are in bondage, and you are not yet past the combate, the Dragon is not yet cast out, and you must know a fuller resurrection, before you can sit downe in peace.

Some of you have got a speech; That those that see two powers within themselves, of darknesse [46] and Light, Love and Envy, sorrow and comfort striving together, sees with two eyes: but you may say, you see every thing and power with a single eye, and nothing you see evill, but all things and actions are good, and as they must be.

Surely this is well, if you become all of you that speake these words, to eat of that Tree of Life; for my part Ile not condemne you. I can rejoyce to see the Resurrection of Christ in any, but I must watch some of you, to see if your conversations be so universally filled with Love, as shall make the darke world startle; and then I can say of a truth, Christ is risen indeed in you.

If your owne eye be darke, that is, if darknesse rule your whole body; then all the actions of your body towards others are in darknesse, and builders up of selfishnesse, which is the one power you yet live in.

But if your eye be truly single, and full of Light, then the Light power wholly rules in you, and the actions of your outward man will be full of Light, and Life, and Love, towards every single branch of the whole Creation.

But some may say, explaine these three particulars in mankinde, that we may know them distinctly, one from another. I Answer, I shall readily doe it.

The first particular is the living Soule, or that estate of simple plaine heartednesse, which hath the Life of the five Sences only, and by that [47] Life preserves that single body, or proprieties.

But the Life of the Spirit, in sound reason lives not yet in the Sences; for pure Reason lives like a corne or wheate, under the clods of Earth, or Beast, and is not yet risen up to rule as King.

This plaine hearted state is set in the midst of many objects, tempting him like the Serpent; and it is open to many crosses, and teares, like the tender grasse, that is soone bruised by the foot of the oxe; it hath not the true rest of Christ in it, though there be much rest and peace in it; for it is changeable.

This is such a state, that though there be selfe-Love, yet there is no hatred towards others in it, but a quiet content to let others live too. As a childe, though he love himselfe (the propriety of a Beast so to doe) yet he envies not others; for Envie, Pride, Covetousnesse, Hypocrisie, rash murdering, anger, hath not yet defiled the Earth. The man is plaine, honest hearted, even Innocent *Adam*.

Like *Nathanaell* in whom there was no guile, and yet *Nathanaell* knew not Christ, that Anoynting spirit as yet ruled not as King in him; for he was open to temptation, and change, and many teares.

Like *Peter*, a man of the same plaine hearted temper, full of Love to Christ and others; yet selfish, he was without guile, and was loving, without knowledge, therefore open to temptation, and change, and teares.

[48] Now, though Christ Commended *Nathanael,* and prayed for *Peter,* that his faith or strength might not fayle him, yet they were both strangers to the Spirit, which was given them afterwards.

And as Christ told his Disciples, I have chosen you twelve, and one of you is a Devill; that is, eleven of you are plaine, honest, simple hearts, in whom there is no guile; you have sincerely in love to me, forsaken all your friends, and riches to follow me: so that Covetous-nesse doth not reigne, Imagination doth not fright you, with what shall we eate, and what shall we drinke, and wherewith shall be cloathed hereafter? As they themselves said, Master, we have for-saken all to follow thee, and what shall wee have &c.

So that here is no subtlety, but downe right simplicity without guile, and these are like wax, prepared for any stamp.

But now *Judas* the twelfth man was a Devill, he was defiled and falne by temptation, that is, he was one that followed Christ for selfe ends; not simply, like most preachers, and covetous, bitter hearted Professors, that will covenant before hand, what they must have be-fore they follow Christ; And when they heare they must part with all to follow Christ, then they are sorrowfull. This is *Iudas,* a Devill, the power of covetousnesse, the curse that hath defiled mankind, and he strives to spread himselfe, that he may [49] defile all. But Christ who is the blessing appeares to destroy this curse.

And when plaine hearted *Peter* told Christ, that though all for-sooke him; yet he would not; alas, saith Christ, *Peter,* thou art plaine hearted, and thou know'st not the wiles of the tempter; thou wilt be overcome and made to denie me. I know thy strength; for I that am the light and life of the world, doe not yet live in thee; Thou art a downe right living Soule, a plaine innocent harmelesse man; but thou art not yet Anoynted, nor cannot be, till I be gone from you; And then Ile send you the comforter, that shall lead you into all truth, and abide with you for ever.

Therefore, when I am taken from you, stay you quiet at *Ierusalem,* til you receive power from on high, which is the Fathers promise to you, and that power ruling in you, shall keep you from being over-come by temptation.

And you see *Peters* strength proved weaknesse, though there was simple hearted innocencie in *Peter's* love to Christ's body; yet his love was changeable; for when the tryall came, *Peter* denyed Christ.

And this plaine heartednesse is the first time of the Beast, or selfe, which is full of peace, while a man is in it; but it is a state like wax, flexible and easie to take any impression.

Therefore the two powers of Light and Darknesse, Christ and the Devill; strives who shall rule in this living soule first; And these two powers are [50] *Iacob* and *Esau*, flesh and spirit, strugling within the wombe of the living Earth, who shall rule first; And darknesse first prevailes, and rules within, enslaves, and causes sorrow, and through his deceit, drawes the man to seeke content in objects without. But then followes Christ the restoring power, and delivers the living soule againe from that bondage, and sets him downe in himselfe, which is the rest and strength of Love unchangeable, who doth cast out all feare.

Now while the darke power rules; the man is as *Iudas*, a Devill, a betrayer of Christ, therefore when Christ begins to redeeme; he kills that darknesse, and brings mankinde back to that plaine hearted estate of simplicitie, in which the Devill found the man when he deceived him; and makes him meeke, humble, flexible, loving plaine hearted, without guile, free from Envie, like the state of a little child; *Except a man be borne againe, and become as a little child, he cannot enter into heaven;* that is, into peace; The power of the Devill must first be cast out, before Christ will appeare to sit downe in rest.

This plaine hearted estate is that which *Paul* spake of; A man must first become a foole, that he may be wise; that is, voide of guile, or hypocriticall deceit, which the power of darknesse is full of; and these are the foolish things of the world, whereby God will destroy the imaginary wise.

This plaine heartednesse without envie or guile, is the Virgine-state of Mankinde; And this Virgine [51] is she that must beare a sonne, and call his name *Emanuell*, God with us.

This chaste Virgine-state, that hath no outward Lover, and that is not defiled, but cleansed from deformity, is this Virgine chaste state, in whom the Sonne of righteousnesse will arise, and take the man into union with himselfe; he rules as King, and Mankinde, the living soule, is freely subject with delight.

So that this Innocencie, or plaine heartednesse in man, was not an estate 6000. yeare agoe onely; But every branch of mankinde passes through it, & first is defiled by imaginary covetousnesse, and thereby is made a Devill; and then he is delivered from that darknesse, by Christ the restorer, and by him made one with the Father and the Son.

In one word then, the innocencie of mankinde, which is the Image of God, is plaine heartednesse without guile, quiet, patient, chast, loving, without envy: yet through weaknesse is flexible, and open to temptation and change; This is the living soule, which God breathed the breath of life into; This is the Garden of *Eden,* it is the spirits house or mansion, and in the body of Mankinde the spirit hath many mansions or dwelling places; this is the field or heaven, wherein *Michaell* and the Dragon fights the great battell of God Almighty.

Many men live in their innocencie longer then others, some are tempted sooner then others, but all must be tempted, and tried by the evill one; that so way may be made for Christ to shew his power; for [52] the Office of Christ, the blessing, is to restore and deliver from death and bondage, and to set man downe in life and unchangeable rest.

Therefore temptations and falling from innocency must be, that so man may be drawne up into the life and strength of the righteous God, or ruler, from whom he shall never fall again; this is the mysterie of God, God manifest in the flesh, or righteousnesse ruling King in man.

So that this innocent estate is the Image of God, but not the strength and life of God; It is wise, but not wisdome it selfe; it is just but not Justice; it is loving, but not Love it selfe. It rejoyces, but it is not Joy it selfe; It is patient, but not Patience it selfe; It is chaste, yet not Chastity; It is plaine hearted without guile, yet not sincerity it selfe; It is filled with rest and peace, while he injoyes himselfe within, and doth not make a league with Satan, or outward objects; for then he falls and meets with sorrow.

Therefore he is said to be made in the Image of God, because this Innocencie is an estate very good, and there is no evill in it; yet it is changeable, subject to be overcome by temptation.

But now God, or the righteous spirit is unchangeable; for he is Wisdome, Justice, Love, Patience, Sincerity, Chastity, Joy, and Peace it selfe, nor cannot be overcome by any temptation.

And this is the mysterie and wisdome of God, to let that innocent nature of man fall, and be defiled by his owne invention; that so, he may declare his [53] power, in redeeming him from that defilement, and in taking him up into unity of the God-head, to remaine in that fountaine of Life and rest, and never to be deceived againe; and this is a redemption indeed; not only to deliver from bondage, but likewise to destroy the tempter; that he shall never appeare to draw man into bondage againe; this is the worke of the Lamb, and the mysterie of God. This worke is that which makes us to have fellowship with the Father, and his Sonne Jesus Christ; This worke puts those songs of prayse and halalujahs into our mouths and hearts, to him that sits upon the throne, and to the Lamb for evermore.

This is the first estate of mankinde, or the living soule in his innocencie, and you need not looke back six thousand yeares to finde it; for every single man and woman passes through it; and when the restorer rises up, they shall be able to say, this is truth.

The second estate of mankinde, is the time of the curse, while he reignes, which is the power of darknesse, or Dragon, that deceives the plaine hearted, simple man; making him to covet after content in objects without him, and to looke for a God without, and so fills him with anger, envie, hypocrisie, vexation, griefe; and brings him into bondage within himselfe. Now this curse reignes in these three particulars.

In the lust of the Eye; In the lust of the Flesh, and in pride of Life.

The lust of the eye is covetousnesse, after any object [54] the man sees, thinking within himselfe, that if he can obtaine such and such objects, he shall be at rest and filled with delight; And this is an unsatisfied roving Lust, and is a self-lover, hurting others; for this Lust of the eye, would draw all to it selfe; and leave all others naked; and when he cannot enjoy those objects; Then Envie and anger arises, vexes, frets and torments the man mightily; But if he obtains, he rejoyces; but his joy is the joy of envie, which doth perish againe, and ends in vexation.

The second is the Lust of the flesh; And this is an excessive, or immoderate degree of covetousnesse, which doth waste and consume the objects that his eye lusted after, not to preserve mankinde, or his body, but to satisfie excessive Beastly desire; he eates and drinks excessively; cloathes himselfe vaine gloriously, or runnes into the immoderate use of women; And so those objects which are for the preservation and delight of Mankinde, he immoderately uses, and by his excesse, destroyes himselfe and them too.

The third is the pride of Life, and this is the very height of covetousnesse, called vaine glory, or secret pride of heart, lifting up himselfe above others, making others bow to him; looking upon himselfe as a God above others, who indeed are his equalls, vexing and fretting, and ready to kill them if any refuse to give him that honour he would have. *Hamons* proud heart is mightily troubled, if *Mordecay* will not bow, This is the pride of Life.

[55] As *Nebuchadnezar* said, is not this great *Babell* which I have built for the glory of my Majesty? so lifting up himselfe above others; this is the power of pride; But now humility stayes, and lets others lift him up.

Looke through the whole body of darknesse, and every branch of him may be applyed to one of these heads.

And while these Lusts rule; the whole body of darknesse reignes as King in the man; As Envy, Pride, Covetousnesse, evill surmisings, hypocrisie, uncleane lust of the flesh, Gluttony, Drunkennesse; And the man hath lost his Innocencie, and is become a Devill; he is a prisoner to his lusts, and is in bondage within himselfe; he enjoys nothing with sweet content.

For let him have what he would have, still he is unsatisfied, and discontent dwells in his heart upon every crosse; he lives without God in the world, and feeds upon husks like the swyne: that is, his delight reaches to outward things only; to riches, honours, pleasures, and women, they are the husks he feeds on, which dies and rots; take these away, and he hath lost his Kingdome; And in this deceived estate, mankinde is a compleat Devill, and is become a very decree of himselfe and others, as experience makes it appeare.

The third estate of Mankinde, is the day of Christ, or the rising up, and reigne of the blessing, which is the restoring power, delivering mankinde from this bondage of Lust, and subduing this power of darknesse, [56] and drawing mankinde into union with the Father, making all things new, and so making peace.

And this he doth, first, by bringing mankinde back againe, to his estate of Innocencie and plaine heartednesse, and so in the eye of the world is a foole, before he be made wise.

Then secondly, he rises up in power and glory, and makes man one with himselfe, and sets him downe in rest never to fall againe.

CHAP. VI. *What the Curse is, that doth defile the Man.*

EVERY branch of Mankinde, is under one of these three estates, First, either in his Innocency; or secondly, under the power of the Curse; or thirdly, under Grace; or the power of the blessing. Now, no man hath, or can have true peace, till he be able to see this cleare distinction within himselfe; he that sees nothing but one power, nor never saw any other but one power in him, that man as yet is a slave to the Devill, But he that hath seene the two powers, to oppose each other within him, and then at last the blessing prevailes, and casts the other murderer out, and sits downe and rules King of righteousnesse, and Prince of Peace. This is Heaven, and he that sees this one power of righteousnesse and peace [57] rule, and sees the other quite falne; this man now is come to eate of the Tree of Life, and shall live for ever; and is truly entered into the one power, or new *Ierusalem*.

Whosoever lives in this life, his actions will be actions of peace, preservation, Love and life to all. But if there appeare actions of darknesse in any, whereby any part of the Creation is capable of destruction by those actions; truly then, that one power in that man is but the curse, which may be called the Power likewise; but it is but the one power of darknesse.

When a man sees the darknesse rule in others, and in himselfe; he sees himselfe in bondage, and is troubled; Now the Seed begins to arise, to bruise the Serpents head.

Lots righteous soule, or the pure Creation, man, as he is more or lesse restored from bondage, he is grieved to see the bad conversation of the wicked power, as he rules in himselfe and others; And there are many *Lots* at this day, whose righteous soule is grieved, to see how the Devill and curse rules and destroyes the Earth. The Devill rules the world; Imaginary selfe-loving Covetousnesse rules the King in the Earth; It is seen plaine, and he goes on boldly without feare;

hardnesse of heart riseth apace, proud murdering flesh growes secure, though his Judgement be near at hand.

Stand still, and you shall see the downefall of *Pharaoh* and his company. As there are time, times, and dividing of times alloted to the reigne [58] of the Beast, in outward Government; which is first the power of Magistracie, medling with matters of Conscience, in restraining or punishing, before the universall Bishop was raised; this is the first time.

Then the time of universall Bishop, till reformed Episcopacy came in, this is the second time; Then the time of reformed Episcopacie, till the variety of Independant and Presbyterian Churches, or State-Government came in; is the third time, and these two latter are called times.

And now *England* is under the dividing of time, and it is a forerunner to the rest of the Nations, and this is the Image of the Beast; and this is the variety of Churches, and differences in Religion, that is amongst men; every one pleading his priviledge, or else it is called the dividing of time, in regard the Government of the Land is taken out of the hands of one man, and put into the hands of many; this is the dividing of time, or the halfe day of the Beast, in respect of outward government.

Even so there are time, times, and dividing of time within the heart of man, which is the occasion of that outward division of times.

The first time is the state of simple plaine heartednesse, or Innocencie; when the five Sences acts in their owne light, which is the pure light of a Beast, but knowes not the power of the Seed, or of the creating spirit; but is a stranger to the spirit, and yet this state is the Image of the spirit; for this is wise, and loving and just; but not Wisdome, Love, [59] and Justice it selfe; and being tempted, it breaks out into folly, envie, and unjustice, and this is the first time of the Beasts reigne within a man.

Then the pleasure of sinne enters, or a league is made betweene that living Earth and outward objects, and the man being deceived, lookes altogether without him for good, for pleasure and for content, and followes all the pleasures of his five Sences with greedinesse; and here he would be a ruler, and some body over others; and in this estate man doth what he will, and his heart never smites him for it; he can lie, and cheat, and whore, and oppresse others, and thinks all is good, for nothing troubles him; this is the state of prodigality or presumption. And this is *Esau*, the hairy mans Kingdome; And this is the first step of his fall, eating the Aple.

Then there followes a time of trouble of minde, arising for that pleasure of selfe-seeking delight, and this is called trouble for mispent time, whereby he meets with many rubs in his good name, in his health of body, and in his outward livelihood amongst fellow-creatures, and now he begins to rebate of his wildnesse and folly; and the Beast or sensitive power begins to be a little tamer, and more moderate; yet Covetousnesse (that Beast) reignes still, and that with more force within, yet this is a cooler time of the day then the former was, for he begins to consider what he doth; yet here is no rest, and this is the third time, and so these two latter degrees makes times; this is the second step of his fall.

Then comes in the dividing of time, within a man, [60] and this is, when the Law in the members fights against the Law of the minde; when a man sees his folly and the bondage of his nature, he sees himselfe a prisoner to his Lusts, and this light in him strives against darknesse in him; he sees Pride striveing against Humility, Envy against Love, contentednesse against anger, uncleannesse of flesh against chastity, sorrow against comfort, and so cries out, *Oh wretched man that I am, who shall deliver me from this body of death*, or bondage to which I am a slave? this is the third step of mans darknesse.

Well, this is the dividing of time within thee; this is the time of the battell within thee, between *Michaell* the Prince of Peace, and the red Dragon, the selfish, imaginary, covetous, murdering power, there is no quiet rest in this estate neither; nay, this dividing of time is the sharpest and hottest time.

And now one step further in the first degree of time, and then the man enters into rest; And this is, when the Seed, or blessing in thee kills that Serpent, and casts him out, and takes possession of thee, and rules in righteousnesse in thee; for now all enemies are subdued under the Anoyntings feet, and he now delivers up the Kingdome to his Father, who is the one spirit of righteousnesse and peace, in whom there is no sorrow; And this God, or Almighty ruler, becomes all in all, the alone King in that living Soule, or Earth; or the five living Sences.

[61] Now this spirit of freedome being rising up in some already, in part, assures the Creation, and gives those bodies as pledges, that he will rise up in the whole, and restore all mankinde to himselfe.

And thus those three particulars in mankinde is considered; first, the pure creation of the Living soule; the single life of the five Sences, which is called the Earth. *Oh Earth, Earth, Earth, &c.*

Secondly, the curse that hath taken mankinde, or this living Earth prisoner; and this is the power of darknesse, called sinne or bondage, and this is called likewise flesh, or carnall man; *If you by the Spirit mortifie the deeds of the flesh you shall live.*

Now the created flesh is not to be mortified, or killed by us, but preserved; therefore the curse therein is called flesh, and deeds of the flesh, because it is a meere selfish power, that would have ease, and honour, and would be counted a God, and would rule over all, to the enslaving of all to himselfe; this is the reprobate, that shall have no peace, for all peace shall be taken from this flesh.

Thirdly, the blessing, who is the seed of Life, or Christ, the righteous and rationall spirit; arising up to rule, and treading unreasonablenesse under his feet, this is the restorer, or Saviour of the captived, or the imprisoned Earth, which sets mankinde free from bondage within himselfe.

And when this power riseth up to rule, he doth not rule to enslave others to him by the murthering sword, but he drawes all men in Love to him; and [62] the union and communion of Love by him is established, in, and among the Creation.

And thus you see there are time, times, and dividing of time within the heart; and though you be come to the dividing of time, yet you are not come to the Mount of God, to true rest, till dividing of time run his course likewise.

But yet here is great comfort to burdened soules, that lies groning under the darknesse of this divideing of time within them, and that are mightily opprest by men that rules in darknesse, and oppression over them; To you I say rejoyce, your Redeemer is come, he rides upon the clouds, and he will speedily appeare for your deliverance, as he hath done for some of your brethren already, who are witnesses, that he is rising and spreading himselfe in the Earth, casting out death, hell, and bondage, and establishing life, peace, and liberty in mankinde, and in the whole creation.

Therefore whatsoever your condition is, murmur not at it, but waite, he that is come to others will come to you, and not tarrie; His power and name is Love, and he will conquer all by Love and patience; And the sonnes of strangers and enemies shall come and fall downe to him and say, thou art the alone, righteous power; take thee our Crownes, Scepters, Swords, doe thou rule, for thou art worthie.

This is the day of Sions glorie; This is the everlasting fire, that is unquenchable; this is the powerfull day of the Lord; this is the Lambe that was [63] slane, and is now risen againe; This is the well beloved sonne of the Father, in whom he delights; This is the promised Seed, the blessing of the whole Earth, who hath been hinted at, and pointed at by Prophecie, but never fully manifested in the whole creation.

But now he begins to appeare, to draw all men after him, to cast out the curse, and to set the Creation in peace; therefore thou weeping soule, cast off this sackcloth, and mourning weeds, thy redeemer is come, and he calls thee to follow him, acting love and patience.

This power of Christ takes away all peace from the flesh, and will not suffer any part of the creation to lie under a false peace any longer; And we see that while he appeares but weakly, how the peace of covetous flesh is disturbed and filled with much murmuring against the Light.

Oh, say men, if this power of universall love be advanced; this will destroy all propriety, and all trading, and bring every thing into confusion. It is true, he shall be advanced for that end, to confound the wisdome and power, and peace of the flesh that the Creation may be no longer deceived, but now at length may come into him, and rest quiet for ever.

Oh, saith Imaginary, covetous, proud, selfe-seeking flesh; If I take not the sword, to restraine the unrulinesse of mankinde; we shall not live one by another; But his intent is not in Love to peace, but that he may rule over all himselfe, and beat downe [64] others under him; And indeed this power is the cause of all warres; for if this murdering selfe-honouring power were once cast out; Love would live in peace, and know warre, division and sorrow no more.

CHAP. VII. *What the blessing is that restores him againe.*

BUT how came mans fall in at the first? I Answer. The outward objects of riches, honors, being set before the living soule, Imaginary covetousnesse, which is the absence of the true Light, moves the man to close with those objects, and to seeke content without him; and through this darke night power, warres, divisions, and discontent arises in mankinde, to teare and devoure it selfe; and so it is said to mankinde, that his destruction is of himselfe; And the misery of mankinde came in by these degrees.

First, when whole mankinde walked in singlenesse and simplicity each to other; Some bodies were more strong then others, as the elder brother was stronger then the younger, and the stronger did work for the weaker, and the whole Earth was common to all without exception; But this singlenesse and simplicity was subject to corruption and change; And the change came in thus.

[65] The stronger, or elder brother seeing the outward objects before him, thereupon imagines, and saith, why should I that doe all the worke, be such a servant to these that doe least worke, and be equall with them? It is fit I should have some larger part of the Earth then they, and be in some more esteeme then others, and that they should acknowledge me in some degree above them.

This Imagination is the Serpent that deceives the man; and as lust is thus conceived within, and the heart, or the living Soule consenting to these imaginary inventions, presently death is brought forth, and Mankinde falls from single simplicity to be full of divisions, and one member of Mankinde is separated from another, which before were all one, and looked upon each other as all one.

This is the first step of the fall, consent within being moved by outward objects of pleasure, riches, and honour for one to be above another; whereas it was the honour of the elder to help the younger, and not to tread him downe.

Secondly, it breaks forth into outward action; for this imaginary invention, in the elder brother moves him to set about, to inclose parcells of the Earth into severall divisions, and calls those inclosures proper or peculiar to himselfe, and that the younger, or weaker brother should lay no claime to it, and the younger brother lets it goe so; and presently their nakednesse appeares, that is, the imaginary covetousnesse of the heart is uncovered, and laid open to the view hereby.

[66] This dividing of the Earth into parcells, was long before it grew a strong setled custome; for plaine heartednesse did much oppose the growth of this imaginary covetousnesse, or Serpent; for when contention began to arise amongst *Abrahams* servants and *Lots*, about the Earth; one side would have so much, and the other side so much; Well, said single hearted *Abraham*, let there be no strife betweene us, for we are brethren; Let us spread farther; and so the one went East, and the other West, and gave more roome in the Earth each to other, and then they were quiet; this is the first breaking forth into action, to make division.

Then next to this, mankinde began to buy and sell these inclosures of Land, one of another, which the creating spirit of righteousnesse gave them no command to doe; for by reason of this bargaining, the younger, or weaker brother is more forcibly shut out of the Earth, and so here is a foundation laid, to steale the Earth by craft, and to murder one another by the sword.

For now saith the Buyer, this parcell of Land is mine. I have paid the fruit of my labours for it, to be properly my owne. But the younger brother comes in, and saith, the land is our portion by creation as well as yours, and we give no consent to be shut out; therefore what authority had you to buy, or the other to sell; by thus doing you cheat us, and cast us out of the Earth; And from hence now divisions and wars begins to arise betweene the brothers.

[67] And so the elder brother *Cain* kills the younger brother *Abel*; *Cain* was subtle and covetous, and *Abel* single hearted, and molested *Cain*, and opposed him in his selfe-seeking Principle, or imaginary invention, to raise himselfe to be above others; thereupon anger ariseth in *Cain*, and he kills his brother, and removes him out of the way, though Conscience tormented him afterwards for it.

And by this murdering power, over-awing one another, the cheating Art of buying and selling, and of dividing the Land into parcells, prevailes amongst mankinde; till at last *Moses* was raised, who was the perfectest man in his time, and he seeing mankinde was run into this division,

He endeavors to keep peace, and to prevent war and bloodshed, he makes a Law, wherein there was much equity betweene man and man, called ten Commandements, wherein every man is limited in his owne propriety; so that if another coveted his Neighbours wife, Land, house, or servant, it was his sinne, and was to be accursed or punished, by a generall consent of all the people; And they all said Amen to this Law; and said they would observe it, and doe it.

Yet saith *Moses*, though this be a Law, setling peace for the present; yet I am not he that shall restore you to your first singlenesse and Innocencie; for a Prophet shall the Lord your God raise up like me, that shall doe that restoring worke; and him [68] shall you heare; and he shall deliver *Jacob* from his sinne, and Israell from his transgression.

And here he points out Christ, who is the power of universall Love; and tells them that whosoever will not heare the voyce of that restoring Prophet, shall be cut off from amongst the people.

And yet this buying and selling, and *Moses* Law of equity to preserve peace, was part of the fall, for it could not keep them in peace together, but still mankinde did molest one another, and rise higher in divisions, and fell to further contention, Covetousnesse, and Pride amongst themselves.

The stronger brother goes further in his imaginary ambitious invention, and makes warre against the younger, or weaker brother, and takes their inclosures by force from them; and either kills them, or turnes them out of the Land, which they had bestowed labour upon; and so did break *Moses* Law, which said, thou shall not kill, thou shalt not steale.

And now divisions and enmity is risen to the height, and the power of the Sword is the very strength of the curse, and is the murderer; for this takes not away propriety from others, by labour, or by buying and selling; but by cruell violence and force, casting downe one, setting up another by force, and now Mankinde is in the extremity of division.

And they that enjoy the land, they or their fathers got it by the Sword, and they keep possession [69] by the Sword, and no man regards the Law of righteous Creation, or of *Moses* Law of Equity; for every man seeks himselfe, and thinks it equity for others to regard him, and is offended at those that doe not regard him; and the whole Earth is filled with this devouring self-righteousnes.

Therefore high time for the great Prophet, which *Moses* spake of to arise, to restore falne man, or else no flesh shall be saved; for one is bent to destroy another; And all is for the Earth who shall enjoy it.

And doth not the nakednesse of man appeare very manifest, that some parties are truly like *Dives*, that fares deliciously every day, goes in rich apparell, silke, and gold upon their clothes; Chests full of silver, houses full of corne, and other fruits of the Earth; And yet sees others starve for want before their faces; And these very rich men notwithstanding makes a profession of Christ, as though they were his servants; Oh doth not these men openly declare their hypocrisie, and discovers their owne nakednesse, that all the world may see, that they are proud, covetous, envious, and the power of darknesse it selfe, and so open enemies and traytors to Christ; All the title they have to their Land is by the power of the sword. Did Jesus Christ doe so? Oh no, No; he was universall Love; and bids every one doe as they would be done by.

This power of the sword doth not only kill and rob, but by his Lawes made and upheld by his [70] power; he hedges the weake out of the Earth, and either starves them, or else forces them through poverty to take from others, and then hangs them for so doing.

They that have the greatest power of the sword in their hands, doe kill, and take away the labours of others, and say it is righteous; but if a weaker hand doth but take from others to supplie necessaries, the other calls this unrighteous, and hangs them for it; surely the King of righteousnesse is not so partiall a God, as to call one and the same action good in his hand, that is the stronger, and bad in his hand, that is the weaker brother.

No, no; This is the righteousnesse of the man of sinne; this is the righteousnesse of the Scribes, Pharisees, and *Iudas*, that counts every thing righteous that pleases them, and every thing unrighteous that displeases them; This is the extremity of the curse, and yet this is the Law that every one now adayes dotes upon; when the plaine truth is, the Law of propriety is the shamefull nakednesse of Mankinde, and as farre from the Law of Christ, as light from darknesse.

And yet Souldiers and Lawyers, and all that crie up this power of propriety, which is both brought in, and upheld by the murdering sword, would be called Saints and members of Christ.

Truly you are all deceived, you are members and actors of the curse, which is the destruction and bondage of the Creation; you are that power [71] that hedges some into the Earth, and hedges others out, and takes to your selves by the power of the killing sword; A liberty to rule over the labours and persons of your fellow-creatures, who are flesh of your flesh, and bone of your bone; And you doe the very same things, in a higher degree and nature, for which you hang other men for, punishing others for such actions as you call sinne, and yet you live in the daily action your selves; taking the Earth from the weaker brother, and so killing him by poverty or prison all day long.

Now this enmity that brought in this division; first of inclosing; then of buying and selling, then of killing one another for the Earth, is the curse within of imaginary covetousnesse, and it was bred by the presentment of outward objects, tempting the five Senses, or the living Soule.

And all the strivings that is in Mankinde, is for the Earth, who shall have it; whether some particular persons shall have it, and the rest have none, or whether the Earth shall be a common treasury to all without respect of persons.

And this is the battell, that is fought between the two powers, which is propriety on the one hand, called the Devill, or covetousnesse, or community on the other hand, called Christ, or universall Love. And as Christ doth cast covetousnesse out of the heart, so propriety is cast out from amongst men, and mankinde will not only become single hearted againe, but will walke in the light of pure Reason [72] and Love, and never fall againe into divisions, but shall be so acquainted with the wyles of Satan, that he shall utterly reject, and abhor his imaginary inticement; As Jesus Christ rejected the temptation of objects; And that Satan, or tempter without prevailed not, because the Anoynting was in him, that was stronger then flesh.

Now this same power in man, that causes divisions and war is called by some men the state of nature, which every man brings into the world with him.

But this Law of darknesse in the members is not the state of Nature; for nature, or the living soule is in bondage to it, and grones under it, waiting to be delivered from it, and is glad to heare of a Saviour.

Looke upon a childe that is new borne, or till he growes up to some few yeares, he is innocent, harmelesse, humble, patient, gentle, easie to be entreated, not envious; And this is *Adam,* or mankinde in his

Innocency; and this continues till outward objects intice him to pleasure, or seeke content without him; And when he consents, or suffers the imaginary Covetousnesse within to close with the objects, Then he falls, and is taken captive, and falls lower and lower.

First, into the slavery of that power of lusts within, leading him forth to act all manner of selfishnesse, with greedinesse to the destruction of others.

[73] And then falls from this delight into trouble of minde, and touch of Conscience, and inward torment, and so falls deeper and deeper into Hell, till the Seed or blessing rise up in him to worke deliverance, and then carrie him back againe, and lead him into the wayes of truth.

And thus we see how mankinde came to fall from his innocencie; and that was by closing to outward objects for content, with inward imaginary Covetousnesse, to finde life in those objects without him.

And mans recovery will be to reject outward objects; and to close with the spirit of truth, life, and peace within, preferring this Kingdome within, before the outward Kingdome.

It is said that Christ was tempted in all things, like as we are tempted. Now how are we tempted? but by presentment of outward objects before us, and when the life of the five Sences closes therewith, thinking to finde content therefrom, we are deceived, and so fall from innocencie.

As for example, if objects of riches be laid before me, and my inward covetousnesse close therewith, I fall; or if the beauty of the female sex be set before me, If my inward lust close therewith excessively, running after variety of strange flesh, I fall.

But if covetousnesse and lust be killed, or doth not breath in me, then, though those objects be tendered to me, I reject them; and so I fall not; And [74] now Satan or the tempter, which are the outward objects finds nothing in me.

And thus it was said of Jesus Christ, that when the Tempter came to him he found nothing in him, that is, Jesus Christ had not an imaginary covetous power in him, to seeke a Kingdome, or happinesse without himselfe, in those objects of pleasure, riches, and honours of the world, but preferred the Kingdome within him before that without him.

And so he was said to have no sinne, because there was nothing in him that consented to the temptation without; he made use of outward objects in moderation, for the safety and peace of his body, but desired nothing in excesse, or immoderately.

The power of darknesse which is Covetousnesse, and Imagination which is the devouring Dragon, had no place in Heaven, that is, in him; for the Dragon was cast out, and the Godhead did dwell bodily in him, in the fulnesse of righteousnesse and peace.

Now I desire any man to shew by experience, any other Devill, or darke power, then these two, that is, The objects without, and the powers of the curse within, joyning in consent together, to enslave the Earth, or the living Soule, which is the innocencie of the five Sences.

While these two joyne together, and meet in consent, Mankinde enters into sorrow, and hath [no] true rest,

But when the power of Lust is killed within, by [75] the blessing, or the seed rising up, then outward objects troubles not, nor enslaves the man. For then a man is content with his present condition, and seeks for a Kingdome within, which moth and rust cannot corrupt, nor theeves breake through and steale; If he have riches, he dotes not upon them, he knowes not how to use them; If he be poore, he is quiet and content; If he be at liberty he is content, if in prison he is content.

So then kill Covetousnesse, or that imaginary darknesse within; And the Devill is kill'd when the Tempter comes, he shall finde nothing in you; he that is free within, is moved to excesse, or unrationall action by no outward object; but he that is not free within, is moved by every object.

And this is the Reason why many people are so angry, and bitter, and flies upon their neighbours with reviling, and reproachfull words, or envious actions, because they are slaves to their flesh; they are in bondage within, they know not liberty; It is the night time with them, the sonne of Love, righteousnesse, and peace is not yet risen up in them.

Therefore they that are at liberty within, in whom the Seed is risen to rule, doe conquer all enemies by Love and patience, and make use of any outward object with moderation, and knows no excesse.

The powers of the curse, he subdues others by the murdering sword, and thereby enslaves others to him; as we see the government of all Nations [76] is this, and the darke power in every mans heart is this; which indeed is the Devills Kingdome that yet rules.

But now the blessing, he subdues his enemies by Love, and saves, and gives life and freedome to his enemies; he first brings mankinde back to pure creation, and then rises up, and rules King of righteousnesse within, and so keeps the man, that the curse never enslaves him againe, and so he puts the man into a better condition then he was in before.

This Seed or Christ then is to be seen within, to save you from the curse within, to free you from bondage within; he is no Saviour that stands at a distance; therefore your publick Ministers bewitches you, by telling you of a Saviour at a distance.

The enmity which burdens you is within, Even the Law of your members that wars against the law of your minde; so that the members are the creature; And that curse wars within them, and so troubles and enslaves the members.

Therefore your Saviour must be a power within you, to deliver you from that bondage within; the outward Christ, or the outward God, are but men Saviours, such as *Moses, Ioshua,* and Judges were, and such as Kings are, and these Gods sometimes proves Devills. Surely such Preachers as tells you your God and Saviour is without, they know not the spirit, they are servants to the curse, their [77] Kingdome is all without, and therefore would have you to seeke for a Kingdome without that lies in objects; for that Kingdome of Christ within they know not.

And here I shall end with this question. What are the greatest sinnes in the world? I answer. These two; First for a man to lock up the treasuries of the Earth in Chests and houses; and suffer it to rust or moulder, while others starve for want to whom it belongs, and it belongs to all; This is the greatest sinne against universall Love; this is the destroying sinne, this is *Achans* sinne; this is the action of Covetousnesse.

The second sinne is like to this, and is the same in nature with the other; And this is for any man, or men, first to take the Earth by the power of the murdering sword from others; and then by the Lawes of their owne making, doe hang, or put to death any who takes the fruits of the Earth to supply his necessaries, from places or persons, where there is more then can be made use of by that particular family, where it is hoorded up.

And he said, sonne of man, seest thou what they doe? Thou shalt see greater abominations. Ezekiel. 8. 6.

FINIS.

THE LAW OF FREEDOM IN A PLAT-
FORM *or* TRUE MAGISTRACY
RESTORED

T HE title page is dated 1652 and the Dedicatory
Epistle to Oliver Cromwell, November 5,
1651. Thomason dated his copy February 20, 1652.
Winstanley's name appears both on the title page
and at the end of the Epistle, and the initials J. W.
at the end of the address to the reader.

Copies are to be found in the following collections: The Bodleian, The Congregational Library
(London), The Guildhall Library, The Thomason Library at the British Museum, and the Library of the University of Chicago.

The text is reproduced from the copy in the Library of the University of Chicago.

[3] TO HIS EXCELLENCY OLIVER CROMWEL,

GENERAL OF THE COMMONWEALTHS

ARMY IN ENGLAND, SCOTLAND, AND

IRELAND

SIR,

God hath honored you with the highest Honor of any man since *Moses* time, to be the Head of a People, who have cast out an Oppressing *Pharaoh:* For when the *Norman* Power had conquered our Forefathers, he took the free use of our English Ground from them, and made them his servants. And God hath made you a successful Instrument to cast out that Conqueror, and to recover our Land and Liberties again, by your Victories, out of that *Norman* hand.

That which is yet wanting on your part to be done, is this, To see the Oppressors power to be cast out with his person; And to see that the free possession of the Land and Liberties be put into the hands of the oppressed Commoners of *England*.

For the Crown of Honor cannot be yours, neither can those Victories be called Victories on your part, till the Land and Freedoms won be possessed by them who adventured person and purse for them.

Now you know Sir, that the Kingly Conqueror was not beaten by you onely as you are a single man, nor by the Officers of the Army joyned to you; but by the hand and assistance of the Commoners, whereof [4] some came in person, and adventured their lives with you; others stayd at home, and planted the Earth, and payd Taxes and Freequarter to maintain you that went to war.

So that whatsoever is recovered from the Conqueror, is recovered by a joynt consent of the Commoners: therefore it is all Equity, That all the Commoners who assisted you, should be set free from the Conquerors power with you: As *Davids* Law was, *The spoyl shall be di-*

vided between them who went to war, and them who stayd at home.

And now you have the Power of the Land in your hand, you must do one of these two things: First, either set the Land free to the oppressed Commoners, who assisted you, and payd the Army their wages: and then you will fulfil the Scriptures and your own Engagements, and so take possession of your deserved Honor.

Or secondly, you must onely remove the Conquerors Power out of the Kings hand into other mens, maintaining the old Laws still: And then your Wisdom and Honor is blasted for ever; and you will either lose your self, or lay the Foundation of greater Slavery to posterity then you ever knew.

You know that while the King was in the height of his oppressing Power, the People onely whispered in private Chambers against him: But afterwards it was preached upon the house tops, That he was a Tyrant and a Traytor to *Englands* peace; and he had his overturn.

The righteous Power in the Creation is the same still: If you, and those in power with you, should be found walking in the Kings steps, can you secure your selves or posterities from an overturn? Surely No.

The Spirit of the whole Creation (who is God) is about the Reformation of the World, and he will go forward in his work: For if he would not spare Kings, who have sat so long at his right hand, governing the World, neither will he regard you, unless your ways be found more righteous then the Kings.

You have the eyes of the People all the Land over, nay I think I may say all neighboring Nations over, waiting to see what you will do: And the eyes of your oppressed friends, who lie yet under Kingly power, are waiting to have the possession given them of that Freedom in the Land, which was promised by you, if in case you prevailed. Lose not your Crown; take it up, and wear it. But know, that it is no Crown of Honor, till Promises and Engagements made by you be performed to your friends. *He that continues to the end, shall receive the Crown.* Now you do not see the end of your work, unless the Kingly Law and Power be removed as well as his person.

[5] *Jonah's* Gourd is a remembrancer to men in high places.

The worm in the Earth gnawed the root, and the Gourd dyed, and *Jonah* was offended.

Sir, I pray bear with me; my spirit is upon such a lock that I must speak plain to you, lest it tell me another day, If thou hadst spoke plain, things might have been amended.

The Earth wherein your Gourd grows is the Commoners of *England*.

The Gourd is that Power which covers you, which will be established to you by giving the People their true Freedoms, and not otherwise.

The root of your Gourd is the heart of the People, groaning under Kingly Bondage, and desiring a *Commonwealths* Freedom in their English Earth.

The worm in the Earth, now gnawing at the root of your Gourd, is Discontents, because Engagements and Promises made to them by such as have power, are not kept.

And this worm hath three heads: The first is a spirit waiting opportunities till a blasting wind arise to cause your Gourd to wither; and yet pretends fair to you, &c.

Another spirit shelters under your Gourd for a livelyhood, and will say as you say in all things; and these are called honest, yet no good friends to you nor the *Commonwealth*, but to their own bellies.

There is a third spirit, which is faithful indeed, and plain-dealing, and many times for speaking truth plainly he is cashiered, imprisoned, and crushed: And the Oppressions layd upon this spirit kindles the fire, which the two former waits to warm themselves at.

Would you have your Gourd stand for ever? Then cherish the root in the Earth; that is, the heart of your friends, the oppressed *Commoners* of *England*, by killing the Worm. And nothing will kill this worm, but performance of professions, words, and promises, that they may be made free men from Tyranny.

It may be you will say to me, *What shall I do?* I answer, You are in place and power to see all Burthens taken off from your friends, the *Commoners* of *England*. You will say, *What are those Burthens?*

I will instance in some, both which I know in my own experience, and which I hear the people dayly complaining of, and groaning under, looking upon you and waiting for Deliverance.

Most people cry, We have payd Taxes, given Freequarter, wasted our Estates, and lost our Friends in the Wars, and the Taskmasters multiply over us more then formerly. I have asked divers this question, *Why do you say so?*

[6] Some have answered me, That Promises, Oaths, and Engagements have been made as a Motive to draw us to assist in the Wars; That priviledges of Parliament and Liberties of Subjects should be preserved, and that all Popery, and Episcopacy, and Tyranny should be rooted out; and these promises are not performed: Now there is an opportunity to perform them.

For first, say they, The current of succeeding Parliaments is stopt, which is one of the greatest Priviledges (and peoples Liberties) for Safety and Peace; and if that continue stopt, we shall be more offended by an hereditary Parliament, then we were oppressed by an hereditary King.

And for the Commoners, who were called Subjects, while the Kingly Conqueror was in power, have not as yet their Liberties granted them; I will instance them in order, according as the common whisperings are among the people.

For say they, The burdens of the Clergy remains still upon us, in a three-fold nature.

First, If any man declare his Judgment in the things of God, contrary to the Clergies report, or the mind of some high Officers, they are cashiered, imprisoned, crushed, and undone, and made sinners for a word, as they were in the Popes and Bishops days; so that though their names be cast out, yet their High Commission Courts Power remains still, persecuting men for Conscience sake, when their actions are unblameable.

Secondly, In many Parishes there are old formal ignorant Episcopal Priests established; and some Ministers, who are bitter Enemies to Commonwealths Freedom, and Friends to Monarchy, are established Preachers, and are continually buzzing their subtle principles into the minds of the people, to undermine the Peace of our declared Commonwealth, causing a disaffection of spirit among neighbors, who otherwise would live in peace.

Thirdly, The burden of Tythes remains still upon our Estates, which was taken from us by the Kings, and given to the Clergy, to maintain them by our labours: so that though their preaching fill the minds of many with madness, contention, and unsatisfied doubting, because their imaginary and ungrounded Doctrines cannot be understood by them, yet we must pay them large Tythes for so doing; this is Oppression.

Fourthly, If we go to the Lawyer, we find him to sit in the Conquerors Chair, though the Kings be removed, maintaining the Kings Power to the height, for in many Courts and cases of Law, the Wil of a Judg & Lawyer rules above the letter of the Law, and many Cases and Suits are lengthened to the great vexation of the Clients, and to the lodging of their Estates in the purse of the unbounded Lawyer: So that we see, though other men be under a sharp Law, yet many of the great Lawyers are not, but still do act their will, [7] as the Conqueror did; as I have heard some belonging to the Law say, *What cannot we do?*

Fifthly, Say they, If we look upon the Customs of the Law it self, it is the same it was in the Kings days, only the name is altered; as if the Commoners of *England* had paid their Taxes, Free-quarter, and shed their blood, not to reform, but to baptize the Law into a new name, from *Kingly Law*, to *State Law;* by reason whereof, the spirit of discontent is strengthened, to increase more Suits of Law, then formerly was known to be: And so as the Sword pulls down Kingly Power with one hand, the Kings old Law builds up Monarchy again with the other.

And indeed the main Work of Reformation lies in this, to reform the Clergy, Lawyers, and Law; for all the Complaints of the Land are wrapped up within them three, not in the person of a King.

Shall men of other Nations say, That notwithstanding all those rare wits in the Parliament and Army of *England*, yet they could not reform the Clergy, Lawyer, and Law, but must needs establish all as the Kings left them?

Will not this blast all our Honor, and make all Monarchial Members laugh in their sleeves, to see the Government of our Commonwealth to be built upon the Kingly Laws and Principles?

I have asked divers Souldiers what they fought for; they answered, they could not tell; and it is very true, they cannot tell indeed, if the Monarchial Law be established without Reformation. But I wait to see what will be done; and I doubt not but to see our Commonwealths Government to be built upon his own Foundation.

Sixthly, If we look into Parishes, the burdens there are many.

First, For the Power of Lords of Manors remains still over their Brethren, requiring Fines and Heriots; beating them off the free use of the Common Land, unless their Brethren will pay them Rent; exacting obedience, as much as they did, and more, when the King was in Power.

Now saith the people, By what Power do these maintain their Title over us? Formerly they held Title from the King, as he was the Conquerors Successor: But have not the Commoners cast out the King, and broke the band of that Conquest? Therefore in equity they are free from the slavery of that Lordly Power.

Secondly, In Parishes where Commons lie, the rich *Norman* Freeholders, or the new (more covetous) Gentry, over-stock the Commons with Sheep and Cattle; so that inferior Tenants and poor Laborers can hardly keep a Cow, but half starve her; so that the poor are kept poor still, and the Common Freedom of the Earth is kept from them, and the poor have no more [8] relief then they had when the King (or Conqueror) was in power.

Thirdly, In many Parishes two or three of the great ones bears all the sway, in making Assessments, over-awing Constables and other Officers; and when time was to quarter Souldiers, they would have a hand in that, to ease themselves, and over-burden the weaker sort; and many times make large sums of money over and above the Justices Warrant in Assessments, and would give no accompt why, neither durst the inferior people demand an accompt, for he that spake should be sure to be crushed the next opportunity; and if any have complained to Committees or Justices, they have been either wearied out by delays and waiting, or else the offence hath been by them smothered up; so that we see one great man favored another, and the poor oppressed have no relief.

Fourthly, There is another grievance which the people are much troubled at, and that is this; Country people cannot sell any Corn or other fruits of the Earth in a Market Town, but they must either pay Toll, or be turned out of Town: Now say they, This is a most shameful thing, that we must part with our estates in Taxes and Free-quarter to purchase the Freedom of the Land, and the Freedom of the Towns, and yet this Freedom must be still given from us, into the hands of a covetous *Norman* Toll-Taker, according to the Kings old burdensom Laws, and contrary to the Liberty of a free Commonwealth.

Now saith the whisperings of the people, The inferior Tenants and Laborers bears all the burdens, in laboring the Earth, in paying Taxes and Free-quarter beyond their strength, and in furnishing the Armies with Souldiers, who bear the greatest burden of the War; and yet the

Gentry, who oppress them, and that live idle upon their labours, carry away all the comfortable livelyhood of the Earth.

For is not this a common speech among the people, We have parted with our Estates, we have lost our Friends in the Wars, which we willingly gave up, because Freedom was promised us; and now in the end we have new Task-masters, and our old burdens increased: and though all sorts of people have taken an Engagement to cast out Kingly Power, yet Kingly Power remains in power still in the hands of those who have no more right to the Earth then our selves.

For say the people, If the Lords of Manors and our Task-masters hold Title to the Earth over us from the old Kingly power, behold that power is beaten and cast out.

And two Acts of Parliament are made. The one to cast out Kingly power, back'd by the Engagement against King and House of Lords. The other to make *England* a free Commonwealth.

[9] And if Lords of Mannors lay claim to the earth over us, from the Armies Victories over the King; then we have as much right to the Land as they, because our labours, and blood, and death of friends, were the purchasers of the Earths freedome as well as theirs.

And is not this a slavery, say the People, That though there be Land enough in *England*, to maintain ten times as many people as are in it, yet some must beg of their brethren, or work in hard drudgery for day wages for them, or starve, or steal, and so be hanged out of the way, as men not fit to live in the earth, before they must be suffered to plant the waste land for their livelihood, unlesse they will pay Rent to their brethren for it? wel, this is a burthen the Creation groans under; and the subjects (so called) have not their Birth-right Freedomes granted them from their brethren, who hold it from them by club law, but not by righteousness.

And who now must we be subject to, seeing the Conqueror is gone?

I Answer, we must either be subject to a Law, or to mens wils. If to a Law, then all men in *England* are subjects, or ought to be, thereunto: but what Law that is to which every one ought to be subject is not yet established in execution. If any say the old Kings Laws are the Rule, then it may be Answered, That those Laws are so full of confusion, that few knows when they obey and when not, because they were the Laws of a Conqueror to hold the people in subjection to the will of the Conqueror; therefore that cannot be the rule for every one: besides, we dayly see many actions done by State Officers, which they have no Law to justifie them in, but their Prerogative will.

And again if we must be subject to men, then what men must we be subject to, seeing one man hath as much right to the earth as another, for no man now stands as a Conqueror over his Brethren by the Law of righteousness?

You will say, We must be subject to the Ruler; it is true, but not to suffer the Rulers to call the Earth theirs and not ours, for by so doing they betray their trust, and run into the line of Tyranny, and we lose our freedome, and from thence Enmity and Wars arise.

A Ruler is worthy double honour when he rules well, that is, when he himself is subject to the Law, and requires all others to be subject thereunto and makes it his work to see the Laws obeyed, and not his own will, and such Rulers are faithfull, and they are to be subjected unto us therein, for all Commonwealths Rulers are servants to, not Lords and Kings over the people. But you will say, Is not the Land your brothers? and you cannot take away another mans Right by claiming a share therein with him.

I Answer, It is his either by creation right, or by right of Conquest: If [10] by Creation right he call the earth his and not mine; then it is mine as well as his, for the Spirit of the whole Creation, who made us both, is no respecter of persons.

And if by Conquest he call the earth his and not mine, it must be either by the Conquest of the Kings over the Commoners, or by the Conquest of the Commoners over the Kings.

If he claim the earth to be his from the Kings Conquest, The Kings are beaten and cast out and that title is undone.

If he claim Title to the earth to be his from the Conquest of the Commoners over the Kings, then I have right to the Land as well as my brother, for my brother without me, nor I without my brother, did not cast out the Kings, but both together assisting with person and purse, we prevailed, so that I have by this Victory as equall a share in the earth which is now redeemed as my brother, by the Law of righteousnesse.

If my brother still say he will be Landlord (through his covetous ambition) and I must pay him Rent, or else I shall not live in the Land, then does he take my right from me, which I have purchased by my money in Taxes, free quarter and blood. And O thou Spirit of the whole Creation, who hath this Title to be called *King of Righteousness, and Prince of Peace;* judge thou between my brother and me, Whether this be righteous, &c.

And now, say the people, is not this a grievous thing that our brethren that will be Landlords right or wrong, will make Laws, and call for a Law to be made to imprison, crush, nay put to death, any that denies God, Christ, and Scripture; and yet they will not practise that golden Rule, *Do to another as thou wouldst have another do to thee,* which God, Christ, and Scriptures, hath Enacted for a Law? are not these men guilty of death by their own Law, which is the words of their own mouth? is it not a flat denyall of God and Scripture?

O the confusion and thick darkness that hath over-spread our Brethren is very great, I have no power to remove it, but lament it in the secrets of my heart; when I see Prayers, Sermons, Fasts, Thanksgiving, directed to this God in words and shews, and when I come to look for actions of obedience to the Righteous Law, suitable to such a profession, I finde them men of another Nation, saying, and not doing; like an old Courtier saying *Your Servant,* when he was an Enemy. I wil say no more, but groan and waite for a restoration.

Thus Sir, I have reckoned up some of those burdens which the people groan under.

And I being sensible hereof was moved in my self, to present this Platform of Commonwealths Government unto you, wherein I have declared a full [11] Commonwealths Freedome, according to the Rule of Righteousness, which is Gods Word. It was intended for your view above two years ago, but the disorder of the Times caused me to lay it aside, with a thought never to bring it to light, &c. Likewise I hearing that M. *Peters* [1] and some others Propounded this request, That the Word of God might be consulted with to finde out a healing Government, which I liked well, and waited to see such a Rule come forth, for there are good rules in the Scripture if they were obeyed and practised: thereupon

I laid aside this in silence, and said, I would not make it publick; but

---

[1] Hugh Peters was a member of a commission of twenty-one to amend the laws. He published a pamphlet, *Good Work for a Good Magistrate,* in 1651. Note Winstanley's very qualified approval of searching the Scriptures for just law; for him the glory of the Jewish commonwealth was that it had no beggars.

this word was like fire in my bones ever and anon, *Thou shalt not bury thy talent in the earth*, therefore I was stirred up to give it a resurrection, and to pick together as many of my scattered papers as I could finde, and to compile them into this method, which I do here present to you, and do quiet my own spirit.

And now I have set the candle at your door, for you have power in your hand, in this other added opportunity, to Act for Common Freedome if you will; I have no power.

It may be here are some things inserted which you may not like, yet other things you may like, therefore I pray you read it, and be as the industrious Bee, suck out the honey and cast away the weeds.

Though this Platform be like a peece of Timber rough hewd, yet the discreet workmen may take it, and frame a handsome building out of it.

It is like a poor man that comes cloathed to your door in a torn country garment, who is unacquainted with the learned Citizens unsetled forms and fashions; take of the clownish language, for under that you may see beauty.

It may be you will say, If Tythes be taken from the Priests and Impropriators, and Copy-hold Services from Lords of Mannors, how shal they be provided for again; for is it not unrighteous to take their estates from them?

I Answer, when Tythes were first enacted, and Lordly power drawn over the backs of the oppressed, the Kings and Conquerors made no scruple of Conscience to take it, though the people lived in sore bondage of poverty for want of it; and can there be scruple of conscience to make restitution of this which hath been so long stoln goods? It is no scruple arising from the Righteous Law, but from covetousness, who goes away sorrowfull to heare he must part with all to follow Righteousness and Peace.

But though you do take away Tythes, and the Power of Lords of Mannors, yet there will be no want to them, for they have the freedome of the Common stock, they may send to the Storehouses for what they want, and live more free then now they do, for now they are in care and vexation by servants, [12] by casualties, by being cheated in buying and selling, and many other incumbrances, but then they will be free from all, for the common Storehouses is every mans riches, not any ones.

Is not buying and selling a righteous Law? No, It is the Law of the Conqueror, but not the righteous Law of Creation: how can that be righteous which is a cheat? for is not this a common practise, when he hath a bad Horse or Cow, or any bad commodity, he will send it to the Market, to cheat some simple plain-hearted man or other, and when he comes home, will laugh at his neighbours hurt, and much more &c.

When Mankinde began to buy and sell, then did he fall from his Innocency; for then they began to oppress and cozen one another of their Creation Birth-right: As for example; If the Land belong to three persons, and two of them buy and sell the Earth, and the third give no consent, his Right is taken from him, and his posterity is engaged in a War.

When the Earth was first bought and sold, many gave no consent: As when our Crown Lands, and Bishops Lands were sold, some foolish Soldiers yeelded, and covetous Officers were active in it, to advance themselves above their Brethren: but many, who payd Taxes and Free-quarter for the purchase of it, gave no consent, but declared against it, as an unrighteous thing, depriving posterity of their Birth-rights and Freedoms.

Therefore this buying and selling did bring in, and still doth bring in, discontents and wars, which have plagued Mankinde sufficiently for so doing. And the Nations of the world will never learn to beat their swords into plowshares, and their spears into pruning hooks, and leave of warring, until this cheating device of buying and selling be cast out among the rubbish of Kingly power.

But shall not one man be richer then another?

There is no need of that; for Riches make men vain-glorious, proud, and to oppress their Brethren; and are the occasion of wars.

No man can be rich, but he must be rich, either by his own labors, or by the labors of other men helping him: If a man have no help from his neighbor, he shall never gather an Estate of hundreds and thousands a year: If other men help him to work, then are those Riches his Neighbors, as well as his; for they be the fruit of other mens labors as well as his own.

But all rich men live at ease, feeding and clothing themselves by the labors of other men, not by their own; which is their shame, and not their Nobility; for it is a more blessed thing to give then to receive: But rich men receive all they have from the laborers hand, and what they give, they give away other mens labors, not their own; Therefore they are not righteous Actors in the Earth.

[13] But shall not one man have more Titles of Honor then another?

Yes: As a man goes through Offices, he rises to Titles of Honor, till he comes to the highest Nobility, to be a faithful Commonwealths man in a Parliament House. Likewise he who findes out any secret in *Nature*, shall have a Title of Honor given him, though he be a young man. But no man shall have any Title of Honor till he win it by industry, or come to it by age, or Office-bearing. Every man that is above sixty years of age shall have respect as a man of Honor by all others that are younger, as is shewed hereafter.

Shall every man count his Neighbors house as his own, and live together as one Family?

No: Though the Earth and Storehouses be common to every Family, yet every Family shall live apart as they do; and every mans house, wife, children, and furniture for ornament of his house, or any thing which he hath fetched in from the Storehouses, or provided for the necessary use of his Family, is all a propriety to that Family, for the peace thereof. And if any man offer to take away a mans wife, children, or furniture of his house, without his consent, or disturb the peace of his dwelling, he shall suffer punishment as an Enemy to the *Commonwealths* Government; as is mentioned in the *Platform* following.

Shall we have no Lawyers?

There is no need of them, for there is to be no buying and selling; neither any need to expound Laws; for the bare letter of the Law shall be both Judg and Lawyer, trying every mans actions: And seeing we shall have successive *Parliaments* every year, there will be Rules made for every action a man can do.

But there is to be Officers chosen yearly in every parish, to see the Laws executed according to the letter of the Laws; so that there will be no long work in trying of Offences, as it is under Kingly Government, to get the Lawyers mony, and to enslave the Commoners to the Conquerors prerogative Law, or Will. The sons of contention, *Simeon* and *Levi*, must not bear Rule in a free *Commonwealth*.

At the first view, you may say, this is a strange Government: but I pray judg nothing before tryal. Lay this Platform of Commonwealths Government in one scale, and lay Monarchy, or Kingly Government, in the other scale, and see which give true weight to righteous Freedom and Peace. There is no middle path between these two; for a man must either be a free and true Commonwealths man, or a Monarchial tyrannical Royalist.

If any say, This will bring poverty; surely they mistake: for there will be plenty of all Earthly Commodities, with less labor and trouble then now it is under Monarchy. There will be no want, for every man may keep as [14] plentiful a house as he will, and never run into debt, for common stock pays for all.

If you say, Some will live idle; I answer, No: It will make idle persons to become workers, as is declared in the *Platform;* There shall be neither Beggar nor idle person.

If you say, This will make men quarrel and fight:

I answer, No: It will turn swords into plowshares, and settle such a peace in the Earth, as Nations shall learn War no more. Indeed the Government of Kings is a breeder of Wars, because men being put into the straits of poverty, are moved to fight for Liberty, and to take one anothers Estates from them, and to obtain Mastery. Look into all Armies, and see what they do more, but make some poor, some rich; put some into freedom, and others into bondage: And is not this a plague among Mankinde?

Well, I question not but what Objections can be raised against this *Commonwealths Government;* they shall finde an Answer in this *Platform* following. I have been something large, because I could not contract my self into a lesser volume, having so many things to speak of.

I do not say, nor desire, That every one shall be compelled to practise this *Commonwealths Government;* for the spirits of some will be Enemies at first, though afterwards will prove the most cordial and true friends thereunto.

Yet I desire, That the *Commonwealths* Land, which is the ancient Commons and waste Land, and the Lands newly got in, by the Armies Victories, out of the oppressors hands, as Parks, Forests, Chases, and the like, may be set free to all that have lent assistance, either of person or purse, to obtain it; and to all that are willing to come in to the practice of this Government, and be obedient to the Laws thereof: And for others, who are not willing, let them stay in the way of buying and selling, which is the Law of the Conqueror, till they be willing.

And so I leave this in your hand, humbly prostrating my self and it before you, and remain

Novemb. 5.   A true Lover of Commonwealths
   1651.   Government, Peace, and Freedom,

Jerrard Winstanley.

[15] TO THE FRIENDLY AND UNBYASSED READER

READER,

I T *was the Apostles advice formerly, to try all things, and to hold fast that which is best. This Platform of Government which I offer, is the Original Righteousness and Peace in the Earth, though he hath been buried under the clods of Kingly Covetousness, Pride and Oppression a long time.*

Now he begins to have his Resurrection, despise it not while it is small; though thou understand it not at the first sight, yet open the door, and look into the house, for thou mayst see that which will satisfie thy heart in quiet rest.

To prevent thy hasty rashness, I have given thee a short Compendium of the whole.

First, Thou knowest that the Earth in all Nations is governed by buying and selling, for all the Laws of Kings hath relation thereunto.

Now this Platform following declares to thee the Government of the Earth without buying and selling, and the Laws are the Laws of a free and peaceable Commonwealth, which casts out every thing that offends; for there is no pricking Briar in all this holy Mountain of the righteous Law, or peaceable Ruler.

Every Family shall live apart, as now they do; every man shall enjoy his own wife, and every woman her own husband, as now they do; every Trade shall be improved to more excellency then now it is; all children shall be educated, and be trained up in subjection to parents and elder people more then now they are: The Earth shall be planted, and the fruits reaped, and carried into Store-houses by common assistance of every Family: The riches of the Store-houses shall be the Common Stock to every Family: There shall be no idle person nor Begger in the Land.

And because offences may arise from the spirit of unreasonable ignorance, therefore was the Law added.

515

For if any man abuse his neighbor, by provoking words, by striking his person, by offering offence to his neighbors wife or children, or to his house or furniture therein, or to live idle upon other mens labours, there are Laws to punish them sharply, and Officers to see those Laws executed, according to the right Order of Commonwealths Government, for the peace of every family in the Land.

[16] *This Commonwealths Government unites all people in a Land into one heart and mind: And it was this Government which made* Moses *to call* Abrahams *seed, one house of* Israel, *though they were many Tribes and many Families: And it may be said, Blessed is the people, whose earthly Government is the Law of Common Righteousness.*

While Israel *was under this Commonwealths Government, they were a terror to all oppressing Kings in all Nations of the World; and so will* England *be, if this righteous Law become our Governor: But when the Officers of* Israel *began to be covetous and proud, they made a breach, or as* Isaiah *said,* The Rulers of the people caused them to err; *and then the Government was altered, and fell into the hand of Kings, like other Nations, and then they fled before their enemies, and were scattered.*

The Government of Kings, is the Government of the Scribes and Pharisees, who count it no freedom, unless they be Lords of the Earth, and of their Brethren: But Commonwealths Government is the Government of Righteousness and Peace, who is no Respecter of persons.

Therefore Reader here is a tryal for thy sincerity; Thou shalt have no want of food, rayment, or freedom among Brethren in this way propounded: See now if thou canst be content, as the Scriptures say, Having food and rayment, therewith be content, and grudg not to let thy brother have the same with thee.

Dost thou pray and fast for Freedom, and give God thanks again for it? Why know that God is not partial; for if thou pray, it must be for Freedom to all; and if thou give thanks, it must be because Freedom covers all people, for this will prove a lasting Peace.

Every one is ready to say, They fight for their Country, and what they do, they do it for the good of their Country. Well, let it appear now that thou hast fought and acted for thy Countries Freedom: But if when thou hast power to settle Freedom in thy Country, thou takest the possession of the Earth into thy own particular hands, and makest thy brother work for thee, as the Kings did, thou hast fought and acted for thy self, not for thy Country; and here thy inside hypocrisie is discovered.

But here take notice, That common Freedom, which is the Rule I would have practised, and not talked on, was thy pretence; but particular Freedom to thy self was thy intent. Amend, or else thou wilt be shamed, when Knowledg doth spread to cover the Earth, even as the waters cover the Seas. And so Farewell.

J. W.

[17] THE LAW OF FREEDOM IN A PLAT-FORM; *or*, TRUE MAGISTRACY RESTORED

CHAP. I.

THE great searching of heart in these days, is to finde out where true Freedom lies, that the Commonwealth of *England* might be established in Peace.

Some say, It lies in the free use of Trading, and to have all Pattents, Licenses, and Restraints removed: But this is a *Freedom* under the Will of a Conqueror.

Others say, It is true Freedom to have Ministers to preach, and for people to hear whom they will, without being restrained or compelled from or to any form of worship: But this is an unsetled Freedom.

Others say, It is true Freedom to have Community with all Women, and to have liberty to satisfie their lusts and greedy appetites: But this is the *Freedom* of wanton unreasonable Beasts, and tends to Destruction.

Others say, It is true *Freedom*, that the elder Brother shall be Landlord of the Earth, and the younger Brother a Servant: And this is but a half Freedom, and begets murmurings, wars, and quarrels.

All these, and such like, are Freedoms: but they lead to Bondage, and are not the true *Foundation-Freedom* which settles a Commonwealth in Peace.

True Commonwealths Freedom lies in the free Enjoyment of the Earth.

True *Freedom* lies where a man receives his nourishment and preservation, and that is in the use of the Earth: For as Man is compounded of the four Materials of the Creation, *Fire, Water, Earth*, and *Ayr;* so is [18] he preserved by the compounded bodies of these four, which are the fruits of the Earth; and he cannot live without them: for take away the free use of these, and the body languishes, the spirit is brought into bondage, and at length departs, and ceaseth his motional action in the body.

All that a man labors for, saith *Solomon*, is this, That he may enjoy the free use of the Earth, with the fruits thereof. *Eccles.* 2. 24.

Do not the Ministers preach for maintenance in the Earth? the Lawyers plead causes to get the possessions of the Earth? Doth not the Soldier fight for the Earth? And doth not the Landlord require Rent, that he may live in the fulness of the Earth by the labor of his Tenants?

And so, from the Thief upon the high way to the King who sits upon the Throne, do not every one strive, either by force of Arms, or secret cheats, to get the possessions of the Earth one from another, because they see their Freedom lies in plenty, and their bondage lies in poverty?

Surely then, oppressing Lords of Manors, exacting Landlords, and Tythe-takers, may as well say, their brethren shall not breathe in the ayr, nor enjoy warmth in their bodies, nor have the moyst waters to fall upon them in showres, unless they will pay them Rent for it: As to say, Their brethren shall not work upon Earth, nor eat the fruits thereof, unless they will hire that liberty of them: for he that takes upon him to restrain his brother from the liberty of the one, may upon the same ground restrain him from the liberty of all four; *viz.* Fire, Water, Earth, and Ayr.

A man had better to have had no body, then to have no food for it; therefore this restraining of the Earth from brethren by brethren, is oppression and bondage; but the free enjoyment thereof is true Freedom.

I speak now in relation between the Oppressor and the oppressed; the inward bondages I meddle not with in this place, though I am assured that if it be rightly searched into, the inward bondages of the minde, as covetousness, pride, hypocrisie, envy, sorrow, fears, desperation, and madness, are all occasioned by the outward bondage, that one sort of people lay upon another.

And thus far natural experience makes it good, That true Freedom lies in the free enjoyment of the Earth.

If we look into the old Scriptures,

We finde, That when *Israel* had conquered the Nations, he took possession of the Enemies Land, and divided it by lot among the Tribes, counting the Enjoyment of the Earth their perfect Freedom.

In the beginning of their wars they first sent Spies to view the Land of [19] *Canaan*, (*Numb*. 13. 23. to 33.) for the enjoyment of that was the Freedom they aymed at; for being so long in the barren wilderness, and children multiplying upon them, they wanted Land to live upon. *Deut*. 1. 28.

And when the Spies returned, and shewed them the fruits of the Land, and had declared what a fruitful Land it was, they were encouraged and restless till they were come thither; and when they heard bad tydings of the Land, their hearts fell, and they were discouraged.

And when the spirit of wisdom, courage and providence in them had subdued those Gyants, and had given the house of *Israel* the Land of *Canaan*, the Rulers and chief Officers of *Israels* Army did not divide the Land among themselves; but being faithful spirited men, they forthwith divided the Land by lot, to every Tribe his portion without exception.

And when *Israel* intreated the King of *Syhon*, to suffer him to pass through his land, he would not suffer him, but gathered all his people together and fought with Israel; And the Lord gave *Syhon* into *Israels* hand: And he took possession of his land.

So that we see by Scripture proof likewise, the land is that which every one place their freedom in.

If we look into the practise of Kings, and Conquerors,

Since the Scriptures of *Moses* were writ, we finde they placed their freedom in the enjoyment of the free use of the earth.

When *William* Duke of *Normandy* had conquered *England*, he took possession of the earth for his freedom, and disposed of our *English* ground to his friends as he pleased, and made the conquered *English* his servants, to plant the earth for him and his friends.

And all Kings, from his time to King *Charles*, were successors of that conquest; and all Laws were made to confirm that Conquest.

For there are his old Laws and Statutes yet to be read, that do shew how he allowed the conquered *English* but three pence, and four pence a day for their work, to buy them bread of their Task-masters; but the freedom of the earth he and his friends kept in their own hands.

And as Kings, so the old Gentry, and the new Gentry likewise, walking in the same steps, are but the successors of the *Norman* victory.

But are not the *Normans* and their power conquered, by the *Commoners* of *England*; And why then should we not recover the freedom of our land again, from under that yoak and power?

Then further, The *Norman* Conqueror made Laws, whereby this *English* earth should be governed, and appointed two national Officers to see those Laws performed.

The first Officer was the *Lawyer*; And his work is conversant about [20] nothing but the disposing of the earth, and all Courts of Judicature, and Suits of Law, is about the ordering of the Earth; according to his Law made by him and his party.

The next Officer was the national Clergie; and their work was to perswade the multitude of people to let *William* the Conqueror alone with a quiet possession and government of the earth, and to call it his and not theirs, and so not to rebell against him.

And they were to tell the people, that if they would acknowledge *William* Duke of *Normandy* and his Successors, to be their Lord, King and Ruler, and would be obedient to his Government; then they should live in the Haven, that is, in peace; and they should quietly enjoy their land which they rented, their houses and fruits of their labors without disturbance.

But if they would not acknowledg him to be their Lord, King, and Ruler, nor submit to his Government, then they should be cast into Hell; that is, into the sorrows of prisons, poverty, whips, and death: and their houses and riches should be taken from them, &c.

And this was a true prophetical and experimental Doctrine: for do we not see, that the Laws of a King, while a King, had the Power of life and death in them? And he who fell under the power of this Lord, must pay the uttermost farthing, before he was released.

And for their pains for thus preaching, the King established by his Laws, that they should have the tenth of the encrease of all profits from the Earth, (1 *Sam*. 8. 15.) placing their freedom where he placed his own, and that is in the use of the Earth brought into their hands by the labors of the enslaved men.

But in after times, when this National Ministry appeared to the people to be but hirelings, and as the people grew in knowledg they discovered their hypocrisie more and more, as they do in these days: Then this Clergy (the spirit of the old Pharisees) began to divine and to deceive the people by a shew of holiness, or spiritual doctrine, as they call it, difficult to be understood by any but themselves; perswading the people to beleeve or fancy, That true Freedom lay in hearing them preach, and to enjoy that Heaven, which they say, every man who beleeves their doctrine, shall enjoy after he is dead: And so tell us of a Heaven and Hell after death, which neither they nor we know what wil be: So that the whole world is at a loss in the true knowledg thereof, as *Solomon* said, *Who shall bring him to see what shall be after he is dead? Eccles.* 3. 22. & 6. 11.

The former hell of prisons, whips and gallows they preached to keep the people in subjection to the King: but by this divined Hell after death, they preach to keep both King and people in aw to them, to uphold their trade [21] of Tythes and new rased Maintenance: And so having blinded both King and people, they become the god that rules: This subtle divining spirit is the Whore that sits upon many waters: This is *Nahash* the Amonite, that would not make peace with *Israel*, unless *Israel* would suffer him to put out their right eyes, and to see by his. 1 *Sam.* 11. 2.

For so long as the people call that a Truth which they call a Truth, and believe what they preach, and are willing to let the Clergy be the Keepers of their eyes and knowledg; that is as much as *Nahash* did, put out their eyes to see by theirs, then all is well, and they tell the people they shall go to Heaven.

But if the eyes of the people begin to open, and they seek to find knowledg in their own hearts, and to question the Ministers Doctrine, and become like unto wise-hearted *Thomas*, to believe nothing but what they see reason for:

Then do the Ministers prepare War against that man or men, and will make no Covenant of Peace with him, till they consent to have their right eyes put out, that is, to have their Reason blinded, so as to believe every Doctrine they preach, and never question any thing, saying, *The Doctrine of Faith must not be tryed by Reason:* No, for if it be, their Mystery of Iniquity will be discovered, and they would lose their Tythes.

Therefore no marvel though the National Clergy of *England* and *Scotland*, who are the Tything Priests and Lords of blinded mens spirits, stuck so close to their Master the King, and to his Monarchial oppressing Government; for say they, *If the people must not work for us, and give us Tythes, but we must work for our selves, as they do, our Freedom is lost:* I, but this is but the cry of an *Egyptian* Taskmaster, who counts other mens freedom his bondage.

Now if the Earth could be enjoyed in such a maner as every one might have provision, as it may by this *Platform* I have offered, then will the Peace of the Commonwealth be preserved, and men need not act so hypocritically as the Clergy do, and others likewise, to get a living: But when some shall enjoy great possessions, and others who have done as much or more for to purchase Freedom, shall have none at all, and be made slaves to their brethren, this begets offences.

The glory of Israels Commonwealth is this,
They had no Begger among them.

As you read, when they had conquered the *Canaanites,* and won that Land, by the purchase of the blood and labour, and by a joynt assistance throughout the whole Tribes of *Israel;* the Officers and Leaders of the people did not sell the Land again to the remainder of their Enemies, nor [22] buy and sell it among themselves, and so by cheating the people set up a new Oppression upon a new account; Neither did they fall a parting the Land before the crowning Victory was gotten: But they forbore the disposing of the Land till the War was over, and all the Tribes stuck close together till all the fighting work was done.

And when they saw the Enemies heart was broke, and that now they were the Masters of the field, then they quietly took possession of the Land as a free reward for all their hazards and labour.

The Officers and Leaders were careful to keep Promise and Engagements to the people, and there was no treachery found in them, as to inrich themselves with the Commonwealths Land, and to deprive others of the price of their Blood, and Free-quarter, and Taxes.

But they made Canon with all the Crown Lands therein, and all other forfeited Lands, which was gotten by a joynt Assistance of person and purse of all the Tribes. The Scriptures say, They made this Canon Land a common Treasury of livelyhood to the whole Commonwealth of *Israel,* and so disposed of it, as they made provision for every Tribe, and for every family in a Tribe, nay for every particular man in a family, every one had enough, no man was in want, there was no beggery among them.

They did not divide this Land only to particular men who went out to War, but they who stayd at home had an equal share; they did not make one brother a Lord of Manor and Landlord, and other brothers to be servants to them: But seeing the Enemies were beaten, not by the Counsellors only, nor by the Leaders of the Army only, but by the common Souldiers also; and not only by them, but by the Laborers who staid at home to provide Victuals and Free-quarter: Therefore did the Counsellors and chief Officers of the Army agree to make provision for every one that assisted, either by person or purse; and this was pure Righteousness.

And to those families in a Tribe which had many persons in it, to them they allotted more Land; and to those families which had less number of persons, they allotted less Land: So that not only the Tribes in general, but every family and person in a Tribe, younger brother as well as elder brother, he who wrought at home to provide food, as well as he that went to War, all had sufficient, there was no want, the Oppression of Beggary was not known among them; all burdens were taken of, and *Israel* in all his Tribes and Families was made a free Commonwealth in Power, as well as in Name. 1 *Sam.* 30. 24. *Josh.* 16. 17. & 18. *Chapters.*

And thus the Land was divided, and the whole Land was the Common Stock, every one had a brotherly freedom therein, for the freedom of the one was the freedom of the other, there was no difference in that they were [23] men of true faithful and publick spirits, not false-hearted.

And so likewise when *Esther* prevailed with King *Ahasuerus* for freedom, she did not seek her own freedom and interest, but the freedom of all her kindred and friends; for common Freedom was that which men of righteous spirits always fought after.

All that I shall say is this, O that those who pretend to set up a Gospel-Commonwealth in *England*, *Scotland*, and *Ireland*, would not be worse then *Moses*, but rather exceed *Moses*, knowing that if this our English Commonwealths Government carry perfect Freedom in his hand, then shall the Law go forth from *England* to all the Nations of the World.

This Foundation being layd from the Example of *Israels* Commonwealth, and Testimony of Gods Word, I shall proceed how the Earth shall be governed for the Peace of a Common-wealth: But by the way, to prevent mistake, I shall insert

A short Declaration to take of Prejudice.

Some hearing of this Common Freedom, think there must be a Community of all the fruits of the Earth whether they work or no, therefore strive to live idle upon other mens labours.

Others, through the same unreasonable beastly ignorance, think there must be a Community of all men and women for Copulation, and so strive to live a bestial life.

Others think there will be no Law, but that every thing will run into confusion for want of Government; but this Platform proves the contrary.

Therefore because that transgression doth and may arise from ignorant and rude fancy in man, is the Law added.

That which true Righteousness in my Judgment calls Community, is this, To have the Earth set free from all Kingly Bondage of Lords of Manors, and oppressing Landlords, which came in by Conquest; as a Thief takes a true mans purse upon the high-way, being stronger than he.

And that neither the Earth, nor any fruits thereof, should be bought or sold by the Inhabitants one among another, which is a slavery the Kingly Conquerors have brought in, therefore he set his stamp upon silver, that every one should buy and sell in his name.

And though this be, yet shall not men live idle; for the Earth shall be planted and reaped, and the fruits carried into Barns and Store-houses by the assistance of every family, according as is shewed hereafter in order.

Every man shall be brought up in Trades and labours, and all Trades shall be maintained with more improvement, to the inriching of the Commonwealth, more then now they be under Kingly Power.

[24] Every Tradesman shall fetch Materials, as Leather, Wool, Flax, Corn, and the like, from the publike Store-houses to work upon without buying and selling; and when particular works are made, as Cloth, Shooes, Hats, and the like, the Tradesmen shall bring these particular works to particular shops, as it is now in practise, without buying and selling. And every family as they want such things as they cannot make, they shall go to these shops, and fetch without money, even as now they fetch with money, as hereafter is shewed how in order.

If any say, This will nurse Idleness; I answer, This Platform proves the contrary, for idle persons and beggers will be made to work.

If any say, This wil make some men to take goods from others by violence, and call it theirs, because the Earth and fruits are a Common Stock; I answer, The Laws or Rules following prevents that ignorance: For though the Store-houses and publike Shops be commonly furnished by every families assistance, and for every families use, as is shewed hereafter how: yet every mans house is proper to himself, and all the furniture therein, and provision which he hath fetched from the Store-houses is proper to himself; every mans wife and every womans husband proper to themselves, and so are their children at their dispose till they come to age.

And if any other man endeavor to take away his house, furniture, food, wife, or children, saying, every thing is common, and so abusing the Law of Peace, such a one is a Transgressor, and shall suffer punishment, as by the Government and Laws following is expressed.

For though the publike Store-houses be a common Treasury, yet every mans particular dwelling is not common, but by his consent, and the Commonwealths Laws are to preserve a mans peace in his person, and in his private dwelling, against the rudeness and ignorance that may arise in Mankind.

If any man do force or abuse women in folly, pleading Community, the Laws following do punish such ignorant and unrational practise; for the Laws of a Commonwealth are Laws of moderate diligence, and purity of Manners.

Therefore I desire a patient reading of what hereafter follows; and when you have heard the extent of Commonwealths Government or Freedom, then weigh it in the ballance with Kingly Government or Bondage, and see whether brings most Peace to the Land, and establish that for Government.

For you must either establish Commonwealths Freedom in Power, making provision for every ones Peace, which is Righteousness; or else you must set up Monarchy again.

Monarchy is twofold; either for one King to rule, or for many to rule by Kingly Principles; for the Kings Power lies in his Laws, not in the Name: [25] And if either one King rule, or many rule by Kings Principles, much murmuring, grudges, troubles and quarrels may and will arise among the oppressed people upon every gained opportunity.

But if Common Freedom be found out, and ease the oppressed, it prevents murmurings and quarrels, and establishes Universal Peace in the Earth.

Therefore seeing the Power of Government is in the hands of such as have professed to the World a godly Righteousness, more purely then that of oppressing Kings, without doubt their faithfulness and wisdom is required to be manifested in action, as well as in words.

But if they who profess more Righteousness and Freedom in words then the Kings Government was, and yet can find out no Government to ease the people, but must establish the Kings old Laws, though they give it a new name; I will leave the sentence, worthy such a profession and such a people, to be given by the heart of every rational man: And so I shall proceed how the Earth should be governed for the Peace of a Commonwealth.

CHAP. II. *What is Government in general.*

GOVERNMENT is a wise and free ordering of the Earth, and the Manners of Mankind by observation of particular Laws or Rules, so that all the Inhabitants may live peaceably in plenty and freedom in the Land where they are born and bred.

In the Government of a Land there are three parts, *viz.* Laws, fit Officers, and a faithful Execution of those Laws.

First, There must be suitable Laws for every occasion, and almost for every action that men do; for one Law cannot serve in all seasons, but every season and every action have their particular Laws attending thereupon for the preservation of right order: As for example;

There is a time to plow, and the Laws of right understanding attends upon that work; and there is a time to reap the fruits of the Earth, and the Laws of right observation attending thereupon.

So that true Government is a right ordering of all actions, giving to every action and thing its due weight and measure, and this prevents confusion, as *Solomon* speaks, *There is a time for all things;* a time to make Promises and Engagements, and a time to see them performed; a right order in times of War, and a right order in times of Peace; every season and time having its Law or Rule suitable, and this makes a healthful Government, because it preserves Peace in a right order.

[26] Secondly, There must be fit Officers, whose spirits are so humble, wise, and free from Covetousness, as they can make the established Laws of the Land their Will; and not through pride and vain-glory,

make their Wills to rule above the Rules of Freedom, pleading Prerogative.

For when the right ordered Laws do rule, the Government is healthful; but when the Will of Officers rule above Law, that Government is diseased with a mortal disease.

Thirdly, There must be a faithful Execution of those Laws; and herein lies the very life of Government: For a right order in Government lies not in the Will of Officers without Laws, nor in Laws without Officers, nor in neither of them without Execution: But when these three go hand in hand, the Government is healthful; but if any one of these be wanting, the Government is diseased.

There is a twofold Government, a Kingly Government, and a Commonwealths Government.

What is Kingly Government or Monarchy?

Kingly Government governs the Earth by that cheating Art of buying & selling, and thereby becomes a man of contention, his hand is against every man, and every mans hand against him: and take this Government at the best, it is a diseased Government, and the very City *Babylon*, full of confusion: and if it had not a Club Law to support it, there would be no order in it, because it is the covetous and proud will of a Conqueror, enslaving a conquered people.

This Kingly Government is he who beats pruning hooks and plows, into spears, guns, swords, and instruments of War; that he might take his younger brothers Creation birth-right from him, calling the Earth his, and not his brothers, unless his brother will hire the Earth of him, so that he may live idle and at ease by his brothers labours.

Indeed this Government may well be called the Government of high-way men, who hath stoln the Earth from the younger brethren by force, and holds it from them by force; he sheds blood not to free the people from Oppression, but that he may be King and Ruler over an oppressed people.

The Scituation of this Monarchial Government

Lies in the will of Kings, *alias* Conquerors, setting up Lords of Manors, exacting Landlords, Tything Priests, and covetous Lawyers, with all those pricking bryars attending thereupon, to be Taskmasters to oppress the people, lest they should rise up in riches and power to disthrone him, and so to share the Earth with him, redeeming their own Creation rights again, which this Kingly Government withholds from Mankind in all Nations; for he is [27] the great Man of Sin, who is now revealed, who sits in the Temple of God, ruling above all that is called God, and both by force and cheating policy takes the Peoples Freedoms from them. *Exod.* 1. 8. 2 *Thes.* 2. 8, 9.

This Kingly Government is he that makes the elder brethren free-men in the Earth, and the younger brethren slaves in the Earth, before they have lost their Freedom by transgression to the Law.

Nay he makes one brother a Lord, and another a servant, while they are in their Mothers womb, before they have done either good or evil: This is the mighty Ruler, that hath made the Election and Rejection of Brethren from their birth to their death, or from Eternity to Eternity.

He calls himself the Lord God of the whole Creation, for he makes one brother to pay rent to another brother for the use of the Water, Earth, and Ayr, or else he will not suffer him by his Laws and Lawyers to live above ground, but in beggery, and yet he will be called righteous.

And whereas the Scriptures say, That the Creator of all things (God) is no Respecter of persons, yet this Kingly Power doth nothing else but respect persons, preferring the rich and the proud; therefore he denies the Scriptures, and the true God of Righteousness, though he pray and preach of the Scriptures, and keep Fasts and Thanksgiving-days to God, to be a cloak to hide his Oppression from the people, whereby he shews himself to be the great Antichrist, and Mystery of Iniquity, that makes War with Christ and his Saints under pretence of owning him.

The great Law-giver of this Kingly Government,

Is Covetousness, ruling in the heart of Mankind, making one brother to covet a full possession of the Earth, and a lordly Rule over another brother, which he will have, or else he will inslave or kill his brother; for this is *Cain*, who killed *Abel:* and because of this, he is called *the great red Dragon, the god of this world, the Oppressor, under which the whole Creation hath groaned a long time, waiting to be delivered from him.*

The Rise of Kingly Government is twofold.

First, By a politick wit, in drawing the people out of Common Freedom into a way of Common Bondage; for so long as the Earth is a Common Treasury to all men, Kingly Covetousness can never raign as King: Therefore his first device was, to put the people to buy and sell the Earth and the fruits one to another; for this would beget discontents, and muddy the waters.

And when this spirit of Monarchy hath drawn the people into the way of buying and selling, and the people begin to vex one another, then began his opportunity to raign.

For in that man wherein this Kingly spirit seats himself, he tells the people [28] that are wronged, *Well, I'le ease you, and I'le set things to rights:* And then he went about to establish buying and selling by Law, whereby the people had some ease for a time, but the cunning Machavilian spirit got strength thereby to settle himself King in the Earth.

For after some time the people through ignorance began to multiply Suits of Law one against another, and to quarrel and fight: Now saith this subtle spirit, *Come follow me,* to one sort of people that are oppressed, *and stick to me, and we will fight with those who wrong you; and if we conquer them, then we will govern the Earth as we please, and they shall be our servants, and we will make them work for us.*

Thereupon one sort of people followed one head, and another sort of people followed another head, and so Wars began in the Earth, and mankind fell a fighting, one part conquering and enslaving another: And now Man is faln from his innocency, and from the glory of the spirit of common Freedom, Love and Peace, into Enmity; every one striving to be King one over another; every one striving to be a Landlord of the Earth, and to make his brother his servant to work for him.

But still here is disorder, therefore this subtle spirit of darkness goes further, and tells the people, *You must make one man King over you all, and let him make Laws, and let every one be obedient thereunto:* And when the people consented thereunto, they gave away their Freedom, and they set up Oppression over themselves.

And this was the rise of Kingly Power; first, by Policy, drawing the people from a common enjoyment of the Earth, to the crafty Art of buying and selling: Secondly, to advance himself by the power of the Sword, when that Art of buying and selling had made them quarrel among themselves.

So that this spirit of Monarchy it is the spirit of Subtilty and Covetousness, filling the heart of Mankind with enmity and ignorance, pride and vain-glory, because the strong destroys the weak; and so one Scripture calls this *the Power and Government of the Beast*, another Scripture calls it *the god of this world, or the Devil:* For indeed the Monarchial spirit is the power of darkness, for it is the great thick Cloud, that hath hid the light of the Sun of Righteousness from shining in his full strength a long time.

And though this Kingly spirit doth call buying and selling a righteous thing, thereby to put the simple younger brother upon it, yet he will destroy it as he pleaseth, by Pattents, Licenses, or Monopolizing.

Or else he will at his pleasure take away the riches which his younger brother hath got by trading, and so still lift up himself above his brother.

And as he rise to the Throne by the crafty Art of buying and selling, and by the Sword, so he is maintained upon the Throne by the same means.

[29] And the people now see, That Kingly Power is the Oppressor, and the Maintainers thereof are called Oppressors by the ancient Writers of the Bible.

This Kingly Power is the old Heaven, and the old Earth, that must pass away, wherein unrighteousness, oppression and partiality dwells.

For indeed we never read, that the people began to complain of Oppression, till Kingly Government rose up, which is the power of covetousness and pride; and which *Samuel* sets forth to be a plague and a curse upon the people in the first rise of it.

He will take your sons and your daughters to be his servants, and to run before his charets, to plant his ground, and to reap his harvest: He will take your fields, your Vineyards and Oliveyards, even the best of them, and give to his servants as pleaseth him: He will take the tenth of your seed, and of your vineyards, and give to his Officers, or Ministers. 1 *Sam*. 8.

And this was that *god*, who appointed the people to pay Tythes to the Clergy.

And many other Oppressions did the Kingly Government bring upon the People, as you may read at large in *Samuel*.

Read 1 *Sam*. 8. from Vers. 10. to 19.

The Winter's past, the Spring time now appears,
  Be gone thou Kingly Tyrant, with all thy Cavaliers.
Thy day is past, and sure thou dost appear
  To be the bond-mans son, and not the free-born Heir.

Matt. 15. 13.

What is Commonwealths Government?

Commonwealths Government governs the Earth without buying and selling; and thereby becomes a man of peace, and the Restorer of ancient Peace and Freedom: he makes provision for the oppressed, the weak and the simple, as well as for the rich, the wise and the strong: He beats swords and spears into pruning hooks and plows; he makes both elder and younger brother Free-men in the Earth. *Micah* 4. 3, 4. *Isai.* 33. 1. & 65. 17. to 25.

All Slaveries and Oppressions, which have been brought upon Mankinde by Kings, Lords of Manors, Lawyers, and Landlords, and the Divining Clergy, are all cast out again by this Government, if it be right in power, as well as in name.

For this Government is the true Restorer of all long lost Freedoms, and so becomes the joy of all Nations, and the Blessing of the whole Earth: for this takes off the Kingly Curse, and makes *Jerusalem* a praise in the Earth. Therefore all you, who profess Religion and spiritual [30] things, now look to it, and see what spirit you do profess, for your profession is brought to tryal.

If once Commonwealths Government be set upon the Throne, then no Tyranny or Oppression can look him in the face and live.

For where Oppression lies upon brethren by brethren, that is no Commonwealths Government, but the Kingly Government still; and the mystery of Iniquity hath taken that peace-makers name to be a cloke to hide his subtil covetousness, pride, and oppression under.

O *England, England,* wouldst thou have thy Government sound and healthful? then cast about, and see, and search diligently to finde out all those burthens that came in by Kings, and remove them; and then will thy Commonwealths Government arise from under the clods, under which as yet it is buryed, and covered with deformity.

If true Commonwealths Freedom lie in the free Enjoyment of the Earth, as it doth, then whatsoever Law or custom doth deprive brethren of their Freedom in the Earth, it is to be cast out as unsavory salt.

The scituation of Commonwealths Government

Is within the Laws of common Freedom, whereby there is a provision for livelyhood in the Earth, both for elder and younger brother; and not the one enslaving the other, but both living in plenty and freedom.

The Officers, Laws, and Customs hereafter mentioned, or such like, according to such a method, may be the Foundation and Pillars of Commonwealths Government.

This Government depends not upon the Will of any particular man, or men; for it is seated in the spirit of Mankinde, and it is called the *light,* or *son of righteousness and peace.* The Tyrants in all ages have made use of this mans name, while he hath lien buryed, to cover their cheating mystery of Iniquity: for if common Freedom were not pretended, the Commoners of a Land would never dance after the pipe of self seeking wits.

This Commonwealths Government may well be called the *antient of days;* for it was before any other oppressing government crept in.

It is the Moderator of all oppression; and so is like *Moses* and *Joseph* in *Pharaohs* Court, and in time will be the Restorer of long lost Freedoms to the Creation, and delights to plant Righteousness over the face of the whole Earth.

The great Lawgiver in Commonwealth Government

Is the spirit of universal Righteousness dwelling in Mankinde, now rising up to teach every one to do to another as he would have another do to him, and is no respector of persons: and this spirit hath been killed [31] by the Pharisaical Kingly spirit of self-love, and been buryed in the dung-hill of that enmity for many years past.

And if these be the days of his resurrection to power, as we may hope, because the name of *Commonwealth* is risen and established in *England* by a Law, then we or our posterity shall see comfortable effects.

In that Nation, where this Commonwealths Government shall be first established, there shall be abundance of peace and plenty, and all Nations of the Earth shall come flocking thither to see his beauty, and to learn the ways thereof; and the Law shall go forth from that *Sion,* and that Word of the Lord from that *Jerusalem,* which shall govern the whole Earth. *Micah* 4. 1, 2.

There shall be no Tyrant Kings, Lords of Manors, Tything Priests, oppressing Lawyers, exacting Landlords, nor any such like pricking bryar in all this holy Mountain of the Lord God our Righteousness and Peace; for the righteous Law shall be the Rule for every one, and the Judg of all mens actions.

David desired rather to be a door keeper in this house of God, or Commonwealths Government, then to live in the tents of wickedness, which was the Kingly oppressing Courts.

If any go about to build up Commonwealths Government upon Kingly principles, they will both shame and lose themselves; for there is a plain difference between the two Governments.

And if you do not run in the right channel of Freedom, you must, nay you will, as you do, face about, and turn back again to Egyptian Monarchy: and so your names in the days of posterity shall stink and be blasted with abhorred infamy for your unfaithfulness to common Freedom; and the evil effects will be sharp upon the backs of posterity.

Therefore seeing *England* is declared to be a free Commonwealth, and the name thereof established by a Law; surely then the greatest work is now to be done, and that is to escape all Kingly cheats in setting up a Commonwealths Government, that the power and the name may agree together; so that all the Inhabitants may live in peace, plenty, and freedom, otherwise we shall shew our Government to be gone no further but to the half day of the Beast, or to the dividing of Time, of which there must be an over-turn. *Dan.* 7. 25. *Rev.* 12. 14.

For Oppression was always the occasion why the spirit of Freedom in the people desired change of Government.

When *Samuels* sons took bribes, and grew rich upon the common purse, and forgot to relieve the oppressed, That made the people forsake the Government by Judges, and to desire a Kingly Government. 1 *Sam.* 8. 3, 4.

[32] And the Oppressions of the Kingly Government have made this Age of the World to desire a *Commonwealths Government*, and the removal of the *Kings;* for the spirit of Light in Man loves Freedom, and hates Bondage.

And because the spirit in Mankinde is various within it self; for some are wise, some are foolish, some idle, some laborious, some rash, some milde, some loving and free to others, some envyous and covetous, some of an inclination to do as they would have others do to them: but others seek to save themselves, and to live in fulness, though others perish for want,

Therefore because of this was the Law added, which was to be a Rule and Judg for all mens actions, to preserve common Peace and Freedom; as *Paul* writ, *The Law was added because of Transgression*, one against another.

The Haven gates are now set ope for English Man to enter:
The Freedoms of the Earth's his due, if he will make adventure.

C H A P. I I I. *Where began the first Original of Government in the Earth among Mankinde?*

THE Original Root of Magistracy is *common Preservation*, and it rose up first in a private Family: for suppose there were but one Family in the World, as is conceived, Father *Adams* Family, wherein were many persons.

Therein *Adam* was the first Governor or Officer in the Earth, because as he was the first Father, so he was the most wise in contriving, and the most strong for labor, and so the fittest to be the chief *Governor.* For this is the golden Rule,

Let the wise help the foolish, and let the strong help the weak. Psa. 35. 10. *Rom.* 15. 1, 2.

But some may say here, That *Adam* was under no Law, but his Will was a Law to him and his houshold; therefore from the root from whence Magistracy first rose, it is clear, That Officers are to be under no Law, but their own Wills, and the people are to be subject thereunto. I answer:

The Law of Necessity, that the Earth should be planted for the common preservation and peace of his houshold, was the righteous Rule and Law to *Adam,* and this Law was so clearly written in the hearts of his people, that they all consented quietly to any counsel he gave them for that end.

[33] Therefore not *Adams* Will onely, but the Will of his People likewise, and the Law of common Preservation, Peace and Freedom, was the righteous Law that governed both *Adam* and his houshould.

But yet observe, That from the Father in a Family was the first rise of Magisterial Government, because Children wanting experience of their own preservation, therefore such as are experienced, are to propound the Law of Government to them: and therefore from *Adam* to this day, the Law of common Preservation is the Rule and Foundation of true Magistracy: and it is the work of all Magistrates to help the weak and the foolish.

There are two roots from whence Laws do spring.

The first root you see is common Preservation, when there is a principle in every one to seek the good of others, as himself, without respecting persons: and this is the root of the tree Magistracy, and the Law of Righteousness and Peace: and all particular Laws found out by experience, necessary to be practised for common Preservation, are the boughs and branches of that Tree.

And because, among the variety of Mankinde, Ignorance may grow up; therefore this Original Law is written in the heart of every man, to be his guide or leader: so that if an Officer be blinded by covetousness and pride, and that ignorance rule in him, yet an inferior man may tell him where he goes astray; for common Preservation and Peace is the Foundation Rule of all Government: and therefore if any will preach or practise Fundamental Truths, or Doctrine, here you may see where the Foundation thereof lies.

The second Root is Self preservation: when particular Officers seek their own Preservation, Ease, Honor, Riches, and Freedom in the Earth, and do respect persons that are in Power and Riches with them, and regard not the Peace, Freedom, and Preservation of the weak and foolish among Brethren.

And this is the root of the Tree Tyranny, and the Law of Unrighteousness, and all particular Kingly Laws found out by covetous Policy to enslave one brother to another, whereby bondage, tears, sorrows and poverty are brought upon many men, are all but the boughs and branches of that Tree, Tyranny; and such Officers as these are fallen from true Magistracy, and are no Members thereof, but the Members of Tyranny, who is the Devil and Satan.

And indeed this Tyranny is the cause of all Wars and Troubles, and of the removal of the Government of the Earth out of one hand into another, so often as it is, in all Nations.

[34] For if Magistrates had a care to cherish the peace and liberties of the common people, and see them set free from Oppression, they might sit in the chair of Government, and never be disturbed.

But when their sitting is altogether to advance their own interest, and to forget the afflictions of *Joseph,* or their brethren that are under bondage: this is a forerunner of their own downfall, and oftentime proves the plague to the whole Land.

Therefore the work of all true Magistrates is to maintain the common Law, which is the root of right Government, and preservation and peace to every one; and to cast out all self-ended principles and interests, which is Tyranny and Oppression, and which breaks common peace.

For surely the disorderly actings of Officers break the peace of the Commonwealth more, then any men whatsoever.

All Officers in a true Magistracy of a Commonwealth are to be chosen Officers.

In the first Family, which is the Foundation from whence all Families sprang, there was the Father, he is the first link of the chain Magistracy. The necessity of the children that sprang from him doth say,

Father, do thou teach us how to plant the Earth, that we may live, and we will obey. By this choyce, they make him not onely a Father, but a Master and Ruler. And out of this root springs up all Magistrates and Officers, To see the Law executed, and to preserve Peace in the Earth, by seeing that right Government is observed.

For here take notice, That though the children might not speak, yet their weakness and simplicity did speak, and chose their Father to be their Overseer.

So that he who is a true Commonwealths Officer, is not to step into the place of Magistracy by policy, or violent force, as all Kings and Conquerors do; and so become oppressing Tyrants, by promoting their self-ended Interests, or Machiavilian Cheats, that they may live in plenty, and rule as Lords over their Brethren.

But a true Commonwealths Officer is to be a chosen one, by them who are in necessity, and who judg him fit for that work.

And thus a Father in a Family is a Commonwealths Officer, because the Necessity of the young children choose him by a joynt consent, and not otherwise.

Secondly, In a bigger Family, called a Parish, the body of the people are confused and disordered, because some are wise, some foolish, some subtil and cunning to deceive, others plain-hearted, some strong, some weak, some rash, angry, some milde and quiet-spirited. By reason [35] whereof offences do arise among brethren, and their common peace is broken.

Therefore as Necessity hath added a Law to limit mens manners, because of Transgressions one against another,

So likewise doth the necessity of common peace move the whole body of the Parish to choose two, three, or more, within that circuit, to be their Overseers, to cause the unruly ones, for whom onely the Law was added, to be subject to the Law, or Rule, that so peace may be preserved among them in the planting of the Earth, reaping the fruits, and quiet enjoyment.

Thirdly, In every County, Shire, or Land, wherein the Families are encreased to a larger Commonwealth, the necessity of the people moves them still to choose more Overseers and Officers to preserve common peace.

And when the people have chose all Officers, to preserve a right Order in Government of Earth among them; then doth the same necessity of common Peace move the people to say to their Overseers and Officers,

Do you see our Laws observed for our preservation and peace, and we will assist and protect you: And this word *assist* and *protect*, implies,

The rising up of the people by force of Arms to defend their Laws and Officers against any Invasion, Rebellion, or Resistance, yea to beat down the turbulency of any foolish or self-ended spirit that endeavors to break their common Peace.

So that all true Officers are chosen Officers, and when they act to satisfie the necessity of them who chose them, then they are faithful and righteous servants to that Commonwealth, and then there is a rejoycing in the City.

But when Officers do take the possessions of the Earth into their own hands, lifting themselves up thereby to be Lords over their Masters, the people, who chose them; and will not suffer the people to plant the Earth, and reap the fruits for their livelyhood, unless they will hire the Land of them, or work for day-wages for them, that they may live in ease and plenty, and not work,

These Officers are fallen from true Magistracy of a Commonwealth, and they do not act righteously; and because of this, sorrows and tears, poverty and bondages are known among Mankinde; and now that City mourns.

And surely if it be carefully looked into, the necessity of the people never chose such Officers, but they were either voluntary Soldiers of Officers chosen by them, who ran before they were called; and so by policy [36] and force they sat down in the chair of Government, strengthening one sort of people to take the free use of the Earth from another sort; and these are sons of bondage, and they act in darkness: by reason whereof the Prophet *Esay* cries out, *Darkness hath covered the Earth, and thick darkness the people, for the Leaders of the people have caused them to err:* I fear so, O *England, &c.*

All Officers in a Commonwealth are to be chosen new ones every year.

When publique Officers remain long in place of Judicature, they will degenerate from the bounds of humility, honesty, and tender care of brethren, in regard the heart of man is so subject to be overspred with the clouds of covetousness, pride, and vain-glory: for though at the first entrance into places of Rule they be of publique spirits, seeking the Freedom of others as their own; yet continuing long in such a place, where honors and greatness is coming in, they become selfish, seeking themselves, and not common Freedom; as experience proves it true in these days, according to this common Proverb,

Great Offices in a Land and Army have changed the disposition of many sweet spirited men.

And Nature tells us, *That if water stand long, it corrupts;* whereas running water keeps sweet, and is fit for common use.

Therefore as the necessity of common preservation moves the people to frame a Law, and to chuse Officers to see the Law obeyed, that they may live in peace:

So doth the same Necessity bid the People, and cries aloud in the ears and eyes of *England,* to chuse new Officers, and to remove the old ones, and to chuse State-Officers every year: And that for these Reasons;

First, To prevent their own evils: for when pride and fulness take hold of an Officer, his eyes are so blinded therewith, that he forgets he is a servant to the Commonwealth, and strives to lift up himself high above his Brethren, and oftentimes his Fall proves very great:

witness the Fall of oppressing Kings, Bishops, and other State-Officers.

Secondly, To prevent the creeping in of Oppression into the Commonwealth again: for when Officers grow proud and full, they will maintain their greatness, though it be in the poverty, ruine, and hardship of their Brethren; Witness the practice of Kings and their Laws, that have crushed the Commoners of *England* a long time.

[27, i. e., 37] And have we not experience in these days, that some Officers of the Commonwealth are grown so mossy for want of removing, that they will hardly speak to an old acquaintance, if he be an inferior man, though they were very familiar before these Wars began? &c.

And what hath occasioned this distance among friends and brethren, but long continuance in places of honour, greatness and riches?

Thirdly, Let Officers be chosen new every year in love to our posterity; for if Burthens and Oppressions should grow up in our Laws and in our Officers for want of removing, as Moss and Weeds grow in some Land for want of stirring, surely it will be a foundation of misery, not easily to be removed by our posterity, and then will they curse the time that ever we their fore-fathers had opportunities to set things to rights for their ease, and would not do it.

Fourthly, To remove Officers of State every year will make them truly faithful, knowing that others are coming after who will look into their ways; and if they do not do things justly, they must be ashamed when the next Officers succeed: And when Officers deal faithfully in the Government of the Commonwealth, they will not be unwilling to remove: The Peace of *London* is much preserved by removing their Officers yearly.

Fifthly, It is good to remove Officers every year, that whereas many have their portions to obey, so many may have their turns to rule, and this will encourage all men to advance Righteousness and good Manners in hopes of Honor; but when money and riches bears all the sway in the Rulers hearts, there is nothing but Tyranny in such ways.

Sixthly, The Commonwealth hereby will be furnished with able and experienced men, fit to govern, which will mightily advance the Honor and Peace of our Land, occasion the more watchful care in the Education of children, and in time will make our Commonwealth of *England* the Lilly among the Nations of the Earth.

Who are fit to choose, and fit to be chosen Officers in a Commonwealth.

All uncivil livers, as drunkards, quarrelers, fearful ignorant men, who dare not speak truth, lest they anger other men; likewise all who are wholly given to pleasure and sports, or men who are full of talk; all these are empty of substance, and cannot be experienced men, therefore not fit to be chosen Officers in a Commonwealth, yet they may have a voyce in the choosing.

Secondly, All those who are interested in the Monarchial Power and Government, ought neither to choose nor be chosen Officers to manage Commonwealths Affairs, for these cannot be friends to common Freedom: And these are of two sorts.

[38] First, Such as have either lent money to maintain the Kings Army, or in that Army have been Souldiers to fight against the recovering of common Freedom, these are neither to choose, nor be chosen Officers in the Commonwealth as yet, for they have lost their Freedom; yet I do not say that they should be made servants, as the conquered usually are made servants, for they are our brethren and what they did, no doubt, they did in a conscionable zeal, though in ignorance.

And seeing but few of the Parliaments friends understand their Common Freedoms, though they own the name *Commonwealth*, therefore the Parliaments party ought to bear with the ignorance of the Kings party, because they are brethren, and not make them servants, though for the present they be suffered neither to choose nor be chosen Officers, lest that ignorant spirit of revenge break out in them to interrupt our common Peace.

Secondly, All those who have been so hasty to buy and sell the Commonwealths Land, and so to entangle it upon a new accompt, ought neither to choose nor be chosen Officers, for hereby they declare themselves either to be for Kingly Interest, or else are ignorant of Commonwealths Freedom, or both, therefore unfit to make Laws to govern a free Commonwealth, or to be Overseers to see those Laws executed.

What greater injury could be done to the Commoners of *England*, then to sell away their Land so hastily, before the people knew where they were, or what Freedom they had got by such cost and bloodshed as they were at? And what greater ignorance could be declared by Officers, then to sell away the purchased Land from the Purchasers, or from part of them, into the hands of particular men to uphold Monarchial Principles?

But though this be a fault, let it be bore withall, it was ignorance of brethren; for *England* hath layn so long under Kingly slavery, that few knew what Common Freedom was: And let a restoration of this redeemed Land be speedily made by them who have the possession of it.

For there is neither Reason nor Equity, that a few men should go away with that Land and Freedom which the whole Commoners have paid Taxes, Free-quarter, and wasted their Estates, Healths and Blood to purchase out of Bondage, and many of them are in want of a comfortable livelyhood.

Well, these are the men that take away other mens Rights from them, and they are Members of the covetous generation of Self-seekers, therefore unfit to be chosen Officers, or to choose.

Who then are fit to be chosen Commonwealths Officers?

Why truly, choose such as have a long time given testimony by their actions to be Promoters of Common Freedom, whether they be Members in [39] Church fellowship, or not in Church fellowship, for all are one in Christ.

Choose such as are men of peaceable spirits, and of a peaceable conversation.

Choose such as have suffered under Kingly Oppression, for they will be fellow-feelers of others bondages.

Choose such as have adventured the loss of their Estates and Lives to redeem the Land from Bondage, and who have remained constant.

Choose such as are understanding men, and who are experienced in the Laws of peaceable and right ordered Government.

Choose men of courage, who are not afraid to speak the Truth; for this is the shame of many in *England* at this day, they are drowned in the dung-hill mud of slavish fear of men; these are covetous men, not fearing God, and their portion is to be cast without the City of Peace amongst the Dogs.

Choose Officers out of the number of those men that are above forty years of age, for these are most likely to be experienced men; and all these are likely to be men of courage, dealing truly, and hating Covetousness.

And if you choose men thus principled, who are poor men, as times go, for the Conquerors Power hath made many a righteous man a poor man; then allow them a yearly Maintenance from the Common Stock, until such time as a Commonwealths Freedom is established, for then there will be no need of such allowances.

What is the reason that most people are so ignorant of their Freedoms, and so few fit to be chosen Commonwealths Officers?

Because the old Kingly Clergy, that are seated in Parishes for lucre of Tythes, are continually distilling their blind Principles into the people, and do thereby nurse up Ignorance in them; for they observe the bent of the peoples minds, and make Sermons to please the sickly minds of ignorant people, to preserve their own riches and esteem among a charmed, befooled and besotted people.

CHAP. IV. *What are the Officers Names in a free Commonwealth?*

IN a private Family, a Father, or Master, is an Officer.

In a Town, City, or Parish,
- A Peace maker.
- A four-fold Office of Overseers.
- A Souldier.
- A Task-master.
- An Executioner. [40]

In a County or Shire,
- A Judg.
- The Peace-makers of every Town within that Circuit.
- The Overseers and Soldiers attending thereupon.

This is called either the Judges Court, or the County Senate.

In a whole Land,
- A Parliament.
- A Commonwealths Ministry.
- A Post-master.
- An Army.

All these Officers are like links of a Chain, they arise from one and the same root, which is necessity of Common Peace, and all their works tend to preserve Common Peace, therefore they are to assist each other, and all others are to assist them, as need requires, upon pain of punishment by the breach of the Laws: And the Rule of right Government being thus observed, may make a whole Land, nay the whole Fabrick of the Earth, to become one family of Mankind, and one well governed Commonwealth; as *Israel* was called *one house of Israel*, though it consisted of many Tribes, Nations and Family.

The Work of a Father or Master of a Family.

A Father is to cherish his children till they grow wise and strong, and then as a Master he is to instruct them in reading, in learning languages, Arts and Sciences, or to bring them up to labour, or employ them in some Trade or other, or cause them to be instructed therein, according as is shewed hereafter in the Education of Mankind.

A Father is to have a care that as all his children do assist to plant the Earth, or by other Trades provide necessaries; so he shall see that every one have a comfortable livelyhood, not respecting one before another.

He is to command them their work, and see they do it, and not suffer them to live idle; he is either to reprove by words, or whip those who offend, for the Rod is prepared to bring the unreasonable ones to experience and moderation:

That so children may not quarrel like beasts, but live in Peace, like rational men, experienced in yielding obedience to the Laws and Officers of the Commonwealth, every one doing to another as he would have another do to him.

The Work of a Peace-maker.

In a Parish or Town may be chosen three, four or six Peace-makers, or more, according to the bigness of the place; and their work is twofold.

[41] First, In general to sit in Councel to order the Affairs of the Parish, to prevent troubles, and to preserve Common Peace, and here they may be called Councellors.

Secondly, If there arise any matters of offence between man and man, by reason of any quarrels, disturbance, or foolish actings, the offending parties shall be brought by the Souldiers before any one or more of these Peace-makers, who shall hear the matter, and shall endeavor to reconcile the parties, and make peace, and so put a stop to the rigor of the Law, and go no further.

But if the Peace-maker cannot perswade or reconcile the parties, then he shall command them to appear at the Judges Court at the time appointed to receive the Judgment of the Law.

If any matters of publike concernment fall out wherein the Peace of the City, Town or Country in one County is concerned, then the Peace-makers in every Town thereabouts shall meet, and consult about it; and from them, or from any six of them, if need require, shall issue forth any Order to inferior Officers.

But if the matters concern only the limits of a Town or City, then the Peace-makers of that Town shall from their Court send forth Orders to inferior Officers for the performing of any publike service within their limits.

Thirdly, If any proof be given that any Officer neglects his duty, a Peace-maker is to tell that Officer between them two of his neglect; and if the Officer continue negligent after this reproof, the Peace-maker shall acquaint either the County Senate, or the National Parliament therewith, that from them the offendor may receive condign punishment.

And it is all to this end, that the Laws be obeyed; for a careful Execution of Laws is the Life of Government.

And while a Peace-maker is careful to oversee the Officers, all Officers and others shall assist him, upon pain of forfeiture of Freedom, or other punishment, according to the Rules following.

One thing remember, That when any offendor is brought before any of these chief Peace-makers, then this is to be noted, that the offender hath rejected mercy once before by refusing to yield obedience to the Overseers, as is explained further hereafter.

The Work of an Overseer.

In a Parish or Town there is to be a fourfold degree of Overseers, which are to be chosen yearly.

[42] The first is an Overseer to preserve Peace, in case of any quarrels that may fall out between man and man: for though the Earth with her fruits be a common Treasury, and is to be planted and reaped by common Assistance of every family, yet every house, and all the furniture for ornament therein, is a propriety to the Indwellers; and when any family hath fetched in from the Store-houses or shops either

Clothes, food, or any ornament necessary for their use, it is all a propriety to that family.

And if any other family or man come to disturb them, and endeavor to take away furniture, which is the ornament of his neighbors house, or to burn, break, or spoyl wilfully any part of his neighbors houses, or endeavor to take away either the food or clothing which his neighbor hath provided for his use, by reason whereof quarrels and provoking words may arise:

This Office of Overseers is to prevent disturbance, and is an Assistance to the Peace-maker; and at the hearing of any such offence, this Overseer shall go and hear the matter, and endeavor to perswade the offendor, and to keep peace; and if friendship be made, and subjection be yielded to the Laws for the Peace of the Commonwealth, the offendor is only to be reproved for his rashness by this Overseer; and there is an end.

But if the offender be so violent, that he will not refrain his offence to his neighbor at this Overseers perswasion, but remain stiff and stubborn, this Overseer shall then give out an Order to the Souldier to carry the body of the offendor before the Councel of the Peace-makers, or before any one or more of them.

And if the offendor will not yield obedience to the Laws of Peace by the perswasion of the chief Peace-makers neither, then this is to be noted to be the second time that this offendor hath refused mercy.

Then shall the Peace-maker appoint him a day, and command him to appear before the Judges Court, either in the City or Country, where the offence is given, and there he shall receive sentence according to the rigor of the Law.

And if an Overseer should make peace, and do not send the offender to the Peace-makers Court, yet this shall be noted the first time of such a ones disobedience to the Laws.

And all this is to prevent quarrels and offences; and the chief Peace-makers or Counsellors may not always be at hand at the beginning of such disturbance, therefore this Overseer is an Assistance thereunto, and is a Member of that Court.

One man shall not take away that Commodity which another man hath first layd hands on, for any Commodity for use belongs to him that first layd [43] hands on it for his use; and if another come and say, I will have it, and so offences do arise, this Overseer shall go to them, or give order to the Souldier to bring the offender to him, and shall endeavor to make peace, either by giving the Commodity to him who first layd hands on it, or else by taking the Commodity from both, and bid them go to the Store-houses and fetch more, seeing the Store-houses are full, and afford plenty of the same Commodities, giving the offender a sharp reproof for offering to break the Peace, noting this to be the first time that such a one offered violence to break the Laws of Peace.

And all persons whatsoever shall assist the Overseers herein; and if any person strike or affront by words this Overseer, he shall give order to the Souldier to carry him before the Peace-makers, and from them the offender shall receive a Command to appear before the Judges Court, where he shall receive the sentence of the Law without mitigation.

For when a Peace-maker or Councellor doth appoint an offender to appear before the Judges Court, such an offender hath refused mercy twice.

All this is to be done in case of small offences; but if any offence be offered by any which comes within compass of death, there shall be no Peace-maker to be a Mediator aforehand, but the offendor shall be tryed by the Law.

The second Office of Overseership is for Trades.

And this Overseer is to see that young people be put to Masters, to be instructed in some labour, Trade, Science, or to be waiters in Store-houses, that none be idly brought up in any family within his Circuit.

Likewise this Overseer is to assist any Master of a family by his advice and counsel in the secrets of his Trades, that by the experience of the Elders, the young people may learn the inward knowledg of the things which are, and find out the secrets of Nature.

And seeing there are variety of Trades, there are to be chosen Overseers for every Trade, so many Overseers as the largeness of the Town and City requires; and the employment of this Overseer is not to work (unless he will himself) but to go from house to house to view the works of the people of every house belonging to his Trade and Circuit, and to give directions as he sees cause, and see that no youth be trained up in idleness, as is said.

And if this Overseer find any youth more capable and fit for another Trade then his own, he shall speak to some Overseers of another Trade, who shall provide him a Master, with the consent of his father, and appoint him what family to live in.

And if the father of a family be weak, sick, or naturally foolish, wanting [44] the power of wisdom and government, or should be dead before his children should be instructed; then the Overseers of this Trade, wherein the Father was brought up, are to put those Children into such Families, where they may be instructed, according to the Law of the Commonwealth.

One man may be an Overseer for twenty or thirty Families of Shoomakers; another for Smiths, another for Weavers of Cloth, another for the Keepers of Storehouses or Shops: for every Trade is to have an *Overseer* for that particular Trade.

And truly the Government of the Halls and Companies in *London* is a very rational and well ordered Government; and the *Overseers of Trades* may very well be called *Masters, Wardens, and Assistants* of such and such a Company, for such and such a particular Trade. Onely two things are to be practised to preserve peace.

The first is, *That all these Overseers shall be chosen new ones every year.* And secondly, *The old Overseers shal not chuse the new ones,* to prevent the creeping in of Lordly Oppression: but all the Masters of Families, and Freemen of that Trade, shall be the chusers, and the old *Overseers* shall give but their single voyce among them.

And as there are to be *Overseers for Trades* in Towns and Cities;

So there are to be chosen *Overseers* in the Country Parishes, to see the Earth planted; and in every Parish in the Country may be chosen four or six *Overseers of Husbandry,* to see the Ground planted within their Circuits, and to see that the work of Husbandry be done orderly, and according to Reason and skill.

Some *Overseers* to look after the *Shepherds,* and appoint out such men as are skilled in that work. Some *Overseers* to look after the *Herdsmen.* Some *Overseers* of them who look to *Horses.* And some for the *Daries.* And the work of these *Overseers* is to see that every Family send in their assistance to work, both in plowing and dressing the Earth, in that season of the year, in *seed time;* and in reaping the fruits of the *Earth,* and housing them in *Storehouses* in time of *Harvest.*

Likewise they are to see, that all *Barns* belonging to any Family, or more publique *Storehouses* belonging to a Parish, be kept in sufficient repair. Likewise they are to see, that every Family do keep sufficient *working tools* for common use, as *Plows, Carts, and furniture,* according as every Family is furnished with men to work therewith: likewise Pickaxes, Spades, Pruning-hooks, and any such like necessary instrument.

Likewise it is the work of this *Overseership* to see, that *Schoolmasters, Postmasters, and Minsters,* do their several Offices, according to the Laws.

[45] Likewise this Overseership for Trades shall see, That no man shall be a House-keeper, and have Servants under him, till he hath served under a Master seven years, and hath learned his Trade: and the reason is, that every Family may be governed by stayd and experienced Masters, and not by wanton youth.

And this Office of Overseership keeps all people within a peaceable harmony of Trades, Sciences, or Works, that there be neither Beggar nor idle person in the Commonwealth.

The third Office of Overseership is to see particular Tradesmen
bring in their Works to Storehouses and Shops, and to
see the Waiters in Storehouses do their duty.

As there are particular Trades requiring strength, and some men are strong to perform such works; so there are some weak in body, whose employment shall be to be Keepers of Storehouses and Shops, both to receive in Commodities, and deliver out again, as any particular Family, or man, wants and comes for them.

As for example:

When Lether is tanned, it shall be brought into the Storehouses for Lether; and from thence Shoomakers, and Harness-makers, and such like, may fetch it as they need.

So for Linnen and Woolen Cloth, it is to be brought by the Weavers into the Storehouses or Shops, from whence particular Families of other Trades may fetch as they need: And so for any Commodity, as in the Law for Storehouses is declared.

Now the work of this Overseership is of the same nature with the other for Trades; onely this is to be imployed onely about the Oversight of Storehouses and shops.

And they are to see that particular Tradesmen, as Weavers of Linnen and Woolen Cloth, Spinners, Smiths, Hatters, Glovers, and such like, do bring in their Works into the shops appointed: And they are to see that the Shops and Storehouses within their several Circuits, be kept still furnished.

That when Families of other Trades want such commodities as they cannot make, they may go to the Shops and Storehouses where such commodities are, and receive them for their use, without buying or selling.

And as this Officer sees the particular Tradesmen to furnish the shops and Storehouses, so they shall see that the Keepers of the shops and Storehouses be diligent to wait, both to receive in, and deliver out again, according to the Law, any commodity under their charge.

[46] And if any Keeper of a Shop and Storehouse neglect his duty of his place, through idleness, or vain conversation, or pride, whereby just offence is given, the Overseers shall admonish him and reprove him: If he amend, all is well; if he doth not, he shall give order to the Soldiers to carry him before the Peace-Makers Court: and if he reform upon the reproof of that Court, all is well: but if he doth not reform, he shall be sent unto by the Officers to appear before the Judges Court, and the Judg shall pass Sentence, *That he shall be put out of that House and Employment, and sent among the Husbandmen to work in the Earth: And some other shall have his place and house till he be reformed.*

Likewise this Overseer shall see to it, That the Keepers of Shops and Storehouses do keep their Houses in sufficient repair: and when any house wants repair, the Keepers thereof shall speak to any of the Overseers for Trades, and they shall appoint either Brick-Layers, Masons, Smiths, or Carpenters forthwith to take the work in hand and finish it.

Fourthly, All ancient men, above sixty years of age, are general Overseers.

And wheresoever they go, and see things amiss in any Officer or Tradesman, they shall call any Officer or others to account for their neglect of Duty to the Commonwealths Peace: And these are called *Elders.*

And every one shall give humble respect to these, as to Fathers, and as to men of the highest experience in the Laws, for the keeping of Peace in the Commonwealth.

And if these see things amiss, and do speak, all Officers and others shall assist and protect them, to see the Laws carefully executed: and every one that affronts or abuses these in words or deeds, shall suffer punishment according to the sentence of the Judg.

And all these shall be generall assistances and encouragers of all Officers in the doing the work of their places.

And the Reason of all is this, That many eyes being watchfull, the Laws may be obeyed, for to preserve Peace.

But if any of these Elders should vent their passion, or express envy against any one, and set up his own will above the Law, and do things contrary to Law, upon complaint, the Senators at the Judges Court shal examine the matter; if he be faulty the Judge shal reprove him the first time, but the second time he does so the Judge shall pronounce, That he shal lose his Authoritie and never beare Office nor generall over-sight more while he lives, onely he shal have respect as a man of Age.

[47] *What is the Office of a Souldier?*

A Souldier is a Magistrate as well as any other Officer, and indeed all State Officers are Souldiers for they represent power, and if there were not power in the hand of Officers, the spirit of rudeness would not be obedient to any Law or Government, but their own wils.

Therefore every year shal be chosen a Souldier, like unto a Marshal of a City, and being the chief he shall have divers Souldiers under him at his command, to assist in case of need.

The work of a Souldier in times of Peace, is, to fetch in Offenders, and to bring them before either Officer or Courts, and to be a protection to the Officers against all disturbances.

The Souldier is not to do any thing without Order from the Officers; but when he hath an Order then he is to act accordingly; and he is to receive Orders from the Judges Court, or from the Peace-makers Court, or from Over-seers as need shall require.

If a Souldier hath brought an Offender before a Peace-maker, and if the Offender will not be subject to the Law by his perswasion, and the Peace-maker send him to the Judges Court, if the offence be under matters of death, the offender shal not be imprisoned in the mean time; But the Peace-maker shal command him to appear before the Judges Court at the time appointed, and the Offender shall promise to obey: and this shal be for two Reasons.

First to prevent cruelty of Prisons. Secondly, in the time of his binding over he may remember himself, and amend his wayes, and by testimony of his own actions and neighbours reports, his sentence may be mitigated by the Judge; for it is amendment not destruction that Common-wealths Law requires.

And if this Offender run away from that Country to another, and so both disobey the Peace-makers command, and break his own promise of appearance; then shall the Souldiers be sent forth into all places to search for him, and if they catch him, they should bring him before the Judge, who shall pronounce sentence of death upon him without mercy.

And if any protect him or shelter him, after hue and cry is made after him, all such protectors shal suffer the losse of Freedome for twelve moneths time, as is shewed hereafter what that is.

But if the offence should be matter of death, then the Peace-maker shal take no promise from him for his appearance, but let the Souldier carry him to Prison, till the next Judges Court sits where he shall have his Tryall.

The Work of a Task-master.

The Work or Office of a Task-master is to take those into his oversight as are sentenced by the Judge to lose their Freedome, and to appoint them their work and to see they do it.

[48] If they do their Tasks, he is to allow them sufficient victuals and cloathing to preserve the health of their bodies.

But if they prove desperate, wanton, or idle, and will not quietly submit to the Law, the Task-master is to feed them with short dyet, and to whip them, *for a rod is prepared for the fools back*, till such time as their proud hearts do bend to the Law.

And when he findes them subject, he shal then carry a favourable hand towards them, as to offending brethren, and allow them sufficient diet and clothes in hopes of their amendment, but withall see they do their work, till by the sentence of the Law he be set free again.

The Task-master shal appoint them any kind of work or labour as he pleases that is to be done by man.

And if any of these Offenders run away, there shal be hue and cry sent after him, and he shal dye by the sentence of the Judge when taken again.

The Work of an Executioner.

If any have so highly broke the Laws, as they come within the compasse of whiping, imprisoning and death, The Executioner shal cut off the head, hang, or shoot to death, or whip the offender according to the sentence of Law. Thus you may see what the work of every Officer in a Town or City is.

What is the work of a Judge?

The Law it self is the Judge of all mens actions, yet he who is chosen to pronounce the Law is called Judge, because he is the mouth of the Law, for no single man ought to Judge or interpret the Law.

Because the Law it self, as it is left us in the letter, is the mind and determination of the Parliament and of the people of the Land, to be their Rule to walk by and to be the touch stone of all actions.

And that man who takes upon him to interpret the Law, doth either darken the sence of the Law, and so makes it confused and hard to be understood, or else puts another meaning upon it, and so lifts up himself above the Parliament, above the Law, and above all people in the Land.

Therefore the work of that man who is called Judge, is to hear any matter that is brought before him; and in all cases of difference between man and man, he shall see the parties on both sides before him, and shall hear each man speak for himself without a Fee'd Lawyer; likewise he is to examine any witness who is to prove a matter in Tryal before him.

And then he is to pronounce the bare Letter of the Law concerning such a thing, for he hath his name Judge, not because his will and mind is to Judge the actions of offenders before him, but because he is the mouth to pronounce the Law, who indeed is the true Judge; therefore *to this Law and to this Testimonie* let every one have a regard who intends to live in peace in the Commonwealth.

[49] But from hence hath arose much misery in the Nations under

Kingly Government, in that the man called the Judg hath been suffered to interpret the Law; and when the mind of the Law, the Judgment of the Parliament, and the Government of the Land, is resolved into the brest of the Judges, this hath occasioned much complaining of Injustice, in Judges, in Courts of Justice, in Lawyers, and in the course of the Law it self, as if it were an evil Rule.

Because the Law, which was a certain Rule, was varied, according to the will of a covetous, envious, or proud Judg, therefore no marvel though the Kingly Laws be so intricate, and though few know which way the course of the Law goes, because the sentence lies many times in the brest of a Judg, and not in the letter of the Law.

And so the good Laws made by an industrious Parliament, are like good Eggs layd by a silly Goose, and as soon as she hath layd them, she goes her way, and lets others take them, and never looks after them more, so that if you lay a stone in her nest, she will sit upon it, as if it were an Egg.

And so though the Laws be good, yet if they be left to the will of a Judg to interpret, the Execution hath many times proved bad.

And truly as the Laws and people of Nations have been abused by suffering men Judges to alter the sence by their Interpretation:

So likewise hath the Scriptures of *Moses,* the Prophets, Christ, and his Apostles, been darkened and confounded by suffering Ministers to put their Inferences and Interpretations upon them.

And surely both the Judges for the Law, and the Ministers for Gods Word, have been both unfaithful servants to man and to God, by taking upon them to expound and interpret that Rule which they are bound to yield obedience to, without adding to, or diminishing from.

What is the Judges Court?

In a County or Shire there is to be chosen
    A Judg.
    The Peace-makers of every Town within that Circuit.
    The Overseers, and
    A band of Souldiers attending thereupon.

And this is called the Judges Court, or the County Senate: This Court shall sit four times in the year, or oftener if need be, in the Country, and four times in the year in great Cities: In the first quarter of the year they shall sit in the East part of the County, and the second quarter of the year in the West, in the third in the South, and in the fourth in the North.

[50] And this Court is to oversee and examine any Officer within their County or Limits; for their work is to see, that every one be faithful in his place; and if any Officer hath done wrong to any, this Court is to pass sentence of punishment upon the offender, according to his offence against the Law.

If any grievance lie upon any man, wherein inferior Officers cannot ease him, this Court shall quietly hear his Complaint, and ease him; for where a Law is wanting, they may prepare a way of ease for the offender till the Parliament sit, who may either establish that conclusion for a Law, if they approve of it, or frame another Law to that effect; for it is possible that many things may fall out hereafter, which the Law-makers for the present may not foresee.

If any disorder break in among the people, this Court shall set things to rights: If any be bound over to appear at this Court, the Judg shall hear the matter, and pronounce the letter of the Law, according to the nature of the offence.

So that the alone work of the Judg is to pronounce the sentence and mind of the Law: and all this is but to see the Laws executed, that the Peace of the Commonwealth may be preserved.

What is the work of a Commonwealths Parliament in general?

A Parliament is the highest Court of Equity in a Land, and it is to be chosen every year; and out of every City, Town, and certain limits of a Country through the Land, two, three, or more men are to be chosen to make up this Court.

This Court is to oversee all other Courts, Officers, persons and actions, and to have a full Power, being the Representative of the whole Land, to remove all grievances, and to ease the people that are oppressed.

A Parliament hath his rise from the lowest Office in a Commonwealth, *viz.* from the father in a family: For as a fathers tender care is to remove all grievances from the oppressed children, not respecting one before another; so a Parliament are to remove all burdens from the people of the Land, and are not to respect persons who are great before them who are weak; but their eye and care must be principally to relieve the oppressed ones, who groan under the Tyrants Laws and

Power: The strong, or such as have the Tyrant Power to uphold them, need no help.

But though a Parliament be the Father of a Land, yet by the Covetousness and Cheats of Kingly Government the heart of this Father hath been alienated from the children of the Land, or else so over-awed by the frowns of a Kingly Tyrant, that they could not or durst not act for the weakest childrens ease.

[51] For hath not Parliaments sat, and rose again, and made Laws to strengthen the Tyrant in his Throne, and to strengthen the rich and the strong by those Laws, and left oppression upon the backs of the oppressed still?

But I'le not reap up former weaknesses, but rather rejoyce in hope of amendment, seeing our present Parliament hath declared *England* to be a free Commonwealth, and to cast out Kingly Power; and upon this ground I rejoyce in hope, that succeeding Parliaments will be tender-hearted Fathers to the oppressed children of the Land.

And not only dandle us upon the knee with good words and promises till particular mens turns be served, but will fill our bellies, and clothe our backs with good actions of Freedom, and give to the oppressed childrens children their birth-right portion, which is Freedom in the Commonwealths Land, which the Kingly Law and Power, our cruel step-fathers and step-mothers, have kept from us and our fathers for many years past.

The particular work of a Parliament is four-fold.

First, As a tender father, a Parliament is to impower Officers, and give out Orders for the free planting and reaping of the Commonwealths Land, that all who have been oppressed, and kept from the free use thereof by Conquerors, Kings, and their Tyrant Laws, may now be set at liberty to plant in Freedom for food and rayment, and are to be a protection to them who labour the Earth, and a punisher of them who are idle. But some may say, What is that I call Commonwealths Land?

I answer, All that Land which hath been withheld from the Inhabitants by the Conqueror, or Tyrant Kings, and is now recovered out of the hands of that Oppression by the joynt assistance of the persons and purses of the Commoners of the Land; for this Land is the price of their blood; it is their birth-right to them and their posterity, and ought not to be converted into particular hands again by the Laws of a free Commonwealth.

And in particular, this Land is all Abby Lands, formerly recovered out of the hands of the Popes Power by the Blood of the Commoners of *England,* though the Kings withheld their rights herein from them.

So likewise all Crown Lands, Bishops Lands, with all Parks, Forrests, Chases, now of late recovered out of the hands of the Kingly Tyrants, who have set Lords of Manors and Task-masters over the Commoners, to withhold the free use of the Land from them.

So likewise all the Commons and waste Lands, which are called Commons, because the poor was to have part therein; but this is withheld from the Commoners, either by Lords of Manors, requiring quit Rents, and overseeing the poor so narrowly, that none dares build him a house upon [52] this Common Land, or plant thereupon, without his leave, but must pay him rent, fines, and heriots, and homage, as unto a Conqueror; or else the benefit of this Common Land is taken away from the younger brethren by rich Land-lords and Freeholders, who overstock the Commons with Sheep and Cattel, so that the poor in many places are not able to keep a Cow, unless they steal grass for her.

And this is the bondage the poor complain of, that they are kept poor by their brethren in a Land where there is so much plenty for every one, if Covetousness and pride did not rule as King in one brother over another, and Kingly Government occasions all this.

Now it is the work of a Parliament to break the Tyrants bands, to abolish all their oppressing Laws, and to give Orders, Encouragements and Directions unto the poor oppressed people of the Land, that they forthwith plant and manure this their own Land, for the free and comfortable livelyhood of themselves and posterities.

And to declare to them, it is their own Creation rights, faithfully and couragiously recovered by their diligence, purses and blood from under the Kingly Tyrants and Oppressors Power.

The work of a Parliament, secondly,

Is to abolish all old Laws and Customs, which have been the strength of the Oppressor, and to prepare, and then to enact new Laws for the ease and Freedom of the people, but yet not without the peoples knowledg.

For the work of a Parliament herein is three-fold.

First, When old Laws and Customs of the Kings do burden the people, and the people desire the remove of them, and the establishment of more easie Laws,

It is now the work of a Parliament to search into Reason and Equity, how relief may be found out for the people in such a case, and to preserve a common Peace; and when they have found out a way by debate of Councel among themselves, whereby the people may be relieved, they are not presently to establish their Conclusions for a Law.

But in the next place, they are to make a publike Declaration thereof to the people of the Land who choose them for their approbation; and if no Objection come in from the people within one moneth, they may then take the peoples silence as a consent thereto.

And then in the third place, they are to enact it for a Law, to be a binding Rule to the whole Land: For as the remove of the old Laws and Customs are by the peoples consent, which is proved by their frequent petitioning and Requests of such a thing; so the enacting of new Laws [53] must be by the Peoples consent and knowledg likewise.

And here they are to require the consent, not of men interested in the old oppressing Laws and Customs, as Kings used to do, but of them who have been oppressed. And the Reason is this:

Because the people must be all subject to the Law, under pain of punishment; therefore it is all reason they should know it before it be enacted, that if there be any thing of the Councel of Oppression in it, it may be discovered and amended.

But you will say, If it must be so, then will men so differ in their judgments, that we shall never agree. I answer:

There is but Bondage and Freedom, particular Interest, or common Interest; and he who pleads to bring in particular interest into a free Commonwealth, will presently be seen and cast out, as one bringing in Kingly Slavery again.

And men in place and office, where greatness and honor is coming in, may sooner be corrupted to bring in particular Interest, then a whole Land can be, who must either suffer sorrow under a burthensom Law, or rejoyce under a Law of Freedom.

And surely those men, who are not willing to enslave the People, will not be unwilling to consent hereunto.

The work of a Parliament thirdly,

Is to see all those burthens removed actually, which have hindered, or do hinder, the oppressed People from the enjoyment of their Birth-Rights.

If their Common Lands be under the Oppression of Lords of Manors, they are to see the Land freed from that Slavery.

If the Commonwealths Land be sold by the hasty Councel of subtil, covetous, and ignorant Officers, who act for their own particular Interest: and so hath entangled the Commoners Land again, under colour of being bought and sold,

A *Parliament* is to examine what Authority any had to sell or buy the Commonwealth Land, without a general consent of the People; for it is not any ones, but every ones Birth-Right: And if some through covetousness and self-interest gave consent privately, yet a *Parliament*, who is the Father of a Land, ought not to give consent to buy and sell that land, which is all the childrens Birth-Right, and the price of their labors, monies, and blood.

They are to declare likewise, that the bargain is unrighteous, and that the Buyers and Sellers are Enemies to the Peace and Freedom of [54] the Commonwealth: For indeed the Necessity of the people chose a *Parliament* to help them in their weakness; and where they see a danger like to impoverish or enslave one part of the people to another, they are to give warning, and so prevent that danger; for they are the Eyes of the Land: And surely those are blinde Eyes that lead the People into Bogs, to be entangled in Mud again, after they are once pulled out.

And when the Land is once freed from the Oppressors Power and Laws, a *Parliament* is to keep it so, and not suffer it by their consent to have it bought or sold, and so entangled in bondage upon a new account.

And for their faithfulness herein to the People, the People are engaged by Love and Faithfulness to cleave close to them, in defence and protection. But when a *Parliament* have no care herein, the hearts of the People run away from them like sheep who have no Shepherd.

All grievances are occasioned either by the covetous Wills of State-Officers, who neglect their obedience to the good Laws, and then prefer their own Ease, Honor, and Riches before the Ease and Freedom of the oppressed People. And here a *Parliament* is to cashier and punish those Officers, and place others who are men of publique spirits in their rooms.

Or else the Peoples Grievances arise from the practise and power that the Kings Laws have given to Lords of Manors, covetous Landlords, Tythe-takers, or unbounded Lawyers, being all strengthened in their oppressions over the People by that Kingly Law. And when the people are burthened herewith, and groan, waiting for deliverance, as the oppressed people of *England* do at this day; it is then the work of a *Parliament* to see the people delivered, and that they enjoy their Creation-Freedoms in the Earth: They are not to dally with them, but as a Father is ready to help his children out of misery, when they either see them in misery, or when the children cry for help; so should they do for the oppressed People.

And surely for this end, and no other, is a *Parliament* chosen, as is cleared before: for the Necessity of common preservation and peace is the Fundamental Law both to Officers and People.

The Work of a Parliament fourthly, is this.

If there be occasion to raise an Army to wage War, either against an Invasion of a Forreign Enemy, or against an Insurrection at home; it is the work of a *Parliament* to manage that business for to preserve common [55] Peace. And here their work is three-fold:

First, To acquaint the people plainly with the cause of the War, and to shew them the danger of such an Invasion or Insurrection; and so from that cause require their assistance in person, for the preservation of the Laws, Liberties, and Peace of the Commonwealth, according to their Engagement when they were chosen, which was this: *Do you maintain our Laws and Liberties, and we will protect and assist you.*

Secondly, A *Parliament* is to make choyce of understanding, able, and publique spirited men to be Leaders of an Army in this case, and to give them Commissions and Power in the name of the Commonwealth, to manage the work of an Army.

Thirdly, A Parliaments work in this case is either to send Embassadors to another Nation which hath invaded our Land, or that intends to invade; to agree upon terms of peace, or to proclaim War; or else to receive and hear Embassadors from other Lands for the same business, or about any other business concerning the peace and honor of the Land.

For a *Parliament* is the Head of a Commonwealths power, or as it may be said, it is the great Councel of an Army, from whom originally all Orders do issue forth to any Officer or Soldier.

For if so be a *Parliament* had not an Army to protect them, the rudeness of the people would not obey their proceedings: and if a Parliament were not the Representative of the People, who indeed is the body of all Power, the Army would not obey their Orders.

So then, a *Parliament* is the Head of Power in a Commonwealth, and it is their work to manage publique affairs in times of War, and in times of Peace; not to promote the Interest of particular men, but for the Peace and Freedom of the whole Body of the Land, *viz.* of every particular man, that none be deprived of his Creation Rights, unless he hath lost his Freedom by Transgression, as by the Laws is expressed.

The work of a Commonwealths Ministry, and why one day in seven may be a Day of Rest from Labor.

If there were good Laws, and the People be ignorant of them, it would be as bad for the Commonwealth as if there were no Laws at all.

Therefore according to one of the Laws of *Israels* Commonwealth made by *Moses*, who was the Ruler of the People at that time:

It is very rational and good, that one day in seven be still set apart for three Reasons.

First, That the People in such a Parish may generally meet together to [56] see one anothers faces, and beget or preserve fellowship in friendly love.

Secondly, to be a day of rest, or cessation from labor; so that they may have some bodily rest for themselvs and cattel.

Thirdly, that he who is chosen Minister (for that year) in that parish may read to the people three things.

First the affairs of the whole Land, as it is brought in by the Postmaster, as it is related in his office, hereafter following.

Secondly, to read the ·Law of the Common-wealth: not onely to strengthen the memory of the Ancients, but that the young people also, who are not grown up to ripeness of experience, may be instructed, to know when they do well, and when they do ill; ·for the Laws of a Land hath the power of freedom and bondage, life and death in its hand, therefore the necessary knowledge to be known, and he is the best Prophet that acquaints men therewith. That as men grow up in yeers, they may be able to defend the Laws and Government of the Land. But these Laws shall not be expounded by the Reader, for to expound a plain Law, as if a man would put a better meaning, then the letter it self, produces two evils.

First the pure *Law* and the minds of people, will be thereby confounded, for multitude of words darken knowledge.

Secondly the Reader will be puffed up in pride, to contemn the *Lawmakers*, and in time that will prove the father and nurse of Tyranny, as at this day is manifested by our Ministry.

And thirdly, because the mindes of people, generally love discourses, therefore that the wits of men both young and old may be exercised, there may be speeches made in a three-fold nature.

First to declare the acts and passages of former ages and Governments, setting forth the benefit of freedom, by well ordered Governments, as in *Israels Common-wealth,* and the troubles and bondage, which hath always attended oppression and oppressors; as the State of *Pharaoh,* and other Tyrant Kings, who said the earth and people were theirs, and onely at their dispose.

Secondly Speeches may be made, of all Arts and Sciences, some one day, some another; As in Physick, Chyrurgery, Astrology, Astronomy, Navigation, Husbandry, and such like. And in these Speeches may be unfolded the nature of all herbs and plants from the Hysop to the Cedar, as *Solomon* writ of.

Likewise men may come to see into the nature of the fixed and wandring stars, those great powers of God in the heavens above; and hereby men will come to know the secrets of Nature and Creation, within which all true [57] knowledg is wrapped up, and the light in man must arise to search it out.

Thirdly, Speeches may be made, sometimes of the Nature of Mankind, of his darkness and of his light, of his weakness and of his strength, of his love and of his envy, of his sorrow and of his joy, of his inward and outward bondages, and of his inward and outward freedoms, &c. And this is that which the Ministry of Churches generally aim, but only that they confound their knowledg by imaginary study, when any one takes upon him to speak without experience.

Now this is the way

To attain to the true knowledg of God (who is the Spirit of the whole Creation,) as he hath spread himself forth in every form, and more eminently in man; as *Paul* writ, *The Creation in all the several bodies and forms are but the Mansions or fulness of him who hath filled all things with himself.*

And if the Earth were set free from Kingly Bondage, so that every one were sure to have a free livelyhood, and if this liberty were granted, then many secrets of God, and his Works in Nature, would be made publike, which men now adays keep secret to get a living by; so that this Kingly Bondage is the cause of the spreading of ignorance in the Earth: But when Commonwealths Freedom is established, and Pharisaical or Kingly Slavery cast out, then will *knowledg cover the Earth, as the waters cover the Seas,* and not till then.

He who is the chosen Minister for that year to read, shall not be the only man to make Sermons or Speeches: but every one who hath any experience, and is able to speak of any Art or Language, or of the Nature of the Heavens above, or of the Earth below, shall have free liberty to speak when they offer themselves, and in a civil manner desire an audience, and appoint his day: yet he who is the Reader may have his liberty to speak too, but not to assume all the power to himself, as the proud and ignorant Clergy have done, who have bewitched all the World by their subtle Covetousness and pride.

And every one who speaks of any Herb, Plant, Art, or Nature of Mankind, is required to speak nothing by imagination, but what he hath found out by his own industry and observation in tryal.

And because other Nations are of several languages, therefore these speeches may be made sometimes in other Languages, and sometimes in our Mother Tongue, that so the men of our English Commonwealth may attain to all Knowledges, Arts and Languages, and that every one may be encouraged in his Industry, and purchase the countenance and love [58] of their neighborhood, for their wisdom, and experimental knowledge in the things which are.

And thus to speak, or thus to read the *Law* of Nature (or God) as he hath written his name in every body, is to speak a pure language, and this is to speak the truth as Jesus Christ spake it, giving to every thing its own weight and measure.

By this means, in time men shall attain to the practical knowledge of God truly; That they may serve him in spirit and truth; and this knowledge will not deceive a man.

I, but saith the zealous, but ignorant Professor,

This is a low and carnal ministry indeed, this leads men to know nothing, but the knowledge of the earth, and the secrets of nature, but we are to look after spiritual and heavenly things. I answer.

To know the secrets of nature, is to know the works of God; And to know the works of God within the Creation, is to know God himself, for God dwels in every visible work or body.

And indeed if you would know spiritual things, it is to know how the spirit or power of wisdom and life, causing motion, or growth, dwels within, and governs both the several bodies of the stars and planets in the heavens above; and the several bodies of the earth below; as grass, plants, fishes, beasts, birds, and mankinde; for to reach God beyond the Creation, or to know what he will be to a man, after the man is dead, if any otherwise, then to scatter him into his Essences of fire, water, earth and air, of which he is compounded, is a knowledge beyond the line, or capacity of man to attain to while he lives in his compounded body.

And if a man should go to imagine, what God is beyond the Creation, or what he will be in a spiritual demonstration after a man is dead, he doth as the proverb saith, build castles in the air, or tells us of a world beyond the Moon, and beyond the Sun, meerly to blinde the reason of man.

Ile appeal to your self in this question, what other knowledg have you of God, but what you have within the circle of the Creation?

For if the Creation in all its dimentions be the fulness of him, that fills all with himself, and if you your self be part of this Creation, where can you finde God but in that line or station wherein you stand?

God manifests himself in actual knowledge, not in imagination; he is still in motion, either in bodies upon earth, or in the bodies in the heavens, or in both; in the night and in the day, in Winter, in Summer, in cold, in heat, in growth, or not in growth.

But when a studying imagination comes into man, which is the devil, for it is the cause of all evil, and sorrows in the world; that is he who puts [59] out the eyes of mans Knowledg, and tells him, he must beleeve what others have writ or spoke, and must not trust to his own experience: And when this bewitching fancy sits in the chair of Government, there is nothing but saying and unsaying, frowardness, covetousness, fears, confused thoughts, and unsatisfied doubtings, all the days of that mans reign in the heart.

Or secondly, Examine your self, and look likewise into the ways of all Professors, and you shall finde, That the Enjoyment of the Earth below, which you call a low and a carnal Knowledg, is that, which you and all professors (as well as the men of the world, as you call them) strive and seek after.

Wherefore are you so covetous after the World, in buying and selling? counting your self a happy man, if you be rich, and a miserable man if you be poor. And though you say, *Heaven after death is a place of glory, where you shall enjoy God face to face,* yet you are loth to leave the Earth to go thither.

Do not your Ministers preach for to enjoy the Earth? Do not professing Lawyers, as well as others, buy and sell the Conquerors Justice, that they may enjoy the Earth? Do not professing Soldiers fight for the Earth, and seat themselves in that Land, which is the Birth-Right of others, as well as theirs, shutting others out? Do not all professors strive to get Earth, that they may live in plenty by other mens labors?

Do you not make the Earth your very Rest? Doth not the enjoying of the Earth please the spirit in you? and then you say, God is pleased with your ways, and blesseth you. If you want Earth, and become poor, do you not say, God is angry with you, and crosseth you?

Why do you heap up riches? why do you eat and drink, and wear clothes? why do you take a woman, and lie with her to beget children? Are not all these carnal and low things of the Earth? and do you not live in them, and covet them as much as any? nay more then many which you call men of the world?

And it being thus with you, what other spiritual or heavenly things do you seek after more then others? And what is in you more then in others? If you say, there is; then surely you ought to let these earthly things alone to the men of the world, as you call them, whose portions these are, and keep you within the compass of your own sphere, that others seeing you live a life above the world in peace and freedom, neither working your self, nor deceiving, nor compelling others to work for you, they may be drawn to embrace the same spiritual life by your single-hearted conversation. Well, I have done here.

[60] *Let us now examine your Divinity,*

Which you call heavenly, and spiritual things, for herein speeches are made not to advance knowledge, but to destroy the true knowledge of God; for Divinity does not speak the truth, as it is hid in every body, but it leaves the motional knowledge of a thing as it is, And imagins, studies, or thinks what may be, and so runs the hazzard true or false: And this Divinity is always speaking words to deceive the simple, that he may make them work for him, and maintain him, but he never comes to action himself to do as he would be done by; for he is a monster who is all tongue and no hand.

This divining Doctrine, which you call spiritual and heavenly things, is the thief and the robber; he comes to spoile the Vinyard of a mans peace, and does not enter in at the door, but he climbes up another way: And this Doctrine is two fold.

First he takes upon him to tell you the meaning of other mens words, and writing by his studying or imagining what another mans knowledge might be, and by thus doing darkens knowledge, and wrongs the spirit of the Authors who did write and speak those things which he takes upon him to interpret.

Secondly he takes upon him, to foretell what shall befall a man after he is dead, and what that world is beyond the Sun, and beyond the Moon, &c. And if any man tell him there is no reason for what you say, he answers you must not judge of heavenly and spiritual things by reason, but you must beleive what is told you, whether it be reason or no: There is a three-fold discovery of falsehood in this Doctrine.

For first it is a Doctrine of a sickly and weak spirit, who hath lost his understanding in the knowledge of the Creation, and of the temper of his own Heart and Nature, and so runs into fancies, either of joy or sorrow.

And if the passion of joy predominate, then he fancies to himself a personal God, personal Angels, and a local place of glory which he saith, he, and all who beleives what he saith, shall go to, after they are dead.

And if sorrow predominate, then he fancies to himself a personal Devil, and a locall place of torment, that he shall go to after he is dead, and this he speaks with great confidence.

Or Secondly, this is the Doctrine of a subtle running spirit, to make an ungrounded wise man mad. That he might be called the more excellent man in knowledge; for many times when a wise understanding heart is assaulted with this Doctrine of a God, a Devil, a Heaven, and a Hell, Salvation and Damnation after a man is dead, his spirit being not strongly grounded in the knowledge of the Creation, nor in the temper of his own heart,

[61] He strives and stretches his brains to find out the depth of that doctrine and cannot attain to it; for indeed it is not knowledg, but imagination: and so by poring and puzling himself in it, loses that wisdom he had, and becomes distracted and mad: and if the passion of joy predominate, then he is merry, and sings, and laughs, and is ripe in the expressions of his words, and will speak strange things; but all by imagination. But if the passion of sorrow predominate, then he is heavy and sad, crying out, *He is damned, God hath forsaken him, and he must go to Hell when he dys, he cannot make his calling and election sure:* And in that distemper many times a man doth hang, kil, or drown himself: so that this divining Doctrine, which you call *spiritual and heavenly things,* torments people always when they are weak, sickly, and under any distemper; therefore it cannot be the Doctrine of Christ the Saviour.

For my own part, my spirit hath waded deep to finde the bottom of this divining spiritual Doctrine: and the more I searched, the more I was at a loss; and I never came to quiet rest, and to know God in my spirit, till I came to the knowledg of the things in this Book: And let me tell you, They who preach this divining Doctrine are the murtherers of many a poor heart, who is bashful and simple, and that cannot speak for himself, but that keeps his thoughts to himself.

Or thirdly, This Doctrine is made a cloke of policy by the subtil elder Brother, to cheat his simple younger Brother of the Freedoms of the Earth: For saith the elder Brother, *The Earth is mine, and not yours, Brother; and you must not work upon it, unless you will hire it of me: and you must not take the fruits of it, unless you will buy them of me, by that which I pay you for your Labor: for if you should do other-*

wise, God will not love you, and you shall not go to Heaven when you dye, but the Devil will have you, and you must be damned in Hell.

If the younger reply, and say, *The Earth is my Birth-Right, as well as yours, and God who made us both, is no Respecter of persons: Therefore there is no Reason but I should enjoy the Freedoms of the Earth for my comfortable Livelyhood, as well as you, Brother.*

I, but saith the elder Brother, *You must not trust to your own Reason and Understanding, but you must beleeve what is written and what is told you; and if you will not beleeve, your Damnation will be the greater.*

I cannot beleeve, saith the younger Brother, *that our righteous Creator should be so partial in his Dispensations of the Earth, seeing our bodies cannot live upon Earth without the use of the Earth.*

[62] The elder brother replies, What, will you be an Atheist, and a factious man, will you not believe God?

Yes, saith the younger brother, if I knew God said so I should believe, for I desire to serve him.

Why, saith the elder brother, this is his Word, and if you will not believe it, you must be damned; but if you will believe it, you must go to Heaven.

Well, the younger brother being weak in spirit, and having not a grounded knowledg of the Creation, nor of himself, is terrified, and lets go his hold in the Earth, and submits himself to be a slave to his brother, for fear of damnation in Hell after death, and in hopes to get Heaven thereby after he is dead; and so his eyes are put out, and his Reason is blinded.

So that this divining spiritual Doctrine is a cheat; for while men are gazing up to Heaven, imagining after a happiness, or fearing a Hell after they are dead, their eyes are put out, that they see not what is their birthrights, and what is to be done by them here on Earth while they are living: This is the filthy Dreamer, and the Cloud without rain.

And indeed the subtle Clergy do know, that if they can but charm the people by this their divining Doctrine, to look after riches, Heaven and Glory when they are dead, that then they shall easily be the Inheritors of the Earth, and have the deceived people to be their servants.

This divining Doctrine, which you call spiritual and heavenly, was not the Doctrine of Christ, for his words were pure knowledg, they were words of life; for he said, *He spoke what he had seen with his Father*, for he had the knowledg of the Creation, and spake as every thing was.

And this Divinity came in after Christ to darken his Knowledg; and it is the language of the Mystery of Iniquity and Antichrist, whereby the covetous, ambitious and serpentine spirit cozens the plain-hearted of his portions in the Earth.

And Divinity cozens a plain heart two ways: First, If a man have an Estate, according to the Kings Laws, he is made by this charm to give it, or bazle [i. e., waste] it away to the Priests, or to religious uses, in hopes to get Heaven when he is dead.

Or secondly, A man by running to hear Divinity Sermons, and dancing after his charming pipe, neglects his labour, and so runs into debt, and then his fellow professors will cast him into prison, and starve him there, and there Divinity will call him a hypocrite and wicked man, and become a Devil to torment him in that Hell.

But surely Light is so broke out, that it will cover the Earth, so that the Divinity Charmers shall say, *The people will not hear the voyce of our charming, charm we never so wisely:* And all the Priests, and Clergy, and Preachers [63] of these spiritual and heavenly things, as they call them, shall take up the lamentation, which is their portion, *Alas, alas, that great City Babylon, that mighty City Divinity, which hath filled the whole Earth with her sorcery, and deceived all people, so that the whole world wondered after this Beast; how is it faln, and how is her Judgment come upon her in one hour?* And further, as you may read, *Rev.* 18. 10.

The Office of the Post-master.

In every Parish throughout the Commonwealth shall be chosen two men (at the time when other Officers are chosen,) and these shall be called Post-masters: And whereas there are four parts of the Land, East, West, North, South, there shall be chosen in the chief City two men to receive in what the Post-master of the East Country brings in, and two men to receive in what the Post-master of the West brings in, and two for the North, and so two for the South.

Now the work of the Country Post-master shall be this, They shall every Moneth bring up or send by tydings from their respective Parishes to the chief City, of what accidents or passages fall out, which is either to the honor or dishonor, hurt or profit of the Commonwealth; and if nothing have faln out in that Moneth worth observation, then they shall write down peace or good order in such a Parish.

And when these respective Post-masters have brought up their Bills or Certificates from all parts of the Land, the Receivers of those Bills shall write down every thing in order from Parish to Parish in the nature of a Weekly Bill of Observation.

And those eight Receivers shall cause the Affairs of the four quarters of the Land to be printed in one Book with what speed may be, and deliver to every Postmaster a Book, that as they bring up the Affairs of one Parish in writing, they may carry down in Print the Affairs of the whole Land.

The benefit lies here, That if any part of the Land be visited with Plague, Famine, Invasion, or Insurrection, or any casualties, the other parts of the Land may have speedy knowledg, and send Relief.

And if any accident fall out through unreasonable action, or careless neglect, other parts of the Land may thereby be made watchful, to prevent like danger.

Or if any through industry or ripeness of understanding have found out any secret in Nature, or new invention in any Art or Trade, or in the Tillage of the Earth, or such like, whereby the Commonwealth may more flourish in peace and plenty; for which Vertues those persons received honor in the places where they dwelt,

[64] When other parts of the Land hear of it, many thereby will be encouraged to employ their Reason and industry to do the like, that so in time there will not be any Secret in Nature, which now lies hid (by reason of the iron age of Kingly oppressing Government) but by some or other will be brought to light, to the beauty of our Commonwealth.

The Rise of a Commonwealths Army.

After that the necessity of the People in a Parish, in a County, and in a Land, hath moved the People to chuse Officers to preserve *common peace*, the same necessity causeth the People to say to their Officers,

Do you see our Laws observed for our common preservation, and we will assist and protect you.

This word *assist* and *protect*, implies the rising of the people by force of Arms, to defend their Laws and Officers, who rule well, against any Invasion, Insurrection or Rebellion of selfish Officers, or rude people;

yea to beat down the turbulency of any foolish spirit that shall arise to break our common Peace.

So that the same Law of Necessity of common Peace, which moved the people to chuse Officers, and to compose a Law for to be a Rule of Government: The same Law of Necessity of Protection doth raise an Army; so that an Army, as well as other Officers in a Commonwealth, spring from one and the same root, *viz.* from the Necessity of common Preservation.

An Army is two-fold, viz. *A Ruling Army, or a Fighting Army.*

A ruling Army is called Magistracy in times of Peace, keeping that Land and Government in Peace by Execution of the Laws, which the fighting Army did purchase in the field by their Blood out of the hands of Oppression.

And here all Officers, from the father in a family, to the Parliament in a Land, are but the Heads and Leaders of an Army; and all people arising to protect and assist their Officers, in defence of a right ordered Government, are but the Body of an Army.

And this Magistracy is called the rejoycing of all Nations, when the Foundation thereof are Laws of common Equity, whereby every single man may enjoy the fruit of his labour, in the free use of the Earth, without being restrained or oppressed by the hands of others.

Secondly, A fighting Army, called Souldiers in the field, when the necessity of preservation, by reason of a forraign Invasion, or inbred Oppression, do move the people to arise in an Army to cut and teer to pieces, either degenerated Officers, or rude people, who seek their own Interest, and not common Freedom, and through treachery do endeavor to destroy [65] the Laws of common Freedom, and to enslave both the Land and people of the Commonwealth to their particular wills and lusts.

And this War is called a Plague, because that cursed enmity of Covetousness, pride, and vain-glory, and envy in the heart of Mankind did occasion the rise of it, because he will not be under the moderate observation of any free and right Order, unless he himself be King and Lord over other persons and their labours.

For now the people do arise to defend their faithful Officers, against such Officers as are unfaithful, and to defend their Laws and Common Peace.

The use or work of a fighting Army in a Commonwealth

Is to beat down all that arise to endeavor to destroy the Liberties of the Commonwealth: For as in the days of Monarchy, an Army was used to subdue all who rebelled against Kingly Propriety; so in the days of a free Commonwealth, an Army is to be made use of to resist and destroy all who endeavor to keep up or bring in Kingly Bondage again.

The work of this fighting Army is twofold.

The first is to withstand the Invasion, or coming in of a forraign Enemy, whose Invasion is for no other end, but to take away our Land and Earth from us, to deny us the free use thereof, to become Kings and Landlords over us, and to make us their slaves.

As *William* the Conqueror, when he had conquered *England*, he gave not only the Land in parcels to his Souldiers, but he gave all men, their wives and children, within such a Lordship, to his Lords of Manors, to do with them as they pleased: And for this cause now doth an Army arise to keep out an Invasion of a Forraigner, that by the defence of our Army, who is part of our selves, the rest of our brethren in the Commonwealth may plow, sow, and reap, and enjoy the fruits of their labours, and so live in peace in their own Land.

Or secondly, If a Land be conquered, and so enslaved as *England* was, under the Kings and conquering Laws, then an Army is to be raised with as much secrecy as may be, to restore the Land again, and set it free, that the Earth may become a Common Treasury to all her children, without respecting persons, as it was before Kingly Bondage came in, as you may read, I *Sam.* 8.

This latter is called Civil Wars, and this is the Wars of the Commoners of *England* against King *Charls* now cast out, for he and his Laws were the successive Power of that *Norman* Conquest over *England*.

[66] And now the Commoners of *England* in this age of the World are rise up in an Army, and have cast out that Invasion of the Duke of *Normandy*, and have won their Land and Liberties again by the Sword, if they do not suffer their Councels to befool them into slavery again upon a new accompt.

Therefore you Army of *Englands* Commonwealth look to it; the

Enemy could not beat you in the field, but they may be too hard for you by policy in Councel, if you do not stick close to see Common Freedom established.

For if so be that Kingly Authority be set up in your Laws again, King *Charls* hath conquered you and your posterity by policy, and won the field of you, though you seemingly have cut off His Head.

For the strength of a King lies not in the visible appearance of his body, but in his Will, Laws and Authority, which is called Monarchial Government.

But if you remove Kingly Government, and set up true and free Commonwealths Government, then you gain your Crown, and keep it, and leave peace to your posterity, otherwise not.

And thus doing makes a War either lawful or unlawful.

An Army may be Murtherers and unlawful.

If an Army be raised to cast out Kingly Oppression, and if the Heads of that Army promise a Commonwealths Freedom to the oppressed people, if in case they will assist with person and purse, and if the people do assist, and prevail over the Tyrant, those Officers are bound by the Law of Justice (who is God) to make good their Engagements: And if they do not set the Land free from the branches of the Kingly Oppression, but reserve some part of the Kingly Power to advance their own particular Interest, whereby some of their friends are left under as great slavery to them, as they were under the Kings; Those Officers are not faithful Commonwealths Souldiers, they are worse Thieves and Tyrants then the Kings they cast out, and that Honor they seemed to get by their Victories over the Commonwealths Oppressor they lose again, by breaking Promise and Engagement to their oppressed friends who did assist them.

For what difference is there between a professed Tyrant, that declares himself a Tyrant in words, Laws and deeds, as all Conquerors do, and him who promises to free me from the Power of the Tyrant if I'le assist him; and when I have spent my estate and blood, and the health of my body, and expect my bargain by his Engagements to me, he sits himself down in the Tyrants Chair, and takes the possession of the Land to himself, and calls it his, and none of mine, and tells me he cannot in Conscience let me enjoy the Freedom of the Earth with him, because it is another mans right?

[67] And now my health and estate is decayed, and I grow in age, I must either beg or work for day wages, which I was never brought up to, for another; when as the Earth is as freely my Inheritance and birthright, as his whom I must work for; and if I cannot live by my weak labors but take where I need, as Christ sent and took the *Asse colt* in his need, there is no dispute, but by the Kings and Laws, he will hang me for a thief.

But hear O thou Righteous Spirit of the whole Creation, and judg, who is the thief. Him who takes away the freedom of the *common-earth* from me, which is my Creation rights, and which I have helped to purchase out of the hands of the Kingly Oppressor by my purse and person, and which he hath taken for wages of me:

Or I, who takes the *Common-earth* to plant upon for my free livelyhood, endeavouring to live as a free *Commoner*, in a free *Commonwealth*, in righteousness and peace.

Such a souldier as this engagement breaker is neither a friend to the Creation: nor to a particular *Common-wealth*, but a self lover and a hypocrite, for he did not fight, to set the Earth free from the bondage of the Oppressor as he pretended by his Engagements; but to remove that power out of the others hand into his own. And this is just like the beasts who fight for mastery and keeps it, not releaving, but still Lording and Kinging over the weak. These are Monarchial souldiers, not *Common-wealths* souldiers; and such a souldier is a murderer and his warfare is unlawful.

But souldiers of true noble spirits, will help the weak, and set the oppressed free, and delight to see the *Common-wealth* flourish in freedom, as wel as their own gardens. There is none of this true nobility in the Monarchial Army, for they are all self lovers; the best is as a briar, and the most upright amongst them is as a thorne held; speak you Prophets of old if this be not true.

A Monarchial Army lifts up mountains, and makes vallies, *viz.* Advances Tyrants, and treads the oppressed in the barren lanes of poverty.

But a *Commonwealths Army* is like *John Baptist*, who levels the Mountains to the Valleys, pulls down the Tyrant, and lifts up the

Oppressed: and so makes way for the spirit of Peace and Freedom to come in to rule and inherit the Earth.

And by this which hath been spoken, an Army may see wherein they may do well, and wherein they may do hurt.

[68] C H A P . V . *Education of mankinde, in Schools and Trades.*

MANKINDE in the days of his youth, is like a young Colt, wanton and foolish, till he be broke by Education and correction, and the neglect of this care, or the want of wisdom in the performance of it hath been, and is, the cause of much division and trouble in the world.

Therefore the Law of a *Common-wealth* does require, that not onely a father, but that all Overseers, and Officers should make it their work to educate children in good manners, and to see them brought up in some trade or other, and to suffer no children in any Parish to live in idleness, and youthful pleasure, all their days, as many have been; but that they be brought up like men, and not like beasts: That so the *Common-wealth* may be planted with laborious and wise experienced men, and not with idle fools.

Mankinde may be considered in a fourfold degree, his childhood, youth, manhood and old age; his childhood and his youth, may be considered from his birth till forty yeers of age; and within this compass of time, after he is weaned from his mother, who shall be the nurse her self, if there be no defect in Nature, his parents shall teach him a civil and humble behavior toward all men. Then send him to School, to learn to read the Laws of the *Common-wealth*, to ripen his wits from his childhood, and so to proceed in his learning, till he be acquainted with all Arts and Languages: and the reason is threefold.

First, By being acquainted with the knowledge of the affairs of the world; by this traditional knowledge they may be the better able to govern themselves like rational men.

Secondly, they may become thereby good *Common-wealths men,* in supporting the government thereof, by being acquainted with the nature of government.

Thirdly, If *England* have occasion to send Embassadors to any other Land, we may have such as are acquainted with their Language; or if any Embassador come from other Lands, we may have such as can understand their speech.

But one sort of Children shall not be trained up onely to book learning, and no other imployment, called Schollars, as they are in the Government of Monarchy, for then through idleness, and exercised wit therein, they spend their time to finde out pollicies to advance themselves, to be Lords and Masters above their laboring brethren, as *Simeon* and *Levi* do, which occasions all the trouble in the world.

Therefore, to prevent the dangerous events of idleness in Scholars, it is reason, and safe for common peace, that after Children have been brought up at Schools, to ripen their wits, they shall then be set to such [69] Trades, Arts and Sciences, as their bodies and wits are capable of; and therein continue till they come to fourty years of age.

For all the work of the Earth, or in Trades, is to be managed by youth, and by such as have lost their Freedoms.

Then from fourty years of age till fourscore, if he live so long, which is the degree of manhood and old age; they shall be freed from all labor and work, unless they will themselves.

And from among this degree of Mankind shal be chosen all Officers and Overseers, to see the Laws of the Commonwealth observed.

For as all men shall be Workers or Waiters in Storehouses till they be fourty years of age, so none shall be chosen a publique Officer till he be full fourty years of age: for by this time Man hath learned experience to govern himself and others: for when young wits are set to govern, they wax wanton, &c.

What Trades should Mankinde be brought up in?

In every Trade, Art, and Science, whereby they may finde out the Secrets of the Creation, and that they may know how to govern the Earth in right order.

There are five Fountains from whence all Arts and Sciences have their influences: he that is an actor in any or in all the five parts, is a profitable son of mankinde: he that onely contemplates and talks of what he reads and hears, and doth not employ his Talent in some bodily action, for the encrease of fruitfulness, freedom, and peace in the Earth, is an unprofitable son.

The first Fountain is the right planting of the Earth to make it fruitful, and this is called Husbandry: And there are two branches of it;

As first, planting, digging, dunging, liming, burning, grubbing, and right ordering of Land, to make it fit to receive seed, that it may bring forth a plentiful crop: And under this Head all Millers, Maltsters, Bakers, Harness-makers for Plows and Carts, Rope-makers, Spinners, and Weavers of linnen, and such like, are all but good Husbandry.

The second Branch of Husbandry is Gardening, how to plant, graft, and set all sort of fruit-trees, and how to order the ground for flowers, Herbs and Roots for pleasure, food, or medicinal. And here all Physicians, Chyrurgeons, Distillers of all sorts of Waters, Gatherers of Drugs, Makers of Wines, and Oyl, and Preservers of fruits, and such like, may learn by Observation, what is good for all bodies, both man and beasts.

The second Fountain is Mineral employment, and that is to search into the Earth to finde out Mynes of Gold and Silver, Brass, Iron, Tin, Lead, Cannel, Coal, and Stone of all sorts, Salt-peter, Salt, and Allom-springs, [70] and such like: And here all Chymists, Gunpowder-makers, Masons, Smiths, and such like, as would finde out the strength and power of the Earth, may learn how to order these for the use and profit of Mankinde.

The third Fountain is the right ordering of Cattel, whether by Shepherds or Herds-men; and such may learn here how to breed and train up Cows for the Daries, Bulls and Horses for the saddle or yoke. And here all Tanners, Hatters, Shoomakers, Glovers, Spinners of Wool, Clothiers, Taylors, Dyers, and such like, may learn how to order and look to these.

The fourth Fountain is the right ordering of Woods and Timber trees, for planting, dressing, felling, framing of Timber for all uses, for building houses or ships. And here all Carpenters, Joyners, Thro-sters [2], Plow-makers, Instrument-makers for musick, and all who work in wood and timber, may finde out the Secret of Nature, to make Trees more plentiful and thriving in their growth, and profitable for use.

The fifth Fountain, from whence Reason is exercised to finde out the Secrets of Nature, is [to] observe the rising and setting of the Sun, Moon, and the Powers of the Heavens above; and the motion of the Tydes, and Seas, and their several effects, powers, and operations upon the bodies of Man and Beast. And here may be learned Astrology, Astronomy, and Navigation, and the motions of the Winds, and the

[2] Turners.

causes of several Appearances of the Face of Heaven, either in Storms, or in Fareness.

And in all these five Fountains here is Knowledg in the practice, and it is good.

But there is Traditional Knowledg, which is attained by reading, or by the instruction of others, and not practical, but leads to an idle life; and this is not good.

The first is a laborious Knowledg, and a Preserver of common Peace, which we finde God himself acting; for he put forth his own wisdom in practise, when he set his strength to work to make the Creation: for God is an active Power, not an imaginary Fancy.

The latter is an idle, lazy contemplation the Scholars would call Knowledg, but it is no knowledg, but a shew of Knowledg, like a *Parrat* who speaks words, but he knows not what he saith: This same shew of knowledg rests in reading or contemplating, or hearing others speak, and speaks so too, but will not set his hand to work: And from this Traditional Knowledg and Learning rise up both Clergy and Lawyer, who by their cunning insinuations live meerly upon the labor of other men, and teach [71] Laws which they themselves will not do, and layes burdens upon others which they themselves will not touch with the least of their fingers; and from hence arises all oppressions, wars, and troubles in the world, the one is the son of contention, the other the son of darkness, but both the supporters of bondage, which the Creation groans under.

Therefore to prevent idleness and the danger of Machivilian cheats, it is profitable for the Common-wealth, that children be trained up in Trades and some bodily imployment, as well as in learning Languages, or the Histories of former ages.

And as boyes are trained up in Learning and in Trades, so all Maides shall be trained up in reading, sewing, kniting, spining of Lynnen and Woollen, Musique, and all other easie neat works, either for to furnish Storehouses with Lynnen and Woollen cloth, or for the ornament of particular houses with needle work.

And if this course were taken, there would be no Idle person nor Beggers in the Land, and much work would be done by that now lazie generation for the enlarging of the common Treasuries.

And in the manageing of any Trade, let no young wit be crushed in his invention, for if any man desire to make a new tryall of his skil in any Trade or Science, the Overseers shall not hinder him, but incourage him therein; that so the Spirit of knowledge may have his full growth in man, to finde out the secret in every Art.

And let every one who finds out a new invention have a deserved honour given him, and certainly when men are sure of food and raiment, their reason will be ripe, and ready to dive into the secrets of the Creation, that they may learn to see and know God (the Spirit of the whole Creation) in all his works; for fear of want, and care to pay Rent to Task-masters, hath hindred many rare Inventions.

So that Kingly Power hath crushed the Spirit of Knowledg, and would not suffer it to rise up in its beauty and fulness, but by his Club Law hath preferred the spirit of Imagination, which is a Deceiver, before it.

There shal be no buying and selling of the Earth, nor of the fruits thereof.

For by the Government under Kings, the cheaters hereby have cozened the plain hearted of their creation birth-rights, and have possessed themselves in the earth and cals it theirs and not the others, and so have brought in that poverty and misery which lies upon many men.

And whereas the wise should help the foolish, and the strong help the weak; the wise and the strong destroys the weak and the simple.

And are not all children generally simple and weak and know not the [72] things that belong to their peace till they come to ripe age, but before they come to that understanding, the cunning ones who have more strength and policy, have by this hypocriticall, lying, unrighteous and cheating Art of buying and selling, wrung the freedoms of the earth out of their hands, and cozened them of their birth-rights.

So that when they come to understanding, they see themselves beggers in the middest of a fruitfull Land, and so the Proverb is true, *Plain dealing is a jewel, but he who uses it shal dye a begger.* And why?

Because this buying and selling is the nursery of cheaters, it is the Law of the Conqueror, and the Righteousness of the Scribes and Pharisees, which both killed Christ and hindred his Resurrection, as much as darkness can to put out light.

And these cunning cheaters commonly become the Rulers of the earth, and then the City Man-kind mourns, for not the wise poor man, but the cunning rich man, was always made an Officer and Ruler, such a one as by his stolen interest in the earth would be sure to hold others in bondage of poverty and servitude to him and his party.

And hence arise oppression and tyranny in the earth upon the backs of the weak younger brethren, who are made younger brothers indeed, as the Proverb is, by their cunning elder brother; and as *Daniel* said, *The basest of men under Kingly government were set to Rule, who can command but not obey, who can take other mens labors to live at ease, but not work themselvs.*

Therefore there shal be no buying and selling in a Free Commonwealth, neither shall any one hire his brother to work for him.

If the Common-wealth might be governed without buying and selling here is a Platform of Government for it, which is the ancientest Law of Righteousness to Mankind in the use of the Earth, and which is the very height of earthly Freedoms. But if the minds of the people, through Covetousness and proud Ignorance, wil have the Earth governed by buying and selling still, this same Platform, with a few things subtracted, declares an easie way of Government of the Earth for the quiet of peoples minds, and preserving of Peace in the Land.

> *For, as like a Tradesman, I ask the highest price,*
> *Yet I may fall (if you will rise) upon a good advice.*

How must the Earth be planted?

The Earth is to be planted, and the fruits reaped, and carried into Barns and Store-houses by the assistance of every family: And if any man or family want Corn, or other provision, they may go to the Store-houses, and fetch without money: If they want a Horse to ride, go into the fields in Summer, or to the Common Stables in Winter, and receive one from the Keepers, and when your Journey is performed, bring him where [73] you had him, without money. If any want food or victuals, they may either go to the Butchers shops, and receive what they want without money; or else go to the flocks of sheep, or herds of cattel, and take and kill what meat is needful for their families, without buying and selling. And the reason why all the riches of the earth are a common stock is this, Because the earth, and the labours thereupon, are managed by common assistance of every family, without buying and selling; as is shewn how more largely, in the Office of Overseers for Trades, and the Law for Store-houses.

The Laws for the right ordering thereof, and the Officers to see the Laws executed; to preserve the peace of every family, and the peace of every man, and to improve and promote every Trade, is shewed in the work of Officers, and by the Laws following.

None will be an enemy to this freedom, which indeed is to do to another as a man would have another do to him, but Covetousness and Pride, the spirit of the old grudging snapping Pharisees, who gives God abundance of good words, in their Sermons, in their Prayers, in their Fasts, and in their Thanksgivings, as though none should be more faithful servants to him then they: nay, they will shun the company, imprison, and kill every one that will not worship God, they are so zealous.

Well now, God and Christ hath enacted an everlasting Law, which is Love; not onely one another of your own minde, but love your enemies too, such as are not of your minde: and, having food and raiment, therewith be content.

Now here is a trial for you, whether you will be faithful to God and Christ, in obeying his Laws; or whether you will destroy the man-childe of true Freedom, righteousness and peace, in his resurrection.

And now thou wilt give us either the tricks of a Souldier, Face about, and return to *Egypt*, and so declare thy self to be part of the Serpents seed, that must bruise the heel of Christ; or else to be one of the plainhearted sons of promise, or members of Christ, who shall help to bruise the Serpents head, which is Kingly oppression; and so bring in everlasting righteousness and peace into the earth. Well, the eye is now open.

Store-houses shall be built and appointed in all places,
and be the common Stock.

There shall be Store-houses in all places, both in the Country and in Cities, to which all the fruits of the earth, and other works made by Tradesmen, shall be brought, and from thence delivered out again to particular Families, and to every one as they want for their use; or else to be transported by Ship to other Lands, to exchange for those things which our Land will not or does not afford.

[74] For all the labours of Husbandmen and Trades-men, within the Land, or by Navigation to or from other Lands, shall be all upon the common Stock.

And as every one works to advance the Common Stock, so every one shall have a free use of any commodity in the Store-house, for his pleasure and comfortable livelihood, without buying and selling, or restraint from any.

And having food and raiment, lodging, and the comfortable societies of his own kinde; what can a man desire more in these days of his travel?

Indeed, covetous, proud, and beastly-minded men desire more, either to be by them to look upon, or else to waste and spoil it upon their lusts; while other brethren live in straits for want of the use thereof.

But the Laws and faithful Officers of a free Commonwealth, do regulate the unrational practice of such men.

There are two sorts of Store-houses; general and particular.

The general Store-houses are such houses as receive in all commodities in the gross; as all Barns, and places to lay Corn and the fruits of the earth at the first reaping: and these may be called Store-houses for Corn, Flax, Wool; for Leather, for Iron, for linen and woollen Cloth, or for any commodity that comes into our hand by Shipping; from whence particular Family or Shop-keepers may fetch as they need, to furnish their lesser shops.

So likewise herds of Cattel in the field, flocks of Sheep, and Horses, are all common Store-houses; so that from the Herds and Flocks every Family may fetch what they want for food or pleasure, without buying and selling.

So likewise all Publike Dayries are Store-houses for Butter and Cheese: yet every Family may have Cows for their own use, about their own house.

And these general Store-houses shall be filled and preserved by the common labour and assistance of every Family; as is mentioned in the Office of Overseer for Trades.

And from these Publike Houses, which are the general stock of the Land, all particular Trades-men may fetch materials for their particular work as they need, or to furnish their particular dwellings with any commodities.

Secondly, there are particular Store-houses or shops;

To which the Trades-men shall bring their particular works; as all instruments of Iron to the Iron-shops, Hats to shops appointed for them; Gloves, Shooes, linen and woollen Cloth in smaller parcels, to shops appointed for every one of them; and the like.

[75] Even as now we have particular trade in Cities, and Towns, called Shopkeepers, which shall remaine still as they be, only altered in their receiving in, and delivering out: for whereas by the Law of Kings or Conquerers, they do receive in and deliver out by buying and selling, and exchanging the Conquerers picture or stampe upon a piece of Gold or Silver, for the fruits of the earth; Now they shall (by the Laws of the Commonwealth) receive into their Shops, and deliver out againe freely, without buying and selling.

They shall receive in, as into a Storehouse, and deliver out againe freely, as out of a common Store-house, when particular persons or Families come for any thing they need, as now they do, by buying and selling under kingly government.

For as particular Families and tradesmen do make several works more then they can make use of; As Hats, Shooes, Gloves, Stockings, Linnen and Woolen cloth: and the like, and do carry their particular work to Store-houses,

So it is all reason and equity, that they should go to other Store-houses, and fetch any other commodity which they want, and cannot make: for as other men partakes of their labors, it is reason they should partake of other mens.

And all these Store-houses and Shops shall be orderly kept by such as shall be brought up to be waiters therein, as is mentioned in the Office of Overseers for trades.

For as there are some men more ingenious to work, so other men are more ingenious in keeping of Store-houses and Shops, to receive in and deliver out commodities. And all this easie work, may be called waiting at such and such a Store-house. As some may waite at Corn-houses, some at linen and woolen houses, some at Leather, some at iron-shops; and every general and particular commodity shall be known where they are, by their houses and shops as it is at this day; so that Townes and Cities, and every Family almost are but Store-houses of one commodity or other, for the uses of the Commonwealth, or to transport to other lands.

Now this same free practice, will kill covetousness, pride, and oppression: for when men have a Law to buy and sell, then, as I said before, the cunning cheaters get great estates by others mens labors; and being rich thereby, become oppressing Lords over their brethren; which occasions all our troubles and wars in all Nations.

Come hither now, all you who chalenge your brethren to deny Christ, as though you were the only men that love Christ, and would be true to him. Here is a trial of your love: can you be as ready to obey the law of liberty [76] which is the command of Christ, as you would have others to obey your Kingly laws of bondage? It may be you will either storme, or go away sorrowful; does not Christ tell you, that if you have food and rayment, you should therewith be content? and in this common freedome, here will be food and rayment, ease and pleasure plentiful, both for you and your brethren; so that none shall beg or starve, or live in the straits of poverty; and this fulfils that righteous law of Christ, *Do as you would be done by:* for that law of Christ can never be performed, till you establish Commonwealths freedome.

Therefore now let it appear, seeing the child is come to the birth, whether you will receive Christ, who is the spreading spirit of freedom, righteousness, and peace; or whether you will return to Monarchy, to embrace that Egyptian bondage still. Well, here is life and death set before you, take whether you will; but know, that unless your righteousness exceed the righteousness of the Kingly and Lordly Scribes and Pharisees, you shall never enjoy true peace in your spirit.

CHAP. VI. *The Kings old laws cannot govern a free Commonwealth.*

THEY cannot govern in times of bondage, and in times of freedom too: they have indeed served many masters, Popish and Protestant: they are like old souldiers, that will but change their name, and turn about, and as they were; and the reason is, because they are the prerogative will of those under any Religion, that count it no freedom to them, unless they be lords over the minds, persons, and labors of their brethren.

They are called the Kings laws, because they are made by the Kings. If any say they were made by the Commoners; It is answered, They were not made by the Commoners, as the Commoners of a free Commonwealth are to make laws.

For in the dayes of the Kings, none were to chuse nor be chosen Parliament men, or law makers, but Lords of Mannors, and Freeholders, such as held title to their inclosures of Land or Charters for their liberties in trades under the King, who called the land his, as he was the Conquerer, or his successor.

All inferior people were neither to chuse, nor to be chosen; and the reason was, because all freeholders of land, and such as held their liberties by Charter, were all of the Kings interest; and the inferior people were successively of the rank of the conquered ones, and servants and slaves from the time of the conquest.

[77] And further, when a Parliament was chosen in that manner, yet if any Parliament man in the uprightness of his heart, did endeavor to promote any freedome, contrary to the Kings will, or former customes from the Conquest he was either committed to prison by the King, or by his house of Lords, who were his ancient *Norman* successive councel of war; or else the Parliament was dissolved and broke up by the King.

So that the old laws were made in times under kingly slavery, not under the liberty of Commonwealths freedome, because Parliament men must have regard to the Kings prerogative interest, to hold his Conquest, or else indanger themselves.

As sometimes it is in these dayes: some officers, dare not speak against the minds of those men who are the chief in power, nor a private souldier against the minde of his officer, lest they be cashiered their places and livelihood.

And so long as the promoting of the Kings will and prerogative was to be in the eye of the law makers, the oppressed Commoners, could never enjoy Commonwealths freedome thereby.

Yet by the wisdome, courage, faithfulness, and industry, of some Parliament men, the Commoners have received here a line, and there a line of freedome inserted into their laws; as those good lines of freedome in *Magna Charta* were obtained by much hardship and industry.

Secondly, they were the Kings laws, because the Kings own creatures made the laws; or Lords of Mannors, Freeholders &c. were successors of the *Norman* souldiers from the Conquest, therefore they could do no other but maintaine their own, and their kings interest.

And do we not see, that all laws were made in the dayes of the Kings to ease the rich Landlord? but the poor laborers were left under bondage still; they were to have no freedome in the earth, by those pharisaical laws: for when laws were made, and Parliaments broke up, the poor oppressed Commoners had no relief, but the power of Lords of Mannors, withholding the free use of the Common land from them, remained still: for none durst make use of any Common land, but at the Lords leave according to the will and law of the Conquerer, therefore the old laws were called the Kings laws.

And these old laws cannot govern a free Commonwealth, because the land now is to be set free from the slavery of the *Norman* Conquest; and the power of Lords of Mannors, and *Norman* freeholders, is to be taken away, or else the Commoners are but where they were, if not faln lower into straights then they were: and the old laws cannot look with any other face then they did; though they be washed with Commonwealths water, [78] their countenance is still withered: therefore it was not for nothing that the Kings would have all their Laws written in French and Latine, and not in English, partly in honour to the *Norman* Race, and partly to keep the common people ignorant of their Creation-freedoms, lest they should rise to redeem themselves: and if those Laws should be writ in English, yet if the same Kingly principles remain in them, the English language would not advantage us any thing, but rather increase our sorrow, by our knowledge of our bondage.

What is Law in general.

Law is a Rule, whereby Man and other creatures are governed in their actions, for the preservation of the common peace. And this Law is twofold:

First, it is the power of Life (called the Law of Nature within the creatures) which does move both man and beast in their actions; or that causes grass, trees, corn, and all plants, to grow in their several seasons: and whatsoever any body does, he does it as he is moved by this inward Law. And this law of Nature moves twofold, *viz.* unrationally, or rationally.

A man by this inward Law is guided to actions of generation and present content, rashly, through a greedy self-love, without any consideration, like foolish children, or like the bruit beasts: by reason whereof, much hurt many times follows the body. And this is called *the law in the members warring against the law of the minde.*

Or when there is an inward watchful oversight of all motions to action, considering the end and effects of those actions, that there be no excess in diet, in speech, or in action break forth, to the prejudice of a mans self or others. And this is called *the light in man, The reasonable power, Or the law of the minde*.

And this rises up in the heart, by an experimental observation of that peace and trouble which such and such words thoughts and actions bring the man into. And this is called *the record on high;* for it is a record in a mans heart above the former unreasonable power. And it is called *the witness or testimony of a mans own conscience*.

And it is said, To the law and to the testimony, &c., for this moderate watchfulness is still the law of Nature in a higher resurrection then the former: it hath many terms which for brevity sake I let pass.

And this twofold work of the law within man strives to bring forth themselves in writing to beget numbers of bodies on their sides. And that power that begets the biggest number alwayes Rules as King and Lord in the creature, and in the creation, till the other part overtop him, even as light and darkness, strive in day and night to succeed each other; or as it is said, *the strong man armed, keeps the heart of man, till a stronger then he come, and cast him out*.

[79] And this written law, proceeding either from reason or unreasonableness, is called the letter; whereby the creation of mankinde, beasts, and earth is governed according to the will of that power which rules. And it is called by his opposite, *the letter that kils*, and by those of the same nature with it, it is called *the word of life*.

As for example, if the experienced, wise, and strong man bears rule, then he writes down his minde to curb the unreasonable law of covetousness and pride in unexperienced men, to preserve peace in the Commonwealth. And this is called *the historical or traditional law*, because it is conveyed from one generation to another by writing; as the laws of *Israels* Commonwealth were writ in a book by *Moses*, and so conveyed to posterity.

And this outward law is a bridle to unreasonableness; or as *Solomon* writ, *it is a whip for the fools back*, for whom only it was added.

Secondly, since *Moses* time, the power of unreasonable covetousness and pride hath sometimes rise up, and corrupted that traditional law.

For since the power of the sword rise up, in Nations to Conquer, the written law hath not been to advance Common freedom and to beat down the unreasonable self-will in mankind, but it hath been framed to uphold that self-will of the Conquerer, right or wrong; not respecting the freedome of the Commonwealth, but the freedome of the Conquerer and his friends only. By reason whereof, much slavery hath been laid upon the backs of the plaine dealing man; And men of publick spirits, as *Moses* was, have been crushed, and their spirits damped thereby; which hath bred, first discontents, and then more wars in the Nations.

And those who have been favorites about the Conquerer, have by hypocrisie and flattery pleased their king, that they might get what they can of the earth into their possession; and thereby have increased the bondage of the painful laborer, if they could but catch him to act contrary to the Conquerers will, called law. And now the City mournes: and do we not see, that the laws of Kings have been alwayes made against such actions as the Common-people were most inclinable to, on purpose to ensnare them into their Sessions and Courts, that the Lawyers and Clergy, who were the Kings supporters, might get money thereby, and live in fulness, by other mens labors?

But hereby the true nature of a wel-governed Commonwealth hath been ruined, and the will of Kings set up for a law, and the law of righteousness, law of liberty trod under foot and killed.

This traditional law of Kings, is that letter at this day which kils true freedom, and it is the fomenter of wars and persecution.

[80] This is the souldier, who cut Christs garment into pieces, which was to have remained uncut and without seame; this law moves the people to fight one against another for those pieces, *viz.* for the several inclosures of the earth, who shall possess the earth, and who shall be Ruler over others.

But the true ancient law of God, is a Covenant of peace to whole mankinde; this sets the earth free to all; this unites both Jew and Gentile into one brotherhood, and rejects none: this makes Christs garment whole againe, and makes the kingdomes of the world to become Commonwealths again. It is the inward power of right understanding, which is the true law that teaches people in action, as well as in words, to do as they would be done unto.

But thus much in general, what law is: hereafter followes what those particular laws may be, whereby a Commonwealth may be governed in peace, and all burdens removed; which is a breaking forth of that law of liberty, which will be the joy of all Nations, when he arises up, and is established in his brightness.

Short and pithy laws are best to govern a Commonwealth.

The laws of *Israels* Commonwealth were few, short and pithy; and the government thereof was established in peace, so long as officers and people were obedient thereunto.

But those many laws in the dayes of the Kings of *England*, which were made some in times of Popery, and some in times of Protestantism, and the proceedings of the law being in French and Latine, hath produced two great evils in *England*.

First, it hath occasioned much ignorance among the people, and much contention; and the people have mightily erred through want of knowledge, and thereby they have run into great expence of money by suits of law, or else many have been imprisoned, whipped, banished, lost their estates and lives by that law which they were ignorant of, till the scourge thereof was upon their backs; this is a sore evil among the people.

Secondly, the peoples ignorance of the laws, hath bread many sons of contention: for when any difference fals out between man and man, they neither of them know which offends the other; therefore both of them thinking their cause is good, they delight to make use of the law; and then they go and give a Lawyer mony to tell them, which of them was the offender. The Lawyer being glad to maintain their own trade, sets them together by the ears, till all their moneys be near spent; and then bids them refer the business to their neighbors, to make them friends; which might have been done at the first.

[81] So that the course of the Law and Lawyers hath been a meer snare to entrap the people, and to pull their Estates from them by craft; for the Lawyers do uphold the *Conquerors Interest, and the peoples Slavery:* so that the King seeing that, did put all the *affairs of Judicature* into their hands: And all this must be called *Justice,* but it is a sore Evil.

But now if the Laws were few and short, and often read, it would prevent those Evils; and every one, knowing when they did well, and when ill, would be very cautious of their words and actions; and this would escape the Lawyers craft.

As *Moses* Laws in *Israels* Commonwealth: *The People did talk of them when they lay down, and when they rose up, and as they walked by the way; and bound them as bracelets upon their hands:* so that they were an understanding people in the Laws wherein their peace did depend.

But it is a sign that *England* is a blinded and a snared generation; their *Leaders* through pride and covetousness have caused them to err, yea and perish too, for want of the knowledg of the Laws, which hath the power of Life and Death, Freedom and Bondage, in its hand. But I hope better things hereafter.

What may be those particular Laws, or such a method of Laws,
whereby a Commonwealth may be governed.

1. The bare letter of the Law established by act of *Parliament* shall be the Rule for *Officer and People*, and the chief Judg of all Actions.

2. He or they who add or diminish from the Law, excepting in the Court of *Parliament*, shall be cashiered his Office, and never bear Office more.

3. No man shall administer the Law for Mony or Reward; he that doth shal dye as a Traytor to *the Commonwealth:* for when Mony must buy and sell Justice, and bear all the sway, there is nothing but *Oppression* to be expected.

4. The Laws shall be read by the Minister to the people four times in the year, *viz.* every *quarter*, that every one may know whereunto they are to yeeld Obedience; then none may dye for want of knowledg.

5. No accusation shall be taken against any man, unless it be proved by two or three witnesses, or his own confession.

6. No man shall suffer any punishment, but for matter of fact, or Reviling words: but no man shall be troubled for his judgment or practise in the things of his God, so he live quiet in the Land.

7. The accuser and accused shall always appear face to face before any Officer, that both sides may be heard, and no wrong to either party.

[82] 8. If any Judg or Officer execute his own Will contrary to the Law, or which there is no Law to warrant him in, he shall be cashiered, and never bear Office more.

9. He who raises an accusation against any man, and cannot prove it, shall suffer the same punishment the other should, if proved. An Accusation is when one man complains of another to an Officer; all other accusations the Law takes no notice of.

10. He who strikes his Neighbor, shall be struck himself by the Executioner blow for blow, and shall lose eye for eye, tooth for tooth,

limb for limb, life for life: and the reason is, that men may be tender of one anothers bodies, doing as they would be done by.

11. If any man strike an Officer, he shall be made a servant under the Taskmaster for a whole year.

12. He who endevors to stir up contention among neighbors, by tale-bearing or false reports, shall the first time be reproved openly by the Overseers among all the people: the second time shall be whiped: the third time shall be a servant under the Taskmaster for three Months: and if he continues, he shall be a servant for ever, and lose his Freedom in the Commonwealth.

13. If any give reviling and provoking words, whereby his neighbors spirit is burthened, if complaint be made to the Overseers, they shall admonish the offender privately to forbear: if he continues to offend his neighbor, the next time he shall be openly reproved and admonished before the Congregation, when met together: if he continue, the third time he shall be whipt; the fourth time, if proof be made by witnesses, he shall be a servant under the Taskmaster for twelve Months.

14. He who will rule as a Lord over his brother, unless he be an Officer commanding obedience to the Law, he shall be admonished as aforesaid, and receive like punishment, if he continue.

Laws for the planting of the Earth, &c.

15. Every houshold shall keep all Instruments and Tools fit for the tillage of the Earth, either for planting, reaping or threshing. Some households, which have many men in them, shall keep Plows, Carts, Harrows, and such like: other housholds shall keep Spades, Pick-axes, Axes, pruning hooks, and such like, according as every Family is furnished with men to work therewith.

And if any Master or Father of a Family be negligent herein, the Overseer for that Circuit shall admonish him between them two; if he continue negligent, the Overseers shall reprove him before all the people: and if he utterly refuse, then the ordering of that Family shall be given [83] to another, and he shall be a servant under the taskmaster till he conform.

16. Every family shall come into the field, with sufficient assistance, at seed time to plow, dig, and plant, and at harvest time to reap the fruits of the Earth, and carry them into the Store-houses, as the Over-

seers order the work, and the number of workmen. And if any refuse to assist in this work, The Overseers shall ask the reason, and if it be sickness, or any distemper that hinders them, they are freed from such service; if meer idleness keep them back, they are to suffer punishment, according to the Laws against Idleness.

Laws against Idleness.

17. If any refuse to learn a trade, or refuse to work in seed-time, or harvest, or refuse to be a Waiter in Store-houses, and yet will feed and clothe himself with other mens labors; The Overseers shall first admonish him privately; if he continue idle, he shall be reproved openly before all the people by the Overseers; and shall be forbore with a moneth after this reproof: If he still continues idle, he shall then be whipt, and be let go at liberty for a moneth longer; if still he continue idle, he shall be delivered into the taskmasters hand, who shall set him to work for twelve moneths, or till he submit to right Order: And the reason why every young man shall be trained up in some work or other, is to prevent pride and contention; it is for the health of their bodies, it is a pleasure to the minde, to be free in labors one with another; and it provides plenty of food and all necessaries for the Common-wealth.

Laws for Store-houses.

18. In every Town and City, shall be appointed Store-houses for flax, wool, lether, cloth, and for all such commodities, as come from beyond Seas, and these shall be called general Store-houses, from whence every particular family may fetch such commodities as they want, either for their use in their house, or for to work in their trades; or to carry into the Country Store-houses.

19. Every particular house and shop in a town or city, shall be a particular Store-house or shop, as now they be; and these shops shall either be furnished by the particular labor of that family according to the trade that family is of, or by the labor of other lesser families of the same trade, as all shops in every town are now furnished.

20. The waiters in Store-houses, shall deliver the goods under their charge, without receiving any money, as they shall receive in their goods without paying any money.

21. If any waiter in a Store-house neglect his office, upon a just

complaint the Overseers shall acquaint the Judges Court therewith, and from thence [84] he shall receive his sentence to be discharged that house and office: And to be appointed some other laboring work under the taskmaster; and another shall have his place: For he who may live in freedom and will not, is to taste of servitude.

Laws for Overseers.

22. The onely work of every Overseer, is to see the Laws executed; for the Law is the true magistracy of the Land.

23. If any Overseer, favour any in their idleness, and neglect the execution of the Laws, he shall be reproved the first time by the Judges Court; the second time cashiered his Office, and shall never bear office more, but fall back into the rank of young people and servants to be a worker.

24. New Overseers, shall at their first entrance into their office, look back upon the actions of the old Overseers of the last year, to see if they have been faithful in their places, and consented to no breach of Law, whereby Kingly bondage should any ways be brought in.

25. The Overseers for Trades, shall see every family to lend assistance to plant and reap the fruits of the Earth; to work in their Trades, and to furnish the Store-houses; and to see that the Waiters in Store-houses be diligent to receive in, and deliver out any goods, without buying and selling, to any man whatsoever.

26. While any Overseer is in the performance of his place, every one shall assist him, upon pain of open reproof (or cashiered if he be another Officer) or forfeiture of freedom, according to the nature of the business in hand, in which he refused his assistance.

Laws against buying and selling.

27. If any man entice another to buy and sell, and he who is enticed doth not yield, but makes it known to the Overseer; the enticer shall lose his freedom for twelve moneths, & the Overseer shal give words [of] commendation of him that refused the enticement, before all the Congregation, for his faithfulness to the *Commonwealths Peace.*

28. If any do buy and sell the Earth or fruits thereof, unless it

be to, or with strangers of another nation, according to the Law of Navigation, they shall be both put to death as traytors to the peace of the *Common-wealth*; because it brings in Kingly bondage again: and is the occasion of all quarrels and oppressions.

29. He or she who calls the Earth his, and not his brothers, shall be set upon a stool, with those words written in his forehead, before all the Congregation; and afterwards be made a servant for twelve moneths under the taskmaster; If he quarrel, or seek by secret perswation, or open rising in arms, to set up such a Kingly propriety, he shall be put to death.

[85] 30. The Storehouses shall be every mans substance, and not any ones.

31. No man shall either give hire, or take hire for his work; for this brings in Kingly bondage: If any Freemen want help, there are young people, or such as are common servants, to do it, by the Overseers appointment: He that gives, and he that takes hire for work, shall both lose their Freedom, and become servants for twelve Months under the Taskmaster.

Laws for Navigation.

32. Because other Nations as yet own Monarchy, and will buy and sell; therefore it is convenient, for the peace of our Commonwealth, That our ships do transport our English goods, and exchange for theirs, and conform to the Customs of other Nations in buying and selling: Always provided, That what goods our ships carry out, they shall be the Commonwealths goods; and all their Trading with other Nations shall be upon the common Stock, to enrich the Storehouses.

Laws for Silver and Gold.

33. As Silver and Gold is either found out in Mynes in our own Land, or brought by shipping from beyond Sea, it shall not be coyned with a Conquerors stamp upon it, to set up buying and selling under his name, or by his leave; for there shall be no other use of it in the Commonwealth, then to make dishes and other necessaries for the ornament of houses, as now there is use made of Brass, Pewter, and Iron, or any other Metal in their use.

But if in case other Nations, whose commodities we want, will not exchange with us, unless we give them money, then pieces of Silver and Gold may be stamped with the Commonwealths Arms upon it, for the same use, and no otherwise.

For where money bears all the sway, there is no regard of that golden Rule, *Do as you would be done by:* Justice is bought and sold: nay, Injustice is sometimes bought and sold for money: and it is the cause of all Wars and Oppressions. And certainly the righteous Spirit of the whole Creation did never enact such a Law, That unless his weak and simple men did go from *England* to the *East Indies,* and fetch Silver and Gold to bring in their hands to their Brethren, and give it them for their good-will to let them plant the Earth, and live and enjoy their livelyhood therein, [they should not have the use of the land.]

Laws to choose Officers.

34. All Overseers and State-Officers shall be chosen new every year, to [86] prevent the rise of Ambition and Covetousness; for the Nations have smarted sufficiently by suffering Officers to continue long in an Office, or to remain in an Office by hereditary succession.

35. A man that is of a turbulent spirit, given to quarreling, and provoking words to his neighbor, shall not be chosen any Officer while he so continues.

36. All men from twenty years of age upwards shall have freedom of voyce to choose Officers, unless they be such as lie under the sentence of the Law.

37. Such shall be chosen Officers, as are rational men of moderate conversation, and who have experience in the Laws of the Commonwealth.

38. All men from forty years of age upwards shal be capable to be chosen State Officers, and none younger, unless any one by his industry and moderate conversation doth move the people to choose him.

39. If any man make suit to move the people to choose him an Officer, that man shall not be chose at all that time: If another man perswade the people to choose him who makes suit for himself, they shall both lose their freedom at that time, *viz.* they shall neither have a voyce to choose another, nor be chosen themselves.

Laws against Treachery.

40. He who professes the service of a righteous God by preaching and prayer, and makes a Trade to get the possessions of the Earth, shall be put to death for a Witch and a Cheater.

41. He who pretends one thing in words, and his actions declare his intent was another thing, shall never bear Office in the Commonwealth.

What is Freedom?

Every Freeman shall have a Freedom in the Earth, to plant or build, to fetch from the Store-houses any thing he wants, and shall enjoy the fruits of his labours without restraint from any; he shall not pay Rent to any Landlord, and he shall be capable to be chosen any Officer, so he be above forty years of age, and he shall have a voyce to choose Officers though he be under forty years of age: If he want any young men to be Assistance to him in his Trade or houshold employment, the Overseers shall appoint him young men or maids to be his servants in his family.

Laws for such as have lost their Freedom.

42. All those who have lost their Freedom, shall be clothed in white woolen cloth, that they may be distinguished from others.

43. They shall be under the Government of a Task-master, who shall appoint them to be Porters or Laborers, to do any work that any Freeman wants to be done.

44. They shall do all kind of labour without exception, but their constant [87] work shall be Carriers or Carters, to carry Corn, or other provision, from Store-house to Store-house, from Country to Cities, and from thence to Countries, &c.

45. If any of these refuse to do such work, the Task-master shall see them whipt, and shall feed them with coarse dyet: And what hardship is this? For Freemen work the easiest work, and these shall work the hardest work: And to what end is this, but to kill their Pride and Unreasonableness, that they may become useful men in the Commonwealth?

46. The wife or children of such as have lost their Freedom, shall

not be as slaves till they have lost their Freedom, as their parents and husbands have done.

47. He who breaks any Laws shall be the first time reproved in words in private or in publique, as is shewed before; the next time whipt, the third time lose his Freedom, either for a time or for ever, and not to be any Officer.

48. He who hath lost his Freedom shall be a common servant to any Freeman, who comes to the Task-masters, and requires one to do any work for him; always provided, that after one Freeman hath by the consent of the Task-masters appointed him his work, another Freeman shall not call him thence till that work be done.

49. If any of these Offenders revile the Laws by words, they shall be soundly whipt, and fed with coarse dyet; if they raise weapons against the Laws, they shall dye as Traytors.

Laws to restore Slaves to Freedom.

50. When any slaves give open testimony of their humility and diligence, and their care to observe the Laws of the Commonwealth, they are then capable to be restored to their Freedom, when the time of servitude is expired, according to the Judges sentence; but if they remain opposite to the Laws, they shall continue slaves still another term of time.

51. None shall be restored to Freedom till they have been a twelve Moneth laboring servants to the Commonwealth, for they shall Winter and Summer in that condition.

52. When any is restored to Freedom, the Judg at the Senators Court shall pronounce his Freedom, and give liberty to him, to be clothed in what other coloured cloth he will.

53. If any persons be sick or wounded, the Chyrurgeons, who are trained up in the knowledg of Herbs and Minerals, and know how to apply plaisters or Physick, shall go when they are sent for to any who need their help, but require no reward, because the Common Stock is the publique pay for every mans labour.

[88] 54. When a dead person is to be buried, the Officers of the Parish and neighbors shall go along with the Corpse to the grave, and see it layd therein, in a civil manner; but the publique Minister nor any other shall have any hand in reading or Exhortation.

55. When a man hath learned his Trade, and the time of his

seven years Apprenticeship is expired, he shall have his Freedom to become Master of a family, and the Overseers shall appoint him such young people to be his servants as they think fit, whether he marry, or live a single life.

Laws for Marriage.

56. Every man and woman shall have the free liberty to marry whom they love, if they can obtain the love and liking of that party whom they would marry, and neither birth nor portion shall hinder the match, for we are all of one blood, Mankind; and for portion, the Common Store-houses are every man and maids portion, as free to one as to another.

57. If any man lie with a maid, and beget a child, he shall marry her.

58. If a man lie with a woman forcibly, and she cry out, and give no consent; if this be proved by two Witnesses, or the mans confession, he shall be put to death, and the woman let go free; it is robbery of a womans bodily Freedom.

59. If any man by violence endeavor to take away another mans wife, the first time of such violent offer he shall be reproved before the Congregation by the Peace-maker, the second time he shall be made a servant under the Task-master for twelve Moneths; and if he forcibly lie with another mans wife, and she cry out, as in the case when a maid is forced, the man shall be put to death.

60. When any man or woman are consented to live together in marriage, they shall acquaint all the Overseers in their Circuit therewith, and some other neighbors; and being all met together, the man shall declare by his own mouth before them all, that he takes that woman to be his wife, and the woman shall say the same, and desire the Overseers to be Witnesses.

61. No Master of a family shall suffer more meat to be dressed at a dinner or supper, then what will be spent and eaten by his houshold, or company present, or within such a time after, before it be spoyled. If there be any spoyl constantly made in a family of the food of Man, the Overseer shall reprove the Master for it privately; if that abuse be continued in his family, through his neglect of family government, he shall be openly reproved by the Peace-maker before all the people, and ashamed for his folly; the third time he shall be made a servant

for twelve Moneths under the Task-master, that he may know what it is to get food, and another shall have the oversight of his house for the time.

[89] 62. No man shall be suffered to keep house, and have servants under him, till he hath served seven years under Command to a Master himself; the reason is, that a man may be of age, and of rational carriage, before he be a Governor of a family, that the Peace of the Commonwealth may be preserved.

Here is the righteous Law, Man, wilt thou it maintain?
It may be, is, as hath still, in the world been slain.
Truth appears in Light, Falshood rules in Power;
To see these things to be, is cause of grief each hour.
Knowledg, why didst thou come, to wound, and not to cure?
I sent not for thee, thou didst me inlure.
Where knowledge does increase, there sorrows multiply,
To see the great deceit which in the World doth lie.
Man saying one thing now, unsaying it anon,
Breaking all's Engagements, when deeds for him are done.
O power where art thou, that must mend things amiss?
Come change the heart of Man, and make him truth to kiss:
O death where art thou? wilt thou not tidings send?
I fear thee not, thou art my loving friend.
Come take this body, and scatter it in the Four,
That I may dwell in One, and rest in peace once more.

CHAP. V.

CHAP. VI.

APPENDIX

OTHER WORKS CONNECTED WITH THE
DIGGERS

O F the pamphlets following, the first two, *Light Shining in Buckingham-shire* and *More Light Shining in Buckingham-shire*, were attributed to Winstanley by Gooch (*English Democratic Ideas in the Seventeenth Century*, 1927, p. 187) and by Bernstein (*Cromwell and Communism*, 1930, p. 132). Undoubtedly they belong to the literature of the more extreme Levellers and were written by someone who was disappointed by what he took to be the conservative tone of the Agreement of the People, as it was revised by the Army Council in December, 1648. Hence there is at least a relationship between the views here expressed and those of the "true Levellers" at St. George's Hill. Nevertheless, a comparison of the two pamphlets with Winstanley's writings of about the same date makes it practically certain that he could not have been the author. This conclusion is supported by the fact that Winstanley regularly signed his pamphlets, when they were not manifestoes issued in the name of the group.

Light Shining in Buckingham-shire was dated by Thomason December 5, 1648. *The New Law of Righteousnes*, which was the first statement of Winstanley's communism, was dated January 26, 1649. *More Light Shining in Buckingham-shire* was dated by Thomason March 30, 1649, and the digging at St. George's Hill began on April 1. Both the pamphlets from Buckinghamshire were certainly written by one author, since the second refers to the preceding as its "first part". It is incredible that, if Winstanley had written in March, he would not have referred to his revelation or to the project at St. George's Hill, especially since this project was contemplated by him when he wrote *The New Law of Righteousnes*. There is nothing in either *Light Shining in Buckingham-shire* or *More Light Shining in*

Buckingham-shire to suggest that the author had any plan for the communal tilling of the commons, though he objected strongly to enclosures. The formation of communistic groups was the essence of Winstanley's revelation. Moreover, *The New Law of Righteousnes* makes it clear that the antecedents of his communism were religious. It grew directly from his belief, first, that the Saints were set apart from the world and were guided by an inner light, and second, that a national revival of religion was imminent. The author of the two pamphlets from Buckinghamshire was chiefly interested in politics; his purpose was to show that the "kingly power" was contrary to Scripture and, in England, a result of the Norman Conquest. These were common Leveller arguments that Winstanley afterward borrowed.

In my judgment these two pamphlets should be read in conjunction with the third pamphlet printed below, *A Declaration from the Wel-affected of the County of Buckinghamshire*, which Thomason dated May 10, 1649, and which contains an endorsement of the planting of the commons, presumably at St. George's Hill. This pamphlet came from the Hundreds of Desborough, Burnham, and Stoke, that is, the southern part of the County, across the River from Surrey. According to *The Kingdom's Faithfull Scout*, under date of May 9, 1649, the resolutions with which the pamphlet concludes were adopted at a meeting of Levellers held in Aylesbury. This suggests the hypothesis that there was a group of extreme Levellers here from whom *Light Shining in Buckingham-shire* and *More Light Shining in Buckingham-shire* had emanated.

It is not improbable that Winstanley had at least been in communication with this group before he received his revelation. The title, "true Levellers", which he adopted for the group of Diggers, suggests a secession. In publicizing his movement he certainly drew extensively on the Leveller argument against the "Norman power". The itinerary of the Digger agents who were sent out to collect funds in the spring of 1650 (above, p. 441) shows that they expected to find sympathizers in the central counties, while the digging at Wellingborough shows that Winstanley's movement had imitators there.

A TRANSCRIPTION OF THE TITLE PAGES

A declaration of the grounds and reasons why we the poor inhabitants
of the town of Wellinborrow, in the County of Northampton,
have begun and give consent to dig up, manure and sow corn
upon the common, and waste ground, called Bareshanke, belonging to the inhabitants of Wellinborrow, by those that have subscribed, and hundreds more that give consent . . . London,
Printed for Giles Calvert, 1650.
Signed: Richard Smith, John Avery, Thomas Fardin, Richard Pendred, James Pitman, Roger Tuis, Joseph Hichcock, John Pye,
Edward Turner.
    (*A broadside*)

A declaration of the wel-affected in the County of Buckinghamshire:
being a representation of the middle sort of men within the
three Chilterne Hundreds of Disbrough, Burnum, and Stoke,
and part of Alisbury Hundred, whereby they declare their resolution and intentions, with a removall of their grievances. Printed
in the year, 1649.
    8 p.

The Diggers mirth, or, Certain verses composed and fitted to tunes,
for the delight and recreation of all those who dig, or own that
work, in the Commonwealth of England. Wherein is shewed
how the kingly power doth still reign in severall sorts of men
. . . Set forth by those who were the original of that so righteous a work, and continue still successfull therein at Cobham in
Surrey. London, Printed in the year, 1650.
    16 p.

Light shining in Buckingham-shire, or, A discovery of the main
grounds; originall cause of all the slavery in the world, but

cheifly in England; presented by way of a declaration of many of the wel-affected in that county, to all their poore oppressed country-men of England: and also to the consideration of the present army under the conduct of the Lord Fairefax . . . Printed in the year 1648.

13 p.

A mite cast into the common treasury: or, Queries propounded (for all men to consider of) by him who desireth to advance the work of publick community. Robert Coster . . .

8 p.

More light shining in Buckingham-shire: being a declaration of the state and condition that all men are in by right. Likewise the slavery all the world are in by their own kinde, and this nation in particular, and by whom. Likewise the remedies, as take away the cause, & the effect will cease. Being a representation unto all the people of England, and to the soldiery under the Lord General Fairfax. The second part . . . London, Printed in the year, 1649.

16 p.

LIGHT SHINING IN BUCKINGHAM-
SHIRE

THE title page is dated 1648, and Thomason
dated his copy December 5. The pamphlet is
anonymous.

Copies are to be found in the following collec-
tions: The Advocate's Library (Edinburgh), The
Bodleian, Brown University Library, Cambridge
University Library, Harvard College Library, The
Huntington Library, The Seligman Library at
Columbia University, The Thomason Library at
the British Museum; there is another copy at the
British Museum.

The text is reproduced from the copy in the
Seligman Library.

[1] LIGHT SHINING IN BUCKINGHAMSHIRE,

or A Discovery of the main ground, original Cause of all the Slavery in the world, but cheifly in England: presented by way of a Declaration of many of the welaffected in that County, to all their poore oppessed Country men of England, &c.

JEHOVAH ELLOHIM Created Man after his own likenesse and image, which image is his Sonne Jesus, *Heb.* 1. verse 2. who is the image of the Invisible God: now Man being made after Gods image or likenesse, and created by the word of God, which word was made Flesh and dwelt amongst us; which word was life, and that life the light of men, 1 *Joh.* 2. this light I take to be that pure spirit in man which we call Reason, which discusseth things right and reflecteth, which we call conscience; from all which there issued out that golden rule or law, which we call equitie: the summe of which is, saith Jesus, *whatsoever yee would that men should doe to you, doe to them, this is the Law and the Prophets;* and *James* cals it the royall Law, and to live from this principle is calld a good conscience: and the creature Man was priviledged with being Lord over other inferior creatures, but not over his own kinde; for all men being a like priviledged by birth, so all men were to enjoy the creatures a like without proprietie one more than the other, all men by the grant of God are a like free, and every man individuall, that is to say, no man was to Lord or command over [2] his own kinde: neither to enclose the creatures to his own use, to the impoverishing of his neighbours, see the Charter, 1. *Gen.* from 26. *vers.* to the end of the Chapt.

611

and see the renewing of the Charter to *Noah* and his Sons, *Gen.* 9. from the 1. *vers.* to the 18.

But man following his own sensualitie became a devourer of the creatures, and an incloser, not content that another should enjoy the same priviledge as himself, but incloseth all from his Brother; so that all the Land, Trees, Beasts, Fish, Fowle, &c. are inclosed into a few mercinary hands; and all the rest deprived and made their slaves, so that if they cut a Tree for fire they are to be punished, or hunt a fowle it is imprisonment, because it is gentlemens game, as they say; neither must they keep Cattle, or set up a House, all ground being inclosed, without hyring leave for the one, or buying room for the other, of the chiefe incloser, called the Lord of the Mannor, or some other wretch as cruell as he, and all must be summoned to a Court Leet, there to acknowledge Fealty and Service, and that with Oathes if required (at least wise if Jurymen) to their Tyrant called Lord of the Mannor; and if a Tenant admitted, if Coppy-holder, he must take an Oath to become a true Tenant, rather Slave, as afore said; now all this Slavery of the one and Tyranny of the other was at first by murther and cruelty one against the other; and that they might strengthen themselves in their villany against Gods ordinances and their Brothers freedomes and rights: They had alwayes a Commander in chiefe, which was the most blindest and desperatest wretch, and he was their chiefe and head, as *Nimerod,* and he became their King; so that I dare make plainly appear by Scripture and Reason, that Kings were not of Gods institution at first, but it arose from the Heathens, *viz.* those that lived after their own beastly lusts: and when *Israel* would have a King, their onely ground was to be like other Nations; and God told *Samuel* saying, they have not cast off or rejected thee but me, that I should not reigne over them. Read the whol 8. Chapter of the 1 of *Samuel* &c. where observe the Slavery that the people are in that have a King, and amongst the whole Catologe observe the Tenth of Stocks, &c. [3] and see the 12. Chapter from the 16. verse forward, what judgements God sent in their Harvest for asking a King, and afterwards observe what misery befell, for they were in continuall Wars abroad, and at last divided into divisions and had two Kings: Then what wofull civill Wars and murthering one another for the Kingdome: I refer you to the whole book of Kings to judge; doe but read that of their first King *Abimelecks* cruelty which was *Gidions* bastard; *Judges* 8. and 21. read the 9. of *Judges*, &c. there he kils his brother with a company of light fellows; and as Kings are the root of Tyrany, so likewise they were the first that brought in wars, see *Gen*. 14. for their greatnesse must be upheld by murther and cruelty, as aforesaid, in so much that in *Revel*. 13. mention is made of an ugly beast with seven heads and ten horns, which horns did persecute the Saints: now in *Revel*. 17. horns are there declared to be Kings, so that Kings are of the Beast, which is a power that makes all subject to it, but onely the Saints, &c. *Revel*. 13. and 7. And saith the Scripture, the Beast hath its power from the Dragon, *Revel*. 13. and 4. and the Dragon in *Revel*. 20. and 2 is the Devill and Satan, so that it is plain, that Kings are of the Beast, and the Beast is of the Devill; and it is as plain, they that worship the King worship the Beast, and they that worship the Beast worship the Devill, *Revel*. 13. and 4. vers. Now let us a little behold our English Powers, all that which is called Magistracie is from the Kings Pattent, and his is from the Devill; for the Kings Predecessors, The outland-ish bastard *William* came to be King by Conquest and murther, now murtherers are, saith *Jesus*, the Divels children, for saith he, the Devill was a murtherer from the beginning and he abode not in the Truth: now Kings are utterly against the truth, and persecutors of the Saints; for saith *Jesus*, they shall bring you before Kings, so that Kings are enemies unto the Kingdome of Christ.

Secondly, Behold now from licence or grant comes all our in-closures and tradings, as priviledge to buy and sell, and to enjoy, occupy and possesse lands; it is from taking the Beasts mark: now observe the rich possessers, incroachers, inclosers, see your holdings, your Pattents, and Charters, and Licence is from the [4] King, and all tenures and holdings of lands is from your King, yea al Writings, Indentures, Bands, Leases, &c. is in the name and authority of him; nay your money is not lawfull, if it be not the Kings coyn, and his picture and superscription on it.

So that observe, the King is made by you your God on earth, as God is the God of heaven, saith your Lawyers: therefore all Lawes, Writs, Summons, Warrants, Patents, &c, must be in his name; nay, the Parliament will settle nothing without him, yea all Honours must be from him. Now then mark if this be not all from the Dragon: and the Priests to verifie this, saith in their thing called Prayer, he is supreme head of their Church, Ecclesiastical as Civil, next under thee and thy Christ, so that he is their third person of their Trinity, and so their God, Defender of their faith. Now here is the blasphemy in *Rev.* 13. *vers.* 5. And in the Scotish Covenant, one Article of their Religion is concerning his sacred Majesty, &c. and Kings are the only chief upholders of Babylon: see how they weep at her down fall, *Rev.* 18. when buying and selling ceaseth, &c.

Now friends, what have we to do with any of these unfruitfull works of darknesse? Let us take *Peters* advice, 1 *Pet.* 4. 3. *The time past of our life may suffice that we have wrought the will of the Gentiles, when we walked in lascivious lusts, excesse of wine, revellings, banquetting, and abominable idolatry.* And let us not receive the Beasts mark, least that the doom in *Rev.* 14. 9, 10. befall none of us: but let us oppose the Beastly powers, and follow the Lamb whithersoever he goeth.

Now here is the chief ground why wicked men stand so for a King; it is to uphold all their confused cruelties and incests as aforesaid: and herein upholding him, they uphold that power that set him up, (by our Saviours rule) and by justifying him, they justifie that power that set him a work in all his tyranny; and they and the Parliament in treating with him, treat with him that authorised him; and in receiving him, receiveth him that set him on work, that is to say the Devil. Then see how we are cheated.

Now the enlightened Saints are commanded to abandon [5] the unfruitfull works of darknesse. But all this power aforesaid is, 1. of darknesse; therefore to be resisted.

2. Christ hath called the Saints to light; therefore they are to walk as children of light.

3. The Saints are to have no fellowship with Belial: but the power aforesaid is of Belial, therefore have no fellowship with it.

4. The said power is to be resisted: and see the promise, for saith James, *Resist the Devil, and he will flee from you.* And this we have experience of, that whensoever the Kings power was manfully resisted, he fled from the resisters.

And therefore those called the Levellers, their principles to free all alike out of slavery, are most just and honest in reference to the matter of freedome: for it is the end of the redemption by Jesus, to restore all things.

And to do this, the removall of the Kingly power will be a main forwardnesse: and indeed the Kingly power is the being of Tyranny; for if no King, no Lord, no Patent, &c. 2. If the execution of Lawes were not in his name, as all Assurances, Writs, Commissions, Patents, Warrants, &c. then he should down if he would, for any use or need they had of him.

[1.] Therefore rich men cry for a King, because the poor should not claim his right that is his by Gods gift.

2. The horsleech Lawyer cryes for a King, because else the supream power will come into the peoples Representatives lawfully elected, and so all Trials would be done in the country, in every Town &c. by the same Neighbourhood, and so the Law would no more be bought nor sold, and then farewel caterpiller-Lawyer.

3. The things, Lord, Barons, &c. cry for a King, else their tyranical House of Peers falls down, and all their rotten honour, and all Patents and Corporations, their power being derived from him, if he go down, all their tyranny fals too. The like of Lord of Manors, Gentlemen, &c. besides the Priests of all men must cry for a King; for by his power and oppressing Courts, all his Judges, Justices, &c. and himself too is their sworn creature, and they are the Priests pack-horses that [6] carry the whore of Babylons ware about, and they want but bels about their neck they may be the better heard, &c. Now if the King go down, what will become of the Priests ware think you? and Tythes goes down.

The like of all base Conventions of men of what kinde so ever. But now the honest man that would have liberty, cryes down all interests whatsoever, and to this end he desires common right and equity, which consists of these particulars following.

1. A just portion for each man to live, that so none need to begge or steale for want, but every one may live comfortably.

2. A just Rule for each man to go by, which Rule is to be found in Scripture.

3. All men alike under the said Rule, which Rule is, To do to another as another should do to him: So that eye for eye, tooth for tooth, hand for hand, &c. and if any one stole, to restore double, &c.

4. The government to be by Judges, called Elders, men fearing God and hating covetousnesse; Those to be chosen by the people, and

to end all controversies in every Town and Hamlet, without any other or further trouble or charge.

And in the Scriptures, the Israelites Common-wealth is an excellent pattern, if led up to that in *Gen.* 1. and *Gen.* 9. mentioned in the beginning.

Now in Israel, if a man were poor, then a publike maintenance and stock was to be provided to raise him again: So would all Bishops lands, Forrest lands, and Crown-lands do in our Land, which the Apostate Parliament men give one to another, and to maintain the needlesse thing call'd a King. And every seven years the whole Land was for the poor, the fatherlesse, widows and strangers, and at every crop a portion allowed them.

Mark this, poor people, what the Levellers would do for you. Oh why are you so mad as to cry up a King? It is he and his Court and Patentee men, as Majors, Aldermen, and such creatures, that like Cormorants devoure what you should enjoy, and set up Whipping-posts and Correcting-houses to [7] enslave you. Tis rich men that oppresse you, saith *James*.

Now in this right Common-wealth, he that had least had no want: therefore the Scripture call them a Family, and houshold of Israel. And in the 2. of the *Acts*, amongst those that received the Gospel, they were gathered into a family and had all things common; yet so, that each one was to labour and eat his own bread. And this is equity, as aforesaid: for it is not lawfull nor fit for some to work, and the other to play; for it is Gods command, that all work, let all eat: and if all work alike, is it not fit for all to eat alike, have alike, and enjoy alike priviledges and freedoms? And he that did not like this, is not fit to live in a Common-wealth. See *Gen.* 9. And therefore weep and howl, ye Rich men, by what vain name or title soever: God will visit you for all your oppressions; You live on other mens labours, and give them their bran to eat, extorting extreme rents and taxes on your fellow-creatures. But now what will you do? for the People will no longer be enslaved by you, for the knowledge of the Lord shall enlighten them, &c.

And now (according to my knowledge,) I shall discover your pedegree from your King to your Gentleman, and it is thus:

William the Bastard sonne of *Robert* Duke of *Normandy*, with a mighty Army of his fellow-Tyrants and Theeves and Robbers, enters

Sussex, kils the inhabitants the *Britains* and their King, that were in an Army to withstand his cruelty and defend their rights, robs and destroyes all places and persons at his pleasure, setleth Garisons of Normans to enslave the Britains, takes all Land and causeth them to hold it by Copyhold, to pay fines and harets at his pleasure, &c. It is too tedious to relate all Polls, Tolls, Taxes &c. that he made our Forefathers pay. Let the Reader view the Chronicle.

But amongst all unnaturall, unreasonable, tyrannicall and cruel Laws he made, as that of Curfer [1], of Felony, That the child must suffer for the Father, &c. And all his tyrannical Lawes he caused to be in an Outlandish tongue. So that here I take [8] this power to be that little horn in *Dan.* 7. 24. because I never heard or read of the like cruelty that any Tyrant did the like, for to cause his cruel Laws to be in an unknown tongue. Now the poor people knew not when they offended or no.

2. For the execution of those Lawes, the people to come to what place he will appoint, at 4 Terms and times in a year.

And 3. to buy their Lawes at the Lawyers unconscionable rate, for he set up and devised the Lawyers. Now as I shall make it appear that this is the horn, so the Caterpillers Lawyers will prove the eyes: which Lawyers are as profitable as magots in meat, and Caterpillers in Cabages, and Wolves amongst Lambs, &c.

And amongst those, see their Preferment (as its called) to suck the People; as Attorny, Counsellor, Barrester, Sergeant, and accordingly Fees to rob, and they take Oaths; and out of this rubbish stuffe are all our Creatures called Judges, and they likewise all to be sworn. And then places of preferment (so called) to tyrannize, and to be the head Tyrants, Sycophants, Wolves, Lyons, Leopards, &c. as Dutchy General, Attorney-Generall, Lord-lubber Keeper, Lord Privy-Seal, Lord Treasurer, Lord Barons of the Exchequer, and I know not what great Catchpoles besides these; all to be sworne to their dread Soveraign Tyrant Beast, &c. And so being right whelps brought up to rend, devoure, rob, spoile, tyrannise &c. over the poor people; then their dread Tyrant, as he hath received power and dignity from the Dragon or Devil as aforesaid, doth shatter, breath out, and all-to-bedaggel them with it, with hairy skind Robes, resembling

---

[1] Curfew; commonly believed in the seventeenth century to have been introduced as a measure of Norman oppression.

the subtle nasty Fox with his dirty tayl. And because the Lord Keeper, Privy Seal, and Treasurers long tails should not daggle in the dirt, they must have another Sycophant slave apeece to carry up for them with their hats off doing homage to their breech. Oh height of all basenesse! What, will they creep in one anothers arses for honour? Why, oh, his Majesties breath of Honour it may be blows out There, and therefore he holds up his gown that it might blow him that holds it up, and makes him be called Sir. Likewise those men thus honoured must have a gue-gaw silver Mace carried before them, With a Crosse a top on it, to [9] shew they have their Title from the Defender of the Popish Faith; the Lord Keeper having a fools-bable like a Purse carried before him: now all these Lawyers, Lyers and twelve Judges: Besides with their cowtred [2] Caps; and Serjeants with their womanish Coifs and Peticots on their Shoulders, with their Barresters, Atturnies, &c. Howbeit, they rob and devoure the people, striving who shall most play the knave and couzen; so that he may clime up into high places of profit: for all those upholding their Kings Prerogative, their Tiranny is unquestionable, that is the reason that they maintain the King can doe no wrong; that he is a God on earth, as God is God in Heaven, and that he is the life of the Law; all Writs, Warrants, Commissions, &c. His name gives the beeing to them: that he is the fountain of our honour and magestracy: yea and that he is supreme head Ecclesiasticall and Civil; also that he is to be accountable to none but God, and all this the better to hide their tyrany; for they being all from him, and all their Commissions; if you question them, then you must question him from whom their power was derived: but they say, he is not to be accountable, &c. so that by this means they uphold all their Tyrany; and there is no way, but to take down the Kingly Power and then their [power] wil down too, & not before: Now these Lawyers are the Eys of the Beast, for the twelve Judges sit in the tyranicall House of Peers, another sort of the Kingly creatures to advice them in all tyrany, and how to keep the Norman yoake about the peoples necks.

The next thing to shew is from whence came all our Nobility and Gentry, even from that outlandish *Norman* Bastard, who first being his Servants and under Tyrants; secondly, their rise was by cruell

---

[2] Probably 'coltered', referring to the shape.

murther and theft by the Conquest; thirdly, their rise was the Countries ruine, and the putting them down will be the restitution of our rights againe; these are called Dukes, Earls, Barons, Marquesse, Lords, &c. And from this Bastard is all our royall blood, therefore to be utterly disesteemed: O then behold, O *England* thy vanity in Idolizing the King and his Children!

Thy Priests have guld, bewitched, cheated, and betrayed thee [10] into these tyrants hands with their sorceries onely for their own filthy lucre and bellies sake, because they have the greatest part of the spoile for their preaching up the King to be the Supream head, Defender of the Faith, Gods anointed; and that if thou doest resist his power thou resisteth the ordinances of God: now all this is but as bridles in thy jaws, and blindes over thy eyes, that thou must be ruled by the Church, and they are thy enemies, and thou must beleeve them; and keep thy self a good Subject to thy Prince, the condition is good: and by all these and a thousand tricks more they doe but mould thee to slavery this five hundred years and more, and by this means the King and his Creatures ride thee in thy Estates and Persons and Labours.

And the Priests [rule] over thy Conscience and soule, and keeps thee in all ignorance and malice; and for so doing thy Priests are thy Princes and beare rule, and for their so bewitching thee they come by their Impropriations and fat Benefits: and it is for those fat Benefits that makes them turn changelings, either to King or Parliament, which will best furnish their kiching [i. e., kitchen]. Therefore shake off those locus and be no more deluded by them, but hearken to the voice of God in the Scriptures and his Saints, and pay no more Tiths to those Priests, nay cast off those abominable deceivers.

All Charters, Pattents, and Corporations was devised onely to uphold the Kings Tyranny, Greatnesse, and Interest; and because the people did rise in many parts for their Priviledges and Right; and he being in straights and knowing not how to uphold his tyranny, devised a way to set the people one against another, by making some Free, some Forreigners, &c. and so deviseth these Patents and Charters in all populous Cities and Towns throughout the Realm to uphold his Interest.

Now as for these bewitching Charters, see how they run in *J.* 1.

Out of our Princely grace, bountie, meer motioned princely favour,
Doe give and grant to this our Citie or Town, &c. To be a body
Corporate, to consist of a Major, Baliffs and Burgesses, &c.

[11] Why? Mark, the better to serve us and our successors (this is the end of their grant) then all Towns and Customs whatsoever is due to us and our successors? We bequeath to the same body Corporate (and every businesse must be sworn, to be the Kings creatures) then out of that pack, they have power to choose twelve Aldermen for a Common-counsell, and they all be sworn again: Then out of this stuffe, all the Burgesses to choose a thing called a Major, and she all to be sworn to the Kings: then she shall be a Just-asse of Peace and Coram [3], and have a silver Hartichoak or toy call'd a Mase, carried before her; and she and her twelve Aldermen following after in their Cunnie skin Gowns, as so many fools in a Mid-summer Aile: and those petty-tyrants shall domineer over the Inhabitants by vertue of their Patent, and enclose all, letting and setting of the Poores lands to, and moneys, stocks of moneys to their own use: and claime a Priviledge from their Charters and Patents that they scorn to be accountable to others, but to their Prerogative Masters; so that you see all tyrany shelters it self under the Kings wings: is it not time then to throw down the King, and bring his Person to his answer: these Patents and Charters is the maine wheele and prop that upholds the Kings tyrany; for by this means the Prerogative people, strives to uphold the King and Lords interests, to get favours of them, to hold up their own knavery and deceit; and doth choose such Burgesses for the Parliament, as will be for the King, as Caterpiller Lawyers, Coliers [i. e., cheats] or lords of the Mannor, Impropriators, or such like; and it is from those Patent Towns that the House of Commons if fil'd with so many kingified Prerogative self interest, proud and cheating Varlets as now it is: and untill those Corporations be thrown down, we can expect never any hope of freedome by a Parliament: see how *Londons* Common-Counsell stir up their Hackneys with Petitions and Mutineys, for a Treaty with our Conquered enemy, &c.[4]

---

[3] Quorum; the Justices of the Peace collectively.

[4] The Presbyterian party in London sent several petitions to Parliament asking for a treaty with the King. The reference here is probably to the last petition of this sort, laid before the Houses by the Common Council on August 31, 1648. On September 18 negotiations began at Newport between Charles and the Parliamentary Commissioners

Therefore let Burgesses hence forth be no more so chosen, but from all the wel-affected in generall.

The next thing is to shew you, as I conceive, how we came by a Parliament, 2. what is a Parliament, 3. what good may [12] be expected by a Parliament as it now stands?

Our fore-fathers the *Brittains,* being altogether in slavery, did rise in many parts, and would not endure the slavery afore said; then the tyrant and his brood, not able to overcome, grants a Parliament as followeth; the People to parly, treat, or declare their minde: to this end, to choose men to treat, as followeth, 1. The Freeholders in every County to choose two, which should be cal'd Knights for the County; and his Patentee Towns, each to choose two more, which should be cal'd Burgesses, and those should sit for the Country, and be cald a House of Commons; and have a firmitive voice, to affirm what they would have done, and the major part to carry it.

2. Provided, that he would have a House of Peers to sit for him from his Prerogative without Election, by his Patent, and those to have an Negative voice to thwart the Commons if they please, and if they assented to the Commons, then it should be an Ordinance; if they did not, then all the Commons did should be null; and if the Commons and Lords, or the most part, did assent, then the King to have a Negative voice; and no Laws to be made or repealed without his consent; and if he consented to it, then it should be an Act, and no otherwise.

3. Before any sitting to Vote, they are to take these Oaths as followeth,

1. That he is their lawfull King: 2. They will not alter the Government as it now stands: 3. And they will not deprive his Successor: and in King *Henry* the eight time, when they came to be Priest ridden, that he is Head of the Church, Ecclesiasticall and Civil, Suprem head &c. Defender of the Faith, and such blasphemies: and these oathes, as it is manifest, they have ever since taken.

Now observe our Worthy Parliament; first the King is to hard for the People to cheat them: for first, the greater number of the

---

and continued, off and on, for about two months. On November 18, Ireton's *Remonstrance of the Army* was adopted by the Council of Officers and presented to Parliament on the 20th. Thus the decision passed out of the hands of Parliament and into those of the Army, as the author of the pamphlet says below (p. 622). See S. R. Gardiner, *The Great Civil War* (1891), Vol. III, chs. 46 and 47.

Commons are chosen by his Patentee Burgesses Major & Aldermen: and the County, but two in a Countie and those the Freeholders, which had their freedome of the Normans, and all the people else shut by from choosing, and if 2. The King hath a House of Patentee Lords to ballance them with their Negative voice.

[13] 3. The King hath a Negative voice, and that is the third State to Ballance them himselfe.

4. In the House of Commons itself, the King hath the bigest part, even neer two to one for most, all the Burgesses be for him, and the major part carrying it by voice. Now what is this but a meer cheat, and observe all the Cronicles from Bastard *William* to *Charles* and upwards, and since, and it will appear that Kings got more by treaties, then ever their Sword could have done, and kept it longer, because now their tyranny was settled by a Law, and the People sworn to those Laws; they thinking they have gained freedome when indeed they have given away their freedome by their Parliaments, as aforesaid: and now we see, had not God moved this Army to prevent this Treaty, this Parliament had utterly cheated and betrayed us into our implacable enemies hands again; and had settled the whole *Norman* power again over us, notwithstanding all this light to the contrary, Treasure spent, Bloodshed, &c. Besides the many Oathes the Commons took to free us; so that *Charles* had like to be set up into his tyranicall Power again; but now blessed be God, the Net is broke, and we are escaped. And for all our tyrany the Priests are our Inchanters, and those that preached it up for their own bellyes sakes.

Now King, Lords, Commons three States, as it hath been cal'd, the little Horne (as I conceive) in *Daniel* the seventh; for it altereth from all other tyranicall Powers in the world whatever: secondly, the King is head of their Church, as aforesaid: thirdly, they alter one tyranicall way, and set up another: and can make up a thing cal'd Religion by one Parliament, and throw it down the next Parliament and set up another; so here is changing times &c. and trampling under feet. And the base Priests, the Ecclesiasticall State, preacheth all those Powers and Constitutions to be *Jure divino*. O wretches, wretches, the black gard of Satan, what will become of them.

FINIS.

1. Kings 12. 16. *So when all Israel saw that the King harkened not unto them, the People answered the King, saying; What Portion have we in David: neither have we inheritance in the Son of Jesse. To your tents O Israel.*

of Kingston to Sir —— Hind, and that of Thornton for

only three, and to—— released the King to ——. William Barton

successor to Hind, which . . . . .

To you, now O Lord . . . . .

MORE LIGHT SHINING IN BUCK-INGHAM-SHIRE

THE title page is dated 1649, and Thomason dated his copy March 30. The pamphlet is anonymous.

Copies are to be found in the following collections: The Advocate's Library (Edinburgh), The Bodleian, Brown University Library, The Thomason Library at the British Museum; there is another copy at the British Museum.

The text is reproduced from the copy in the Thomason Library.

[3] MORE LIGHT SHINING IN BUCKING-HAM-SHIRE.

The Apostle saith, *Whatsoever things were written, were for our learning.*

IT is recorded in Scripture, that man being created male and female after Gods own Image or likeness, *viz.* his Son Jesus, who is said to be the Image of the invisible God, and the first born of every Creature, and by whom all things were made, and to whom all things were to subject, for he being Lord over all the inferior Creatures; God endowed with that excellent Rule of right Reason, which is the pure influence of the Almighty, whereby he should walk in subjection to his Creator and Father, and in Equity towards his own kind, *viz.* to do to another, as the other should do to him, and none to lord or force any arbitrary power one over another, or to assume any priviledge above his brethren; for all men by Gods donation are all alike free by birth, and to have alike priviledg by vertue of his grant: *Gen.* 1. 26. to the end, and *Gen.* 9. 1. to 18. So that as all inferior creatures are given unto man, *viz.* mankind, and that for all necessaries as he should need: So it is as plain, that every man hath a right and propriety in the creatures, one as well as the other; so that for any to inclose them wholly from his kind, to his own use, to the impoverishment of his fellow creatures, whereby they are made his slaves, is altogether unlawful, and it is the cause of all oppressions, whereby many thousands are deprived of their rights which God hath invested withal, whereby they are forced to beg or starve for want; for all grounds being inclosed, and all other things monopolized into a few Mercinarys hands, wherby thousands that would, and desire to live in a lawful Calling [4] lawfully, are of all people most oppressed, because not suffered to keep any thing about them, because of the incroachers before named, who will either hunt it or pownd it, &c. neither can they enjoy the benefit of their own labor,

627

although God commands they should, because of those forenamed
oppressors, who have not only inclosed, monopolized, incroached, in-
hanced all the creatures into their hands, but do likewise extort away
the labours of their poor brethren, and take out the bread out of
their mouths, and from their poor wives and children, by their unreasonable, unlawful, unjust and wicked Rates, Taxes, Powls, Towls,
Customs, so that the flower of those industrious mens labors are
boulted out from them, and only the Bran left them to feed on; and
if any seem for all this to maintain his family through his extream
industry, then the other Cormorants force offices on him, &c. thereby
to more inslave him and that with most wretched oaths, &c. Oh it
would be too tedious to relate all the slavery they are put to, and
sworn [to] perform, as that at their Court-leets, there to appear to
do homage, and acknowledg themselves slave to their Tyrants, called
Lords of Mannors; and if they hold any Lands, what extream Rents
are they forced to pay for it, to their extorting Landlords? besides
above the 3^d part of their labor taken from them by the impropriators,
besides paying quitrents, as it is called, whereby in some, as the Lords
of the Mannors, are petty Tyrants and Kings; so they hold all from
a supream Lord, who was none of Gods setting up, viz. a King,
whom they upholding as the only dread Soveraign Lord, and allowing him a great and intolerable Revenue, as Lands, Customs, Poles,
Toles, Tithes of all sorts, and quitrents, &c. with Fines, Harriets, and
Charters, Patents, Monopolies, &c. by which means they can be Farmers under him, and petty tyrants over the people: and to secure themselves from being made deliver up their usurped powers and interest;
they have their Commissions, Grants, Pattents holding in his name,
and they protecting him from being questioned and his power thrown
down; he doth defend, uphold, maintain and allow them to rend,
tear, devour, rob, spoyl, extort and tyrannize over the poor people,
&c. and to this end doth invest them with strange names and titles,
such as the Scripture owns not, or never did allow of, as Dukes,
Princes, [5] Earls, Marquesses, Viscounts, Lords, Barons, Sirs, Es-
quires, Gentlemen, &c. and priviledges accordingly, as to hunt, hawk,
&c. all which vain titles are forbidden by our Saviour as heathenish:
for it arose from mans own sensuality, darkness, and wickedness, and
murder, for *Nimrod* was the first King, and he was such a bloody

wretch, that he was called a Hunter, *Gen.* 10. 8, 9, 10. that is, a Hunter of his own kind in the presence of the Jehovah even against Gods Ordinance, so wicked was he; and *v.* 10. *The beginning of his Kingdom was Babel, viz.* Confusion, out of Gods way, by which confusion he raised up a pack of Tyranny; after many Kings more, and they divided each against others; and striving who should be the greatest Incloser and Tyrant, fell together by the ears, and caused the people to murder one another; so that it was Kings that first brought in Wars. Read the 14. Chap. of *Genesis,* where observe the first murderings and thefts: and the rise of Dukes was from wicked *Esau.* Read the 36. of *Genesis;* these the Kings call their Cozens: In short, the whole Scriptures declare Kings to be no better then Tyrants and Vsurpers: And although God granted the *Israelites* a King, yet it was in his anger, saith the Scripture, *Hosea* 13. 11. and he took him away in his wrath. And although some good men were Kings, yet it was not in regard to their Office, but Persons, for in that they were Kings they were Tyrants, and did extreamly extort from the people; for see how *Solomon* extorted from the people, 1 *Kings* 4.: first see his Princes, from *verse* 1. to the 7. then see his Officers to get provision monethly, from *verse* 7. to the 20. then see his provision for his Court, 22, 23. *verses,* as in one day 30 measures of fine flour, 60 measures of meal, 10 fat Oxen, 20 pasture Oxen, 100 Sheep, besides Harts, Roes, Bucks, fallow Deer, and fatted fowl. See 27. *verse,* how his Officers provided, &c. and 26. *verse,* do but note the horses that he kept, as forty thousand stalls of horses for Charets, & twelve thousand horsemen; then see in the 28. *v.* the people bring, as the Officers appointed, in *v.* 27. Barly and Straw for the horses, and Dromedaries, &c. which was such an oppression, that the people, when they came to crown *Rehoboam,* would condition to have it removed, 1 *King.* 12. 1. to 7. and he refused to take off those burdens, to *v.* 16. then in *v.* 16. the people refused to chuse him King. [6] And then did they not chuse *Jeroboam* King? read the *chap.* and did not *David* command *Mephibosheth,* that he and *Ziba* should divide the Land, 2 *Sam.* 19. 29. *viz. Mephibosheths* Land; now *Ziba* was but the others servant, read 2 *Sam.* 16. from Vers. 1. to Vers. 4. there *Ziba* slandereth his Master *Mephibosheth;* and *David* giveth away *Mephibosheths* whole estate unto *Ziba,* Vers. 4. And when *Mephib-*

osheth comes to clear himself from his servants slander, *David* restores to himself his own again: So that the slanderer must have the
honest mans goods. What Justice is this?

Their Offices were tyrannical, only God did many times for his
names sake let them have now and then a good man in the place, out
of special favor, and no otherwise; for the Kingly Power, even to
Israel, at first, was confirmed upon, as a plague, and no otherwise, as
a reward of their own wickedness; and thunder and rain was sent
in their Wheat-harvest, to convince them That their wickedness was
great in desiring a King: read 1 *Sam*. 12. 17, 18. And in Vers. 19. the
people desireth *Samuel* to pray for them, and confesseth, that of all
their sins they had added this sin, in asking a King. And in Vers. 20.
Samuel told them they had done all this wickedness, &c. And Vers.
25. tells the people, That if they would still do wickedly, both they
and their King should perish.

Now their wickedness was in two Respects:

1. In desiring to have a King to be like other Nations, 1 *Sam*. 5. 8.
viz. the Gentiles and Heathens that followed their own sensuality:
Now those *Israelites* not to be like other people.

2. In advancing a man, one of their own kinde, in the place of a
God, and so to idolize their own flesh above God: For do but observe what the Almighty saith unto *Samuel*, 1 *Sam*. 8. 7. *They have
not*, saith the Lord, *rejected thee, but they have rejected me, that I
should not reign over them:* And see Vers. 8. and forward, What a
tyrannical Government Kings are. From Vers. 11. to the end of the
Chapter.

*And he said, This will be the manner of the King that shall reign
over you; he will take your sons, and appoint them for himself, for
his charets, and to be his horsemen, and some shall run before his
charets.*

[7] *And he will take your Daughters to be Confectionaries, Cooks,
and Bakers.*

*And he will take your fields, and vineyards, and your oliveyards,
and give to his officers, and to his servants.*

*And he will take your men-servants, and your maid-servants, and
your goodliest young men, and your asses, and put them to his work.*

He will take the tenth of your sheep, and you shall be his servants.

And you shall cry out in that day, because of your King which ye have chosen, and the Lord will not hear you in that day.

Which Scriptures do declare, That Kings are the heads of all Tyrants; and that wicked men, shrouding themselves under him, have not only protection by him to Tyranny, but likewise you see he will give them large gifts, but out of other mens estates: For, saith the Scripture, *he will take your vineyards and oliveyards, the best of them, and give them to his servants.* This is the Reason why those men will be the Kings slaves, because the people may be slaves to them, and they to tyrannize: And in Vers. 15 & 17. there comes in your Tithes of Labor and Stock; Kings were the Authors of it.

2. They do not only incroach away mens estates, but likewise make slaves of men: see Vers. 12. He will make Them plow his grounds, and reap his harvest, and make his instruments of War; so that Kings are the cause of Wars: For of necessity they must keep up Armies, else the people will never be such slaves as to obey them. Then they make Captains of thousands, and Captains of hundreds; Here is the rise of Nobility and Gentry: And men, for to get his favor, will be willing to enslave their own kinde, as to be Captains; O the height of all slavery! What? slaves to Kings, that so the people may be their slaves? So it is, as Kings are the worst of men, yet others will execute their wills: If *Ahab* and *Jezebel* will take *Naboths* Vineyard, do but send a Letter to the chief of the City, and they will stone him. Let but *Charls* send out a Commission for Aray, and how many will execute it? yea, if he will raise an Armie to murther and plunder us, he need but set up his Standard, and thousands will rise for him; Priests will preach in his behalf, and that he is the Lords annointed, [8] though it is with the Popes grease, and he Antichrists hackney, and hath his power from the Beast, *Revel.* 13. That hath his authority from the Dragon, who is the Devil and Satan, whose first predecessor was the *Norman* Bastard *William,* who came to be King by cruel murther, as shall be proved hereafter: so that as the creature, man, is enslaved to his kinde, and all Monopolizings, Encroachings, Inhancings, Licenses, Patents, Grants, Prerogatives, Priviledges, unjust and unnatural, arbitrary and wicked, compacted, unreasonable and all unjust interests, are unlawful, and the Scriptures do every where protest against it, calling it *Oppressions;* and pronounceth Judgments against it, calling the Abettors, Promoters, and

Actors of the same, though men call them *Kings*, *Lords*, *Generals*, *Parliaments*, *Councels*, *Consuls*, *Judges*, or by what name else they are known, dignified, or distinguished, as the Priests call it, to be but *Lions*, *Bears*, *Wolves*, *Leopards*, *Foxes*, *Bulls*, *Beasts*, *Dogs*, *Whelps*, from their Natures: For being led by their sensuality, avarice, and lusts, and making all others their slaves, to serve them with cap and knee, &c. to labor, drudg, trudg, work, moyl for them, &c. as if they were born only to be their slaves, and they to use them as their Beasts, Horse, &c. yea, and beholding to them for it too; that so they may be their Dog-keepers, or to wait on their horses, Lackeys to run before them, and be Postillions, Pillions, &c. Yea, and to make them hold their Lands, Houses, Cottages, &c. at what terms, holdings, slaveries they please, forcing fines and harriates at every change, &c. And the better to keep them in slavery, have utterly denyed them to have any power or voyce to chuse their Law-makers, or Law-executioners: And lest they should have some Justice done by some in Authority, they have devised such a multitude of Courts and Terms, so that those great Cormorants can remove the suite out of one Court into another; and Law being *bought* and *sold* by the wicked encroaching Norman, shameless, cheating, hack-ney Lawyers, being worse then the devil, who scorns to take a peny Fees to torment any, but will do it freely. By all which means those poor men are kept in slavery, both in person and estates; and not only so, but are rated and taxed by the aforesaid Task-masters, whereby they bear out those rich, idle Vermin. But yet this is not all; [9] but if those great *Nimrods* fall out, and being moved one against the other, who shall most inslave the people, and suck them most, and being compacted into parties, and their lusts moving them to Wars, then the poor harm-less men must be invited to fight the others battels, and to this end, *Pharaoh*-like, they have their Juglers, who can play the Hocus Pocus, and invent a thing they call Religion, like *Jeroboams Calves*, who was the first invented State Worship: then a Convocation or Synod of Divisers [i. e., schemers], who being more cunninger then their Mas-ters, they quickly get above them, and can outreach them by their wills and subtilness, they quickly juggle them together with Oaths, Cove-nants, &c. then they do as the lowbel [1]-men amongst Larks, carry a false light and gloss of Scripture, and with their preaching and noises, thump-ing and bumping the Pulpit cushions, cudgel them into a conceit to raise

---

[1] A bell used to frighten birds into a net.

up a way of maintenance for the Church Devines, as Tythes, &c. this being done, and their god bellies fil'd, then like so many Beagles they open their mouths, and with full cry, having the scent of such a great benefit, &c. lay on like Thatchers: Oh rise, help your King, help your Parliament: Oh your Lives, Liberties and Religions lyeth at stake: Thus were the poor men made murder each other, and those that were unwilling to go were pressed & forced by both sides, a most wicked practise; & when they come home again, as very slaves as at the first, and no care taken for widows, fatherless, sick, lame, &c. as is fit, but many, I fear, perish for want, and others that take for need hanged, or if they are in debt, made lie in prison and rot: for all which wickedness, although they have made Laws, Ordinances, &c. for the same ends, and so they hold all their incloseness by a Law, yet mark what the Scripture saith of it, *Wo be to them that decree wicked decrees.* And for their incloseness, *Wo be to them that joyn house to house, that the poor hath no place, &c.* And for their oppression, *It is not of the Lord, that the people should labor in the fire.* Mark what became of *Pharaoh,* and the *Ægyptians,* for their oppressing the *Israelites:* And was not the old world drowned for using violence? for what all those miseries befell the *Israelites* and *Judah?* for in all the Scriptures was not oppression one of the chief grounds.

From whence we observe, That all those oppressors before [10] named do live altogether out of Gods way, and in Rebellion to his Laws: first, because they live without a Calling, and so are idle, being Vagabonds, and wasters of the creatures, by drunkenness, pride, gluttony, and so but Vermin in a Common-wealth, and by their own Law ought to be put into a house of Correction, and to be made work.

1. They are Rebels against Gods Command, for saith he, *In the sweat of thy face thou shalt eat bread:* By *Thou* is meant all mankind, none exempted.

2. *Those that will not work, let them not eat,* saith the Scripture.

3. Christ bids pray, *Give us our dayly bread.*

Now none is our bread but what we work for, for, as said before, *In the sweat of thy face thou shalt eat bread;* therefore those that work not, have no right to eat: and as they are Rebels, so are they Thieves, because when a man hath got bread, *viz.* necessaries by his labor, it is his bread; now the other that sweats not at all, yet makes this man to pay him tribute out of his labor, by Rates, Taxes, Rents, &c. it is theft, and so against the Commandment, *Thou shalt not steal.*

4. He is a Traytor against the Jehovahs anointed, *viz.* Jesus Christ, who alone is Lord and King over man, and all men are equals.

1. Now for one man to be Lord or King over another, and force on his Commands of his own authority, he takes on him the place of Jesus, and so is a Rebel and Traytor to the Crown and Dignity of Christ.

2. For man to reject the Laws of God, which binds him, *to do to another as another should do to him,* and force on his own Arbitrary Laws, such a one is a Rebell in the highest degree, and his power is of the Beast, and so of the Devil, and he and his followers are said to go into perdition, and shall be tormented for ever and ever.

3. For man to inclose all Lands and Creatures from his kind, is utterly unnatural, wicked, and treacherous; for if man shall eat bread by his sweat, then he must needs have ground to sow corn; therefore to inclose all grounds from him, is to starve him, for if no corn, no bread, and if no ground, no corn; then this is theft in the highest degree. Mark this you great Cormudgings, [11] you hang a man for stealing for his wants, when you your selves have stole from your fellow brethren all Lands, Creatures, &c. Now mark what saith the Scripture, *Pull out the beam out of thine own eye, then shalt thou see to pull out the mote out of thy brothers eye:* So first go hang your selves for your great thefts of incloseness and oppressness, and then afterwards that you can go hang your poor brethren for petty thefts, as for a sheep, corn, &c.

So that from those grounds we conclude, first, What God entitleth man with, that is to say, with alike priviledges.

2. All men are to enjoy alike Freedoms, and none more then the other, so that they are equal, and none have to do to command another, no more then another him, but in a Joynt union and agreement; that any be set up, it is but a trusted humane power, and they but servants to the whole, and may be removed at pleasure.

3. Man is to subject himself to one Soveraign Lord Jesus, and is to go by the Rule of Equity, and no otherwise.

4. From all which grounds all men have right to the Creatures, &c. one as well as the other.

This being so, we now conclude that people for the general living out of Gods way, and most they enjoy is contrary to his Commands, so all that power, by which they hold it, is an unlawful power: and secondly, without a Reformation they must never look to have Gods Justice, in plagueing of, by Wars, Pestilences, Dearths, &c. to cease from them.

Now for the power, 1. Let us examine from whence it is. 2. How it arose. 3. What it is. 4. Who are the chief upholders of it. 5. Who are under it. 6. How it may be removed.

First, From whence it is; Let us consider the Scriptures at the rising of it, and that was by oppressions and murders, and this arose out of the wickedness of mans heart, *viz.* out of his lust, which is from that beastly corruption and body of sin in him, *which*, saith the Scripture, *is not subject to the Law of God, neither can be*. This was that which stirred up *Cain* to kill *Abel*, *Lamech* to be avenged seventy seven times: This made men war, as *James* saith: This made *Nimrod* to become a Hunter of his kind; and as it puffed up men to be Kings, so again those Kings to be Tyrants, and kill, &c. *Gen.* 14. for saith the Scripture, *It arose from the earth*, that is, earthly affections [12] which is from the lusts of the flesh, the lust of theeves, and the pride of life, as *John* saith: and as it compacted it self into a visible Monarchy, and so into Kingdoms, the devil doth acknowledg them to be his, and offered them to Jesus, if he would have worshipped him.

Secondly, Jesus doth utterly disown them, calling them the worlds Kingdoms, and said *His Kingdom was not of this world*. Now that the Devil owns these powers to be his, and Jesus doth disown them, and distinguisheth his Kingdom from them, then whose must they be? and from whence have Kings, Dukes, Lords, Gentlemen, &c. Tyrants, as they are called, their power & Tythes? that not from Jesus Christ, for Christ doth utterly forbid all his Subjects to be called Lords, &c. as a heathenish thing, and of the world, and heathens were the Devils worshippers, and the devil is called the prince and god of this world, for in heaven he hath nothing to do there; then if the devil be prince of the world, then all these powers are from him, *viz.* those powers aforesaid, and so the Tythes of Superiority, as King, Lord, &c. are from the devil: now that their buildings are of the devil, no marvel then that they strive to uphold his interest.

Thirdly, For the rising of it, *Daniel* doth describe it under the notion of four several beasts, each distinct from other in quality, but because the beast which *John* describes is the last, which is to remain until the Kingdom of Christ throweth it down. Read the 13 of the *Revelations*, there this Beast is described with seven heads and ten horns, his rise is out of the Sea, *viz.* waters, and waters are the people, and out of the foming beastliness of this Sea came out this Monster, his natures are like the Lyon, Bear, Leopard, what more crueler beasts then any one of these, but all their cruel qualities are in him, his heads are two males, a Monster, and seven in Scripture is perfection, *viz.* perfect wickedness, and ten horns to support him, *viz.* Kings; so that kingly power is of this Beast, and this Beast is of the Dragon, for he gives him his power and authority.

Fourthly, For the chief upholders of this power, the Scripture declares to be Kings, for Kings are the horns of it, that upholds its power, &c. and by whom it persecutes. Now by Kings in Scriptures are meant any supream powers that are by force, &c. therefore *Herod* was called a King, and yet a [13] Tetrarch. And in *Joshua*, there mention is made of thirty two Kings in the Land of *Canaan*, and yet but Governors of Cities, Castles, &c. therefore *Nebuchadnezzar* is said to be a King of Kings. And here in *England*, those called *Earls, Dukes, Marquesses, Vicounts, &c.* what were they but petty Kings? and had they not a tyrannical House of Peers, that had a *negative voyce* with the King? and did he not call them his Couzens? and by whom we were cozened of our Liberties: and blessed be God, their power is down. And as these are Kings, so besides there are Vice-kings, *viz.* those that are Deputies, as Mayors in Cities and Towns corporate, that are *Kings of Patents*, which Patents are meer Monopolies, and serve to inhance Trading and Commodities in a few mens hands, to beggar the whole; these take Towls and Customs of their Brethren; so that if a man pitch a sack of corn, one of these men comes like a Beggar with a dish, and then carrieth it to the *King of beggars*, that is the Mayor: Those Vice-kings have twelve Peers too, whereby they domineer over the whole Town, city, &c. Then there are the *Hedg-kings, viz.* those called *Lords of the Mannors*, those fellows can keep a *Court-leet*, and enslave all within their Territories; These are *Kings* of all those Cuckcows in their Liberties, whereby fools are made to pay Lead, Silver, quit-rents, &c. These all claim proprieties as aforesaid.

But now all this power came by murther at the first, by *William the Norman Conqueror*, as it is declared in the *first part* that was set out before [2]. So that although the Emperial King is removed, and his Power, what are we the neer, so long as those other petty kings remain?

[2] *Light Shining in Buckingham-shire.*

and all that Power, Courts, &c. are in force still, though in another name, as Lord-keepers, &c. Cannot the Lawyer cozen and cheat as much in that name as in the Kings? Is this all the Reformation the Parliament will do? and will the Army be such fools, as to let those beastly Courts, Terms, &c. remain, with all those wicked Laws in force? which are the very nerves of the beast, the upholding of all the diabolical interests, as I said before; for it is by murther that all those interest-parties hold that priviledg as they do: and it is those wicked *Norman Laws* that do authorize them: Sure the Souldiers will not suffer this to continue, but put down the Terms; and set aside buying and selling [14] Law. Sure if the Parliament do not do it, as it is plain they will not, if not forced, then why may not the Souldiers as well pull the Judges out of *Westminster Hall*, and take all their rusty Records, Laws, &c. and make a fire on them? that so we may have honest, godly Laws, according the Scriptures and Reason. Would it not be a notable booty for the Soldiers, when so many cheating Lawyers are together at the Term, to drive them out, or else strip their long-tail'd Gowns over their ears? O Souldiers! you could never do a better peece of service, then to put down the Lawyers, and all their Courts, with all Patents, Grants, &c. whatsoever is of the *Norman* and beastly power: For as Kings are the chief upholders, so the Lawyers are their hackneys, that with their quirks and deceits do deceive the poor people, and keep them in bondage to those *Kings*. Are they not their Stewards in all their Court-leets, and elsewhere? Therefore suffer not one Term more, and we in the Country likewise assist with what power we can. So let us acquit our selves like men, and be no more slaves to none; this were excellent indeed. And those proud hypocritical Officers that are amongst you, that are against our Freedom, and would do the work of the Lord by halves, put them out, and chuse honester in their rooms; and the onely way is to take down their great pay: let them serve as you do, or with a moderate allowance. So likewise stand for the taking down all Tythes: and forasmuch as the Priests serve not the Lord Jesus, but their own bellies, being Antichristian; O then suffer them not to have any forced Maintenance, but as people will freely give them; and let none be persecuted for his Conscience; then you will do us good indeed, and we shall say, God is amongst you of a truth. Now as we have discovered the Beastly power, and who upholds it, which are *Kings, Lords, Terms, and Lawyers*, O then stand to us that we may never have any more *Kings* at all, neither no other arbitrary Tyrants, or tyrannical Offices that thereunto belongeth: for all the whole world is under this power of wickedness. Now mark what saith the Scripture, *That all who worship the beast shall be tormented.* And it is plain, so long as the people [are] subject to it, they worship the devil: Therefore no marvel if there are heavy Judgments in the Nations, so long as they continue thus in rebellion against God.

[15] Lastly, How it may be removed, is, to give all liberty for godly men to declare against it. 1. Therefore take away all binding Laws, penalties, &c. that men may freely preach against it, even in all publike meetings, that so the Priests may no more delude the people. 2. Utterly abolish these wicked Laws, Terms, &c. with all Patents, Corporations, Grants, Monopolies, &c. For why may not all Controversies be ended by Arbitration of our own Neighbourhood, by the rule of Equity at home, then to be thus abused by the Lawyers? And why may not every man as freely speak, preach that God hath made out to him, as the Priests? And if the Priests will not be quiet, but still stir up strife, let them be set aside, as needless and unprofitable, who keep the people in blindness, as they have done, in preferring a wicked man in the place of a God, as they did *Charls Stuart.*

Lastly, Above all, look to the poor; let not all the Bishops Lands, Crown Lands be swallowed up, nor Commons, Parks, Woods, Forrests, &c. for your great ones gape for to inclose them: but let all be for the poor, until more comes: and all, whosoever, that have oppressed the poor, let them make restitution fourfold. And think on prisoners that perish in prison by merciless Creditors & Jaylors, that they may not be mewd up, and starved, until they are poysoned there. And likewise a way to prevent cozening and cheating one another; and that all Tryals be in every Hundred by twelve men of the same neighbor-hood, and all buying and selling Law put down, as aforesaid: And let a free Trade be in the Nation; All Monopolies, Patents, &c. utterly taken away. And for the rule to go by that which is declared the Rule of Equity, *to do to all men as they should do to others, &c.* and all other false tyrannical rules taken away, and all Laws to be out of the Scriptures, seeing there is but one Law-giver, who is able both to save and destroy. And for Law Executioners, to be only such, who are right godly, honest, wise, moderate, judicious, reasonable, and faithful men, and those chosen by free Election of the People; and so all that bulk of Officers that are by Pattents, as all Judges, Iustices, Sheriffs, Bailies, Mayors, &c. and all other Offices that are not elected by the people, but were forced on us with out our Election, and against our consents, by a Patent: And [16] forasmuch as the throwing down the Kingly power, all those fell with it; and we looked never to have them more revived, seeing that all power is arbitrary that is not out of the peoples voluntary Election, the people being declared the supream Authority under God; and whom they chuse, to be the lawful Magistrate: yet nevertheless, as if the Parliament intended still to keep the old arbitrary and tyrannical *Norman Laws, Terms* and *Courts*, still to enslave us; and *Lawyers, Patentee Officers* to torment, have made an Act that all *Patents, Grants, Courts, &c.* shall continue as they formerly did, only Writs in the *Judges* and *Keepers names* [3], although in our *Petitions* we utterly denyed the same: and they have appointed *Commissioners* to be *Justices* without *any election from us.* Likewise the *Grandees in the Army* have preferred a thing called *An Agreement of the People* [4], which is too low and too shallow to free us at all: for it doth not throw down all those *Arbitrary Courts, Powers and Patents,* as aforesaid: And what stock or way is provided for the *poor, fatherless, widows, and impoverished people?* And what advancement of encouragement for the *laboring and industrious,* as to take off burthens, is there? By all which, and by *Arbitrary Powers* erected anew, we see, that they minde their own *interest, gain, and rotten honor* more then our *absolute Freedom*: This being so, we are enforced to appeal to all our *dear brethren* in *England,* and *Souldiers in the Army,* to stand every one in his place, to oppose *all Tyranny* whatsoever, and by whomsoever, intended against us.

[3] On February 17, 1649, Parliament authorized justices of the peace, sheriffs, and officers of courts to continue acting until new commissions were issued, and authorized indictments, actions, writs, etc., in the name of the Keepers of the Liberty of England by Authority of Parliament.

[4] In November, 1648, Lilburne and Ireton agreed that the Agreement of the People should be revised by a supposedly representative committee. Lilburne published this revision under date of December 10, 1648. The understanding with Ireton, as Lilburne supposed, included the acceptance of the committee's draft as final and the submission of it to the people for ratification. In fact, it was amended by the Council of Officers and presented to the House of Commons on January 20, 1649, with a mild request that the House consider it. Lilburne published his version of the bargain with the officers in *The Legal Fundamental Liberties of the People of England, Revived, Asserted, and Vindicated,* June 8, 1649. This is reprinted by A. S. P. Woodhouse in *Puritanism and Liberty* (1938), pp. 342 ff.: The Agreement of the People as formulated by the committee, with the changes made by the officers, is reprinted, *ibid.,* pp. 355 ff.

Reader, You may expect in the third Part to have an Anatomizing of all Powers that now act, &c.

And in the fourth the Grounds and Rules that all men are to go by.

Farewel.

FINIS.

A DECLARATION OF THE WEL-AFFECTED IN THE COUNTY OF BUCKINGHAMSHIRE

THE title page is dated 1649, and Thomason dated his copy May 10. The pamphlet is anonymous. According to *The Kingdom's Faithfull Scout*, May 4 to 11, the resolutions at the end were adopted by a Levellers' meeting at Aylesbury (Bucks.). This meeting would have been one small item of the great Leveller disturbance of that spring, which reached its culmination, so far as the Army was concerned, in the mutiny of Scrope's regiment and their defeat at Burford on May 14.

There are copies in the Harvard College Library and in the Thomason Library at the British Museum.

The text is reproduced from the copy in the Thomason Library.

A DECLARATION OF THE WELL-AFFECTED IN THE COUNTY OF BUCKINGHAM-SHIRE.

Wε have for this eight years waited with much patience, and great expence of Treasure, besides the loss of many our dear friends, in the pursuance of our just Rights, and Freedoms, which God had invested us withall, and the whole Nation, and kept from us by the Arbitrary Powers, & tyrannicall Factions of the Nobility, Courtiers, Episcopal Priests, and wicked cheating Lawyers, besides Impropriators, Patentee-men, Lords of Mannors, and all illegall Courts, &c. and other diabolicall Interest parties, that had all their Licences, Patents, Grants, Commissions, from the late King, whose first Predecessor was that out-landish Bastard, *William* the *Norman* Conqueror; from whence doth proceed the originall of all our slavery, both in Tenures, Termes, tyrannicall Laws, Customs, &c. whereby we, the lower sort of People, are made slaves to the wills of *Tyrants*, by reason the Law, being in an outlandish *Tongue*, and withall bought and sold by the Lawyers, who judge the Causes according to the Purse, and will do no Justice without money; so for filthy [4] lucre, will stand to justifie and maintain any unjust, and wicked, and tyrannicall Custome, or illegall persecutions of any Tyrants whatsoever, although to the utter deprivation and undoing of the poor widdows, fatherless, &c. and to the advancing the *Wills* of merciless *Tyrants;* and which said parties, especially the Lawyers, was the chief instruments of procuring all that miserable effusion of bloodshed, and ruine in this Nation, by the Judges giving their Verdict for ship-moneys, and other Monopolies over all sorts and trades, and which doth still strive to hinder all good, and godly, honest and just Reformation, they striving rather to uphold their own theft and deceit, then admitting any just composure and agrement of the People, lest all trials should be by twelve men of the

643

neighbourhood in every Hundred, without expence and charge, which would be the ruine of their needless Calling, and a full ease to the People, who are now vexed and undone by their Removes, Demurs, and needless journeys to their *Termes*, whereby they live upon the only Dissentions, and Differences of the People, and by whose Subtilties, Counsels, and Delusions, the whole Nation hath been inslaved ever since the foresaid Conquest, by whose strategems all the middle sort, and poor People hath been pursued by merciless Priviledges, great men, as Lords, Gentlemen, and extorting Lords of Mannors, whereby all wicked Customs, as Fines, Hariots, Quit-rents, and Headsilvers [i. e., poll-taxes], with all slavish and base Tenours, Tyths, Impropriations, and Patents, Prerogative Charters; the said Lawyers being alwayes Judges and Stewards of those Arbitrary Courts, and are chosen by those Prerogative Borough towns to be Burgesses of Parliament, which have been the great obstructors and hinderers of all our Liberties, Freedoms, and naturall Rights.

But when we received so many Promises, Declarations, and Remonstrances from the Parliament, that so soon as God should make them capable, and overthrow their enemies that were in arms against them, they would make us [5] the absolute freest People in the world, removing all Oppressions; all which did engage us to assist them: and finding them to apostatize from their principles in their *Treaties*, the Army promising to stand by us that we might have our Freedoms; but finding both the Parliament and Army to break their promises, and to be as Arbitrary as those that were before them, in maintaining all the foresaid oppressions upon us, with new vexations, as *Excise*, *Taxes*, *Free-quarter*, &c. suffering their Committees to domineer over us, the same *Terms*, *Lawyers*, *Courts*, remain as corrupt as formerly, *Tithes*, slavish *Tenures*, *Tolls*, *Patents*, &c. still in force, our friends most unjustly, and *Starchamber-like* imprisoned by a new Committee, called the *Councel of State*, which was never desired to be set up or allowed to tyrannize over the People, yet no less then four of our worthy friends, as Mr. *Lilburn*, Mr. *Walwin*, Mr. *Prince*, Mr. *Overton*, must be by them sent to the *Tower* at their pleasure [1], for not answering Interoga-

---

[1] Lilburne, Walwyn, Prince, and Overton were committed to the Tower by the Council of State on March 28, 1649, for publishing the *Second Part of England's New Chains*, as tending to incite mutiny in the Army. Lilburne was tried and acquitted the following October, and the men were released on November 8, 1649. See S. R. Gardiner, *The Commonwealth and Protectorate* (1894), Vol. I, ch. 2.

tories; the Parliament approve of it, some of our friends cast into other prisons, as Captain *Bray* [2], and an honest faithful souldier [3] murthered, and shot to death by the audatious and perfidious proud *Officers* of the Army, who in a Councel of War condemns him, the General refusing to pardon or repleeve him, the *Janisary* souldiers murther him; so that even the old conquest of *William* the *Norman* is now revived again; the forenamed *Lawyers*, with the *Impropriators*, *Lords* of *Mannors*, *Patentee men*, and chiefe *Officers* of the *Army*, with the *Judges*, wicked *Peers*, *&c.* being compacted all in one, and minding utterly to betray, inslave, and undo us, more then those former *Tyrants* before them, doth still keep up the *Kingly* power, altering the title, and all that Diabolicall Interest that doth belong unto it, &c. so that *Quitrents*, *Fines*, and *Hariots*, *Tolls* and *Customs* are still forced upon us, and the *Impropriators* suing us for *Tythes;* no right Justice to be had for the meaner and poor people, many undone, ready to famish and starve, yet no effectuall [6] course taken for them, as their need requires, all our honest petitions slighted and disregarded.

All which tyranny, oppression, and arbitrary proceedings of theirs makes us doubt of any true Reformation, or just Freedom and Liberty to come from them, so long as those wicked Lawyers and impropriators, &c. are amongst them, and untill all those Lawyers and Impropriators be purged out from amongst them it will be to little purpose to make any more addresses to them.

Likewise finding the Grandees of the Army to be the men that hinder both the honest soldiery, that stands for absolute Freedom, and doth imprison, and put them to death, that are for just principles of common Right and Equity, so that those honest men are by those proud Commanders persecuted by the name of Levellers.

By all which, we see those chief Commanders are grown to an extream height of avarice, pride, hypocrisie and apostacy, meer arbitrary Politicians prefering their filthy lucres, and diabolical interests, gain

[2] William Bray had been tried by court martial as a leader of the Leveller mutiny in Henry Lilburne's regiment, at Ware on November 15, 1647. He was returned to duty after acknowledging error. In 1649 he was excluded from the General Council of the Army and lodged a complaint against Fairfax which was so violent that the House of Commons voted it scandalous. He was committed to Windsor Castle on March 19, 1649, and remained in custody until October, 1651.

[3] Robert Lockyer was executed on April 27, 1649, as the ringleader of the mutiny in Whalley's regiment. His funeral was the occasion of a great Leveller demonstration in London.

and ugly honor, more then the common Freedom of us and the sol-diery, for a great part of them to be so barbarous, as to subject them-selves to those Commanders wils, although it be to murther their fel-lows that are godly, honest, and consciencious, &c.

All which, both by Parliament, and Grandees of the Army, there can be but little good expected from them, and bootlesse for us any longer to wait for their delivering us, notwithstanding their flattering delu-sions, and hypocritical Fasts, making us believe they would take off our oppressions, when they lay more on us, not at all removing the Roman power, but allowing Law to be bought and sold still, and yet will not suffer our imprisoned friends to have it for their money, but to lye in prison during pleasure, &c. inventing new wayes to try them; others tryed, sentenced, condemned, kild, &c. even by a Court Martial, contrary to the diabolical *Norman* Laws themselves.

[7] And therefore we declare our intentions, that the World may take notice of our Principles, which are for common right and freedom. And therefore,

1. We do protest against all Arbitrary Courts, Terms, Lawyers, Impropriators, Lords of Mannors, Patents, Priviledges, Customs, Tolls, Monopolizers, Incroachers, Inhancers, &c. or any other interest-parties, whose power are Arbitrary, &c. as not to allow, or suffer our selves to be inslaved by any of those parties, but shall resist, as far as lawfully we may, all their Arbitrary proceedings.

2. We protest against the whole Norman power, as being too intol-lerable a burden any longer to bear.

3. We protest against paying Tythes, Tolls, Custom, &c.

4. We protest against coming to Westminster Terms, or to give any mony to the Lawyers, but will endeavor to have all our contro-versies ended by 2, 3, or 12 men of our own neighborhood, as before the *Norman* Conquest.

[8] 5. We protest against any trial by a Martial Court, as Arbitrary, Tyrannical, and Wicked; and not for a free people to suffer in time of Peace.

6. We shall help to aid and assist the poor, to the regaining all their Rights, dues, &c. that do belong unto them, and are detained from them by any tyrant whatsoever.

7. And likewise will further and help the said poor to manure, dig,

&c. the said Commons, and to fell those woods growing thereon to help them to a stock, &c.

8. All wel-affected persons that joyn in community in Gods way, as those [in] *Acts* 2, and desire to manure, dig, and plant in the waste grounds and Commons, shall not be troubled or molested by any of us, but rather furthered therein.

9. Wee desire to go by the golden rule of equity, viz. *To do to all men as we would they should do to us*, and no otherwise; And as we would tyrannize over none, so we shall not suffer our selves to be slaves to any whosoever.

FINIS.

are the said Commons, and to fell those woods growing thereon to help them to a stock, &c.

8. All well-affected persons that joyn in community in Gods ways as these [in] Acts, and desire to manure, dig, and plant in the waste grounds and Commons, shall not be troubled or molested by any of us, but rather furthered therein.

9. Wee desire to go by the golden rule of equity, viz., To do to all men as wee would they should do to us, and no otherwise; And as wee would tyrannize over none, so we shall not suffer ourselves to be slaves to any whosoever.

FINIS.

A DECLARATION of the Grounds and Reasons why we the Poor Inhabitants of the Town of Wellinborrow, in the County of Northampton, have begun and give consent to Dig up, Manure and Sow Corn upon the Common, and Waste Ground, called Bareshanke, Belonging to the Inhabitants of Wellinborrow, by those that have Subscribed, and Hundreds more that give Consent.[1]

WEE FIND in the Word of God, that God made the Earth for the use and comfort of all Mankind, and set him in it to till and dresse it, and said, That in the sweat of his brows he should eat his bread; and also we find, that God never gave it to any sort of people, that they should have it all to themselves, and shut out all the rest, but he saith, The Earth hath he given to the children of men, which is every man.

2. We find, that no creature that ever God made was ever deprived of the benefit of the Earth, but Mankind; and that it is nothing but covetousnesse, pride, and hardnesse of heart, that hath caused man so far to degenerate.

3. We find in the Scriptures, that the Prophets and Apostles have left it upon Record, That in the last days the oppressor and proud man shall cease, and God will restore the waste places of the Earth to the use and comfort of Man, and that none shall hurt nor destroy in all his holy Mountain.

[1] A Broadside in the Thomason Library at the British Museum. Thomason dated it March 12, 1650.

649

4. We have great Encouragement from these two righteous Acts, which the Parliament of England have set forth, the one against Kingly Power, the other to make England a Free Common-wealth.

5. We are necessitated from our present necessity to do this, and we hope that our Actions will justifie us in the gate, when all men shall know the truth of our necessity: We are in Wellinborrow in one Parish 1169 persons that receive Alms, as the Officers have made it appear at the Quarter Sessions last: we have made our Case known to the Justices, the Justices have given Order that the Town should raise a Stock to set us on work, and that the Hundred should be enjoyned to assist them; but as yet we see nothing is done, nor any man that goeth about it; we have spent all we have, our trading is decayed, our wives and children cry for bread, our lives are a burden to us, divers of us having 5. 6. 7. 8. 9. in Family, and we cannot get bread for one of them by our labor; rich mens hearts are hardened, they will not give us if we beg at their doors; if we steal, the Law will end our lives, divers of the poor are starved to death already, and it were better for us that are living to dye by the Sword then by the Famine: And now we consider that the Earth is our Mother, and that God hath given it to the children of men, and that the common and waste Grounds belong to the poor, and that we have a right to the common ground both from the Law of the Land, Reason and Scriptures; and therefore we have begun to bestow our righteous labor upon it, and we shall trust the Spirit for a blessing upon our labor, resolving not to dig up any mans propriety, until they freely give us it; and truly we find great comfort already, through the goodnesse of our God, that some of those rich men amongst us, that have had the greatest profit upon the Common, have freely given us their share in it, as one Mr John Freeman, Thomas Nottingam and John Clendon, and divers others; and the Country Farmers have proffered divers of them to give us Seed to sow it, and so we find that God is perswading Japheth to dwell in the tents of Shem: and truly those that we find most against us are such as have been constant enemies to the Parliaments Cause from first to last.

Now at last our desire is, That some that approve of this work of Righteousnesse, would but spread this our Declaration before the great Councel of the Land, that so they may be pleased to give us more encouragement to go on, that so they may be found amongst the small number of those that considers the poor and needy, that so the Lord may deliver them in the time of their troubles, and then they will not be found amongst those that *Solomon* speaks of, which withhold the Corn (or the Land) from the Poor, which the people shall curse, but blessing shall be upon the heads of those Rulers that sell Corn, and that will let the poor labor upon the Earth to get them Corn, and our lines shall blesse them, so shall good men stand by them, and evil men shall be afraid of them, and they shall be counted the Repairers of our Breaches, and the Restorers of our Paths to dwell in. And thus we have declared the truth of our necessity; and whosoever will come in to us to labor with us, shall have part with us, and we with them, and we shall all of us endeavor to walk righteously and peaceably in the Land of our Nativity.

RICHARD SMITH. JOHN AVERY. THOMAS FARDIN.
RICHARD PENDRED. JAMES PITMAN. ROGER TUIS.
JOSEPH HICHCOCK. JOHN PYE. EDWARD TURNER.

LONDON, Printed for Giles Calvert, 1650.

A MITE CAST INTO THE COMMON TREASURY

THE pamphlet has no title-page. Thomason dated his copy December 18, 1649. Robert Coster's name appears under the title at the beginning of the text. Coster signed the Letter to Fairfax written in December, 1649, the Appeale to all Englishmen, and the Letter taken at Wellingborough.

There are copies in the Harvard College Library and in the Thomason Library at the British Museum.

The text is reproduced from the copy in the Thomason Library.

[1] A MITE CAST INTO THE COMMON TREAS-

URY: *or*, Queries propounded (for all men to

consider of) by him who desireth to advance the

work of publick Community: Robert Coster

WHETHER all men (by the grant of God) are not alike free, and all to enjoy the Earth with the fulness thereof alike (*Geneses* 1. from the 26. verse, to the end of the Chapter, and the 9. Chap. from the 1. to the 18. verse), untill they sell their Birth-right and Inheritance, for a proud idle life: the 2. of the *Thessalonians*, and the 3. Chapter, from the 6. to the 13. verse?

2. Whether the Scriptures, in many places, do not complain of mans Lording over his own kind (as in *Isaiah* 3. 15. [2] *Luke* 22. 24, 25, and 26. verses. *Mat.* 23. chap. from the first to the 13. verse), Calling such men for their nature and cruelty, *Lyons, Wolves, Foxes, Doggs* (*Isaiah* 56. 10, 11. *Ezek.* 22. 27. The men call some of them, Lords of Mannors, Ministers, and Lawyers)?

3. Whether particular propriety was not brought into the roome of publick Community by Murther and Theft; and accordingly have been upheld and maintained? In which Acts of cruelty, whether those devouring Creatures before mentioned, have not been chief, and whether such naked shameless doings do not lie lurking under fig-leave Clothing, such as Sabboth, Fasting, and Thanksgiving dayes, Doctrines, Formes, and Worships?

4. Whether the Lords of Mannors, do not hold their Right and Title to the Commons, meerly from the Kings Will, (which Will proving a Burthen to the Nation, caused the King to loose his head) and whether the strongest point in their Law for the keeping up their Title, be not, *Take him Jaylor?*

5. Whether the Common People of *England* may not seize upon

the Land, which is called after their own name, to wit, the Commons, for to dresse and improve it for their best advantage; for these Reasons following, without paying fines, Quit-rents, Heriots, or swearing Fealty (or any other cursed and diabolicall payments whatsoever) to any Tyrant soever?

First, Because the great Creator of all things, ordained that the earth with the fulness thereof should be a common Treasury of Livelihood for all, and that none should Lord over his own kind; but that all should love as Brethren, and so glorifie the Creator in the work of his hands.

Secondly. Because the Common People of *England*, have (these six or seven hundred years) been shut out from having any benefit of the Earth, except that which they have bought by their slavish payments. And all this by & through the meanes of that illegitimate Lord and Master propriety, which was ushered into the Creation, by those two grand [3] disturbers of our Peace, Murther and Theft; and therefore now it is high time for them (the Common People) to lay hold upon the wast Land, that so they may receive some benefit freely, and may no longer live in a starving condition: and this cannot with reason be denyed by the Gentry and Clergy, if they consider what cruelty they have acted towards their fellow-Creatures these many years, who have a priviledg to the Earth equall with themselves.

Thirdly. Because there is no Statute-Law in the Nation that doth hinder the common people from seizing upon their own Land (but onely the mercinary wills of men) and therefore where there is no Law, there is no transgression.

Fourthly. Because oppression and cruelty doth bear so much sway in the Nation, that poor men will be necessitated to make a breach of the Lawes of the Nation, if they are not suffered to labour the Earth for their maintenance.

Whether it would not prove an Inlet to Liberty and Freedom, if poor men which want Imployment, and others which work for little wages, would go to digging and manuring the Commons, and most [i. e., waste] places of the Earth; considering effects that this would produce?

As 1. If men would do as aforesaid, rather then to go with Cap in hand, and bended knee, to Gentlemen and Farmers, begging and in-treating to work with them for 8 d. or 10 d. a day, which doth give them an occasion to tyrannize over poor people (which are their fellow-Creatures) if poor men would not go in such a slavish posture, but do as aforesaid, then rich Farmers would be weary of renting so much Land of the Lords of Mannors.

2. If the Lords of Mannors, and other Gentlemen who covet after so much Land, could not let it out by percells, but must be constrained to keep it in their own hands, then would they want those great baggs of money (which do maintain pride, Idleness, and fulness of bread) which are carried into them by their Tenants, who go in as slavish a posture as may be; namely, with Cap in hand, and bended knee, crouching and creeping from corner to corner, while his Lord (rather [4] Tyrant) walkes up and down the Roome with his proud lookes, and with great swelling words questions him about his holding.

3. If the Lords of Mannors, and other Gentlemen, had not those great bagges of mony brought into them, Then down would fall the Lordliness of their spirits, and then poor men might speak to them; then there might be an acknowledging of one another to be fellow-Creatures.

For what is the Reason that great Gentlemen covet after so much Land? Is it not because Farmers and others creep to them in a slavish manner, proffering them great summes of money for such and such percells of it, which doth give them an occasion to tyrannize over their fellow Creatures which they call their Inferiours?

Secondly. And what is the Reason that Farmers and others are so greedy to rent Land of the Lords of Mannors? Is it not because they expect great gaines, and because poor men are so foolish and slavish as to creep to them for imployment, although they will not give them wages enough to maintain them and their Families comfortably: All which do give them an occasion to tyrannize over their fellow-Creatures, which they call their Inferiors.

All which considered, if poore men which want Imployment and others which work for little wages, would go to dresse and improve the common and wast Lands, whether it would not bring down the prizes of Land, which doth principally cause all manner of things to be deare?

Whether a Livelihood be not the right and propriety of every man; Looke in the first Query.

Whether this be not intruded into by those which do impoverish their fellow-Creatures by their buying and selling, and by their inclosing and appropriating the Earth, with the fruits thereof unto themselves (purposely to uphold their Lordly spirits) as most men do; and so (in plain *English*) rob and steale from their fellow Creatures, their proper right and Inheritance?

Whether those Scriptures which say, Love thy Neighbour [5] as thy selfe; and do unto all men as you would they should do unto you: and He that hath this Worlds goods, and seeth his Brother in want, and yet shutteth up the bowells of Compassion from him, how dwelleth the love of God in him? *Matt.* 7. 12; *John* the first, Chapt. the 3, verse the 17.

And many such Scriptures; Whether they are not least spoken of, and lesse practised among men now a dayes, although in them is contained the whole Law and Prophets?

> *The Nation is in such a state as this,*
>   *to honour rich men because they are rich.*
> *And poor men, because poor, most do them hate,*
>   *O, but this is a very cursed State.*
> *But those which act from love which is sincere,*
>   *will honour truth where ever it doth appear.*
> *And no respecting of persons will be with such,*
>   *but Tyranny they will abhorre in poor or rich.*
> *And in this state is he whose name is here,*
>   *your very loving friend,* Robert Costeer.

THOUGH *we have been sad*
    yet now are glad
      To see such a joyfull time,
Our Misseries they,
Are passing away,
And truth beginneth too clime.
   We shall
be freed from thrall
When Righteousnesse reigneth as King,
  The Glory so bright
  Shall darken the light
  Which comes from the Man of sinne.

Though men do us hate,
  yet we in this state
Do suffer joyfully,
  Though stripes we receive,
  We do them forgive,
  Which acts such cruelty.
    For we
with them must agree,
Who seeketh our blood to spill,
  And thus we may
  Their cruelty slay,
  Yea thus we shall envy kill.

The Poore long
  have suffered wrong,
By the Gentry of this Nation,
  The Clergy they
  Have bore a great sway
  By their base insultation.
    But they shall
Lye levell with all
They have corrupted our Fountaines;
  And then we shall see
  Brave Community,
  When Vallies lye levell with Mountaines.

[7]   *Tyranny have*
          made many a slave
      Within this Land of ours,
          But he must packe
          For his Power doth cracke
          And the day it will be ours.
              The Priests ball,
          and after him call
      Saying, you must with us abide,
          For if you do goe
          Then cometh our woe,
          And we shall have no more Tythe.

      The Gentry are
          fil'd with the like care,
      How they shall their Power maintaine,
          For they know
          If Tyranny go,
          They must packe to France *or to* Spaine.
              Therefore they
          will this gallant stay,
      And hide him under a backe Gowne,
          Or else in a Coach
          Will keepe him very close,
          Fearing he should be found.

      The time indeed
          that this cursed seed
      Doth as closely in all men;
          But chiefly in those
          Who are Englands *foes,*
          And we do very well know them.
              But the light
          that shineth so bright
      Reveileth this wickednesse,
          And it must go
          I very well know
          To a Land of forgetfullnesse.

[8]
The time is nigh
   that this mystery
Shall be no more obscure,
   And then we shall see
   Such community
   As shall alwayes indure.
     The Rich and Poore
   shall love each other
Respecting of Persons shall fall,
   The Father alone
   That sits in his Throne
   Shall honoured be of all.

The glorious State
   which I do relate
Unspeakable comfort shall bring,
   The Corne will be greene
   And the Flowers seene
   Our store-houses they will be fill'd
     The Birds will rejoyce
   with a merry voice
All things shall yield sweet increase
   Then let us all sing
   And joy in our King,
   Which causeth all sorrowes to cease.

FINIS.

                 F I N I S .

A DIGGER SONG[1]

You noble Diggers all, stand up now, stand up now,
    You noble Diggers all, stand up now,
    The wast land to maintain, seeing Cavaliers by name
Your digging does disdaine, and persons all defame
    Stand up now, stand up now.

Your houses they pull down, stand up now, stand up now,
    Your houses they pull down, stand up now.
Your houses they pull down to fright poor men in town,
    But the gentry must come down, and the poor shall wear the crown.
       Stand up now, Diggers all.

With spades and hoes and plowes, stand up now, stand up now,
    With spades and hoes and plowes stand up now,
Your freedom to uphold, seeing Cavaliers are bold
    To kill you if they could, and rights from you to hold.
       Stand up now, Diggers all.

Theire self-will is theire law, stand up now, stand up now,
    Theire self-will is theire law, stand up now.
Since tyranny came in they count it now no sin
    To make a gaole a gin, to sterve poor men therein.
       Stand up now, stand up now.

The gentrye are all round, stand up now, stand up now,
    The gentrye are all round, stand up now.
The gentrye are all round, on each side they are found,
    Theire wisdom's so profound, to cheat us of our ground.
       Stand up now, stand up now.

[1] *The Clarke Papers*, Vol. II, pp. 221 ff. Reprinted by permission of the Royal Historical Society.

The lawyers they conjoyne, stand up now, stand up now,
    The lawyers they conjoyne, stand up now,
To arrest you they advise, such fury they devise,
    The devill in them lies and hath blinded both their eyes.
        Stand up now, stand up now.

The clergy they come in, stand up now, stand up now,
    The clergy they come in, stand up now.
The clergy they come in, and say it is a sin
    That we should now begin, our freedom for to win.
        Stand up now, Diggers all.

The tithe they yet will have, stand up now, stand up now,
    The tithes they yet will have, stand up now.
The tithes they yet will have, and lawyers their fees crave,
    And this they say is brave, to make the poor their slave.
        Stand up now, Diggers all.

'Gainst lawyers and gainst Priests, stand up now, stand up now,
    Gainst lawyers and gainst priests stand up now.
For tyrants they are both even flatt against their oath,
    To grant us they are loath, free meat, and drink, and cloth
        Stand up now, Diggers all.

The club is all their law, stand up now, stand up now,
    The club is all their law, stand up now.
The club is all their law to keep men in awe,
    But they no vision saw to maintain such a law.
        Stand up now, Diggers all.

The Cavaleers are foes, stand up now, stand up now,
    The Cavaleers are foes, stand up now;
The Cavaleers are foes, themselves they do disclose
    By verses not in prose to please the singing boyes
        Stand up now, Diggers all.

THE DIGGERS MIRTH

THE title page is dated 1650, and Thomason dated his copy April 4. The first song is described as a Christmas carol, and publication is said to have been delayed with the intention of adding more songs to the collection. Though no author is given, the title page states that the book is issued by the Diggers at Cobham.

The only copy known to me is in the Thomason Library at the British Museum.

[3] THE DIGGERS CHRISTMASS-CAROLL.

This for a Christmasse-Caroll was invented,
Which here unto your view is now presented;
'Twas writ at that time which you Christmasse call
And had come forth then; but this is all
The reason why it came not forth before,
Because we thought for to have added more.
    Accept of this therefore with all thy heart,
    Thou maist hereafter see a Second part.
       To the Tune of the *Spanish Gypsie*.

1.

Y OU PEOPLE which be wise,
   Will Freedom highly prise;
   For experience you have
What 'tis to be a slave:
   This have you been all your life long,
   But chiefly since the Wars begun.

2.

When great Men disagree
About Supremacy,
Then doe they warn poor men
To aid and assist them
   In setting up their self-will power,
   And thus they doe the poor devour.

3.

[4]   Yet they cunningly pretend
They have no other end
But to set the poor Free
From all their slavery:
   And thus they do the poor deceive,
   In making them such things believe.

4.

Their blinde Guides will not spare,
These things for to declare;
Yea they aloud will cry,
Stand for your liberty;
    The Gospel that lyes at the stake;
    Rise therefore 'tis time to awake.

5.

The Priests very sensible be,
If the poor their Liberty see;
Their Tythe-plundring trade will fall,
And then farewell Tythes all.
    Then would they not be finely fed,
    But they must work for their own bread.

6.

[5]   The King an Army did gain,
His power for to maintain;
That Army did pretend
For to be *England*'s friend,
    In saving of their Libertie
    Which lay at stake and like to die.

7.

Another Army then
Was raised by mighty Men,
That Army to oppose,
Looking on them as Foes:
    Likewise these powers did agree
    To make the English Nation free.

8.

A Covenant they did take,
And promises they did make
All burthens to remove,
And to unite in love;
    Yet we cannot see that good hour,
    The taking down of Kingly power.

9.

[6]   The Nation willingly
      Did maintain this Army,
      Their Freedom for to gain;
      But as yet all in vain:
          For still a Kingly power doth stand
          In many persons of this Land.

10.

      A Kingly power I say
      Doth in most men bare sway,
      But chiefly in Lords of Mannors,
      And in the Priests and Lawyers:
          This Kingly power is their Self-will,
          Which in this manner they do fulfill.

11.

      The Priests they tyrannize,
      By taking of the Tythes;
      The poor they much oppresse
      By their pride and idlenesse:
          No Scripture warrant they can show,
          Why any of these things they do.

12.

[7]   Therefore I pray consider,
      And lay your heads together;
      For you will never thrive,
      Whilst Priests do gain the Tythe.
          But let them work as well as you,
          For Reason bids them so to do.

13.

      They neither plow nor sow,
      Nor do they reap or mow,
      Nor any seed do finde,
      But Priests the people grinde:
          The tenth of all things they do crave;
          And thus each man is made a slave.

14.

The Lawyers they are next,
By whom the poor are vext;
Their practice is most base,
For they will plead mens Case,
　　According to the length o' th' Purse,
　　And so the Lawyers prove a Curse.

15.

[8]　　Another trick they have,
The Nation to inslave;
Mens quarrels they'll maintain,
Their Moneys for to gain:
　　Therefore if Lawyers you uphold,
　　They'l cheat you of your silver & gold.

16.

Therefore my brethren dear,
The Lawyers quite Cashiere;
Go not to them for Law,
For they your sides will claw;
　　They'l tell you that your case is good,
　　When they doe mean to suck your blood.

17.

Therefore be rul'd by me,
And do not Lawyers Fee,
But end your suits at home,
Lest you be overthrown;
　　For if Lawyers gain your estate,
　　You may repent when 'tis too late.

18.

[9]　　Besides the Priests and Lawyers,
There be the Lords of Mannors,
Who lay claim to waste Land,
Which by blood-shed was gain'd;
　　For Duke *William* the *Norman* King,
　　By much bloodshed this land did win.

19.

When he this Land had gain'd,
He presently Ordain'd,
That his chief Souldiers should
This Land by parcels hold,
    Owning him to be the Supream,
    In paying tribute unto him.

20.

From hence came Lords of Mannors,
With Fines, quit-Rents and Heriots,
And all such cursed things,
Which are payed to these Kings:
    And thus the people be brought down
    By Lords of Mannors who wear the Crown.

21.

[10]   The Lords of Mannors, I say,
Do bear a mighty sway;
The Common Lands they hold,
Herein they are too bold:
    They will not suffer men to till
    The comon Lands, by their good wil.

22.

But Lords of Mannors must know,
Their title to Commons is low;
For why their title came in
By WILLIAM the Norman King.
    But now the *Norman* successor is dead,
    Their Royalty to th' Commons is fled.

23.

Therefore let me advise
All those which Freedom prise,
To Till each Heath and Plain,
For this will Freedom gain:
    Heriots and Fines this will expell,
    A bondage great men know full well.

24.

[11]   For we do plainly see,
The Sword will not set's free,
But bondage is increased;
Because our wealth is wasted
    By paying Taxes and Free-quarter,
    Expecting Freedom would com after.

25.

But Freedom is not wonn,
Neither by Sword nor Gun:
Though we have eight years stay'd,
And have our Moneys pay'd:
    Then Clubs and Diamonds cast away,
    For Harts & Spades must win the day.

A HINT OF THAT FREEDOM WHICH SHALL COME,
WHEN THE FATHER SHAL REIGN ALONE IN HIS SON.[1]

THE Father he is God alone,
    nothing besides him is;
All things are folded in that one,
    by him all things subsist.

He is our light, our life, our peace,
    whereby we our being have;
From him all things have their increase,
    the tyrant and the slave.

And when the Father seeth it good,
    and his set time is come;
He takes away the tyrants food,
    and gives it to the Son.

[13]   Then *Esau's* potage shall be eat,
    for which he sold his right;
The blessing *Jacob* shall obtain,
    which *Esau* once did slight.

And *Jacob* he shall then arise
    although he be but small
Which *Esau* once did much despise
    and *Esau* down must fall.

For there must rise a root of *Jess*,
    a righteous branch indeed;
Who setteth free him that's oprest
    and *Esau* down must tread.

And *Esau* shall the blessing seek,
    and with tears shall it crave;
Which he did set unto the meek,
    which once he made a slave.

---

[1] This song is reprinted by A. S. P. Woodhouse in *Puritanism and Liberty* (London, 1938), p. 385.

[14]   But sing, O *Jacob*, for thy time
      of freedom now is come;
  And thou thy self judg *Esau*,
      the which hath done the wrong.

  For to the Son the Father hath
      all Judgment given now;
  And *Esau* shall be justly judg'd,
      which *Jacob*'s seed hath plow'd.

  And thou that as a Lord hast Raign'd
      over Gods Heritage;
  Thy part thou hast already play'd,
      therefore come off the Stage.

  For when thou think'st thy self most safe
      and riches thou hast got;
  Then in the middest of thy peace,
      torment shall be thy lot.

[15]   And of this long time thou hast been told,
      but much thou didst it slight;
  Therefore *Esau* we must be bold
      now for to claim our right.

  For now the Father's pointed time,
      which he did fore-intend
  To set up Freedom, and pull down
      the Man which did offend:

  The time, I say, it is now come,
      in which the Lord will make
  All Tyrants servants to the Son,
      and he the power will take.

  This worldly strength wherewith thou didst
      all times thy self repose;
  Shall prove but as a broken reed,
      for thou the field shalt lose.

[16]   For there shall rise a mighty Stone,
      which without hands is cut;
Which shall the Kingly powers break
      he shall be free from shot.

The first that which this Stone shall smite
      shall be the head of Gold;
A mortal wound he shall them give
      now minde thou hast been told.

FINIS.

AN INDEX OF PERSONS MENTIONED IN THE DIGGERS' PAMPHLETS

GENERAL INDEX